P9-DJA-213

NETWORK THERAPY FOR ALCOHOL
AND DRUG ABUSE

NETWORK THERAPY FOR ALCOHOL AND DRUG ABUSE

A New Approach in Practice

MARC GALANTER, M.D.

BasicBooks
A Division of HarperCollins*Publishers*

Library of Congress Cataloging-in-Publication Data
Galanter, Marc, 1941–
    Network therapy for alcohol and drug abuse: a new approach in
practice/Marc Galanter.
        p. cm.
    Contents: Includes bibliographical references and index.
    ISBN 0–465–00099–1
    1. Substance abuse—Treatment.   2. Social networks—Thera-
peutic use.   3. Self-help groups.   I. Title.
    RC564.G34 1993
    616.86'0651—dc20   92–23309
                                                                   CIP

Copyright © 1993 by Marc Galanter. Published by BasicBooks, A
Division of HarperCollins Publishers, Inc.

All rights reserved. Printed in the United States of America. No part
of this book may be reproduced in any manner whatsoever without
written permission except in the case of brief quotations embodied in
critical articles and reviews. For information, address BasicBooks, 10
East 53rd Street, New York, NY 10022-5299.

Designed by Ellen Levine

93 94 95 96 CC/HC 9 8 7 6 5 4 3 2 1

To Wynne, Cathryn, and Margit

Contents

Acknowledgments

ANYONE WHO WRITES about a new treatment approach is wise to acknowledge the people who laid the groundwork for the effort, as they deserve much of the credit for making the idea possible. In my case, certain teachers were particularly influential in promoting a clear-thinking orientation to patients' needs and persistence in the pursuit of a good outcome. In general psychiatry, they were Christian Beels, Edward Hornick, David Mann, and Lawrence Rockland. When I entered the field of addiction, systematic approaches to treatment and clinical research were still uncommon, and people who were highly influential in my thinking included innovators like Griffith Edwards, Benjamin Kissin, Mansell Pattison, and Melvin Selzer. In addition, the contributions of Jack Mendelson, Abraham Wikler, and Leon Wurmser influenced my understanding of addiction.

The opportunity to teach and carry out research in the field of alcohol and drug abuse was the product of my good fortune to serve on the faculty at New York University School of Medicine and at the Albert Einstein College of Medicine, both of which were fertile ground for innovative thinking and for the dissemination of new ideas. At NYU and Bellevue Hospital, Robert Cancro promoted an open atmosphere where varied orientations could flourish. I probably would not have been involved in the addiction field without the Federal Career Teacher Program in Alcoholism and Drug Abuse; the program allowed me flexibility in developing an academic commitment in an underserved area, and it nurtured teaching in the addiction field nationally.

When it came to developing new ideas in addiction, however, I have learned as much from my colleagues in academic medicine as from the scholars who preceded them. Other doctors who have presented problems and discussed them with me provided an important stimulus for thought. These include faculty in my division at New York University, our fellows and residents in training, and friends and associates around the country. My wife, Wynne, gave me valuable insights into family interactions as well and provided thoughtful advice about the development of this book.

Many people have been important to the operation of my academic office; without Debra Lalande and Kristin Frillmann this manuscript could not have been assembled.

Finally, no medical or psychological conception emerges from theory alone. In fact, the most important contributors to the development of this book were my patients whose problems demanded new approaches, and their families and friends who helped them. These people cannot be credited by name or even accurately described. I am most appreciative, however, for having worked along with them to overcome the painful and confusing issues they confronted.

PART I

RETHINKING THE TREATMENT OF ADDICTION

CHAPTER 1

The Need for a New Approach

MOST MENTAL HEALTH PROFESSIONALS are ill prepared to help the alcoholic or drug abuser achieve recovery, even though addicted people and their families regularly turn to them for help. Furthermore, few alcoholics or addicts are willing to attend Alcoholics Anonymous (AA) meetings until they've suffered very long; most drop out before becoming involved with the organization. A pointed question inevitably arises: How can we engage and treat these troubled people more effectively?

To answer this question, it is necessary first to provide a clear portrait of addiction from both psychological and pharmacological perspectives. Then I will show how family, friends, and self-help groups can be engaged in parallel with individual therapy. They can provide effective support for the rehabilitation of addictive illness in network therapy, an innovative format for treatment. Through social support we can overcome the denial and relapse that compromise the care of the substance abuser.

It may be helpful here to give an operational definition of *network therapy*. It is an approach to rehabilitation in which selected family members and friends are enlisted to provide ongoing support and to promote attitude change. Network members are part of the therapist's working team, not subjects of treatment. With addicted patients, the goal of this approach is the prompt achievement of abstinence with relapse prevention, and the development of a drug-free adaptation to daily life.

The problem of providing effective care is illustrated well by the case of a patient I recently encountered.* I was contacted by Paul, a physician practicing at a local hospital. He was concerned that Nancy, whom he hoped to marry, was alcoholic. He explained that when they were getting to know each other, there were periods when Nancy had seemed to be unavailable. Only after they moved in together did he realize the reason for these periods of absence: Nancy would regularly go on drinking binges. Sometimes she did not go in to the law office where she worked. Once when she was drunk she had threatened to kill herself.

Paul turned to her parents, but they preferred to minimize the issue, apparently not wanting to tarnish their daughter's image. He pleaded with Nancy to go to AA; she said she would think about it.

Nancy had been in treatment for a few years with a reputable psychiatrist, whom I later found out had tried to discourage her drinking. This therapist had encountered a problem that is common to those confronted with addicted patients. Although it must have been clear to this psychiatrist that his pleas were doing little good, he was unwilling to speak with Paul because of the need to preserve the "integrity" of Nancy's analysis.

A few weeks after Paul and I met, Nancy came to see me at Paul's behest. I tried to get her to look at her problem. She, however, said that she was quite comfortable in her analysis and that it was offering her valuable insights. Furthermore, she did not think it useful for me to speak directly with her doctor. When I pointed out that her continued drinking argued for additional intervention, or at least for some visits to Alcoholics Anonymous, she contended that her relationship in therapy should be enough to deal with her problems.

For many alcoholics, years of treatment have meant that they achieved "insight" but continued drinking. Stories of therapy like Nancy's abound at meetings of Alcoholics Anonymous. Ironically, though, these addicted people could have been treated effectively by those same therapists if the psychology of addiction had been better understood and more effective care implemented.

Let me elaborate here on the option of introducing a social network in the context of such therapy. It is safe to say that most effective addiction treatment entails self-help, peer support, or both, and that

*Patients' names and the details of their lives have been changed to prevent identification.

4

these are hard to come by in professional office practice. To address this strategic deficit, I developed an approach that engages the support of a small group—some family members, some friends—to meet with a substance abuser and therapist at regular intervals to secure abstinence and help with the development of a drug-free life. This approach did not come easily; it evolved through careful attempts to manage many patients over the course of their rehabilitation.

Nancy's resistance to seeking help for her alcoholism was typical of the way denial shows itself over the course of the disease. A few months after I initially saw her, she became annoyed at her psychiatrist for "pestering her" about going to AA, and she dropped out of treatment. The drinking continued unabated, and later that year she lost her job at the law office because of her unreliability. Paul was ready to walk out as well, but he said he would give her one more chance if she would see "the doctor who said you have to stop drinking." Nancy came in saying that her problem was that she needed "to get a handle on the depression" she had felt since losing her job.

I was not about to let her ventilate her feelings in isolation—I would have fallen into the same trap as her first therapist. I told her that since drinking played a role in her problem, it was important that we get some support for her, someone to help her look at her situation. I asked her to bring Paul and a friend of hers to our next session to discuss the issue. This was the beginning of her network therapy.

The two network members were certainly more revealing about the extent of Nancy's alcoholism than she had been. They described how it had often left her in awkward social situations and how she was incapacitated the day after her heavy drinking. I encouraged Paul and the friend to voice their feelings and concerns, to soften her inclination to avoid the problem. The impact of this network session moved Nancy to acknowledge that she had a problem with alcohol. The network members helped me to prevail on her to accept the idea of abstinence.

Together, the four of us developed a regimen to support her recovery, one that included individual sessions as well as meetings with this network. To this we added AA meetings. In later sessions the network members urged her to attend the meetings when she expressed misgivings about them. Nancy and I continued to meet with her network while she focused on ways to protect her abstinence and on the psychological issues that would allow her to achieve a full recovery.

She had a few slips back into drinking while in treatment; at one point she wanted to give it all up. Her network was behind her continued abstinence, though. We all consulted together at these times of crisis.

With each slip we would work together to understand what drinking cues—situations and emotional states—led to the relapses. We would then plan together how Nancy could handle these cues when they came up again.

As time went on and Nancy's abstinence was secured, our network sessions were held less frequently, but they were not called off and her individual therapy continued. In network sessions, the three of us would act as a sounding board for her recovery. We also provided the assurance that if Nancy slipped again, even after treatment was over, there would be a resource to draw on to secure her return to sobriety.

We drew on one particularly meaningful relationship to bolster Nancy's abstinence. We often spoke with her sister on my speaker phone during our network sessions. Although her sister lived in a remote city, Nancy had a particularly trusting relationship with her, and the sister had been very distressed for years over her drinking problem. This relationship was one that added strength to the bonds of affiliation that supported Nancy's recovery.

We will later consider a variety of devices that enhance the effectiveness of the network, like introducing relapse prevention techniques into network sessions, using formal written agreements, and managing medication intake. There are many tortuous turns on the road toward recovery, clearly more than can be conveyed in the brief recounting of this case. In studying these turns, however, we shall begin to understand the psychological issues confronting the addict, and we can review a new and effective approach to treatment.

The Perspective of Time

To clarify why progress in outpatient treatment has come slowly, I will share my own experience. I had a peculiar introduction to the addiction field, having started out as an instant expert, designated twenty years ago by the National Institute of Mental Health as a Career Teacher in alcoholism and drug abuse. Expertise, or even competence, at treating addiction was so uncommon then that the federal government was eager to support a young faculty member in each of a number of medical schools in the hope that their academic commitment would lead them to become involved in that major public health area.

I took this mission seriously. I began to search the medical literature for articles or books on treating addiction, but I found almost nothing. True, there was some interesting research on biochemical mechanisms and on the organ damage caused by addiction. In fact, I had written some of it. But there was nothing on how to resolve a drinking or drug problem for a patient who came for help.

Soon my colleagues began to send me addicted patients to treat, and I felt obliged to do the best I could. After all, there was no one else around who could manage them—or wanted to, for that matter. Initially, I would suggest to the alcoholics I saw that they go to AA; they would not go. Or I would tell them to stop drinking and reason with them, and they would politely ignore my request. I would get pill addicts to cut back, and they would soon resume their use.

Since that time, researchers in addiction have begun to develop a systematic understanding of how drug and alcohol dependence wreak their effects on thinking and behavior, and many dedicated people have entered the field. In this book, we will examine their observations and show as well how current understanding can be applied to treatment.

But it is now two decades since I was appointed an instant expert. Are treatment approaches for people like Nancy elaborated in the professional literature? In fact, there are still very few descriptions in psychological texts of a comprehensive approach that the therapist can apply to addicted patients. Detoxification regimens, research approaches, and hospital programs are available, but they do little to clarify the day-to-day struggle that must be staged while recovery is achieved with a patient who is living in the community. Few therapists venture beyond recommending to the alcoholics who come for help that they attend AA or that they take a long break from their jobs and family and go away to a rehabilitation hospital. Beyond this, psychiatrists, psychologists, and social workers simply apply their usual approaches to treatment, hoping that they will be useful. And because usual therapy rarely solves the problem, it is assumed by many that hospitalization is the only safe treatment for addicted people. It is not. An astute application of what we now know about addiction can avert hospitalization for the large majority of substance abusers, without sacrificing a good outcome.

Behavioral techniques for managing impulses for drug seeking have recently emerged from psychology and physiology, but these approaches were known to few clinicians until recently. For this reason, we will integrate the concepts of relapse prevention that emerge from that context with the use of a supportive network for self-examination. Similarly, the relationship between addiction and the symptoms of depression and anxiety has been poorly understood for quite some time and is only now being researched in depth. This theme, too, is essential to the understanding of addictive behavior and to the development of

7

an effective approach to the treatment of substance abuse. All these issues must be brought together for effective treatment.

How does network therapy fit into our evolving understanding of addiction? Addicted persons generate great conflict and resentment among their family and friends. On the one hand, persons close to the addict have long been angered by his or her lack of responsiveness and by a history of disappointment. On the other hand, they are remorseful over the addict's unhappiness and the losses that the person has suffered. The tension between anger and guilt makes it all but impossible for individuals close to addicted people to approach them in an objective way. At one time they overreact and castigate them, and at another time they shrink from asserting their concerns, to the point of enabling addictive behavior.

In recent years, professionals have begun to consider the orchestration of family dynamics to move the addicted person toward recovery. One important approach has been a technique for intervention with the reluctant substance abuser, which brings the family together to plan a confrontation designed to impress the addict with the immediate need for hospitalization. With aid from a professional, family members can thereby work together to have a meaningful impact, spurring the patient into action. Multiple family therapy groups for substance abusers have also come into use; they create a setting where a diversity of issues are melded together to neutralize individual resentments. The sense of community engendered in such groups can be supportive, and at the same time can foster compliance with an expected norm of abstinence.

Furthermore, therapists have only marginal potential for influencing patients outside the office. If a patient has a slip into drug abuse, the therapist may not be apprised—and if he or she knows, the therapist has little influence. Therapists on their own are limited in the degree to which they can make demands on the patient's life, and the patient is free to walk away from the therapeutic situation if it is uncomfortable, that is to say, if it challenges a serious relapse to addiction. All these factors make the engagement and orchestration of family and friends into the therapy with a substance-abusing patient an invaluable resource, one that offers remarkable opportunity for the modification of traditional psychotherapeutic techniques to treat the substance abuser.

CHAPTER 2

An Introduction to Network Therapy

Emergence of the Network Concept

Let us now consider how several influential therapeutic perspectives relate to the treatment of addiction. This setting will help put the network approach into perspective.

INSIGHT-ORIENTED THERAPY

There are many schools of psychotherapy, over 140 by one recent count,[1] but most practitioners base their treatment on an empathic exchange that is insight-oriented. Sadly, this modality, as traditionally practiced, has been found to have limited usefulness for treating addiction. In one study, nine in ten traditionally practicing psychiatrists acknowledged that they were unable to treat alcoholism effectively.[2] One physician who was an expert in alcoholism treatment pointed out that "numerous alcoholics, including alcoholic physicians and psychiatrists, have volunteered their experiences relevant to the impossibility of achieving psychotherapeutic results during the use of alcohol."[3]

To understand this unfortunate situation, we can turn to George Vaillant, who researched the life history of alcoholics; he underlined the denial and disordered chemistry evident in alcoholics who were entering psychotherapy. He wrote, "The greatest danger of this is wasteful, painful psychotherapy that bears analogy to someone trying to shoot a fish in a pool. No matter how carefully he aims, the refracted image always renders the shoot wide of its mark."[4] He also reported on a sample of men who were found to have long remitted from patterns of severe alcoholism.[5] Whereas 41 percent attributed their positive outcomes to will power, and others acknowledged the additional assistance of institutions such as hospitals, clinics, and Alcoholics Anonymous (AA), only 7 percent ascribed their remissions to psychotherapy. An extensive report was recently issued by the quasi-governmental Institute of Medicine on the treatment of alcoholism; psychotherapy was hardly mentioned, and no studies on its efficacy for alcoholism recovery were cited. Many AA members, speaking at their meetings, testify bitterly to years of drinking while they were in individual therapy. In their view, psychotherapy is seen not only to be ineffective, but often harmful. One patient of mine rued the years of analysis he underwent while continuing to drink; he lost the fidelity of his children, and his marriage ended in divorce.

In light of these observations, one might question whether there is a role for the thousands of mental health practitioners in the treatment of substance abuse. Can they contribute to the addiction field in a meaningful way? Yes, but they must first confront a central paradox in their therapeutic technique. In the setting of psychotherapy a willing patient makes use of a capacity for insight, while a relatively passive practitioner disavows active intervention in the patient's decision making. But this traditional stance undermines the ability of the practitioner to take the steps necessary to initiate abstinence when treating an addict or to terminate an episode of drinking when it occurs. Without an active, interventionist orientation, the therapist's role in addiction treatment is vitiated.

The need for effective direction is not restricted to the psychotherapy setting. A large collaborative study was carried out on the effectiveness of disulfiram (Antabuse) in the treatment of alcoholism, one in which patients were supposed to take the drug each morning.[6] Any drinking that day would produce a reaction of severe discomfort, due to the interaction of Antabuse with alcohol. Because of this reaction, the patients could effectively prevent a slip by simply taking their disulfiram each day. Yet, they experienced very little improvement in their outcome relative to alcoholics who received similar treatment without disulfiram.

Is disulfiram ineffective in deterring the use of alcohol? The answer, of course, lies in whether patients actually take the drug, since they can choose to "forget" it any morning. Without active intervention to assure that patients take the drug, it is relatively ineffective. (Network therapy as an adjunct to individual treatment can markedly enhance the effectiveness of this medication, as will be shown.)

Any approach to addiction rehabilitation must allow therapists to ensure that substance abusers will comply with the treatment plan. To this end, we will see how insight-oriented therapy must be modified so that the patient's own natural network of social relations is engaged to play an active role in altering his or her long-standing pattern of behavior. Psychotherapy need not rely solely on the substance-abusing patient—who is vulnerable to a slip at any juncture—or on the therapist's fruitless attempts to interpret and reconstruct the patient's denial. By turning to family, friends, and peers to address the addictive problem, an addiction treatment can draw on those whom the patient would rely on for assistance with other problems.

THE FAMILY PERSPECTIVE

Since family ties are, by and large, the strongest and most durable threads in the social fabric, much thought has been given to the relationship between them and addictive illness. We will consider first an approach that restructures the family system as a whole, and then one directed solely at specific members of the family.

Ludwig von Bertalanffy examined complex biological systems, and he tried to understand the operation of their separate components in terms of how they operated together.[7] He conceived of these systems as being organized to ensure their own internal stability and to protect themselves from outside disruption; he suggested that organs, cells, and other components evolved to carry out cooperative functions. This idea was intriguing for clinicians who were studying family interactions.[8] They had begun to notice that their own attempts to bring about an improvement in a troubled family member, such as a schizophrenic child, often produced a readjustment among the others that would protect the family system's usual mode of interaction. In fact, family members seen together in therapy would often repeatedly take steps, intentionally or not, to preserve their preexisting relationships, even at the expense of the recovery of a sick member. Like a living organism, they formed a system preserving its own homeostasis.

Psychiatric researcher Peter Steinglass and his colleagues introduced this idea of maintaining homeostasis in order to explain how some families preserve a pattern of substance abuse in one of their members.[9] They brought families of alcoholics into a residential research unit to examine their behavior, first while the alcoholic member was sober, and later while he or she was drinking. They found that an alcoholic apparently might get drunk to help members of the family secure intimacy, relief from tension, or solutions to problems.

For example, an alcoholic woman outpatient reported that she had got drunk just when her child was suffering from a fever; the behavior was puzzling, given her commitment to mothering.[10] On closer examination it became clear that she was unable to assert herself with her husband while sober. She had to drink to summon the courage to overrule him while he was ignoring her anxiety over their child's illness; he had refused to let her call the pediatrician. She could act on her own and seek medical assistance only when emboldened by her drunken state. For the family system to be able to meet certain challenges, this woman had to be an alcohol abuser.

Other investigators have offered support for this systems model as well. Some have examined the actions that spouses label as attempts to control an alcoholic's drinking but that actually aggravate a drinking problem; hiding liquor bottles or summoning relatives may have such an effect.[11] In such ways a covert agenda can operate within a family to undermine the announced desire to get an alcoholic to stop drinking. Further support for the systems model is evident in the work of Theodore Jacob and his colleagues who have studied how families adapt to the impact of different patterns of alcoholism.[12] They found that families apparently adapt better to continuous drinking, even if very heavy, than to intermittent drunkenness. The continuous drinkers fight less, are less likely to lose a job, and neglect their families less than do the binge drinkers. Consumption that is heavy may actually minimize stress in the family system by stabilizing relationships, as long as it is consistent and not unduly disruptive.

These findings suggest that it may be useful to conceive of the family as an integrated system in order to gain a fuller perspective on the alcoholic's behavior. In practice, however, it is easier to define specific roles for certain individual members, even lending them the quality of easily recognizable archetypes. This approach is certainly inherent in the disease concept of addiction, in which pathology is seen to reside within the patient, leaving problems of compulsive use, withdrawal symptoms, and impulsivity as principal forces in shaping the behavior of the afflicted person.

A bridge between the systems model and the concept of archetypal roles may be seen in transactional analysis, as described by Claude Steiner; he outlined the interactional games that alcoholics can play and the consequent roles into which the people they relate to are cast.[13] For example, in the game Drunk and Proud, an alcoholic husband may typically seek out guilt-free expression of his aggression by using the drunken state as a vehicle for excusing hostile and inappropriate behavior, such as unruliness or philandering at a party. He follows this behavior the next day by manipulating his wife with an apology and insistence that the future will bring reform. He thereby sets her up for one of two ineffectual roles, either the prosecutor ("I don't believe you") or the patsy ("OK, I'll believe you").

Steiner illustrates how the professional, in treating the alcoholic, can be cast into these roles as well, thus losing influence. One alcoholic was forced by his irate girlfriend to seek counseling. He kept his appointments faithfully. Early on he told his therapist that he was sober, although he would sometimes begin sessions with a wink. After some months, the girlfriend, incensed, called the therapist and told him that his patient was drinking more than ever. The therapist, now the patsy, realized that the alcoholic patient had been dissembling with his wink, not acknowledging the drinking in sessions.

Archetypes have also been developed for the roles that other family members commonly play.[14] For example, the alcoholic's child may be cast as the baby who responds to the family's problems by acting out immaturely to secure the relief of tension within the family, or as the mascot, a go-between for the alcoholic in conflictual relations. Perhaps the classic archetype is that of the spouse as the enabler who covers up for the alcoholic, making excuses to an irate employer for absences, or issuing a series of threats that, in their emptiness, only reinforce the perception that ill consequences need not be feared.

The concept of enabling has been broadened somewhat in recent years to imply that a spouse's psychological dependence on the relationship can parallel the alcoholic's dependence on drink. Such spouses are labeled co-dependent, and their problems are described as "a progressive pattern of self-defeating behavior that develops in response to living in a committed relationship with a chemically dependent person or other dysfunctional person."[15] The concept of the co-dependent spouse can be useful, but it illustrates as well the problem of indiscriminately casting family members into roles. The co-dependency label has been worn thin by those who have used it to refer to dysfunctional aspects of almost any relationship, and co-dependency has been reified by some into a disease in itself ("a personality disorder"),[16] conveniently suggesting its candidacy for reimbursement by health insurers, if nothing more.

All this can argue for an active but flexible approach to understanding the substance abuser's family without relying too much on the labeling of individual members. Unfortunately, though, the application of the family model to the long-term treatment and rehabilitation of addiction has been relatively limited. Most therapists in office practice remain uncertain about how to reconstruct family systems. The techniques that have been developed generally require formal training or the availability of structured support services, such as clinics and hospitals. They may not be readily available to the practitioners who most often encounter the substance-abusing patient. Consider the use of interventions and of systematic family therapy. Both provide valuable models, but require adaptation to be more easily applied.

The intervention technique, developed by Vernon Johnson, has gained popularity as a way of initiating treatment.[17] As originally applied at the Johnson Institute in Minneapolis, it entails a carefully orchestrated preparation of the substance abuser's family before the patient is contacted. The intervention takes place in the presence of the therapist, often in an office where the patient has been brought on some pretense. The alcoholic is confronted with evidence of the problem by each family member and then is given the ultimatum of either entering the hospital for rehabilitation or suffering rejection, (for example, the person's spouse may move out).

In its traditional form, this approach may be more than a lone therapist is prepared to undertake. For one thing, alcoholics are prone to depression and suicide, and a failed intervention is not without risk for the dejected alcoholic. The technique is further limited in that it was developed to ensure the immediate placement of the patient into a rehabilitation hospital, a move that is not always desirable to the patient. On the other hand, the intervention technique would be considerably more useful if some of its principles were adapted to a less threatening approach that would be more suitable to outpatient care. We shall consider such an network option in a later chapter.

A New Approach to Treatment

EXPANDING THE BASE OF INFLUENCE

Some time ago, early in my work in the substance abuse field, I encountered the work of Ross Speck and Carolyn Attneave,[18] who had developed an approach to mental health treatment that relied on social networks. Their interventions involved the engagement of a large number of members from the social circle of a disturbed person in order to orchestrate a practical treatment plan for rehabilitation. These networks could involve as many as a dozen or more family members and friends.

Attneave, a native American, was influenced by her experience of the potency and curative value of the larger tribal unit in dealing with mental illness. She and Speck drew on the philosophy of community psychiatry as well, which was seen as a vehicle for engaging the social context of a mentally ill person in order to avoid removing that person to a remote treatment setting, such as a state hospital. Their conception was appealing because it did not rely on institutionalizing the mentally ill, even those who were severely disturbed, instead creating a supportive envelope by drawing on the strength of relatives and friends for rehabilitation.

Indeed, the native American population includes some of the few subcultures in North America that have a long history of strong social ties; many reside in the communities where their forebears grew up. The use of community ties in the treatment of alcoholism within this population would understandably be appealing. For example, practices of the Native American Church, an indigenous religious sect among the Cheyenne and Arapaho of the Southwest, have been used in generating a sense of spiritual community to treat alcoholics.[19]

Another example of the potential role of the social network in altering addictive behavior is seen in the potent influence of contemporary new religious movements, which I have studied. Cultic groups like the Hare Krishna movement and the Unification Church of Sun Myung Moon were able to eliminate serious alcohol and drug problems among their members within a familylike social context.[20] The groups' ability to manage members' behavior was striking; management depended on intense cohesiveness and communality rather than coercion. It became clear that social networks could be effective as a vehicle for attitude change and for altering a member's perspective on reality. These changes are certainly important for rehabilitating an addicted person.

In the public alcoholism clinic I directed, patients without families to support them had to be repeatedly confronted by their peers in group therapy with the realities of their addiction, so that denial would not erode their capacity to deal with reality. A social network is apparently necessary for stabilizing the cognitive components of the patients' recovery, for allowing them to deal with a new reality, and for providing the essential support for accepting the new reality.

I reflected that a cohesive network could confront the denial that the addict brings into individual treatment and introduce the perspective of abstinence in the therapist's consulting room. Because of the social ties in such a network, the patient might be reluctant to run from treatment. With this in mind, I began to have substance abusers bring their spouses to sessions, and then other members of their social networks as well. Spouses, friends, and relatives added detail on the severity of addiction that the patient could not or would not initially offer. It became clear to me that the substance abusers' unreliable histories were of limited value without input from a corroborating family member or peer. These network members became invaluable later for establishing a realistic and supportive context for recovery.

Another issue contributed to my developing the network therapy approach. In recent years we have witnessed the proliferation of in-patient rehabilitation facilities for substance abusers in the United States and abroad. Such programs, many lasting a month or more, are useful in that they terminate the patient's access to alcohol and drugs immediately and then create a safe environment for detoxification and education. But they do present problems. Family and social ties are disrupted while patients are hospitalized. These settings also deny patients the opportunity to learn to deal with the conditioned cues for relapses; the real temptations do not present themselves while the patient is in the hospital.

As an alternative, it seemed reasonable to support a patient's rehabilitation by means of the social ties available in the community. A person's immediate network might include his or her spouse, some friends, or family. Components of the network are merely parts of the natural support systems that usually operate without professional involvement. But when the members of the network can be brought to act in concert, their influence serves as a therapeutic device. Network therapy can complement individual or group therapy, and AA as well.

To reiterate, network therapy may be defined as an approach to rehabilitation in which specific family members and friends are enlisted into the treatment to provide support and to promote attitude change. For addicted patients, the goal of this approach is the prompt achievement of abstinence, with the prevention of relapse and the development of a drug-free adaptation. We can now take a look at how the network format plays out in some actual sessions.

KEN'S CASE

Ken worked regularly as a bank executive, and although he was a stable community member, he had been drinking heavily for many years. He generally dozed off in his easy chair each evening, and he was often intoxicated when his family needed him. Ken apparently got drunk at some business lunches as well, and he had been passed over for promotions.

I initially spoke with Ken on the phone; learning of his wife's concern, I asked him to bring her along to our initial session. In our first session, I allowed his wife, Jean, to elaborate on the particulars of his drinking so that Ken could not minimize it, as he would have done if left to his own devices. Jean revealed that not only had the problem hurt their relationship, but it had strongly affected their grown son, who had long been disillusioned and resentful over his father's erratic behavior. She reported that the son was willing to do whatever he could to help his father achieve sobriety.

Ken was a thoughtful and deliberate man, relatively quiet; his position as a bank executive suited him well. I surmised that in a structured work situation he could effectively manage relationships with his co-workers. Jean, on the other hand, was volatile and assertive. She interrupted him freely, leaving him unsure of how to react. At times, he fell into a passive, silent stance, apparently annoyed. It was clear that Ken's problems dealing with Jean would play a role in his response to treatment.

Jean's observations about Ken's drinking problems were straightforward, though, and her description of their son's distress was compelling. What was lacking was Ken's ability to express himself in the session unless I protected his right to speak. The couple's style of interaction was no doubt expressed at home in a retreat into alcohol that gave him both respite from his wife and a means to avenge her taking front stage.

The tone of the session was established by Jean's description of the effects of Ken's drinking. No doubt Ken on his own would have revealed less. I explained that his problem, practically speaking, could be addressed only through abstinence. Jean clearly agreed, and I elaborated at some length on the need for abstinence to avoid relapse.

As is typical when a spouse is engaged in this way, Ken was beginning to feel some social pressure as well as the force of logic. He agreed to stop drinking, "at least for now," and to go to several AA meetings as well. I then explained the importance of having additional members in our nascent support network to help him avoid relapse. Ken was not enthusiastic, but with some coaxing from Jean, said he would bring his good friend Bill the next week and his twenty-three-year-old son the week after that.

All five of us met at the second session. As I do in all network sessions, I began by asking the patient to recount his experiences related to drinking since the last network meeting. This helps to keep responsibility for reporting and for maintaining abstinence in the patient's hands, rather than making him a passive member of the network. Patients are kept honest this way because the other members have been observing.

Ken reviewed the status of his abstinence. I then clarified how we were all there to support the goal of his abstinence and to share all information related to his drinking. Everyone agreed that they were eager to see him overcome his compromising alcohol problem. Intuitively, people lean toward being supportive with someone they care for who is in an awkward position. I promoted this mood, since the network's strength lies in its being perceived positively by the patient, who has ample inclination to become defensive and despairing.

Ken's friend Bill, in particular, was important to this mood. His contribution illustrates the value of extending the network to include peers. The relationship between the two went back to their college days, and it was frank and caring. While Ken's ambivalence toward Jean would allow him to disappoint her and return to drinking, the idea of disappointing or deceiving Bill was not as easy for him to entertain.

The next session was held with Ken alone, and he spent much time complaining about his wife's continual demands. I acknowledged the problems in their interaction, but underlined the need for him to develop a more active stance if he wanted to effect a change at home. The suggestion that he could become more assertive, validated by my own acquaintance with his wife's style, appealed to him. But our encounter also went smoothly because Ken did not reveal that he had drunk a glass of wine at a dinner party two days before, contrary to our understanding.

We met next with the network, and Jean was late. Ken was more at ease in her absence. I began by asking him to recount all alcohol-related events. With his son and Bill present, Ken apparently felt obliged to acknowledge that he had taken a glass of wine with dinner on a few social occasions. In fact, Ken reported with a smile that Jean had been sitting next to him at those times and had not commented on the matter; he did not seem to mind incriminating her.

I decided that it was necessary to express my dismay at Ken's slip forcefully enough to convey to the group that any drinking at all meant that he was headed for trouble. "Look, I know you are all concerned with getting the alcohol problem in hand, but if we let this sort of thing happen, you can rest assured that Ken will be back where he started in no time." In directing the statement to the entire group, I diffused the message and implied instruction, implying that the problem was not just

18

Ken's. In addition, I did not want to be too hard on Ken myself because so much of his drinking was associated with his digging in his heels when he felt put upon by his wife. The presence of other network members was therefore valuable in allowing me to avoid being the sole enforcer of his abstinence.

At this point Jean arrived, apologizing demonstratively for being detained at work. I reviewed the exchange up to that point and asked her immediately, "What happened? We're supposed to keep in touch with each other. Why didn't you give me a ring when Ken started drinking?" My tone was one of surprise. I wanted to direct some of the pressure toward Jean, to show Ken that he did not have to fall back on negativity as the odd man out, as the only network member who was incriminated.

Jean was a bit defensive. She explained, "I wasn't sure what to do. When I first came here I decided to pull back and not intrude on Ken's problem. I thought it should be up to him to do the job."

"I understand your point, but we all have to be clear on how the network works. It's obviously Ken's job to stay abstinent, but the rest of you will be supporting him on this and sharing any information related to drinking." I explained again how open communication is maintained among network members on anything related to alcohol, and I reminded the network members to call me if Ken drank so that we could all discuss his drinking in the group. "Now we should get a sense from Ken about how he started drinking again so we can work on how to prevent it in the future."

By implication, I did not consider continued drinking a legitimate option. In the network, use of the addictive agent in any manner, controlled or not, is never treated as acceptable.

We spoke at some length about what happened at the dinner parties where Ken had drunk, but he finally said, "Having a good dinner without wine is like taking the spice out of life. You can't expect me to go without a fine wine forever. After all, I don't plan to go back to heavy drinking." It was true that Ken had a taste for fine wines, but like so many other rationales for drinking, this one had to fall away if his alcoholism was to be addressed. So I went into my usual routine about the need to abstain completely, explaining the vulnerability associated with taking one's first drink.

Ken seemed unimpressed. It appeared as if he had found a way to assert himself in the group and maintain some autonomy, knowing full well that all those present wanted him to stop drinking. His behavior reflected the intriguing interface between the physiology of addiction and personality problems, as both came into play here. The compulsive nature of addiction that prevented him from limiting his drinking to a reasonable level was the central problem that we were facing, given his alcoholism. On the other hand, his style of engaging in the treatment was greatly influenced by his personality. He would passively take control over the people around him by holding his ground when they wanted something from him. Unless I could get him to give up the "occasional" glasses of wine, it was clear that he would be facing relapse.

Ken's son, who had said little in our first session together, spoke at this point. "Dad, we only want the best for you. You know how much trouble you've had from drinking. Can't we get the family together?" He went on to describe the loneliness he had felt when he was young and Ken was emotionally absent. But there was an angry edge in his voice, one that reflected a lack of forgiveness, and perhaps other burdens not related to his father.

The young man had made his point convincingly about the drinking, but Ken reacted to his anger. "You've got your own agenda in life, and I have mine." Ken lectured to his son a bit; he was not prepared to be scolded by him. I could see that he was affected by Albert's appeal, but he was still holding his own against the group. The exchange illustrates how important it is to discourage recrimination in the network meetings.

As it happened, Bill had suffered the effects of alcoholism in his own family. He was careful about drinking himself, wanting to avoid the possibility of becoming alcoholic. I asked him for his thoughts. Bill put no pressure on Ken, but told the story of his own father. He said that he could not himself say what Ken should do, but he remembered well the two years when his father had stopped drinking. "I've always looked back sadly to that time. My sister and I had two parents for a change, and my mother didn't have to live in fear of his getting drunk and hitting her." Bill went on for a good while, clearly affected by his own memories of the troubled relationship he had with his father. "It ended abruptly one day when he came home drunk and said that he thought he could handle his liquor. That was the last I really knew of him as a father."

Everyone was silent for a moment. I did not know Ken well enough to see whether Bill's message had gotten through to him, but the session was coming to an end. Not wanting to appear coercive, and realizing Ken's recalcitrance, I said only, "Let's hope things will go well over the next week. What Bill said carries an important message. The chance to achieve abstinence doesn't come often; try to make use of it."

At our next meeting, which was held with the network, I asked Ken to report on events related to drinking since we got together last. This is a ritual for all network sessions. The tale he told was peculiar, and it revealed less than it withheld. "I spent both days last weekend watching ball games with Bill and some other friends. He never said anything outright, but I noticed that he didn't have a single beer. I know this is a big sacrifice for him because he always has a can or two, and that way he can assure himself a good time. I guessed that Bill was willing to suffer a big inconvenience to make a point to me, and that he was supporting me."

What did Ken mean by this? There did not seem to be anything so striking about Bill's not having any beers over the course of a few ball games. Bill was apparently not a heavy drinker, and certainly he could have handled abstinence easily. And Ken said nothing about what *he'd* done over the weekend. Had he drunk at all? Ken seemed to be holding back information, maintaining control over the meeting by not letting us know what had taken place.

Jean chimed in. "We're going away on vacation for a week, and there are a lot of things that we're going to have to deal with. We'll be in restaurants at times, and there will be wine available." She looked to me. "I'm not sure what to do. We'll be traveling with another couple, and we have to tell them whether we're going to be drinking or not." Jean continued at some length, ignoring Ken's response to Bill. I was pleased that the network did not include this couple alone, communicating as poorly as they did.

Ken's implicit message now seemed clearer after Jean's display. He was affected by Bill's willingness to help without being intrusive. He was resentful of Jean. He needed to be on his own and to have an opportunity to embark on his abstinence program without her immediate involvement. I decided to support his need and wanted to convey that I was not going to fall into a pattern of intrusion. "Jean, those are very good points you're making, but I think we ought to put them aside for a moment. It might be useful to let Ken reflect a little on his situation."

Ken rambled on a bit in his own way, about drinking and the taste of wine. "I must say," he noted obtusely, "I've managed without any supplement to meals for the last few days. It may not be so bad after all." He seemed to be saying that he could now eat a good meal without a glass of wine, if he had to. It was an awkward dance indeed that this couple had played out over the years, as he withdrew to avoid her assertiveness and she only became more aggressive—frightened, as well—in the face of his confusing style.

Ken's son seemed to take a cue from Bill and me and now spoke less angrily: "Dad, we're here to help you. Just let me know if there's anything you want me to do. You know I'm behind you."

It did not seem wise to push Ken too hard. As long as Jean was kept at bay he seemed to be moving toward accepting our plan. Finally, after several minutes of amicable exchange between Ken and Bill, I felt safe asking him to stay away from alcohol over the course of his week out of town with Jean.

"I guess I can do it if you think it's necessary."

"What should I do?" Jean chimed in. "What should I tell him about not drinking?" I wanted to remove Jean from the circuit, but at the same time did not want to leave Ken without some accountability. I suggested, "Why don't you let Ken be in charge of his abstinence regimen? You can just report back your observations when you both return. That way the drinking issue won't be too entangled in your relationship. We'll have him get in touch with Bill over the course of the week."

Bill, an excellent complement to Ken's personality, and sensitive as well, offered to be available whenever Ken might call. I said this was a great idea, but preferred that there be a formal understanding as to when they would be in touch. Structure was clearly needed here. We set up a time for them to speak by phone. It seemed clear by this point that Ken would not want to betray Bill's support and have to report to him that he had been drinking. He agreed as well to go to two AA meetings over the course of the week away.

Ken did remain abstinent for that week away, and his therapy was ultimately successful. Clearly, the network had been essential to his maintaining stability early on. Had he been left to his own devices in individual therapy, his original slip into drinking would have placed him directly at odds with the goals of the treatment, and it would have likely driven him into an escape, from me and AA as well; alternatively, he would have continued to drink and hide it.

Furthermore, Ken's treatment had to be directive, given his long history of drinking; that is to say, he had to be told what he should do when it came to the risk of a slip. But something more than a psychiatrist's presence was needed to ensure that he would stay engaged and be responsive to such intervention. The network provided this cohesiveness and support. And the network also served as a setting for examining the cues to drinking that led Ken to feel craving—the social events, the evenings at home with no agenda. Such learning experiences, as we shall see, are integral to securing abstinence. Network members can be most helpful in identifying times when an alcoholic person is inclined to drink.

Working with Ken and his family alone would have posed a difficult problem in itself. His relationship with his wife had clearly been aggravated by the passive withdrawal associated with his drinking. His treatment would have potentially been cast in a punitive role, effectively placing me in alliance with Jean in trying to impose ourselves on him. His response would likely have been rebellious, if passive, as it had been toward her over the years. His son and he had been at odds for quite a while as well, and they were not ready to reconcile at this point. The fidelity of his family was vital, but the accompanying feelings needed to be softened.

By broadening the base of participation in the network, it was possible to bring in important input from Bill to balance out these family roles. Bill's presence shifted the focus of the exchange from Ken's past failings in the family to his problems and opportunities outside the family. He also offered Ken the chance to assume the role of a caring and sympathetic friend and to feel more active, rather than victimized. Through the involvement of a friend, we reframed the context—from Ken within his family to a group that included a peer from outside, as well.

Forces That Shape the Network

COHESIVENESS

Social cohesiveness has been defined as the product of all forces that act to keep members engaged in a group, and it can be an important therapeutic instrument.[21] It is generally evident and well focused in indigenous mental healing rituals in preindustrial societies. In religious ceremonies of northeast Africa, for example, schizophrenics are managed by focused community support using indigenous religious rituals. Cohesiveness is evident in industrialized society as well among traditional groups, as in *espiritismo*, a healing ceremony for conversion symptoms and other illnesses among Puerto Rican immigrants in the United States.[22]

Intense social cohesiveness was amply apparent among members of the new religious movements of the 1970s, which represented in some ways a revival of preindustrial community structure. Members of groups such as the Unification Church and Hare Krishna movement wanted to remain closely associated with each other and to "protect" their compatriots from onslaughts by their parents, who were eager to withdraw them from the group. Along with colleagues, I measured the emotional well-being of selected members, using standardized scales, and found it to be directly proportional to the intensity of their feelings of cohesiveness toward the group: those who were intensely engaged measured high in emotional well-being, and those who felt alienated experienced distress. Similarly, conversion into the sect, and hence social engagement, produced an appreciable decline in emotional distress among recruits. This relationship between the two measured variables, emotional well-being and cohesiveness, apparently served as an implicit motivation for persons to stay close to the group and effectively promoted their compliance with its expectations.

Although community ties in our contemporary society are generally weak, the kinds of intimacy and social support that characterize traditional societies can potentially be generated by engaging a small network of persons close to the patient. If the relationship between cohesiveness and emotional well-being is harnessed within the therapeutic context, and if the patient can come to experience closeness to the therapy network as a vehicle for well-being, then the resulting social forces can move the patient toward accepting the group's expectations as abstinence becomes the ticket to sustaining closeness.

The purpose of network therapy is to create an atmosphere that will allow an alcohol or drug abuser to experience relief from distress by participating in a cohesive social group and by moving toward a drug-free outlook. For example, after the patient has achieved an initial sobriety, network sessions often acquire a bit of a social quality. The group becomes friendly and close-knit, and stories, even jokes, may carry over from one session to the next. I had a patient once whose network members were quite inclined to help but not very interested in psychologizing about his problems. The ambience of closeness was sufficient for the network to be effective.

COGNITION

In order to act out a pattern of behavior that is clearly self-destructive, addicts must adopt a pattern of denial. This denial is supported by a variety of distorted perceptions—persecution at the hands of employers, failings of a distraught spouse, a presumed ability to control the addiction. Such a cognitive set is not only unwarranted, it is also at variance with the common sense views of those around the addict. Intimate and positive encounters with them in the network produce an inherent conflict between the addict's views and the views of network

24

members. The addict must resolve this conflict of perspectives (or cognitive dissonance)[23] to feel accepted in the group. The network therefore creates an ongoing pressure on the addict to relinquish the trappings of denial.

Typically, addicts deal with this conflict by defensive withdrawal, but if their network is properly managed, cohesive ties in the group will engage them and draw them into an alternative outlook. Gradually, they come to accept that their distress can be relieved by means of a change in attitude, as denial and rationalization are confronted in a supportive way. Over a period of time, engagement in the network allows addicts to restructure the perspective in which the addiction has been couched.

This cognitive restructuring can be achieved in a variety of cohesive networks that engage addicted people and sustain their involvement, ultimately leading them to conversion. Faith healing communities engage troubled or sick people in an alternative perception of their experiences and illness, relieving distress by introducing a new outlook on its meaning.[24] Pain or anxiety is reinterpreted by traditional healers in light of the group's world view. Illness can then be seen as a visitation from without. This gives the suffering person respite from guilt and allows for rejection of the symptom and engagement into the supportive community of family and peers. AA provides such a setting as well. The group sustains addicts' involvement, leading them to attend to the views of its members rather than dismissing them. The group's potent influence engages the patient in an alternative world view. Addiction becomes viewed as an illness, a visitation, which must be expunged. Ultimately addicts achieve a quasi-religious conversion.

For addicts, both healthy and faulty attitudes have long coexisted in conflict with each other, and the cognitive dissonance produced by these contradictions has driven them into a defensive stance, fending off any attack on this awkward balance. Yet, in a proper supportive context, a constructive view premised on abstinence and on acknowledgment of the harmful nature of drug use can emerge. Addicts can experience a conversion of sorts.

It is worthwhile considering how such a conversion takes place in the ongoing network. The therapist can establish a positive ambience in the group, and the patient experiences a social context that is actually unfamiliar. As in the twelve-step programs, he or she is now accepted rather than rejected, despite a history of being at odds with family and friends. Feelings of cohesiveness emerge among network members. The patient feels well-being rather than malaise while in the company of sober people. This, too, is unfamiliar. Confronted by a confusing

25

context, the patient is open to the introduction of a new explanatory perspective, one that will help him or her to reconcile these discrepant circumstances. For one woman, four members of her network quickly made clear that she was much more likable at social gatherings before she would begin drinking. Her inclination to present herself as a happy drunk could not sustain itself in the face of two siblings and two friends who attested to the contrary.

Attribution theory, developed by the social psychologist Fritz Heider,[25] posits the following: under confusing circumstances people are more open to the introduction of unfamiliar or previously unacceptable ideas from their social environments, as long as these ideas lend clarity to the context. They may attribute new meaning to an unfamiliar feeling when it is artfully introduced. This new meaning can resolve the uncertainty raised by a distressing or uncertain context in which they find themselves. Engagement into a new perspective is particularly effective when it is offered in a supportive group setting. Thus, in times of political turmoil, a new political philosophy can be introduced if it explains people's distress, provides an easily understood solution to their problems, and is introduced in the context of zealous social supports. Group rallies and small group encounters of supportive peers are particularly useful for such indoctrination.

In the case of the addict, such new meaning can be introduced into the support network by the therapist, who creates a mood of acceptance, even hope. Within the context of the network session, then, old defenses may be eroded and new ideas introduced as the therapist promotes a new perspective for the patient, namely: abstinence may indeed be the best option for the relief of distress and the reordering of a disrupted life.

An understanding of the nature of conversion in a large, zealous group (even a religious sect) is helpful in clarifying the way in which such transformations in attitude come about in the treatment network. In studies of zealous self-help groups (AA is an example) that I carried out with my colleagues, we found that people who came into the group context experiencing the greatest emotional distress were most open to responding to a new set of attitudes presented by the group. When engaged into a discussion where they felt supported, and thereby relieved of distress, participants could come to accept a new and initially unappealing perspective as the price of continued acceptance. In AA, strong support is offered, but the inductee must accept the perspective of abstinence in order to experience relief to its fullest.

In network therapy, the same dynamic is achieved when the therapist implicitly orchestrates attitudes within the group that are supportive and conducive to engagement. Conflicts among members that would compromise a positive view of rehabilitation and abstinence are resolved or avoided. It is therefore important to screen potential network members, in discussion with the patient, to avoid those who might undermine an appropriate consensus. For example, addicted friends are typically threatened by the patient's emerging orientation toward abstinence and tend to subvert a consensus in the network.

COERCION

Every society has methods of forcing reluctant members to comply with its norms of behavior. Formal social controls, such as those effected by the state, generally ensure compliance with legal restrictions. They are, however, less influential overall than the informal controls embodied by a community of mutual understanding, mediated by family and friends. No society can codify and enforce all the many proprieties it expects of its members.

In the case of the therapeutic network, which operates by informal controls, a variety of measures, implicitly coercive in nature, are available. Although these measures clearly do not carry the force of law, they do allow for an intervention that can force the hand of the addicted patient at times when drug use might take place. Family and friends have considerable influence to draw on, and if encouraged by participation in a socially sanctioned forum such as a professional setting, they feel more comfortable in applying that influence. Actions such as the withdrawal of affection, the expression of group disapproval, and the disruption of social interactions that are desirable to the patient can be highly coercive. More important, these steps need not actually be taken in order to enforce compliance. The threat of action may be enough, particularly when it is clear that the patient cannot avoid the network's judgment by being manipulative.

The network modality is effective in converting idle threats into effective coercion. While standing alone, network members are generally ambivalent about taking action against a substance-abusing peer because they experience sorrow, as well as anger, over the person's plight. In the network, on the other hand, the therapist converts these motives into justified action, sanctioned by a professional; potentially coercive behavior is now understood to be for the patient's own good.

Since network members also act in concert, the sum of their interventions is much greater in impact than the parts. They are now less hesitant to express disapproval over inappropriate behavior because they need not fear that others will back off when confronted by the angry, defensive alcoholic. The cooperative tone initiated by the therapist encourages mutual supportiveness and conjoint action.

It should be noted, however, that formal coercion is rarely, if ever, promoted in the network, and angry words are discouraged by the therapist as well. The prime goal of this modality is to provide support so that the patient is motivated from within to achieve abstinence. The natural response of disappointment alone has great coercive potential, given the cohesive and supportive nature of the setting. Once a balanced network has been properly established, the patient will be reluctant to invoke its disapproval.

On the other hand, it may be valuable at times for the patient to be engaged in an explicit agreement in which coercive measures are named. At a point when the patient is clear thinking and abstinent, for example, he or she may well agree to a plan that would otherwise be refused. Thus, the initially sober addict may be asked to agree to participate in an emergency network session upon the request of the therapist. If he or she later has a slip, the leverage of this agreement, when backed up by an understanding with the network, can help to ensure that the session will take place. The availability of such a device can be invaluable in pressing the addict to comply with the expectations of treatment at a crucial juncture.

Who Should Be Treated?

APPROPRIATE PATIENTS FOR NETWORK TREATMENT

Recent research suggests the importance of defining the treatment approach and setting that is most suitable for a particular patient. The form of treatment can be based on the drug of choice and the social and psychological circumstances of the patient. The problem of matching is difficult, however, since a patient can present different needs at different times. Indeed, an extensive research literature has developed around the means of matching patients to treatments.[26]

The network approach can be used to address a large variety of addicted patients and can be augmented with other modalities. With regard to the severity of addiction, however, the following criteria should be met.

1. The substance abuser should be unable to limit consumption of the drug to a reasonable or predictable level, despite repeated attempts to do so; this has been called the phenomenon of loss of control.

2. The person should also have consistently demonstrated a vulnerability to relapse to the agent of abuse; a number of attempts to stop or
to cut back should have failed. This approach is therefore not necessary
for abusers who have demonstrated the ability to set appropriate limits
on their alcohol or drug use. Such patterns of abuse (as opposed to
dependence or addiction) can be treated as psychological symptoms
with a more traditional psychotherapeutic approach, or with behaviorally oriented advice. They do not require the more restrictive model of
network therapy.

3. On the more severe end of the addiction spectrum, the network
modality cannot be used to initiate and then carry out a full course of
treatment for patients whose addiction is apparently unmanageable on
an outpatient basis, even with proper social supports. Patients excluded
in this fashion include long-term intravenous opiate addicts, alcoholics
who have not been able to stop drinking for even a brief period of time,
and addicts with unusual destabilizing circumstances, such as homeless-
ness, severe personality disorders, or psychosis.

These severely affected patients may need special supportive care,
such as inpatient detoxification, long-term residential treatment, or drug
substitution (namely, methadone maintenance). After discharge from an
inpatient facility, however, the more severely disabled patient still requires careful aftercare in order to avoid relapse, and although hospitalization typically involves engagement in a twelve-step program,
thoughtful professional follow-up is important as well. This follow-up
can take the form of network therapy, and we know that combining AA
and professional care enhances the impact of AA itself.[27] Under these
circumstances, the patient's family or network should be brought into
treatment with the therapist while the addicted person is still in the
hospital. In this way, the beginnings of a support network can be
established while the patient is still in a stable, protected setting.

THE OUTCOME OF TREATMENT

In an attempt to gain perspective on the overall effect of network
therapy, I reviewed my experience with the addicted people whom I had
treated for at least three sessions during the last twelve years. Results
of this evaluation, published in greater detail elsewhere, can be summarized here.[28]

The average age of these sixty patients was thirty-seven; most were
unmarried (63 percent), employed (72 percent), and male (77 percent).
They were dependent on a variety of agents, alcohol and cocaine (42

percent) being the most common. A smaller number were abusers of opiates, marijuana, or nicotine. The two most common types of patient were single young people dependent on cocaine or alcohol and middle-aged, married, alcoholic men.

Almost all of the patients (92 percent) were treated with a support network, rather than alone. A majority of the networks included mates (62 percent) or peers (51 percent). Parents, siblings, and children participated less often. The younger patients were more likely to have their parental families represented, although I never set up their networks without including someone of the patient's age.

Several forms of treatment were used in addition to network therapy. All the patients were seen in individual therapy. Almost a third (30 percent) went to more than ten twelve-step meetings, which was a sizable group, since alcohol was not the principal drug of abuse for many of the patients. Seven of the sixty patients were treated with antidepressants, and four of them were hospitalized because they could not maintain sobriety as outpatients.

The results of treatment were gratifying. The large majority of patients (77 percent) achieved a major or full improvement. This meant that they were abstinent or had virtually eliminated substance use, and their life circumstances were materially improved and stable. Using these criteria for improvement, patients with mild to moderate severity of drug use were more likely to achieve success than those with severe dependence (93 percent versus 61 percent). Interestingly, a patient's drug of choice was not associated with relative success, nor was regular AA attendance.

The majority of patients whose primary drug was alcohol were offered disulfiram (Antabuse), observed by a network member (sixteen of twenty-one). Disulfiram use was associated with a major or full improvement in almost all cases (fourteen of the sixteen). On the other hand, refusal to take disulfiram was typically associated with only moderate improvement (for four of six), probably because these were patients who had rejected the initial proposed treatment option. In a sense, acceptance of the proposed treatment modality is a strong predictor of a better outcome.

CHAPTER 3

Understanding Addiction

T HE CAUSES OF RELAPSE to alcoholism and drug dependence are rarely clear to the family of an addict, to the therapist, or to the addict. Yet no effective approach to addiction can be considered without some understanding of why people repeatedly revert to their destructive patterns of abuse.

Fortunately, in recent years much has been learned about this problem. Beyond the realm of conflict and motivation we can examine the particular psychological vulnerability on which addictive drugs usually act. We will also consider a model of motivation that is quite different from those used in most current psychotherapies, and we will begin to see why the therapies applied by most mental health workers fare poorly in treating the substance abuser.

What Makes a Drug Addictive?

All addictive agents have two principal characteristics: they generate craving—a desire for repeated use—and they produce discomfort when they are withdrawn.[1] With regard to the first trait, we say that an addicting drug is a reinforcer, that is to say, it produces a reaction in the central nervous system that leads the exposed person to take it more often. For example, drinking alcohol initially produces euphoria and a release of tension; caffeine produces mild stimulation, perceived in a positive way. These responses are likely to lead the user to further consumption.

By analogy, consider a classic laboratory situation: a mouse is placed in a cage where a pellet of cheese is released whenever it presses a lever. In this, we have what medical researchers call an animal model for self-administration of a reinforcing drug. Cheese for the mouse can be compared with alcohol, cocaine, or caffeine for a potential addict. Because eating the cheese produces a reinforcement, the mouse is likely to press the lever with greater frequency as time goes on. Furthermore, even if the cheese is released only occasionally, after a while the mouse will continue to press with regularity, as it has been conditioned, or trained, to do so. One might say that the mouse has come to crave pressing the lever. In this we have used an anthropomorphic term to describe the mouse's motivation, but the experiment does suggest why people continue to use drugs even after the initial rewards are long lost.

The analogy is more compelling if we imagine the mouse in its cage, separated from the lever by a grid. It will claw at the barrier, seemingly driven by the desire to do whatever it takes to repeat the action that once provided it with cheese.

This example of reinforcement can be compared with the situation presented by addictive drugs. Alcohol, for example, can produce the reward of relief from tension for a period of time, and can thereby lead a drinker to turn to it with regularity. Under the right circumstances, the drinker will begin to suffer its ill effects, and the person's life may be gravely compromised. Nonetheless, because of the reinforcing qualities of alcohol, the drinking continues; the incipient alcoholic may crave alcohol in its absence, just as the mouse was compelled to press the lever even when cheese pellets were no longer released.

These are examples of operant conditioning. An immediate response to the reinforcement in this case is much more influential in deterring behavior than a later aversive (or negative) consequence. Thus, the hangovers or job loss that take place long after the drug is used do not effectively counter the immediate positive response to the drug.

If these reinforcing properties of drugs of abuse were the only ones that affected people's addictive behavior, however, our problems with addiction would be more manageable. With proper support we might steel the addict's will to avoid drugs and successfully convey the message to stay away from them for a reasonable period of time until alternative interests emerged. In the end, everyday countervailing forces such as a spouse's anger or the desire to get a promotion at work would prevail. Our addict would remain abstinent.

What makes recovery from addictive drugs particularly problematic is their capacity to bring about a relapse to dependence long after the addicted person has become free from the drug. To understand this vulnerability we must look at the withdrawal reaction, an unpleasant state engendered by the body when addictive drugs are withdrawn after a long period of use. Withdrawal is most clearly evident after a binge of drug taking; reactions include alcoholic shakes, cocaine crashes, and heroin sweats. Withdrawal is reflected more subtly in the psychology of the addiction, however, and that psychology has important implications for recovery.

An understanding of the apparent lapse in motivation related to withdrawal will help to explain the inscrutable process of relapse. The substance abuser will forswear alcohol or drugs many times, yet a stable recovery is foiled by the many slips back to alcohol or drug use. The withdrawal model helps explain why addict, family member, and care-giver are repeatedly frustrated in their attempts to avoid a return to drugs. Traditional approaches to psychotherapy must be reconstructed to address the character of relapse.

THE PROBLEM OF RELAPSE

The problem of return to addiction is seen with all drugs of abuse, in all social classes, and in many psychological circumstances. Eddie was old enough to remember a time in the 1950s when heroin was first marketed widely in Harlem, and thus became readily available at modest cost. He was a teenager at the time, working at his first job as a shipping clerk. Like many other youths in that community he was able to get a fix of the drug on occasion; at first his work and social life suffered little apparent disruption. As the drug became more expensive and his addiction became entrenched, Eddie found that he had to resort to petty theft to sustain his habit. Eventually, his criminal activity became more flagrant and he was ultimately imprisoned a number of times. Each time he was in jail he promised himself to stay away from the drug when he was released.

I got to know Eddie while he was in treatment at our hospital years later. He was a pleasant and appealing middle-aged man. He was now stabilized on methadone maintenance and had recently begun work. His interactions with our staff and my discussion with a family member revealed no grave flaws of character that would have repeatedly led him toward a self-destructive course.

I once asked Eddie to think back to the last time he had been released from prison and had then relapsed. What had taken place to upset his commitment to abstinence? He recalled that he had been out of jail for several days and was making the effort to stay straight. One afternoon, unexpectedly, he found himself running off to find a pusher who he knew was still in the neighborhood. He realized in retrospect that this had meant a relapse to drugs, and ultimately a return to criminality and imprisonment.

Did he know whether anything of note had happened on that day? Could he remember the events immediately preceding his running off to buy heroin? He was lost in thought for a moment. "I just had gone to call my girlfriend. We were going together up to the time I was in jail, but something had come between us. I was standing in a phone booth. What she said on the phone made it clear that things were not going to hold together between us. I had a sinking feeling; I felt miserable. I just went off and got the stuff. I didn't really think about it. It was kind of automatic."

His response was in keeping with a pattern of reacting to stress that he had fallen into over his years of access to heroin, but he was not fully aware of the pattern. Eddie's relapse would have been very hard to address in a traditional therapy. An acutely depressed or anxious patient generally reacts to a disappointment with a more protracted period of dejection, one that is remembered by the patient and brought up in a session.[2] Furthermore, the patient's acting on disappointment is preceded by a decision to act. The typical distressed patient is therefore amenable to examining his or her motives in treatment. Eddie's relapse to drug taking, on the other hand, was rapid and not associated with conscious deliberation. It was not likely to have been brought up by him spontaneously in a session with a therapist.

How, then, do we understand the peculiar, refractory pattern that led to his relapse? By actively probing, we found that two circumstances that were previously associated with drug taking had happened to coincide on this occasion: Eddie's exposure to his old spot for acquiring the drug and his need to relieve a feeling of intense disappointment. In combination, these cues led to his seemingly automatic and unthinking return to drug-seeking behavior. This "collapse" in function, which is typical of the relapse to addiction, is generally not associated with weighing the consequences of the act. Furthermore, Eddie did not experience any distress as he went to buy the heroin, nor did he consider at the time that the consequences of his relapse would be much more serious than the dejection that he felt over his girlfriend. As it turned out, after shooting up on that occasion he did so again a day later; within the week he was using heroin daily and returning to his previous pattern of addiction and criminality.

Addicted people confront many different social problems, many different addictive agents, and a wide range of ongoing emotional distress. Nonetheless, they share two compelling features: they are vulnerable to a relapse to drug use with little warning, and they experience loss of control in a way that is almost mysterious. These are two clinical hallmarks of addiction. It appears that certain subjective and environmental cues precipitate these phenomena, but the uncontrollable nature of the process cannot be explained without recourse to a model that weds the biological and psychological mechanisms that underlie addiction.

CONDITIONED ABSTINENCE

To understand the problems of relapse and loss of control we can first describe them. Identification reveals that the addict must avoid those persons, places, and things that have previously led him or her to use drugs or alcohol. Members of Alcoholics Anonymous focus on the vulnerability to relapse produced by exposure to the cues previously associated with drinking. It serves as a valuable shibboleth for members of that fellowship and for other addicts as well. Similarly, AA's aphorism "one drink and you're drunk" characterizes and describes the phenomenon of loss of control.[3]

On the other hand, description is not enough. The mechanisms that underlie these phenomena, what makes them take place, must be identified if we are to understand what the addictive process really is, develop new approaches to treatment, and aid the clinician and substance abuser in developing a flexible and effective approach to addictive disease. We must go beyond a common sense appreciation of related behavior, beyond an understanding of people's usual mode of motivation as we intuitively appreciate it, and beyond distinctions between physiology and psychology. Sadly, both therapists and clinical researchers have found it difficult to make the last advance, so most addicted people encounter limited expertise in the consulting room.

One model that is important to understanding relapse is the conditioned abstinence (or conditioned withdrawal) response. This conception was originally introduced by Abraham Wikler, a physician researcher who had studied both the physiology of addiction and the puzzling behaviors of his addicted subjects.[4] Wikler worked at the federal Addiction Research Center in Lexington, Kentucky, in the decades after World War II. Narcotic antagonists used in the treatment of addiction were studied at the center. Because these drugs can displace conventional opiates like heroin and morphine from opiate receptor sites in the central nervous system, antagonists are invaluable as agents for combating overdoses. Addicts whose consciousness and vital functions have been compromised by an overdose of heroin can be treated, their lives often saved, by administrating an antagonist. The antagonist eliminates the excessive dose by occupying the body's opiate receptor sites and dislodging the excessive amount of heroin, while displaying no opiate activity of its own. Indeed, the sight of a heroin addict in coma, near death, being restored promptly to alertness by the administration of a narcotic antagonist is one of the most remarkable experiences in emergency room medicine.

Significantly, addicts who have been continuously taking opiate drugs are not only restored to a noncomatose state: the acute loss of heroin activity at the opiate receptor site can also result in their abruptly going into withdrawal, much as if they had not received a dose of heroin.

In studying the narcotic antagonist nalorphine, Wikler made a surprising observation, whose import he appreciated only later. As expected, addicts maintained on morphine could be thrown into withdrawal by the injection of a single dose of nalorphine. Wikler and his colleagues did not only administer doses of nalorphine, however: they occasionally substituted a placebo to check on the pharmacological effectiveness of the antagonist. On these occasions, they did not expect to precipitate withdrawal, since the placebo was inert, by definition. Nonetheless, the subjects would experience appreciable cramps, nausea, tearing, and even widened pupils on the placebo, just as they did with the active antagonist itself.

Wikler shrewdly observed that his patients had been conditioned by the presentation of the syringe and needle along with the antagonist. Like Pavlov's bell, these stimuli had been paired with the unconditioned stimulus, the antagonist nalorphine. With repeated trials of the nalorphine, the stimulus paired with it, namely the injection paraphernalia, could alone precipitate withdrawal. Wikler concluded that withdrawal reactions to narcotic agents could be conditioned, and he postulated that this withdrawal might even lead to relapse. When an abstinent addict is exposed to drug-related stimuli, the conditioned withdrawal reaction will prompt feelings of drug withdrawal, which the addict subjectively experiences as drug craving. This craving can then lead the addict to seek out drugs.

This model helps to explain Eddie's relapse. As he described it, he had experienced the reemergence of withdrawal feelings at the street corner where he had previously purchased drugs many times—times when he had felt in need of a fix. Similarly, Wikler's subjects experienced the emergence of withdrawal feelings in the experimental setting where they had experienced withdrawal in previous nalorphine trials. Both they and Eddie had been conditioned to experience withdrawal in response to a particular stimulus configuration, Eddie at the street corner, they in the setting where nalorphine was administered.

If the addict can gradually become conditioned to respond to a set of cues that can trigger a relapse, we ask a question: What natural responses, analogous to the salivation of Pavlov's dog, are involved? To answer, we must consider the biological nature of drugs of abuse. All such drugs have the potential for eliciting withdrawal reactions. This potential reflects the body's ability to neutralize the direct effects of these drugs by producing an adaptive, physiological response in a direction opposite to the drug's effect, a response that assures that the body will not be overwhelmed by the drug itself. That is not to say that the human body evolved to stave off cocaine, alcohol, or heroin as part of some sort of natural war on drugs. Instead, we find that the drugs that can elicit an addiction apparently tap innate homeostatic, stabilizing mechanisms in the body. These mechanisms are related to the neurotransmitters intrinsic to the body's function. Thus, alcohol and heroin, which are by and large sedative drugs, elicit in the body a natural adaptive response of excitation likely related to the GABA and endorphin neurotransmitter systems, respectively.[5] Cocaine is a stimulant, which elicits in the body an adaptive response of sedation and depression, engaging the dopaminergic and noradrenergic neurotransmitter systems.[6] These adaptive responses, which are clinically evident as withdrawal, are generally seen only when the direct effects of the drug have worn off and the body's adaptation predominates. Thus, an alcoholic develops seizures only after a long drinking binge, a cocaine addict crashes and sleeps only after a day or two of cocaine use.

How are these withdrawal phenomena conditioned so that they emerge in response to environmental cues? Consider Eddie's vulnerability to relapse. When he was first exposed to heroin as a youth, he had not yet acquired a conditioned withdrawal reaction. At that point, exposure to his street corner would have had no particular effect on his subjective or mental state. But the administration of opiates produces a contrary response. If Eddie took heroin enough times at that street corner, then his body would have generated its response in association

37

with the stimulus configuration of the street corner on many occasions. However, the response would have been masked by the direct effect of heroin at the receptor site. Ultimately, exposure to the street corner itself would produce that withdrawal response—just as exposure to the bell produced salivation in Pavlov's dog, and just as Wikler's subjects were conditioned to the nalorphine placebo. Eddie's innate homeostatic response would have become conditioned, without his knowledge, and left him vulnerable to conditioned withdrawal feelings whenever he was exposed to the associated stimulus of the street corner.

It is not yet clear whether there exist receptor sites for alcohol to allow for conditioned withdrawal in the alcoholic. We have good evidence that there are receptor sites for benzodiazepine drugs, which are cross-tolerant to alcohol; that is to say, these drugs produce effects similar to alcohol, can relieve the symptoms of alcohol withdrawal, and are addictive themselves. The benzodiazepines include such commonly used drugs as chlordiazepoxide (Librium), diazepam (Valium), and alprazolam (Xanax). There is now evidence, initially elaborated in Steven Paul's laboratory at the National Institute of Mental Health, that agents that block the benzodiazepine receptor can also block the effects of alcohol.

We have other evidence that the adaptive response to alcohol emerges in the body shortly after the onset of drinking, and not only when a person goes into frank withdrawal following a long alcohol binge. Henri Begleiter and his colleagues, for example, studied the nature of the withdrawal process as evidenced in changes in the evoked response, a measure of brain excitability, and found that the characteristic behavior of hyperactivity observed during the withdrawal period is reflected in evoked response activity in the brain soon after the beginning of a drinking episode.[7] Just as the effects of narcotic antagonists provide evidence that withdrawal is a biological response to opiates, so does this measure of brain excitation suggest an adaptive biological response to the sedative qualities of alcohol, a response that can be conditioned.

The phenomenon of conditioned abstinence has been subject to considerable investigation, and it has been further validated.[8] What is needed is an integration of this model into a practical approach to the problems that face the patient and therapist in a typical clinical encounter.[9]

"ONE DRINK AND YOU'RE DRUNK"

This AA aphorism merits further examination with regard to alcohol-ism. As discussed before, addiction to alcohol entails a vulnerability to loss of control over the quantity of alcohol consumed by an alcoholic after the first drink. For the severe alcoholic, the vulnerability is absolute; for the mild abuser, it may sometimes be overcome with careful management.[10] This loss of control can be understood by recourse to the model of conditioned abstinence that we have just examined.

The conditioned cues that most commonly precipitate drug use are those that have been immediately associated with ingestion of the drug. For the alcoholic this is the taste of liquor, the handling of the glass, and the immediate sensation of intoxication. For the heroin addict, these are the sight and manipulation of the works—the needle, syringe, and spoon used to prepare and administer the drug—as well as the initial rush after ingestion. For cigarette smokers these include the sight of the cigarette and the odor of its smoke. For crack cocaine smokers, these are the rocks and the pipe. With each repeated administration, the addicted person becomes conditioned to experience the beginnings of the withdrawal response, subjectively experienced as drug craving. The addict may preempt the craving by immediately taking the next dose of the drug.

Because of this, each exposure to the drug of abuse—each drink, each shot of heroin, each cigarette—serves as a cue to further drug ingestion. Without a first drink the alcoholic may experience no immediate compelling cue to further drinking. After that first drink, the stirrings of conditioned withdrawal have been initiated, and vulnerability to the second and the third is awakened.

The addicted person does not as a rule allow himself or herself to experience the withdrawal that may emerge in the face of such conditioned cues. Instead, a chain of behaviors unfolds in which drug seeking and ingestion take place in order to avert an uncomfortable feeling of withdrawal. Although it may be true that some persons may be exposed to an addictive agent without becoming conditioned in this way, we have little empirical data allowing us to predict the course of this process in a given individual, so that it is hard to judge just who will become addicted.

LESS WELL RECOGNIZED ADDICTIONS

Dependence on sedatives is a widespread addictive behavior, since almost all prescribed sedating drugs have a potential for addiction. One paradoxical aspect of this problem is that persons who had for years slept well without sedatives may become dependent on them once they have been prescribed for an acute problem, such as a period of anxiety related to a family crisis. Such persons may find themselves unable to fall asleep without a nighttime dose, even after the crisis has abated. They ask their physicians to prescribe these drugs on an ongoing basis. The physicians become quite uncomfortable supporting an apparently addictive habit, one that might well escalate.

Sleeping pills are reinforcers: they produce relaxation and generate a withdrawal reaction. Furthermore, they are generally administered in the same setting each night, a situation ripe for establishing a habituated craving. After some weeks, the setting where the drug is ingested becomes a cue for the conditioned abstinence syndrome, or drug craving. When the patient tries to sleep without the pill the conditioned abstinence is experienced as malaise and activation. Those responses perpetuate the insomnia, which can now be relieved only by the administration of the sedative drug each night.

The situation can become very problematic. One patient who was using increasingly large doses of sleep medication at bedtime was gruff and assertive. He owned his own business, and he was not disposed to relinquishing control over his life or his medications. He suffered from a chronic heart condition, and although he had undergone cardiac bypass surgery he was still prone to symptoms of angina. Each time he tried to skip his dose of nighttime sedative or cut back on it, the chest pains would reemerge. The anxiety he felt, which was associated with the conditioned withdrawal and lack of control over the situation, clearly precipitated his attack. This pattern was unwittingly aggravated by his wife, a physician, who would take an electrocardiogram when he felt the pain to make sure he was not having a heart attack; that only heightened his anxiety.

Nicotine addiction is one of the country's leading causes of death. Although the immediate subjective effects of nicotine are relatively subtle, it is important to remember that a one-pack-a-day smoker receives some 70,000 doses of the drug each year, administered rapidly to the brain.[11] Clearly, even mildly reinforcing qualities experienced almost immediately upon inhalation carry a remarkable potential for habituation.

Caffeine addiction also illustrates the subtle interface between conditioned craving and pharmacological withdrawal. Pharmacological withdrawal follows a decline in the actual level of the drug in the body after large amounts of it have been taken over a long period of time. It is not a conditioned response per se. Caffeine withdrawal has been demonstrated in the laboratory to occur within less than a day after terminating regular coffee use.[12] With more than 80 percent of American adults consuming caffeine,[13] this drug is easily available to its regular consumers. Nonetheless, given a period of abstinence during sleep and the associated preparation time of morning coffee, many heavy consumers of caffeine undergo malaise awaiting their morning dose. Because of this, it is hard to distinguish between pharmacological and conditioned withdrawal. On the one hand, the morning setting and arrival in the kitchen are clearly conditioned cues regularly associated with caffeine taking. On the other hand, the coffee drinker may be undergoing pharmacological withdrawal as well.

Another problematic addiction is that of eating. This is particularly true of the large portion of the American public, including 37 percent of women, that is dieting at a given time. It is both compelling and distressing that reviews of weight loss studies reveal surprisingly poor long-term outcome. Indeed, body weight variance has been shown by researchers such as Albert Stunkard to be strongly correlated with genetic predisposition.[14] Like other everyday addictions, however, food craving and overeating behavior are precipitated by conditioned cues associated with previous ingestion, such as the sight of an open refrigerator, the ambience of a restaurant, and feelings of loneliness. All these cues can precipitate eating in the unsuccessful dieter, and thus undermine a plan for weight reduction. Attempts at weight loss, however, present one unique and confounding problem that other struggles against addictive behavior do not. Because we must eat *something*, because abstinence from food is not an option, the dieter is always in the position of the alcoholic who has taken a first drink.

Preventing Relapse

Most psychotherapists assume that patients will describe their symptoms in the therapy session as they seek relief from distress. Sadly, this assumption is of limited value in treating addicted people, and will fail on two counts. The first is the outright denial that characterizes addiction. The second is the conditioned cues that lie beyond the awareness of the addicted person. The addict may at times be aware of circumstances that lead to a slip, perhaps the general context of being offered a drink or some cocaine. By the time of the next therapy session, however, the addicted patient will have long since denied or lost touch with the cues that precipitated the drug taking. The patient will talk about the consequences of the slip, attributing it to some other available cause, perhaps family or circumstances. Such a misattribution of causation is expected in the face of unexplained and unsettling experience.[15] In any case, the addict in relapse will not spontaneously offer an understanding of how the slip came about unless the cues that precipitated it were so glaring that awareness of them breaks through a cloud of forgetfulness.

A therapist must therefore be able to elicit lost or forgotten information related to a drinking relapse. The patients must be encouraged to become aware of the cues to which they are subject. To do this, therapists treating substance abusers must change the way they approach these patients and tailor their techniques to the needs of the illness. They must draw on empathy and understanding, skills they have acquired from training in psychotherapy, but they must be willing to use these skills in new ways.

To ascertain the cues that precipitate conditioned withdrawal, craving, and relapse, the therapist will have to enter into areas with no immediate, compelling emotional content for the patient. Using this approach, which I have termed guided recall,[16] the patient is asked about locations, casual companions, and seemingly unrelated events associated with the period of time when conditioned cues were first encountered. The therapist might ask, "To whom did you speak earlier that afternoon? Was there anything unusual about the call?"

Patients must understand the reasons for such probes and must be engaged in a mutual exploration. They must learn to search for associations themselves in the future, and they must be motivated to ferret out drug-related cues. Together therapist and patient will ascertain that a given stress, such as an argument, can generate conflict which in turn precipitates a drinking episode.

Often the patient needs to forget in the session, to deny the circumstances of drug use, in order to protect the addiction. The therapist must unearth the relevant details and engage the patient so as to reveal the cues that can lead to further slips. Eric, a lawyer, was initially ambivalent about abstinence. He had, however, acknowledged that his drinking was appreciably disruptive to his family, and he had agreed to stop.

In one session, after three months of treatment, he reported somewhat sheepishly, "Alice said I should tell you I had a drink the other night." We had an agreement that he would report a slip.

I commended him on his going along with the understanding: "That's really good that you can discuss it. What happened?"

"Not much, just a drink after work. It really didn't affect me." It became clear that summoning up details of the episode would fly in the face of his need to deny. We needed to know more, though.

"Where did you actually take the drink?"

"After work."

"Where, exactly?"

"My secretary gave it to me as I was leaving."

This was unexpected. It emerged that the secretary, Lana, kept a bottle in her desk, and she often had a drink at the end of the day. Before Eric had begun treatment, they would often have a moment of conversation over a few drinks before they went home. Lana was an older woman who had always watched out for his interests.

We discussed other such occasions of drinking after work in the past. It turned out this had happened once since he came for treatment as well, unreported. He acknowledged that the drinking cue was a hard one to overcome unless it was eliminated entirely. We agreed that he would ask Lana not to keep liquor in the office. The cue and the temptation would be removed. I confirmed this at our next session. Patients must be kept out of harm's way.

FOCUSING ON DRINKING CUES

From a behaviorist standpoint, it is important to extinguish the conditioned responses that lead to relapse, so that the addict's abstinence can be protected. We know from behavioral theory that an aversive stimulus can extinguish a conditioned response if it is applied repeatedly each time the response is emerging. Although the therapist cannot trail behind the alcoholic to administer a shock when the sight of a liquor bottle or a transient disappointment elicits craving, a number of aversive maneuvers can be used to extinguish the conditioned effect of drug cues. One approach, which has been used for some time in some hospitals in both the United States and Russia, is based on eliciting vomiting with apomorphine immediately after hospitalized alcoholic patients are given their favorite alcoholic beverage, usually in a naturalistic setting such as a bar.[17]

Extinction of conditioned craving is also evident in the use of disulfiram (Antabuse) in the treatment of alcoholism.[18] Disulfiram has virtually no clinical effect unless its ingestion is followed by the consumption of alcohol. In that case, it produces an extremely unpleasant, but not dangerous, reaction of headache, facial flushing, chest discomfort, and nausea. The drug has been used for several decades to aid in the treatment of alcoholism. With rare exceptions, patients who take a 250 mg pill every morning will not drink, because they are well aware of the ill consequences of consuming alcohol while the compound is in their system, on average several days. Disulfiram is particularly useful in treating alcoholics when its ingestion is monitored by a family member—as we do in network therapy. Under those circumstances, patients are not only abstinent, they also experience much less craving than those treated without disulfiram.

The apparent role of disulfiram in relation to conditioned abstinence is quite revealing. Because alcoholics are aware that grave consequences will immediately befall them if they drink, they are alerted to anticipating conditioned cues. At first they consciously attend to any that may arise; later they anticipate cues by habit. They thereby experience an aversive response to these cues when they are encountered, so that the threat of the alcohol–disulfiram reaction serves to extinguish craving and drug seeking and provides a stable basis for working in therapy to establish an alcohol-free lifestyle.

In the psychotherapy setting as well, patients must be made aware of relapse cues in order to avoid being controlled by them.[19] In this regard, the concept of cognitive labeling is useful. The impact of a conditioned stimulus can be manipulated if the stimulus is tagged with some label in the addict's mind, one that helps the person remember to avert the conditioned abstinence response. If the street-corner context that precipitates heroin craving is consciously associated with some threat, the addict can recognize it better in the future and can act to avoid that setting. If addicts are alerted to the fact that certain disappointments lead them to drink, they can become aware of the conditioned sequence and be forewarned. The goal of therapy must therefore include both making addicted people aware of the conditioned cues to which they are subject and labeling the cues in such a way that recovering addicts begin to find them aversive.

A variety of techniques employ the labeling of conditioned cues to address the vulnerability of the substance abuser to relapse. Often these are referred to under the rubric of relapse prevention. Alan Marlatt and Helen Annis, for example, have developed profiles of the kinds of cues to which a drinker may be vulnerable and have suggested procedures for training an abuser to address these cues.[20] William Miller and his associates have gone so far as to spell out techniques in a manual that can be read and applied by drinkers themselves, with little or no professional supervision.[21] Some researchers have applied the techniques in the laboratory to heroin and cocaine craving as well.[22]

The Inventory of Drinking Situations developed by Annis is an example of these structured approaches. Her questionnaire addresses groups of situations that might serve as drinking cues. Some reside in the drinker, such as unpleasant emotions and the desire to test control over alcohol. Others are interpersonal situations, such as pressure from others to drink and pleasant social occasions. Annis proposes that the patient score the relevance of each of those circumstances and that the therapist develop homework assignments to help the patient manage these situations more effectively. The inventory is a relatively easy one to use and may be helpful, particularly for a relatively inexperienced therapist for whom the concept of conditioned cues is a new one. Ultimately, however, the approach needs to be broadened to allow a therapist flexibility in dealing with the patient's own pattern of denial relative to his or her psychology. Furthermore, a therapist must deal with the patient's social rehabilitation as well.

Relapse prevention techniques based on managing conditioned cues have generally been studied in tightly structured research settings, and the approaches prescribed in these projects are not likely to appeal to therapists who use the typical open-ended format of psychotherapy. The application of the techniques will therefore probably evolve in a way similar to that of earlier approaches to behavior modification—for example, techniques for phobia treatment and systematic desensitization have been adapted for use in more established therapeutic settings.[23] Some authors have already amalgamated relapse prevention and AA philosophy.[24]

A patient who had been abstinent for two years reported that he had had a passing thought of ordering a cold beer while he was in a bar at a resort hotel the week before. He was practiced at looking out for such cues. We were able to examine the related stimuli; we focused on his past associations to drinking for relaxation and his desire to be part of a convivial drinking group.

Cues of this type are often associated with seemingly unremarkable circumstances, even though the consequences may be severe. It was some time before it became apparent that one patient's slips into cocaine use were associated with her frequenting a certain bar where she had purchased and used the drug before. Although she was generally not aware of any craving before she went to the bar, even the act of walking by later led her to seek out the drug. We spent some time reviewing the issue of her vulnerability to that bar, and we agreed that in the future she would not follow a route that took her near it.

Since conditioned cues are often related to a subjective state, they may at times be precipitated by addicts' own maladaptive behavior patterns, ones that cause them remorse. One patient experienced three major relapses to drinking, each of which led to considerable difficulty at his job. In time, it became apparent that the most compelling aspect of his turning to alcohol was the experience of an intense sense of rejection and consequent anger if he felt criticized by people on whom he depended. Even his priest's well-intentioned attempt to absolve him of the harm he had done his family was perceived as an assault on his worth as a person; that eventuated his going off to buy a drink upon leaving the church. This response was an issue that had to be examined by recourse to understanding his relationship with his parents, who were both rejecting in their own ways. What was emphasized first, however, was the recognition of this reactive pattern and the need to avert his turning to drinking when it arose.

A few more guidelines may help clarify the therapeutic use of cognitive labeling.

Early Cues

The entire sequence of conditioned cues must be elicited, as it often stretches far back in time, hours or days before the patient becomes tempted to relapse. An apparent cue may be preceded by another that is not at first apparent. For example, one recovering patient had a slip at a restaurant where she was exposed to numerous drinking cues. The stage for this had been set, however, by a disappointment in relations with her boyfriend the day before. This was not obvious at first.

First Priority

It is important to anticipate conditioned cues in detail, and then to discuss their management. Otherwise, patients may be caught unaware in the future and will be subject to an uncontrolled conditioned response of drug seeking. A woman who was considering adopting a child was deeply concerned with the process, and the issue was clearly foremost in her mind. To secure her abstinence, however, I first asked her to discuss a potential drinking situation that was coming up. I brought up drinking before dealing with the adoption, to emphasize the importance of avoiding relapse.

No Blaming

Recrimination has no place in the process of cognitive labeling, on the part of the patient, the therapist, or the family. Patients themselves, if properly motivated, will introduce aversive stimuli to aid in extinguishing conditioned clues. The therapist must therefore present to both patient and family a model of relapse that explains how the self-control of an addict is compromised by drug cues. At times I have had to work with family members in a conjoint session to help them moderate their judgmental views.

Dreams

Patients may have dreams that overtly portray fears of relapse and vulnerability. These are often revealing of cues experienced the day or two before. One abstinent patient dreamed of drinking down a bottle of vodka while feeling dread at the same time; at a party the night before he had encountered an alcoholic friend who had recently relapsed. The friend had aroused fears and temptations of relapse in him.

Multiple Modalities

Twelve-step groups such as AA and a family support program should be engaged into this broader process. No single modality in isolation can be viewed as sufficient.

CHAPTER 4

Psychopathology, Old and New

Problems That Lead to Addiction

Psychological problems may precede and contribute to the onset of alcohol or drug abuse. Obversely, substance abuse can erode the ability of a person to adapt to stress and may produce new and debilitating psychological problems. The interface between substance abuse and mental illness therefore is so complex that it is poorly addressed by the definitions currently used in the mental health field. Psychiatry often confounds rather than clarifies this interaction.

Our current nomenclature is faulty for addressing the relationship between substance abuse and psychiatric disorders.[1] One reason for this is that the system separates out the substance abuse disorders from other psychiatric problems, such as anxiety states, paranoia, and the like. This separation makes life easier for those who prepare medical nomenclature, as it avoids the confusion of complex definitions. But in relation to the way an addicted person actually experiences difficulties, it often makes little sense. The shortcomings are evident in descriptions both of discrete symptoms, such as depression and anxiety, and of the more diffuse problems of adaptation, such as antisocial or dependent personality disorders.

Consider depression, an illness based on specific psychiatric symptoms. We generally apply this diagnosis to label a primary, characteristic disorder of mood; but depression is found in many alcoholics when they

are first diagnosed. Depression may also be seen after they are detoxified. Scales for measuring depression by its symptoms have been widely
used to delineate this combined syndrome.[2] Some clinicians borrow
from the terminology of freestanding mood disorders to define alcohol-
related depression, as if the syndromes were the same. Others are
inclined to say that the alcohol-related depressive picture does not
qualify as a mood disorder in itself.

Since the depressed alcoholic and the patient with primary depression
have overlapping symptoms, opinions vary among expert psychiatrists
regarding the relationship between the two syndromes. Marc Schuckit,
for example, has tried to lend clarity to the debate by arguing for the
separate genetic and physiologic origins of the two syndromes.[3] Roger
Meyer has defined a typology of six possible relationships between
psychiatric illnesses such as depression and alcoholism.[4] Much of the
problem here has emerged from the use of a diagnostic manual designed
to describe discrete phenomena; unfortunately, reality has not tailored
itself to this system.

Most clinicians treat depressive symptoms in substance abusers in
accordance with their own philosophies. Those inclined to psychopharmacology prescribe antidepressants for their alcoholic patients after a
short period of depression, then concentrate on addressing mood-
related symptoms. Others rely more on AA or stress the need for
continuing abstinence, assuming that the depression is part of the healing process of recovery from addiction. Since the depressive feelings of
alcoholics tend to be self-limited, the ultimate resolution of symptoms
is often seen as a confirmation of the clinician's perspective.

Labeling can, however, be damaging. For example, one alcoholic
patient may barely meet the standard criteria for a major depressive
disorder while another falls short of them. Is the former suffering from
two discrete diseases and the latter from just one? Might the alcoholism
treatment of the patient diagnosed as depressive be disrupted by addressing the depression as a separate problem? Might the patient relapse
to drinking, stop going to AA meetings, then drop out of treatment
because the psychiatrist has concentrated on the mood disorder? Sadly,
yes; this is not an uncommon occurrence. A diagnostic distinction that
does not address the patient's actual problems can do more harm than
good. The best clinicians do not allow the patient's alcoholism treatment
to suffer while they are managing depression. Yet semantic distinctions
lead many clinicians to lose track of the fragility of the alcoholic's
abstinence when active, continuous attention to it is necessary.

Problems of psychiatric nomenclature are not restricted to specific symptom pictures such as depression. The mental health field has been casting about for quite some time with little success to explain the self-destructive ways in which addicts handle their lives. For the first half of this century at least, psychoanalysts were of the view that the peculiar behaviors of alcoholics were due to characteristic personality defects of early origin. Otto Fenichel wrote in 1945 in his classic work *The Psychoanalytic Theory of Neurosis:* "There are a few points that are specific for alcoholism . . . difficult family constellations created specific oral frustrations in childhood. These frustrations gave rise to oral fixations . . . [and]—more or less repressed—homosexual tendencies."[5] Fenichel bolstered this position with nineteen references to the psychoanalytic literature. History provides a cautionary note about the place of canard in explaining addiction.[6]

The *American Handbook of Psychiatry,* a major professional resource throughout the 1960s, included drug addiction under the rubric "some other character disorders," pointing out, "There is a high degree of narcissism and intense oral fixation, and diffusion of instincts may occur—giving the impression that their energy has not been sufficiently neutralized."[7] Indeed, alcohol and drug dependence were classified in the diagnostic manual of the American Psychiatric Association alongside "other personality disorders" and "sexual deviations" until its third revision in the mid-1970s.[8]

More recently, there has been a turning away from the concept of the addictive personality, in good part because of prospective studies on young people who later develop alcoholism. Mary Kammeier and her associates,[9] for example, examined the scores of students who took the Minnesota Multiphasic Personality Inventory, a standardized test of psychopathology and adaptation, when they entered college. The researchers compared those who were later hospitalized for alcoholism with those who were not. They found no remarkable differences between the two groups on their earlier profiles. Nonetheless, the lack of a distinctive profile does not mean that psychological problems do not contribute to addiction. Instead, it may mean that the relationship between the personality and addiction is complex and characteristic of a person's adaptation. What relationship should then be inferred between psychiatric problems and addiction?

There are some useful ways to understand how addicts' personalities, conflicts, and symptoms interact with their addictive problems. This interaction is based on how substance abusers cope with stress—the stress of being an addict, of individual character structure, and of the problems of life.

Genetics, social circumstances, and simple drug availability all clearly play a role in the origin of alcohol and drug abuse. Nonetheless, the observant clinician will regularly be able to identify specific psychological issues that predated the patient's addictive illness and played a role in its initiation. A well-conceived course of therapy, with the various modalities it subsumes, can then be applied to treating these problems so as to bolster a stable recovery.

Three problems in particular can contribute to the genesis of drug dependence. People can use psychoactive drugs to self-medicate for emotional distress, and repeated use can result in dependence. People may also address long-standing personality disorders by taking drugs, in an attempt to deal with conflicts that they cannot resolve more constructively in their daily lives. Unresolved problems with rebelliousness may, for example, be acted out in patterns of abuse that are unintentionally self-destructive. Finally, unmet narcissistic needs for affection or recognition may be fulfilled in the intoxicated state; alcohol can provide consolation and succor for the short term in a life that seems empty.

SELF-MEDICATION

Many painful feelings can be dispelled by drugs of abuse, at least for the short term. Alcohol can relieve anxiety and help the user forget daily tensions. Stimulants can relieve depression, and opiates can dispel all malaise as they generate a blissful and untroubled state.

The role that self-medication plays is a complex one. George Vaillant, for example, examined six major prospective studies on the origins of alcoholism and found little relationship between psychiatric difficulties in early life and the emergence of alcoholism in later years.[10] The findings appeared to demonstrate that in our society, where exposure to alcohol is normative, the potential for getting addicted need not be driven by a pathological inclination to seek out alcohol. The same would be true for exposure to heroin or cocaine in the ghetto at certain points in history, when almost all youths were likely to be presented with the opportunity for drug use. The usual stresses and disappointments of everyday life coupled with continuing exposure to the drug may lead to addiction, at least in physiologically vulnerable individuals.

We have seen a recent and startling emergence of substance abuse among persons suffering from major mental illness. The trend clearly suggests that under certain circumstances psychopathology can indeed predispose to drug dependence. This problem has reached alarming

51

proportions in the general psychiatric population. In chairing New York State's Task Force on Dual Psychiatric and Addictive Illness, I collaborated with a number of colleagues in reviewing the medical literature on this topic and surveyed psychiatric facilities across the state.[11] A remarkably high prevalence of substance abuse among general psychiatric patients was reported, 31 percent in general hospitals and 41 percent in state hospitals.

State and federal officials have only recently begun to respond to this issue. They have effectively acknowledged that many of the treatment programs for general psychiatric patients who are not designated addicts have become repositories for those with dual diagnoses. Often the hospitals are sites for active drug use and drug dealing as well. We found, in fact, that many patients persist in taking drugs that they know to exacerbate their symptoms.[12]

Conversely, psychiatric symptoms occur regularly in patients attending programs designated for drug abuse treatment, and numerous studies have shown very high rates of diagnosed psychopathology in persons being managed for alcohol and heroin addiction.[13] In one such report, for example, Edward Khantzian, who has examined the self-medication issue in detail, found that 71 percent of narcotic addicts had mood or anxiety disorders diagnosed by standard criteria.[14]

These findings illustrate the importance of determining ways in which psychiatric difficulties may antedate and even precipitate addictive disorders in certain patients. They do not, however, militate against the necessity of taking steps to secure abstinence and avoid conditioned cues. Nor do they diminish the importance of self-help groups like AA, even though these groups generally skirt the issue of psychopathology. The tools of addiction treatment are as important as ever for these patients, even though they are often ignored in conventional treatment.

The diversity of patients who fall into patterns of self-medication is illustrated by Armand. Unlike most of the diagnosed substance abusers who self-medicate, he was able to stop compulsive drinking with relative ease, and suffered no relapse on follow-up. In a sense, Armand illustrates abusive self-medication in its pure form, without an addictive diathesis. He was thirty-six and unemployed when he came for consultation for attacks of panic. He had first experienced symptoms while in college. Over the years, he had become subject to anxiety at home and become overwhelmed when he set foot outside the house.

Armand had drunk moderate amounts of alcohol from time to time in an attempt to relieve acute episodes of anxiety. As he recently embarked on one more attempt to seek employment, however, he began to drink more heavily in order to deal with the stress of transporting himself from his home to his workplace. Soon he was consuming almost a fifth of hard liquor each day. He was feeling some relief in the short term, but was racked by anxiety nonetheless. After several months his drinking and anxiety symptoms led to the end of his job, and it became apparent to him that he was "becoming an alcoholic, and headed for even worse trouble than before," as he later told me. He became increasingly worried about this possible fate and decided that he had to stop drinking, which he did successfully over the course of the next week.

From the day he stopped drinking, Armand did not take another drop of alcohol for the several years about which I got a corroborated follow-up. He did not attend AA, nor did he discuss his problem with alcohol with me very often from the time he first appeared for a consultation, three months later. Armand had been self-medicating in response to a discrete psychiatric illness, and there was a clear-cut relationship between the severity of his symptoms and his drinking behavior until he opted for abstinence. Since we know that there are differences between people in their physiological predispositions to alcohol dependence, it is not surprising that some drinkers, like Armand, might respond to long-standing distress by recourse to the heavy use of alcohol without becoming chronically dependent.

Drug use in the context of illness takes on an aversive nature, and the unpleasant connotations surrounding drug use at such times can undermine the reinforcing nature of the drug after the problem remits. A person who associates an addictive drug with a past episode of painful psychiatric illness may therefore experience the drug in a much more negative light than someone who used it to enhance a feeling of well-being. This association no doubt contributes to the very low rates of addiction among patients who have been medicated with narcotics during periods of physical illness, even for an extended time. In Armand's case, his anxiety syndrome undoubtedly imparted connotations to heavy drinking which he preferred to forget, such as the fear of losing control of his emotions.

Patients who self-medicate heavily and develop abusive patterns are not necessarily seen by psychiatrically trained professionals. For example, Fred Quitkin[15] has suggested that some addicted patients might experience an effective resolution to their substance abuse if treated with proper medication for anxiety or depression. We still await careful epidemiological studies to ascertain the prevalence of such syndromes.

PERSONALITY DISORDERS

For many substance abusers, alcohol and drugs have a straightforward value: they relieve tension or serve as a sedative. They may also acquire a symbolic and more subtle role in a person's life. Sometimes this role expresses the mythology of the society. It can reflect a quest for virility, particularly among male adolescents, or it can confer the right to abrogate accepted standards of behavior when used to justify regressed behavior or sexual intimacy. At other times, however, drug use may have a more idiosyncratic meaning for abusers, one associated with their own earlier conflicts, and hence their personality structure.

There are important implications in conceiving of substance abuse as the symbolic expression of internal conflict. For one thing, this helps explain why we have not found commonalities in the psychopathology of addicted people.[16] Addicts may repeatedly enact characteristic interpersonal games and long-term adaptive patterns[17] that serve as the means of dealing with new life situations, but these games vary greatly among individuals and reflect the diversity of human nature. Whereas discrete personality disorders have been neatly classified in our diagnostic nomenclature, perhaps too neatly, the lifelong patterns enacted by substance abusers rarely become clear without a considerable exploration of their histories. Furthermore, substance use and abuse can play a role in the adaptive patterns of the well adapted with minor character pathology as well as of the poorly adapted with full-blown personality disorders.

Behavior that gains expression through drug use can initially represent a successful means of avoiding intrapsychic conflict, and a pathological pattern may emerge only after drug use begins to lead to ill consequences of its own, often years later. Thus, an inhibited teenager who sees herself as a responsible parent surrogate may have trouble socializing with her peers, but she may be able to play the temptress at parties when she gets drunk. Only years later, after repeated reliance on this device, might she become dependent on alcohol as an adaptive tool and then find her capacity to function in daily life compromised. Such dependence may well not arise unless she has a physiological predisposition for alcoholism.

This model suggests the difficulties that a therapist confronts in attempting to move a patient toward stable abstinence. In many cases, it is necessary to address underlying conflicts which have long been part of the patient's adaptive style. The therapeutic work necessary to deal with a personality disorder then becomes important to the success of the treatment. A patient's adaptive style can also materially interfere with the therapeutic process if not addressed, and it can undermine the resolution of the substance abuse pattern. Because of this, the patient's adaptive pattern must be carefully observed, with constant attention being given to the interaction between therapist and patient.

Two research studies have clarified the value of psychotherapy in resolving conflicts associated with addiction. Therapy that provides insight into maladaptive behavior has proven itself useful relative to medication treatment and as an adjunct to addiction management. In one multicenter study, a comparison of treatment modalities conducted by Irene Elkin and her associates demonstrated the value of both interpersonally oriented and cognitively based therapies in treating depression.[18] These psychological treatments were found to be as effective as antidepressant medication on eighteen-month follow-up, and all modalities were considerably more effective than placebo treatment. This study was arguably the most carefully controlled demonstration to date of the potency of psychological intervention in effecting symptom relief, particularly because it addressed an illness often thought to be rooted in biological vulnerability. It showed that a carefully conceived psychological treatment paradigm could reshape deeply rooted symptomatic behavior as effectively as a specific biological agent.

In a second study, George Woody and his colleagues showed that psychotherapy, when used as an adjunct to methadone maintenance, can play an effective role in the rehabilitation of street heroin addicts.[19] The psychotherapy was useful in supporting improved psychological function and adaptation to work, as well as allowing for lower methadone doses, and it yielded less illicit drug use as well. Insofar as this treatment was directed at addicts' managing their personal conflicts more effectively, this study can be said to have demonstrated the utility of psychotherapy in a difficult population—persons with long histories of serious addiction and long at odds with the society around them.

The experience of one patient, Cindy, illustrates how a long-term disorder of drug abuse can reflect the acting out of earlier conflicts and how psychotherapy, if well conceived, can play a role in recovery. The severity and nature of her problems met the diagnostic criteria for antisocial personality disorder, including early truancy and running away from home, and later stealing and social instability. If she had had a greater disposition toward impulsivity and aggressiveness, her situation, bad as it was, might have been even worse. Furthermore, if she had come from a more economically and culturally disadvantaged background, her prognosis might have been more ominous.

Cindy was a thirty-three-year-old, single advertising copywriter who came to treatment because of an inhibition in her creative outside writing, an activity that she had previously pursued with success. She had been in therapy for this problem for several months, with little success. Her first therapist had been quite impressed by her childhood history of abuse and her ongoing problematic sexual behavior. Ultimately, she was referred to me by another consultant who felt that an addiction specialist might have a way to treat her "special problems" as a supposedly recovered addict.

At her first visit, Cindy described her commitment to writing fiction. She produced short stories and nonfiction pieces under pseudonyms and was successfully published. For the past two years, however, her productivity in this sphere had been declining. She had not met deadlines on commissions, and she was coming to be viewed as unreliable by publishers. Furthermore, she was beginning to have some difficulty with her copywriting at the ad agency. Her inhibition in writing had begun shortly after she had broken up with the latest in a series of live-in boyfriends. This relationship, like others before, could only be described as mutually destructive; it was characterized by bitter recrimination and drug use by both parties. Ironically, however, Cindy's poor relationships had motivated her to keep writing, as her need to put distance between herself and her boyfriend kept her at her desk. In the absence of an object for her resentment, her ability to write at home had declined.

Cindy's problematic relations with men had begun in her early teens. They reflected the acting out of a central conflict between her need for dependency and a great anger that derived from her relationship with her parents, her father in particular. He was a successful lawyer, respected in the community, but he drank heavily. In secret he was a merciless abuser of his two daughters, and to a lesser extent of his wife. Cindy and her sister were regularly beaten with the back of his hand, with his fist, or with a piece of garden hose; the bruises would be picked up by today's school officials, who are more attentive to the issue of child abuse. She was often locked in the basement for hours on end, and was more than once treated in an emergency room for a laceration. Stories of the father's brutality had been kept secret by the family, and even now they might have seemed to be fantasy when recounted if they were not fully corroborated by her older sister, whom Cindy brought to one of our sessions.

Cindy adapted to this intolerable abuse by developing a pattern of rebellious self-destructiveness, one that would serve over time to validate her angry and mistrustful feelings. She ran away from home at intervals after the age of twelve; at fifteen, she did not return. Unfortunately, this pattern also involved associating with drug-abusing members of a motorcycle gang, snorting heroin daily for a year, and breaking and entering to secure money for the group. While a teenager, Cindy also went through periods of promiscuity; she was raped on one occasion by members of her dubious circle of friends. Still, she was very bright and had a good deal of initiative. Remarkably, she found her way to college a few years after being sent to a juvenile home. She supported herself while going to school, and was graduated shortly before her twenty-sixth birthday.

Cindy's remarkable history and her troubled adaptation could have easily served as distractions from a current problem with drug abuse. When she entered treatment, though, I questioned her at length about her supposed abstinence from drugs. The theme of drug use was, in fact, closely intertwined with her current life circumstances. She would often acquire ounces of cocaine and then parcel the drug out in small amounts to a number of "trusted" clients. She had also been more actively involved in the sale of heroin some years before, and now would still host the importer, an old friend, for an evening or two while he was in town to make his sales. These dealings did not provide her much income, but they gave her the opportunity to live on the edge of danger and to act out her rebellion against duly constituted authority.

Another problem presented by Cindy's drug exposure was the possibility of relapsing to more serious drug dependence at any point. She would try out some of the drugs being dealt, and this in turn would sometimes trigger further use. It became clear that the drug involvement, as a continuing theme in her life, reflected the same anger, the same need to violate social norms, as she had expressed since youth. It also played a role in consolidating her identity as a renegade, in her losing a job two years before, and in her entering some highly compromising relationships.

I had to conduct Cindy's therapy along two principal lines, one directed at resolving the issues that had led to an inhibition in her writing and the other at assuring the stability of a drug-free adaptation. As this process was being initiated, I asked her to bring in two good friends to our third session, ones who were not drug abusers. Along with us, they would help to put the issue of her drug use into perspective. Although their role in a future network was not clear at first, the friends' contributions clarified the considerable vulnerability to relapse into drug abuse that Cindy faced, for like other substance abusers, she could not help but understate the seriousness of her problem. For example, they told of the drug subculture she was exposed to. She had attended parties with acquaintances from the arts, many of them involved in drugs, and would occasionally accept cocaine or heroin when it was offered there.

Cindy and the friends agreed that we would meet at intervals to discuss how she could extract herself from these circumstances. We further agreed that she would begin to attend Narcotics Anonymous meetings; she and I would examine what reservations she might have about these meetings in later sessions. Importantly, she saw these interventions as helpful when introduced in collaboration with her friends, and she was willing to take steps with them to reorient her problematic adaptation.

The network proved itself invaluable soon thereafter when Cindy had been exposed to drugs and had slipped. She began speaking about no longer needing treatment. I brought up the issue in a scheduled meeting with her and her network, and one member pointed out to her that this might be a time to stick with the therapy, as he knew of her having snorted heroin the week before. Cindy's friend the heroin importer had come through town. The friend reminded Cindy that she had left her last therapy after such an occasion of drug use; this was a revelation. The exchange led Cindy to reconsider her wish to "graduate" from treatment, and it was a turning point as well in her deciding to avoid compromising social events.

Cindy and I began to consider the antecedents of her problems, in particular her repressed feelings about the abuse she had experienced in childhood. Remarkably, she spoke about these experiences, as well as the delinquent activities that ensued from them, with a blandness reminiscent of the repression of Freud's nineteenth-century hysterics. She seemed almost surprised by her own recollections. Cindy had clearly lost contact with the anger and remorse that she had no doubt felt on some level in response to her childhood brutalization.

The conflicts underlying Cindy's problems had been discussed at length in a previous unsuccessful therapy while she continued to take mood-altering agents. The drugs had stabilized her self-destructive adaptation, protecting her from reality by means of repression and denial. The experience had undermined constructive change and conflict resolution in other spheres, and it damaged the alliance between her and a previous therapist. Her drug use and abuse should have been addressed from the outset.

Cindy's case also illustrates the expression of childhood conflict in drug-related antisocial behavior. It underlines how both drug-related problems and character pathology must be addressed. By showing concern over issues that Cindy raised herself, I was able to gain access to her problem of drug use, and do so promptly, even though this problem was ego-syntonic for her, that is to say, not causing her conscious distress.

The use of the social network in this situation was invaluable in providing a realistic context for the therapy. It was equally important in defusing the emotional charge of a strategic intervention so that I was not perceived as an imposing authority figure. Had Cindy's compatriots not been involved in the treatment, she would have seen me as abusive and demanding in suggesting that she give up her drug-related lifestyle, and would have reacted with unconscious anger as she had to other men and to authorities. Her friends undercut the emergence of such a transference and facilitated our addressing her problems forthrightly.

NARCISSISM

Often the drug state can initially fill an emotional void within the abuser, a void that originates early in life. This conception fits in well with the self psychology of Heinz Kohut, who emphasized the role of narcissism in normal development.[20] Disorders of narcissism, often acquired from inadequate or lost parental support, can be related to the addictive process. They can, in Kohut's words, "leave a dreadful feeling of fragmentation of the self that the addict counteracts by his addictive behavior."[21]

A lack of parental support and sustenance can generate an intense feeling of unmet need in the child; recent observations on self psychology make clear that this can take place both early and late in childhood. Ironically, alcoholic parents are often themselves responsible for such problems, as they may be absent physically or emotionally when the child needs sustenance. An alcoholic mother may regularly leave her child to eat by himself and watch television alone while she is incapacitated by her drinking. With his need for approval regularly ignored, he may grow up unable to feel secure. Such a gap can be met with the illusion of warmth and acceptance offered by the intoxicated state. In time, a person meeting these narcissistic needs through alcohol or drugs may become habituated to the intoxicated state as a source of support, and then become entrained in a pattern of conditioned alcohol-seeking behavior.

This issue is reflected in the case of one patient whose dependency on alcohol for personal fulfillment became apparent over the course of his treatment. Charles was a fifty-eight-year-old executive who came to seek help for his drinking problem largely because of pressure from his second wife, a woman twenty-five years his junior. He was isolated from intimate relationships. For almost all his waking hours he operated in his rarified corporate atmosphere, and almost all of his social engagements were related to business. His two grown children saw relatively little of him, in part because of his gruff attitude and in part because of their resentment over his divorce from their mother, which he had precipitated largely by his heavy drinking.

As I got to know him, Charles's difficulty with intimacy became clear. He described both his parents as emotionally remote, offering him little support in his youth for pursuits other than those which reflected his aggressive ambition. He had admired his father, a successful local political figure, and aspired as a child to attain his own recognition in a broader community, a mission that seemed to be the prime basis of his father's interest in him. The boy clearly achieved this goal while in high school: he graduated first in his class, and had an unusually successfully extracurricular career. He was president of the high school student body, a star athlete, and an officer in a local civic youth group. The narcissistic disorder he suffered clearly related to the fact that his value as a child was predicated on his achievements, rather than on unconditional acceptance by his parents. At one point in his therapy he bitterly observed that he would have meant little to them without his record of success. This was particularly true for his father; Charles recalled his father's coldness when his winning record at athletics was interrupted by an occasional loss.

There was an interesting parallel between the isolated state that Charles had created for himself in adulthood and the nature of his adaptation in adolescence. During his teens, despite his considerable apparent success, Charles had no close relations. He avoided social functions. His excuse was that he was "not good at social dancing"; this seemed unlikely because Charles was a talented athlete. His academic, civic, and athletic successes served as the basis for his fulfillment, apparently filling a void in his sense of self.

Upon arrival at college, Charles felt less certain of himself. Reliance on his father's approval was no longer a viable option. Comfort came instead from getting drunk at the fraternity house and being part of a group.

This issue was reflected in his current work situation as well. He was apparently outgoing and engaging at work, where he knew that relations were limited in their personal demands. He was, for example, able to engage overseas clients and maintain highly effective working relations with colleagues by phone and by occasional meetings. After these meetings, however, he would lapse into isolated drinking.

The influence I could bring to bear on Charles as he gradually eliminated occasional slips from his pattern of recovery was enhanced by his reaction to me in the therapy. It reflected two kinds of transferences, which Kohut describes in relation to treating problems of narcissism. In the first place, Charles needed an admiring audience, and to an extent found one in me, as I could reflect back his own success and therapy contributed to his sense of self-esteem. He would reveal to me at intervals the importance of his business dealings, clearly pleased with the respect I accorded them—indeed, he was very talented in his work. In addition, my own role was idealized. I was defined as an esteemed figure in my field, and he derived comfort, much as he had in earlier life with his father, knowing that his merit as a patient was reflected in mine as an expert. All this enabled him to take the risk of engaging in an expression of his own personal needs, something that he would have otherwise shunned.

How Addiction Takes Its Toll

Addiction can result in a variety of functional deficits, some caused by toxic effects of drugs and alcohol on the brain and others by compromised psychological adaptation. We will first consider alcohol's effect on the brain, which is particularly important for some patients during the initial weeks of abstinence. Because of subtle losses in intellectual function, the detoxified alcoholic may have difficulty initiating a drug-free life and adapting to the demands of treatment.

ALCOHOL AND MEMORY

Memory losses are noted primarily among the heaviest drinkers, particularly those who have been hospitalized. It is important that clinicians who treat patients coming out of short-term detoxification take care to notice their deficits and tailor the treatment accordingly. Unfortunately, many clinicians do not manage to do so, in part because these patients may not lose much verbal fluency, and in part because patients are particularly vulnerable to denying their problems at this stage of remission. Furthermore, undue emphasis has been placed in the medical field on the uncommon but flagrant severe memory loss, leaving physicians and therapists inattentive to ubiquitous but less dramatic problems.

Attempts have been made to characterize the most common forms of memory loss in recovering alcoholics. It has been demonstrated, for instance, that their ability to associate faces with names is appreciably compromised.[22] Furthermore, the capacity of hospitalized alcoholics to recall alcohol-related educational material is limited as well. This problem is worst among patients who are examined during the first week after cessation of drinking.[23] Many such patients simply do not recall well what the hospital staff tells them; the staff members assume that the material is absorbed. Memory deficits are correlated with demonstrable changes in brain structure as well, as evident in computerized tomography, where hallmarks of cerebral atrophy are found. Importantly though, considerable improvement in structural deficits is observed as early as the first month after cessation of drinking,[24] and this improvement has been shown to continue for as long as a year after the initiation of abstinence.[25]

Evidence of a protracted abstinence syndrome has long been considered relevant to the treatment of addiction. This conception was introduced by William Martin in relation to opiate addiction[26] and was elaborated as well for alcoholism.[27] The syndrome is a constellation of physiological derangements observed over the long term after withdrawal from drugs of addiction. Protracted abstinence syndrome is contrasted with the acute abstinence syndrome, which includes more evident withdrawal symptoms. The acute syndrome is thought to be associated with the low-grade malaise reported by many substance abusers long after they have stopped taking their drug. Such physiological derangements are difficult to distinguish from the many psychological consequences of stopping addictive drugs. Physiological components should therefore be kept in mind as we examine the emotional compromise suffered by addicted people. Often the effects on mood of withdrawal from drugs are erroneously ascribed to poor attitude alone.

SECONDARY DEPRESSION

Martin Keeler, an alcohol researcher, once posed the following question as the title of a study on persons hospitalized for alcohol problems: "Are all recently detoxified alcoholics depressed?"[28] Not only is depressed mood one of the most common psychological problems confronting the detoxifying substance abuser, but about half of the actively employed men and women who are alcoholic and drinking experience symptoms of depression severe enough to interfere with their functioning.[29] A conservative estimate of the portion of alcoholics who commit suicide (3 percent) is one hundred times higher than that for the general population.[30] Disappointment and regret, let alone depression, also introduce a vulnerability to relapse among addicted people who are inclined to seek relief from unhappiness in a familiar way.

Cocaine abuse, which is characterized by "crashes" after heavy continuous use, is also regularly complicated by depression. Among military veterans recently seeking psychiatric assistance, for example, 75 percent of those who had gone through cocaine withdrawal reported depression complicated by sleep disturbances and fatigue. In our own studies the large majority of persons hospitalized for problems associated with cocaine dependence had experienced depression and suicidal ideation; these two symptoms were the most frequent psychiatric ones confronted by these patients, more common than aggressive behavior or paranoia.[31] Recent evidence, in fact, suggests that chronic cocaine use may cause long-term, even permanent, damage to the regulation of neurotransmission.[32]

In light of the frequency of depressive symptoms, clinicians must regularly confront the issue of managing depression over the course of treating the substance abuser. Ron, for example, was a forty-year-old actor who had become depressed some time after he stopped a pattern of heavy and damaging drinking and bouts of cocaine use. His situation would lead some clinicians to rely on medication and others to turn to psychotherapy; some would use AA as the primary intervention, and others would see AA only as an adjunct to professional care. As Ron's experiences make clear, however, combined approaches are often important in the period following alcohol and drug use.

Over the weeks after Ron became abstinent, I noted a decline in his mood. He became increasingly sullen and captive to feelings of hopelessness. Initially, it was not clear whether Ron's depression was typical of a primary major mood disorder or merely a severe variant of the depression often seen when people achieve abstinence. The former diagnosis might suggest a more aggressive pharmacological intervention. Since Ron had begun drinking heavily in adolescence, it was not possible, based on history, to draw on a prior drug-free experience to distinguish between the two possibilities. Ron had also become quite withdrawn for periods of as much as two weeks in recent years while drinking and taking cocaine, but these withdrawals always took place after a binge. Earlier in his life, too, he had become withdrawn at times after drinking heavily.

Furthermore, Ron was living with a woman, Janet, with whom he fought bitterly. He was often cold, almost to the point of being sadistic in ignoring her. When Janet wanted attention, she would repeatedly lash out at him for ignoring her and intrude herself into his relationships with his friends. When I had seen them together she had accused Ron of being uncaring; that was understandable from her perspective, but Ron would only become more withdrawn and angry in response to her histrionics and constant criticism. I felt that if there were any relationship capable of undermining a recovery from depression, this couple had attained it. Ron, however, was emotionally dependent on his girlfriend, and he was afraid to leave her. He persisted in the relationship despite his doubts.

Ron's withdrawal from auditions and meetings with his agent was quite in keeping with his sullenness and inclination to isolate himself in the face of distress, as he had done repeatedly after bouts of drinking and rounds of cocaine use over previous years. He and I had spoken at length about his turning the corner on this compromising pattern of behavior, but the corner had not yet been turned, and withdrawal to varying degrees was both a result of and an aggravating factor in his problems for the months that we had been meeting.

After several weeks of Ron's depression and ensuing social isolation, I decided that psychotherapy and AA alone were not resolving his symptoms, and I put him on an antidepressant medication. I had hoped that he might have returned consistently to auditions and classes, as he had insisted he would; this would have offered him the opportunity for social interactions other than the damaging ones with his girlfriend. As it turned out, his response to medication as several more weeks went by was modest, even with changes in dosage and drug.

Ron's support network had been instrumental in his initial abstinence, and I thought that the group might be able to assist him in getting out of the house. For weeks of his depression, though, the group was unable to meet. Finally, in the fifth week of Ron's antidepressant regimen, two of his network members came in. With their support, Ron was moved to act. He went back to teaching an acting class, and he moved out of his apartment for a while, leaving behind his girlfriend and their destructive exchanges. Within a week he began feeling better, and his improvement held over the next month.

Ron's treatment had engaged almost all of the arrows in my quiver. We had repeatedly discussed the cognitive and psychodynamic components of his perceived helplessness, and we agreed on the need to alter his behavior and avoid a passive withdrawal whenever he felt depressed.

His network members were valuable in getting him out of the house and away from a noxious situation. It is not clear, but the medication may have helped to lift the depression. Furthermore, Ron was receiving support from fellow AA members, who reassured him that his dejected state would improve. In retrospect, I would be loathe to forgo any of the multiple modalities we had used.

Many clinicians are reluctant to involve more than the patient alone, and more than one or two modalities, in the private practice situation. This stance derives both from the medical model, in which illness is seen to be rooted in the individual, and the psychoanalytic tradition, in which patients are seen in absolute privacy and isolation. Drawing on a limited range of modalities, however, is ill advised in treating addiction.

We have been acquainted with enlisting multiple modalities in the clinic setting for some time. This approach was given conceptual strength by clinical researchers like Mansell Pattison, who examined a variety of treatment programs to ascertain which modalities were practiced and how they could best be offered in combination.[33] Similarly, George Hunt and Nathan Azrin developed community-based reinforcement techniques, which acknowledge the importance of broader social adjustment in recovery from alcoholism; they emphasized supporting the alcoholic in improved engagement in community activities.[34] It is time for office-based therapists to act more aggressively in orchestrating the many resources that are at their disposal. Being wedded to one modality or another is not helpful to the clinician or the addicted patient.

THE COLLAPSE OF PSYCHOLOGICAL DEFENSES

Perhaps the most distressing, even crippling, consequence of addiction is the way it undermines a person's capacity to employ mature psychological defenses, the adaptive skills necessary to manage and face everyday stress. A detoxified alcoholic sales representative rationalizes her long-standing failure to be promoted by blaming her product line; although she is now sober, she still externalizes responsibility rather than accepting that the problem lies within herself. A young man stops his multiple drug abuse. He had avoided intimate relations since he began using drugs in his early teens; now he complains, "All women are self-centered when you get to know them. If the right one's out there, I haven't run into her yet."

Denial, the maladaptive defense most characteristic of addictive illness, ensures that substance-abusing persons will be unaware of the quantities of drugs they have consumed, as well as of the consequences of their abuse. A hospitalized alcoholic in liver failure will say in earnest that she drinks only infrequently on social occasions and that she anticipates no trouble remaining abstinent. An alcoholic man is shocked a year after he stopped drinking when his college-age son describes the sexual advances he had repeatedly made toward the boy's female friends. Even in sobriety the father had never acknowledged to himself the existence of these distressing behaviors.

These troubling distortions arise among patients who are otherwise coherent and astute in their social judgment. Because of this pattern, clinicians have long failed to make sense of the compromised communications and fallacious histories they encounter in addiction treatment. Some ascribe the primitive defenses to emotional immaturity or alcohol's toxicity, as if somehow such labels obviate the need to understand the underlying mechanisms. To understand the addict's shifting sense of causation, we must consider the ways in which mature psychological defenses become stunted or even collapse, how reality testing and the ability to moderate emotional distress can be lost.

Persons who use an intoxicant repeatedly, for whatever purpose, will begin to introduce the drug into their daily routine at times when it helps them deal with feelings of distress. Although use of the drug may be initiated in response to peer pressure or social custom, the regular user will inevitably, if inadvertently, begin to draw on it to relieve distress. Continued use for the relief of distress is then reinforced by the pharmacological effects of the drug, since it serves as a reward for its own use. Soon habituation takes place, and conditioned withdrawal leads to drug seeking whenever distress emerges. Over time, the drug use begins to provide an alternative way to address problems. A man is habituated to drinking after work rather than trying to work out a constructive solution to his feeling rejected on the job or rather than sublimating his need for acceptance by joining his wife in preparing dinner. A teenager becomes habituated to smoking marijuana before going out with friends rather than struggling with her need to overcome the fear of appearing awkward in unfamiliar circumstances. Substance abusers become habituated to avoiding tough choices. Fueled by their dependence and an addictive agent, they forget the conflicts they have put out of mind and begin to believe their own rationalizations.

Sadly, as these patterns become generalized they are applied to a variety of life stresses. In this regard young people are particularly vulnerable. Those who began substance abuse in early adolescence regularly emerge from their addiction with the very troubling inability to cope with the major life tasks they should have mastered in their late teens and early adulthood. They are frightened by the possibility of working out conflicts over sexual and intimate relations, and they are often governed in these relationships by the need to avoid their fears of inadequacy. They have not developed a capacity to undertake school and work tasks with a sense of responsibility, having muted their fear of this challenge with continual use of drugs. They have not emerged in a constructive fashion from childlike relations with their nuclear families. They have become habituated to seeking the tension relief of the drug state when confronted with the onerous demands of emerging maturity.

Adults also experience a surprising regression in the face of day-to-day difficulties once they have come to rely on addictive agents to confront those problems. Steeped in rationalizations, they fail to deal well with the anger they feel toward their children, becoming inhibited in asserting their parental role or suffering from outbursts of temper. They shrink from the challenges of a promotion on the job if advancement threatens long-standing feelings of insecurity.

. But beyond this, people with a long history of addiction appear to buckle in the face of stress, to experience a collapse in their coping capacity when confronted with challenges or disappointments that require them to face adversity and react with deliberation. In this regard, the model of affect regression is useful, as applied to the understanding of addiction by the psychoanalyst Leon Wurmser.[35] In working closely with substance abusers, Wurmser was impressed by the total and radical transformation of feelings that they often experience, *"overwhelming feelings* of anger and rage, of shame and guilt, or boredom and emptiness, or loneliness and depression." A rapid regression into such states could serve as the onset of a transient, disabling condition that would prevent an addicted person from coping with stress. No doubt, these regressions reflect frailty in the defenses of the addicted person borne out by years of using a drug when confronted by conflict.

The collapse into such states is further compounded by a profound loss of self-esteem and a sense of hopelessness associated with the emergence of unmanageable feelings. To protect against this unpleasant state, addicts fall back on defenses that are emotionally self-protective but of limited value in dealing realistically with circumstances. They may externalize responsibility for their plight. They may undertake splitting, seeing the world in terms of good and bad, supporters and oppressors, rather than appreciating the complexity of people around them. Furthermore, they may reflexively dissociate from their feelings and lose access to them. Although such responses may seem extreme, they are regularly encountered in the treatment of addicted patients. It may be difficult for the therapist to gain access to such states, since patients must defend against confronting them because they would be vulnerable to painful feelings.

Affect regression may occur in a seemingly well adapted substance abuser. For example, I treated an alcoholic executive, an even-tempered man who prided himself on his self-control; his desire to protect his status at work had been the principal reason he had decided to stop drinking. After being abstinent for several months, he was confronted by an unexpected situation: he received a memo suggesting that he might not be given the portion of corporate stock he anticipated for his annual dividend. His self-esteem was closely tied in with his standing among his peers at work; this news, which he interpreted as a threatened loss of status, came as a disappointment. He put the memo down and left the office to get a bottle of liquor. Within minutes he was intoxicated.

I spoke with him a few days later and tried to discern how he had suffered such a reversal in his abstinence after several months. Only by means of a careful reconstruction did I learn that the drinking episode took place immediately after his reading the memo. To protect himself from his intense reaction, he had virtually lost awareness of the relationship between the two events. As we spoke further, he was finally able to recall a sudden, piercing sense of remorse and fear, with no clear limits. He realized that he had moved immediately to secure the liquor and take a drink.

This affect regression, or collapse into a primitive feeling state, reflected an acquired disability in adaptive capacity. In this case, the immediate transformation of this regressed state into drug-seeking behavior illustrates the degree to which a sudden loss of mature coping skills can take place, and the rapidity with which it can result in habitual dysfunctional behavior.

Affect regression takes place on a more global level in the chronically addicted. Lisa was a twenty-six-year-old woman whose decline into multiple drug dependence had begun in high school. On first evaluating her, I was struck by her apparent immaturity and need for constant emotional nurturance. She was distraught and demanding when not the center of attention. She had succeeded in putting together a coterie of drug users who were attentive to her and generally available. Lisa followed the Grateful Dead with them; like many youthful drug abusers, she had come to experience this rock group as a symbolic replacement for the traditional values she ignored. The group's concerts on the road had become a combination of religious pilgrimage and mobile drug supermarket for her. The scene was also a proscenium on which she could attract attention by her juvenile antics, all geared to assuring her the constant attention and seeming admiration she needed.

Lisa was continually demanding favors of her family in a way that reflected a loss of all perspective on social propriety. It was clear that if they were to be involved in her recovery, they would have to be responsive to her demands for attention and willing to reorganize their schedules in accordance with her expectations. Yet these demands did not end when she stopped her alcohol and cocaine use. Although she no longer used her father's credit card to cater occasional parties and rent limousines, as she had done while addicted, Lisa still expected unlimited access to his support. In no way was she prepared to assume responsibility for her own upkeep, certainly not to undertake constructive employment.

But throughout, Lisa was racked by fears of abandonment, and in this pattern her potential for affect regression was apparent. She suffered an intense fear of loneliness. Being alone and away from the phone produced intolerable anxiety.

It took quite a while to discern whether these deficits in adaptation reflected permanent failings in her character or whether they were the product of the drug use. Lisa's episodic petulance and fear of facing life on her own were so deeply etched into her lifestyle that it seemed unlikely that she could move toward a mature and responsible adaptation. Nonetheless, after months of sobriety, she began to shed the worst of the deficits. The terror that she felt at not having her narcissistic and dependent needs met on demand abated. She began, for example, to establish a more orderly financial relationship with her parents, rather than demanding money as the impulse for a given purchase arose.

Lisa's vulnerability to an ongoing regression in defensive style lessened as we discussed her management of threatening situations in the context of her sobriety. After several months of treatment, she began to spend time at the family's place of business to acquaint herself with its operation. At first she expected the staff to attend to her every wish. A snub by one longtime employee incurred Lisa's rage. With time, however, she began to realize the inappropriateness of her outbursts, and she understood the need to assert control over these seemingly unmanageable feelings. She trained herself to walk away in silence, a behavior she should have learned a dozen years before in the normal course of maturation. Later, she was able to deal appropriately with the offending employee, even befriend her.

Lisa had initially met the conventional diagnostic criteria for a border-line personality disorder. In light of this, her presentation and her diagnosis might well have caused confusion; that disability would not have remitted as hers did. Over time, Lisa began to acknowledge that issues that she had initially avoided confronting were in fact not so threatening and could be faced in the context of her treatment. She illustrated well that the innate potential of addicted people to adapt successfully cannot be judged on the basis of how they initially present.

PART II

NETWORK THERAPY IN ACTION

CHAPTER 5

Establishing the Network

THERAPISTS SET FORTH certain ground rules about treatment in their first encounter with a patient; they describe the format of an initial evaluation, specify the length of the sessions, and give some indication of their preferred therapeutic modalities. The first encounters will also indicate an implied agreement that is equally important in determining the nature of the ensuing treatment. Some therapists will tend to control exchanges; a clinician in this pattern will reel off a series of structured questions. Other therapists will imply that treatment will be less structured. They may begin: "Tell me what brought you here," and then allow the patient to speak at length. The patients may assume that they will be allowed to pursue issues of their choosing.

Another influence on the implied contract is the problem the patient brings to the therapeutic encounter. Problems generally encompass symptoms and personality traits that can operate independent of the patients' volition. The obsessive compulsive, the hysteric, or the victim of unmanageable marital strife will act as if driven by the problems. In a sense, the therapist opens a three-way negotiation between himself or herself, the patient, and the problem; the therapist must ensure that the undertaking is framed from the outset to achieve a positive outcome.

We now consider substance abusers upon entering treatment. We have seen so far that the addictive problem is one over which they have marginal control. Furthermore, because of the covert conditioning process and the defenses of denial and rationalization which have overtaken them, they are unable to provide a balanced picture of the way in which the disease has impinged on their behavior. Therapists must therefore establish from the outset an implicit contract in which certain controls, necessitated by the nature of the addict's presentation, are introduced. If a loosely structured encounter is allowed to continue for long, an implicit collusion between patient and therapist will allow the pathology to gain the upper hand. There will be little opportunity to place constraints on the substance abuse pattern later on. The patient who is allowed to enter treatment believing that drinking is condoned will immediately perceive the therapeutic contract as one in which this behavior is permitted. Subsequent attempts to reverse this implied understanding will be seen as a violation of the tacit agreement. The exchange that follows is typical of what may ensue when the therapist has allowed an alcoholic patient to continue drinking, having hoped that insight into his problems would lead to a remission.

The patient misses a session, and the therapist suspects that he was compromised by drinking over the weekend. She screws up her courage and tries to confront him at their next encounter. "It sounds to me like your drinking has gotten out of hand. I think we should talk about you stopping the alcohol completely."

"Not really, I was just exhausted from my last sales trip and needed to unwind over the weekend with a few drinks."

"Well, it's time to change course; I want you to think about it carefully. Next time we should talk about your going to AA."

The patient withdraws from treatment, saying to himself, "That doctor doesn't understand me; she doesn't appreciate the work pressure I'm under," or "The bills for therapy sessions are piling up too high; she said it wasn't working anyway, so why should I go?"

The patient had been inadvertently led to believe that his need to drink compulsively was being accepted. On an unconscious level, under pressure to rationalize his continued abuse, he misconstrued the therapist's initial reluctance to intervene in his drinking as a tacit acceptance of it; several more sessions without a clear agreement on abstinence had further consolidated this conclusion. He therefore reacted to the confrontation as if an understanding had been violated, and he felt betrayed. But his resentment was actually fueled by his defensiveness over continued drinking, and as a consequence he angrily summoned up a rationalization for terminating the treatment.

His therapist was surprised at the abrupt termination, but she had sensed trouble in the air. In beginning the last session, she was aware of her own hesitation to bring on a confrontation over the drinking, knowing that her patient would not be pleased when told about AA. The therapeutic alliance was therefore headed for disruption from the outset, as the drinking was never likely to get better through an airing of the patient's conflicts.

An active, strategically planned approach is necessary from the beginning of any encounter with an alcoholic or addict unable to control the abuse. Furthermore, the therapist should make clear that the addiction will be taken in hand and that the patient's initial motivation for treatment will be directed at ensuring abstinence. The patient is led to appreciate that the business of rehabilitation and restructuring of his or her life will be pursued faithfully.

The Alcoholic Couple

The first conceptual step beyond individual therapy is to introduce the patient's spouse as an integral part of treatment. The benefits of taking this step are those of network therapy with larger groups as well. Inside the therapy session, the presence of the spouse provides the therapist with support and with an ally against the patient's denial. Outside the office, the participating spouse has access to the patient's behavior. In most cases, the spouse alone cannot command the full strength of a larger network, but there are certain circumstances in which spousal involvement may suffice. Let us consider how network therapy can be initiated with the spouse and see how this approach contrasts with traditional patient treatment.

I have been teaching psychiatric residents for some years to reorient themselves to a simple network approach, one that entails a reasonably cooperative patient and spouse. The trainees in this clinical situation confront the same problems of reframing treatment as do practitioners in the mental health field as a whole.

INTRODUCING THE NETWORK CONCEPT

It is ironic that many mental health professionals go through apprenticeships in clinical care that make them less well prepared to treat the substance abuser. For example, psychiatrists begin in acute care services, where a pragmatic and assertive approach to treatment is adopted. (This approach is appropriate for managing the psychological defenses employed by addicted patients, as well.) Later, in clinics, however, they are trained to assume a more passive posture with nonpsychotic patients, letting these patients set the stage for their own therapy to an apprecia-ble extent. The psychiatric resident soon identifies with a professional stance that is less conducive to initiating treatment for addiction, and comes to consider it less desirable to take an active role in directing the patient's treatment. If the patient is coherent and is not suffering severe depression, the therapist views being directive as inelegant, even de-meaning.

In the treatment of substance abuse we cannot be certain that patients will retain their motivation to be treated, even until the initial appoint-ment. They are not like depressed people, whose symptoms drive them to appear promptly for evaluation. Alcoholics may get drunk at any time and decide they can handle the alcohol problem alone. More needs to be done from the outset to engage them. For example, the patient's spouse can be involved in an initial phone call, so that the idea of a support network is established early on. The network will be needed to secure abstinence.

Here is an illustration of how a woman might be engaged in the initial stage of her husband's therapy. After receiving a referral, I generally interview the alcoholic patient briefly over the phone to discuss his problem and to spell out the need for him to initiate treatment with a clear mind, in the absence of intoxicants. I ask him what pitfalls he might face on trying to be abstinent the day of our appointment. This question alerts him to the need to look for triggers of his drinking and introduces the idea that toughing it out on his own will not provide a solution.

Perhaps it emerges that he often has a few drinks after work, before going home. In that case I would develop an understanding with the patient that some means should be provided to secure the period be-tween the end of his workday and our evening appointment time. I ask him if he might go out to dinner with his wife that evening to keep him from going directly from the office to a bar. I suggest that his wife meet him at the office so that he will not make a detour for a drink along the way to the restaurant.

Generally, he will be agreeable, and I ask if I might speak briefly with his wife to confirm our plan. Inevitably, she will be exasperated by his long-standing alcohol problem, and therefore supportive of any reason-able attempt to help him stop drinking. The patient, his wife, and I talk together for a while on the phone, and we identify other relevant triggers for drinking. Our agreement is now reasonably well secured, and the wife will meet her husband at his office before the appointment to go out to dinner.

A number of things are accomplished in this way. We have tacitly introduced the idea that abstinence is integral to treatment of the patient. We have set the tone for her being engaged in providing assistance, and we have secured her support for the patient's being present—sober—at the first appointment. Importantly, we have introduced the idea of mutuality and support in dealing with the illness; the husband and wife are not being cast in the roles of felon and victim.

This brief exchange with a patient can be considered in terms of the three group forces described in chapter 2: cohesiveness, cognition, and coercion. Looking at the components of this exchange in these terms will expose the strategy involved in network therapy.

Cohesiveness

A patient seeking help from a therapist generally feels helpless and isolated. The substance abuser, especially, has often been the object of scorn and rejection from family, peers, and perhaps employer. Although this pain may be hidden behind a facade of bravado, it gnaws at the addict. A rejecting attitude may be projected onto the therapist in an initial encounter, as the very institution of therapy can be seen to represent the social establishment, which disapproves of substance abusers.

Whatever the history of conflict in the couple, one cannot underestimate the intensity of family ties and their potential for influence. Clearly, they exceed the strength of affiliation that a patient feels toward the therapist at the outset of treatment. The therapist begins by directing the couple's mutual behavior so as to draw on the strength of their tie and to circumvent the ambivalence the partners may feel toward each other.

The patient therefore needs to be given evidence of acceptance. In our example I took the time to query him in some detail on his situation, indicating a concern beyond the formalities of making an appointment. Drawing the patient into an exchange with his wife created a sense of community within the family for dealing with the problem of drinking, one built around helping the patient, rather than accusing him of past misdeeds. I wanted to promote cohesiveness by engaging the couple in a conjoint plan, providing them with hope for dealing with the problem through cooperative effort.

Cognition

A framework of understanding that is central to recovery has been introduced to the patient; over time, this can be made integral to the therapeutic alliance. The importance of abstinence was brought up as a prelude to the first session. Abstinence will form the basis of a later agreement, but the patient is not required to accept it as a permanent commitment at first. He need only cooperate in attempting abstinence during the day of his first appointment.

The patient is also introduced to the idea of broadening the base of support to include other people. He begins to see the possibility of deriving assistance from persons close to him in a way that is not overly threatening and that does not require him to reveal personal matters unrelated to his drinking. The telephone exchange began cognitive training to help the patient recognize triggers for drinking; the couple were asked to examine circumstances that might lead the patient to a slip on the day of his session. This technique will be used more often as therapy progresses.

Coercion

Narrowing the range of options in which the patient's behavior takes place helps to eliminate certain undesirable outcomes. It does not mean forcing constraints that the patient is unwilling to consider, nor does it mean using overt threats, except perhaps the threat of the therapist's withdrawal from treatment. An overtly coercive approach is fraught with risk, as the therapist has no authority over the patient's behavior; the therapist's principal therapeutic tools are cooperation and good will.

Nonetheless, a framework has been constructed over the course of the phone call in our example that delimits the patient's latitude to drink unabated. Denial has been undermined by bringing his wife into the phone conversation and allowing her to mention some details about his drinking that he might have otherwise neglected. She provides some insurance for his attending the initial session because she has some influence if his denial should mount before that time.

Given the framework developed on the phone, and a reasonably cooperative patient, we can turn to the first session held in the office. The session is directed at making the option of abstinence acceptable to the patient. A history must be obtained and a treatment plan formulated. Taking an open-ended psychodynamic history, however, would put the therapist at a certain disadvantage. The patient should not be allowed to set the stage by rationalizing and minimizing the problem. The patient who gets away with this will later have to defend the initial distortions in order to save face.

Having taken a brief history over the phone, corroborating the report of the referring physician, I have clarified that the man has a serious alcohol problem. A few short questions and my own observation of the patient can rule out a concomitant psychiatric or medical disorder that would require immediate attention. The patient and his wife can be approached early in treatment with the strategy in mind of creating an atmosphere of collaboration and securing the patient's commitment to abstinence. For example, he can be asked to describe briefly the circumstance of his referral, and his wife can be brought in to react. If she seems reasonably supportive, but frank, she can be allowed to express her distress over this serious problem and to describe its impact on the family. It is important to maintain an air of good feeling, but at the same time the problem should not be minimized. A consensus should be established in the consulting room that the drinking is unmanageable.

The couple can then be asked about the patient's health. Anything that can be brought in to substantiate the ill consequences of drinking will be of benefit. The wife may point out some alcohol-related health problems that the patient himself would not raise, such as hypertension, accidents, or abnormal liver chemistries. Ultimately, a formulation must be presented to argue why the patient should stop drinking.

The strategy of treatment planning cannot be uncertain; the goal of abstinence must be established with assurance, anticipating that the patient will comply. The therapist must operate with sensitivity to ensure that the exchange will lead in the right direction, getting the spouse to support the plan. The therapist must adopt an approach that he or she is comfortable presenting.

At this point I tell the couple of the failures of traditional therapy in treating alcoholism, and how many patients have relapsed and drunk over the course of long and fruitless treatments at the hands of well-meaning psychiatrists. I dredge up the tales of disgruntled alcoholics reporting at AA meetings how they had continued drinking through their therapies. I point out that I have spent a good deal of time developing a technique that is effective and that the alternative is to expose a patient to the risk of relapse and further difficulty. Furthermore, should the patient relapse, there is no assurance of a return to sobriety and stability.

Some addicted patients have come for consultation and then refused to undertake a path of abstinence. Their stories are depressing, and many suffer permanent scars of relapse before they seek help again, if they ever do. After this little lecture, I ask the wife to speak up and express her support of undertaking a definitive treatment, then move to elicit the patient's assent.

By this time, the patient is generally responsive and will usually agree to go along with abstinence. Now is the time to propose a disulfiram regimen and to describe its usefulness. I tell the patient and his wife how this medication effectively prevents drinking for at least two days after each dose, because the patient is alerted to avoid the nausea, flushing, palpitations, and dizziness of an alcohol—disulfiram reaction. A cooperative patient taking disulfiram will sustain abstinence because this potential reaction serves as a reminder whenever the vulnerability to drinking is there. After disulfiram has been taken for at least a year, abstinence is well established. The patient will then be in a position, in consultation with me, to decide whether he wants to continue with the medication or whether he feels he can remain sober without it.

The principal problem with disulfiram is that patients discontinue the medication and then start drinking a few days later; they do not combine alcohol with the medication and risk the drug interaction. Disulfiram taken at the patient's discretion therefore has a limited beneficial effect. The nature of denial is such that it can easily lead to forgetting; omitting disulfiram on one day opens the door to subsequent forgetting and then drinking.

No one can force the patient to take the pills, but he needs only two factors to ensure that he takes them. The first is his own motivation, which will persist as he remains sober on disulfiram. The second is a nonthreatening device to remind him to take his pill each day, so that he does not forget out of residual denial or some drinking trigger he encounters. I therefore arrange for him to take the pill in the morning, when he is least likely to be interested in drinking, in front of his wife. It is not her job to remind him. It is *his* job to let her see him taking the pill; the responsibility is his own. I do not want to generate any new marital conflicts by having her impose new demands on him.

I give her a list on which to write down the time she observes him taking his pill. She will bring the list to sessions when the three of us meet together, and she is to leave a message on my answering machine if he doesn't take the pill or if he drinks. The list helps her remember to observe.

I keep some disulfiram pills in the office so that I can have a new patient take the first dose during the initial session, assuming that there are no medical problems. Then the patient will not be tempted to drink the next day or to forget to start the regimen. I plan for a group phone call in a day or two to make sure that everything has gone smoothly. I ask the patient to go for a medical check-up within a few days and to attend an AA meeting before our next appointment. The three of us will meet within a week, and I may have an individual session with the patient before then.

Several aspects of the therapeutic agenda have been moved forward in the session with the patient and his wife. Cohesiveness within our small network is promoted by bringing the couple and the therapist together in a long-term mutual task that eliminates recrimination. The patient is given an active role in the treatment plan, and his wife is given the opportunity to support him in that capacity. I demonstrate concern by staying in close contact with them on the ensuing day or two, by being available by phone, and by reviewing the disulfiram list. A collaboration has been initiated.

On a cognitive level, the possibility for denial has been minimized by recourse to the wife as informant. The exchange has been framed to minimize the opportunity for the patient to elaborate on past rationalizations. The context of communication has been secured for a realistic acceptance of the severity of his drinking. Furthermore, the disulfiram that he will be taking leads him to stay alert to drinking cues. He will maintain an awareness of his vulnerability so as to avert an alcohol–disulfiram reaction.

With regard to coercion, as defined broadly, the patient's latitude for a return to drinking has been markedly limited. He was brought into this session in an abstinent state and was therefore able to take his first dose of the medication without a reaction. Although there is a mechanism to help him remember to take the disulfiram in the future, the initiative to take the pill each morning rests in his hands. It is not in the hands of his spouse. Although this distinction may seem subtle, the patient comes to know that he is engaged in a treatment that is primarily his own, and that he is not coerced by his wife. But with his compliance being monitored, he will be reasonably likely to continue to take the drug. He will become less vulnerable to the cues for alcohol use and less likely to lapse into rationalization, because he will be implicitly aware of the possibility of undergoing a reaction. Under these circumstances, I have consistently found that patients experience a marked diminution of craving for alcohol.

PROBLEM PATIENTS

On approaching a therapist, most substance abusers are willing to invest some effort in a cooperative venture, if the approach is properly explained. The patient's spouse can then be expected to be of help, and both partners can be made to appreciate that collaboration along the lines of a network format will serve their respective interests. But some couples will not cooperate. Their reluctance to participate in this approach usually stems from specific problems that must be clarified and effectively addressed. Some issues can be dealt with in a straightforward way—for example, a previous bad experience in treatment, misinformation about addiction, or the residue of arguments over the problem. Sexual issues may have to be addressed as well, such as the potency and libido problems associated with acute intoxication and with chronic heavy drinking.

Patients may balk at certain parts of the package they are offered and still participate successfully in treatment. Some are unwilling to attend AA meetings at first, but may commit to do so if they have difficulty sustaining abstinence. Others may have been abstinent for a week or two on their own; perhaps they attended AA prior to coming for treatment. These patients might be seen in network treatment alone; disulfiram may not be necessary. The patient who refuses these supports for abstinence may need a network that includes family and friends, not the spouse alone, since greater social pressure may be needed should the patient lapse into drinking.

Certain patients will resist any plan that would effectively terminate their drinking. Some present themselves for treatment with no intention of taking action; they want only to placate someone else. Others may be so dependent on alcohol that they are unable to achieve even a brief period of abstinence to begin treatment. For these patients a referral for hospitalization, typically for longer than the week needed for detoxification, will be necessary.

Between the problems that are remedied relatively easily and those that cannot be resolved at all lie a variety of situations that present the clinician with an intriguing technical challenge for initiating a collaboration with the substance abuser and spouse. The network approach offers both the conceptual challenge and the opportunity to understand addiction and its impact on the patient's life.

CONTAINING THE REBELLIOUS PATIENT

A patient's outright refusal to comply with treatment most often reflects the denial of addiction, but rebellious behavior can result as well from a character trait that operates independent of denial, and the nature of that trait may determine the viability of the treatment. Some people will balk at the imposition of any authority over them, and the therapist inevitably comes to represent such authority on two counts: by carrying the sanction of society to give instructions, and by representing the unpalatable imposition of abstinence. Tim, for example, was ornery but likable. He had spent much of his childhood and adolescence being told by his mother, "You are just like your father." Indeed, like his father, he was rebellious. He was often suspended from high school, and he had his share of encounters with the police for rowdiness while drinking. Tim had applied himself to his career as an illustrator, and by the time I saw him he had achieved considerable success. He was unwilling to operate in a corporate setting, though, and he relied on freelance work exclusively. Furthermore, a client who offended him might well be shut out. I was particularly impressed by his refusal to get a driver's license, even though he used his wife's car on city streets with some regularity.

Tim wanted to terminate his long-standing drinking pattern, which had led him to consume a quart of Scotch each day, particularly while working at home; he was motivated by the fact that his wife, Sharon, was six months pregnant with their first child. He appeared for treatment saying that he wanted to take disulfiram; in keeping with his independent nature, he had researched the medication on his own. He was willing to come to therapy each week, and at intervals with Sharon, but it rankled him to have her watch him take the drug each morning; it was not his style to conform with any regimen that was not of his own construction.

I doubted that Tim would be willing to reinstitute a treatment regimen if he were to start drinking again. It seemed clear that his recalcitrant nature would be exacerbated by the denial inherent in a relapse, and he would not likely listen to me or his wife. It seemed unwise to set up a situation in which I might have to tangle with the recalcitrant side of his personality during drinking bouts, and I felt it was necessary to secure his confirmed use of disulfiram.

He and I both stuck to our guns on the issue of disulfiram observation by Sharon, and all but came to the point of arguing over it. I sensed, however, that Tim was not inclined to walk out, as there was a certain affinity between us, and we were both committed to his recovery. I needed only to find a way to break our deadlock by changing the equation of the dispute.

I looked at Sharon. She was a proud and successful woman who had refused to marry Tim until three months into her pregnancy, and he respected her for her independence. Apparently moved more by concern for their unborn child than by her own self-interest, she turned to her husband and said, with distress in her voice, "Come on, Tim, let's give the doctor a chance. If he thinks it's what you need, you might as well give it a try."

Tim became more sheepish, perhaps realizing that it was not Sharon's nature to implore him to address her interests. He responded grudgingly that he would comply, a concession made clearly to her, not to me. In time he came to see the regimen as a reasonable part of his responsibility toward his new family.

It is important to stress that the cohesiveness inherent in his emerging family unit was central to Tim's acceptance of the regimen. Had the two of us been there alone to deliberate, there would have been little more that I could have summoned to bolster my position. As on so many occasions with families, however, a sense of mutuality, a commitment that would never be felt toward a therapist, could be elicited to move a difficult situation forward.

THE ENABLING SPOUSE

The stereotypical enabling spouse is the distraught wife who drives her drunken husband home from the party after he makes a pass at her best friend, makes excuses to his boss when he misses work the next day, and changes the sheets on their bed so he can comfortably sleep off his bottle of rum. AA and Al-Anon emphasize the need for an alcoholic to hit bottom without being buoyed up by an enabler; these groups therefore instruct this woman to stop picking up after her errant mate. In Al-Anon, in particular, she is told to develop an independent set of interests and to stop meddling in her husband's drinking problem, since her attempts to help may do more harm than good.

In the context of network therapy, on the other hand, the spouse is a vital participant in treatment. The husband or wife is therefore offered an active role in addressing the patient's drinking habits but is not responsible for maintaining the patient's abstinence or for covering up for the patient. To use the spouse in treatment it is important to understand the motivations behind enabling, so that they can be addressed from the outset. Among these are a range of most basic feelings—love, respect, fear, and shame.

Joseph was a prominent clergyman whose alcohol dependence had grown more severe in recent years. At times his drinking was evident in his slurred speech at social events, and he often became intoxicated while working in his study at night. The problem came to a head when he arrived intoxicated and almost incoherent for a scheduled sermon while he was on a speaking tour; he had to be ushered out of the church by a colleague shortly after he had mounted the podium.

When I later met with him and his wife, Patricia, I saw that she had been unable to acknowledge the growing evidence of his alcoholism because of her affection and respect for him. Such behavior was shameful in her eyes. It contrasted, in a way she could not accept, with the reverent image that she had of him. Furthermore, during the previous year she had become more actively involved in her own career, and it seemed clear to me when we spoke that she felt guilty about the possibility that her seeming "abandonment" of Joseph and their children might have contributed to his growing disability. In this couple, the wife was not likely to do more in the treatment than simply observe her husband's taking disulfiram.

Unlike Joseph, who had been rudely awakened to the implications of his alcoholism and had decided to confront his problem on his colleagues' advice, Patricia tended to minimize the problem. In fact, when he stopped taking his disulfiram and had a slip two months into the treatment, she did not report his lapse to me as she should have. She later explained that she had felt that it would be unfair to speak ill of him. She had been blinded by love and respect, which had fueled her denial of the problem.

In a situation such as this one, the denying spouse should be reminded of the importance of complying with the regimen. In a supportive way, the patient and spouse can be led to examine the triggers that led to relapse and the reasons they were inhibited in notifying the therapist of the slip. Sometimes it is comforting for a guilt-laden spouse to focus on having failed in an obligation of reporting—to take the blame.

Feelings of shame can also motivate a spouse to hide the consequences of the addict's compulsive behavior. Shame can generate denial, which in turn is protected by keeping the problem out of the treatment setting. The spouse who is blinded by shame may be unable to cooperate in a therapeutic plan that requires accepting the nature of the addiction and planning realistically to address the vulnerability it represents.

Sally came from a heavy-drinking family whose members had avoided the ravages of alcoholism, and she herself could consume several martinis without losing control when her clan gathered. Her husband, Jack, did not hold his liquor as well and, try as he might, would frequently end up intoxicated and dysfunctional at social events. He drank heavily in the evenings upon returning from work as well, and was often unavailable as a meaningful presence in the family.

We initially undertook a trial of controlled drinking, with a clear understanding on the part of the couple that Jack would move on to abstinence if he could not manage the limited drinking. Indeed, he proved unable to limit his consumption on repeated occasions, and he agreed to stop drinking. For her part, Sally proved a reluctant participant in the treatment. She pointedly let her husband know that he should be able to manage his alcohol. "What's wrong with you, anyway? You're not a vagrant," was one of her less kind reminders. She also missed many of our joint sessions. It became clear to me over time that she was embarrassed to have a family member who could not hold his liquor and who therefore could not drink with her family; appearances and status were very important to her. Indeed, Jack already had one strike against him: his origins were humbler than hers, and her family assets augmented his income to support their well-appointed household.

Jack was the object of her projective identification. That is to say, she saw in him an imperfect figure vulnerable to derision—as she feared she was. She was defensive about her own imperfections and felt humiliated by her husband's inadequacies. This resentment, grounded as it was in her long-standing character pathology, was more than I could resolve in the context of the network. Sally threatened the stability of her husband's abstinence, though, and it therefore seemed wise to have her join us at intervals to minimize her subverting the treatment. In network therapy, it is best to have access in the network to family members who present an active and unavoidable threat to the patient's stability.

THE UNLOVING SPOUSE

Some spouses have serious misgivings about their marriages— owing to the patient's substance abuse or to conflicts in the relationship—and these misgivings may present strategic problems in developing a collaborative plan. In such cases it is essential to underline the practical value of participating in the treatment in order to avoid running against the grain of a spouse's desire to maintain distance. The network is not a forum for rebuilding a spouse's character; neither is it one for reintroducing love into a spiritless marriage. Priorities must be organized around practical aid for the patient's recovery.

A fifty-two-year-old man, David, sought help for his drinking problem primarily because his wife, Samantha, did not seem to care for him;

by virtue of a remission he hoped to secure her affection. She was sixteen years his junior, and their marriage had produced five children in rapid succession. He persuaded her to come to the initial session, but she arrived twenty minutes late, citing an excuse that was not compelling. Samantha was clearly annoyed at having to be present and stated that she could not come again, as she had to tend to the children and organize after-school activities. Unlike her husband, who was stolid and graying, she was clearly youthful. She commented icily that she preferred "not to be associated with his treatment, or get too involved in his life, at that."

David had few people available as alternative network members, and I decided that it was unwise to retreat from involving Samantha, even though it would be hard to engage her support. Instead of accepting her nonparticipation, I expressed great regret that she was being compromised by the plan, having to travel a considerable distance, and stated my own appreciation that she had gone out of her way to be of help. I commended her, almost lavishly, on how valuable she was in the session, and never suggested that she was being much less than cooperative. Although it is usually the patient who has to be impressed by the importance of the network, in this case it was clear that his wife had to be convinced that she was needed to bolster the imperfect nature of her husband's therapy. I was willing to swallow my own pride to secure David's sobriety.

I gave Samantha the opportunity to clarify some of the ill consequences of her husband's alcoholic behavior at home, particularly in relation to his withdrawal from the children. This might have defined further her alienation from him, but in this case it provided her with a rationale for her effort on the children's behalf. Even though their marriage was loveless in many respects, it was likely to persist because of the brood at home, and if David achieved more stable abstinence, their own relationship would likely improve to some degree, and her motivation to participate would be greater.

I conceded that demands on her time militated against a major commitment on her part, but asked if she might not come back two weeks hence. She agreed to do so. My concessions to her anger and frustration had apparently allowed her to see another side of the issue of participating in the treatment, and the opportunity to ventilate had mollified her as well. Furthermore, she probably saw that she and the children could derive some practical benefit from David's enhanced functioning.

The therapist must construct a cognitive framework with the spouses to ensure an understanding of why the treatment will address their interests and why their efforts are justified, even though feelings may have to follow behind. In this case, the ambivalent wife had to be brought to the point of considering that she had a practical stake in cooperating.

THE THERAPIST AS ENABLER

One particularly awkward situation for managing the substance abuser arises when another therapist inadvertently serves as an enabler by allowing continued drug use on the patient's part. Ironically, the enabling therapist can inadvertently assume a role that is inaccessible and subverting. For their own reasons, such therapists can be difficult to engage into any enlightened treatment plan. The enabling therapist's status as an independent professional severely limits the consultant's latitude for constructive influence. Engaging a spouse may serve as a vehicle for rectifying the situation, since he or she may be the only countervailing force available.

The patient of the enabling therapist is generally involved in an insight-oriented therapy or psychoanalytic treatment, which has the seductive goal of getting at the "real roots" of the addiction. That therapy may well provide the patient with an understanding of certain conflicts; yet continued use of an addictive drug during treatment undermines almost any chance of meaningful change. When such patients come to me for consultation, I point out that they might have to terminate the ongoing treatment to begin one that actively addresses their addiction. This step is particularly appropriate after a long course of treatment during which alcohol or drug use has persisted. Input from a long-suffering spouse may be the only corroboration that the patient's situation has not improved over the course of treatment. The spouse's involvement may be invaluable if he or she can be encouraged to insist on more effective care.

The situation is even more awkward when a patient is referred by a therapist whose judgment I trust. At such times, I temper my approach, while clarifying the situation with the other therapist and obtaining a corroborative history from the patient and spouse together. Sometimes I recommend giving the original therapy more time, since some patients do resolve their addiction while in a traditional therapy. Unfortunately, though, we have no evidence that successful outcomes in traditional therapy are more common than success for those who decide to overcome the addiction entirely on their own.[1]

If the patient has had a relatively brief course of treatment and would like to continue with it, I might therefore suggest that the patient add AA to the current regimen; I advise the other therapist to promote AA attendance and to consider disulfiram. I recommend that the patient return for a second consultation a few months hence, in order to see whether a more focused plan is indicated.

In light of the patient's potential collusion in a therapy that can subvert abstinence, however, it is important that there be an outside source of support. I generally secure participation of the spouse to ensure that a proper follow-up is not "forgotten." If the spouse can remind an errant addict of the scheduled return to the consultant, there is effective leverage that otherwise might not exist. Clearly, it is best to fix the date of the follow-up appointment with patient and spouse at the time of the initial consultation.

We must now consider the use of a larger network in framing the patient's management, since a spouse alone rarely provides sufficient social leverage to ensure the cohesiveness, cognitive input, and coercive potential necessary to an effective therapeutic vehicle. The network's base must be broadened, since network therapy is often the only alternative to protracted hospitalization.

The Larger Network

Enlarging the membership of the network beyond the spouse alone offers a valuable range of options, in terms of both the personalities of those selected and the logistical options that are generated. The unpredictable interactions that unfold create a fascinating arena for the professional. If the patient is reasonably willing, the approach is limited largely by the therapist's imaginativeness and facility at building an effective coalition.

Why does network therapy need more than the spouse? By the time patients come for treatment, their spouse has generally lost influence, and the patients have developed rationalizations to avoid responding to their distress. Guilt is sealed over with defensiveness. The spouse is called a nag, and may be tagged the cause of the drinking, rather than its victim. Furthermore, the absence of input from outside the marriage allows the patient to claim that his or her spouse's observations emerge from some long-standing conflict in the marriage; the patient dismisses legitimate issues that the spouse raises.

For example, consider the sedation induced by benzodiazepines (like diazepam, Valium), as reported by a patient's husband, in the first interview. The patient, however, needing to rationalize her continued use of the drug, can dismiss her husband's observations. The therapist might say, "Alicia, your husband said that you sometimes sit in your chair and gaze at magazines for hours on end without turning a page."

"That was only once or twice, and it wasn't a problem."

Her husband is distressed: "Honey, that isn't so. It happens almost every night."

Sadly, Alicia dismisses her husband with an ad hominem argument. "Jack, that's easy for you to say. Where are you while I take care of the kids all day? How can you blame me for wanting time to relax at night?"

Once an issue has been framed in this way, the therapist cannot readily reverse the pattern of rationalization and the patient's way of nullifying her husband. An additional member or two in the network, however, could agree with the thrust of the therapist's and husband's position, even before Alicia has expanded on her rationalization, and prevent the situation from getting out of hand. Her friend might have interceded before the patient dismissed her husband's comment: "After all, we're all worried that you'll have an accident when you nod off while you're driving." Alternatively, the therapist might have solicited the friend's observation right off: "Were *you* ever worried about the way Alicia was acting when she seemed dazed?"

There is another problem posed by working with a spouse as sole network member. Undue burden is placed on the spouse whenever considerable initiative is needed to deal with a slip. The spouse may be unable to shoulder this burden adequately because of his or her guilt or anger, whereas other network members can provide relief from the pressure. They may offer emotional support simply by sharing a concern. Sometimes a sympathetic comment, even a glance, from a network member can balance the sense of failure felt by a spouse when the patient has spoken dismissively. A slip can be redefined as a misfortune, rather than as cause for guilt; the therapist may be reluctant to do so, for fear of alienating the patient.

The spouse presents only one type of relationship and draws on only one role in the patient's life. With more diverse interactions included in the network, and more varied personalities, the treatment will be more effective.

A friend can make constructive demands on the patient when the therapist and spouse cannot. For example, patients dependent on CNS depressants generally experience considerable difficulty in terminating their use because of the anxiety they feel on cutting their dose to zero.

This was evident with Gina, who had been taking small amounts of an opiate-based cough syrup containing hydrocodone (Hycodan) for some years. Although she took only two teaspoons on returning home from work and two more before retiring, it was clear that the actual termination of her drug use would be very difficult for her. Although Gina insisted she could "handle stopping herself," I asked that we add at least one member to the network in addition to her husband.

When it came time for her to stop the cough syrup, she developed an elaborate rationale for deferring the termination, and it was clear that I could not have circumvented this defense on my own. In addition, her husband and she had a rather tense relationship, and his influence was limited. Fortunately, her next-door neighbor, a close friend of hers, was our other network member, and she was able to gently join in our chorus. She insisted that deferring the termination would only produce more difficulties later on. The friend represented an accountability to common sense and a relationship of trust that neither the husband nor I could achieve.

OTHERS IN THE NETWORK

A variety of issues must be addressed to ensure that network members will exert meaningful influence, free from undue tension. For this reason, the therapist must pay careful attention to the patient's social context from the beginning. My experience with Cameron illustrates how a network is constructed. Cam was referred to me because his excessive and chronic cocaine use had damaged his nasal septum. He had been involved in moderate drug use while in high school, and in college he sometimes binged on cocaine on weekends. Now he was twenty-seven, and his addiction was drawing off most of his financial resources. But the magnitude of his problem was not known to his family, as he had moved away from his hometown to pursue graduate studies and take a new job. Cam did not have nearby family or long-standing friends where he now lived, except for his girlfriend, Sheila, whom he had been seeing for a year. He was at a loss to provide a roster of potential network members, but we agreed that it would be suitable for Sheila to join us in the next session.

Whenever a new member is introduced into the network, I ask the patient to review relevant aspects of the addiction to date. This recounting is essential to undercut denial; patients cannot fully convey the nature of their problem in the initial months of treatment because they need to protect their denial and to avoid compromising their image in the eyes of those close to them. Furthermore, network members themselves are rarely aware of the full scope of the problems that they will be addressing as they become collaborators in treatment. In Sheila's case, this recounting was important because she was exposed to Cam's use of cocaine to enhance their sexual relations. She had no awareness of the extent of the damage to his nasal septum, and she was unaware that his addiction had spread to daytime hours, leading him to frequent binges that compromised his studies.

The three of us considered who else might join in the network. Cam had an older sister with whom he had a good relationship, but she was unfortunately out of the country for an extended time. Although I often engage family members over a speaker phone during sessions, the remoteness of his sister made her involvement impractical. His younger brother, Todd, on the other hand, for whom he felt considerable affection, was in college ninety miles away, and he had a car. Cam was reluctant to inconvenience him, but Sheila became an ally in pointing out that his brother would undoubtedly want to help. Her contribution allowed Cam to make use of assistance that he might otherwise have been reluctant to accept.

I pressed Cameron further about whether other people who were close to him might be available. He acknowledged the concern felt for him by an older cousin in town, Terry, whom he saw every month or so. Cam feared, however, that the cousin would be disapproving and that her participation could be "like having my mother in the room." Here again, Sheila was useful. She suggested to Cam that the cousin had limited contact with his family, and although she was not a friend as such, she had been quite supportive to him on his arrival in the city.

The participation of his cousin and brother illustrates the value of having a variety of relationships entrained in the network. Terry, for example, who was fifteen years older than Cam, later infused a sense of propriety and career orientation; because I made clear that her role was to be supportive—to be available rather than to remonstrate—she tried hard to ensure that her participation was not oppressive. Cam's brother, like Sheila, carried little authority, as he was seven years younger than Cam. He did, however, elicit unambivalent affection and concern from Cam. Cam did not want to let Todd down.

This case illustrates as well the vigilance necessary in avoiding tension among potential network recruits. Early on, Cam mentioned the availability of a woman friend of his. There was little discussion of the topic, but it was clear to me that Cam's relationship with the woman left Sheila uncomfortable. I curtailed the discussion of the participation of the other woman without going into detail, realizing that Sheila's role in the group was vital and that her comfort in participating had to be protected.

Throughout our initial discussion with Sheila I did not address the dynamics of the couple's relationship in any depth. Although the therapist must use a keen eye in evaluating relations in the network, members are not exposed to a therapeutic discussion of interpersonal process or conflicts. Dealing with such issues can create agendas that conflict with the development of a team spirit, and if such issues do arise they should be addressed with the goal of support rather than relational change. In this respect, network therapy is quite different from family systems therapy, and it is easier for the nonspecialist to apply.

The here-and-now approach used to promote intimate interchanges in group therapy has little place in the network.[2] It has been well demonstrated that opening up intense interpersonal reactions and conflicts can be invaluable as part of the long-term management of personality defects in group treatment. The pragmatic work of dealing with alcoholic denial and the alliance building necessary in network therapy, however, have to leave issues like these unstated. Network members do not have the opportunity to explore interpersonal process in depth, nor can they achieve resolution of the issues that might be raised, since they meet at infrequent intervals and have another agenda, namely, supporting the patient's abstinence. Instead, the therapist must develop a feeling of congeniality and cooperativeness, relying on his or her acquired skills to promote constructive relationships in a task-oriented setting.

As we were establishing the network, I called Cameron's brother on the phone during a meeting with Cam and Sheila, and I was able to reach him and secure his agreement to join us a week later. Cameron and Sheila also agreed to contact his cousin to see whether she could be at our next meeting, the following Monday. Cam, Sheila, and I had worked out a plan to remove him in the interim from sources of cocaine—the couple would spend the weekend in the country.

At the third session, Cameron undertook the difficult task of informing his cousin of the circumstances surrounding his addiction, with active support from me. I set the stage by underlining the nature of addiction as a disease and describing the inability of persons who were dependent on a drug to limit their consumption. I had the responsibility to ensure that the cousin's participation would be supportive, and I took this responsibility seriously. At a few points during Cameron's presentation, when it appeared that his cousin was puzzled or distressed, I again put his experience in a context that would both relieve her displeasure and focus her attention on her role as a collaborator in a partnership, rather than as a member of a tribunal.

To bolster the emerging relationships, I called Cam's brother again in his dorm room during this session, and we informed him of what we had discussed. I also secured an agreement with Cam that the network members could contact me if they had any concern about his welfare, and that I could be in touch with them. Such an understanding can be invaluable if the patient has a slip.

On a number of occasions Cameron might well have abandoned me and the therapy if the others had not been there to keep him engaged. He had two minor slips over the course of the first few months; he discussed them with Sheila at home shortly after they occurred, and they met with the network and dealt with the associated circumstances. Reporting to the network was important in helping Cameron stay abstinent.

Cameron's situation did call for intervention in one of the relationships. There was a good measure of sadomasochism in the relationship between Cameron and Sheila, and he took a certain pleasure in foisting his distress on her when he felt a craving for drugs, as he did regularly. For example, he would make her feel that she had to help him out but that she could not do anything concrete. "Sheila, I don't know if I'm going to make it through the day today. . . . No, there's really nothing you can do."

I discussed the issue with Cam, but there remained a continuing pressure on Sheila that might well destabilize her role in the network. Finally I had the three of us meet alone to discuss the style of Cam and Sheila's interaction. This was as close as I would likely come to dealing with interpersonal conflicts in the network on a psychological level. The discussion was not as subtle as the psychoanalytic exchange: "Cam, I think you're driving Sheila nuts," I said to put the problem in context for Sheila. To Sheila I said, "You have to understand that he's letting off steam. Be supportive, but don't feel you have to resolve his feelings for him."

Recruitment Problems

Sometimes it takes sacrifice to include an important member of the patient's social constellation. At other times, a loss of support may be accepted so that the balance within the network is not compromised.

The following examples illustrate how such decisions are made and describe some of the problems raised by players on the emerging team.

TROUBLE WITH PARENTS

Parental divorce commonly raises issues regarding a patient's family. Yet the divorce does not have to dictate the makeup of the network; it may even yield a certain latitude in the selection of network members. Richard, for example, was only twenty when he came for treatment, and it seemed natural to consider a role for his parents in the therapy. He was in active rebellion against them, though, and it became clear as we spoke that much of his involvement in drugs had arisen from a need to assert his separateness in a way that would both anger and frustrate them. His parents were divorced and both had remarried. When I pressed him to consider the participation of some members of the parental generation, he chose to include the new spouses. Although it was obvious that this would be quite unsettling to his parents, I agreed to go along with his choice; he knew that the stepparents were not hostile toward each other. Furthermore, he agreed that at some point we would be in contact with his natural parents as well. The stepparents, along with one of Richard's sober friends and a cousin, worked out well and constituted a stable group. Because his congenial relationship with them was not troubled by the ambivalence that he felt toward his natural parents, he could discuss his addiction comfortably in their presence.

Furthermore, the possibility of conflict between the various parental figures was muted because the focus in network sessions is always kept on the patient's rehabilitation and welfare. If there is potential competition between members, it is translated into a desire to appear supportive and to play the role of a good member. Because of this, certain tensions within the group can actually operate to enhance the network's function as a therapeutic instrument. Offers of emotional support and social assistance, as well as promptness in participation, all give expression to members' need to be seen as constructive.

Some young adult patients find it highly unpalatable to include their parents in their network. This view must be respected, but it can pose problems when parents are paying for therapy. There is considerable risk in having no ongoing contact with the parents in such a case. Since the patient's ambivalence can emerge more openly during the course of treatment, leading him or her to become more isolated from parents or display hostility toward them, they may come to see the therapy as undermining their relationship with their child. Withdrawal of financial

95

support for the therapy, if nothing else, can become a serious threat to ongoing treatment. It is therefore important that some precedent for communication between therapist and parents be established. This can take the form of one or two conjoint sessions with the parents once the therapy has been well established.

LOVERS

A lover, particularly one who lives with the patient, is a natural candidate for membership in the network. Unfortunately, though, such relationships are often unstable. The lover's participation may be valuable at the outset of treatment, but the severance of a relationship can be quite disruptive later on and can destabilize the network and its role as a bulwark of abstinence. I am therefore reluctant to include boyfriends or girlfriends whose relationship with the patient does not have a reasonable longevity as well as apparently good prospects for continuation.

Another issue arises with such network members. It is unfair to place a weighty burden on someone whose interests may later be compromised. The problem arises particularly for the young woman who puts herself out to help an addicted boyfriend whose sociopathic inclinations allow him to violate her trust without qualm. Even if the woman is willing to participate at considerable sacrifice, the therapist must be cautious not to allow her to suffer abuse by virtue of her desire to see the relationship succeed. I have encountered a number of male patients who seem to experience much less remorse at abandoning or betraying a faithful girlfriend than I did in hosting the network sessions while they did so. Such circumstances raise the issue of the therapist's responsibility to network members. Although network members are not patients, they respond to the therapist as a professional in whom they place their trust. Yet many addicts readily disappoint those who trust them.

One patient of mine was quite accomplished and apparently respectable, but he had sociopathic traits that complemented his heavy drug abuse habit. His girlfriend participated faithfully in his treatment for some months, along with two of his friends, while he continued to avoid fully commiting to our plan. Her commitment to him was heartfelt, and she remained faithful when he had to go for long-term residential treatment in a remote state, followed by a move to a halfway house there for several months. She was in therapy herself throughout this period, and she knew that it was not advisable to give up an independent social life—and she was reluctant to embark on new relationships. But I was troubled by the compromises that she had made in her own life, and I wondered what part I might have played in initiating her potentially self-destructive course of action. I was not sure that the patient would ever reciprocate the earnest commitment his lover had made to him.

DRUG ABUSERS IN THE NETWORK

Given the role of the network in securing patient compliance, the inclusion of members who are substance abusers is inevitably destructive. Their identification with patients' drug dependence often leads them to undermine a suggested treatment approach and to compromise attempts to avoid or respond to slips. Patients should therefore be queried in detail to ensure that the people they suggest as network members do not have alcohol or drug problems.

Sometimes network members' substance abuse is not apparent to the patient. In the case of Betsy, it was not possible to include only family or close friends in the network. One member, Alice, was surprisingly noncompliant as we discussed the proposed treatment plan in our first network meeting. Betsy had been snorting heroin and cocaine for many years, and it was clear to me that she would have to undergo observed urinalyses to detect a relapse. All members but Alice concurred with this option; she insisted that these urinalyses would be an infringement on Betsy's rights and would be dehumanizing, whatever the intended benefit. The issue was discussed at some length in the group, and the dissenting member was effectively overruled, although she had shaken Betsy's commitment for a time; she clearly would have been more agreeable had Alice not put her opinion forth so aggressively. The dissenter was absent at the next meeting, and I was relieved that she did not appear again. Some time later, it emerged that she had been snorting cocaine regularly herself and had recently suffered a major decline in function.

ANGRY MEMBERS

Some participants' intense anger compromises their ability to feel compassion for the patient and to follow an agreed-upon course of action. If it is evident from the outset that a potential member presents such a problem, it is wise to offer the option of withdrawing. Unfortunately, though, the anger often does not emerge at its worst until it has been provoked by some difficulty the patient experiences with relapse—at such a time the anger is most disruptive.

97

One network member, the brother-in-law of a patient, was clearly tense and angry from the outset of treatment. His own rigidity and demanding nature led him to insist on helping but also made him intolerant of the patient's "weakness" in having become addicted. To be helpful, he offered the patient an opportunity to sleep over at his office, to help him avoid exposure to the threat of drugs. Unfortunately, the patient was unable to live up to his agreement to remain abstinent, and he arrived intoxicated at his brother-in-law's office. Despite my attempts to convey the uncontrollable nature of the addiction to the brother-in-law, he was unable to contain his anger in the ensuing sessions, and he became abusive of his troubled relative more than once. I realized that his departure from the network would be for the best, particularly since the patient was unable to draw a useful lesson from these exchanges. I spoke with the patient, then explained the situation to the brother-in-law on the phone. He was glad to leave.

Another patient agreed to see me for her drinking problem when her brother joined forces with their mother to initiate the treatment. The brother had always been ashamed of the patient. She had never married and was something of an eccentric, and his distaste and resentment were amply apparent when we met. Some time later the patient experienced difficulties in maintaining her abstinence; her brother refused to continue attending, having confirmed his bias that the patient could not attain a recovery and achieve the respectability he wanted. We added two sober friends of the patient to her network in place of the brother, and they were not only more sympathetic to her plight but also more accepting of her lifestyle.

From these situations, it becomes apparent that some close relations should be allowed to feel that they can support the patient's effort without being part of the network. It is useful for the therapist to wait before deciding which parties should become members of the group. Although it requires some finesse, it is possible to sign up certain network members while offering others who attend the initial meetings the option for bowing out with an excuse that allows them to avoid feeling guilty or embarrassed about appearing to abandon a close relation.

Unwilling Patients

The most tenuous of networks is typically initiated by a call from someone seeking help for an addicted friend or relative. The fact that the patient has not made the call means that he or she has not taken the initiative to make a limited first step to deal with the problem. Under these circumstances I always suggest that the caller encourage the patient to call me so that the patient can assert some ownership in the treatment process. If the friend or relative believes that the patient is unwilling to call me, I will ask that a larger network come to the initial interview to discuss the patient's problem. Reliance on a spouse, for example, to draw an alcoholic into treatment under these circumstances represents a problem beyond one of noncompliance. It gives the alcoholic an opportunity to refuse the option of bringing in family and friends, thereby paralyzing the initiation of a network that would be necessary to introduce both supportive and coercive measures.

This lesson was made clear when I was misled by George's initial description to underestimate the resistance that would be offered by his wife. George was thoughtful, lucid, and caring, and his wife was a woman who had apparently faced adversity in an admirable manner and had gone on to pursue career training despite medical disabilities. She had become addicted to opiates after several surgical procedures that had left her in chronic pain. I asked George to bring her in, only to find out after two sessions that she would not cooperate in relinquishing her covert sources of medication; nor would she consider a course that would lead to abstinence, even with appropriate management of her pain by an expert in the field. Thanks to my strategic error, she was able to say that she did not want her husband to communicate with two family friends who would have been invaluable in framing a therapeutic network. She said further that she was not interested in coming any more. Her husband now felt that he could no longer approach the friends and ask them to meet with us, since his wife expressly told him not to bring them in.

Sadly, the threat to this woman's dependence on her drugs had generated a paranoia and secretiveness on her part that led her to refuse consultation from an expert in pain medication, to assert destructive control over the therapeutic context, and to render me without leverage in my attempt to initiate treatment. George alone was not prepared to take further action.

To address circumstances like these, Vernon Johnson developed an intervention technique which has been widely disseminated by the Johnson Institute, an addiction treatment and training center in Minneapolis.[3] This approach begins when friends or family solicit assistance for an addict who has refused help. The therapist, who is trained in framing an intervention, assembles a group close to the patient and interviews members in depth with regard to their understanding of the patient's disability. Over some sessions, they are trained to confront the patient with their objective observations of the consequences of his or her addictive illness. A time is set to bring the patient to an office, unaware that a confrontation is coming. With the support of the therapist, each group member tells the patient what they have seen of the problem. The patient is told that he or she must either enter the hospital for treatment or suffer withdrawal of the group's support and involvement. The alternative to treatment may be abandonment by the spouse or some other highly coercive measure. The object is to make avoidance of treatment so unpalatable that the addicted person will relent and enter a rehabilitation facility.

The technique has achieved some popularity, largely because it does not allow the patient to define the terms of an initial encounter so as to avoid treatment. The confrontation inherent in this intervention approach is explicit and pointed, but supportive as well, so that it is difficult for the patient to rationalize away the material with which he or she is confronted. Furthermore, the entire undertaking is coupled with the immediate availability of hospitalization that will sequester the patient for an extended period, so that the reemergence of denial will not lead the patient to go off to buy liquor or drugs.

Coercive techniques can be troubling, though, because of the risk inherent in framing a cataclysmic consequence as an alternative to treatment. The outcome of addiction treatment is never certain, and substance abusers are frequently depressed, often more so than their family members are aware. They may respond with self-destructive behavior in ways that are not anticipated beforehand. Furthermore, techniques that threaten the continuity of marital ties are very problematic: marriages may be much more positive than is apparent when addiction is at its worst. For this reason I have always tried to frame interventions that avoid the threat of an outright disruption in family relations. Even so, in some cases coercive pressure may be necessary to initiate treatment.

A CASE OF ARM TWISTING

Patients can be drawn into a modified intervention approach by relying on the natural affiliative feelings in a patient's family, even when coercion suitable to the circumstances is applied. As we shall see in Andrew's case, financial pressure was used. Coercive pressure was important here at the outset so that the patient's denial of his illness could be gradually undermined, ultimately allowing him to recognize the need for abstinence.

The First Week

Mindy came to my office as an emissary for her family. She reported that they needed help with her thirty-two-year-old brother, Andrew. He was a partner in the family's importing business and a part-time jazz musician who had been using cocaine heavily for some years. She did not think the drug had compromised him seriously until recently, but for the last four months he had retreated to his apartment for days on cocaine binges. At these times, his main communication with the outside world was to call nearby grocers and liquor stores for supplies. Mindy thought that he had begun going downhill six months before, after his girlfriend moved out on him and his jazz quartet broke up. We later found out that both events took place because of his cocaine use.

I asked about his background, and Mindy explained that Andrew had always been interested in a career in music. He was ambivalent about his involvement in the family business. He had completed business school largely at the urging of his parents, while he was also playing jazz professionally. I went over the family membership with her and asked her to bring in her husband, father, and brother, and to invite Andrew as well.

The Second Week

Mindy brought the family members in as requested, but Andrew said he could not make the appointment. We knew his calendar was empty. All present were involved to some degree in the family business, but the father, an overbearing man and a widower, held the pursestrings. All had hoped that Andrew would keep the family enterprise operating success-fully because of his natural enthusiasm and talents. Although he had been playing a valuable part in the business until several months before, he had recently become a poor candidate for this role. I thought to myself that Andrew had found a way to avenge his father's oppressive-ness, but I did not voice this opinion. Strategy, not psychodynamics, was most relevant here.

We examined carefully what leverage the group had to get Andrew to participate, but there was little in the way of personal pleas or concern for the business that he had not recently dismissed. In the absence of a clear alternative, I proposed that his father be prepared to limit Andrew's access to financial resources, and discussed with the group how this might be carried out. They were willing to consider the option, and were relieved that a professional could develop with them some means to force their troubled family member out of his seclusion.

Mindy and her husband were apparently on the best terms with Andrew, so I suggested that they meet with him and tell him that the family had consulted with a doctor who was prepared to speak with him and help him out. We chose a specific appointment time they would propose to him. They could explain further that if he were unwilling to come in and talk, the family was prepared to limit the support that had allowed him to seclude himself as he had. If appropriate, my emissaries could make clear some of the particulars we had discussed, such as suspending credit cards and cash remittances.

As we finished the session, I was concerned about the father's role. He was a mercurial man, and very angry at his son. He was assertive enough to back up the intervention, but he had long interfered in Andrew's life, and he might yet be a wild card in trying to move the plan forward.

Two days later, Mindy called to say that Andrew had agreed to come in. She and her husband were apparently able to convey the message without being overbearing. Andrew showed up at the appointed time and seemed willing to get help for his "depression." Although he acknowledged occasional use of cocaine, he denied that it was a problem. He did indeed appear unhappy, perhaps having recently crashed from cocaine. He said further that he would be willing to meet me for sessions, and agreed to get together with the family as well, but would in no way consider going into a hospital. I was pleased that he had a diffuse appreciation that he needed help, even if he was in denial of his addiction.

The Third Week

The whole family came in with Andrew, and he said he was willing to see me. He still insisted that he could easily stop his "slight" cocaine use. On the basis of previous discussions we worked out a plan: Andrew would come to sessions twice weekly, sometimes with the family, and would go for observed urinalysis twice a week as well, in order to demonstrate that he had stopped using the cocaine. The family would continue paying Andrew's rent and would provide access to charging food at the local grocery. The family would give Andrew $200 twice a week but would withhold a payment if he missed either a therapy session or a urinalysis. This rate of support was comparable to what he had been drawing for the last few months. My thought was that it would let him know that the family's intent was serious, without appearing too punitive. I explained that continued reimbursement of his credit cards was a sign of the family's trust that he would continue in treatment, and that the urinalyses would validate that he had not fallen into cocaine use. He assured me that drugs would not be a problem.

I chose to have payments withheld for a missed urine report, but not for a positive urine report, because Andrew seemed to be desirous of getting out of his rut, even though his denial prevented him from acknowledging the role of the cocaine. My assumption was that the awareness of positive urines alone, coupled with carefully managed family support, would address his denial. The object was to invoke some coercion to ensure his participation but not to punish him for his addiction or force him into hiding.

Nonetheless, I reflected to myself on the remarkable ways that denial could manifest itself. Andrew's agreement to the plan seemed almost bland, as if he had no cocaine problem whatever. Things were going a bit too smoothly.

Mindy called later that week. Dad was refusing to pay the $200 to his "drug addict son" despite our agreement, because he disapproved of Andrew's attitude. The father was clearly far from an ideal network member. This need to control was compatible with his past style: Andrew had told me when we met alone that he had planned to major in music in college, but his father had threatened to cut off his support if he did not prepare himself for a career in business. Andrew had complied at the time, but he had gone on a drug binge shortly thereafter. I told Mindy to reason with her father as well as she could. I later called him myself and finally convinced him to live up to the agreement.

The Fourth Week

Andrew and I met alone again. He discussed his difficulties with his girlfriend and his interest in continuing with a career in music, even if he were to return to the family business. He also acknowledged that he might have a problem with cocaine. We began to develop the basis of a therapeutic alliance. His first urine test was positive for cocaine (and benzodiazepines), possibly only from use prior to the agreement with the family; the second was negative. Andrew was coming into work every day.

The family met later that week, but Andrew did not show up; his third urine was reported positive. Since my understanding with Andrew and his network was that all drug-related information would be shared, I discussed this with the family. Instead of focusing on the father's evident anger, I used the opportunity to educate the group on the nature of addiction and pointed out that we should simply stick to our agreement, and Andrew would receive $200 less from the family this week.

The Fifth Week

Andrew came in and said he hadn't been able to face the whole family the last time, particularly his father. I made an effort to convince him that his father was better managed by our meeting with him at intervals, rather than by leaving him on his own to be disruptive. I tried to get Andrew to see that I could be his ally in dealing with the family but that he would have to stay away from cocaine to give me a credible position from which to represent his interests. His next urine was negative.

Andrew and I met together with the network, and the session went well, in that I was able to encourage his family to express support for his return to work and their faith in his contribution to the business. Although he remained somewhat depressed, Andrew seemed pleased that there might be a role for him if he emerged from his difficulties. He denied, however, that he had used cocaine the week before, shrugging his shoulders when I asked him how the urinalysis was positive. Needless to say, I was concerned with his stance, but the family either was reluctant to confront this denial at the moment or was not fully aware of the meaning of a positive urine. It was essential to avoid condoning the denial, though, so I said to them, "This is hard to deal with, but of course a urine positive for cocaine means that Andrew used the drug." Then, turning to Andrew, I continued, "Even so, I understand that you're trying to stay away from the coke now."

Despite its rocky beginnings, the therapy held together. At times the father and children were at each others' throats in arguments that spilled over from the business. Andrew had a number of slips, but the fiscal arrangement and his pride in a growing role in the business helped him stay in treatment. After two months, he was able to acknowledge his use of cocaine when it did occur, and soon thereafter he became consistently abstinent.

Needless to say, at many points over the course of such an intervention the balance between trust and coercion must be delicately managed. In considering this balance, it is useful to look at the roles of both therapist and patient as they evolved. The therapist has to develop a position that is seen as both fair and effective, since it is necessary to persuade network members that they must participate in a new way. Intense feelings have to be managed as well, as evidenced in my negotiation with Andrew's angry and controlling father. The therapist must carefully assess which family members are his or her most reliable allies. In this case, I deputized Mindy and her husband early on to contact Andrew.

Having dealt with irrationality, having elicited support, and having brought in the patient, the therapist must take a more neutral position as an ally of both patient and family. In this case, I encouraged Andrew to appreciate that I could arbitrate between him and his overbearing parent. Whatever the circumstances, the therapist must also instill hope that there can be a successful rehabilitation and a more promising life for the patient. Hope bolsters everyone's morale in the face of bewildering conflicts and intermittent failures.

The role of the patient is more complex: the patient maintains the irrational denial while participating in treatment. Andrew's denial took months to remit, while he and I were implicitly working together to stabilize a new perspective on his addiction. It may seem paradoxical, but as long as a secure and supportive network has been constructed for the patient, continuing denial need not prevent an implicit collaboration and the forward movement of the treatment.

To consider the "conversion" of a denying but compliant addict, it is useful to turn to the model of self-perception theory, as developed by Daryl Bem.[4] Bem pointed out that people come to "know" their attitudes and emotions in large part by inferring them from their own behaviors. The voluntary acting out of a behavior begins, in time, to lead the actor to adopt the psychology and motivations attendant on such behavior; a child is taken to church each Sunday and in time comes to see himself or herself as a Methodist or a Catholic. So, too, for the patient in a family context supportive of a sober perspective. As the patient complies with those attitudes and stops using drugs, he or she begins to perceive himself or herself as an abstinent, recovering person. Gradually, denial remits and a more healthful perspective, previously submerged but nonetheless influential, can emerge.

The role of fiscal constraints, as employed in this case, must also be considered; this step cannot be undertaken lightly. I elected this option for Andrew because it appeared to be the only means available for engaging him. The framework was adopted only after particulars had been developed with the family, and it did not involve any greater limitation on him than was necessary to secure participation. Yet the understanding was explicit enough for Andrew to appreciate that he might be compromised if he did not adhere to the agreement. Although I took care to minimize ill will on his part by not dwelling on the financial issue, it was clear to me that the treatment would have been vulnerable for several months at least if this leverage had not been used.

It is important to understand, however, that coercion need not engender rebellion and animosity. Coerced parties sometimes identify with the views of people who demand their compliance; this paradoxically positive response may help us understand how many patients do indeed comply with a coercive intervention. An interesting, if exaggerated, example of this phenomenon is seen in the Stockholm syndrome, originally described in relation to hostages held against their will.[5] Such persons often assume the views and ideologies of their captors and even defend the captors who have imposed their will on them. The syndrome may partially explain why a noncompliant patient can be engaged in treatment under pressure, then come to espouse the views of the treating party and the social network. This is particularly true when the network's views are directed at the patient's best interests and supported by the broader society.

Nonetheless, coercive constraints can certainly have an impact on the therapeutic alliance and can foster the evolution of a negative transferential stance. A contaminated transference, however, is better than freedom to use drugs: continuing drug abuse will always vitiate the benefits of therapy.

With these issues in mind, it is important that coercion be seen as an expression of the family's concern, not a sadistic invention of the therapist. That is why I made sure that it was Mindy and her husband who approached Andrew with our initial proposal. The family was compelled to make clear their commitment to implementing the plan, so that I would not later be cast as the reinforcer of good behavior. It also made clear to Andrew that the plan had emerged from the family, not from me alone. Even with such safeguards, the issue of coercion does continue to play a role in the patient's thinking over the long course of treatment.

CHAPTER 6

Intersection with Other Therapies

Q UESTIONS WILL ARISE about the relationship between net-work therapy and other treatments: How is it different from approaches like individual, family, or group therapy? Can it be combined with these other therapies? We can answer these questions by contrasting the basic techniques of network therapy with those of other treatments. The exercise will also highlight just how networks are used and where this approach fits into the broad array of psychotherapies.

Network versus Individual Therapy

The strategically oriented approach used in the network carefully targets behaviors and then develops a strategy to change them through direct intervention. Thus, a young adult patient may be encouraged to rely on his mother for help if he needs her help to sustain his abstinence; the therapist's interpretation of his need to rebel may be delayed for months. The mother's usefulness is more important at this stage than the patient's self-realization.

The nondirective approach to individual therapy, in contrast, is based largely on subjective and empathic exchange. Individual therapy lies at the opposite end of the therapy spectrum from network therapy; traditional psychotherapy plays down symptoms and diagnoses and eschews behavioral management. Furthermore, the nondirective approach is

107

based on the assumption that a relatively comfortable alliance between therapist and patient will soon emerge, based on mutual understanding. In actuality, a reliable alliance is unlikely to emerge early in the recovery of addicts; abstinence must be secured, even though addicts are ambivalent about making abstinence a goal.

DIRECTIVE VERSUS EXPRESSIVE THERAPY

The nondirective, empathic model has been influential in encouraging an open interchange between clinician and patient and in freeing therapy from an overreliance on intellectual trappings and behavioral management. As described by Carl Rogers, congruence between therapist and patient on an emotional level is central to assuring that the sweep of a patient's feelings can carry their communication.[1] The two might be likened to a pair of skaters engaged in a dance on ice: there is little sense that one imposes his or her will on the natural flow of the other's movement; mutuality above all is evident. In treatment where mutuality exists, "the therapist is able to participate in the patient's communication," make "comments [that] are always in line with what the patient is trying to convey," and use a "tone of voice [that] conveys the complete ability to share the patient's feelings."[2]

Clearly, the appropriateness of this mutuality depends on the degree of understanding and collaboration that can be expected in the exchanges between therapist and patient. It posits that patients' moods and communications can be trusted to promote mutuality, that they do not need to hide their problems from the therapist or from themselves. For addicts, sadly, these assumptions do not apply, and therapists must take a more directive stance. The therapist must avoid being drawn into a process of seduction, in which the inclination to empathize with the patient leads to misconstruing motive and behavior, and to becoming an enabler in the addiction.

From the perspective of therapy based on mutuality, therapists treating addiction are in a difficult position. To address the addiction requires compromising one of the most effective means of establishing a therapeutic alliance, namely an empathic, untrammeled exchange with the patient. But the situation is not so bleak; individual sessions are held to discuss issues that are not necessarily related to maintaining abstinence and undoing the denial of illness. Two parallel tracks are therefore developed in the treatment. On one the network is used strategically to stabilize abstinence—sometimes running contrary to the immediate flow of the patient's desires and feelings. On the second is treatment based on a more unstructured, empathic exchange. In the second context trust can be built in developing new goals for a a sober life.

The network can protect the therapist because its members may be seen as the enforcers of abstinence. One patient was berated by his brother in a network session for his callousness in ignoring the impact of his alcoholism on his wife. I allowed some of this to be expressed, to serve as a lesson; the patient seemed bewildered, but chastened. In the individual session, I encouraged the patient to express his feelings about being scolded, and I listened to his expressions of frustration. We then considered the event with regard to his announced goal of becoming more sensitive to those close to him. In the empathic individual setting he was able to deal with his resentment toward his brother and gain an understanding of his own attitude.

According to Rogers, the therapist concerned with maintaining parity in the relationship with the patient "follows the patient's line of thought," "treats the patient as equal," and "sees the patient as a co-worker on a common problem."[3] Rogers's directives of parity are not just taken at face value in network therapy. The network therapist must surely be aware of the patient's line of thought and anticipate what its meaning (perhaps its subversive intent) may be. The therapist's first priority, however, is to consider the patient's meaning from a strategic standpoint, relative to its anticipated effect on abstinence.

It is important that patients be accepted as partners in the treatment, but only within constraints defined by the therapist. As addicts, they had previously set their own agenda—one of sustaining addiction—and in that regard autonomy served them poorly. An understanding must therefore be established, within specific guidelines, that they trade the options that might allow them to promote addiction for respect as collaborators in planning. Network therapy relies more heavily on active collaboration between therapist and patient than most other treatments do. The patient is expected to assume a role of active partnership in nurturing and organizing the network and ensuring its continuity, in anticipating and averting slips, and in establishing goals for later rehabilitation.

THE RULES OF THERAPY

We can now consider some specific principles of network therapy and contrast them with insight-oriented psychotherapy as it is generally practiced by social workers, psychologists, and psychiatrists.

- Network therapy: the therapist is prepared to set the session's agenda.
- Insight therapy: patients introduce issues of their own choice.

In network therapy, the therapist selects issues for discussion whenever it is necessary. If the patient seems headed for a slip, the therapist addresses that issue first. Similarly, when the network meets, the patient's review of substance-related experiences is always the first item of business. In traditional therapy, on the other hand, salient issues emerge as the patient expresses what first comes to mind and associates to those reflections.

- Network therapy: a display of feelings can serve as a defense against dealing with addiction.
- Insight therapy: the expression of feelings is a vehicle for resolving symptoms.

For the nonaddicted patient, the unleashing of strong feelings is important in understanding the genesis of symptoms. For the addicted person, ventilation of feelings can be a guise for leading the therapeutic exchange away from important issues of sobriety. Such expressions are encouraged only if they do not distract the treatment from its principal goal, and an affective display may even be cut short if it is defensive in nature.

One patient addicted to minor tranquilizers became tearful in a session over her boss's mistreatment of her. I sensed that she might have taken some pills after the event, and I interrupted to ask her directly if she had. I would have preferred to wait until she had fully expressed her feelings, but the issue had come up late in the session. It was important that the agenda of drug use not be put off until our next meeting, as that might have allowed for further erosion in her abstinence.

- Network therapy: insight can serve as a smokescreen to avoid addiction problems.
- Insight therapy: insight is encouraged and unconscious conflicts are interpreted.

The resolution of unconscious conflict must be regarded with extreme caution early in network therapy. Discussion of conflicts in the session can operate like a prism in the hands of the addicted person, distorting the actual nature of the drug abuse and misleading the patient and

110

therapist into allowing continued substance abuse. Both therapist and patient must be aware of this, so that they avoid unproductive deliberations over childhood experience while the patient continues to drink.

In contrast, the resolution of unconscious conflict is one of the principal tenets of insight-oriented psychotherapy, since maladaptive behavior is presumed to be tied into these conflicts and to stem from early relationships. Long-standing relationship issues are typically introduced by the patient into new relationships. As the therapist addresses these conflicts, the theory goes, the patient will benefit in real-life behavior and find relief from distress. For the addict, however, abstinence must come first.

- Network therapy: addiction-related material is always shared with the network.
- Insight therapy: exchanges in the consulting room are kept confidential.

In network therapy, constraints of confidentiality are not applied to issues associated with drug use, as it is important that members of the network be aware of any circumstances that would aid them in participating in the addiction treatment. The therapist must let the patient know early on that information will be openly exchanged. Discussions that do not bear on drug use are kept in confidence by the therapist. This should be made clear in the earliest sessions with the network.

I have forgotten on occasion to make the terms of communication clear. I was once left with a patient who was off on a drinking binge, and I was uncertain about whether I should reach out to his family for help. I did not feel that I had the prerogative to call his wife because a prior understanding had not been clearly established. We should have reached such an agreement when we were initially discussing the format of treatment. Now that the patient was drinking heavily, my request to speak to his wife inevitably ran up against his pressure to continue drinking. Fortunately, we were able to make a proper agreement on communication once his slip came to an end.

This entire approach contrasts with traditional, expressive therapy, where it is important that patients feel comfortable about revealing behaviors that they would not want family or friends to know about, including problems with substance abuse. In particular, patients' shame over their perceived failings is not allowed to compromise the capacity to associate freely in the session or to share confidences with the therapist. In the network setting it is the responsibility of the therapist to ensure that the issue of shame is minimized or dispelled by defining a sense of mutuality and collaboration from the outset.

- Network therapy: the actions of the patient and network members are orchestrated in whatever way necessary to ensure the patient's abstinence.
- Insight therapy: the therapist does not prescribe behavior.

In insight therapy, symptom relief is said to derive from the resolution of conflict and from the expression of feelings in an interpretive setting. In the network it is essential that the therapist be able to prescribe behaviors that will avert relapses to drug use. Both the patient and members of the network therefore must be open to embarking on a behavioral regimen to aid in the implementation of the treatment. For example, the patient and network members should be willing to meet together outside the therapy office at a time when the patient is vulnerable. In another context, the therapist may instruct the patient to write a doctor who has prescribed sleeping pills, requesting that the doctor stop prescribing. The network should be drawn into supporting such behavioral direction from the therapist.

- Network therapy: social pressure is an integral part of treatment, often the only means of ensuring abstinence.
- Insight therapy: outside parties are not solicited to influence the patient's behavior.

The baldfaced use of social pressure or guilt inevitably incurs the patient's resentment; in an outpatient setting, the resulting rebelliousness can understandably be hard to control. But indirect pressure may be necessary to get alcoholics and drug abusers to enter treatment. In ongoing treatment as well, addicts' inability to give up a highly conditioned addictive behavior often necessitates the use of this leverage if stability is to be sustained. Social pressure in its mildest form can entail exploring with the patient in an individual session how loved ones will be compromised if drinking continues. In a more stringent version, the family can be engaged to ensure that a return to addiction will lead to their implicit withdrawal of support or to the patient's embarrassment. The highly influential bonds that hold members of the network together in their intimate relations have the potential of invoking great remorse. The patient is under some pressure not to let down loved ones and friends, disappointing them by a return to drug use. Such remorse can be a major motivation for remaining abstinent and can serve as a deterrent.

I met with an alcoholic woman and her husband because the family had pressed her to stop drinking. Knowing that her resentment toward her spouse was undermining her motivation, I arranged that we include her younger sister, who was enrolled in college in a remote city, in the next session. We did this by speaker phone. It was clear to me that the patient did not have the heart to let down her sister, who had been hoping for years that she would finally agree to meet with a therapist to address her drinking problem.

- Network therapy: unconscious anger and conflict are dealt with by encouraging mutuality and support. The motives of people in the network are not interpreted.
- Insight therapy: transference reactions are interpreted to aid in addressing the patient's conflict.

Patients cannot be put in the awkward situation of having psychological defenses scrutinized in front of family members about whom they have mixed feelings. Furthermore, since the interpretation of behavior is of value to a person only in the context of an ongoing therapy, network members themselves are rarely, if ever, offered interpretations that would put their motivations in question. Their attitudes toward the therapist are left unexposed, and the difficulties they may have in relating to the group are dealt with supportively. The positive side of their contributions is pointed out; addressing their misgivings and resentments would imply undue criticism.

Thus, a controlling father vying for a dominant role in the group is engaged in a friendly and respectful manner. It is never implied that his demanding behavior might reflect his competitive nature. A self-centered sibling is heard out as well, even though she displays little genuine concern for the patient; her unsympathetic nature might later help the network to confront the addicted patient. We want only to help the father or sibling play a constructive role in the immediate situation of the network.

Network Therapy versus Therapies with Families and Groups

Like family and group therapy, the network approach brings several people together to address a psychological problem. But the approaches are different. Group therapists may focus on the individual patient or try

113

to shape the group overall. They can direct attention to the individual's symptoms, or they may facilitate interaction among members so they learn from each other. Therapists may consider the group as a backdrop for a series of focused interventions, or they may manipulate its dynamics for therapeutic ends. Therapists working with a network, however, support group cohesiveness but focus always on the individual patient and the addiction.

APPROACHING THE FAMILY

Pioneers in family therapy have developed a variety of approaches. In his psychodynamic approach to family therapy, Nathan Ackerman relied heavily on the importance of members' insights and on the possibility of resolving problems engendered by conflicts and losses that members experience earlier in life.[4] For him, the reconsideration of early family experiences and reflection on the past were important therapeutic tools. This approach was evident as well in the technique developed by Murray Bowen, who led participants in sessions to review their family backgrounds in detail in order to help them achieve autonomy and differentiate themselves from each other.[5] Needless to say, these approaches relied heavily on the premise that a family's current problems are rooted in pressures that arose in their families of origin. In a sense, the consulting office was populated by those present and by the ghosts of their extended families.

In network therapy, we avoid focusing on the patient's family history in the network sessions themselves, since an involvement in family conflicts can be disruptive to the network's primary task of helping to maintain the patient's abstinence. To bring up history would establish an additional agenda and set of goals, potentially obliging the therapist to assume responsibility for resolving conflicts that are not necessarily tied to the addiction. Family and interpersonal dynamics can be addressed with the patient alone.

One patient brought his estranged wife and his brother to my office as we embarked on treating his prescription drug abuse. The tension between patient and spouse was considerable, as both were competitive and controlling in their own ways. She interrupted too often to offer her opinions, and he was dismissive of her, to the point of sitting with his back to her. His brother tried his best to remain neutral.

By listening with interest and respect to both husband and wife, letting each play a positive role in framing the treatment, I could tap their initiative and their desire to shine in the session. Thus I could draw on the wife's knowledge as historian of the patient's drug use, and all three participants were able to focus on the task of considering more members to add to this nascent network. The traits that might have served as grist for a family therapist, including the patient's troubled relationship with his parents, were not discussed. Instead the character traits of those present were engaged in the network's tasks of history taking and of building the membership.

One of the most elegant contributions of the family therapy movement is the conception of families as social systems whose imbalances can generate psychological symptoms in members who are seemingly uninvolved in the immediate conflict. Salvador Minuchin played a central role in the evolution of this concept. His structural approach has served as a touchstone for those learning to work with the systems model.[6] Minuchin looked at subsystems within the family, like those of the parents and of the children, and developed "road maps" of the family terrain to delineate tacit coalitions among family members and the boundaries between the family's subsystems. Dysfunction was not seen to reside in a symptomatic member, even if that person was labeled as pathological. Instead it emerged from systemic forces sufficiently intense to produce severe pathology far removed from an actual source of conflict. A child's life-threatening anorexia could derive from imbalances in the parental subsystem, parents' impact on the children's role in the family, and the expression of parents' tensions in one child.

This conception of the origin of symptoms can be valuable in understanding the emergence of substance abuse in a given child within a family. A structural approach may be indicated, indeed preferred, in dealing with an emerging drug problem in many younger adolescents. However, long-standing addiction in an adult may not be terminated by restructuring the family system. A chronic pattern of abuse in the adult may well have achieved an autonomy of its own over many years, as drug-seeking behavior became conditioned and firmly lodged. Internal cues such as mood fluctuations, quite unrelated to family circumstances, or external cues such as social settings associated with drug use, precipitate relapses in a manner independent of relations at home. The patient must therefore be engaged in a way that will abort these conditioned vulnerabilities, and a supportive matrix must be constructed to ensure continued behavioral constraints.

Is this better done by restructuring family relations or by avoiding family conflicts and organizing the family to support abstinence? My observation, after working with persons who have suffered from years of addiction, is that it is more effective to assemble a task-oriented network whose members are strategically best suited to the behavioral task. The dynamics of the group should be understood, but used only tacitly and supportively. A perceptive manager might do the job of leadership well, even in the absence of an intellectual understanding of family dynamics.

Shifting the focus away from the nuclear or marital family is particularly relevant for patients who have uncertain commitments to both sets of relations. They may be in rebellion against their parents or uncertain about continuing in their marriage, so that peers or lovers may be more important to them than members of a traditional family constellation. Moving the emphasis to a collaborating network therefore allows for more flexibility and provides both patient and therapist more latitude. A network might include the patient's spouse, but the introduction of a sister and a friend as well means that ambivalence in the marital relationship will not seriously undermine the network's activities.

One type of family therapy that does bear considerable similarity to network format is the strategic family approach.[7] Like a network therapist, Jay Haley focuses directly on the presenting problem, rather than on the dynamics of the family system. Treatment is begun with a careful examination of the nature of the symptoms, their time course, and the events that take place as they emerge. As in other behaviorally oriented therapies, the focus is a relatively narrow one, and an understanding of behavioral sequences associated with the problematic situation is of primary importance. Indeed, this identification of the circumstances surrounding the emergence of the problem can be likened to the ferreting out of conditioned cues that lead to the addict's sequence of drug use. Both approaches assume that the sequences will suggest options for bringing about the problem's resolution. As he developed this strategic model, Haley observed that certain behaviors within a family can unintentionally promote the very symptoms they are designed to suppress; this is clearly similar to the conception of the alcoholic's spouse unwittingly serving as an enabler.

Some of the techniques used in strategic family therapy, however, are different from those we apply in treating substance abuse. A strategic therapist may offer "paradoxical interpretations," prescribing behaviors that would seem to aggravate, rather than relieve, the target symptom.[8] The therapist might give parents an assignment to do just those things that have provoked arguments with their symptomatic child, with some new dimension added to assert control over the symptom—for example, setting aside thirty minutes after dinner each night to argue. By

116

sponses has been developed by Irvin Yalom, who emphasizes the need to ensure benefit from group interaction by actively promoting and then mining the strong feelings that emerge between members.[12] He promotes the expression of unstated feelings between members and has them examine their responses. The technique is valuable in resolving the problems that patients have in ongoing relationships with family and friends.

Yalom also studied the use of here-and-now group therapy with alcoholics. He found them responsive to the approach, as verified by a positive outcome on a number of psychological measures. His patients, however, generally relied on AA or other addiction treatment to secure abstinence.[13] Thus, while his approach can be quite useful with interpersonal relations in alcoholic patients, it does need to be coupled with other techniques that are themselves directed at the goal of abstinence. Yalom's work, in fact, suggests that an expressive group therapy might well be a useful collateral to network sessions in the treating of alcoholism.

THE ECOLOGICAL MODEL

One last approach bears considerable similarity to network therapy. It has been termed ecological because it deals directly with the broader environment in which a person's addiction is lodged. Specific interventions are undertaken outside the immediate therapy setting in order to bring about change in the broader living circumstances that have supported the patient's problematic behavior. One option is to run a behaviorally oriented clinic for alcoholics, and also to monitor their work and family situations, using home visits as part of the treatment.[14] This approach promotes rehabilitation through dealing directly with the environmental reinforcers of the alcoholic lifestyle. The ecological approach is also reflected in the intervention techniques developed by Vernon Johnson, who brought in family and friends so that they might plan on confronting the recalcitrant alcoholic and draw up a series of consequences they would apply outside the family session if the patient did not agree to enter treatment (chapter 5).[15]

The family therapy movement per se has been associated with the ecological model. Minuchin's work with delinquent boys and their families articulated this perspective.[16] He posited that family structure is integrated into the pathology of the patient on the one hand and the social problems of the community on the other.

Like the ecological approach, network therapy reaches out to engage community players and works to restructure the circumstances in which the patient's problem is embedded. It recognizes that the addict cannot relinquish addictive behavior unless the environmental cues that precipitate it are understood and assistance brought in to ensure that the cues are addressed.

In sum, a network session is quite different from those typical of many models of individual, group, and family therapy, in that it avoids emphasis on emotional expressiveness, interpretation of conflict, and formal restructuring of family and peer relations. Instead, it is free to focus on the social supports and behavioral change necessary to protect the patient's abstinence. This straightforward and directive approach does not derive from ignorance of the dynamics inherent in these aforementioned perspectives. It is born instead out of respect for the remarkable tenacity of the behaviors associated with alcohol and drug dependence and the value of meaningful, coordinated support from family and friends in altering those behaviors.

Combining Treatments

We have considered how different therapies address the addict's needs. Most come up short as usually practiced. Can network therapy be combined with any of them for a more favorable outcome?

A therapist can certainly hold network sessions as a complement to individual therapy. The approaches together can relieve the tensions that arise in moving an addicted person to abstinence. Individual sessions can be used to help patients to realize that they have a stake in a sober life and to develop a better adaptation. Indeed, sobriety must be embedded in a new and meaningful adaptation in order for it to persist. In the network, emphasis is placed on providing practical support and a sounding board for sobriety. But the network will not deal with sensitive aspects of a patient's intimate relations or adaptive problems; these are discussed more privately. A patient can also be engaged by a network therapist in group therapy, while separate meetings are held with the patient and a support network to ensure abstinence outside the office. It is important that a therapy group not be accepting of alcohol or drug use, though, or it will undermine the patient's recovery.

Carrying out network therapy with a patient who is being treated individually by a different therapist is more difficult. In subtle ways, the other therapist may inadvertently undermine the network's task. Behaviors related to addiction might be viewed as adaptive by a therapist naive to addiction treatment. For example, the other therapist might condone socializing with heavy drinkers or might allow the patient to hold on to the idea that a return to drinking is possible once "current circumstances" are in hand. The main sticking point of a two-therapist format is agreement on the need to maintain absolute abstinence.

I have referred some patients who are in network therapy for treatment in other modalities with carefully selected therapists. One family that was supposed to be playing a supportive role was riddled with strife and intense ambivalence. Issues that might have been easily addressed became the subject of intense conflict and explosive anger. For example, should anyone drink at home when Dad is around? In this case, I opted to rely more heavily on the patients' friends for network support and had the family come in only at intervals, mainly to keep them from undermining the father's abstinence and generating resentment. I referred them for family treatment with another therapist to address the broader goal of living more amicably with each other.

CHAPTER 7

The Role of Alcoholics Anonymous in Network Treatment

MORE THAN A MILLION addicted people in America, and almost two million worldwide, are AA members. Most of them attribute their recovery, if not their very lives, to this fellowship. In recent years, AA members are increasingly involved in professional therapy as well, and the relationship between that treatment and the AA fellowship is often complex. In framing the format of network therapy it is essential to examine how it interfaces with AA.

The experience of one patient will help to introduce the unique role that this group can play in the course of network treatment. It also gives a sense of how an alcoholic person can become engaged in the program as a complement to network support.

One Patient's Tale

Ron came to me on the heels of great personal tragedy. Three weeks before, his wife of twenty years had committed suicide with an overdose of sleeping pills while he was away on business. Only a few months before that, they had moved into town, and they had no relatives or close friends nearby. The childless couple had left their close friends behind when they moved.

Ron's marriage had been fraught with difficulties for some time, much of it due to his heavy and destructive drinking. Indeed, the move itself had been suggested by his superiors at work because his heavy drinking had affected his job performance. His boss had hoped that the new posting would yield a fresh outlook, but in actuality this was an unlikely cure for the alcoholism that was at the root of his problem.

Ron came to me in the hope of finding respite from intense remorse. His anguish was accentuated by an awareness that he and his wife had argued bitterly during the fateful days preceding her suicide. This realization motivated him to "consider cutting back on the drinking," as he said. As usual, I embarked on an implicit negotiation over the components of a recovery regimen. Ron was willing to have the one person in town whom he knew well, Steve, an old business colleague, join us the next day, and he agreed to refrain from drinking until that time. He had no interest in going to AA, as he was "not really an alcoholic." The situation was less than ideal, but not impossible.

Ron agreed to start on a regimen of taking disulfiram under observation after we met with Steve the next day. He would have to take two of his observed doses each week at sessions with me, and the third at his friend's house.

After Ron had remained sober for a few months, I was still troubled by the fact that he would neither admit to being alcoholic nor accept that he had to remain abstinent for the long term to protect himself from relapse. At one point, he acknowledged in a session of our small network that he had been particularly upset during the few weeks preceding, and he had been taking minor tranquilizers to relieve his tension. He knew that these drugs were addictive in themselves. In fact, he reported his use with some anguish, because the cocktail of drugs that his wife had used in her suicide had included this very medication, and he could see his slip as continuing the saga of ruination in which he had played so active a part.

This pattern of drug use was potentially a dangerous one; furthermore, the rational and interpretive exchanges that Ron and I were having might not prevent more use of the tranquilizer as a prologue to drinking, given his shaky commitment to abstinence. I took the occasion to work with Steve to press Ron to attend some AA meetings to underline the need for absolute abstinence.

As with some other addicted patients, the actual exposure to the meetings ignited a fascination for them in Ron. We got together with his friend the next week, and Ron reported on two meetings he had attended, saying, "I think AA could be a good thing for me. Maybe it'll help to deal with my spiritual problems." Admittedly, the burden of guilt was great for Ron, and the opportunity to experience some relief was valuable. But AA did more than that. For the first time, Ron was able say, "I think I am an alcoholic." Steve and I were relieved to hear his report.

Ron also told us of some occasions before his wife's death when his drinking had been severe. He had never before acknowledged these in our meetings. He told of times when he was away on business and had to skip conferences because he knew he was too drunk to carry on. Finally, and tearfully, he spoke of his inability to respond to his wife's pleas for help during the period right before her suicide, as he had spent the evenings drinking while he was on the road. But Ron could also take some distance from the AA meetings as his involvement progressed. He appreciated that there was a certain artificiality to the intense feelings that were regularly expressed, and he knew that there was still no history or depth in his relationships with the people at the meetings. He would sometimes talk about the group's "bumper sticker philosophy," but he would acknowledge that it offered him meaning and direction that he felt he sorely needed.

As Ron became more involved, his commitment to the group's principles came to infuse much of what he said. I chose not to comment on this, just as I would not interpret the nature of a patient's religious commitments. Ron would discuss his remorse over his wife's death in the context of the forgiveness that he associated with AA, and Steve and I would listen, pleased that he found solace in the fellowship. At times I would help him explain the AA approach in our conjoint sessions. Sometimes he would cite ideas or shibboleths that seemed arcane; I had no idea whether they had any currency at meetings beyond the ones he attended. Often he would turn to AA's "serenity prayer," saying that it allowed him to deal with the most difficult problems he encountered. (It reads: "God, grant me the serenity to accept the things I cannot change, courage to change the things I can, and wisdom to know the difference.")

But Ron could not fully resolve his remorse over his wife's death, and he had to confront these feelings to progress in his evolution as an AA member. One day he came in speaking about his difficulty in "working the steps." He said, "I can't accept the idea of a higher power. I feel guilty and I can't reconcile myself to the idea of religion."

Ron had come from a fundamentalist Protestant background in the Midwest, and had been infused with the conception of a punitive deity throughout his childhood. This was coupled with his parents' inclination to turn to religion to express their disapproval of him. He spoke to me

124

in a tortured way. "I feel guilty, and I can't get the idea out of my mind that God is berating me."

Unlike the issue of abstinence, this moral confrontation I dealt with relatively passively, encouraging Ron to express his concerns and work out a way of dealing with his guilt within himself. He struck on a solution one day, and reported it to me at our next meeting. A fellow AA member had told him, "You don't have to look at God as somebody who's going to force things on you. If you don't like what he says, tell him to go to hell. You can speak up as well as he." Ron seemed reassured by this unusual advice, feeling that he might have the right to assert himself against religious authority, something that he had been denied in his youth.

AA was also valuable in helping Ron deal with the conditioned cues associated with craving for alcohol. After a year of treatment, Ron, his friend, and I agreed that he would stop taking disulfiram. As is often the case, he became cognizant of exposure to alcohol. One weekend, he was at a cocktail party with some business clients, and he noticed himself contemplating the appealing taste of a mixed drink. He quickly cut this short, but nonetheless realized it was something to be discussed. His sponsor suggested an approach, sometimes used by AA members, in which he was to summon up the image of vomiting on any occasion in which the thought of drinking came to him. The approach implicitly reflected the model of introducing an aversive stimulus to extinguish drinking cues (chapter 3).

When Ron, his friend, and I met to discuss drinking issues, we talked about the sequence of cues associated with his response to the alcohol at the party. These related to his anxiety about business dealings, historically a cue to heavy drinking. We looked at ways to address this malaise. Ron revealed that he sometimes noticed himself dwelling on the sight of liquor bottles and reading the details in liquor advertisements in magazines. We agreed together that he would specifically avoid attending to any such stimuli, and we also reviewed the discussion on dealing with cues that he had had with his AA sponsor.

Eventually, Ron became an AA sponsor himself. His management of a new member was an issue that he realized had psychological import, and he recognized his inclination to be overly caring and supportive in this role. He had been highly indulgent of his wife and her needs when he wasn't drinking; his protectiveness may have contributed to her dwelling on her own problems over the years. We looked at his style of interacting with the person he sponsored, and at his willingness to provide small sums of money to help the young man establish himself—a risky business indeed with an unstable recovering alcoholic. Interestingly, Ron's own sponsor had commented on this same issue.

Ron's treatment was successful, and his commitment to abstinence was stabilized in large part because of the role that AA played in his recovery. Because he was socially isolated when we began treatment, we had little social network to draw on. The basis for undermining the denial of his addiction was compromised. Yet other patients have more stable supports and enjoy great gains from their involvement in AA nonetheless. How AA achieves such effects need not be a mystery, although the process is often regarded as such. If carefully examined, the psychological basis of AA's remarkable influence can be understood, and its interaction with professional therapy can be appreciated as well.

AA as a Treatment Modality

How effective is AA? To what extent should the patient in network therapy be pressed to attend? Certainly, the organization has flourished, and its members tell dramatic stories of progress. Nonetheless, in an era when professional treatment is increasingly accessible, this question deserves attention. Indeed, some experts on alcoholism treatment have questioned how much we really know about the long-term outcome of membership;[1] Griffith Edwards, a researcher on alcoholism treatment, has pointed out that claims for the universality of AA can easily be exaggerated.[2] A classic review of alcoholism treatment studies suggested that compared with alcohol clinic treatment, AA seems to be applicable to a narrower range of patients.[3]

Chad Emrick, who has conducted the most careful analysis of research on AA, evaluated the characteristics of members and the long-term impact of the group.[4] He concluded that no one can predict with certainty which alcoholics are more likely to affiliate with AA from their initial evaluation, although it does appear that people with more severe compulsive drinking and with anxiety and negative feelings associated with their drinking are more likely to join after an initial encounter. Age, race, sex, religion, and a variety of other demographic factors do not consistently predict enlistment or outcome. About 40 to 50 percent of those who do join AA become long-term, active members, and may have several years of total abstinence while with the organization. Overall, we find that the outcome in AA is similar to that with well-focused professional care alone. But patients treated by professionals do have a better outcome if they attend AA as well.

AA probably does about as well as focused professional care. Moreover, the organization has clearly touched many more alcoholics to date than have other approaches, professionals included—at no cost to the general public. The movement has also had a profound influence on the attitude of our society toward alcoholism and other addictions. It has allowed countless alcoholics to acknowledge their dependency with less shame and to appreciate that they can seek help without fearing outright rejection by society. On this count, any patient in addiction treatment has something to learn from involvement with a twelve-step movement.

HOW DOES AA WORK?

Most AA members prefer to take the movement's remarkable success on faith, explaining it in terms of "fellowship" and "spiritual values," and leave it at that. Although these terms do indeed convey much of the group's character, they do not explain in psychological terms the unusual effectiveness of this group. One reason the issue has been neglected is that contemporary psychology tends to shy away from the study of zealous, inspirational groups. Objective researchers are reluctant to look at spiritual and religious phenomena, as William James aptly pointed out nearly a century ago.[5] A group like AA differs from religious movements in many ways, but we can learn a great deal about its operation by looking at how social support mechanisms and religious experience interact. Over the years, I have studied a number of religious sects and have found similarities between them and zealous self-help groups. The latter include a parents' movement to combat their children's drug abuse, a mental health self-help group, and AA itself.[6] What emerges is a fascinating interaction between the psychological needs of members and the operation of the group as a social system.

ENGAGEMENT

An atmosphere of intense supportiveness is very important during the phase of recruitment into a zealous self-help group, since the feeling of being accepted in these settings has a strong, seductive effect. Among the people joining religious movements, those who suffer the most emotional distress are most likely to join later on; they have the most to gain on an emotional level.[7] Similarly, any alcoholic coming to an AA meeting for the first time will be welcomed warmly if he or she makes any attempt to make contact with an established member.

A strong consensus in the group regarding the value of its ideology is important. In many self-help groups, as in religious groups, the philosophy of the leader is consistently touted as a potential solution to worldly problems of anomie, depression, and even international strife. This transcendent perspective among members suggests that alternative explanations, and certainly the convert's errant attitudes, will now have little value. Thus, Bill W., the founder of AA, and the AA *Big Book* are held in reverence by all members whom a recruit encounters. Recruits are repeatedly told that the tales in this book should be read carefully until their message gets through.

Encounters in meetings are generally carefully arranged to place the control over discussion in the hands of established members, and members often constitute an absolute majority of those present. AA certainly does not brook testimonials to drunkenness from the podium. Attendees are not supposed to speak up if they are still drinking, and only those who have long been sober serve as sponsors. With continuing control over the "context of communication,"[8] and intense social support, the ideas that the group seeks to convey seem increasingly credible to the initiate.

Alcoholics exposed to AA are therefore engaged under the following circumstances:

- If their distress is great enough and the group's message is relevant to their needs
- If they are maintained in the controlled meeting environment long enough, or if they visit frequently enough
- If the cohesiveness of the recruitment setting is sufficiently engaging for them
- If the absolute nature of the group's message stands unquestioned

It is important to make clear that this process is also found in groups with very different missions, such as evangelical religious sects.

TRANSCENDENT EXPERIENCE

An intense spiritual commitment is an essential force in AA, energizing both the recruitment process and members' continuing commitment. Although AA does not define itself as a religious entity, it clearly maintains a strong religious orientation. Many aspects of the program are tied in to the member's relationship to a "higher power," lending the movement an absolute and quasi-religious character without formally making a claim to divine inspiration. In our Western society, those exposed to the group know full well that this higher power is associated with a Judeo-Christian tradition in which an omniscient and omnipotent deity brooks no idolatry or debauchery. Granted, the phrase "as we understand Him" has been appended to the references to God in two of the steps. Nonetheless, when long-standing members discuss a higher power, the religious connotations of this concept are generally intense. It would be a mistake if this commitment were underestimated or challenged in a therapy session, as it is closely tied to an unquestioning commitment to abstinence.

The spirituality of AA is allied with the induction of an alternative emotional state. This serves to create an "aha" experience that can help rivet the novice to the acceptance of a new world view. It can generate an intensity of feeling that has characterized dramatic transformations in attitude from the conversion of St. Paul to the intense emotional reactions of born-again Christians to persons learning transcendental meditation. It is also a phenomenon that works in more muted form.

Many AA members describe experiences they had upon joining that reflect the spiritual awakening that Bill W. underwent, as they come to feel their own intense belief. The strong feelings of mutuality and supportiveness that emerge at each AA meeting, often described by AA members as necessary to their equanimity, reflect this phenomenon. These feelings are highly engaging for those who respond, as a visit to an AA meeting will attest.

EMOTIONAL COMMITMENT

The ability of zealous groups to engage and retain members is quite striking, given the fact that those they recruit usually start out at odds with their philosophy. In reviewing our own research findings, I was impressed by a finding that helped to explain this capacity, one that I termed the relief effect:[9] members of these groups experience a decrease in emotional distress upon becoming involved and staying engaged, and, conversely, they suffer an increase in distress if they become alienated. We systematically studied the emotional state of recruits to a variety of zealous groups at given points in membership and found that recruits' levels of anxiety and depression were highest before joining and became high again if they were alienated from other members. On the other hand, anxiety and depression declined markedly during the period right after joining and was low as well through adversity and disruption, as long as their feelings of affiliation were strong.[10]

The weight of these findings strongly suggests that as people are recruited into zealous groups, their psychological stability comes to be dependent on the degree of affiliation they feel toward the group. This reactivity is the product of their intense responsiveness to the supportive nature of the group and their growing dependency on it for a feeling of self-worth. They are rewarded, or operantly reinforced, with a decrease in distress for complying with the group. They are effectively "punished" with the extinguishing stimulus of emotional distress when they do not maintain a close affiliation. This relief effect for emotional distress means that recruits become operantly conditioned by their own response to the group to stay tied to it for the long term and to adhere to its principles. It is as if their feelings were on a spring, tied to the group.

In looking at AA from this perspective, we can understand better how the movement has been so influential in maintaining alcoholics' attendance at meetings that combat their long-standing inclination to drink, and in keeping them faithful to its transcendent philosophy of abstinence. Most alcoholic people who have reached the point of giving up the drug are quite miserable, and AA offers them succor and relief. If they affiliate, the meetings' social setting and the forces of cohesion and belief leave them emotionally dependent on the movement and vulnerable to distress if they stay away. Over repeated instances of operant reinforcement, they become conditioned to an emotional dependency on the movement.

This conditioned dependency is reflected in many ways. For example, it may be evident in the comments of highly committed members who have been out of town and have missed some meetings. They are typically eager to return because they "just don't feel right," or they are "anxious and ill at ease" for not having been in the company of other members, even for a few days. Nor is attendance at meetings alone sufficient for committed members to feel properly affiliated. They have to maintain abstinence as well, just as members of zealous religious groups must adhere to the norms of their peer group in order to feel properly affiliated. When they fall out of compliance with the expectations of the group, they feel alienated, and their alienation is then translated into feelings of malaise. The spring is pulled taut.

Repeated exposure to this process produces an operantly conditioned, "lock-step" compliance with the demands of the group. In AA, this means maintaining abstinence and "working the steps," that is, working through a prescribed sequence of spiritually intense stages in their sobriety and growing involvement with the group.

The Diversity of Members' Experiences

To understand how these principles of group psychology are played out in patients in network therapy, we can consider how some patients became engaged in AA and how that affiliation related to their experiences in therapy.

SUPPORT WHEN NEEDED

AA can serve as a transitional object, a bridge between dependence on drugs or alcohol and a life that is independent and substance-free. Addicted people have come to depend on their drugs to address immediate emotional needs, and they become habituated to seeking relief from frustration through intoxication. Because of this, giving up a drug means an implicit loss in support. Some of this loss is replaced by the therapist and some by the concern and attention of network members. Nonetheless, a considerable emotional gap is often left. As George Vaillant points out, this is generally filled with a substitute dependence until greater autonomy is achieved.[11] Alcoholics Anonymous is probably the most effective of the alternative dependencies.

Sylvan illustrated how AA can serve as a transitional object for the initial stage of sobriety. He was from a generation of gays that had emerged from the city's cafe society, and he came to me asking for assistance with a disabling alcohol problem. Although he agreed to stop drinking and using cocaine as we met together with a few of his friends, he was reluctant to go to AA meetings, as he felt they were for "ordinary, straight" folks seeking pedestrian help. He insisted that "meetings" and "rehabs" were not stylish in his subculture, and as an openly gay person, he did not think that involvement in them was appealing. I was aware, as well, that Sylvan had had enough emotional demands placed on him by his parents while he was a teenager to make him shrink away from subjecting himself to what he perceived to be a heavy dose of social pressure.

All this changed when Sylvan encountered an acquaintance, also homosexual, whom he respected. The friend had undertaken "ninety meetings in ninety days," the suggested intensive introduction to the AA fellowship. The friend suggested that Sylvan attend an AA group comprised of gay members, and Sylvan soon attached himself to the group. He systematically went to the ninety meetings over the course of three months, acknowledging that he thought this would help him get through a difficult period. Indeed, it did.

After this initiation, Sylvan dropped out of AA, saying that he had gotten what he needed at the time, although the friend remained involved for the long term. Sylvan clearly seemed to have benefited from the group's support and concern for his abstinence. AA had provided a transition into stability when he felt he needed it, and he later did well with the therapy alone.

Angela also used AA as a transitional object early on in her treatment. Her parents, who were not in the network, had demanded that she attend one AA meeting a week as a precondition to their paying for therapy. Although their demand was an awkward imposition, she did indeed go to AA meetings for a few months with some regularity. She never worked the steps or acquired a sponsor, but nonetheless she continued to make use of meetings occasionally when she felt threatened by the possibility of drinking, even after her treatment had come to an end. AA was a support when it was needed.

A SPIRITUAL CONVERSION

Another pattern of association with AA resembles the classic experience of spiritual conversion, and is very different from the limited engagement just described. This type of transformation is common among long-term members who continue to attend regularly for many years. It entails the coalescence of the forces of social cohesiveness and belief described above. The resulting intense commitment can produce a striking change in a person's attitudes and a reliability in maintaining abstinence.

Ryan had been in treatment for several months but was occasionally still slipping into episodes of drinking. At one point, a representative of his corporation's employee assistance program contacted me to report that Ryan's drinking at the office had affected an important business meeting. I discussed this ominous communication with Ryan and his wife, making the point that his reluctance to accept total abstinence could cost him his job. Although he had reluctantly gone to a few AA meetings, I pressed him to become involved, so that he would avert another slip. He was not very enthusiastic, but he was willing to go along, given the circumstances.

Ryan began going to meetings with some regularity and, as the weeks went by, would speak with reverence about AA and about "making a commitment." He recounted with pride how he had "qualified," or spoken of his recovery experiences at a meeting. AA catch phrases began to appear in his speech, so that he would say, "Easy does

132

it," to illustrate a point about avoiding conflicts at home, rather than elaborating on the complexity of how he had dealt with his wife and children.

At times, Ryan seemed transfixed, exhibiting a lack of guile that was quite unlike him. He began to go to meetings every day in response to the suggestion of his sponsor, and soon he avowed to his wife and me that meetings had become an essential part of his life. He would some-times speak like a religious convert, suggesting contrition after years of sinning, and made clear that he would never again even consider having a drink. He spoke about the "honesty in the program," as he saw it, which would demand that he relinquish his passing infidelities. His commitment was such that I had to help his puzzled wife deal with it. I was able to follow up Ryan's experience for a number of years after his treatment came to an end. His daily attendance at AA never waned, and his working the AA twelve steps provided him with a sense of purpose in life that he cherished.

Intense responses are not always long lasting. One patient agreed to go to an AA meeting while I was trying to convince him to steer clear of his occasional cocaine use. I was struck, even touched, by the dramatic quality of his response to the fellowship. He spoke of the intense intimacy of the setting, the warmth that he felt from its members, and the compelling value of permanent abstinence that they had so convinc-ingly espoused. He had acquired overnight the same appearance that Ryan had taken on over the course of weeks. I eagerly encouraged him to attend more.

The idiosyncrasy of response to such zealous groups is often obscure. The patient returned from his next meeting, at the same chapter, and reported to his network and me that he was unimpressed, although this AA meeting had been no different from the last. He had decided that the fellowship was really not for him, he told us, and he chose not to return. This closed the door on his willingness to consider AA or Narcotics Anonymous, despite the network's repeated requests. I was unable to learn why his attitude had changed so dramatically between the two meetings.

MEETING A PSYCHOLOGICAL NEED

A very different aspect of engagement is reflected in the way spiritu-ally oriented groups can address the psychological problems of individ-ual members. Sometimes the group ameliorates long-standing symp-toms that a recruit has been unable to deal with. One man had suffered from anxiety for many years; he regularly turned to alcohol to allay the symptoms. Although he often traveled by plane, he became anxious on flights and drank heavily to relieve his distress. Presentations at meetings also caused him considerable discomfort, which he learned to anticipate and relieve with alcohol. He was tense in general.

AA helped to address his drinking problem, and his attendance at AA meetings soon corresponded to a decline in his distress. The value of AA as a tranquilizer of sorts was underlined by a statement he made to me after he had been out of town one week. "Missing meetings while I was away was a big problem. I didn't get to one for five days last week, and I just couldn't take that old 'button-pushing.' I kept barking at Jennie [his wife] and was unpleasant at work. I knew something was unsteady inside of me that was making me more irritable at every turn. But getting back to a meeting made me feel like my old self again. I'll have to make a meeting every day on the next trip."

Affiliation with a zealous group ameliorates neurotic distress by means of the relief effect, the product of the social support and cohesiveness. Any disaffiliation can yield a loss of support sufficient to generate anxiety, so that a missed meeting generates sufficient motivation to ensure continuing attendance. In the case of this last patient, the relief from distress not only provided a sense of well-being but actually yielded a decline in the symptoms that had constituted a diagnosed anxiety disorder. This relief showed. His wife pointed out in the network meetings that his demeanor had changed appreciably since he became involved in AA.

AA meetings often provide an arena in which members' personality is expressed. Thus, alcoholics with intense needs for dependency can find succor in the group, and if they are afraid of being rejected for what they might say, they are welcome to participate in a relatively passive way. Others find an opportunity for self-assertion, as AA offers the chance to contribute actively in a larger arena than people generally have available. This can be most meaningful, since most people have little chance to express their altruistic impulses in an organized group, and therefore feel empowered by the social role they can play in meetings.

Conversely, character disorders may become evident in a problematic response to the program. That can be discussed in therapy. Vivian became active in the governance of AA and served as a representative from her chapter at the AA intergroup administrative meetings. She took the opportunity to act out some of the anger she felt over the physical abuse that her mother had subjected her to when she was young, and she found it hard to temper her antagonistic attitude. On a number of occasions, she came into conflict with her AA sponsor, who also participated in these administrative meetings, and even challenged the sponsor's prerogative to attend certain out-of-town AA functions. Soon the sponsor began to remove herself from the supportive relationship that Vivian wanted of her.

As we discussed the matter in therapy, Vivian could not easily understand how her own behavior reflected an improper response to the sponsor's role as a mentor in the fellowship. In order to approach the issue, we had to deal at some length with the rage Vivian felt toward her mother, and I was able to discuss with her individually the antagonistic attitude she often directed at her mother in network meetings. In time, she began to treat her sponsor with more of the deference appropriate to their relationship.

Discussions of patients' interaction with other AA members can help them clarify interpersonal problems they encounter outside the fellowship. In Vivian's case, the exchange was productive and ultimately well received. But just as I would not question in a therapy setting the underpinnings of a patient's religious beliefs, I do not intrude myself into their commitment to the core of AA belief and practice. Such questions are best left to patients, their sponsors, and other members.

THE SYMBOLISM OF A HELPING HAND

A doctor or social worker in a hospital may tend to the needs of an alcoholic person, but they elicit little of the commitment that one sees among AA members. This difference is due in part to the belief system of AA, in which acceptance of a higher power is a rationale for mutual commitment. Members of AA might as well be members of the same novitiate or soldiers in the same embattled platoon. The pedestrian aspects of a social agency clearly have no counterpart to this social structure. The concept of a higher power not only reflects the relationship between AA and its religious antecedents, it also represents an absolute expectation of idealism. There is no parallel in the workaday world of professionals, who are paid for their efforts. This AA idealism can raise an act of simple support into one that is transforming in nature.

The symbolic importance of such assistance was evident in Maggie's description of how she stopped drinking. She had been hospitalized at a rehabilitation center for a month. She and another patient gave the staff so much trouble that they were reprimanded by their counselor and told that their prognosis was poor. Maggie left the rehab feeling that she had seen enough of its philosophy of daily AA meetings. She was uncertain about whether she would drink again, but she did have a glass of wine just to "try it out." Her errant friend had been discharged several days before her. Maggie called his house and reached his wife, only to find out to her horror that he had died shortly after discharge from an overdose of alcohol and pills.

Maggie was grief stricken, and could think only of a return to the bottle to help her forget her pain. Several days of drinking passed, and she could not bring herself to face her relatives and sober friends. She decided to take herself to an AA meeting, having no one to turn to for company. Intoxicated as she was, she exchanged words with some women at the meeting. Later she could not remember their faces, let alone their names. As she recalled, they offered to take her home after the meeting.

She next remembered waking up the following morning, uncertain about whether the strangers from the meeting might have assaulted her, or ransacked her apartment, or just left the place as they had found it. Looking around, she saw that the apartment had been put in order. Items that she had strewn about when she packed for the hospital were neatly arranged, and the dishes were washed. Clean clothes had been taken from the closet and were laid out at her bedside.

Twelve years later, Maggie told me that she never took another drink after that night, although she did not encounter any of these members of the AA fellowship thereafter, as well as she could recall, and went only infrequently to AA meetings. The help, given anonymously, had wrought a profound effect on her. The experience was as close to a spiritual one as she was likely to encounter, and I preferred not to intrude on the resulting recovery through my analysis of the situation.

The experience that followed her pivotal AA meeting had apparently transformed her view of the fellowship from suspicion to trust, and with that transformation Maggie had been able to accept the message it offered. This organized altruism, embodied in the twelfth step, introduces into the fellowship the tradition of Christian charity, one that has become less common in our world of anomie and lost community. This message can have a profound effect on the alcoholic who feels dejected and alone.

PATIENTS WHO RESIST AA

Almost every alcoholic embarks on a plan for recovery with unconscious ambivalence, and usually with a conscious desire to drink at some future time—perhaps even the next day. The influence of the therapy network and the pressure that it can generate to get a patient to agree to attend several AA meetings is most valuable, since therapists on their own have limited influence in this regard. A spouse who is encouraged to go to some meetings with a patient, a friend in the network who expresses interest in their content, a network member who reports that AA was useful to his own relative, all are invaluable in moving the person through the initial stages of resistance. The ambivalent response of individual patients to this situation presents an intriguing glimpse of how a given personality style can interfere with the process of engagement.

Fear of Passivity

A patient may avoid attending AA meetings out of a fear of passivity. Iris, an epileptic alcoholic, had seen her independence compromised over the course of many years while she was forced to rely heavily on her physicians and family as they struggled to deal with her disability. Not only did she often find herself at the mercy of those around her because of her seizures, but she came to rely very heavily as well on her domineering father, who continued to infantilize her far beyond her adolescent years.

Alcohol provided her with a vehicle for rebelling against this feared passivity when she was in college, and she said to me more than once that she had had enough of being at the mercy of her father. But Iris was also clearly drawn to being dependent on others, as passivity had acquired a seductive quality in her youth. It became clear that her rebellious behavior was a way of staving off the attractiveness of being cared for. This counterdependency underlay her initial reluctance to attend AA meetings, as she was afraid of becoming dependent on them.

I would not deal with issues like these in the network, as they reflected conflicts that were too troubling for Iris. Instead I solicited support from the network members on the practical value of going to AA meetings. Fortunately, one member was herself a recovering alcoholic; she was more than willing to accompany Iris to AA initially and to acclimate her to the program. Iris learned that there are a variety of possible accommodations to AA and that the fear of engulfment that she experienced could be addressed by tailoring her own adaptation to the program. She consistently kept herself from an intense involvement—instead of going each day, she would attend a regular weekly meeting and drop in at an additional one when she felt the need. This pattern kept her at enough of a distance to avoid the issue of her own potential for submitting passively to the group's regimen.

Fear of Humiliation

Another reason for avoiding AA is the fear of humiliation, of suffering an injury to one's narcissism by exposure to potential slight or embarrassment. Indeed, protected pride could well have been the hallmark of Charles's adaptation, as his refined image and impeccable professional reputation were more to him than just a way of managing his career. Like his upright and stiff posture, these were ways of avoiding embarrassment.

In his therapy as well, Charles was unwilling to reveal himself in a way that would compromise his pride. His sessions with the network and individually were stilted, and he had little to offer about the unpleasant and threatening issues that underlay his drinking. He would have no truck with AA, and he refused to attend even one meeting. Members of his network and I were of no avail in influencing him, and his avowal that he had nothing to say to a group of strangers was one that we could not circumvent; his treatment proceeded without any encounter with the fellowship. Fortunately he was willing to comply with a regimen of taking disulfiram, observed by his wife; he held her at enough of a distance emotionally so that she posed relatively little threat to him.

Conflicts about Anger and Retribution

To some people any affiliation may seem like a potential threat. Emmett projected the image of a punishing parent onto AA, making it an object of dread. His adolescence was replete with behaviors that could only be called psychopathic, although his upper-middle-class, liberal background would have suggested a more temperate attitude. He was a very angry and abusive adolescent, involved in many fistfights and in petty crime. He spent part of his college years in jail for not complying with police investigations into a drug ring he was involved in.

For Emmett, the line between exposure and punishment was a thin one, and he was constantly vulnerable to doing battle with any party whom he saw as an authority. If confronted by teachers, police, or a therapist, he provoked punishment through his hostile, sometimes passive-aggressive behavior, while at the same time living in fear of their anger. This pattern clearly derived from a very troubled relationship

138

with his father, who had been cruel and derisive toward him throughout his youth.

Not surprisingly, Emmett was reluctant to become involved in AA throughout the very rocky period of his own recovery. I felt, though, that he might be willing to attend if he could overcome his view of the organization as an agent of punishment. I was aware that he could form close ties with friends whom he trusted, and he did continue to see me and to assemble his therapy network, admittedly between bouts of anger.

In time, Emmett agreed to go to AA meetings, encouraged by a friend who was in the fellowship. At first he was unable to speak up at all, and he did not qualify at a meeting for the longest time. As his therapy progressed, though, he began to appreciate better his own provocative style, and the world around him began to appear less menacing. He tried participating more actively in the fellowship, and soon he became a deeply committed member and a strong advocate. Now he used catchwords and maxims from AA to lecture to his network and me as he asserted his newfound status as a member of a select group. Emmett's conversion to a full acceptance of AA reflected his ability to split the world in two, into good and evil, accepting and rejecting. Whereas AA had initially represented a punitive and threatening force, it came later to gain the unqualified acceptance that Emmett had sought but fearfully fended off. He now embraced AA fully, and even used it as a vehicle for asserting control over his life to avoid feeling threatened by those around him.

We see that AA generates cohesiveness and a consensus, as does network treatment. Because of the intense commitment AA engenders, however, it offers a reliable influence for abstinence that the network alone may not provide. On this count, patients who become engaged in AA have a materially better chance of remaining abstinent, and hence of achieving a successful recovery.

PART III

PRINCIPLES OF NETWORK THERAPY

CHAPTER 8

Maintaining Abstinence

HAVING CONTRASTED NETWORK THERAPY with other modalities, we can now look at how this approach addresses the psychology of addicted persons over the course of their therapy. We will consider the middle game of treatment, played out after the patient is initially engaged but before abstinence has been stabilized. In this context, the fragile beginnings of abstinence must be stabilized and relations within the network secured. The network approach can therefore be conceived around three issues:

1. Maintaining abstinence
2. Supporting the network
3. Securing future behavior

The dispute over whether alcoholics can ever return to normal, social drinking has attracted a great deal of attention. The question is important: the clinician must be clear whether the standard of abstinence is absolute and how aggressively it can be applied to all patients. Should any drinking ever be allowed? What is the impact of a transient slip?

From a theoretical standpoint, some arguments have been advanced for the feasibility of nonabstinent goals. Alcoholism is a syndrome with behavioral manifestations that can reflect the willful misconduct of the drinker. That is to say, the alcoholic's difficulties are clearly not the product of uncontrollable biological factors alone. The syndrome is clearly distinguished from purely neurological diseases, like epilepsy or dementia. This has led some people—nonclinicians—to oppose the concept of alcoholism as a disease; and some behavioral psychologists have undertaken research into techniques to train less severe alcoholics for limited drinking.[1] Approaches to limited drinking range from structured behavioral regimens and the examination of cues that precipitate excessive drinking, to educational approaches, and even to manuals that the alcoholic applies on his or her own.[2]

Nonetheless, it is quite telling that in recent years the goal of controlled use by addicted persons has largely been abandoned in the United States for the treatment of alcohol dependence, and certainly for the treatment of dependence on drugs like cocaine and heroin. In fact, some early studies that suggested the feasibility of controlled drinking have been reexamined and questions have been raised of whether their findings justify the inference that controlled drinking is viable.[3] The very low incidence of good nonabstinent positive outcomes has been further corroborated in a thorough follow-up of 1,289 alcoholics who had required hospitalization in St. Louis, conducted by John Helzer and his colleagues.[4] Less than 2 percent met the criteria of stable, moderated drinking by the end of the five-to-eight-year period of follow-up.

Probably more influential, though, has been the consensus of practitioners in the field. I know of no established clinical program for alcoholism in the United States that offers controlled drinking as the announced goal of alcoholism treatment. Senior clinicians, as well, such as Griffith Edwards, Sheldon Zimberg, Stanley Gitlow, and Donald Gallant, have also adopted this stance.[5] I have followed up patients who were unwilling to embark on an abstinent treatment regimen and decided to control their drinking or drug use on their own. Later I have been regularly distressed to hear of highly disadvantageous outcomes, ranging from broken homes and compromised careers to fatalities from the toxic effects of alcohol or drugs, sometimes suicide. Alcoholics Anonymous, which is responsible for the recovery of more alcoholic patients than any other current approach, eschews the concept of controlled drinking. The astute alcoholic, family member, or clinician is wise to avoid swimming against this tide.

Despite all this, we know that some treated alcoholics, on follow-up, are apparently found to be drinking less, albeit with some problems. Edward Gottheil and George Vaillant, for example, both carefully examined the outcome for treated alcoholics and community-based alcoholics, respectively.[6] They found that a portion of them were drinking but to a lesser degree than they had at first contact. The problem in considering controlled drinking in a given patient, however, is that only a very small portion of bona fide alcoholics actually learn to moderate their drinking. Although we know that they are likely to be among the less severe drinkers, we do not know how to predict which patients these might be, nor do we have any way of determining which ones who initially limit their drinking will relapse weeks or months later into their earlier pattern of alcoholism. In a given case, a clinician would be ill advised to allow a patient to elect a treatment goal whose outcome is most likely to be bad.

In light of all this, a strategy must be framed to make abstinence a primary goal of treatment. To this end, intervention can take place with varying degrees of intrusiveness. On the most limited level, a proper accounting of the circumstances surrounding addictive behavior must be obtained, and the patient must be confronted with his or her denial. Beyond this, pressure and behavioral controls are introduced.

Getting at the Real Story

To plan well for continued abstinence requires taking an accurate history. Such information is obtained much more reliably if the patient's network can supplement what the patient provides. The rationalizations of the addict alone will leave the therapist unaware of essential aspects of his or her history. This is well illustrated by the many patients who are treated for depression or anxiety and then are later found to suffer from occult alcoholism.

Larry's treatment required a series of interventions designed to ensure that the right information was available regarding his drinking. He came to see me because he was depressed and less able to travel, problems that had emerged after he experienced a series of panic attacks while commuting to work by train. These episodes left him anxious over leaving the house, and frightened in particular of using any train or subway. His symptoms abated after he was treated with a combination of antidepressant medication and desensitization, both couched in a supportive psychotherapy. Several weeks into his treatment, though, he described some arguments with his wife, and I came to suspect that his drinking was more of a problem than he had acknowledged in his initial evaluation. We discussed the matter, and he said he sometimes got drunk when they argued.

I decided to ask him to bring his wife in. That step might seem unremarkable, but it was actually awkward in the context of his ongoing therapy. Over the course of individual treatment, patients and their therapists tend to develop a sort of cocoon. Mutual protectiveness becomes part of an implicit contract, and an attempt by the therapist to change the singular nature of this liaison can be experienced as a violation of the intimacy achieved. This is particularly true if the introduction of an outsider relates to an issue around which the patient feels defensive, like drinking.

Larry was very protective of our sessions, and I realized my request to bring in his wife would have to be made carefully so that his resistance would not compromise the plan. If I were to say: "Larry, the arguments you describe make me think that you might be having a problem with your drinking. What would you think about bringing Janet in so the three of us can discuss this together?" Larry might respond, "I don't think that's such a good idea. Janet has been on the warpath recently." It is hard to back a patient off from such a position. Then if I replied, "But the information she would give us could be quite helpful," he could answer, "I don't think she would have much to offer, and I don't think I'd be comfortable with her here." That would end the discussion.

When a collateral is needed for information, the therapist is wise to anticipate the patient's reluctance and to take charge of the terrain from the outset, introducing the topic with some emotional intensity and assertiveness. I therefore had to let Larry know that as his therapist, presumably acting wisely on his behalf, I *expected* his cooperation. "You know, Larry," I said for a start, "these stories make me think you've got a problem with alcohol, one that can seriously undermine your interests. The only way to approach this sensibly is to bring in your wife and for us all to talk it over. I've found that there's no other way to get a clear picture of the situation. I'd like you to speak with her and have her join us at our next session." I then discussed with him travel and even babysitting logistics to obviate any excuses. If he had not spoken with Janet by the next time, I was prepared to get him to call her up on the spot and make arrangements for her to come in. My point is that you don't leave things to chance if a collateral is needed to acquire information relevant to abstinence. You devise a strategy that will ensure the person's presence.

Larry's wife did come in the next week. As I expected, she provided information that reflected a good deal more of a problem than Larry had been able to acknowledge. His drunkenness had caused them considerable trouble, even in the last two weeks. One evening he had a blackout and forgot where he had left the car; they had not been able to locate it until the next afternoon. On another occasion he had broken down the door to their bedroom during an argument while he was drunk. What is more, for some years he had drunk himself to sleep in front of the television on most evenings.

Larry clearly had a problem with drinking, but it was not clear whether he had to be abstinent or whether he might moderate his consumption. Here, too, proper information had to be obtained to make the decision. I decided to use a diagnostic test developed by Marty Mann, one of the pioneers in AA, and a very astute student of alcohol problems. She had described it to me in my days in the addiction field. She sometimes based her assessment of whether abstinence would be necessary on the characteristic loss of control seen in true alcoholics— their inability to define limits to their drinking once they had taken their first drink. A period of abstinence alone would not be a sufficient test, since alcoholics often sustain abstinence successfully, even for weeks, before they relapse. The person being evaluated is therefore instructed to designate a lower limit to the alcohol he or she will consume each day during one month, perhaps one drink or two. This means that the person will have to test his or her control once the drinking cue of alcohol is introduced. The patient then chooses a daily upper limit, as well, intending to consume no more than that limit, perhaps six, even eight or ten, drinks. An alcoholic who begins drinking will prove unable to stay under this prescribed upper limit for thirty days. If a person can stay within the limit, he or she can learn to control drinking.

The approach is a useful one, but Larry illustrated how information for such an evaluation requires the input of another person. By the tenth day of this test, Larry's reports were quite positive, although he did say that he had "about" six drinks on a few occasions; his upper limit had been six, not about six. I had my suspicions, but I decided to wait until we had his wife come in at the midpoint of the test to give her reading of his performance.

Janet contradicted Larry on two counts; they seemed subtle to him, but clearly reflected an entirely different perspective. She reported that on several social occasions Larry seemed to have drunk more than his prescribed six drinks; she had kept an eye on him while he made trips to the bar in their living room. Even more important was the quantity of vodka that Larry consumed with each "drink." For the purpose of this test, we had defined a drink as an ounce and a half of hard liquor, four ounces of wine, or twelve ounces of beer, all equivalent in alcohol content. She pointed out that Larry poured his vodka into a tumbler rather than a shot glass; he would pour in what looked like several ounces, and then add a few ice cubes. On my request, before the next session, Larry measured out the amount of liquor equivalent to what he usually poured into his tumbler. It turned out to be four or five ounces. His drinking problem was clearly greater than he had estimated.

This experience with Larry underlines some important points about securing abstinence. We see clearly that collateral information is essential; if a person needs to be evaluated for an alcohol or drug problem at all, he or she cannot be assumed to be a reliable informant. In opening up necessary sources of information regarding drinking, the exclusivity of the therapist–patient encounter cannot become an obstruction. Furthermore, one meeting with a collateral will not guarantee clarity about the patient's drinking.

Collateral information is necessary also to protect the abstinence of addicted people who are assumed to have been long recovering. Cindy had been given my name at a point in her life when she was snorting heroin on most days; she was considering entering treatment for her drug problem. Now, two years later, she came in with a writing block that complicated her work as a freelance author.

Cindy had apparently succeeded in overcoming a difficult problem with addiction, and she was now motivated to move on and enhance her capacity to work productively. The clarity of her presentation left me inclined to take her reported abstinence at face value. Furthermore, I was touched—even shocked—by the difficulties she had experienced as a child. It was not surprising that she had turned to drug abuse when she had entered adolescence. It would be nice for a change to treat someone who had overcome a serious addictive problem on her own.

Nonetheless, I felt obliged to disrupt our exchange and ask her to bring in some friends to serve as a network for ensuring her abstinence. I had encountered enough problems with the emergence of drug use in supposedly stable patients to want a measure of protection for the recovery that she had achieved. She agreed to bring in two friends. As the four of us spoke, there seemed to be a comfortable and somewhat self-congratulatory quality to the initial exchanges about her recovery.

After half the session had passed, though, I turned to one member of the network and asked him if he was certain of the security of her recovery. He looked at her, then told her pointedly, "I'm not so sure about that. You hang around with a pretty wild crowd. I've been to some of their parties and seen some heroin and coke passed around." Cindy looked a little sheepish, and her friend continued, apparently willing to confront her for her own good. "I know you sometimes try out some of the drugs they offer."

148

Cindy acknowledged, "Well, maybe sometimes." It emerged that her use of drugs on such occasions had been infrequent for the past year, perhaps on only two or three occasions, but it had taken place.

"Do you have any other concerns?" I asked the friend.

He looked to her for permission to speak. After she gave it, he said, "Well, Cindy sometimes has house guests who transfer heroin from Europe to the States. I don't think she's tried any of it, though."

"Maybe you can say some more about this," I said to Cindy, wondering now what the whole story might be. She did indeed host some drug dealers once or twice a year, friends from a time when she had been into a good deal more trouble, but she no longer got any financial benefit from the encounters. It later emerged that this activity reflected a pattern of antisocial behavior carried over from her highly rebellious adolescence. Although she did not consume the drugs that dealers were bringing to her home, the vulnerability to drug use was still there and had to be addressed. Cindy clearly had something of a secret life, a remnant of her former pattern of drug use. The very symbolic nature of this secrecy—keeping it from authority figures, as she had kept her addiction from her parents—necessitated having access to her collaterals. I would not have wanted this drug exposure to compromise a recovery that was progressing in a constructive way.

It is worth noting here that the diagnostic manual of the American Psychiatric Association allows for the designation of different levels of severity for alcohol and drug dependence, but it has no category for full recovery. Addiction can be in remission, but there is no acknowledged cure. It is always useful to corroborate a patient's report, even late into sobriety.

Getting the Addict to Go Along

STRATEGIC PRESSURE

We can next consider the introduction of social pressure in the network setting as a means of ensuring abstinence. Influence, as we shall see, can be introduced with varying degrees of intensity.

Albie came to me because his family and friends were concerned that his heavy, regular use of cocaine was compromising his competency at work and his social life. In the initial meeting he agreed to bring in a friend and his parents. I was aware that this network had its problems, since Albie had originally become involved in drug use while asserting independence from a domineering father, for whom he now worked. But his family constituted an important part of his social universe, and his adjustment in the workplace was very important to him. In any case, including a senior figure from the workplace in the network would inevitably suggest coercion.

A few days after the network met, Albie and I had a second session. He reported having a slip after a particularly hard day at work, apparently in reaction to an argument with his father at the office. He had been up all night doing cocaine, and he had used some the next day as well, missing work. We examined the circumstances, in particular the cues immediately preceding his calling up his drug supplier; the exchange was useful in helping him define for himself how anger and frustration had led him to crave the drug.

The ensuing session was held with the entire network, in which a variety of conflicting forces had to be orchestrated to establish pressure for Albie's securing abstinence. Albie himself was quite willing to discuss the nature of his slips, but his parents were apparently tortured over this most recent drug use. His mother held back tears, while his father made it clear that he was on the verge of tossing his son out of the family business. Neither parent was contributing in a constructive way, and I suggested that they allow more time before making a judgment about the outcome of their son's attempt at recovery. In addition, I went over the conditioning model of drug-related cues to give them an intellectual hook on which to hang their participation and to justify some temperance. Albie's friend was useful in setting a tone of moderation, leaving the parents reluctant to create too embarrassing an emotional display.

In one respect, the tension in the session encouraged me to assume a positive therapeutic stance, in that it allowed for the triangulation that can emerge in such family settings. I could position myself as an intermediary between the troubled parents and their guilty son, while remaining on the sidelines of their argument. I could thereby address, as a protector, rather than an accuser, the defensiveness and anger that had regularly turned Albie to reactive drug use. The parents' guilt evocation and implied threat were therefore not without utility. They provided an element of coercion, which, if carefully controlled, would help keep Albie on his toes. Moderate pressure is an important tool for securing abstinence.

Over the course of the network sessions, it was possible to educate the parents and to get them to be patient. Albie became more trusting toward me and better able to open up in his individual therapy. He discussed his misgivings about his parents and was able to deal with some of the anger that had previously been channeled into acting out through drug abuse. He could address related adaptive problems as well. He began to understand better some of the hostility he was venting toward his girlfriend, resentment that he had found hard to suppress in previous relationships.

A rather different option for the management of social pressure to promote abstinence came up later with the network, when the status of Albie's recovery emerged as an issue in planning for the family's business. His uncle and father were reorganizing their workplace and had to decide what role to carve out for Albie in the new operation. I was well aware of the practical importance of the matter, as it could have a material effect on Albie's future, and he and I discussed at some length what stresses the new business might bring to bear and whether he would be able to deal with these pressures. Albie had not used cocaine for four months at this point, and I felt I could support a positive view of his future, based on his regular attendance in therapy and on the network's corroboration of his abstinence.

After some discussion, Albie and I decided to have the uncle join us in the network so that the entire family could discuss Albie's role in the business. This idea seemed strategically sound, since his progress had reached the point where the family could begin thinking of him and his ability to assume responsibility in a new way.

I asked Albie to give the network an assessment of his ability to handle a new and demanding role at work. He reviewed his progress in a positive way, and I encouraged the family's planning a more active and ambitious role for him. In response to us both, they expressed a willingness to offer him a more responsible place in the firm. The mood in the office was positive, and it was borne out over the ensuing months; Albie's recovery had been further secured. Again, I was able as therapist to use leverage with both the patient and his family to bolster his abstinence, and to triangulate with the family's demands for stability and the patient's need for support. Nonetheless, behind the change was implicit coercion, because Albie's father would be privy to discussion of his drug use should he experience a slip.

HOW MUCH COERCION?

A patient's resistance to treatment can provoke an intrusive reaction from his or her friends. Network members will therefore sometimes coerce patients to remain abstinent in a heavyhanded way. This was certainly true for Sandy, an aggressive publicist whose friends responded with an assertiveness that complemented his own. I first encountered Sandy's case when three of his friends came to ask what they could do to bring him to his senses and avert his ruination. Sandy was in his early forties and had suffered from alcohol problems dating back to college. He had long considered his drinking to be a measure of his virility, and he was delighted that he could drink all of his buddies under the table. In recent years, however, his periods of effective functioning between protracted drinking bouts had become shorter, and a bender now and again left his small public relations firm without leadership and vulnerable to losing accounts.

With his friends I discussed the course of alcoholism at some length, described options for intervening, and suggested that they press him to come in to see me. I made clear that his tenacious dependence on alcohol might mean that a hospital stay would be necessary to start unless he could comply with a structured ambulatory regimen. When his friends spoke with him, Sandy did agree to come in. In my office he was even willing to acknowledge that he had a drinking problem. But he insisted that he could handle it on his own, as he apparently handled all other problems. He was not prepared to consider any other alternatives I offered, and he saw no reason to take seriously my suggestion that he consider hospitalization, network meetings, or attendance at AA.

A month later, Sandy's drinking again got out of hand. His friends, having been coached on the options open to them, brought him in his sodden state to a local hospital to detoxify and, they hoped, to embark on treatment. Within a few days, Sandy was planning to leave on his own recognizance. Paul, one member of the group, called me, and I told him that I would be pleased to see Sandy again. Paul conferred with his friends, then called back to say that Sandy would come back to my office—or they would bring him in. Paul simply wanted to know how to deliver him to my doorstep.

I was taken aback by his aggressive style, but I could see its value in producing some movement in this reluctant patient. After some discussion with me and then with the two other network members, Paul said that he would arrange for Sandy's discharge from the hospital to be set for a time that I was available, and that he would "guarantee Sandy's delivery, one way or another." In that light, I asked that the entire network come in with Sandy so that we would all be able to discuss ways for him to achieve abstinence. The tone was being set for this nascent network. Sandy would be willing to consider help, but he had to be shoved along to comply.

The network members clearly cared for their alcoholic friend, and they were prepared to go to great lengths to help him out. When I spoke with Sandy I could tell that he was quite attached to them, although he was annoyed that they had involved themselves in his drinking habits. But Sandy was obviously drinking himself into the ground, and there didn't seem to be a better way to go about stopping him.

Sandy's treatment stretched out over three years, and he was sober for the last year continuously. The last part of his therapy was directed at helping him achieve a more comfortable accommodation to life. Throughout the first year, however, he only grudgingly accepted the steps that would secure his abstinence. Each was taken with intense pressure from network members after a relapse. On one occasion, after he had been taking disulfiram for three months, he had to go to London for a week on business. Apparently things did not go too well with his client, and his hubris, which he bore like armor, was damaged. He "forgot" to take disulfiram for a few days. On the plane home, while he was ruminating about his difficulties, he ordered a drink. Then he had some more. Over the course of the flight he became so intoxicated that he had to be taken by wheelchair to a taxi when the plane landed.

After he missed our next scheduled session and did not answer the phone, I made contact with his network members to see if they had heard from him. They were quite concerned, and Paul volunteered to go over to Sandy's apartment to see whether he was there. A few hours later I heard from Paul. Sandy was soused, lying in bed, insisting that he would drink until he saw fit to stop and that he did not want to discuss the matter. I envisioned a protracted bender unless some intervention were developed, so I was contemplating what to do.

Paul solved the problem: "Don't worry. I'll make sure he doesn't drink any more. While he's in this shape I can push him around if I need to."

A vision of shackles and bruised wrists went through my mind. "What do you mean?"

"Look, I'm here. I'll just keep an eye on him. Dennis can take over later tonight when I have to go home."

I mulled over my experience with networks, and concluded that this was not likely to result in too alarming a situation. "Is he cooperative?"

"He isn't really saying much."

"Can I speak with him?"

"He doesn't want to talk to anyone."

The next day, Sandy was willing to talk on the phone and was contrite. He had been moved over to his girlfriend's house in the morning when Dennis and Paul had adjudged him to be sufficiently cooperative to be placed in her custody. He was ready to pick up where

153

he had left off before to his trip overseas, apparently the wiser for his experience.

This intervention was clearly more intrusive than usual. The degree of surveillance established by Sandy's network members rarely came close to that provided in a hospital, and the introduction of constraints like Paul's should be considered only if they can be accomplished with a genuine feeling of supportiveness. Such coercive intervention in the hands of parties that a patient views with ambivalence would clearly be counterproductive; a patient should not be led to mistake assistance for malice. Thus, parents dealing with a late adolescent or young adult child in such a manner would probably compromise his or her trust for the network, and for the therapist as well; they would no doubt elicit all the resentments of adolescent rebellion.

AA members may also intervene actively, and at times may come to the home of an alcoholic person. But they are wisely constrained by the limitations in their relationship with the person and by the need for the fellowship to be perceived as nonintrusive. An AA member would not be likely to coerce or restrain someone.

Many techniques can therefore be summoned up to ensure a patient's abstinence; the degree to which they intrude on him or her varies considerably. In most cases, network members are called on to play a role in the office alone. They typically give information on circumstances that carry the risk of relapse, and they provide support. Beyond that, they may sometimes verbalize strongly held feelings, and they may help to plan living or financial arrangements.

More active pressure is applied less commonly. This step is restrained by the therapist, rather than encouraged. Such interventions should be premised on a clear understanding of the nature of the collaboration between therapist, patient, and network members. For these reasons, considerable clinical judgment is needed in allowing for the use of any coercive measures.

Is Abstinence the Only Option?

In our public clinic, I tend to accept diminished, but still problematic, levels of drinking. We have limited staff support, and the patients are disadvantaged. In private practice, I am less accepting of any alcohol or drug use, and with rare exceptions I will not treat substance abusers who continue to use drugs on which they are dependent. If the alcohol or drug use persists, I might see the patient with a network at infrequent intervals to keep in touch but defer treatment until the patient is ready for abstinence.

Circumstances, however, do infrequently yield an outcome of moderated drinking, and I think it is important here to illustrate how this can emerge in the context of network therapy. An effective strategy, however well applied, cannot guarantee every patient's compliance with the agreed-on goal of abstinence. We can therefore consider two patients who achieved a limitation in their drinking, one with apparent success, the other with more problematic results. For each, treatment began with the intention of sustaining abstinence, but in each case I had to face the following quandary: patients are supposed to accept the goal of abstinence. Under what circumstances, however, should they be treated further even if they renege on this commitment?

The first patient is Jack, whose wife, Sally, was described previously, (chapter 5) as an enabler of his drinking. She was unwilling to tolerate his bouts of drunkenness at social events, but she balked at the prospect of being married to someone who could not hold his liquor and drink in a convivial way with her family. That standard created a problem for Jack, as he had become intoxicated at family events, embarrassing his wife and driving her to torrents of derision. In addition, his problem with drinking had extended into other areas of his life at home. Over the few months preceding his treatment, however, Jack's problem had diminished in response to pressure from Sally. He was drinking somewhat less at home over the course of the evening, and his episodes of unruly intoxication at social events had become less frequent.

Sally's attitude was a roadblock for the treatment. As I embarked on a plan of abstinence with Jack, she subverted it by speaking derisively at home of his "inability to drink." I felt that it was necessary to have her engaged in his network, however, so that I could keep an eye on her. I asked to include an additional party, hoping to temper her contributions. Jack suggested his brother, a sensible and thoughtful person who was well acquainted with his long-standing drinking problem.

It seemed clear to me that to sustain a stable abstinence, particularly with the conflict engendered by his wife, Jack would need the support of disulfiram. He took his pills on his own, stopped drinking, and participated in a constructive way in his individual therapy. After several months, however, it emerged that Jack had begun to skip his disulfiram and was having a few drinks at social events, in good part in response to pressure from Sally. His brother and I were concerned, but Jack insisted that he now wanted to try to drink in moderation. Apparently pressure from Sally had augmented his natural preference as an alcoholic

155

to keep drinking. There did not seem to be a strong strategic base on which to argue for abstinence, since his wife was the very person who had led him to treatment.

Jack seemed to have traits that carry a good prognosis for controlled drinking. He had experienced an improvement in his problem even before the onset of therapy, and he had been successfully abstinent for several months. His work and home lives were stable, and his attitude was reasonably positive. It seemed best to allow him his trial of controlled drinking, with an understanding that he would pursue abstinence if it did not work out.

After careful discussion, we agreed that Jack would drink only at social occasions, and that he would have no more than three drinks of wine, never any hard liquor. This seemed to satisfy him and Sally, as it met the symbolic needs of being a social drinker, rather than someone who could not exercise control over his drinking. We wrote down the particulars of this accord, and agreed as well that Sally and Jack's brother would monitor the agreement and report to me if it were breached. I continued to see Jack for three more months, and met with him and his network on four subsequent occasions over the next year and a half. At these times, much attention was paid to the drinking cues he encountered and how they were managed. I also had occasion to communicate with a different relative of his a few years later, who reported to me that Jack had sustained his moderation in drinking. Freedom from the ill consequences of alcoholism for that long a time is as good an outcome as we see in most studies of alcoholism treatment, and can be considered to be auspicious.

What does this experience illustrate? Jack had begun to limit his drinking prior to embarking on the disulfiram regimen. Clearly he showed the motivation and capacity to move toward stability on his own. In addition, his problems were most evident on occasions when he fell into conflict with his wife, and he and I had been able to discuss this issue in his individual therapy. This may have given him a stronger base for avoiding intoxication as an instrument of rebellion.

Sally also contributed to the stability of his controlled drinking. She set limits on either side of the range within which Jack could drink. She was assertive and highly influential in his thinking, and she was not prepared to tolerate his being either abstemious or rowdy. While he had been implicitly rebelling against it for years, this pincer effect influenced his positive outcome.

Finally, although Jack was successful in achieving a pattern of controlled drinking, his success was not predictable when he initially presented. Others, even persons with similar characteristics, have failed to stabilize in this manner. I would not have suggested this regimen at the outset, although it did evolve successfully after the fact.

Another patient attempted to limit drinking, with a less positive outcome—an outcome clearly related to his less positive attitude, his heavier drinking, and his lack of proper support. From the outset, Harold's circumstances did not suggest a good prognosis: he evidenced poor social adjustment and severe alcoholism. My encounter with him yielded a modified drinking pattern that retained many problems associated with alcoholism.

Harold was in his mid-thirties. He had begun smoking marijuana heavily in high school, trading in the drug as well. He later dropped out of college after succeeding in a summer job which he parlayed into regular work, but he was fired within a year because of his regular drug use. Over the ensuing decade Harold supported himself partly on family assets and partly on the marijuana trade. He drifted toward a heavy reliance on alcohol. By the time his family came to speak with me, he was subject to occasional benders and spent much of his time in a slovenly apartment, drinking through his afternoons and evenings. Some of his binges left him unreachable for a day or two. His mother and two brothers were very frightened for him.

It was clear to me that Harold should be placed on a regimen of abstinence. He did agree to stop drinking, although he would not take disulfiram and only reluctantly agreed to go to a few AA meetings. I was willing to treat him, though, given his announced willingness to be abstinent and to assemble a network. Unfortunately, however, after not drinking for several weeks, Harold began to drink intermittently, insisting that he would stop as soon as he "ran into trouble."

I felt a certain concern for his family, and agreed to continue with this treatment. That may have been a mistake. Nonetheless, I was influenced by Harold's seeming willingness to achieve a stable outcome, and I agreed to go along with this plan. Harold did maintain a lower level of drinking. He had gone from a pint or more of hard liquor each evening to about six ounces. He would have three or four drinks in a bar some afternoons, as well, but much less than he used to drink. He had no more benders. This decline in drinking, along with his therapy, enabled him to set up a more appropriate residence, to manage his resources more sensibly, and to socialize with women more appropriately.

Still, Harold was beset by problems that were embedded in this residual drinking, so that I had to regard his outcome as much less successful than I would have preferred. His characteristic adaptation of withdrawing from conflict and standing as an outsider persisted. Although he saw women, his encounters were characterized by dependency and angry confrontations, followed by withdrawal. Most evenings were still spent at home, moderately intoxicated. Nor did his relationship with his brothers, who had achieved considerable success in life, improve. They had initially joined in his network, but after seeing Harold achieve only modest improvement in his social circumstances, they eventually opted out. Two friends of Harold's, who remained in the network with his mother, were more tolerant of his deviancy. The network and I remained unable to generate a commitment that would move him toward abstinence.

Harold's inclination to maintain unrealistic aspirations as a means of avoiding responsibility was in conflict with any motivation to achieve sobriety. For some time, he had fancied himself as a musician, and although he had an amateur's talent, his aspiration served for him more as a defense against embarking on a realistic career plan than as a true vocation. He likewise refused to affiliate himself with AA to any appreciable extent, although he did attend a meeting every week or two. To stop drinking meant facing reality in its fullest, and his personality disorder did not allow him to pursue that end.

Unlike Jack, who was relatively well adjusted, Harold found the move toward a functional, controlled drinking state to be too threatening to embrace. In the absence of more definitive means of intervening, I was able to bring him only so far. Perhaps I should have been more willing to refuse to see him for a time when he began drinking again.

Harold's outcome reflects the fate of a portion of treated alcoholics who move from a level of destructive drinking to one of heavy, if less dangerous, consumption. These patients may have protracted periods of stability, some for the long term, at such a level. This was evident when we followed up a large number of patients in our public clinic.[7] Some were drinking less and were relatively stable, but they functioned at a level considerably below their potential. Abstinence, if it had been achieved, would have supported a more positive social outcome.

CHAPTER 9

Supporting the Network

IN MANY WAYS, psychotherapy is a sophisticated technology for social influence, one that evolved into its current form over more than a century. From the early psychoanalysis to more recent brief therapies and behavioral approaches, clinicians and researchers in the mental health field have refined psychotherapy to be more efficient and better targeted at specific populations. As a technology, however, psychotherapy is unique in that it makes use of communication and social interaction as its equipment, rather than mechanical or electronic devices. If the verbal approaches used in the psychotherapies were tangible rather than expressive, if they were made up of mechanical parts rather than human speech, we would more readily recognize them as the artifacts of a technological science.

One aspect of the recent evolution in our psychotherapeutic tools has been the engagement of families and small groups as instruments for change and symptom relief. From this perspective, the use of the social network to stabilize abstinence can be seen as the development of a new technological device. The network itself is an instrument for change; as with a mechanical device, its constitution and integrity must be protected, and its smooth function must be ensured.

Keeping the Network Intact

THE PATIENT'S ROLE

The importance of the patient's responsibility in care and protection of the network cannot be underestimated. For one thing, the patient's participation is essential if the network is not to be perceived as an instrument of coercion. If it were seen that way, the patient would soon find it irrelevant in the curbing of temptations and craving, just as nagging friends and family were beforehand. The patient must see the network as an adjunct to his or her own efforts to achieve a stable sobriety.

The network must never suppress the patient's initiative, since recovery is an active process. Addicted people have to be vigilant for problems as soon as they appear on the horizon so as to avoid cues for drinking or taking drugs. It is essential that the patient be engaged in a therapeutic process in which his or her own activity is prized and supported. This important self-help is promoted in Alcoholics Anonymous, and a similar feeling of initiative must be supported in network therapy as well. In contrast, in conventional insight therapy a patient often has no formal responsibility other than talking, paying, and being reasonably civil.

The addict's active role in network therapy includes ensuring that the group's members will be present at appointed sessions and that misunderstandings or tangled personal relations do not impede effective interaction. In this respect, the patient becomes an active collaborator with the therapist, with a defined role in managing the group.

Some patients, like those with executive experience at work, are effective managers of people and can readily summon up a network and sustain ongoing attendance. It is useful to rely on and be appreciative of their considerable skills. Compliments will bolster their self-esteem. This feeling of empowerment is particularly valuable early in recovery, when patients' confidence is typically compromised.

Other patients are good at engaging and sustaining the network because of their own self-absorption, a narcissistic investment in themselves, and they bask in the pleasure they derive from being the focus of attention in any group, whatever its purpose. To interpret this potential character flaw early on would no doubt produce injury to their pride; it would be of no value to them and could potentially undermine the therapeutic alliance. Discussions of network management can be quite useful in the individual sessions, but they must always take place within the framework of supporting patients' self-esteem, particularly while they are emotionally vulnerable.

Edna did not at first seem a good candidate for network management. She was a perceptive and thoughtful woman who had been relegated to a passive position in her family when she took up heavy drinking as a vocation after she stopped work to raise her son. Her only avenue of assertion now was to carp at her husband, Irwin, and her twelve-year-old son. When family problems arose, her opinions were regularly discounted. When I asked her about ameliorating her lot, she said she had no clear idea of how to influence her family, other than to protest their impositions, and this to no avail. We initiated Edna's network with her husband, her widowed father, George, and a friend, Arlene. As it emerged, her role as network manager was important in her becoming more effective with family and friends.

Edna's husband initially assumed that he would arrange for our meetings, monitor her behavior, and generally take her in hand. His intentions were good, but these actions would only have served to reproduce in treatment the existing pattern in the family. I went to great lengths to explain to Edna that it was her responsibility to deal with attendance at network meetings and to direct her own recovery. Rather than balking at the whole idea, she saw this task as an opportunity to assert herself. As a consequence, she saw me as a potential ally in her achieving a new, more active role for herself. I underlined this in our individual sessions by helping her define options for developing a more influential position in the family, based on her continuing abstinence.

Edna's role in securing the attendance of network members served as a laboratory for examining her emerging self-assertion. It helped her understand how she dealt with other people, how she influenced them to adopt her goals, and how she confronted the problems of becoming an initiator with family and friends, a role she had long ceased to play. Since the network was supportive of her abstinence, she had a forum in which her newfound self-assertion was treated with more respect.

In Edna's case we had to deal with a fear of assertion that predated her alcoholism but was exaggerated by her guilt over the failings caused by her drinking. She sometimes withdrew from social activities, began to sulk, and found herself falling out of touch with friends. At these times she looked ahead to days devoid of any social activity while her son was at school and her husband was at work. This dynamic was evident as well in her limited efforts to bolster her relationship with Arlene, the network member, having little to do with her between sessions. Arlene as a consequence was occasionally absent from group sessions. When Arlene failed to show up on one occasion, Edna and I were able to examine the way she related to Arlene, and to other friends as well. This "real-life" evidence of problems she was having was useful in helping her become more effective in engaging her social environment, and led to more effective management of relations with her family as well.

A most compelling example of Edna's need to reach out to those close to her emerged in dealing with her father. Edna had to come to grips with some of the problems in their relationship in order to secure his attendance. Since she was a child, her father had been unable to tolerate any expression of anger on her part. When she became upset, he would glare at her, and she would recoil from asserting herself. She grew up hesitant to say things that would annoy persons close to her, and this was still the case with George. Now he was beginning to express doubts about the need to come to all her network meetings. After all, she had been abstinent for four months, and he told her that it was time for her to handle the drinking issue on her own. It was clear to me that the man had no place in his universe for emotional needs other than his own.

Edna was hesitant to assert herself with her father, and we discussed her need to deal with him on this issue. Her response was fearful. "Why can't you talk to him yourself?" she asked plaintively.

"That's just the point. He's your father, and your interest hinges on the integrity of the group; it's your job to take care of it."

Edna agreed to speak with him, but apparently made a weak case; he seemed not to have been won over. We role-played their next exchange. I took the part of her father and I implied that I did not want to become too involved in her problems.

"Dad, I don't think you're really listening," she said finally, in enacting their anticipated encounter. "I'm not really sure of myself yet, and I still need your help. You can't just walk away when I need you." She was asserting her position with clarity, and she cried while her voice shook with anger.

The experience allowed her to see that she could put her needs forth when she had to, and she was able to secure her father's attendance. Her growing value as an initiator in the network clearly coincided with her opportunity to resolve this long-standing issue.

THE THERAPIST'S ROLE

Although the patient is accorded an active role in managing the network, responsibility for the strategy to maintain the network inevitably rests on the therapist's shoulders. It is the therapist who sustains objectivity and goal directedness throughout, particularly when relapse is threatened.

Every therapy has its practical side, especially the housekeeping issues that are part of the therapist's role. An understanding of this role and of the illness is often reflected as much in these nuts-and-bolts issues as in the overarching theory. In the case of psychoanalysis, for example, an unresponsive therapist's role in furthering free association may be very important theoretically. On a practical level, however, the analyst who allows protracted silences can make a patient overly anxious and unnecessarily resentful of therapy. Practicalities and creature comforts cannot be dismissed.

In the case of network therapy, the practicalities reflect the way in which the therapist must weave disparate threads from social group into a supportive tapestry, and how vulnerable that tapestry is to small tears, if they are allowed to accumulate. The therapist must define a strategy that will actively promote cohesiveness in the group and ensure its continuity.

A few practical points illustrate some mechanics of the therapist's role with the network.

- The therapist should always set the time for the next meeting during the network session, as some members will inevitably forget or confuse appointment times unless they are clearly laid out.*
- Members should be discouraged from rearranging the network's appointment times after the fact, since changes in schedule leave people annoyed, wondering why their own Tuesday night tennis game can't be accommodated if someone else's dinner party was honored.
- Some people will complain, and the patient may wonder about all the time spent on arranging meetings. What good does it do to sit around deliberating over Monday at seven or Wednesday at six? The importance of continuity and of getting appointments secured should always be made clear.

The challenge of maintaining network continuity is better revealed in unanticipated crises than in scheduling details. The therapist's decisions

---

*Network sessions are usually held weekly during the first month of treatment, biweekly for the next month, and then less often. After six months they are held once every month or two. More sessions can be scheduled as needed. Individual sessions continue over the course of treatment. Altogether, therefore, the patient has a session of one kind or another once or twice weekly.

on how or whether to use the network in dealing with a clinical problem can be crucial. This emerged in my experience with Annette, who for years had relied heavily on diazepam (Valium), a tranquilizer with considerable dependency potential, to help her relax in the evening and get to sleep. Annette managed to stop the pills on her own, but she soon became depressed and anxious, and her marriage, already shaky, began to deteriorate. She saw a psychiatrist specializing in psychopharmacology; he found her voracious and unpredictable consumption of the antidepressants and sleep medication he prescribed quite unmanageable. In despair over dealing with her addictive style, the psychiatrist referred her to me.

It seemed clear to me that she needed a support network to manage her compulsive drug taking, even though she was in theory no longer actively addicted. (She was a "dry drunk," in AA terminology.) So I met with Annette's husband, William, a physician, who stated clearly that he was "just tired of tending to her," a reaction that echoed the one expressed by her last psychiatrist. Her husband did, however, agree to join a network along with two of her friends and her brother. Our announced goal was to help this frightened woman manage her acute distress and avoid grasping for pills while I treated her for depression.

One day Annette called me, in the throes of anxiety, as yet unresponsive to the antidepressant medication I was prescribing. She had impulsively increased her dose of the drug in the hope of coping with her insomnia; the drug did produce a side effect of drowsiness. William had unwisely become embroiled in helping her to manage the medication, and was getting very short tempered.

My first impulse was to meet with the couple to stabilize her medication. On reflection, though, I realized that this would not be the best approach. The idea had been appealing because it would have been awkward to get the whole network together within a day or two, and I was tempted to rely on William's understanding of her drugs. Putting pressure on William by meeting with the couple alone, however, might only generate more conflict between them and place additional stress on their marriage. In addition, relying on the two of them would draw Annette's addiction problem into the context of their marital conflict, rather than dissipating it into a broader arena. I therefore asked Annette to undertake the arduous task of summoning up her entire network two days hence, which she did indeed do, as she was suffering and wanted to keep my support.

It has been necessary from time to time to mobilize a network by calling an emergency session. In Annette's case, I reviewed for the assembled group how the years of dependence on drugs had led to a physiological withdrawal syndrome and had undermined her ability to deal with anxiety. We discussed the proper management of her medication and how she could take steps to deal with her acute distress by changing her pattern of activity at home.

The group proved to be very valuable. Annette's older brother summoned up his recollection of her anxious nature, dating back to her youth, and reassured her that her current problems might be no more than an exaggeration of her usual style, and not unique. Her friend pointed out that getting involved in a project at her daughter's school the week before had been an effective antidote to rumination and anxiety; why not try to find more of these constructive options now, she suggested. Both her brother and her friends remonstrated with her over the need for patience until the medication took effect.

Furthermore, the network's activity and input over the course of the session allowed William to sit back and serve as a resource, rather than to feel that he had to tend to his wife's every concern. This change in his role allowed the couple important latitude in mending their troubled relationship, and was further consolidated by ensuing sessions with the network. Eventually the couple reconciled.

THE NETWORK'S ROLE

A strong network is premised on open communication. In order for the network to operate as a therapeutic instrument, all participants, the therapist included, must be free to contact each other about a drug problem whenever the need arises, without necessarily securing permission from the patient. This option should be clear from the outset, as part of a negotiated plan for treatment. The freedom to act will not only be invaluable when a crisis arises; it also emphasizes that the bonds of influence in the network are substantial and that the network roles are taken seriously.

The patient and network members should be encouraged to communicate among themselves and to provide support whenever they feel it advisable. A network member should expect to be called on by the patient for assistance related to drug problems when needed. My experience is that this option is not abused, and the sensitivities inherent in the ongoing social relations are not violated.

In many situations this understanding about open communication proves invaluable. For example, one patient, an actor, was often working on location. He did not always tell me when he would next appear for a session, although he did apologize for his unreliable attendance. If not for the fact that his irregularity could reflect a relapse, I would have been prepared to await his return and to resolve related psychological issues as the treatment progressed. On one occasion, my option of calling a friend of his in network proved important in dealing with a lapse in his attendance. The friend located him at my request, and he and other members of the group were able to help the patient cut his slip short.

The network can substitute for the therapist in his or her absence. I have often arranged for a patient to meet with network members while I was at a conference or on vacation. But such meetings must be carefully scheduled beforehand. The therapist formalizes anticipated network activities, transforming the members from a group of well-wishers to a well-honed instrument for change with delegated authority.

This coverage is particularly useful shortly after treatment has begun, when the patient's abstinence is not fully secured. We have all heard the classic tales of lost souls a-wandering each August as their analysts summer on Cape Cod. In fact, periods of absence pose only minor problems for the majority of patients who are being treated for long-standing problems of personality disorder. In the addiction field, on the other hand, particularly early on in treatment, problems can emerge rapidly and acutely, and a surrogate for the therapist can be invaluable.

Interestingly, network members are generally more effective than a stand-in psychiatrist who is unfamiliar with the patient in averting problems before a relapse has occurred. Most patients are reluctant to contact a professional they do not know unless they are experiencing great distress, and relapse can occur long before distress mounts to painful levels. I am sometimes impressed by network members who are more able than I to elicit a patient's feelings around a troubling issue, or to secure an understanding of the need to adopt a constructive stance. Family and community ties are surprisingly effective in the recovery process, and we have lost much by relegating to professionals so many of the roles they can fulfill.

For the work milieu in the network to be regarded as effective, the therapist's delegation of authority must be authentic. The network must have experience in participating actively in decisions and in arriving at a consensus that is implemented in action; their opinions cannot be solicited after the fact. For this reason, action on many decisions should be reserved for the network, even though the issues can be addressed with the patient alone. For example, if urines have been monitored for drugs of abuse, can the frequency of collection be reduced? A patient's peers may have an excellent sense of the patient's reliability in reporting slips. Is the patient ready to go back to work? Each network member can give input on the patient's readiness for new responsibilities. Some issues can be a matter for extended discussion, and the therapist can present a point of view at times as a peer-participant.

The network can sometimes be a very useful court of last resort. One patient had to be placed on a regimen of observed urinalyses because his combined addiction to snorting heroin and smoking cocaine presented a very high risk for relapse. He was a rebellious young man used to demanding his own way, and after two months of monitoring he decided in a pique that he had had enough of the urinalyses; they had all been negative, and the procedure was inconvenient for him. I was very uncomfortable with this because his period of risk for relapse was not over by any means. I finally persuaded him to wait until our network meeting, which would take place the following week, where he could present his case to the group. After some discussion at the meeting, they agreed with the need for continued monitoring and then prevailed on him to follow their collective advice. The patient was annoyed, but in the end he could not dismiss their consensus out of hand, and he agreed to an extension of the period of observation. Any psychiatrist treating addicted patients knows that the availability of such influential input can be crucial at times when a patient is moved to write his or her own treatment plan, one that carries grave risk.

ADDING AND DROPPING MEMBERS

Because cohesiveness among the network's members is the basis for their effective action, it is very important that the group's membership roster be protected, for both symbolic and practical reasons. Symbolically, the image of a stable, mutually trusting membership helps each of the participants feel important to the group and obliged to continue constructive participation. It sets the tone for members to speak up frankly and to expect that their views will be heard, since they know they all have a long-term investment in the undertaking. Cohesiveness supports their attendance as well, even when they may have their doubts at times about their value to the patient's recovery.

Practically speaking, a working collaboration in the network is very hard to replenish with substitute members, once an understanding among participants has been achieved. The history of the members' mutual involvement in the patient's initial abstinence is not easily recouped by adding someone who did not go through those struggles with the remainder of the group. For these reasons, I am very reluctant to make changes in the network's constituents. Often this means discouraging the patient from acting on changes in his relationship with another member.

Arthur, a homosexual patient, brought in a group of friends as network members. Although their relationships were subject to the vagaries of a relatively unstable gay social set, they were quite supportive of him and helped him achieve stability in his sobriety by means of their sensitivity and, occasionally, by direct persuasion. In one individual therapy session, though, Arthur mentioned casually that he planned to drop one of the members. I questioned Arthur about the nature of their falling out, as I had not noticed his friend's nefarious side. As Arthur explained it, his change of heart seemed to be more the product of shifting loyalties within a social circle than the reflection of a meaningful difference in attitude between them or in their ability to get along. The situation further reflected on a long-standing problem of his own with intimacy and with establishing stable, close relationships.

I was concerned for the stability of the network and saw no value in its being threatened by this apparently transient issue. This did not seem to be the time to deal with the psychology underlying Arthur's pique, however. That would have required protracted effort, and would have raised his hackles. Instead, I pointed out that in my view it was important that we work out how he could reevaluate his stance on this member and resolve those immediate issues he would have to address with this friend in order to achieve a rapprochement. I gave him my rationale for protecting the network, shifting the psychological onus of our discussion to the fragility of network therapy and the need to preserve the stability of the group. Later on the whole episode came to be useful in considering his problems more broadly, but it was first strategically important to ensure that a network member was not dropped because of a problem that could be avoided.

On the other hand, a lover whose relationship has come to an end almost always moves out of the network. In such cases, the lover may retain membership for a time, until it becomes clear that a final break is inevitable. Such situations often introduce a note of misery into the sessions.

One patient's hapless girlfriend appeared on a few occasions, unsure whether the relationship was on or off. The patient let her twist in the wind while he ruminated in individual sessions over whether to continue to see her. Fortunately, the issue of the relationship was not on the table during the network meetings. The girlfriend's pride was maintained, and she still spoke her mind. Spurred on by her own annoyance, she made some telling and rather useful comments about her boyfriend's self-absorption.

Other patients' relationships have headed happily toward marriage, yielding an additional member for the network. Such partners are generally discreet in their initial comments, although they can rock the boat a bit. One spoke up about the role of the patient's parents in his becoming addicted, putting them on the spot, something I would have preferred to avoid. The patient had long been abstinent, and there was no need to open old wounds, or indeed to make a new incision. I passed by the comment so as not to raise the tension level by allowing it to become a subject for discussion.

The Right Atmosphere

The network clearly needs a good working atmosphere to operate effectively. This allows the patient to give up dependence on drugs to trust in the security provided by the network and the therapist. Success entails two principal issues: cognitive factors, that is to say, a new perspective on addiction, and the appropriate interpersonal orientation, a feeling of mutual support.

A NEW PERSPECTIVE ON ADDICTION

Patients and network members alike enter the treatment setting with a very limited understanding of the nature of addiction. They are inclined to blame the substance abuser for the illness. Network members may themselves also feel responsible for the patient's problem, so that they become defensive or angry when the patient runs into trouble. All this confounds effective participation in the treatment process. It is therefore essential to introduce a perspective on addiction that does not cast blame. Focusing on drug dependence as a disease enables the participants to shift the responsibility from the addict to the collaborating treatment team.

Estabalishing an alternative, constructive attitude is an implicit goal in many treatments for addiction. One clinical program set up orientation groups for the spouses of alcoholics who had not volunteered for treatment. This educational intervention was intended to foster a new attitude and offer proper information; there was a decrease in the alcoholic's drinking, even though only the nonaddicted spouse participated.[1]

With opiate addiction, which is clearly a very difficult problem, Thomas Kosten and his associates reported that attitudes associated with denial were more effectively addressed when family members were engaged in therapy; in addition, patients remained in treatment longer.[2] Needless to say, Al-Anon, a self-help approach to changing attitudes for the family members of alcoholics, has long served as a valuable adjunct to AA.

Impressive techniques designed to change the attitudes of patients themselves were reported by Irvin Yalom in his study on group therapy for alcoholism. He developed a treatment approach over a period of experimentation, and then compared it with group therapy for nonalcoholic patients.[3] At first Yalom had considerable difficulty keeping his alcoholic patients involved and compliant with the treatment process. He had to contend with disruptive behavior and absences in times of stress—such as when a member of the group drank or when interpersonal tensions were high—and these disruptions were often disabling to the group. He addressed the issue by introducing techniques to generate a stable and supportive milieu, each of which involved hammering home a perspective on interpersonal relations that would allow members to react constructively to events in the sessions.

Sometimes Yalom would solicit information from members on a questionnaire, then report his findings back to them. At other times, he would instruct members in a didactic way on the meaning and effects of exchanges that had taken place in the group. One approach that he found particularly useful was to provide session summaries that were laced with his own interpretations, so that members could better understand the difficulties they confronted in working together constructively. By means of these devices, he encouraged the therapeutic use of interpersonal relations in the group. He took a firm hold on the flow of communication; he directed it so that intense feelings could be contained and so that he could achieve his therapeutic ends.

The need to introduce a stabilizing perspective on addictive illness in networks was evident in my experience with Iris, an epileptic woman who used her drinking in part to address anxiety over arguments at work. She drowned her sorrows in alcohol each night, weekends as well as weekdays. After our initial meeting, we brought together a network consisting of her sister Eve and two of her friends. Iris was emotionally dependent on her parents, but she ruled out their participation because she regarded them as punitive and intrusive, a perspective that was supported by her sister, who resented them even more. But Eve's involvement in the network was not without problems as well, as she had a temper that was easily ignited, and she often directed her anger at Iris when she lost patience with her sister's drinking. She was particularly angered by Iris's unreliable handling of her seizure medications and her irresponsible style of relating to her friends.

From our first meeting together, it seemed clear that Eve's inclination to censure would set a negative tone for the network unless steps were taken to introduce another perspective, and so I spent a good deal of time helping the group understand the nature of the addictive process. I had to secure a supportive attitude in Eve, in particular. This lesson was also important for Iris herself, in quelling some of the guilt that could generate despair and make it hard for her to abort a slip. I explained at length how the alcoholic's control over drinking is limited, and that setting a clear limit on consumption can be beyond her reach, once a series of cues leads her to drink. Much of the time in our initial sessions was devoted to a description of the nature of conditioned drug seeking and its role in bringing about relapse.

It is essential to ensure open communication as a norm for the network. Members must have the information necessary to act as a group. This was particularly important for Iris, as I had not prescribed disulfiram for her because it interacts with phenytoin (Dilantin), a medication that she was taking for her epilepsy. Beginning each session with a careful recounting of events related to alcohol was all the more essential, since the possibility of her drinking remained real. On more than one occasion Iris did drink after work, and each time I acted promptly with the network to help her reestablish her abstinence.

Iris often became entangled in the conflicts between her employers, an argumentative couple who ran a theatrical talent agency. She had done the same with her parents as a child. Now she often ended up frustrated, angry, and tearful, as she had in her youth. In one individual session, Iris recounted yet another episode of this sort, and then she sheepishly acknowledged that because of it she had "not been doing too well with the drinking." I queried her on this, and she said that on two of the last three days she had had "a few drinks" with a friend after work, but was fortunately able to avoid intoxication. She was apparently unhappy about her failure to maintain abstinence, though, and could understand the need to bring the sequence of drinking to an end.

The situation was problematic, though, because I was leaving town the next day for a week, and I was uncertain of her ability to stay sober until we met again. I said we ought to speak with someone in the network immediately, to establish a plan for the group to meet in the interim. We knew that her sister was probably at home.

"You mean, call my sister right now?" I could see that she was afraid of Eve's passing judgment on her, however much we had inculcated the idea of alcoholism as a disease.

"Well, there's a good chance you could drink again while I'm away, and we do need some help with this."

"Do you really think Eve believes all that crap about me having a disease?" Iris read my mind.

"We've got to try her out. Look, it's my job to keep the right attitude going in the network, and since I'm getting you into this, I'll have to get her to look at this the right way."

I dialed Eve, and the three of us went over the story on my speaker phone. I proposed that Iris meet with her and the other network members over that next weekend. Eve agreed, but she was distressed that such a big deal was being made over the matter. It was clear she felt I was pampering her sister, and I had to draw on the understanding we had achieved in our network sessions: "Eve, it sounds like you're annoyed at Iris for slipping up, but you have to remember that it's part of the disease process."

She was put on the defensive. "Well, you'd think she could have handled a little argument at work."

I skirted an elaborate explanation. "Listen, think over what we've been saying about the nature of alcoholism when we get off the phone, and then do me a favor. Try to get everybody to support Iris on this. I think we can be very helpful if we just let her know we're behind her."

Iris looked at me and rolled her eyes, conveying her doubt that Eve could be so easily reformed, but Eve agreed to be supportive. We discussed a time for the network members to meet that weekend, and Eve volunteered that she would call Iris the next day as well.

I hung up and saw that Iris was annoyed. She insisted that she had been imposed on, saying that the exchange had raised the same feelings of helplessness that she had long felt as a child, as a victim of epilepsy. I knew she was in earnest, and not only resentful of having her drinking contained. We had often discussed the cross of illness that she had borne. I tried to mollify her, pointing out that under the awkward circumstances this was the best we could do, and called her later that evening to make sure that we were at peace with each other. The group met as scheduled.

I am sure that Iris would have had a good deal more trouble with drinking in my absence that next week if we had not taken the issue in hand. This delicate exchange worked out well because careful groundwork on a proper perspective had been laid in the network, so that in a time of crisis, recrimination and guilt could be minimized.

A FEELING OF SUPPORT

Addicts emerge from their protracted period of drug dependence as traumatized survivors. Their ability to sustain abstinence is built on a sense of security that can support a belief in the goal of recovery. Social support within the network is therefore a central factor in the patient's ability to adhere to a plan for treatment.

An interesting parallel can be drawn from the course of posttraumatic stress disorder, a cluster of anxiety-related symptoms that results from highly traumatic experiences, such as wartime injury or sexual assault. The importance of traditional family and social roles in assuring stability in a patient's own identity, adjustment, and hope for the future has been defined as essential in psychotherapy.[4] Research support is found in studies like those conducted by Terence Keane and his associates, who compared Vietnam veterans experiencing the syndrome with those who were well adjusted. They found that the traumatized group, who suffered anxiety, depression, guilt, and sleep disturbance, were likely to be living in a setting marked by absent social supports.[5]

Because of the need for cohesiveness in the network, it is important to make use of every opportunity to enhance communication and to keep the network in touch. Thus, when one of Iris's friends was away on vacation for three weeks early in the treatment, I arranged for her to participate in a network session over the speaker phone. During that session, after the participants in the room had each spoken, I solicited her views over the phone on what we had been discussing. She made some worthwhile observations, as is typical for telephone participants, who feel the need to justify the elaborate arrangement with a meaningful contribution. Her continuing presence was therefore felt, and open communication was maintained.

Ensuring a supportive atmosphere also means avoiding the intrusion of extraneous issues that might undermine the established tone of mutual support. Extraneous conflicts that cannot be easily resolved should be addressed with considerable care, and preferably circumvented. Not all issues opened up in discussion can be brought to resolution, and they can often compete for attention with the primary goal of helping the patient maintain abstinence.

Iris's network's atmosphere was threatened by the considerable animosity that she bore her parents. There was no doubt that her parents, her father in particular, had contributed to her rebelliousness and drinking. Nonetheless, I was always careful to keep the issue of the parents from becoming too much a focus in the network. In particular, I implicitly discouraged Iris's sister from railing against them. Eve's intense resentment of her parents drew on her need to find a release for unrelated conflicts and dissatisfactions in her own life.

The whole parental issue would have thrown us into the quagmire of Eve's psychological problems and would have reverberated in ways that were unpredictable. Better to deal with it superficially in the network and focus more on the circumstances in Iris's current life. She and I were able to discuss her parents in the more insulated setting of her individual sessions.

Other personal problems of the members had to be managed carefully to protect this group's cohesiveness. Suzanne, Iris's friend and a member of the network, was alcoholic herself, but had been abstinent for two years. She offered some interesting and useful insights into the issues that confronted Iris in her sobriety, but she clearly had problems to work out with regard to her own recovery. Although she commented on the problems of staying abstinent, I avoided referring to her expertise as a recovering alcoholic so as not to lean too heavily on an issue about which she lacked objectivity. The network sessions were not to become a therapy setting for Suzanne.

One particularly delicate situation was Eve's potential for an angry display when she felt that Iris was not playing according to the rules, as Eve construed them. Eve remained in danger of being estranged from the group, and on one occasion she did not appear at a meeting. I asked Iris where she was. It turned out that a few days earlier she had revealed to Eve that she had not told her about an episode of drinking that had taken place some weeks previously. Eve had exploded in anger, accusing Iris of lying to her, and saying that she had enough of her "cheating ways." It seemed to me she was particularly incensed that Iris had told her friends but not her.

Iris and her friends were prepared to dismiss Eve as a "bitch" in her absence, someone whose participation they could dispense with in the network. But it was clear to me that Eve had a good deal to offer because of the close ties between her and Iris. I was also oriented to protecting network membership, as usual.

Knowing that Iris and her two friends would understand, I told them that Eve was probably being scapegoated because of her anger over being the odd person out. I tried to help them see why she felt cornered at not being informed of Iris's drinking episode. I asked Iris to speak with Eve about the situation, to mollify her, and to bring her back to the next session. Iris did so. In the ensuing session, I used the issue of notification about drinking as an opportunity to underline for all the members of the network, Eve now among them, the importance of good communication, and to clarify terms under which Iris would tell any given member, and me as well, if she had a slip.

CHAPTER 10

Securing Future Behavior

A THERAPIST TREATING ADDICTION should always be thinking about strategies for shaping future behavior. The patient is told, "one day at a time," but the therapist constructs a framework for long-term sobriety. Marital woes, too, are addressed in terms of the patient's long-term recovery. Much of the art in this therapy therefore consists of weaving together a fabric of interventions, none of them with a certain outcome, but all directed at protecting the patient from the risk of relapse.

Sometimes—although not often—a modest intervention is surprisingly effective for the long term. This is worth considering just to highlight how surprising it may be in a field where elaborate approaches to management are usually necessary. Alan was an alcoholic in his late thirties when he originally met with me over the course of two months. About twenty years later a pharmacist called for approval of his continuing prescription for disulfiram (Antabuse). Alan's prescription record had been handed over by another pharmacy which had recently closed; apparently he had renewed it at intervals over two decades. I was taken aback, never having written for more than one or two renewals, and I told the pharmacist that I had to speak with Alan before approving his prescription. Renewals should not have been made automatically over the years, I told him. He explained, defensively, that there must have been a mistake at the previous pharmacy.

Alan's situation came clearly to mind. His wife and I had deliberated with him at some length as we tried to secure his sobriety, and I barely convinced him to take his disulfiram for a month before he let me know that he could handle things himself, then thanked me and said good-bye. Although we had discussed a plan for his sobriety, his prognosis seemed guarded in the absence of further treatment; his drinking had been disabling, causing him no end of problems in his business and family life. I wondered how long he would take his remaining tablets of disulfiram and stay sober.

Alan, a sales representative, had been so disorganized. He would sit in my office, trying almost pitifully to convey how his work was going. He would pull out a dogeared cluster of envelopes bound by a rubber band. In local taverns he had scrawled names and figures on envelopes. Alan was barely earning a living, disrupted as he was by heavy drinking. How, I thought then, would this man ever keep himself together, refrain from frequent intoxication, and put his life in order?

I called Alan's house to follow up on the prescription matter. His wife was pleased to inform me of his progress. He was doing very well, holding some of the larger accounts in his industry. He had suffered only a few modest bouts of drinking since we originally met, and he had been fully abstinent for the past several years. Alan had sought no more professional help and had never set foot in an AA meeting. She said that he had told her more than once, however, that the Antabuse had been invaluable to him, and he had taken it on numerous occasions when he felt uncertain of his sobriety.

When I reached him in a later call, Alan said he was pleased to hear from me, but he did not seem eager to talk long. He graciously thanked me for my efforts in retrospect. Yes, he was sober. By now he took the disulfiram infrequently, although he liked to have it on business trips when he was exposed to a lot of drinking. A modest renewal would likely carry him for a few years more, he said.

Alan apparently needed an approach he could apply by himself, and he had fortunately devised it by using the material offered him. He had not been too interested in my ministrations, and apparently belonged to the small group of alcoholics who could recover with a minimal, focused intervention. Griffith Edwards, the alcoholism researcher, has studied the impact of physician advice, and demonstrated that it can often be as effective as more extensive treatment.[1] In practice, though, we certainly find that most patients do not fare well with advice alone. As of now we do not know how to predict which few patients might respond to a focused, brief intervention.

A Web of Controls

A variety of constraints can be introduced to ensure a patient's stability during the early days of treatment, and then gradually lifted. These techniques can complement each other quite effectively. This orchestration was illustrated in the treatment of Daryl, whose severe addictive problem made him an uncertain candidate for recovery when he first came for treatment. He had been snorting heroin daily for most of the previous fifteen years, and had been using cocaine heavily for the last eight, most recently in the form of freebase cocaine and crack. Despite his serious drug problem, he had some important strengths that were demonstrated in his work. A talented jazz musician, he performed regularly, and he was also a faculty member in a local music college. Daryl was quite solicitous of his students' development, although his teaching was often compromised by his drug taking.

There was a measure of irony in the events that moved Daryl to seek help, since his long course of treatment was very successful in the end. Initially he asked only for help with his immediate situation; he wanted to bring his drug use down to a more manageable level. He was concerned because his recent descent into unfettered addiction had been precipitous. He was completing a sabbatical at the music school and had been relatively idle. He had engaged in little productive work in recent months. He realized that his ability to return to teaching had become limited, as he had become dependent on crack smoking, which would be much more disruptive to a stable work routine than the heroin addiction alone. Furthermore, his wealthy girlfriend, Jeannette, was thinking about going off to a residential treatment center for help with her own addiction, and he was troubled by the thought of losing her as a companion in drug seeking and as an emotional support.

I first made it clear to Daryl that he had to stop his drug use entirely, and underlined the fact that treatment would be useless otherwise. He was actually willing to cede this point, undoubtedly with the usual ambivalence. Nonetheless, his express agreement allowed us to go ahead, and we focused on securing his abstinence.

The treatment techniques were interwoven into the network over more than two years of his subsequent recovery. All were designed to stabilize his abstinence and secure a more positive lifestyle. Each of these played an important role in securing his long-term sobriety:

1. Establishing a network with drug-free members
2. Undergoing a brief hospitalization

3. Changing his residence
4. Administering an opiate blocking agent (naltrexone) under observation
5. Monitoring his urine for drugs
6. Attending Narcotics Anonymous
7. Coming to network sessions held in my absence
8. Focusing on his passive adaptation in individual therapy.

In this way a rationale can be developed for interweaving a variety of interventions, each directed at managing behavior, each with its own time for introduction and withdrawal.

At the outset, Daryl and I had to put together a network, in particular one that did not include drug abusers. This was a task of no small dimension, since most of his current social ties were to people who were at the very least heavy drug users. I knew that we had to do this quickly, given his imminent vulnerability to his multiple addictions. The effort therefore involved a variety of maneuvers, such as quickly discounting some proposed members who were apparently drug dependent and then including some of Daryl's sober relatives whom he was less close to at present. We later had to tactfully drop one member of the group when she became readdicted after some years of abstinence.

My plan was to hospitalize Daryl briefly as soon as we had assembled the network. The need for this was compelling, and he himself acknowledged it. The combination of two major addictions, one to heroin and the other to cocaine, each relatively independent of the other, was more than could be addressed at once. Daryl's insurance did not cover extended hospital treatment, but would allow for several days' stay, and I admitted him to a local psychiatric hospital to detoxify him from heroin and introduce a blocking agent. My strategy was to use the hospitalization to get Daryl's heroin habit under control. We could then address the cocaine problem more definitively after he got out.

Naltrexone (Trexan) would be a vehicle for his long-term abstinence from heroin. It is an opiate antagonist taken in pill form three times a week. After ingestion, it occupies opiate receptor sites for a few days and blocks heroin and other opiates from producing euphoria.[2] The drug might be used widely, as it effectively eliminates the addict's ability to respond to heroin, and hence removes the principal reason for using narcotics. But, like disulfiram, it is only as effective as the patient. Trials of this drug have shown it to be of limited utility for most addicts, who typically "forget" to take the medicine while on their own recognizance, and go back to heroin use soon thereafter.[3] Heroin addicts are then likely

179

to disappear from treatment. Naltrexone has therefore been used primarily in very reliable patients who are under great pressure to maintain abstinence from opiates.[4] For example, practicing physicians who have been caught abusing narcotics may have this blocking agent prescribed while undergoing monitoring dictated by their state medical boards. In these cases, their urine is regularly tested for abused opiates. Given the authority vested in state medical boards, the physicians generally stay with the naltrexone in order to protect their licenses.

Naltrexone can be used to considerable advantage in a broader range of patients when it is administered the way we have described with disulfiram monitoring. Each dose the patient takes is observed by a network member. The respective roles are clear in this approach. The patient's job is to assume responsibility for taking the naltrexone in front of the observer. The observer's job is only to report to the therapist if the patient does not take a given dose, but never to convince the patient to take his or her medication. The observer thereby provides an effective reminder to the patient to take the naltrexone, but is not a lone enforcer. This approach to monitoring naltrexone use gives the patient responsibility for ingestion, but supports the network's influence because the patient knows that if a missed dose is reported to the therapist, it will be discussed at the next network meeting, thereby ensuring that denial does not undermine naltrexone's continuous long-term use.

Daryl was a good candidate for naltrexone because he had a reasonably stable network, which included his sister, with whom he had an amicable and trusting relationship. I therefore discussed with him and the group a plan to admit him to the hospital for several days to detoxify him from heroin, and to initiate naltrexone administration under his sister's observation as soon as he was drug-free and ready for discharge. We discussed the plan for taking naltrexone at some length with the network while he was on a short pass from the hospital, thereby setting the groundwork for shifting directly into the outpatient format when Daryl left the hospital.

I also discussed with Daryl and his network that observed urinalyses would be needed for a considerable period of time, as it would be many months before his stability was assured. The opiate blocker would leave Daryl relatively free from craving for heroin, but it could not ensure that he would stay away from the drug, since some people do try to use heroin while they are on naltrexone. More important, his addiction to cocaine would necessitate long-term urine monitoring, since the naltrexone gave no protection against nonopiates.

There was little doubt as well that Daryl could not live with Jean-

nette, at least until both had experienced some months of stable abstinence. They had long fed off each other in their addictions, and I was
none too sure that Jeannette would make it to a rehab. At this point, her
wealth and petulance were buffering her from the need to seek an
alternative to her life in addiction. While Daryl was in the hospital, we
therefore arranged that he would move in with his sister for at least a
few months.

The period after hospitalization was fraught with problems. The
presence of Daryl's girlfriend clearly meant a threat of renewed drug use.
After lengthy deliberations in the network, he saw her less often. Nonetheless, we did have to discuss arrangements for a few brief meetings,
and the network members helped to delimit their encounters. Fortunately, Jeannette was willing to let him go off on his own when she saw
that he was giving her less attention than she got from other members
of her social set.

Daryl had not been enthusiastic about connecting with Narcotics
Anonymous, but I pressed him nonetheless to attend at least twice a
week upon leaving the hospital. Like many patients, he went grudgingly, saying that "it wasn't his thing," and he didn't "go for the
religious angle." My feeling in such cases is that some attendance is
worthwhile nonetheless. Being exposed to peer addicts who have re-
nounced drug use can at least introduce the concept of abstinence from
a new perspective. In any case, NA represented at a minimum a scheduled drug-free activity to fill some of Daryl's free hours. In response to
my pressure and the group's support, Daryl went to NA intermittently
for some months, until he persuaded me by his lapses in attendance that
he should not be pressed to go any more. He later acknowledged that
the experience was "useful," but still not his "thing," although he did
attend occasionally when he was under stress.

The urinalyses came up as an issue at one network meeting not long
after Daryl left the hospital. He said he would like to drop the procedure.
It was expensive, as his urines were monitored by another doctor, and
inconvenient, as well, he said. However true this might be, Daryl's shaky
condition made me view his request as an expression of his desire to
protect his addiction. I tried to make my rationale clear. "I know you
want to stop taking the drug and you're trying hard." He was, indeed,
and it was important to give him credit for this even though he was
clearly struggling with his ambivalence.

"But we're all aware you've had some slips with the coke already, and
there certainly could be some more." As long as we continue to examine
the cues that lead to slips, and ensure that the drug use isn't buried, we'll

be on the right track. That's why the urines are so important. They mean that we will always be keeping the drug use in the open, and that you can't forget a slip. This way you'll have to let us know *before* we get a positive urine result, not afterward." With some additional pressure from his network, Daryl agreed to keep up the urine monitoring.

Daryl continued to have serious problems with cocaine over the months following his hospitalization, even though he met regularly with me and his network. The problem was compelling. As long as he was having slips on cocaine, he was vulnerable to denial, which might lead him to hide the cocaine use from me and the network—or, worse, to develop an excuse for dropping out of treatment. A further complication was my plan to leave on vacation for three weeks during this early phase of treatment. It was essential to have a plan to secure what we had accomplished so far. I arranged that during my absence Daryl's sister would get reports on his urinalyses and that the whole network would meet with Daryl each week to review his situation. I felt that the network members would handle Daryl's care better than a physician unfamiliar with his case.

I further decided to press the goal of having Daryl achieve abstinence from cocaine within two weeks of my return from vacation. I thought that by that time he would be ready for an all-out assault on the residual cocaine use. This plan reassured Daryl and the network, and gave them a reason to promote his stability over the period of my absence. My own pronouncement provided me with some reassurance as well. With this set of auxiliary controls in place, no ground was lost during the intervening vacation, and we were indeed able to establish a reasonably secure abstinence soon after my return.

The long course of these interlocking controls in Daryl's treatment is instructive. He continued to take the naltrexone under observation three times a week for a year, either at his sister's house or in my office while meeting with me. After that he took it on his own for almost a year more. He would write down the time each morning when he took the naltrexone and bring in his record for me to review at intervals. Unlike some patients, Daryl was not eager to be relieved of this pharmacological constraint on his drug use. In fact, on one occasion late in the treatment, he himself demurred from terminating the naltrexone, saying that he was not yet sure that he was ready to give up his insurance against relapse.

Daryl underwent observed urinalyses each week for the first four months of treatment, then twice a month for ten months more. After that he went each month until he had been off the naltrexone for several

months. This regimen assured a period of monitoring after he was off
the medication and physiologically able to experience a heroin high.
Each change in the frequency of his urine monitoring was preceded by
discussion within the network; members had to agree that the new
regimen would be safe.

Daryl and I met twice weekly for two and one-half years, sometimes
with the network. Network meetings took place each week for the first
few months, and then less often. Aside from events related to the
addiction per se, perhaps the most important issue Daryl and I confronted in his individual sessions was the passivity that had compromised his life. He had been dependent on his mother as a youth, and then
had been dependent on his addicted girlfriend over the several years
before entering treatment.

Although specific devices such as the opiate antagonist and observed
urinalyses could launch his abstinence, it was important for him to have
a new and active orientation toward life to ensure long-term sobriety.
I struggled with Daryl to help him become more assertive with women
and in his work. With the aid of both sobriety and introspection, he was
able to develop more constructive social relationships and to assume a
more active role in his social life.

These changes came in the form of small triumphs. For example, early
on, Daryl came to appreciate that his choice to not have an answering
machine had psychological meaning. It served to isolate him from an
active social existence and to ensure that he would not establish meaningful ties outside the drug subculture. His buying an answering machine meant that he was now ready to consider at least the risk of entry
into a drug-free social existence. In time, Daryl also undertook an
initiative at the music school that drew on his considerable creative
talents and on an emerging capacity to deal with the institution's poli-
tics. This degree of activity had eluded him for years.

Put It in Writing

Because rationalization undermines so many of the addict's best plans,
it is often useful to put the understandings that underlie treatment into
writing. Written agreement leaves less room later on for confusion
about what the patient should expect and affords the patient a check
against reality if a question arises about what had been agreed on in
treatment. Consequences of violating a plan can range from a written
reminder to the patient to a more stringent contingency imposed from

without. As with other aspects of treatment, the participation of network members in establishing a written understanding enhances its importance to the patient and broadens the options for enforcement.

THE CALLING CARD

In the simplest of written interventions, the patient has well-defined guidelines at hand when he or she encounters a stimulus for drug seeking. To prepare, it is important to review in advance problem situations the patient is likely to deal with and to develop ways for him or her to respond. These can be abbreviated and written on a small card that the patient carries around. The very existence of such written pointers makes rationalization, or "forgetting," a little harder.

I used this technique with Brad, a cocaine addict who owned a rock music rehearsal hall. His social life and business activities were so intertwined with a subculture of drug use that he was regularly exposed to cues for drug seeking, including people using cocaine. In one network session, he reported having a slip at a party when his date, standing at his side, was offered cocaine by a friend. "I wasn't thinking. It was just there, and I said OK when she offered me some."

"Did you know there could be drugs at the party before you went?" I asked.

"I probably could have guessed, but I didn't think about it too much."

We discussed with the group how Brad could manage his activities so that he would stay free from drugs, then we looked at the variety of cues that had brought on this slip. I engaged the group in trying to develop a self-protective approach for him to apply when he was most vulnerable. This was particularly important when he was out on dates, or at parties, since any new acquaintance in his social set could turn out to be a drug user. I summarized our guidelines as follows:

1. Make no dates with anyone you suspect of using cocaine.
2. Don't go into a room where people are using the drug.
3. If cocaine is brought out, leave the room right away.

I wrote the rules on my calling card as we spoke. I then asked Brad to read them back to the group and to put the card in his wallet. The card would provide a reminder to discourage him from acting on the conditioned cues when he encountered them. I encouraged the network members to discuss these guidelines again at the next network session.

It is often surprising to see patients continue carrying these cards with them long after alcohol or drug use has ceased to be an active issue. The card forms an implicit contract, and it can be an important adjunct to the treatment because it introduces some of the strength of the therapeutic relationship into a period of vulnerability. In this way, it acquires the quality of a talisman, symbolically embodying the network's function.

LETTERS TO DOCTORS

Physicians are the principal source of mood-altering medications in our society, and they will inevitably allow some patients to become drug dependent. Most commonly a patient is treated for a problem for which the drug is legitimately prescribed. For example, analgesics may have been used for an acute and painful illness, or minor tranquilizers for anxiety associated with family crisis. Much less commonly, unscrupulous physicians will prescribe drugs to produce dependence, so that they effectively become pushers of these pills, sustaining a lucrative, often illicit business.

Even if addicted patients want to avoid their prescribing doctors, the ready availability of a sanctioned source of drugs is generally more than they can avoid, so that formal means of enforcing an end to the relationship, generally in writing, may be needed. In a number of these prescribing circumstances I have encountered, a letter sent by the patient to the doctor has served to terminate such a cycle of unfortunate prescribing. Physicians are increasingly under the watchful eyes of both state licensing boards and malpractice lawyers, and any written document that might later compromise them with these parties will quickly produce a chilling effect in the prescribing relationship.

The use of amphetamines for dieting was long a source of such abuse. It has now largely disappeared because of constraints imposed by state and federal authorities, as well as the demonstrated ineffectiveness of these drugs for long-term weight loss. In other circumstances, dependency-producing minor tranquilizers are often prescribed carelessly or even illicitly; this practice is unfortunately current today.

Some time back, when amphetamines were more readily available by prescription, I treated Emily for dependence on these pills. She could always turn on impulse to a physician who ran an amphetamine mill, presenting herself as needing to continue her "diet." After she passed some time in a waiting room filled with people, most of them dependent on the drug as well, a nurse took her blood pressure and she was given a prescription by the doctor with hardly a word exchanged.

It became clear that as long as this physician was available as a ready

185

source of the drug, it would be very hard for Emily to avoid an occasional relapse. We therefore composed a letter to him, informing him of her addiction and requesting that he no longer prescribe for her. The letter was written on my stationery and stated as well that she was in treatment with me. Given a potential threat to his practice, he withdrew as a resource for her. (At the time, the reporting of such physicians to state authorities was uncommon. Today I would probably notify the licensing board directly.)

When legitimate prescribers are involved, one generally has to cast a larger net of communication. Patients who draw on ethical physicians are rarely able to obtain from a single source the large quantities of a drug that they need. Leslie's husband called me when he became aware that she was hiding pills around the house and taking them secretly. As I spoke with him, and later interviewed them together, the scope of the problem became apparent. Leslie was taking some thirty Tylenol 3 tablets a day, each of which contains 30 mg of codeine, a dependency-producing opiate drug. To keep up with the many prescriptions she needed, she had to turn at intervals to her orthopedist, internist, and dentist, and then fill prescriptions in three different locations, manipulating pharmacists as well.

Leslie was typical of pill-dependent people who are provided medication that they gradually begin to abuse. Her drug use began with surgery a few years before to correct the chronic back pain produced by a slipped disc. Later she needed extensive oral surgery. Despite her addiction, though, Leslie appeared to be doing relatively well. She maintained a responsible job, and the relationship with her husband was good enough, except for the considerable strife that had recently emerged around her pill taking.

As we discussed treatment options, Leslie made it clear that she did not want to undergo the disruption of hospitalization. She said that she had seen enough of "white walls and Formica countertops" to last her a lifetime. I told the couple that it might be possible to get her free of drugs without hospitalization, but there was little chance of her doing well until we made sure that all of her sources of medication were eliminated. Each one would have to be notified and closed off before we undertook detoxifying her and helping her to remain abstinent.

Leslie realized she had no reasonable alternative, and along with her husband and two sisters, discussed the various physicians with whom she was in contact. This exchange, carried out over a few family sessions, served to bring out some prescribing relationships that she might otherwise not have mentioned. She was less likely to keep back information in the network, as she would not want to be seen later as having betrayed her family members. Ultimately, we drew up a list of four physicians, two dentists, and three pharmacies who had serviced her prescribing, and she sent each one a simple note on my stationery:

> Please be advised that I am now in treatment to terminate opioid dependence (codeine) with Dr. Galanter. Please do not prescribe or dispense any further medications of this type for me.

The letters served as the beginning of a successful course of treatment for Leslie. Their effectiveness was confirmed when I received a phone call from one of the physicians to whom we had written. He asked if it was acceptable to prescribe an unrelated medication, given the letter he had received. I reassured him that it was.

CONTRACT FOR A CATACLYSM

The contingency contract is the most dramatic form of written device. It involves a signed agreement that a contingency, or a threatened intervention, will be applied if the patient uses drugs. This approach was originally developed by behavioral therapists for a variety of applications, then later adapted to the field of addiction.[5] Thomas Crowley applied the technique in his treatment of cocaine addicts when this epidemic was first emerging; many of the people seeking treatment at that time had little hope of a successful outcome.[6] His patients, generally physicians, were quite willing to risk a cataclysmic consequence to stay off the drug.

Crowley's concept was straightforward: patients had to have a resource of great value they could ill afford to lose—a legal practice, a medical license, or a sizable financial asset. To be accepted into treatment, they would sign a contract that guaranteed the loss of that resource if they were ever found to be using cocaine; the agreement was carefully monitored through observed urinalyses. The assumption underlying this treatment model was that if the contingency were threatening enough, the patient, however badly addicted, would refrain from using the drug. Indeed, most of his heavily addicted patients did succeed over the course of this treatment and follow-up, an average of twenty months.

A lengthy contract was signed by the therapist, the patient, and a witness, defining all the particulars, specifically what would happen if the patient ever had a positive urine. An appropriate letter was then prepared, in the case of physicians to a licensing board, that included a signed "confession" of the patient's addiction, and an agreement to relinquish his or her license. The contract included authorization for the treating party to mail the letter if any urine were found positive for cocaine. Such an agreement clearly could not be managed casually, and the terms were spelled out very carefully. For example, it was stipulated that missing a urinalysis without proper excuse would be considered equivalent to having a urine positive for cocaine.

The technique has not been used too widely in this form, since most therapists are not inclined to impose harsh consequences on their patients. Psychotherapists are inclined to see themselves more as enablers of personal growth than as agents of coercion. Nonetheless, the contingency contract can have a place in addiction treatment under certain circumstances. Other treatment options, less compromising to the patient, should first have failed, so that a new idea is in order. Furthermore, there should be enough good will between therapist and patient, with additional support from the network, so that a harsh contingency is not seen as a punitive.

John, an advertising executive, had been in treatment for several months. When he initially presented, his addiction had been severe; he was snorting large amounts of cocaine, five or ten grams on some days, and regularly driving himself into a paranoid state. He would often spend his evenings alone in his apartment with a baseball bat at his side, waiting to fend off an imagined police assault. His best friend, Billy, was fed up with John's drug use, after many attempts to intervene.

As treatment began, I put a network together with John that consisted of Billy; his girlfriend, Mara; and another friend. Treatment appeared to go well at first, and John's consumption of cocaine was cut back dramatically, both in quantity and in frequency. But he never achieved full abstinence. Initially, he seemed to have a minor slip once every week or two, but then his usage became more common, as attested to by Mara and Billy. He refused to attend Narcotics Anonymous meetings.

We spent a good deal of time discussing the cues for drug use, with John's active participation. He appeared to want to apply what he learned, but was not successful. After a time, I elected to put him on an antidepressant as well, as it had been found to have some effectiveness in cutting down on craving, but this too had no apparent effect in preventing his occasional lapses.

At one point, John acknowledged that he had recently been using drugs more often, although not in large quantities. He had been hiding this use from the network members and from me, and he had been lying to us at times. This sort of concealment was fairly uncommon in my experience, as I have found that most people are loathe to betray the trust of the network once a good working relationship has been established and a mutual goal of abstinence has been agreed on.

I began to realize that John's psychological difficulties were complicating his recovery, in that he displayed sociopathic traits that compromised his collaborating with treatment. Throughout his life, he had experienced less remorse than one would expect in betraying the confidence of people close to him. He was inclined as well to cut corners on the standards of behavior associated with the institutions he participated in, therapy included. He had always been resentful of having to obey anyone he perceived to have authority over him, and this behavior extended to his manipulating Mara as well, as he demonstrated a good deal less fidelity toward her than he avowed.

John's background was certainly contributing to his personality disorder. His father had been a chronic alcoholic, abusive to his mother and him. The father had degraded himself as well over the years of John's childhood, shooting himself in the leg on one occasion, and ultimately drowning while he was drunk. John had bitterly resented his father, and he felt no more affection for his stepfather. His behavior had been a problem for both. He began selling marijuana in junior high school as much to place himself out of the pale of legality as to reap any great material benefits. He continued to deal marijuana while in college, although he made enough money from a well-paying part-time job. Later he discovered cocaine as a vehicle for alienating himself.

John's need to hold back on commitments, to protect himself from the risk of placing his trust in others, allowed him to punish people close to him. This was evident in many of his current pursuits. He divided his time between a full-time job in a publishing house and a sideline in real estate. This secondary pursuit did not add much to his income, but it did allow him to feel that he could compromise the system he was in. In therapy, the continued drug use was a way of obliquely punishing his network and me for the misfortunes visited on him in his youth, although in the end he compromised only his own well-being.

I tried to impress on John that he was repeating a pattern of hostile and rebellious nonconformity that had followed him through life. He agreed but was apparently unable, or unwilling, to make the effort necessary to put an end to his habit. I described the option of a contingency contract to John and his network hoping that this would either scare him into compliance or prepare the group to take this step.

It became clear that John's intermittent use of cocaine would continue, and with it the vulnerability of returning to his previous highly compromised state. At this point, I suggested we apply the contingency contract. It would require absolute abstinence, as well as attendance at NA or AA meetings at least once a week. The contingency here was the mailing of a letter to John's direct supervisor, the president of the publishing house, if he used cocaine once more. The letter would state that John was addicted, that his drug use had been responsible for his absences and poor performance in the past, and that he was now resigning. Personal matters at the company were highly contentious, and such a letter would likely cost him his job.

Feeling the same despair as I, John was inclined to consider the option, but then angrily said to me in the network meeting, "And if I don't pull off this trick, then where am I?"

"I think you can do it. If we stick to the terms of the contract, you'll have to go along, and you will." I spoke softly and supportively, knowing that the rest of the group, fed up with John by now, would come down harder on him.

Billy indeed took a hard line, and his voice betrayed the fact that his patience had worn thin: "John, you've dished out enough crap already. If you're serious, you'll come in on it. You can't pull this off on your own, and I'm sick of your lying to us." Mara said as much in her own way. Once again, it appeared that the presence of a network allowed for a losing situation to be changed into a viable one, as they put pressure on John to take a step he had to take.

John was unwilling to sign up for a full year of the contract, a period of time that would be necessary to ensure subsequent sobriety. We therefore wrote the contract for six months, but included a clause stating, "I understand that if I do not extend the contract for an additional six months, I am not continuing in good faith with a proper treatment plan." With the network behind this clause, I felt we could secure a full year's agreement when the time came.

The observed urinalyses, now clearly central to implementing the contract, had to be ensured. We agreed that Billy, whom I had found to be quite reliable, would be responsible for collecting the urines over the course of the year. As spelled out in the contract, Billy would summon John on the days that Billy and I arranged in advance. John would appear at Billy's office, not far from his own, and give a sample of urine under observation. Further terms were defined to avoid any manipulation of the collection schedule.

John's psychology was important here, in that he expressed a desire to comply with the plan, and was willing to participate after the agreement was sealed. The one-year period of contingency indeed worked well, because he could end his drug use when threatened with a most serious consequence. In addition, Billy, with the support of the network, participated steadfastly and worked well with both John and me.

Ten months later, I decided in discussion with the network to eliminate the contingency for the last two months of the contract year, while still maintaining the urinalyses. Apparently John's abstinence was stable enough by this point; and he continued with his therapy sessions, and was able to maintain abstinence without the contract. I saw him for an additional six months after the urinalyses were terminated, and neither he, his network members, nor I could report that there was further drug use.

There are many variations on the contingency contract, although I prefer to rely first on mutuality with the patient and the network and to avoid potentially punitive options. Sometimes, though, the approach can be adapted to smaller problems which might otherwise seem unresolvable. I worked with Rachel and her network to relieve her abuse of alcohol, which had been closely associated with anxiety symptoms she had long experienced. We had developed a successful medication regimen to manage the syndrome as well. As it happened, Rachel had to move to a remote city, and we decided to continue speaking over the phone while her situation stabilized.

One problem in bridging these two geographical locales, however, lay in clarifying the relationship between Rachel's very heavy coffee consumption, some twenty cups a day, and her residual anxiety. At my suggestion, she tried a number of times to stop the coffee drinking. Given the caffeine's addictive nature and her dependent disposition, she was never able to stop completely. She would succeed in cutting back to a few cups a day, then would soon build up to seven or eight again. On one occasion she was free of coffee for several days, but then stopped off at a gas station while traveling on business and found herself having a cup of coffee again, which led to a return to heavy consumption over the ensuing days.

We were never able to get a sense of what her true mood state was because she was never free from coffee or the immediate consequences of cutting back on it, so I decided to devise a contingency that would allow Rachel to eliminate her remaining few cups of coffee. I felt comfortable that she would be honest with me as she had been over the course of her treatment to date.

Contingencies need not always be destructive. They can also be abhorrent. Since Rachel was from a Jewish family that had suffered in the Holocaust, we arranged that she would send me two $500 checks, each made out to an organization that she knew to have neo-Nazi ties, with letters expressing her support for the group. An additional note spelled out our understanding that if she had another cup of coffee, I was to send the first check to the organization, and if she had one more cup the second would be sent. This gave us a backup contingency. With this, Rachel stopped drinking coffee. The contingency plan worked because a clear written agreement was supported by a good working relationship between patient and therapist.

The devices we have discussed in this chapter are ways in which behavior can be managed over the long term to secure protection from the vagaries of the addictive drive. The establishment of a web of protective measures and the use of written agreements illustrate how strategic thinking can be applied to this end. By no means, however, do they exhaust the options that a creative therapist can generate to manage a patient's behavior in planning for a secure recovery.

Summary

We can close this chapter by reviewing some essential points about the network approach for treating addiction.

1. *It is essential to target behavior.* Effective intervention with addicts is clearly an exercise in promptly terminating the consumption of alcohol and drugs. Yet traditional approaches to treatment have not stressed immediate abstinence. Expressiveness and insight, although valuable to the treatment process, have too often substituted for a successful commitment to abstinence.

2. *Patients need to find new meaning in their lives.* A renewed sense of purpose is essential to the process of recovery. The spiritual orientation of Alcoholics Anonymous highlights this issue. Drinking or drug-use cues will always present the recovering addict with the danger of relapse. In an effective treatment, the appeal of the drug use will be extinguished when the patient begins to see signs of a new life as meaningful, and his or her addictive past as undesirable. Only when the symbolic meaning associated with conditioned cues is transformed can long-term abstinence be secured. This transformation can be achieved successfully only with support from family and friends, not by behavior change alone.

3. *An eclectic treatment approach is needed.* The therapist must be prepared to adopt a variety of modalities, using social and family management, psychodynamic psychology, other therapies, and appropriate self-help groups. No single modality will work effectively for all patients, nor will a given modality necessarily work alone. Common sense and judgment often make the difference in successful treatment.

Appendix
The Rules of Network Therapy Summarized

AT ITS HEART, the network approach is meant to be straightforward and uncomplicated by theoretical bias—for the patient, for the network member, and for the therapist. In this light, I have summarized the main points to be observed in treatment by the network therapist.

Select Patients Carefully

1. Network therapy is appropriate for people who cannot reliably control their intake of alcohol or drugs once they have taken their first dose; those who have tried to stop and relapsed; and those who have not been willing or able to stop.

2. People whose problems are too severe for the network approach include those who cannot stop their drug use even for a day or cannot comply with outpatient detoxification and those whose associated problems make cooperation unlikely, such as the homeless or psychotics. Such patients generally need hospitalization.

3. People who can be treated with conventional therapy and without a network include those who have demonstrated the ability to moderate their consumption without problems for extended periods and those who have only had a brief episode of abuse.

Start a Network as Soon as Possible

1. It is important to see the alcohol or drug abuser promptly, as the window of opportunity for openness to treatment is generally brief. A week's delay can result in a person's reverting back to drunkenness or losing motivation.

2. If the person is married, engage the spouse early on, preferably at the time of the first phone call. Point out that addiction is a family problem. For most drugs, you can enlist the spouse in ensuring that the patient arrives at your office with a day's sobriety.

3. In the initial interview, frame the exchange so that a good case is built for the grave consequences of the patient's addiction, and do this before the patient can introduce his or her system of denial. That way you are not putting the spouse or other network members in the awkward position of having to contradict a close relation.

4. Make clear that the patient needs to be abstinent, starting now. (A tapered detoxification may be necessary sometimes, as with depressant pills.)

5. When seeing an alcoholic patient for the first time, begin disulfiram (Antabuse) treatment as soon as possible, in the office if you can. Have the patient continue taking disulfiram under observation of a network member.

6. Start arranging for a network to be assembled at the first session, generally involving the patient's family and close friends.

7. From the first meeting you should consider how to ensure sobriety till the next meeting, and plan that with the network. Initially, their immediate company, a plan for daily AA attendance, and planned activities may all be necessary.

Select Network Members with Care, and Make Sure the Network Atmosphere Is Supportive

1. Include people who are close to the patient, have a long-standing relationship with him or her, and are trusted. Avoid members with substance-abuse problems, as they will let you down when you need their unbiased support. Avoid superiors and subordinates at work, as they have an overriding relationship with the patient independent of friendship.

2. Get a balanced group. Avoid a network composed solely of the parental generation, or of younger people, or of people of the opposite sex. Sometimes a nascent network selects itself for a consultation if the patient is reluctant to address his or her own problem. Such a group will later supportively engage the patient in the network, with your careful guidance.

3. Make sure that the mood of meetings is trusting and free of recrimination. Avoid letting the patient or the network members be made to feel guilty or angry in meetings. Explain issues of conflict in terms of the problems presented by addiction—do not get into personality conflicts.

4. The tone should be directive. That is to say, give explicit instructions to support and ensure abstinence. A feeling of teamwork should be promoted, with no psychologizing or impugning members' motives.

5. Meet as frequently as necessary to ensure abstinence, perhaps once a week for a month, every other week for the next few months, and every month or two by the end of a year.

6. The network should have no agenda other than to support the patient's abstinence. But as abstinence is stabilized, the network can help the patient plan for a new drug-free adaptation. It is not there to work on family relations or to help other members with their problems, although it may do this indirectly.

Keep the Network's Agenda Focused

1. *Maintaining abstinence.* The patient and the network members should report at the outset of each session any exposure of the patient to alcohol or drugs. The patient and network members should be instructed on the nature of relapse and plan with the therapist how to sustain abstinence. Cues to conditioned drug seeking should be examined.

2. *Supporting the network's integrity.* Everyone has a role in this. The patient is expected to make sure that network members keep their meeting appointments and stay involved with the treatment. The therapist sets meeting times and summons the network for any emergency, such as a relapse; the therapist does whatever is necessary to secure stability of the membership if the patient is having trouble doing so. Network members' responsibility is to attend network sessions, although they may be asked to undertake other supportive activity with the patient.

3. *Securing future behavior.* The therapist should combine any and all modalities necessary to ensure the patient's stability, such as a stable, drug-free residence; the avoidance of substance-abusing friends; attendance at twelve-step meetings; medications like disulfiram or blocking agents; observed urinalyses; and ancillary psychiatric care. Written agreements may be handy, such as a mutually acceptable contingency contract with penalties for the violation of understandings.

Incorporate Individual Therapy into the Treatment

1. The patient is seen in individual therapy once or twice a week, and abstinence is the first priority for individual therapy, as well as for network sessions. Insight and expressiveness are important, but they must be subordinate to making sure that abstinence is unthreatened.

2. A search for conditioned cues for drug seeking can be used to understand the potential for relapse and to investigate areas of conflict. It is important to explore the emotional, circumstantial, or substance-related events that bring substance use to mind.

3. Ultimately, individual therapy must be directed at the patient's adopting a new and drug-free lifestyle in which abstinence will be embedded. Long-term recovery is only as stable as the patient's new adaptation to family, friends, and work. Group or family therapy might be used instead of or in addition to individual therapy, but only if abstinence is stressed.

Make Use of AA and Other Self-help Groups

1. Patients should be expected to go to meetings of AA or related groups at least two or three times, with follow-up discussion in therapy.

2. If patients have reservations about these meetings, try to help them understand how to deal with them. Issues like social anxiety should be explored if they make a patient reluctant to participate. Generally, resistance to AA can be related to other areas of inhibition in a person's life, as well as to the denial of addiction.

3. As with other spiritual involvements, do not probe the patients' motivation or commitment to AA once engaged. Allow them to work out things on their own, but be prepared to listen.

Terminate the Network Therapy at the Appropriate Time

1. Network sessions can be terminated after the patient has been stably abstinent for at least six months to a year, after group discussion of the patient's readiness for handling sobriety without a network.

2. Establish an understanding with the network members that they will contact the therapist at any point in the future if the patient is vulnerable to relapse. They can be summoned by the therapist as well. This should be made clear in a network session before termination.

Notes

Chapter 2   An Introduction to Network Therapy

1. M. Parloff, cited in Karasu 1977.
2. Hayman 1956.
3. Gitlow and Peyser 1980, p. 13.
4. Vaillant 1981, p. 49.
5. Vaillant 1980.
6. Fuller et al. 1986.
7. Von Bertalanffy 1968.
8. Jackson 1957.
9. Steinglass et al. 1987.
10. Davis et al. 1974.
11. Orford 1986.
12. Jacob, Dunn, and Leonard 1983.
13. Steiner 1974.
14. Anderson and Liepman 1989.
15. Gorski 1989, p. 16.
16. Ibid., p. 18.
17. Johnson 1986.
18. Speck 1967; Speck and Attneave 1974.
19. Albaugh and Anderson 1974.
20. Galanter 1989.
21. Ibid.; Cartwright and Zander 1962.

22. Singer and Borrero 1984.
23. Festinger, Riecken, and Schachter 1956.
24. Kleinman and Gale 1982; Pattison, Labins, and Doerr 1973.
25. Heider 1958.
26. Emrick 1989.
27. Institute of Medicine 1990a.
28. Galanter in press a, in press b.

Chapter 3   Understanding Addiction

1. Griffiths and Woodson 1988.
2. Actually a generalized anxiety disorder, 300.02 (*DSM IIIR*, American Psychiatric Association 1987).
3. Rudy 1986 discusses the evolution of this concept.
4. Wikler 1973.
5. Gallimberti et al. 1989; Suzdak et al. 1986.
6. Ritz et al. 1987.
7. Begleiter, Porjesz, and Yerre-Grubstein 1974.
8. O'Brien et al. 1977; Siegel et al. 1982; Siegel 1987; Le, Poulos, and Cappell 1979.
9. McAuliffe 1982; Ludwig 1988.
10. Vaillant 1983; Miller and Baca 1983; Institute of Medicine 1990b.
11. Warburton 1988.
12. Griffiths, Bigelow, and Liebson 1986.
13. Gilbert 1976.
14. Stunkard 1988; Stunkard et al. 1990.
15. Heider 1958.
16. Galanter 1983.
17. Stojiljkovic 1969; Galanter 1981.
18. Fuller et al. 1986.
19. Wikler 1973; Ludwig et al. 1978.
20. Marlatt and Gordon 1985; Annis 1986.
21. Miller and Baca 1983.
22. Childress et al. 1988.
23. Beck, Rush, and Shaw 1979.
24. Gorski and Miller 1986.

Chapter 4   Psychopathology, Old and New

1. American Psychiatric Association 1987.
2. Keeler, Taylor, and Miller 1979; Weissman and Myers 1980.

3. Schuckit 1986.
4. Meyer 1986.
5. Fenichel 1945, p. 379.
6. Lisansky 1960.
7. Michaels 1959, p. 362.
8. American Psychiatric Association 1968, pp. 41–46.
9. Kammeier, Hoffman, and Loper 1973.
10. Vaillant 1983.
11. Galanter, Castaneda, and Ferman 1988; Haugland et al. 1989.
12. Galanter 1989.
13. Rounsaville et al. 1982, 1987.
14. Khantzian and Treece 1985.
15. Quitkin et al. 1972.
16. Kammeier, Hoffman, and Loper 1973.
17. Berne 1964.
18. Elkin et al. 1989.
19. Woody et al. 1983.
20. Kohut 1971.
21. Kohut 1977, p. 197.
22. Becker et al. 1983.
23. Becker and Jaffe 1984.
24. Carlen et al. 1986.
25. Grant, Adams, and Reed 1984.
26. Martin and Jasinski 1969.
27. Gallant 1982.
28. Keeler, Taylor, and Miller 1979.
29. Parker et al. 1987.
30. Murphy and Wetzel 1990; Rich, Young, and Fowler 1986.
31. Bunt et al. 1990.
32. Gawin and Ellinwood 1988.
33. Pattison, Coe, and Rhodes 1969.
34. Hunt and Azrin 1973.
35. Wurmser 1977.

Chapter 5   Establishing the Network

1. Institute of Medicine 1990b.
2. Yalom 1985.
3. Johnson 1986.
4. Bem 1972.
5. Strentz 1980.

Chapter 6   Intersection with Other Therapies

1. Rogers 1966.
2. Fiedler 1950, cited in Rogers 1951, pp. 53–54.
3. Ibid. 1966.
4. Ackerman 1966.
5. Bowen 1978.
6. Minuchin 1974.
7. Haley 1977.
8. Palazzoli-Selvini et al. 1978.
9. Hoffman 1981.
10. Bion 1959.
11. Whitaker and Leiberman 1964.
12. Yalom 1985.
13. Yalom 1978.
14. Hunt and Azrin 1973.
15. Johnson 1986.
16. Minuchin et al. 1968.

Chapter 7   The Role of Alcoholics Anonymous in Network Treatment

1. Emrick 1989.
2. Edwards 1982, p. 232.
3. Baekeland 1977, p. 407.
4. Emrick 1989.
5. James 1902 (1929).
6. Galanter 1990.
7. Galanter 1990.
8. Lifton 1961.
9. Galanter 1980.
10. Galanter and Buckley 1978; Galanter et al. 1979.
11. Vaillant 1983.

Chapter 8   Maintaining Abstinence

1. Miller and Caddy 1977; Chick et al. 1988.
2. Marlatt and Gordon 1985; Annis 1986; Chick et al. 1988; Miller and Baca 1983.
3. Pendery, Maltzman, and West's 1982 evaluation of Sobell and Sobell 1976; Edwards's 1985 evaluation of Davies 1982.

4. Helzer et al. 1985.
5. Edwards 1985; Zimberg 1982; Gitlow and Peyser 1980; Gallant 1987.
6. Gottheil et al. 1982; Vaillant 1983.
7. Galanter, Castaneda, and Solomon 1987.

Chapter 9   Supporting the Network

1. Thomas et al. 1987.
2. Kosten et al. 1983.
3. Yalom 1974; Yalom et al. 1978.
4. Boehnlein 1987.
5. Keane et al. 1988.

Chapter 10   Securing Future Behavior

1. Edwards et al. 1977.
2. Martin et al. 1973.
3. Schuckit, 1989.
4. Tennant et al. 1984.
5. Hall et al. 1977.
6. Crowley 1984.

References

ACKERMAN, N. (1966). *Treating the troubled family*. New York: Basic Books.

ALBAUGH, B. J., & ANDERSON, P. O. (1974). Peyote in the treatment of alcoholism among American Indians. *American Journal of Psychiatry, 131,* 1247–1250.

AMERICAN PSYCHIATRIC ASSOCIATION. (1968). *Diagnostic and statistical manual of mental disorders* (2nd ed.). Washington, DC: American Psychiatric Association.

AMERICAN PSYCHIATRIC ASSOCIATION. (1987). *Diagnostic and statistical manual of mental disorders* (3rd ed., rev.). Washington, DC: American Psychiatric Association.

ANDERSON, R. C., & LIEPMAN, M. R. (1989). Chemical dependency and the family. In M. R. Liepman (Ed.), *Family medicine curriculum guide to substance abuse* (vol. 8, pp. 1–34). Photocopied manual, University of Massachusetts.

ANNIS, H. M. (1986). A relapse prevention model for treatment of alcoholics. In W. E. Miller & N. Heather (Eds.), *Treating addictive behaviors: Processes of change.* (pp. 407–421). New York: Plenum.

BAEKELAND, F. (1977). Evaluation of treatment methods in chronic alcoholism. In B. Kissin & H. Begleiter (Eds.), *Treatment and rehabilitation of the chronic alcoholic* (pp. 161–196). New York: Plenum.

BECK, A. T., RUSH, A. J., & SHAW, B. F. (1979). *Cognitive therapy for depression.* New York: Guilford.

BECKER, J. T., BUTTERS, N., HERMAN, A., & D'ANGELO, N. (1983). Learning to associate names and faces: Impaired acquisition on an ecologically relevant memory task by male alcoholics. *Journal of Nervous and Mental Disease, 171,* 617–623.

BECKER, J. T., & JAFFEE, J. H. (1984). Impaired memory for treatment, treatment-relevant information in inpatient alcoholics. *Journal of Studies on Alcohol, 45,* 339–343.

BEGLEITER, H., PORJESZ, B., & YERRE-GRUBSTEIN, C. (1974). Excitability cycle of somatosensory evoked potentials during experimental alcoholization and withdrawal. *Psychopharmacologia, 37,* 15–21.

BEM, D. J. (1972). Self-perception theory. In L. Berkowitz (Ed.), *Advances in experimental social psychology* (vol. 6). New York: Academic Press.

BERNE, E. (1964). *Games people play.* New York: Grove.

BION, W. (1959). *Experiences in groups.* New York: Basic Books.

BOEHNLEIN, J. K. (1987). Culture in posttraumatic stress disorder: Implications for psychotherapy. *American Journal of Psychotherapy, 51,* 519–530.

BOWEN, M. (1978). *Family theory in clinical practice.* New York: Jason Aronson.

BUNT, G., GALANTER, M., LIFSHUTZ, H., & CASTANEDA, R. (1990). Cocaine/"crack" dependence among psychiatric patients. *American Journal of Psychiatry, 147,* 1542–1546.

CARLEN, P. L., PENN, R. D., FORNAZZARI, L., ET AL. (1986). Computerized tomographic scan assessment of alcoholic brain damage and its potential reversibility. *Alcoholism Clinical and Experimental Research, 10,* 226–232.

CARTWRIGHT, D., & ZANDER, A. (EDS.). (1962). *Group dynamics: Research and theory.* Evanston, IL:, Row, Peterson.

CHICK, J., RITSON, B., CONNAUGHTON, J. (1988). Advice versus extended treatment for alcoholism: A controlled study. *British Journal of Addiction, 83,* 159–170.

CHILDRESS, A. R., McLELLAN, A. T., EHRMAN, R., & O'BRIEN, C. P. (1988). Classically conditioned responses in opioid and cocaine dependence: A role in relapse? In B. A. Ray (Ed.), *Learning factors in substance abuse* (NIDA Research Monograph 84, pp. 25–43). Rockville, MD: ADAMHA.

CROWLEY, T. J. (1984). Contingency contracting treatment of drug-abusing physicians, nurses, and dentists. In J. Grabowski, M. L. Stitzer, & J. F. Henningfeld (Eds.), *Behavioral integration techniques in drug abuse treatment* (NIDA Monograph 46). Rockville, MD: Department of Health and Human Services.

DAVIES, D. L. (1962). Normal drinking in recovered alcohol addicts. *Quarterly Journal of Studies on Alcohol, 23,* 94–104.

DAVIS, D. I., BERENSON, D., STEINGLASS, P., & DAVIES, S. (1974). The adaptive consequences of drinking. *Psychiatry, 37,* 209–215.

EDWARDS, G. (1982). *The treatment of drinking problems: A guide for the helping professions*. New York: McGraw-Hill.

EDWARDS, G. (1985). A later follow-up of a classic case series: D.L. Davies' 1962 report and its significance for the present. *Journal of Studies on Alcohol, 46*, 181–190.

EDWARDS, G., ORFORD, J., EGERT, S., ET AL. (1977). Alcoholism: A controlled trial of "treatment" and "advice." *Journal of Studies on Alcohol, 38*, 1004–1031.

ELKIN, I., SHEA, M. T., WATKINS, J. T., ET AL. (1989). National Institute of Mental Health treatment of depression collaborative research program: General effectiveness of treatments. *Archives of General Psychiatry, 46*, 971–982.

EMRICK, C. D. (1989). Alcoholics Anonymous: Membership characteristics and effectiveness as treatment. In M. Galanter (Ed.), *Recent developments in alcoholism* (vol. 7, pp. 37–49). New York: Plenum.

FENICHEL, O. (1945). *The psychoanalytic theory of neurosis*. New York: W. W. Norton.

FESTINGER, L., RIECKEN, H., & SCHACHTER, S. (1956). *When prophecy fails.* Minneapolis: University of Minnesota Press.

FIEDLER, F. E. (1950). The concept of an ideal therapeutic relationship. *Journal of Consulting Psychology, 14*, 239–245.

FULLER, R. K., BRANCHEY, L., BRIGHTWELL, D. R., ET AL. (1986). Disulfiram treatment of alcoholism: A Veterans Administration cooperative study. *Journal of the American Medical Association, 256*, 1449–1455.

GALANTER, M. (1980). Psychological induction into the large group: Findings from a contemporary religious sect. *American Journal of Psychiatry, 137*, 1574–1579.

GALANTER M. (1981). Alcoholism programs in the USSR and Yugoslavia: Effects of social context on treatment modalities. In M. Galanter (Ed.), *Currents in alcoholism* (vol 8, pp. 183–194). New York: Grune and Stratton.

GALANTER, M. (1983). Psychotherapy for alcohol and drug abuse: An approach based on learning theory. *Journal of Psychiatric Treatment and Evaluation, 5*, 551–556.

GALANTER, M. (1989). *Cults: Faith, healing, and coercion.* New York: Oxford University Press.

GALANTER, M. (1990). Cults and zealous self-help movements: A psychiatric perspective. *American Journal of Psychiatry, 147*, 543–551.

GALANTER, M. (IN PRESS, A). Network therapy for addiction: A model for office practice. *American Journal of Psychiatry.*

GALANTER, M. (IN PRESS, B). Network therapy for substance abuse: A clinical trial. *Psychotherapy.*

GALANTER, M., & BUCKLEY, P. (1978). Evangelical religion and meditation: Psychotherapeutic effects. *Journal of Nervous and Mental Disease, 166,* 685–691.

GALANTER, M., CASTANEDA, R., & FERMAN, J. (1988). Substance abuse among general psychiatric patients: Place of presentation, diagnosis, and treatment. *American Journal of Drug and Alcohol Abuse, 142,* 211–235.

GALANTER, M., CASTANEDA, R., & SALAMON, I. (1987). Institutional self-help therapy for alcoholism: Clinical outcome. *Alcohol Clinical and Experimental Research, 11,* 424–429.·

GALANTER, M., RABKIN, R., RABKIN, J., & DEUTCH, A. (1979). The "Moonies": A psychological study. *American Journal of Psychiatry, 136,* 165–170.

GALLANT, D. M. (1982) Psychiatric aspects of alcohol intoxication, withdrawal, inorganic brain syndromes. In J. Solomon (Ed.), *Alcoholism and clinical psychiatry* (pp. 141–162). New York: Plenum.

GALLANT, D. M. (1987). *Alcoholism: A guide to diagnosis, intervention, and treatment.* New York: W. W. Norton.

GALLIMBERTI, L., GENTILE, N., & CONTON, G., (1989). Gamma-hydroxybutyric acid for treatment of alcohol withdrawal syndrome. *Lancet, 2,* 787–789.

GAWIN, F. H., & ELLINWOOD, E. H. (1988). Cocaine and other stimulants: Actions, abuse and treatment. *New England Journal of Medicine, 318,* 1173–1182.

GILBERT, R. M. (1976) Caffeine as a drug of abuse. In R. J. Gibbins, Y. Israel, H. Kalant, et al. (Eds.), *Research advances in alcohol and drug problems* (vol. 3). New York: Wiley.

GITLOW, S. E. & PEYSER, H. S. (EDS.). (1980). *Alcoholism: A practical treatment guide.* New York: Grune and Stratton.

GORSKI, T. T. (1989). *Do family of origin problems cause chemical addiction?* Independence, MO: Herald House.

GORSKI, T. T., & MILLER, M. (1986). *Staying sober: A guide for relapse prevention.* Independence, MO: Herald House.

GOTTHEIL, E., THORNTON, C. C., SKOLODA, T. E., ET AL. (1982). Follow-up of abstinent and non-abstinent alcoholics. *American Journal of Psychiatry, 139,* 560–565.

GRANT, I., ADAMS, K. M., & REED, R. (1984). Aging, abstinence, and medical risk factors in prediction of neuropsychologic deficit among long-term alcoholics. *Archives of General Psychiatry, 41,* 710–718.

GRIFFITHS, R. R., BIGELOW, G. E., & LIEBSON, I. A. (1986). Human coffee drinking: Reinforcing and physical dependence producing effects of caffeine. *Journal of Pharmacology and Experimental Therapy, 239,* 416–425.

GRIFFITHS, R. R., & WOODSON, P. P. (1988). Caffeine physical dependence and reinforcement in humans and laboratory animals. In M. Lader (Ed.), *The psychopharmacology of addiction* (British Association for Psychopharmacology Monograph No. 10, pp. 141–156). New York: Oxford University Press.

HALEY, J. (1977). *Problem solving therapy*. San Francisco: Jossey-Bass.

HALL, S. M., COOPER, J. L., BURMASTER, S., & POLK, A. (1977). Contingency contracting as a therapeutic tool with methadone maintenance clients. *Behavioral Research and Therapy, 15*, 438–441.

HAUGLAND, G., SIEGEL, C., ALEXANDER, M. J., & GALANTER, M. (1989). Results of a hospital survey on the dually disabled patient. In M. Galanter (Ed.), *Task Force on Combined Psychiatric and Addictive Disorders*. New York: New York State Office of Mental Health.

HAYMAN, M. (1956). Current attitudes to alcoholism of psychiatrists in Southern California. *American Journal of Psychiatry, 112*, 484–493.

HEIDER, F. (1958). *The psychology of interpersonal relations*. New York: Wiley.

HELZER, J. E., ROBINS, L. N., TAYLOR, J. R., ET AL. (1985). The extent of long-term moderate drinking among alcoholics discharged from medical and psychiatric treatment facilities. *New England Journal of Medicine, 312*, 1678–1682.

HOFFMAN, L. (1981). *Foundations of family therapy: A conceptual framework for systems change*. New York: Basic Books.

HUNT, G. M., & AZRIN, N. H. (1973). A community reinforcement approach to alcoholism. *Behavior, Research, Therapy, 11*, 91–104.

INSTITUTE OF MEDICINE. (1990A). *Broadening the base of treatment for alcohol problems*. Washington, DC: National Academy Press.

INSTITUTE OF MEDICINE. (1990B). *Prevention and treatment of alcohol problems: Research opportunities*. Washington, DC: National Academy Press.

JACOB, T., DUNN, N. J., & LEONARD, K. (1983). Patterns of alcohol abuse and family stability. *Alcoholism: Clinical and Experimental Research, 7*, 382–385.

JACKSON, D. (1957). The question of family homeostasis. *Psychiatric Quarterly Supplement, 31*, 79–90.

JAMES, W. (1906/1929). *The varieties of religious experience*. New York: Modern Library.

JOHNSON, V. E. (1986). *Intervention: How to help someone who doesn't want help*. Minneapolis: Johnson Institute Books.

KAMMEIER, M. L., HOFFMAN, H., & LOPER, R. G. (1973). Personality characteristics of alcoholics as college freshman and at the time of treatment. *Quarterly Journal of Studies on Alcohol 34*, 309–399.

KARASU, T. B. (1977). The psychotherapies: An overview. *American Journal of Psychiatry 134*, 851–863.

KEANE, T. M., GERARDI, R. J., LYONS, J., & WOLFE, J. (1988). The interrelationship of substance abuse and post-traumatic stress disorder. In M. Galanter (Ed.), *Recent Developments in Alcoholism*. New York: Plenum.

KEELER, M. H., TAYLOR, I., & MILLER, W. C. (1979). Are all recently detoxified alcoholics depressed? *American Journal of Psychiatry, 136*, 586–588.

KHANTZIAN, E. J., & TREECE, C. (1985). DSM III psychiatric diagnosis of narcotic addicts. *Archives of General Psychiatry, 42*, 1067–1071.

KLEINMAN, A., & GALE, J. G. (1982). Patients treated by physicians and folk healers: A comparative outcome study in Taiwan. *Culture Medicine Psychiatry, 6*, 405–423.

KOHUT, H. (1971). *The analysis of self*. New York: International Universities Press.

KOHUT, H. (1977). *The restoration of the self*. New York: International Universities Press, 1977.

KOSTEN, T. R., JALALI, B., HOGAN, I., & KLEBER, H. D. (1983). Family denial as a prognostic factor in opiate addiction treatment outcome. *Journal of Nervous and Mental Disease, 171*, 611–616.

LE, A. D., POULOS, C. X., & CAPPELL, H. (1979). Conditioned tolerance to the hypothermic effect of ethyl alcohol. *Science, 206*, 1109–1110.

LIFTON, R. J., (1961). *Thought reform and the psychology of totalism*. New York: W. W. Norton.

LISANSKY, E. S. (1960). The etiology of alcoholism: The role of psychological predisposition. *Quarterly Journal of Studies on Alcohol, 21*, 314–343.

LUDWIG, A. M. (1988). *Understanding the alcoholic's mind: The nature of craving and how to control it*. New York: Oxford University Press.

LUDWIG, A. M., BENDFELDT, F., WIKLER, A., & CAIN, R. B. (1978). "Loss of control" in alcoholics. *Archives of General Psychiatry, 35*, 370–373.

MARLATT, G. A., & GORDON, J. A. (EDS.). (1985). *Relapse prevention: Maintenance strategies for addictive behavior change*. New York: Guilford.

MARTIN, W. R., & JASINSKI, D. R. (1969). Physiological parameters of morphine in man: Tolerance, early abstinence, protracted abstinence. *Journal of Psychiatric Research, 7*, 1–18.

MARTIN, W. R., JASINSKI, D. R. & MANSKY, P. A. (1973). Naltrexone: an antagonist for the treatment of heroin addiction. *Archives of General Psychiatry 28*, 784–91.

MCAULIFFE, W. E. (1982). A test of Wikler's theory of relapse: The frequency of relapse due to conditioned withdrawal sickness. *International Journal of the Addictions, 17*, 19–33.

MENDELSON, J. H., & MELLO, N. K. (EDS.). (1985). *The diagnosis and treatment of alcoholism*. New York: McGraw-Hill.

MEYER, R. (1986). How to understand the relationship between psychopathology and addictive disorders. In R. E. Meyer (Ed.), *Psychopathology and addictive disorders* (pp. 3–16). New York: Guilford.

MICHAELS, J. J. (1959). Character structure and character disorders. In S. Arieti (Ed.), *The American handbook of psychiatry* (vol. 1, pp. 353–357). New York: Basic Books.

MILLER, W. R., & BACA, L. M. (1983). Two-year follow-up of bibliotherapy and therapist-directed controlled drinking training for problem drinkers. *Behavior Therapy, 14,* 441–448.

MILLER, W. R., & CADDY, G. R. (1977). Abstinence and controlled drinking in the treatment of problem drinkers. *Journal of Studies on Alcohol, 38,* 986–1003.

MINUCHIN, S. (1974). *Families and family therapy.* Cambridge: Harvard University Press.

MINUCHIN, S., MONTALVO, B., GUERNEY, R. B., ET AL. (1968). *Families of the slums.* New York: Basic Books.

MURPHY, G. E., & WETZEL, R. D. (1990). The lifetime risk of suicide in alcoholism. *Archives of General Psychiatry, 47,* 383–392.

O'BRIEN, C. P., TESTA, T., O'BRIEN, T. J., ET AL. (1977). Conditioned narcotic withdrawal in humans. *Science, 195,* 1000–1002.

ORFORD, J. (1986). Critical conditions for change in addictive behaviors. In W. R. Miller & N. Heather (Eds.), *Treating addictive behaviors* (pp. 91–108). New York: Plenum.

PALAZZOLI-SELVINI, M., BOSCOLO, L., CECCHIN, G. (1978). *Paradox and counterparadox.* New York: Jason Aronson.

PARKER, D. A., PARKER, E. S., HARTFORD, T. C., & FARMER, G. C. (1987). Alcohol use and depression among employed men and women. *American Journal of Public Health, 77,* 704–707.

PATTISON, E. M., COE, R., & RHODES, R. S. (1969). Evaluation of treatment: A comparison of three facilities. *Archives of General Psychiatry, 20,* 478–488.

PATTISON, E. M., LABINS, N. A., & DOERR, H. A. (1973). Faith healing: A study of personality and function. *Journal of Nervous and Mental Disease, 157,* 367–409.

PENDERY, M. L., MALTZMAN, I. M., & WEST, L. J. (1982). Controlled drinking for alcoholics? New findings and a reevaluation of a major study. *Science, 217,* 169–175.

QUITKIN, F. M., RIFKIN, A., KAPLAN, J., & KLEIN, D. F. (1972). Phobic anxiety syndrome complicated by drug dependence and addiction: A treatable form of drug abuse. *Archives of General Psychiatry, 27,* 159–162.

RICH, C. L., YOUNG, D., & FOWLER, R. C. (1986). San Diego suicide study: I. Young vs. old subject. *Archives of General Psychiatry, 43,* 577–582.

RITZ, M. C., LAMB, R. J., GOLDBERG, S. R., & KUHAR, M. J. (1987). Cocaine receptors on dopamine transporters are related to self-administration of cocaine. *Science, 237,* 1219–1223.

ROGERS, C. R. (1951). *Client-centered therapy: Its current practice, implications, and theory.* Boston: Houghton Mifflin.

ROGERS, C. R. (1966). Client-centered therapy. In S. Arieti (Ed.), *The American handbook of psychiatry* (pp. 183–200). New York: Basic Books.

ROUNSAVILLE, B. J., DOLINSKY, Z. S., BABOR, T. F., & MEYER, R. E. (1987). Psychopathology as a predictor of treatment outcome in alcoholics. *Archives of General Psychiatry, 44,* 505–513.

ROUNSAVILLE, B. J., WEISSMAN, M. M., WILBER, C. H., ET AL. (1982). Diagnosis and symptoms of depression in opiate addicts: Course and relationship to treatment outcome. *Archives of General Psychiatry, 39,* 151–156.

RUDY, D. R. (1986). *Becoming alcoholic: Alcoholics Anonymous and the reality of alcoholism.* Carbondale: Southern Illinois University Press.

SCHUCKIT, M. A. (1986). Genetic and clinical implications of alcoholism and affective disorder. *American Journal of Psychiatry, 143,* 140–147.

SCHUCKIT, M. A. (1989). *Drug and alcohol abuse: A clinical guide to diagnosis and treatment.* New York: Plenum.

SIEGEL, S. (1982). Pavlovian conditioning and heroin overdose: Reports by overdose victims. *Bulletin of the Psychonomic Society, 22,* 428–430.

SIEGEL, S. (1987). Pavlovian conditioning and ethanol tolerance. In K. O. Lindros, R. Ylikahri, & K. Kiianmaa (Eds.), *Advances in biomedical alcohol research* (pp. 25–36). Oxford: Pergamon Press.

SIEGEL, S., HINSON, R., KRANK, M., & MCCULLY, J. (1982). Heroin "overdose" death: Contribution of drug-associated environmental cues. *Science, 216,* 436–437.

SINGER, M., & BORRERO, M. G. (1984). Indigenous treatment for alcoholism: The case of Puerto Rican spiritualism. *Medical Anthropology: Cross-Cultural Studies in Health and Illness, 8,* 246–273.

SOBELL, M. B., & SOBELL, L. C. (1976). Second-year treatment outcomes of alcoholics treated by individual behavior therapy: Results. *Behavior Research Therapy, 14,* 195–215.

SPECK, R. (1967). Psychotherapy of the social network of a schizophrenic family. *Family Process, 6,* 208–220.

SPECK, R., & ATTNEAVE, C. (1974). *Family networks.* New York: Vintage.

STEINER, C. (1974). *Games alcoholics play.* New York: Ballantine.

STEINGLASS, P., BENNETT, L. A., WOLIN, S. J., & REISS, D. (1987). *The alcoholic family.* New York: Basic Books.

STOJILJKOVIC, S. (1969). Conditioned aversion treatment of alcoholics. *Quarterly Journal of Studies on Alcohol, 30,* 900–904.

STRENTZ, T. (1980). The Stockholm syndrome. *Annals of the New York Academy of Sciences, 347,* 137–150.

STUNKARD, A. J. (1988). Some perspectives on human obesity: Its causes. *Bulletin of the New York Academy of Medicine, 64,* 902–923.

STUNKARD, A. J., HARRIS, J. R., PEDERSON, N. L., & MCCLEARN, G. E. (1990). The body mass index of twins who have been reared apart. *New England Journal of Medicine, 322,* 1477–1482.

SUZDAK, P. D., GLOWA, J. R., DRAWLEY, J. N., ET AL. (1986). A selective imidazobenzodiazepine antagonist of ethanol in the rat. *Science, 234,* 1243–1247.

TENNANT, F. S., RAWSON, A., COHEN, A. J., & MANN, A. (1984). Clinical experience with naltrexone in suburban opiate addicts. *Journal of Clinical Psychiatry, 45,* 42–45.

THOMAS, E. J., SANTA, C., BRONSON, D., & OYSERMAN, D. (1987). Unilateral family therapy with the spouses of alcoholics. *Progress in Behavioral Social Work,* 145–162.

VAILLANT, G. E. (1980). The doctor's dilemma. In G. E. Edwards & M. Grant (Eds.), *Alcoholism treatment in transition* (pp. 13–31). Baltimore: University Park Press.

VAILLANT, G. E., BEAN, M. H., & ZINBERG, N. E. (EDS.), (1981). Dangers of psychotherapy in the treatment of alcoholism. In *Dynamic approaches to the understanding and treatment of alcoholism* (pp. 36–54). New York: Free Press.

VAILLANT, G. E. (1983). *The natural history of alcoholism.* Cambridge: Harvard University Press.

VON BERTALANFFY, L. (1968). *General systems theory.* New York: George Braziller.

WARBURTON, D. M. (1988). The puzzle of nicotine use. In M. Lader (Ed.), *The psychopharmacology of addiction* (British Association for Psychopharmacology Monograph No. 10, pp. 27–49). New York: Oxford University Press.

WEISSMAN, M. M., & MYERS, J. K. (1980). Clinical depression in alcoholism. *American Journal of Psychiatry, 137,* 372–373.

WHITAKER, D. S., & LIBERMAN, M. (1964). *Psychotherapy through the group process.* New York: Atherton.

WIKLER, A. (1973). Dynamics of drug dependence. *Archives of General Psychiatry, 28,* 611–616.

WOODY, G. E., LUBORSKY, L., MCLELLAN, A. T., ET AL. (1983). Psychotherapy for opiate addicts: Does it help? *Archives of General Psychiatry, 40,* 639–645.

WURMSER, L. (1977). Mrs. Pecksniff's horse? Psychology names in compulsive drug use. In J. D. Blaine & D. S. Julius (Eds.), *Dynamics of drug dependence* (NIDA Research Monograph 12, pp. 36–72). Washington, DC: Government Printing Office.

YALOM, I. D. (1974). Group therapy and alcoholism. *Annals of the New York Academy of Sciences, 233,* 85–103.

YALOM, I. D. (1985). *The theory and practice of group psychotherapy.* New York: Basic Books.

YALOM, I. D., BLOCH, S., BOND, G., ET AL. (1978). Alcoholics in interactional group therapy. *Archives of General Psychiatry, 35,* 419–425.

ZIMBERG, S. (1982). *The clinical management of alcoholism.* New York: Brunner/Mazel.

Index

Abstinence: Alcoholics Anonymous and, 125, 126, 130, 131–36, 144; conditioned, 35–41; conversion of addict to, 25–27; establishing importance of, 5–6, 17–18, 76–77, 78–80; partial vs. controlled, 143–45, 147–48, 154–58; problems of maintaining, 143–58, 197; variety of treatment techniques for, 47, 65, 178–83, 193, 198. *See also* Disulfiram (Antabuse)

Ackerman, Nathan, 114

Acute care services, 75

Addiction: addictive personality and, 50–51; collapse of psychological defenses and, 65–70; conditioned abstinence response and, 35–41; criminal behavior and, 33–35; depression and, 48–49; effective treatment of, 4–5; functional deficits caused by, 61–70; implied contract in treatment of, 73–75; individual therapy and, 4, 9–11, 41–43, 44, 55; narcissism and, 50, 51, 59–61, 138, 160–61; nature of, 31–33; personality disorders and, 51, 54–59; problems related to, 48–61; self-medication and, 51–53; vulnerability to relapse and, 35, 38–39. *See also* Network therapy; Relapse; *and names of specific addictive substances*

Addiction Research Center (Lexington, Kentucky), 35–36

Addictive personality, 50–51

Adolescence, drug use in, 95, 157, 189

Affect regression, 68–70

Aggression, in group therapy, 118

Agreements, written, 183–92, 198; on calling cards, 184–85; contingency

217

Coronary Artery Disease and the Myocardial Ischemic Cascade

Editors

U. JOSEPH SCHOEPF
JAMES C. CARR

RADIOLOGIC CLINICS OF NORTH AMERICA

www.radiologic.theclinics.com

Consulting Editor
FRANK H. MILLER

March 2015 • Volume 53 • Number 2

616.075
R129
v.53 no.2

LIBRARY
Milwaukee Area
Technical College
MILWAUKEE
CAMPUS
WITHDRAWN

ELSEVIER

1600 John F. Kennedy Boulevard • Suite 1800 • Philadelphia, Pennsylvania, 19103-2899

http://www.theclinics.com

RADIOLOGIC CLINICS OF NORTH AMERICA Volume 53, Number 2
March 2015 ISSN 0033-8389, ISBN 13: 978-0-323-35665-7

Editor: John Vassallo (j.vassallo@elsevier.com)
Developmental Editor: Donald Mumford

© **2015 Elsevier Inc. All rights reserved.**

This periodical and the individual contributions contained in it are protected under copyright by Elsevier, and the following terms and conditions apply to their use:

Photocopying
Single photocopies of single articles may be made for personal use as allowed by national copyright laws. Permission of the Publisher and payment of a fee is required for all other photocopying, including multiple or systematic copying, copying for advertising or promotional purposes, resale, and all forms of document delivery. Special rates are available for educational institutions that wish to make photocopies for non-profit educational classroom use. For information on how to seek permission visit www.elsevier.com/permissions or call: (+44) 1865 843830 (UK)/(+1) 215 239 3804 (USA).

Derivative Works
Subscribers may reproduce tables of contents or prepare lists of articles including abstracts for internal circulation within their institutions. Permission of the Publisher is required for resale or distribution outside the institution. Permission of the Publisher is required for all other derivative works, including compilations and translations (please consult www.elsevier.com/permissions).

Electronic Storage or Usage
Permission of the Publisher is required to store or use electronically any material contained in this periodical, including any article or part of an article (please consult www.elsevier.com/permissions). Except as outlined above, no part of this publication may be reproduced, stored in a retrieval system or transmitted in any form or by any means, electronic, mechanical, photocopying, recording or otherwise, without prior written permission of the Publisher.

Notice
No responsibility is assumed by the Publisher for any injury and/or damage to persons or property as a matter of products liability, negligence or otherwise, or from any use or operation of any methods, products, instructions or ideas contained in the material herein. Because of rapid advances in the medical sciences, in particular, independent verification of diagnoses and drug dosages should be made.

Although all advertising material is expected to conform to ethical (medical) standards, inclusion in this publication does not constitute a guarantee or endorsement of the quality or value of such product or of the claims made of it by its manufacturer.

Radiologic Clinics of North America (ISSN 0033-8389) is published bimonthly by Elsevier Inc., 360 Park Avenue South, New York, NY 10010-1710. Months of issue are January, March, May, July, September, and November. Periodicals postage paid at New York, NY and additional mailing offices. Subscription prices are USD 460 per year for US individuals, USD 709 per year for US institutions, USD 220 per year for US students and residents, USD 535 per year for Canadian individuals, USD 905 per year for Canadian institutions, USD 660 per year for international individuals, USD 905 per year for international institutions, and USD 315 per year for Canadian and foreign students/residents. To receive student and resident rate, orders must be accompanied by name of affiliated institution, date of term and the signature of program/residency coordinatior on institution letterhead. Orders will be billed at individual rate until proof of status is received. Foreign air speed delivery is included in all *Clinics* subscription prices. All prices are subject to change without notice. **POSTMASTER:** Send address changes to *Radiologic Clinics of North America*, Elsevier Health Sciences Division, Subscription Customer Service, 3251 Riverport Lane, Maryland Heights, MO63043. **Customer Service: Telephone: 1-800-654-2452** (U.S. and Canada); **1-314-447-8871** (outside U.S. and Canada). **Fax: 1-314-447-8029. E-mail: journalscustomerservice-usa@ elsevier.com** (for print support); **journalsonlinesupport-usa@elsevier.com** (for online support).

Reprints. For copies of 100 or more of articles in this publication, please contact the Commercial Reprints Department, Elsevier Inc., 360 Park Avenue South, New York, New York 10010-1710. Tel.: +1-212-633-3874; Fax: +1-212-633-3820; E-mail: reprints@elsevier.com.

Radiologic Clinics of North America also published in Greek Paschalidis Medical Publications, Athens, Greece.

Radiologic Clinics of North America is covered in *MEDLINE/PubMed (Index Medicus), EMBASE/Excerpta Medica, Current Contents/Life Sciences, Current Contents/Clinical Medicine, RSNA Index to Imaging Literature, BIOSIS, Science Citation Index,* and *ISI/BIOMED.*

Printed in the United States of America.

Contributors

CONSULTING EDITOR

FRANK H. MILLER, MD
Chief, Body Imaging Section and Fellowship
Program and GI Radiology; Medical Director
MRI; Professor, Department of Radiology,
Northwestern University, Feinberg School of
Medicine, Northwestern Memorial Hospital,
Chicago, Illinois

EDITORS

U. JOSEPH SCHOEPF, MD
Department of Radiology and Radiological
Science, Heart and Vascular Center, Medical
University of South Carolina, Charleston,
South Carolina

JAMES C. CARR, MD
Department of Radiology, Northwestern
University Feinberg School of Medicine,
Chicago, Illinois

AUTHORS

**Dr. SAEED AL SAYARI, MBBS,
GERMAN BOARD OF RADIOLOGY,
EUROPEAN BOARD OF CARDIAC
RADIOLOGY (EBCR)**
Non-Invasive Cardiac Imaging Fellow,
Cardiothoracic Section, Department of
Radiology and Nuclear Medicine, University of
Basel Hospital, Basel, Switzerland; Specialist
Radiologist, Department of Radiology, Mafraq
Hospital, Abu Dhabi, United Arab Emirates

FABIAN BAMBERG, MD, MPH
Departments of Diagnostic and Interventional
Radiology, University Hospital Tübingen,
Tübingen, Germany; Cardiac MR PET CT
Program, Massachusetts General Hospital,
Harvard Medical School, Boston,
Massachusetts

NICHOLAS I. BATALIS, MD
Department of Pathology and Laboratory
Medicine, Medical University of South
Carolina, Charleston, South Carolina

STEFAN BAUMANN, MD
Department of Radiology, Heart and Vascular
Center, Medical University of South Carolina,
Charleston, South Carolina; First Department
of Medicine, University Medical Centre
Mannheim (UMM), University of Heidelberg,
Mannheim, Germany

RICHARD R. BAYER II, MD
Division of Cardiology, Department of
Medicine, Medical University of South
Carolina, Charleston, South Carolina

DAVID A. BLEUMKE, MD, PhD
Director, Radiology and Imaging Sciences,
National Institutes of Health, Bethesda,
Maryland

**Prof. Dr. JENS BREMERICH, MD,
SWISS AND GERMAN BOARDS OF
RADIOLOGY, EUROPEAN BOARD OF
CARDIAC RADIOLOGY (EBCR)**
Chief of Cardiothoracic Section, Department
of Radiology and Nuclear Medicine, University
of Basel Hospital, Basel, Switzerland

JAMES C. CARR, MD
Department of Radiology, Northwestern University Feinberg School of Medicine, Chicago, Illinois

SALVATORE A. CHIARAMIDA, MD
Heart and Vascular Center, Medical University of South Carolina, Charleston, South Carolina

JEREMY D. COLLINS, MD
Department of Radiology, Feinberg School of Medicine, Northwestern University, Chicago, Illinois

ANDREW M. CREAN, MD
Department of Medicine, University of Toronto; Division of Cardiology, Peter Munk Cardiac Center, Toronto General Hospital, Toronto, Ontario, Canada

CARLO NICOLA DE CECCO, MD
Department of Radiological Sciences, Oncology and Pathology, University of Rome "Sapienza", Latina, Italy; Department of Radiology and Radiological Science, Medical University of South Carolina, Charleston, South Carolina

ULLRICH EBERSBERGER, MD
Heart and Vascular Center, Medical University of South Carolina, Charleston, South Carolina; Department of Cardiology, Heart Centre Munich-Bogenhausen, Munich Municipal Hospital Group, Munich, Germany

THOMAS G. FLOHR, PhD
Siemens Healthcare, Computed Tomography, Forchheim; Institute of Diagnostic Radiology, Eberhard-Karls-University, Tübingen, Germany

CHRISTOPHER J. FRANÇOIS, MD
Associate Professor of Radiology and Medicine, University of Wisconsin – Madison, Madison, Wisconsin

STEPHEN R. FULLER, BSc
Department of Radiology, Heart and Vascular Center, Medical University of South Carolina, Charleston, South Carolina

TOBIAS GEISLER, MD
Department of Cardiology and Cardiovascular Medicine, University Hospital of Tübingen, Tübingen, Germany

UDO HOFFMANN, MD, MPH
Cardiac MR PET CT Program, Massachusetts General Hospital, Harvard Medical School, Boston, Massachusetts

LAURA JIMENEZ JUAN, MD
Department of Medical Imaging, University of Toronto; Department of Medical Imaging, Sunnybrook Health Science Centre, Toronto, Ontario, Canada

Dr. SEBASTIEN KOPP, MD, SWISS BOARD OF RADIOLOGY
Consultant Radiologist, Cardiothoracic Section, Department of Radiology and Nuclear Medicine, University of Basel Hospital, Basel, Switzerland

KAI LIN, MD
Department of Radiology, Northwestern University Feinberg School of Medicine, Chicago, Illinois

FELIX G. MEINEL, MD
Institute for Clinical Radiology, Ludwig-Maximilians-University Hospital, Munich, Germany; Department of Radiology and Radiological Science, Medical University of South Carolina, Charleston, South Carolina

KONSTANTIN NIKOLAOU, MD
Department of Diagnostic and Interventional Radiology, University Hospital of Tübingen, Tübingen, Germany

PUSKAR PATTANAYAK, MD
Post Doc IRTA, Laboratory of Diagnostic Radiology Research, National Institutes of Health, Bethesda, Maryland

MATTHIAS RENKER, MD
Department of Radiology and Radiological Science, Heart and Vascular Center, Medical University of South Carolina, Charleston, South Carolina; Department of Medicine I, Cardiology and Angiology, Giessen University Hospital, Giessen; Department of Cardiology, Kerckhoff Heart and Thorax Center, Bad Nauheim, Germany

JEREMY RIER, DO
Heart and Vascular Center, Medical University of South Carolina, Charleston, South Carolina

CHRISTOPHER L. SCHLETT, MD, MPH
Department of Diagnostic and Interventional Radiology, University Hospital Heidelberg, Heidelberg, Germany; Cardiac MR PET CT Program, Massachusetts General Hospital, Harvard Medical School, Boston, Massachusetts

BERNHARD SCHMIDT, PhD
Siemens Healthcare, Computed Tomography, Forchheim, Germany

U. JOSEPH SCHOEPF, MD
Department of Radiology and Radiological Science, Heart and Vascular Center, Medical University of South Carolina, Charleston, South Carolina

DANIEL H. STEINBERG, MD
Division of Cardiology, Medical University of South Carolina, Charleston, South Carolina

AKOS VARGA-SZEMES, MD, PhD
Department of Radiology and Radiological Science, Medical University of South Carolina, Charleston, South Carolina

RUI WANG, MD
Department of Radiology and Radiological Science, Medical University of South Carolina, Charleston, South Carolina

JULIAN L. WICHMANN, MD
Department of Radiology, Heart and Vascular Center, Medical University of South Carolina, Charleston, South Carolina; Department of Diagnostic and Interventional Radiology, University Hospital Frankfurt, Frankfurt, Germany

BERND J. WINTERSPERGER, MD
Department of Medical Imaging, University of Toronto; Department of Medical Imaging, Peter Munk Cardiac Center, Toronto General Hospital, Toronto, Ontario, Canada

PETER L. ZWERNER, MD
Division of Cardiology, Department of Medicine, Medical University of South Carolina, Charleston, South Carolina

Contents

> On a subcellular level, atherogenesis is characterized by the translocation of proatherogenic lipoproteins into the arterial wall. An inflammatory response involving complex repair mechanisms subsequently causes maladaptive vascular changes resulting in coronary stenosis or occlusion. The chronology of the underlying processes occurring from atherosclerosis to myocardial ischemia affect the selection and interpretation of diagnostic testing. An understanding of the ischemic cascade, atherosclerosis, coronary remodeling, plaque morphology, and their relationship to clinical syndromes is essential in determining which diagnostic modalities are useful in clinical practice.

> While coronary computed tomography (CT) angiography and more refined imaging of the coronary anatomy have driven technical innovation in cardiac CT for the last 10 years, there is now an increasing focus on functional applications of cardiac CT, such as evaluation of the myocardial blood supply or assessment of dynamic myocardial perfusion. Novel techniques show promising results. This article focuses on state-of-the-art CT imaging techniques to visualize the coronary anatomy, describes aspects of radiation dose reduction, and briefly touches on recent approaches to obtain functional information from a CT scan of the heart, in particular dual-energy CT.

> In patients with stable chest pain, coronary CT angiography (CCTA) has demonstrated high accuracy in excluding coronary artery disease and CCTA findings carry prognostic significance for the occurrence of future cardiovascular events. Increasingly, CCTA has been adopted as a triage tool in patients with acute chest pain. In specific clinical scenarios, CCTA further represents a useful tool to exclude an ischemic etiology in patients with cardiac arrhythmias or newly diagnosed heart failure. Several novel techniques are currently being investigated which may extend the ability of CCTA to characterize and quantify coronary artery plaque and assess the hemodynamic significance of stenosis.

Coronary computed tomography angiography (CCTA) is recommended for the triage of acute chest pain in patients with a low-to-intermediate likelihood for acute coronary syndrome. Absence of coronary artery disease (CAD) confirmed by CCTA allows rapid emergency department discharge. This article shows that CCTA-based triage is as safe as traditional triage, reduces the hospital length of stay, and may provide cost-effective or even cost-saving care.

The exact definition and prognostication of vulnerable plaque remain elusive, and multiple imaging modalities aim to identify these plaques. As a noninvasive technique for the diagnosis of coronary artery disease, coronary computed tomography angiography has become increasingly utilized, primarily in patients with an elevated cardiovascular risk profile. Recent advances in technical methods have allowed for improved visualization of the vessel wall and surrounding tissue, allowing for improved characterization of vulnerable plaques by identifying features such as low-density plaques, positive remodeling, and spotty calcification. Quantification and qualification of these plaques may enhance the ability to predict future cardiovascular events.

Coronary computed tomography angiography (CCTA) is an established imaging technique for the noninvasive assessment of coronary arteries. However, CCTA remains a morphologic technique with the same limitations as invasive coronary angiography in evaluating the hemodynamic significance of coronary stenosis. Different computed tomography (CT) techniques for the functional analysis of coronary lesions have recently emerged, including static and dynamic CT myocardial perfusion imaging and CT-based fractional flow reserve and transluminal attenuation gradient methods. These techniques hold promise for achieving a comprehensive appraisal of anatomic and functional aspects of coronary heart disease with a single modality.

Cardiac magnetic resonance (CMR) imaging is increasingly being used to evaluate patients with known or suspected ischemic heart disease, because of its ability to acquire images in any orientation and the wide variety of sequences available to characterize normal and abnormal structure and function. Substantial improvements have been made in the hardware and software used to perform CMR, resulting in better and more consistent image quality. There has been a greater emphasis recently in developing and validating quantitative CMR techniques. This article reviews advances in CMR techniques for assessing cardiac function, myocardial perfusion, late gadolinium enhancement, and tissue characterization with T1 and T2 mapping sequences.

The characteristics of coronary artery disease are gradual thickening of the coronary walls and narrowing of the vascular lumen by the buildup of atherosclerosis plaques. These morphologic changes can be noninvasively detected by coronary magnetic resonance (MR) imaging/MR angiography (MRA). In addition, functional changes, such as coronary wall distensibility and flow changes, may also be evaluated with MR imaging. However, the application of current MR imaging/MRA techniques is limited in clinical practice because of several adverse technical and physiologic factors, such as cardiac and respiratory motion. Many technical innovations have been adopted to address these problems from multiple aspects.

Stress cardiac magnetic resonance imaging can provide valuable information for the diagnosis and management of ischemic heart disease (IHD). It plays an important role in the initial diagnosis in patients with acute chest pain, in the diagnosis of complications post myocardial infarction (MI), in the assessment of the right ventricle after an acute MI, to detect complications due to or after interventions, in prediction of myocardial recovery, to detect inducible ischemia in patients with known IHD, in differentiating ischemic from non-ischemic dilated cardiomyopathy, and in risk stratification.

Cardiac MR imaging (CMR) combines assessment of myocardial function and tissue characterization, and is therefore ideally suited to evaluating patients with ischemic heart disease (IHD). This article discusses evaluation of left ventricular global function at CMR, reviewing the literature supporting global parameters in risk stratification and assessment of treatment response in IHD. Techniques for assessment of regional myocardial function are reviewed, and normal myocardial motion and fiber arrangement discussed. Despite barriers to clinical adoption, integration of this assessment into clinical routine should improve the ability to detect functional consequences of early myocardial structural alterations in patients with IHD.

Assessment of myocardial viability is of ever-evolving interest in cardiovascular imaging, with major societies having incorporated viability imaging as class I or class IIa indications in their guidelines to better guide patient management. As with late gadolinium enhancement cardiac magnetic resonance (MR), assessment of residual myocardial viability or the extent of myocardial infarction is straightforward and this technique may easily be combined with other cardiac MR modules. In clinical routine functional assessment and myocardial perfusion imaging if often used in conjunction allow for a comprehensive assessment of ischemic heart disease.

Puskar Pattanayak and David A. Bleumke

Late gadolinium enhancement (LGE) is a simple, robust, well-validated method for assessing scar in acute and chronic myocardial infarction. LGE is useful for distinguishing between ischemic and nonischemic cardiomyopathy. Specific LGE patterns are seen in nonischemic cardiomyopathy. Patient studies using T1 mapping have varied in study, design, and acquisition sequences. Despite the differences in technique, a clear pattern that has been seen is that in cardiac disease postcontrast T1 times are shorter. Extracellular volume fraction measured with cardiac computed tomography represents a new approach to the clinical assessment of diffuse myocardial fibrosis by evaluating the distribution of iodinated contrast.

PROGRAM OBJECTIVE
The objective of the *Radiologic Clinics of North America* is to keep practicing radiologists and radiology residents up to date with current clinical practice in radiology by providing timely articles reviewing the state of the art in patient care.

TARGET AUDIENCE
Practicing radiologists, radiology residents, and other health care professionals who provide patient care utilizing radiologic findings.

LEARNING OBJECTIVES
Upon completion of this activity, participants will be able to:
1. Review the role of imaging in evaluating and characterizing tissue of the myocardium.
2. Discuss current clinical principles in CT and MRI imaging of Coronary Artery Disease.
3. Review state-of-the-art techniques for assessment of Ischemic Heart Disease.

ACCREDITATION
The Elsevier Office of Continuing Medical Education (EOCME) is accredited by the Accreditation Council for Continuing Medical Education (ACCME) to provide continuing medical education for physicians.

The EOCME designates this enduring material for a maximum of 15 *AMA PRA Category 1 Credit*(s)™. Physicians should claim only the credit commensurate with the extent of their participation in the activity.

All other health care professionals requesting continuing education credit for this enduring material will be issued a certificate of participation.

DISCLOSURE OF CONFLICTS OF INTEREST
The EOCME assesses conflict of interest with its instructors, faculty, planners, and other individuals who are in a position to control the content of CME activities. All relevant conflicts of interest that are identified are thoroughly vetted by EOCME for fair balance, scientific objectivity, and patient care recommendations. EOCME is committed to providing its learners with CME activities that promote improvements or quality in healthcare and not a specific proprietary business or a commercial interest.

The planning committee, staff, authors and editors listed below have identified no financial relationships or relationships to products or devices they or their spouse/life partner have with commercial interest related to the content of this CME activity:
Saeed Al Sayari, MBBS; Nicholas I. Batalis, MD; Stefan Baumann, MD; Richard R. Bayer II, MD; David A. Bluemke, MD, PhD; Jens Bremerich, MD, EBCR; James C. Carr, MD; Salvatore A. Chiaramida, MD; Jeremy D. Collins, MD; Andrew M. Crean, MD; Carlo Nicola De Cecco, MD, PhD; Ullrich Ebersberger, MD; Anjali Fortna; Christopher J. François, MD; Stephen R. Fuller, BSc; Tobias Geisler, MD; Kristen Helm; Udo Hoffmann, MD, MPH; Brynne Hunter; Laura Jimenez Juan, MD; Sebastien Kopp, MD; Sandy Lavery; Kai Lin, MD; Felix G. Meinel, MD; Frank H. Miller, MD; Konstantin Nikolaou, MD; Puskar Pattanayak, MD; Matthias Renker, MD; Jeremy Rier, DO; Christopher L. Schlett, MD, MPH; Karthikeyan Subramaniam; Akos Varga-Szemes, MD, PhD; John Vassallo; Rui Wang, MD; Julian L. Wichmann, MD; Peter L. Zwerner, MD.

The planning committee, staff, authors and editors listed below have identified financial relationships or relationships to products or devices they or their spouse/life partner have with commercial interest related to the content of this CME activity:
Fabian Bamberg, MD, MPH is on the speakers bureau for Bayer HealthCare AG and Siemens AG.
Thomas G. Flohr, PhD has an employment affiliation with Siemens AG.
Bernhard Schmidt, PhD has an employment affiliation with Siemens AG.
U. Joseph Schoepf, MD has research grants from Bayer AG, Bracco, General Electric Company doing business as GE Healthcare, Medrad, Inc. a trademark of the Bayer group of companies, and Siemens AG; has royalties/patents with Meetings By Mail copyright Savarese Associates Ltd., and Springer Science+Business Media.
Daniel H. Steinberg, MD is a consultant/advisor for Boston Scientific Corporation, St. Jude Medical, Inc., and Terumo Medical Corporation; and has a research grant from Edwards Lifesciences Corporation.
Bernd J. Wintersperger, MD, EBCR, FAHA is on speakers bureau and has research grant from Siemens AG, and has stock ownership with Allscripts.

UNAPPROVED/OFF-LABEL USE DISCLOSURE
The EOCME requires CME faculty to disclose to the participants:
1. When products or procedures being discussed are off-label, unlabelled, experimental, and/or investigational (not US Food and Drug Administration [FDA] approved); and
2. Any limitations on the information presented, such as data that are preliminary or that represent ongoing research, interim analyses, and/or unsupported opinions. Faculty may discuss information about pharmaceutical agents that is outside of FDA-approved labelling. This information is intended solely for CME and is not intended to promote off-label use of these medications. If you have any questions, contact the medical affairs department of the manufacturer for the most recent prescribing information.

TO ENROLL

To enroll in the *Radiologic Clinics of North America* Continuing Medical Education program, call customer service at 1-800-654-2452 or sign up online at http://www.theclinics.com/home/cme. The CME program is available to subscribers for an additional annual fee of USD 315.

METHOD OF PARTICIPATION

In order to claim credit, participants must complete the following:

1. Complete enrolment as indicated above.
2. Read the activity.
3. Complete the CME Test and Evaluation. Participants must achieve a score of 70% on the test. All CME Tests and Evaluations must be completed online.

CME INQUIRIES/SPECIAL NEEDS

For all CME inquiries or special needs, please contact elsevierCME@elsevier.com.

RADIOLOGIC CLINICS OF NORTH AMERICA

NOW AVAILABLE FOR YOUR iPhone and iPad

Preface

Coronary Artery Disease and the Myocardial Ischemic Cascade: State-of-the-Art Computed Tomography and MR Imaging

U. Joseph Schoepf, MD   James C. Carr, MD

Editors

The field of cardiovascular medicine continues to see tectonic shifts in its makeup. Paradigms that have governed patient care and management for decades are going overboard in droves. Coronary catheterization and percutaneous intervention, which once formed the centerpiece of cardiac care, are increasingly relegated to niche indications in acute myocardial injury. Optimal medical therapy is taking center stage. Drastic cuts in reimbursement are rendering nuclear myocardial perfusion imaging increasingly uninteresting to many of the private practice providers who once so liberally prescribed and performed these tests. Of the traditional cardiac imaging modalities, evidently only echocardiography has emerged relatively unscathed from recent turmoil.

Thus, the combination of changing medical practice patterns and economic realities has created a perfect storm for reshaping the field of cardiovascular medicine in general and cardiovascular imaging in particular. There is fertile ground for newer modalities to fill the void left by older tests that are falling out of favor. Both cardiovascular CT and MR imaging have seen definitive quantum leaps in their ongoing technical evolution in recent years. Improved speed of acquisition continues to drive the field forward, but in addition, the increasing utilization of quantitative imaging biomarkers will allow more precise characterization of disease for diagnosis and follow-up. Importantly, scores of newer generation clinicians and researchers have been working diligently on creating evidence for the appropriate, beneficial, and cost-effective use of these advanced, modern-era noninvasive tests. Accordingly, cardiac CT and MR imaging stand ready to assume their rightful central role in the management of coronary artery disease. However, it is safe to predict that both cardiac CT and MR imaging will never see the same degree of utilization as their predecessors in the structural and functional evaluation of ischemic heart disease; restricted resources will require much more stringent and judicial use of these modalities in our time. The

Radiol Clin N Am 53 (2015) xv–xvi
http://dx.doi.org/10.1016/j.rcl.2015.01.001
0033-8389/15/$ – see front matter © 2015 Published by Elsevier Inc.

improvements in performance and safety along with more rigorous vetting of their effectiveness for various indications that cardiac CT and MR imaging have undergone will, however, most certainly enhance patient outcomes if they are used more systematically in future.

This issue of the *Radiologic Clinics of North America* is beautiful testimony to the ingenuity that has been driving the implementation of cutting-edge CT and MR imaging techniques in the noninvasive structural and functional assessment of coronary heart disease. Our gratitude goes out to all our expert contributors who took the time from their busy schedules to share their knowledge, experience, and insights with our audience. We are also exceedingly grateful to the team at Elsevier, who again so expertly steered the production of this issue, which we proudly present to our readers.

U. Joseph Schoepf, MD
Department of Radiology and Radiological Science
Heart & Vascular Center
Medical University of South Carolina
Ashley River Tower, MSC 226
25 Courtenay Drive
Charleston, SC 29425, USA

James C. Carr, MD
Department of Radiology
Northwestern University Feinberg School of Medicine
NMH/Arkes Family Pavilion Suite 800
676 North Saint Clair
Chicago, IL 60611, USA

E-mail addresses:
schoepf@musc.edu (U.J. Schoepf)
jcarr@northwestern.edu (J.C. Carr)

Imaging Coronary Artery Disease and the Myocardial Ischemic Cascade
Clinical Principles and Scope

Matthias Renker, MD[a,b], Stefan Baumann, MD[a,c],
Jeremy Rier, DO[a], Ullrich Ebersberger, MD[a,d],
Stephen R. Fuller, BSc[a], Nicholas I. Batalis, MD[e],
U. Joseph Schoepf, MD[a,*], Salvatore A. Chiaramida, MD[f]

KEYWORDS

- Atherosclerosis • Coronary artery disease • Vascular remodeling • Plaque vulnerability
- Myocardial ischemia • Ischemic cascade

KEY POINTS

- Coronary atherosclerosis is a multistage process of chronic inflammation that involves endothelial dysfunction and preferentially develops at areas of low shear stress.
- Positive remodeling indicates an outward expansion of coronary artery plaques that may preserve luminal dimensions and frequently does not present on coronary catheter angiography.
- Significant coronary stenosis may result in an ischemic cascade from subclinical to clinical manifestations comprising hypoperfusion, metabolic alteration, ventricular dysfunction, electrocardiogram abnormalities, and clinical symptoms.
- Plaque vulnerability defines coronary artery lesions susceptible to complications that clinically present as adverse events, typically caused by plaque rupture with subsequent coronary thrombosis.
- Knowledge of patient factors and clinical presentation may help in selecting the appropriate test to produce the correct diagnosis and assess future prognosis.

INTRODUCTION

The spectrum of cardiovascular diseases ranges from congenital over inflammatory, rheumatic, hypertensive, and dysrhythmic to valvular varieties, but most frequently atherosclerosis of the coronary arteries, which is also referred to as coronary artery disease (CAD), represents the underlying pathologic alteration. Characterized by the formation of plaques within the luminal wall layers of the coronary arteries, CAD remains a prevalent disease of high socioeconomic relevance despite

Disclosures: U.J. Schoepf is a consultant for and/or receives research support from Bayer, Bracco, GE Healthcare, Medrad, and Siemens Healthcare. All other authors declare that they have no financial disclosures.
[a] Heart and Vascular Center, Medical University of South Carolina, Ashley River Tower, 25 Courtenay Drive, Charleston, SC 29425-2260, USA; [b] Department of Medicine I, Cardiology and Angiology, Giessen University Hospital, Klinistrasse 33, Giessen 35392, Germany; [c] 1st Department of Medicine University Medical Centre Mannheim (UMM), Theodor-Kutzer-Ufer 1-3, Mannheim 68167, Germany; [d] Department of Cardiology, Heart Centre Munich-Bogenhausen, Munich Municipal Hospital Group, Englschalkinger Strasse 77, Munich 81925, Germany; [e] Department of Pathology and Laboratory Medicine, Medical University of South Carolina, HD281, 165 Ashley Avenue, Charleston, SC 29425, USA; [f] Heart and Vascular Center, Medical University of South Carolina, Ashley River Tower, 25 Courtenay Drive, Charleston, SC 29425, USA
* Corresponding author.
E-mail address: schoepf@musc.edu

Radiol Clin N Am 53 (2015) 261–269
http://dx.doi.org/10.1016/j.rcl.2014.11.010
0033-8389/15/$ – see front matter © 2015 Elsevier Inc. All rights reserved.

the associated mortality having declined substantially in many affluent countries over the past decades.[1] Given the improved prognosis of acute coronary syndromes (ACSs), the prevalence of CAD has increased along with the burden of associated morbidity and consequential costs.[1–3]

Continued technological advances in noninvasive CAD imaging have led to a growing armamentarium of modalities with high diagnostic accuracy for diagnosing and assessing the significance of CAD.[4–6] A comprehensive understanding of the pathophysiology of atherosclerosis of the coronary arteries and myocardial ischemia is required to obtain an accurate diagnosis and direct clinical decision making. As such, this article outlines the clinical principles of CAD and its underlying sequence of events from the initiation of atherosclerosis to development of myocardial infarction.

ATHEROGENESIS
Traditional and Nontraditional Risk Factors

Although the predictive value for CAD risk factors is greater in the overall population, the consideration of risk factors in individuals may still be useful. Important risk factors for CAD are diabetes mellitus, dyslipidemia, hypertension, tobacco smoke inhalation, age, and a familial history of premature CAD or cardiovascular death. Wilkins and colleagues[7] showed that life expectancy free of CAD is substantially longer for subjects with an optimal risk profile than for those with more than 1 cardiovascular risk factor.

Despite the predictive ability of classic risk factors, their absence does not rule out future cardiovascular events. Retrospective analysis of 120,000 patients with CAD revealed that 15.4% of women and 19.4% of men did not have any classic risk factors. This finding emphasizes the importance of defining nontraditional risk factors that further characterize risk and influence decisions regarding preventative treatment.[8] Extensive research is being conducted on inflammatory and lipid-related markers that potentially predict the development of CAD. For example, increased high-sensitive C-reactive protein level has been shown to be associated with increased cardiovascular risk even in the absence of hyperlipidemia.[9] Management of dyslipidemia has emerged as the key therapeutic strategy to reduce both primary and secondary cardiovascular events.[10] Recent study results by Tonelli and colleagues[11] further suggest that the combination of chronic kidney disease and proteinuria represents a nontraditional CAD risk factor conferring risk equivalent to that of diabetes mellitus, an established CAD risk factor.

Mechanisms of Disease

Atherosclerosis represents a systemic, inflammatory process involving medium to larger sized arteries (Fig. 1).[12,13] It is known that chronic endothelial injury is likely to occur at vascular sites characterized by low shear stress (eg, bifurcations).[14,15] In addition, sites that are exposed to turbulent flow possess decreased atheroprotective function and thus are more prone to oxidative stress, endothelial dysfunction, and an exorbitant immunoinflammatory response.[16]

Atherogenesis occurs in both inner layers of the arterial wall: the tunica intima and media. Current thought regarding the genesis of atherosclerosis places increased emphasis on the presence of the following mechanisms:

- Translocation and accumulation of lipoproteins within the intima
- Oxidative modification of lipoproteins
- Foam cell formation via smooth muscle cells (SMCs) or macrophages (fatty streak formation)[9]

It has been shown that the translocation of lipoproteins and lipids into the artery wall represents movement along a concentration gradient rather than an active, receptor-mediated endocytosis.[17] Low-density lipoproteins, very-low-density lipoproteins, lipoprotein (a), apo (B 100), and lipoprotein remnants are considered promoters of atherosclerosis.[18] After lipoproteins bind to the endothelium and are modified, they then migrate to the intimal layer of the arterial wall. The presence of a proatherogenic substrate results in the recruitment of leukocytes (monocytes and T cells) under the direction of chemokines produced by

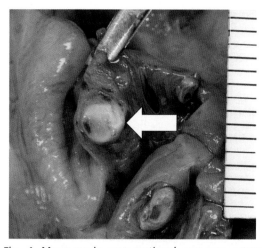

Fig. 1. Macroscopic cross-sectional coronary artery view showing severe lipid-rich atherosclerotic plaque (*arrow*) leading to critical stenosis.

endothelial cells and SMCs. This substrate eventually becomes engulfed by macrophages and/or SMCs to form foam cells. The nascent atheroma or fatty streak is primarily composed of foam cells and is thought to be a partially reversible stage of atherogenesis.[9]

Molecular repair mechanisms intended to restore vascular homeostasis are then activated and induce an inflammatory response, including monocyte adhesion and macrophage phagocytosis of oxidized lipoproteins. However, Allahverdian and colleagues[19] recently challenged the idea that the intimal foam cell population in human coronary atherosclerosis comes from a predominantly myeloid lineage. Their results indicate that SMCs contain a larger burden of excess lipid compounds than was previously known and that many foam cells previously identified as monocyte-derived macrophages in fact descend from SMCs.[19]

Technological advances in imaging techniques represent an exciting area of ongoing research in atherosclerosis and allow the resolution of gross plaque features but also the in vivo characterization of atherosclerotic lesions at the molecular level.[20] In molecular imaging, fluorescence and hybrid techniques such as fluorescence molecular tomography/computed tomography (CT) and PET/magnetic resonance (MR) imaging have the potential to solve specific challenges associated with coronary plaque imaging and facilitate patient care.

ATHEROSCLEROTIC PLAQUE DEVELOPMENT
Morphologic Plaque Features

Further atherosclerotic plaque development occurs with plaque remodeling, destabilization, and increased thrombogenicity, which depend on the balance of antiinflammatory and proinflammatory mechanisms of the adaptive and innate immune systems. The extracellular matrix (ECM) produced by SMCs comprises a significant amount of the atherosclerotic plaque volume.[9] Because the ECM plays a key role in cell migration, proliferation, and plaque modification, either decreased production or increased breakdown of ECM may result in increased vulnerability. Calcification is another feature of advanced atherosclerotic plaques; increasing calcification is generally thought to confer more plaque stability.[8] **Fig. 2** provides a histopathologic example of different morphologic plaque features.

Many of these morphologic features have been described by modern imaging modalities, such as coronary CT angiography, MR imaging, spectroscopy, intravascular ultrasonography (IVUS)–virtual

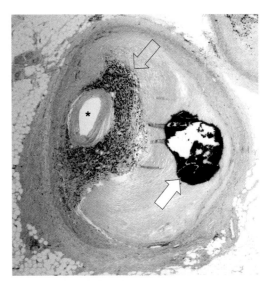

Fig. 2. Microscopic cross-sectional vessel display showing plaque calcification (*white arrow*) and areas of hemorrhage (*open arrow*) with numerous hemosiderin-laden cells around the lumen (*asterisk*).

histology, optical coherence tomography, and thermography. **Fig. 3** shows an example of plaque imaging by use of coronary CT angiography.

Vascular Remodeling

In postmortem studies of human coronary arteries, Glagov and colleagues[21] showed that most atheromatous plaques tend to expand toward the adventitia before concentrically infringing on the vessel lumen. Two distinct phenomena of vascular remodeling can be described through the assessment of the area occupied by the external elastic membrane (EEM), which separates the 2 inner layers of the vascular wall from the outer layer

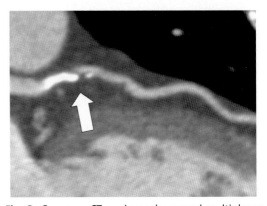

Fig. 3. Coronary CT angiography curved multiplanar reformation of the left coronary artery revealing calcified and noncalcified plaque composition in the midvessel (*arrow*).

(tunica adventitia). Positive remodeling results in expansion of the EEM area, whereas negative re-modeling (**Fig. 4**) results in shrinkage of the EEM area within the cross section of a lesion.

Although both types of vascular remodeling may be present in coronary occlusive stenosis, positive remodeling initially prevented narrowing of the vessel lumen, whereas negative remodeling accelerated this process. In experimental and human post–balloon angioplasty studies, negative re-modeling was the most important determinant of luminal restenosis. Furthermore, negative remod-eling is commonly found in atherosclerotic lesions of the peripheral arteries.[22]

IVUS provides excellent resolution to define the boundaries of tissue interfaces with an abrupt change in acoustic impedance. Thus, IVUS consti-tutes the primary clinical method to investigate the extent and direction of arterial remodeling in vivo. With IVUS, vascular remodeling can be deter-mined from measurements of the EEM area at the site of the lesion of interest and a reference site. MR imaging and CT allow for noninvasive three-dimensional differentiation of tissue struc-tures beyond the arterial lumen and therefore serve as alternative techniques for an accurate assessment of vascular remodeling.[23,24]

Plaque Vulnerability

Muller and colleagues[25] coined the term vulner-able plaque to define the pivotal plaque character-istics that trigger the onset of ACS, hypothesizing that coronary artery thrombosis is caused by an atherosclerotic plaque rupture resulting in obstruc-tion of the lumen. Autopsy studies have revealed that features common to plaques responsible for fatal myocardial infarctions include the presence

of a thin fibrous cap separating the lipid core from the lumen (50–65 μm thick), the presence of a large lipid core, an abundance of inflammatory cells, fewer smooth muscle cells, and spotty calci-fication.[26] Despite plaque rupture being respon-sible for most ACS events, the term vulnerable plaque has evolved to define all plaques suscepti-ble to complications.[27] The 2 major types of vulnerable plaques susceptible to complications are rupture-prone and erosion-prone plaques.[13] Rupture-prone plaques are mainly characterized by lipid-rich cores and thin fibrous caps, whereas erosion-prone plaques are principally character-ized by erosion of the endothelial surface.[13]

Despite significant efforts to definitively charac-terize vulnerable plaques, emerging data indicate that delineating the morphology, composition, and hemodynamic severity of coronary artery pla-ques causing ACS is more complex than was originally thought. Noninvasive and invasive ante-mortem imaging studies along with postmortem pathologic studies indicate the development of ACS to be multifactorial in nature.[26,28,29] It has been shown that rupture of a thin-cap fibroather-oma does not necessarily lead to ACS because asymptomatic plaque fissure is a frequent event leading to plaque progression.[30,31] Yonetsu and colleagues[32] corroborated these findings by showing that about 15% of patients with stable angina presented with plaque fissure. To date, it is largely unknown why plaque fissures lead to ACS in some, but not all, cases.

Although coronary catheter angiography is the reference standard for determining the degree of luminal stenosis, it is insensitive for defining vul-nerable plaques. Likewise, functional tests that depend on the ischemic cascade may be un-remarkable and therefore unable to identify high-risk lesions. Modalities that allow imaging of cross-sectional anatomy may be helpful in iden-tifying vulnerable plaques. Characterization of vul-nerable plaque is an area of rapid development and may occur either invasively (optical coherence tomography, IVUS, near-infrared spectroscopy with IVUS), or noninvasively (CT, MR imaging, PET). An example of near-infrared spectroscopy coregistered with the IVUS technique is provided in **Fig. 5**.

Lesion Severity

Although positive remodeling is capable of pro-ducing luminal stenosis, it may also generate extensive plaque development that does not result in stenosis.[9] Because these lesions do not result in visually obstructive stenosis, not only do pa-tients remain asymptomatic but coronary catheter

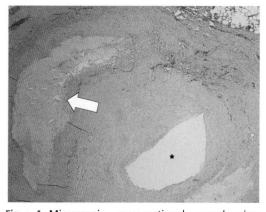

Fig. 4. Microscopic cross-sectional vessel view showing negative coronary artery remodeling, because the vessel lumen (*asterisk*) is compromised by atherosclerotic plaque (*arrow*).

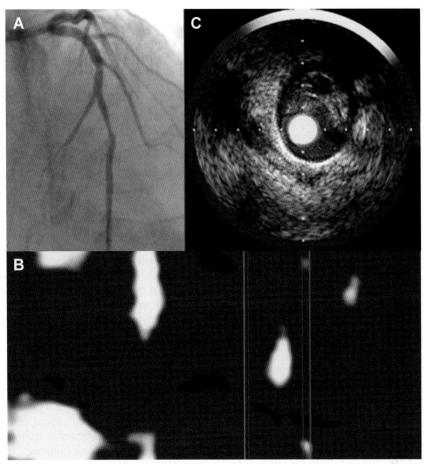

Fig. 5. Coronary catheter angiography reveals stenotic disease within the left anterior descending coronary artery (*A*). Intracoronary near-infrared spectroscopy chemogram shows the presence of lipid core plaque (*B, yellow*). Combining near-infrared spectroscopy and IVUS shows evidence of plaque with a large lipid core (*C*).

angiography may be unrevealing. However, even in the absence of severe luminal stenosis, plaques that undergo positive remodeling may still be responsible for triggering the ischemic cascade or developing ACS.[33] Compilation of serial angiographic studies revealed that only 15% of acute myocardial infarctions had evidence of stenosis greater than 60% on a prior angiogram.[9] This finding was also supported in studies on thrombolysis, because about half of patients undergoing thrombolytic treatment of a first myocardial infarction had less than 50% stenosis of the infarct-related artery once the acute thrombus was lysed.[26]

Through its modes of remodeling, atherosclerosis can cause 2 different manifestations of CAD, characterized either by rapid obstruction in acute coronary syndrome or gradual narrowing in chronic stable angina.[34] The factors that determine positive or negative vascular remodeling and its progression are poorly understood[35]; potential factors include differences in shear stress, endogenous substances that affect vasomotor tone, inflammation, endothelial activation, circumferential location of plaque development, and programmed arterial response.[36]

Assessment of functional lesion characteristics heralded a new era in the diagnosis of CAD. In addition to angiographic estimation of luminal diameter stenosis, catheter-based fractional flow reserve may be used to detect lesion-specific ischemia.[37] CT-based derivation of fractional flow reserve has recently been introduced to noninvasively detect lesion-specific ischemia with promising results.[38] Integrating functional lesion information may provide a more comprehensive approach to lesion severity than anatomic evaluation.

Spatial Plaque Distribution

Another important factor in coronary artery plaque vulnerability is spatial distribution. Clinical observations raised suspicion that most occlusive coronary artery thromboses leading to ACS are clustered in the proximal portions of the major epicardial vessels. Numerous studies have therefore attempted to map the coronary artery tree locations that possess the highest risk for future events. An exemplary study by Gotsman and colleagues[39] found that most coronary artery stenoses causing ST-elevation myocardial infarction are located proximally and at bifurcations. More recently, studies clarified the initial clinical hypothesis and more specifically localized higher-risk lesions to discrete coronary artery segments, mostly within the first 60 mm.[40,41]

Most of the studies characterizing spatial distribution of CAD are based on traditional coronary catheter angiography. Coronary CT angiography has recently been integrated into societal guidelines as an appropriate noninvasive modality for rapid evaluation of symptomatic patients with low to intermediate cardiovascular risk profiles.[42] Through CT, early detection of plaque composition may help to characterize and selectively prevent plaques from culminating in adverse clinical events.

The Ischemic Cascade

Myocardial ischemia is highly linked to atherosclerosis, only occurring otherwise in rare circumstances such as trauma, coronary arteritis, aortic or coronary dissection, thromboembolism, congenital anomalies, vasospasm, cocaine abuse, and iatrogenic causes (eg, as a complication of coronary angiography).[43] The reduction of coronary artery blood flow leads to myocardial hypoperfusion, resulting in an imbalance between myocardial oxygen supply and demand and potentially culminating in a myocardial infarction. The severity and duration of ischemia determine whether the damage is reversible or permanent with subsequent myocardial necrosis. The typical ischemic response induced by hemodynamically significant coronary stenotic lesions results in an ischemic cascade that proceeds from subclinical to clinical manifestations. The cascade is characterized by metabolic abnormalities, diastolic dysfunction, systolic dysfunction, electrocardiographic abnormalities (ST-segment depression), and eventually clinical symptoms (angina pectoris).[44] The chronology of events is typical, but cannot be generalized, because events do not necessarily occur consecutively and clinical findings may not present (eg, terminal ST deviation in non–ST-elevation myocardial infarction).

The underlying pathophysiologic principles and sequential processes of the myocardial ischemic response provide a rationale for choosing an appropriate diagnostic modality (**Fig. 6**). It seems that the earliest abnormality featured in the myocardial ischemic cascade is hypoperfusion, which is then followed by ventricular dysfunction. Thus, stress myocardial perfusion imaging tests (**Fig. 7**) possess favorable sensitivity for an early detection of myocardial ischemia, although wall-motion stress imaging studies show higher specificity.[45–47] As the myocardial ischemic cascade proceeds, electrocardiographic abnormalities may become detectable. However, the diagnostic accuracy of stress electrocardiographic testing is low because these abnormalities are potentially present at rest in the absence of disorder and may be influenced by pharmacotherapy.[48] Therefore, the addition of cardiac imaging improves diagnostic performance and moreover provides incremental prognostic information at the advanced stage of the ischemic process.[49]

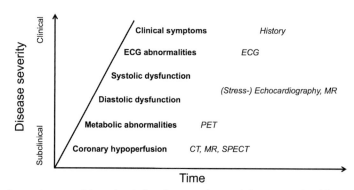

Fig. 6. Sequence of events comprising the ischemic cascade model, arranged with appropriate diagnostic measures. ECG, electrocardiogram; SPECT, single-photon emission computed tomography.

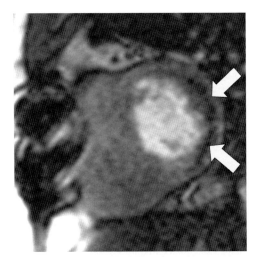

Fig. 7. Perfusion MR imaging during stress shows a myocardial blood pool defect in the left circumflex coronary artery territory (*arrows*).

SUMMARY

Major principles of atherogenesis, the advancement of coronary atherosclerotic lesions, and the subsequent events in the myocardial ischemic cascade are reviewed from a clinical perspective. The concept of plaques being susceptible to clinical complications is emphasized with a discussion of controversial aspects. Implications for choosing appropriate cardiovascular imaging techniques are discussed in the context of the ischemic cascade. Thus, this article provides a framework for improvements in the diagnostic management of patients with known or suspected CAD based on its pathophysiologic development.

REFERENCES

1. Nabel EG, Braunwald E. A tale of coronary artery disease and myocardial infarction. N Engl J Med 2012;366(1):54–63.
2. Fuster V, Mearns BM. The CVD paradox: mortality vs prevalence. Nat Rev Cardiol 2009;6(11):669.
3. Heidenreich PA, Trogdon JG, Khavjou OA, et al. Forecasting the future of cardiovascular disease in the United States: a policy statement from the American Heart Association. Circulation 2011;123(8): 933–44.
4. Shaw LJ, Hausleiter J, Achenbach S, et al. Coronary computed tomographic angiography as a gatekeeper to invasive diagnostic and surgical procedures: results from the multicenter CONFIRM (Coronary CT Angiography Evaluation for Clinical Outcomes: an International Multicenter) registry. J Am Coll Cardiol 2012;60(20):2103–14.
5. Moschetti K, Muzzarelli S, Pinget C, et al. Cost evaluation of cardiovascular magnetic resonance versus coronary angiography for the diagnostic work-up of coronary artery disease: application of the European Cardiovascular Magnetic Resonance registry data to the German, United Kingdom, Swiss, and United States health care systems. J Cardiovasc Magn Reson 2012;14:35.
6. Arnoldi E, Henzler T, Bastarrika G, et al. Evaluation of plaques and stenosis. Radiol Clin North Am 2010;48(4):729–44.
7. Wilkins JT, Ning H, Berry J, et al. Lifetime risk and years lived free of total cardiovascular disease. JAMA 2012;308(17):1795–801.
8. Khot UN, Khot MB, Bajzer CT, et al. Prevalence of conventional risk factors in patients with coronary heart disease. JAMA 2003;290(7):898–904.
9. Braunwald E, Bonow RO. Braunwald's heart disease: a textbook of cardiovascular medicine. 9th edition. Philadelphia: Saunders; 2012.
10. Stone NJ, Robinson J, Lichtenstein AH, et al. 2013 ACC/AHA guideline on the treatment of blood cholesterol to reduce atherosclerotic cardiovascular risk in adults: a report of the American College of Cardiology/American Heart Association Task Force on Practice Guidelines. J Am Coll Cardiol 2014;63: 2889–934.
11. Tonelli M, Muntner P, Lloyd A, et al. Risk of coronary events in people with chronic kidney disease compared with those with diabetes: a population-level cohort study. Lancet 2012;380(9844):807–14.
12. Libby P, Ridker PM, Hansson GK. Progress and challenges in translating the biology of atherosclerosis. Nature 2011;473(7347):317–25.
13. Falk E, Nakano M, Bentzon JF, et al. Update on acute coronary syndromes: the pathologists' view. Eur Heart J 2013;34(10):719–28.
14. Fuster V, Badimon JJ, Badimon L. Clinical-pathological correlations of coronary disease progression and regression. Circulation 1992;86(6 Suppl): III1–11.
15. Chatzizisis YS, Coskun AU, Jonas M, et al. Role of endothelial shear stress in the natural history of coronary atherosclerosis and vascular remodeling: molecular, cellular, and vascular behavior. J Am Coll Cardiol 2007;49(25):2379–93.
16. Berk BC. Atheroprotective signaling mechanisms activated by steady laminar flow in endothelial cells. Circulation 2008;117(8):1082–9.
17. Steinberg D, Parthasarathy S, Carew TE, et al. Beyond cholesterol. Modifications of low-density lipoprotein that increase its atherogenicity. N Engl J Med 1989;320(14):915–24.
18. Sniderman AD, Furberg CD, Keech A, et al. Apolipoproteins versus lipids as indices of coronary risk and as targets for statin treatment. Lancet 2003; 361(9359):777–80.

19. Allahverdian S, Chehroudi AC, McManus BM, et al. Contribution of intimal smooth muscle cells to cholesterol accumulation and macrophage-like cells in human atherosclerosis. Circulation 2014;129(15): 1551–9.

20. Fishbein MC. The vulnerable and unstable atherosclerotic plaque. Cardiovasc Pathol 2010; 19(1):6–11.

21. Glagov S, Weisenberg E, Zarins CK, et al. Compensatory enlargement of human atherosclerotic coronary arteries. N Engl J Med 1987;316(22):1371–5.

22. Pasterkamp G, Wensing PJ, Post MJ, et al. Paradoxical arterial wall shrinkage may contribute to luminal narrowing of human atherosclerotic femoral arteries. Circulation 1995;91(5):1444–9.

23. Gauss S, Achenbach S, Pflederer T, et al. Assessment of coronary artery remodelling by dual-source CT: a head-to-head comparison with intravascular ultrasound. Heart 2011;97(12):991–7.

24. Gharib AM, Zahiri H, Matta J, et al. Feasibility of coronary artery wall thickening assessment in asymptomatic coronary artery disease using phase-sensitive dual-inversion recovery MRI at 3T. Magn Reson Imaging 2013;31(7):1051–8.

25. Muller JE, Tofler GH, Stone PH. Circadian variation and triggers of onset of acute cardiovascular disease. Circulation 1989;79(4):733–43.

26. Libby P. Mechanisms of acute coronary syndromes. N Engl J Med 2013;369(9):883–4.

27. Naghavi M, Libby P, Falk E, et al. From vulnerable plaque to vulnerable patient: a call for new definitions and risk assessment strategies: part I. Circulation 2003;108(14):1664–72.

28. Crea F, Liuzzo G. Pathogenesis of acute coronary syndromes. J Am Coll Cardiol 2013;61(1):1–11.

29. Niccoli G, Liuzzo G, Montone RA, et al. Advances in mechanisms, imaging and management of the unstable plaque. Atherosclerosis 2014;233(2):467–77.

30. Burke AP, Kolodgie FD, Farb A, et al. Healed plaque ruptures and sudden coronary death: evidence that subclinical rupture has a role in plaque progression. Circulation 2001;103(7):934–40.

31. Di Vito L, Prati F, Arbustini E, et al. A "stable" coronary plaque rupture documented by repeated OCT studies. JACC Cardiovasc Imaging 2013; 6(7):835–6.

32. Yonetsu T, Kakuta T, Lee T, et al. In vivo critical fibrous cap thickness for rupture-prone coronary plaques assessed by optical coherence tomography. Eur Heart J 2011;32(10):1251–9.

33. Bech GJ, De Bruyne B, Pijls NH, et al. Fractional flow reserve to determine the appropriateness of angioplasty in moderate coronary stenosis: a randomized trial. Circulation 2001;103(24):2928–34.

34. Libby P. Mechanisms of acute coronary syndromes and their implications for therapy. N Engl J Med 2013;368(21):2004–13.

35. Kaski JC. Atheromatous plaque location and arterial remodelling. Eur Heart J 2003;24(4):291–3.

36. Samady H, Eshtehardi P, McDaniel MC, et al. Coronary artery wall shear stress is associated with progression and transformation of atherosclerotic plaque and arterial remodeling in patients with coronary artery disease. Circulation 2011;124(7): 779–88.

37. Sels JW, Tonino PA, Siebert U, et al. Fractional flow reserve in unstable angina and non-ST-segment elevation myocardial infarction experience from the FAME (Fractional flow reserve versus Angiography for Multivessel Evaluation) study. JACC Cardiovasc Interv 2011;4(11):1183–9.

38. Renker M, Schoepf UJ, Wang R, et al. Comparison of diagnostic value of a novel non-invasive coronary computed tomography angiography method versus standard coronary angiography for assessing fractional flow reserve. Am J Cardiol 2014; 114:1303–8.

39. Gotsman M, Rosenheck S, Nassar H, et al. Angiographic findings in the coronary arteries after thrombolysis in acute myocardial infarction. Am J Cardiol 1992;70(7):715–23.

40. Gibson CM, Kirtane AJ, Murphy SA, et al. Distance from the coronary ostium to the culprit lesion in acute ST-elevation myocardial infarction and its implications regarding the potential prevention of proximal plaque rupture. J Thromb Thrombolysis 2003; 15(3):189–96.

41. Wang JC, Normand SL, Mauri L, et al. Coronary artery spatial distribution of acute myocardial infarction occlusions. Circulation 2004;110(3):278–84.

42. Abbara S, Arbab-Zadeh A, Callister TQ, et al. SCCT guidelines for performance of coronary computed tomographic angiography: a report of the Society of Cardiovascular Computed Tomography Guidelines Committee. J Cardiovasc Comput Tomogr 2009;3(3):190–204.

43. Hamm CW, Bassand JP, Agewall S, et al. ESC guidelines for the management of acute coronary syndromes in patients presenting without persistent ST-segment elevation: the task force for the management of acute coronary syndromes (ACS) in patients presenting without persistent ST-segment elevation of the European Society of Cardiology (ESC). Eur Heart J 2011;32(23):2999–3054.

44. Detry JM. The pathophysiology of myocardial ischaemia. Eur Heart J 1996;17(Suppl G):48–52.

45. Schinkel AF, Bax JJ, Geleijnse ML, et al. Noninvasive evaluation of ischaemic heart disease: myocardial perfusion imaging or stress echocardiography? Eur Heart J 2003;24(9):789–800.

46. Fleischmann KE, Hunink MG, Kuntz KM, et al. Exercise echocardiography or exercise SPECT imaging? A meta-analysis of diagnostic test performance. JAMA 1998;280(10):913–20.

47. Pellikka PA, Nagueh SF, Elhendy AA, et al. American Society of Echocardiography recommendations for performance, interpretation, and application of stress echocardiography. J Am Soc Echocardiogr 2007; 20(9):1021–41.

48. Kligfield P, Lauer MS. Exercise electrocardiogram testing: beyond the ST segment. Circulation 2006; 114(19):2070–82.

49. Berman DS, Hachamovitch R, Shaw LJ, et al. Roles of nuclear cardiology, cardiac computed tomography, and cardiac magnetic resonance: noninvasive risk stratification and a conceptual framework for the selection of noninvasive imaging tests in patients with known or suspected coronary artery disease. J Nucl Med 2006;47(7): 1107–18.

Computed Tomographic Assessment of Coronary Artery Disease
State-of-the-Art Imaging Techniques

Thomas G. Flohr, PhD[a,b,*], Carlo Nicola De Cecco, MD[c,d], Bernhard Schmidt, PhD[a], Rui Wang, MD[d], U. Joseph Schoepf, MD[d], Felix G. Meinel, MD[d,e]

KEYWORDS

- Coronary CT angiography • Cardiac computed tomography • ECG-gated scanning
- ECG-triggered scanning • Iterative reconstruction • First-pass enhancement scanning
- Dual-energy computed tomography • Cardiac perfusion computed tomography

KEY POINTS

- Excellent temporal resolution and spatial resolution are key to clinically robust computed tomography (CT) coronary angiography.
- Electrocardiography-triggered sequential scanning is radiation dose efficient and should be the method of choice for most cardiac CT examinations. Depending on the patient's size and shape, scanning at low x-ray tube voltage (70 - 100 kV) may significantly reduce the radiation dose.
- Coverage of the heart in one heartbeat is possible with large-area detectors or high-pitch spiral scanning.
- Assessment of both coronary artery morphology and the status of myocardial perfusion with CT is a coveted goal. New techniques such as dual-energy cardiac CT or dynamic myocardial perfusion CT show promising results.

INTRODUCTION

Imaging of the heart with computed tomography (CT) is technically demanding. On the one hand, high temporal resolution is required: the shorter the acquisition time of a CT image, the better will the moving anatomy of the heart and the coronary arteries be visualized. On the other hand, spatial resolution has to be excellent, because the coronary arteries have diameters of only a few millimeters, and not only their lumen but also plaque and stenosis need to be evaluated. To image the heart in a phase-consistent way, for example, in the diastolic rest phase, data acquisition has to be synchronized with the patient's electrocardiogram (ECG). Finally, the radiation exposure to the patient should be as low as reasonably achievable.

Multidetector-row CT (MDCT) has been used for cardiac imaging since the advent of 4-slice CT scanners in 1999.[1–6] Available since 2004, 64-slice CT systems are currently considered prerequisite for

Disclosure: T. Flohr and B. Schmidt are employees of Siemens Healthcare, Germany.
[a] Siemens Healthcare, Computed Tomography, Siemensstr. 1, Forchheim, Germany; [b] Institute of Diagnostic Radiology, Eberhard-Karls-University, Tübingen, Germany; [c] Department of Radiological Sciences, Oncology and Pathology, University of Rome "Sapienza", Latina, Italy; [d] Department of Radiology and Radiological Science, Medical University of South Carolina, Charleston, SC 29425, USA; [e] Institute for Clinical Radiology, Ludwig-Maximilians-University Hospital, Munich, Germany
* Corresponding author. Siemens Healthcare, Computed Tomography, Siemensstr. 1, Forchheim 91301, Germany.
E-mail address: thomas.flohr@siemens.com

Radiol Clin N Am 53 (2015) 271–285
http://dx.doi.org/10.1016/j.rcl.2014.11.011
0033-8389/15/$ – see front matter © 2015 Elsevier Inc. All rights reserved.

cardiac imaging in routine clinical scenarios.[7–10] While coronary CT angiography (CTA) and more refined imaging of the coronary anatomy have driven technical innovation in cardiac CT for the last 10 years, there is now an increasing focus on functional applications of cardiac CT, such as evaluation of the myocardial blood supply with first-pass enhancement studies, augmented by the use of dual-energy data acquisition, or dynamic myocardial perfusion assessment. These techniques may have the potential to enhance the application spectrum of cardiac CT, for example by providing means to determine the hemodynamic relevance of coronary artery stenosis. Furthermore, cardiovascular CT plays an increasing role in the support of interventions such as the planning of transcatheter aortic valve replacement procedures.

This article focuses on state-of-the-art CT imaging techniques to visualize the coronary anatomy, describes aspects of radiation dose reduction, and briefly touches on recent approaches to obtain functional information from a CT scan of the heart, in particular dual-energy CT.

CURRENT STATUS OF DATA ACQUISITION TECHNIQUES FOR CORONARY COMPUTED TOMOGRAPHIC ANGIOGRAPHY
Spatial Resolution

State-of-the-art ECG-controlled scanning of the heart with 64 or more slices with 0.5 mm, 0.6 mm, or 0.625 mm collimated slice width provides isotropic submillimeter resolution to visualize the coronary arteries. Despite the significant progress in comparison with older 4-slice or 16-slice technology, spatial resolution is still not fully sufficient for coronary CTA in patients with severe coronary calcifications. Calcium blooming may prevent reliable assessment of the coronary lumen and lead to overestimation of coronary artery stenosis. In a recent multicenter trial,[11] the presence of coronary calcifications with an Agatston score greater than 1000 was the most relevant independent predictor of uninterpretable coronary segments in a coronary CTA. Assessment of stent patency and in-stent restenosis is yet another challenge. Previous studies have shown that image quality is strongly dependent on the material and architecture of the stents, and on the technical properties of the CT system. Using 64-slice CT and first-generation dual-source CT (DSCT), Maintz and colleagues[12,13] found an average lumen visibility of 50% to 59% for most of the commonly used 2.5- to 4-mm coronary stents in a phantom setup, with extreme values of 3.3% for a tantalum stent and 90% for a magnesium stent. Ongoing technical progress may overcome some of the challenges posed by limited spatial resolution. Use of dedicated high-definition scan modes for the evaluation of 25 coronary stents resulted in significantly lower in-stent luminal attenuation and significantly larger mean measured in-stent luminal diameter.[14] Improved in-stent lumen assessment was demonstrated to be possible with third-generation DSCT.[15] Two previously evaluated stents[12,13] presented an in-stent lumen visibility of up to 76% and 83%, respectively, when scanned with a third-generation DSCT system, compared with respective visible diameters of 52% and 56.7% reported previously (**Fig. 1**).

Temporal Resolution

In CT, a partial scan data segment is the minimum amount of scan data needed for image reconstruction in the entire scan field of view (SFOV). A partial scan data segment comprises half a rotation of scan data plus the total detector fan angle. In the isocenter of the CT scanner, where the heart is usually positioned, half a rotation of scan data is sufficient. The data acquisition time per image, referred to as temporal resolution, is therefore half the gantry rotation time. Gantry rotation times down to 0.27 seconds with modern CT scanners result in a temporal resolution down to 135 milliseconds. This time is adequate for a clinically robust visualization of the coronary arteries at moderate heart rates, but may be challenging in patients with high and irregular heart rates. To improve temporal resolution, several approaches have been introduced. From the very beginning of cardiac CT multisegment reconstruction, the combination of smaller scan data segments from multiple consecutive heartbeats, has been

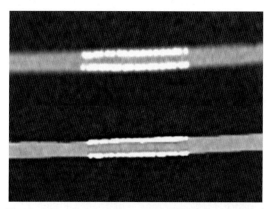

Fig. 1. A 3-mm stent in a contrast-filled tube, scanned on a 64-slice CT system (*top*) and on a third-generation dual-source CT (DSCT) system (*bottom*), applying the highest available spatial resolution. (*Courtesy of* T. Gassenmaier, MD, University of Würzburg, Würzburg, Germany.)

proposed. Multisegment reconstruction may improve image quality at higher heart rates, but requires regular sinus rhythm for robust performance and comes at the expense of increased radiation dose (see, eg, Yoneyama and colleagues,[16] who found an average radiation dose of 4.8 mSv for a 1-beat scan and 7.8 mSv for a 2-beat scan in the CORE320 trial). Algorithmic approaches to correct for the motion of the coronary arteries in the CT images, thereby achieving very good virtual temporal resolution, have been proposed recently,[17–20] although as yet they miss validation in larger clinical studies. As of today, most investigators still propose the administration of β-blockers to patients with heart rates higher than 65 to 75 beats/ min to lower and stabilize the heart rate.

Since 2005, 3 generations of DSCT systems have been made available. DSCT systems are equipped with 2 x-ray tubes and 2 corresponding detectors offset by about 90° (**Fig. 2**).[21]

Unlike single-source CT systems, which achieve a maximum temporal resolution of half the gantry rotation time without use of multisegment reconstruction, DSCT scanners provide a temporal resolution close to a quarter of the gantry rotation time[22]: 83 milliseconds for the first-generation DSCT (SOMATOM Definition; Siemens Healthcare, Forchheim, Germany), 75 milliseconds for the second-generation DSCT (SOMATOM Flash), and 66 milliseconds for the third-generation DSCT (SOMATOM Force). This temporal resolution is independent of the patient's heart rate. Meanwhile, clinical studies have demonstrated the potential of DSCT to reliably perform coronary CTA with little or no dependence on the patient's heart rate.[23–26] In a meta-analysis of 33 studies published between 2006 and 2011 that compare the diagnostic accuracy of first- and second-generation DSCT coronary angiography for the

detection of greater than 50% stenosis with invasive catheter angiography as a reference standard,[27] the investigators found a pooled sensitivity of 98% and a pooled specificity of 88% on a per-patient basis, with no significant differences in sensitivity or specificity in the subgroup of studies with and without heart-rate control. The median radiation dose, however, was smaller in the studies with heart-rate control (1.6 mSv) than in the studies without heart-rate control (8 mSv).

Electrocardiogram-Gated Spiral (Helical) Scanning

During the first years of routine clinical integration of coronary CT angiography, retrospectively ECG-gated spiral (helical) scanning has been the most widely used data acquisition technique. A spiral (helical) CT scan with continuous data acquisition and continuous table movement at low table feed (low spiral pitch) is performed to examine the patient's heart. Simultaneously, the patient's ECG is recorded. After data acquisition, the ECG serves as a guide to select those data intervals in the spiral CT data set that were measured in different heartbeats in the same, user-selected relative heart phase. These data are then used for phase-consistent image reconstruction of the coronary anatomy. **Fig. 3** shows the principle of retrospectively ECG-gated spiral scanning.

This scan mode is versatile because it allows for retrospective optimization of the reconstruction window and image reconstruction in different heart phases. In some approaches, the ECG trace can be retrospectively edited to cope with difficult timing situations.

As a negative aspect, retrospectively ECG-gated spiral scanning of the heart requires highly overlapping spiral data acquisition at low table

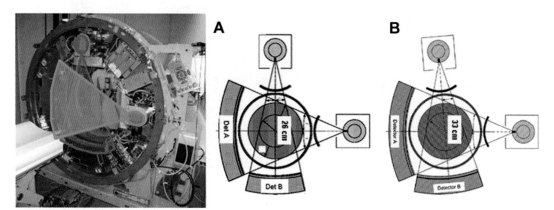

Fig. 2. DSCT with 2 independent measurement systems. (*A*) First generation. (*B*) Second generation. To increase the scan field of view (SFOV) of detector *B*, a larger system angle of 95° was chosen. With the third-generation DSCT, the SFOV of detector *B* was further increased to 35.5 cm.

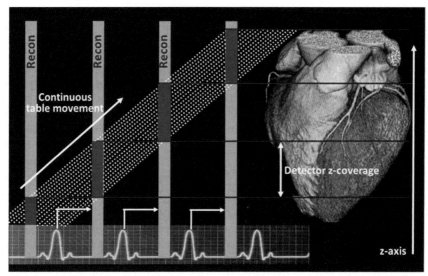

Fig. 3. Principle of retrospectively electrocardiogram (ECG)-gated spiral scanning of the heart. The ECG of the patient is schematically shown at the bottom. The dashed white lines indicate the z-positions of the individual detector rows of a multirow detector relative to the patient. The table moves continuously, and scan data are continuously acquired. After data acquisition, only those scan data with a user-selectable temporal distance to the preceding R wave are used for image reconstruction (indicated as *red boxes*). For a gapless volume coverage of the heart in each cardiac phase, low table feed is required, which has to be adapted to the heart rate of the patient: the higher the heart rate, the faster the table can move. Using a 4-cm detector, the heart is covered in 3 to 4 heartbeats.

feed for phase-consistent imaging and is therefore associated with relatively high radiation dose to the patient, which can be reduced by using ECG-controlled dose-modulation approaches (ECG pulsing). Meanwhile, many CT scanners are equipped with versatile ECG-pulsing algorithms that react flexibly to arrhythmia and ectopic beats, and have the potential to extend the clinical application spectrum of ECG-synchronized dose modulation to patients with irregular heart rates.

Electrocardiogram-Triggered Sequential (Axial) Scanning

As an alternative scan mode, prospectively ECG-triggered sequential scanning in a "step-and-shoot"

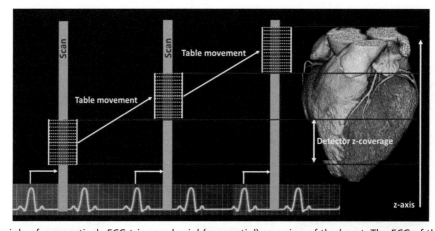

Fig. 4. Principle of prospectively ECG-triggered axial (sequential) scanning of the heart. The ECG of the patient is schematically shown at the bottom. The dashed white lines indicate the z-positions of the individual detector rows of a multirow detector relative to the patient. Axial (sequential) scan data are acquired with a user-selectable temporal distance to the preceding R wave (indicated as *red boxes*). After each axial scan, the table moves to the next z-position. Using a 4-cm detector, the heart is covered in 5 - 7 heartbeats in a "step-and-shoot" technique, because scan data can typically only be acquired every second heart beat.

technique is more commonly used with newer generations of CT systems. During the CT examination, the patient's ECG is used to trigger the start time for the acquisition of axial (sequential) CT images (Fig. 4). The patient table is moved to its defined start position. With a user-selectable temporal distance from an R wave, an axial CT scan without table movement is performed. The CT system acquires scan data covering a subvolume of the patient's cardiac anatomy that corresponds to the total z-width of the detector or is somewhat smaller (for CT systems with large detectors in the z-axis direction that have to cope with cone-beam effects). The table is moved to the next z-position, and the next axial CT scan is performed at the corresponding temporal distance from the next R wave. In this way the heart volume is sequentially covered by axial scans. Because of the time necessary for table movement, only every second heartbeat can be used for data acquisition.

ECG-triggered axial scanning is a dose-efficient scan technique. In a simple technical realization, a partial scan data interval (ie, the minimum amount of data necessary for image reconstruction) is acquired in a user-selected phase of the patient's cardiac cycle. As a consequence, however, retrospective reconstruction in a slightly different phase of the patient's cardiac cycle to minimize motion artifacts is not possible, nor is multiphase reconstructions for evaluation of the heart function. Furthermore, the temporal offset of scan data acquisition to the next R wave has to be extrapolated from previous heart cycles, which is a challenge in patients with irregular heartbeat and arrhythmia. In patients with low and regular heart rate, however, coronary CTA at a low radiation dose of 3 mSv or less is feasible.[28–30]

More refined ECG-triggering approaches provide a wider application spectrum of ECG-triggered sequential CT. The user may choose a wider data acquisition window by adding data to the beginning and end of the partial scan data segment ("padding"), thereby enabling retrospective optimization of the reconstruction phase of the images at the cost of (somewhat) increased radiation dose.[31] Some approaches provide flexible selection of the data acquisition window width similarly to ECG-gated spiral scanning, and even functional evaluation by simultaneous image reconstruction in systole and in diastole is possible. With the use of these techniques ECG-triggered sequential scanning is as versatile as ECG-gated spiral scanning, yet at lower radiation dose and with the benefit of a possible rejection of ectopic beats: advanced algorithms are available which, for example, stop data acquisition when an extrasystole occurs and resume scanning at the same z-position in the next regular heart cycle. This action is not possible with ECG-gated spiral scanning. With the use of advanced arrhythmia rejection, a decrease in radiation exposure by 50% in comparison with retrospectively ECG-gated spiral CT was observed in patients with variable heart rates,

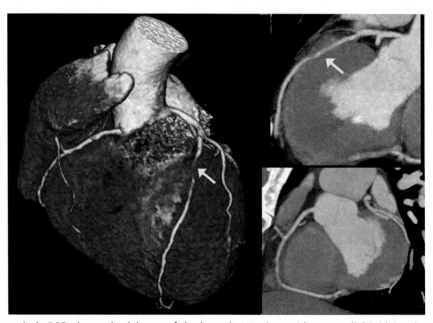

Fig. 5. Prospectively ECG-triggered axial scan of the heart in a patient with myocardial bridging (*arrow*) using a second-generation DSCT. The patient's heart rate varied between 77 and 103 beats/min during data acquisition. Effective radiation dose was 2.5 mSv. (*Courtesy of* Erasmus Medical Center, Rotterdam, the Netherlands; with permission.)

with preserved image quality.[32] Several investigators propose to adapt the width of the data acquisition interval to the patient's heart rate and widen it with increasing heart rate (see, eg, Leschka and colleagues[33]). At high heart rates, absolute end-systolic triggering may be favorable.[34] **Fig. 5** shows a clinical example of state-of-the art ECG-triggered coronary CTA.

Diagnostic coronary CTA at low radiation dose with absolute end-systolic prospective triggering using DSCT has been reported in patients with atrial fibrillation.[35,36] Using an absolute delay strategy, successful coronary CTA in patients with atrial fibrillation has also been demonstrated for 320-row CT.[37]

Already introduced for electron-beam CT and abandoned during the early days of multidetector-row cardiac CT, ECG-triggered sequential scanning of the heart went through a renaissance with the advent of 64-row CT systems providing 40-mm z-axis coverage. ECG-synchronized CT volume imaging of the heart using these systems comprises typically 3 to 4 subvolumes reconstructed from data acquired over multiple consecutive heartbeats (see also **Figs. 3** and **4**).[38] As a consequence of variations of the heart motion from one cardiac cycle to the next, these image subvolumes can be shifted relative to each other, resulting in stair-step or banding artifacts in multiplanar reformations or volume-rendered images. Furthermore, inadequate contrast timing may lead to different contrast enhancement in the subvolumes. Recently, 128-row, 256-slice CT systems with 80-mm z-axis coverage were commercially introduced (Philips ICT; Philips Healthcare, Best, the Netherlands). These systems facilitate examinations of the heart with 2 axial scans, thereby reducing the number of potential steps in the volume image to 1.[39] In a study with 160 consecutive patients, prospectively triggered axial coronary CTA performed on 256-slice CT provided significantly improved and more stable image quality at an equivalent effective radiation dose when compared with 64-slice CT.[40]

As of today, 2 CT vendors provide single-source CT systems with large-area detectors capable of imaging the entire heart in one beat, using one axial scan without table movement. With 320 × 0.5-mm collimation at 0.28 seconds rotation time (Toshiba Aquilion One; Toshiba Medical Systems Corp, Tokyo, Japan) and 256 × 0.625-mm collimation at 0.28 seconds rotation time (GE Revolution; GE Healthcare, Waukesha, WI, USA), these systems can cover 16 cm in the z-axis direction at isocenter, large enough to cover the entire heart in one beat, hence avoiding stair-step and banding artifacts and problems due to inconsistent contrast enhancement in different subvolumes.[41] At the boundary of the SFOV, volume coverage is smaller owing to the cone-beam geometry. Meanwhile, successful use of CT systems with 16-cm detector coverage for coronary CTA has been demonstrated.[42–44] However, a drawback of increasing detector width is that larger portions of the data can be distorted in cases of arrhythmia or ectopic beats during acquisition of scan data. Another challenge of larger detector z-coverage is increased x-ray scatter. Scattered radiation may cause hypodense cupping or streaking artifacts, and the scatter-induced noise may reduce the contrast-to-noise-ratio (CNR) in the images.[45]

Electrocardiogram-Triggered High-Pitch Scanning

DSCT systems offer a different way to approach the coveted goal for cardiac CT: a "snapshot" image of the entire heart in one cardiac cycle. With a single-source CT, the spiral pitch p (p is the table feed per rotation divided by the collimated z-width of the detector) is limited to $p \leq 1.5$ to ensure gapless volume coverage along the z-axis. With DSCT systems, however, the second measurement system, which acquires scan data at the same angular position a quarter rotation later, facilitates a maximum pitch $p = 3.2$ in a limited SFOV that is covered by both detectors.[46] A quarter rotation of data per measurement system (in parallel geometry) is used for image reconstruction, and each of the individual axial images has a temporal resolution of a quarter of the gantry rotation time. The patient's ECG is used to trigger the start of table motion and the start of the high-pitch spiral. **Fig. 6** illustrates the high-pitch technique. Second-generation DSCT provides a maximum table feed of 430 mm/s, sufficient to cover the heart (12 cm) in about 0.27 seconds, at a temporal resolution of 75 milliseconds per image. Using this technique, visualization of the coronary arteries at very low radiation dose (≤ 1 mSv) and with good image quality has been reported for patients with regular heart rates up to 60 to 65 beats/min.[47–50] With third-generation DSCT, offering a maximum table feed of 737 mm/s to cover the cardiac anatomy in about 0.15 seconds at a temporal resolution of 66 milliseconds per image, successful use of this technique has been extended to patients with heart rates up to 70 to 75 beats/min.[51,52] **Fig. 7** presents a clinical example.

RADIATION DOSE AND RADIATION-DOSE REDUCTION

As a consequence of the ongoing discussion of radiation exposure by CT in both the public and

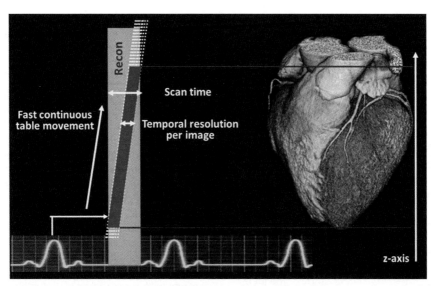

Fig. 6. Principle of prospectively ECG-triggered high-pitch spiral scanning of the heart. The ECG of the patient is schematically shown at the bottom. The dashed white lines indicate the z-positions of the individual detector rows of a DSCT relative to the patient. The table is moved at very high speed, sufficient to cover the entire heart within 1 heartbeat. Note that at each z-position only the minimum amount of scan data necessary for image reconstruction is acquired. The temporal resolution per image is therefore close to a quarter of the gantry rotation time; there is, however, a slight phase shift of the reconstructed images along the z-axis (see the *tilted red box*).

scientific literature, techniques to reduce radiation dose in coronary CTA have gained considerable attention.

Choice of Scan Technique

Radiation exposure of coronary CTA is significantly influenced by the choice of scan technique:

retrospectively ECG-gated spiral scanning or prospectively ECG-triggered axial scanning. In a meta-analysis of 20 studies evaluating the diagnostic accuracy of coronary CTA compared with catheter angiography in 3330 patients with coronary artery disease (CAD) and without tachyarrhythmia, the pooled sensitivity/specificity of

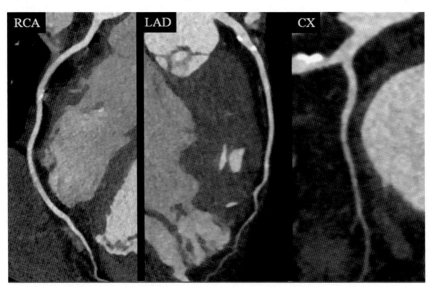

Fig. 7. Prospectively ECG-triggered axial scan of the heart using a high-pitch spiral mode in a 50-year-old patient with a heart rate of 73 beats/min. Curved multiplanar reformations of right coronary artery (RCA), left anterior descending artery (LAD), and circumflex artery (CX). Tube voltage 80 kV, effective radiation dose 0.5 mSv. (*Courtesy of* Universitätsspital Zürich, Zürich, Switzerland; with permission.)

coronary CTA was 98.7%/91.3% with prospective triggering and 96.9%/95.8% with retrospective gating. The pooled effective dose was 3.5 mSv with prospective triggering and 12.3 mSv with retrospective gating.[53] Similar results were reported in the PROTECTION-III study,[54] a prospective, multicenter, multivendor trial, including 400 patients with low and stable heart rates. Prospectively triggered axial scanning resulted in a mean dose of 3.5 mSv, 69% less than with retrospectively gated spiral (helical) scanning (11.2 mSv). To reduce radiation dose to the patient, ECG-triggered axial (sequential) scanning should be used whenever possible. A further reduction in radiation exposure to values below 1 mSv has been demonstrated with ECG-triggered DSCT high-pitch spiral scanning.[51,55,56] However, this technique is limited to patients with low to moderate regular heart rates. In a recent study,[57] the investigators concluded that the use of advanced scanners facilitating prospectively triggered or high-pitch spiral scan modes results in marked dose reduction across a variety of cardiovascular studies, with no compromise in image quality.

Low-Kilovolt Imaging

Another efficient technique to lower radiation exposure is the use of low-kV protocols. Because of the increased iodine contrast at lower x-ray tube kilovoltage, the CNR in contrast-enhanced images increases at low kV if the radiation dose is kept constant.[58,59] By contrast, lower radiation dose is sufficient at low kV to maintain a desired CNR. The potential for dose reduction is more significant for smaller and medium-sized patients. In the PROTECTION-II trial, a study of 400 nonobese patients, the investigators demonstrated reduced radiation exposure by 31% at maintained image quality when using a coronary CTA protocol with 100-kV tube voltage when compared with the standard 120-kV protocol.[60] Even lower radiation exposure can be achieved with the use of 80-kV protocols. Because of current limitations of x-ray tubes, use of 80-kV protocols has so far been limited to small patients.[61] Recent progress in x-ray tube design has led to the introduction of CT systems capable of providing high power reserves at 80 and 70 kV. These systems have the potential to enable coronary CTA at 70 to 80 kV even in obese patients without compromising CNR, and thus reduce radiation dose by 49% to 68%.[62] A promising approach is the combination of low x-ray tube voltage with dose-efficient data acquisition techniques, such as ECG-triggered high-pitch spiral scanning. In a recent study,[63] third-generation DSCT high-pitch coronary angiography at 70 kV

in nonobese patients resulted in robust image quality at significantly reduced radiation dose (0.44 mSv) and contrast medium volume (45 mL).

Iterative Reconstruction

As an add-on to the dose-reduction approaches described, iterative image reconstruction has found its way into routine cardiac CT scanning. In an iterative reconstruction, a correction loop is introduced into the image reconstruction process.[64] Although the technical realization is highly vendor specific, all approaches aim at including the statistical properties of the acquired measurement data into the image reconstruction process in a better way than used for traditional filtered back-projection. As a result, they maintain or even improve high-contrast resolution and reduce image noise in low-contrast areas, which is the prerequisite for a potential reduction in radiation dose. In particular, when combined with other dose-efficient techniques, such as ECG-triggered sequential scanning, ECG-triggered high-pitch scanning, and low-kV data acquisition, iterative reconstruction may enable coronary CTA at very low radiation dose levels. Representative of many published studies demonstrating coronary CTA in selected patients at sub-mSv dose, Stehli and colleagues[65] combined ECG-triggered sequential scanning at 80 kV with model-based iterative reconstruction, Layritz and colleagues[66] used ECG-triggered sequential scanning at 100 kV with SAFIRE (Siemens Healthcare), Yin and colleagues[56] combined ECG-triggered high-pitch spiral scanning at 80 kV with SAFIRE, and Chen and colleagues[44] used ECG-triggered sequential 320-row CT in combination with iterative reconstruction. Schuhbaeck and colleagues[67] demonstrated coronary CTA with a radiation dose as low as 0.06 mSv with sufficient image quality in selected patients, through the combination of low-kV high-pitch spiral acquisition and raw data–based iterative reconstruction. Alternatively, iterative reconstruction may be used to improve the image quality in coronary CTA, for example to improve the performance of automated vessel segmentation algorithms,[68] or to obtain higher diagnostic accuracy for detecting lipid-core plaque.[69] **Fig. 8** shows a representative clinical example of the image quality obtained with state-of-the-art iterative reconstruction.

FUNCTIONAL IMAGING

Coronary CTA can visualize the coronary arteries with excellent image quality. However, as a consequence of still insufficient spatial resolution it tends to overestimate the degree of coronary stenosis,

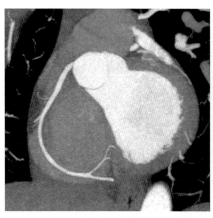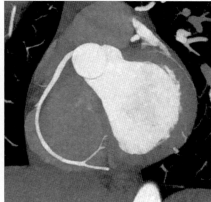

Fig. 8. Prospectively ECG-triggered axial scan of the heart. Curved multiplanar reformation of the RCA. (*Left*) Standard filtered back-projection reconstruction. (*Right*) State-of-the-art iterative reconstruction (ADMIRE, level 4).

and does not provide information about its hemodynamic relevance. Coronary CTA is reliable for ruling out functionally relevant CAD, but is a poor predictor of myocardial ischemia.[70]

Assessment of both coronary artery morphology and the status of myocardial perfusion, using the same imaging modality, at best in a single examination, remains a coveted goal.[71] Therefore, research is ongoing to also provide information about the myocardial blood supply using CT. Bucher and colleagues[72] provide a review of currently available CT techniques for the assessment of myocardial perfusion.

First-Pass Enhancement Scanning

In the most basic approach, a coronary CTA scan is used to also evaluate the blood supply of the myocardium. These first-pass enhancement studies provide a snapshot image of the myocardial blood volume at a single arterial contrast phase; this is not perfusion imaging in a strict sense, even if sometimes incorrectly called cardiac perfusion CT. Hypoattenuation of the myocardium is interpreted as perfusion defect. Because the concentration of the contrast agent in the myocardium is not assessed as a function of time, CT first-pass enhancement scanning depends critically on the timing of the scan. First-pass enhancement scanning has been applied to patients with acute and chronic myocardial infarction.[73,74] To identify reversible ischemia, first-pass enhancement scanning has been performed not only at rest but also with the application of adenosine stress. In the recent CORE320 multicenter study using 320-row CT,[75] 381 patients from 16 centers underwent first-pass rest and first-pass adenosine-stress CT imaging and rest and stress

single-photon emission CT (SPECT) before and within 60 days of invasive coronary angiography. The reference standard for the diagnosis of CAD was a stenosis of at least 50% at invasive coronary angiography. CT first-pass rest and stress myocardial blood volume imaging showed a per-patient sensitivity and specificity for the diagnosis of CAD of 88% and 55%, compared with 62% and 67% with SPECT. In those patients with greater than 50% stenosis on coronary CTA, evaluation of CT first-pass enhancement resulted in sensitivity, specificity, positive predictive value (PPV), and negative predicative value (NPV) of 80%, 74%, 65%, and 86%, respectively.[76]

First-Pass Enhancement Scanning with Dual-Energy Data Acquisition

Recently, single-phase, first-pass enhancement CT imaging has been performed with the use of dual-energy (DE) acquisition techniques. DE CT data can be obtained by using different kV settings of the x-ray tube. In one technical realization, the x-ray tube voltage is rapidly switched between 80 kV and 140 kV, such that consecutive projections of a CT scan are acquired at different kilovoltage (fast kV switching). DSCT systems enable the acquisition of DE data by operating both x-ray tubes at different tube voltages. Optimization of the spectral separation and as a consequence optimization of the quality of DE evaluation is possible by introducing additional prefiltration into the high-kV beam, for example by means of a filter that can be moved into the beam when needed and moved out for standard applications. It has been demonstrated that prefiltering the high-kV beam with 0.4 mm tin improved the DE contrast between iodine and calcium as much as 290%.[77] **Fig. 9**

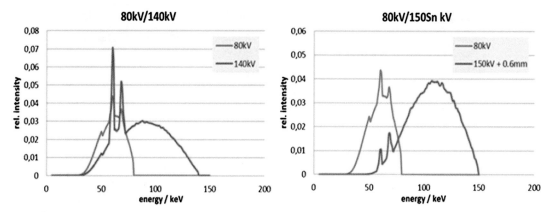

Fig. 9. (*Left*) Standard 80-kV and 140-kV spectra used for dual-energy (DE) imaging. Both spectra overlap signif-icantly. (*Right*) 80-kV spectrum and 150-kV spectrum with additional 0.6-mm tin prefiltration. Note the reduced spectral overlap.

shows the improvement in spectral separation when using 80 kV and 150 kV with 0.6 mm tin pre-filtration (as realized in third-generation DSCT) when compared with the standard 80 kV/140 kV combination.

For the purposes of myocardial blood volume imaging, DE data have been used to create an "iodine map" of the myocardium. Compared with hypoattenuation on single-energy CT images, DE iodine maps are potentially more sensitive for the detection of hypoperfused myocardium,[78] as they allow for a potentially quantitative evaluation of the iodine content, and other sources of hypoat-tenuation (eg, fat) can be ruled out.

ECG-controlled dual-source DE CT has been performed at rest[78,79] and during stress.[80–82] It has been used to detect both fixed perfusion de-fects and reversible ischemia. Vliegenthart and colleagues[83] provide a comprehensive overview of potential clinical applications of DE CT of the heart.

Ko and colleagues[80] investigated the classifica-tion of stenosis severity with first-generation dual-source DE CT in a group of 45 patients with known CAD. On comparing DSCT angiography with inva-sive coronary angiography as a gold standard, the investigators found 91.8% sensitivity, 67.7% specificity, 73.6% PPV, and 87.5% NPV for the detection of significant coronary artery stenosis with CT on a per-vessel basis. When adding dual-source DE CT at rest and during stress for the evaluation of the myocardial blood supply and reclassifying coronary stenosis severity ac-cording to the combined CT information, they re-ported 93.2% sensitivity, 85.5% specificity, 88.3% PPV, and 91.4% NPV.

Fig. 10 presents a clinical example of the use of rest and stress DE CT.

Dynamic Perfusion Computed Tomography

The most refined and clinically most promising CT technique to acquire information about the blood supply of the myocardium is dynamic perfusion scanning. Quantitative dynamic cardiac CT perfu-sion imaging is characterized by time-resolved assessment of the inflow and outflow of the contrast agent in the left ventricle.

Using CT systems with area detector technol-ogy, the entire myocardium can be examined by repeated ECG-controlled scanning without table movement. An alternative technique has been developed for DSCT: ECG-triggered sequential scan data are acquired at 2 alternating table posi-tions using end-systolic timing, with the table mov-ing forward and backward between the 2 positions. Using end-systolic triggering, data acquisition is not affected by extrasystolic events; the volume of the left ventricle is smaller; the total amount of intraventricular contrast is lower, result-ing in reduced artifacts; and myocardial wall thick-ness is higher, providing a more robust basis for assessing perfusion abnormalities. In a recent study, Rossi and colleagues[84] compared the per-formance of a myocardial blood flow (MBF) index derived from dynamic CT perfusion imaging under adenosine stress with that of coronary CTA with both visual and semiautomatic quantitative evalu-ation in the detection of functionally significant coronary lesions in patients with stable chest pain. Fractional flow reserve less than 0.75 was used as a gold standard to characterize coronary stenosis as functionally significant. For intermedi-ate coronary lesions, the specificity of visual CTA (69%) and quantitative CTA (77%) was improved by the subsequent use of the MBF index (89%). Most importantly, a quantitative cutoff value of

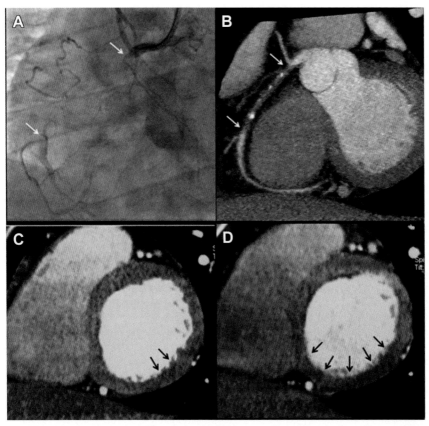

Fig. 10. ECG-gated spiral DE cardiac CT acquisition in a 60-year-old hypertensive man with a history of smoking, using second-generation DSCT at 100 kV/140 Sn kV, rotation time 0.28 seconds. Both conventional catheter angiography (*A*) and CT angiography derived from the rest DE scan (*B*) show chronic total occlusion of the proximal RCA (*arrows*). The DE energy iodine maps at rest (*C*) and during stress (*D*) indicate a reversible perfusion defect (*arrows*). (*Courtesy of* Vancouver General Hospital, Vancouver, Canada; with permission.)

the MBF index to detect functionally significant coronary lesions was defined, namely 78 mL/100 mL/min.

One obstacle for the integration of dynamic cardiac perfusion imaging into routine clinical algorithms is the relatively higher radiation dose of these examinations in comparison with first-pass enhancement scanning. Ongoing technical progress, however, enabling the use of 80 kV or even 70 kV tube voltage for dynamic cardiac perfusion CT, holds promise to reduce radiation dose to values of 5 mSv and less.[85]

Further clinical studies will be needed to evaluate the clinical role of the different approaches to assess the status of the myocardial blood supply with CT, and to demonstrate the potential and limitations of single-phase first-pass enhancement imaging with both single-energy and dual-energy data acquisition, and both without and with pharmacologically induced stress, and quantitative time-resolved perfusion imaging.

REFERENCES

1. Achenbach S, Ulzheimer S, Baum U, et al. Noninvasive coronary angiography by retrospectively ECG-gated multi-slice spiral CT. Circulation 2000;102:2823–8.
2. Becker C, Knez A, Ohnesorge B, et al. Imaging of non calcified coronary plaques using helical CT with retrospective EKG gating. AJR Am J Roentgenol 2000;175:423–4.
3. Kopp AF, Schröder S, Küttner A, et al. Coronary arteries: Retrospectively ECG-gated multi-detector row CT angiography with selective optimization of the reconstruction window. Radiology 2001;221:683–8.
4. Knez A, Becker C, Leber A, et al. Non-invasive assessment of coronary artery stenoses with multi-detector helical computed tomography. Circulation 2000;101:e221–2.
5. Ohnesorge B, Flohr T, Becker C, et al. Cardiac imaging by means of electro- cardiographically gated

multisection spiral CT—initial experience. Radiology 2000;217:564–71.

6. Nieman K, Oudkerk M, Rensing B, et al. Coronary angiography with multi-slice computed tomography. Lancet 2001;357:599–603.

7. Hoffmann MH, Shi H, Schmitz BL, et al. Noninvasive coronary angiography with multislice computed tomography. JAMA 2005;293:2471–8.

8. Leschka S, Wildermuth S, Boehm T, et al. Noninvasive coronary angiography with 64-section CT: effect of average heart rate and heart rate variability on image quality. Radiology 2006;241(2):378–85.

9. Leber AW, Knez A, Ziegler F, et al. Quantification of obstructive and nonobstructive coronary lesions by 64-slice computed tomography—a comparative study with quantitative coronary angiography and intravascular ultrasound. JACC 2005;46(1):147–54.

10. Raff GL, Gallagher MJ, O'Neill WW, et al. Diagnostic accuracy of non-invasive coronary angiography using 64-slice spiral computed tomography. J Am Coll Cardiol 2005;46(3):552–7.

11. Vanhecke TE, Madder RD, Weber JE, et al. Development and validation of a predictive screening tool for uninterpretable coronary CT angiography results. Circ Cardiovasc Imaging 2011;4(5):490–7.

12. Maintz D, Seifarth H, Raupach R, et al. 64-slice multidetector coronary CT angiography: in vitro evaluation of 68 different stents. Eur Radiol 2006;16(4): 818–26.

13. Maintz D, Burg MC, Seifarth H, et al. Update on multidetector coronary CT angiography of coronary stents: in vitro evaluation of 29 different stent types with dual-source CT. Eur Radiol 2009;19(1):42–9.

14. Fuchs TA, Stehli J, Fiechter M, et al. First in vivo head-to-head comparison of high-definition versus standard-definition stent imaging with 64-slice computed tomography. Int J Cardiovasc Imaging 2013;29(6):1409–16.

15. Gassenmaier T, Petri N, Allmendinger T, et al. Next generation coronary CT angiography: in vitro evaluation of 27 coronary stents. Eur Radiol 2014;24(11): 2953–61.

16. Yoneyama K, Vavere AL, Cerci R, et al. Influence of image acquisition settings on radiation dose and image quality in coronary angiography by 320-detector volume computed tomography: the CORE320 pilot experience. Heart Int 2012;7(2):e11.

17. Bhagalia R, Pack JD, Miller JV, et al. Nonrigid registration-based coronary artery motion correction for cardiac computed tomography. Med Phys 2012; 39(7):4245–54.

18. Rohkohl C, Bruder H, Stierstorfer K, et al. Improving best-phase image quality in cardiac CT by motion correction with MAM optimization. Med Phys 2013; 40(3):031901.

19. Apfaltrer P, Schoendube H, Schoepf UJ, et al. Enhanced temporal resolution at cardiac CT with a novel CT image reconstruction algorithm: initial patient experience. Eur J Radiol 2013;82(2):270–4.

20. Fuchs TA, Stehli J, Dougoud S, et al. Impact of a new motion-correction algorithm on image quality of low-dose coronary CT angiography in patients with insufficient heart rate control. Acad Radiol 2014;21(3): 312–7.

21. Flohr TG, McCollough CH, Bruder H, et al. First performance evaluation of a dual-source CT (DSCT) system. Eur Radiol 2006;16(2):256–68.

22. McCollough CH, Schmidt B, Yu L, et al. Measurement of temporal resolution in dual source CT. Med Phys 2008;35(2):764–8.

23. Scheffel H, Alkadhi H, Plass A, et al. Accuracy of dual-source CT coronary angiography: first experience in a high pre-test probability population without heart rate control. Eur Radiol 2006;16(12):2739–47.

24. Matt D, Scheffel H, Leschka S, et al. Dual-source CT coronary angiography: image quality, mean heart rate, and heart rate variability. AJR Am J Roentgenol 2007;189(3):567–73.

25. Ropers U, Ropers D, Pflederer T, et al. Influence of heart rate on the diagnostic accuracy of dual-source computed tomography coronary angiography. J Am Coll Cardiol 2007;50(25):2393–8.

26. Weustink AC, Neefjes LA, Kyrzopoulos S, et al. Impact of heart rate frequency and variability on radiation exposure, image quality, and diagnostic performance in dual-source spiral CT coronary angiography. Radiology 2009;253(3):672–80.

27. Li M, Zhang GM, Zhao JS, et al. Diagnostic performance of dual-source CT coronary angiography with and without heart rate control: systematic review and meta-analysis. Clin Radiol 2014;69(2): 163–71.

28. Earls JP, Berman EL, Urban BA, et al. Prospectively gated transverse coronary CT angiography versus retrospectively gated helical technique: improved image quality and reduced radiation dose. Radiology 2008;246(3):742–53.

29. Stolzmann P, Leschka S, Scheffel H, et al. Dual-source CT in step-and-shoot mode: noninvasive coronary angiography with low radiation dose. Radiology 2008;249(1):71–80.

30. Arnoldi E, Johnson TR, Rist C, et al. Adequate image quality with reduced radiation dose in prospectively triggered coronary CTA compared with retrospective techniques. Eur Radiol 2009;19(9):2147–55.

31. Labounty TM, Leipsic J, Min JK, et al. Effect of padding duration on radiation dose and image interpretation in prospectively ECG-triggered coronary CT angiography. AJR Am J Roentgenol 2010; 194(4):933–7.

32. Lee AM, Engel LC, Shah B, et al. Coronary computed tomography angiography during arrhythmia: radiation dose reduction with prospectively ECG-triggered axial and retrospectively ECG-gated helical 128-slice dual-

source CT. J Cardiovasc Comput Tomogr 2012;6(3):172–83.

33. Leschka S, Scheffel H, Desbiolles L, et al. Image quality and reconstruction intervals of dual-source CT coronary angiography: recommendations for ECG-pulsing windowing. Invest Radiol 2007;42(8):543–9.

34. Lee AM, Beaudoin J, Engel LC, et al. Assessment of image quality and radiation dose of prospectively ECG-triggered adaptive dual-source coronary computed tomography angiography (cCTA) with arrhythmia rejection algorithm in systole versus diastole: a retrospective cohort study. Int J Cardiovasc Imaging 2013;29(6):1361–70.

35. Srichai MB, Barreto M, Lim RP, et al. Prospective-triggered sequential dual-source end-systolic coronary CT angiography for patients with atrial fibrillation: a feasibility study. J Cardiovasc Comput Tomogr 2013;7(2):102–9.

36. Sidhu MS, Venkatesh V, Hoffmann U, et al. Advanced adaptive axial-sequential prospectively electrocardiogram-triggered dual-source coronary computed tomographic angiography in a patient with atrial fibrillation. J Comput Assist Tomogr 2011;35(6):747–8.

37. Kondo T, Kumamaru KK, Fujimoto S, et al. Prospective ECG-gated coronary 320-MDCT angiography with absolute acquisition delay strategy for patients with persistent atrial fibrillation. AJR Am J Roentgenol 2013;201(6):1197–203.

38. Flohr T, Schoepf UJ, Ohnesorge B. Chasing the heart—new developments for cardiac CT. J Thorac Imaging 2007;22(1):4–16.

39. Muenzel D, Noel PB, Dorn F, et al. Coronary CT angiography in step-and-shoot technique with 256-slice CT: impact of the field of view on image quality, craniocaudal coverage, and radiation exposure. Eur J Radiol 2012;81(7):1562–8.

40. Klass O, Walker M, Siebach A, et al. Prospectively gated axial CT coronary angiography: comparison of image quality and effective radiation dose between 64- and 256-slice CT. Eur Radiol 2010;20(5):1124–31.

41. Rybicki FJ, Otero HJ, Steigner ML, et al. Initial evaluation of coronary images from 320-detector row computed tomography. Int J Cardiovasc Imaging 2008;24(5):535–46.

42. Nasis A, Leung MC, Antonis PR, et al. Diagnostic accuracy of noninvasive coronary angiography with 320-detector row computed tomography. Am J Cardiol 2010;106(10):1429–35.

43. Tomizawa N, Maeda E, Akahane M, et al. Coronary CT angiography using the second-generation 320-detector row CT: assessment of image quality and radiation dose in various heart rates compared with the first-generation scanner. Int J Cardiovasc Imaging 2013;29(7):1613–8.

44. Chen MY, Shanbhag SM, Arai AE. Submillisievert median radiation dose for coronary angiography with a second-generation 320-detector row CT scanner in 107 consecutive patients. Radiology 2013;267(1):76–85.

45. Engel KJ, Herrmann C, Zeitler G. X-ray scattering in single- and dual-source CT. Med Phys 2007;35(1):318–32.

46. Flohr TG, Leng S, Yu L, et al. Dual-source spiral CT with pitch up to 3.2 and 75 ms temporal resolution: image reconstruction and assessment of image quality. Med Phys 2009;36(12):5641–53.

47. Achenbach S, Marwan M, Ropers D, et al. Coronary computed tomography angiography with a consistent dose below 1 mSv using prospectively electrocardiogram-triggered high-pitch spiral acquisition. Eur Heart J 2010;31(3):340–6.

48. Lell M, Marwan M, Schepis T, et al. Prospectively ECG-triggered high-pitch spiral acquisition for coronary CT angiography using dual source CT: technique and initial experience. Eur Radiol 2009;19(11):2576–83.

49. Leschka S, Stolzmann P, Desbiolles L, et al. Diagnostic accuracy of high-pitch dual-source CT for the assessment of coronary stenoses: first experience. Eur Radiol 2009;19(12):2896–903.

50. Lell M, Hinkmann F, Anders K, et al. High-pitch electrocardiogram-triggered computed tomography of the chest: initial results. Invest Radiol 2009;44(11):728–33.

51. Morsbach F, Gordic S, Desbiolles L, et al. Performance of turbo high-pitch dual-source CT for coronary CT angiography: first ex vivo and patient experience. Eur Radiol 2014;24(8):1889–95.

52. Gordic S, Husarik DB, Desbiolles L, et al. High-pitch coronary CT angiography with third generation dual-source CT: limits of heart rate. Int J Cardiovasc Imaging 2014;30(6):1173–9.

53. Menke J, Unterberg-Buchwald C, Staab W, et al. Head-to-head comparison of prospectively triggered vs retrospectively gated coronary computed tomography angiography: meta-analysis of diagnostic accuracy, image quality, and radiation dose. Am Heart J 2013;165(2):154–63.

54. Hausleiter J, Meyer TS, Martuscelli E, et al. Image quality and radiation exposure with prospectively ECG-triggered axial scanning for coronary CT angiography: the multicenter, multivendor, randomized PROTECTION-III study. JACC Cardiovasc Imaging 2012;5(5):484–93.

55. Neefjes LA, Dharampal AS, Rossi A, et al. Image quality and radiation exposure using different low-dose scan protocols in dual-source CT coronary angiography: randomized study. Radiology 2011;261(3):779–86.

56. Yin WH, Lu B, Hou ZH, et al. Detection of coronary artery stenosis with sub-milliSievert radiation dose by prospectively ECG-triggered high-pitch spiral CT angiography and iterative reconstruction. Eur Radiol 2013;23(11):2927–33.

57. Chinnaiyan KM, Bilolikar AN, Walsh E, et al. CT dose reduction using prospectively triggered or fast-pitch spiral technique employed in cardiothoracic imaging (the CT dose study). J Cardiovasc Comput Tomogr 2014;8(3):205–14.

58. Siegel MJ, Schmidt B, Bradley D, et al. Radiation dose and image quality in pediatric CT: effect of technical factors and phantom size and shape. Radiology 2004;233:515–22.

59. McCollough CH, Primak AN, Braun N, et al. Strategies for reducing radiation dose in CT. Radiol Clin North Am 2009;47(1):27–40.

60. Hausleiter J, Martinoff S, Hadamitzky M, et al. Image quality and radiation exposure with a low tube voltage protocol for coronary CT angiography results of the PROTECTION II trial. JACC Cardiovasc Imaging 2010;3(11):1113–23.

61. Cao JX, Wang YM, Lu JG, et al. Radiation and contrast agent doses reductions by using 80-kV tube voltage in coronary computed tomographic angiography: a comparative study. Eur J Radiol 2014;83(2):309–14.

62. Meinel FG, Canstein C, Schoepf UJ, et al. Image quality and radiation dose of low tube voltage 3rd generation dual-source coronary CT angiography in obese patients: a phantom study. Eur Radiol 2014;24(7):1643–50.

63. Meyer M, Haubenreisser H, Schoepf UJ, et al. Closing in on the K edge: coronary CT angiography at 100, 80, and 70 kV-initial comparison of a second-versus a third-generation dual-source CT system. Radiology 2014;273(2):373–82.

64. Thibault JB, Sauer KD, Bouman CA, et al. A three-dimensional statistical approach to improved image quality for multislice helical CT. Med Phys 2007; 34(11):4526–44.

65. Stehli J, Fuchs TA, Bull S, et al. Accuracy of coronary CT angiography using a submillisievert fraction of radiation exposure: comparison with invasive coronary angiography. J Am Coll Cardiol 2014;64(8):772–80.

66. Layritz C, Schmid J, Achenbach S, et al. Accuracy of prospectively ECG-triggered very low-dose coronary dual-source CT angiography using iterative reconstruction for the detection of coronary artery stenosis: comparison with invasive catheterization. Eur Heart J Cardiovasc Imaging 2014;15(11): 1238–45.

67. Schuhbaeck A, Achenbach S, Layritz C, et al. Image quality of ultra-low radiation exposure coronary CT angiography with an effective dose <0.1 mSv using high-pitch spiral acquisition and raw data-based iterative reconstruction. Eur Radiol 2013; 23(3):597–606.

68. Spears JR, Schoepf UJ, Henzler T, et al. Comparison of the effect of iterative reconstruction versus filtered back projection on cardiac CT postprocessing. Acad Radiol 2014;21(3):318–24.

69. Puchner SB, Ferencik M, Maurovich-Horvat P, et al. Iterative image reconstruction algorithms in coronary CT angiography improve the detection of lipid-core plaque—a comparison with histology. Eur Radiol 2015;25(1):15–23.

70. Stolzmann P, Donati OF, Scheffel H, et al. Low-dose CT coronary angiography for the prediction of myocardial ischaemia. Eur Radiol 2010;20(1):56–64.

71. Bastarrika G, Lee YS, Huda W, et al. CT of coronary artery disease. Radiology 2009;253(2):317–38.

72. Bucher AM, De Cecco CN, Schoepf UJ, et al. Cardiac CT for myocardial ischaemia detection and characterization-comparative analysis. Br J Radiol 2014;87(1043):20140159.

73. Nikolaou K, Sanz J, Poon M, et al. Assessment of myocardial perfusion and viability from routine contrast-enhanced 16-detector-row computed tomography of the heart: preliminary results. Eur Radiol 2005;15(5):864–71.

74. Nieman K, Cury RC, Ferencik M, et al. Differentiation of recent and chronic myocardial infarction by cardiac computed tomography. Am J Cardiol 2006; 98(3):303–8.

75. George RT, Mehra VC, Chen MY, et al. Myocardial CT perfusion imaging and SPECT for the diagnosis of coronary artery disease: a head-to-head comparison from the CORE320 multicenter diagnostic performance study. Radiology 2014;272(2):407–16.

76. George RT, Arbab-Zadeh A, Miller JM, et al. Computed tomography myocardial perfusion imaging with 320-row detector computed tomography accurately detects myocardial ischemia in patients with obstructive coronary artery disease. Circ Cardiovasc Imaging 2012;5(3):333–40.

77. Primak AN, Giraldo JC, Eusemann CD, et al. Dual-source dual-energy CT with additional tin filtration: dose and image quality evaluation in phantoms and in vivo. AJR Am J Roentgenol 2010;195(5):1164–74.

78. Ruzsics B, Schwarz F, Schoepf UJ, et al. Comparison of dual-energy computed tomography of the heart with single photon emission computed tomography for assessment of coronary artery stenosis and of the myocardial blood supply. Am J Cardiol 2009;104(3):318–26.

79. Wang R, Yu W, Wang Y, et al. Incremental value of dual-energy CT to coronary CT angiography for the detection of significant coronary stenosis: comparison with quantitative coronary angiography and single photon emission computed tomography. Int J Cardiovasc Imaging 2011;27:647–56.

80. Ko SM, Choi JW, Song MG, et al. Myocardial perfusion imaging using adenosine-induced stress dual-energy computed tomography of the heart: comparison with cardiac magnetic resonance imaging and conventional coronary angiography. Eur Radiol 2011;21:26–35.

81. Weininger M, Schoepf UJ, Ramachandra A, et al. Adenosine-stress dynamic real-time myocardial perfusion

and adenosine-stress first-pass dual-energy myocardial perfusion CT for the assessment of acute chest pain: initial results. Eur J Radiol 2012;81(12):3703–10.

82. Ko SM, Choi JW, Hwang HK, et al. Diagnostic performance of combined noninvasive anatomic and functional assessment with dual-source CT and adenosine-induced stress dual-energy CT for detection of significant coronary stenosis. AJR Am J Roentgenol 2012;198:512–20.

83. Vliegenthart R, Pilgrim GJ, Ebersberger U, et al. Dual-energy CT of the heart. AJR Am J Roentgenol 2012;199:S54–63.

84. Rossi A, Dharampal A, Wragg A, et al. Diagnostic performance of hyperaemic myocardial blood flow index obtained by dynamic computed tomography: does it predict functionally significant coronary lesions? Eur Heart J Cardiovasc Imaging 2014;15(1): 85–94.

85. Kim SM, Cho YK, Choe YH. Adenosine-stress dynamic myocardial perfusion imaging using 128-slice dual-source CT in patients with normal body mass indices: effect of tube voltage, tube current, and iodine concentration on image quality and radiation dose. Int J Cardiovasc Imaging 2014;30(Suppl 2):95–103.

Coronary Computed Tomographic Angiography in Clinical Practice: State of the Art

 CrossMark

Felix G. Meinel, MD[a,b,*], Richard R. Bayer II, MD[c], Peter L. Zwerner, MD[c], Carlo Nicola De Cecco, MD[a,d], U. Joseph Schoepf, MD[a,c], Fabian Bamberg, MD, MPH[e]

KEYWORDS

- Coronary CT angiography • Cardiac CT • Coronary artery disease • Chest pain
- Diagnostic accuracy • Prognostic value

KEY POINTS

- Coronary computed tomographic (CT) angiography (CCTA) has high diagnostic accuracy for the noninvasive assessment of coronary artery disease (CAD), and findings at CCTA hold strong prognostic significance.
- CCTA thus plays an important role in the evaluation and management of patients with known or suspected ischemic heart disease.
- The use of CCTA should be informed by established guidelines and appropriate use criteria, which are likely to further evolve and be refined.
- Novel, investigational developments in CCTA are aimed at characterizing and quantifying coronary artery plaque and assessing its hemodynamic significance.

INTRODUCTION

Within the past decade, CCTA has left the early stages of technical development and accuracy assessment and developed into a robust, well-established imaging test with an important role in the evaluation and management of patients with known or suspected ischemic heart disease.[1] The specific indications for CCTA continue to be the subject of debate, and guidelines on its appropriate use are likely to be modified and developed over the years to come. The controversies surrounding CCTA have led to uncertainties on the part of both radiologists and clinicians regarding its appropriate use. This article discusses established and emerging applications for CCTA in light of the available evidence on its accuracy, prognostic value, cost-effectiveness, risks, and benefits. Building on this evidence, the authors provide a practical overview of the appropriate use of CCTA in state-of-the-art clinical practice.

Disclosure statement: Dr U.J. Schoepf is a consultant for and/or receives research support from Bayer, Bracco, GE, and Siemens. The other authors have no conflicts of interest to disclose.

[a] Department of Radiology and Radiological Science, Medical University of South Carolina, 25 Courtenay Drive, Charleston, SC 29425, USA; [b] Institute for Clinical Radiology, Ludwig-Maximilians-University Hospital, Marchioninistraße, Munich 81377, Germany; [c] Division of Cardiology, Department of Medicine, Medical University of South Carolina, 25 Courtenay Drive, Charleston, SC 29425, USA; [d] Department of Radiological Sciences, Oncology and Pathology, University of Rome "Sapienza" – Polo Pontino, Latina, Italy; [e] Department of Radiology, University of Tübingen, Hoppe-Seyler-Straße, Tübingen 72076, Germany

* Corresponding author. Institute for Clinical Radiology, Ludwig-Maximilians-University Hospital, Marchioninistraße, Munich 81377, Germany.

E-mail address: felix.meinel@med.uni-muenchen.de

Radiol Clin N Am 53 (2015) 287–296
http://dx.doi.org/10.1016/j.rcl.2014.11.012
0033-8389/15/$ – see front matter © 2015 Elsevier Inc. All rights reserved.

STABLE CHEST PAIN SYNDROME
Diagnostic Accuracy

A multitude of studies have investigated the accuracy of CCTA for detecting anatomically significant stenosis with 50% or more luminal narrowing with invasive angiography as the reference standard. Across all published meta-analyses on the accuracy of CCTA using at least 64-slice multidetector CT systems, the median sensitivity on a per-patient level was 97.8% with 89.6% sensitivity.[2] The high sensitivity reported across most studies translates into a negative predictive value of 95% to 100%. A fully diagnostic CCTA that demonstrates no significant stenosis can thus exclude obstructive CAD with a high degree of certainty.

These accuracy data were chiefly generated with retrospectively electrocardiography (ECG)-gated CCTA and 64-slice CT. The accuracy of CCTA using more dose-efficient techniques and more advanced CT systems has also been analyzed. Two meta-analyses specifically analyzing studies on prospectively ECG-triggered CCTA revealed a pooled sensitivity of 99% to 100% and specificity of 89% to 91% on the per-patient level.[2,3] Other meta-analyses have investigated the performance of CCTA with specific state-of-the-art CT systems. For 320-slice CCTA, a pooled per-patient sensitivity of 93% and specificity of 86% were reported, translating into a negative predictive value of 90%.[4] For dual-source CT, pooled sensitivity was 98% to 99% and specificity was 88% to 89%, with a negative predictive value of 98% to 99%.[5,6] Thus, there is overall good evidence that the accuracy of CCTA with state-of-the-art equipment and dose-saving techniques is at least equivalent to the more traditional retrospectively ECG-gated CCTA with 64-slice CT.

Prognostic Value

In a meta-analysis analyzing 11 studies including a total of 7335 mostly symptomatic patients with suspected CAD followed for a median of 20 months, the presence of any greater than 50% stenosis at CCTA was associated with a 10-fold higher risk for cardiovascular events, the finding of any CAD inferred a 4.5-fold risk, and each coronary segment involved increased the risk for adverse outcomes by 23%.[7] In a more recent analysis of 17,793 patients from the CONFIRM (Coronary CT Angiography Evaluation for Clinical Outcomes: An International Multicenter) registry, the majority of whom had chronic chest pain, the number of proximal segments with mixed or calcified plaques and the number of proximal segments with 50% or more stenosis were the CCTA parameters with the strongest predictive value for all-cause mortality at a median follow-up of 2.3 years.[8]

Evidence on the more long-term prognostic value of CCTA is beginning to accumulate. Hadamitzky and colleagues[9] followed up 1584 patients for a median of 5.6 years and described annual rates of major adverse cardiac events (MACE) of 0.2% for patients with no CAD and 1.1% in patients with obstructive CAD. In a 2014 study reporting on a median 6.9-year follow-up period in 218 patients, annual MACE rates were 0.3%, 2.7%, and 6.0% in patients with normal CCTA, nonobstructive CAD, and obstructive CAD, respectively.[10] Thus, the available data suggest that (1) the warranty period with an excellent prognosis after a CCTA study negative for any CAD extends beyond 5 years and (2) the presence of any CAD, obstructive CAD, and the burden of atherosclerotic changes at CCTA is strongly predictive for cardiac outcomes in patients with chronic chest pain.

Cost-Effectiveness

A decision analysis model comparing the cost-effectiveness of CCTA and single-photon emission computed tomography (SPECT) in patients with chest pain and no known CAD determined that CCTA is more cost-effective in this setting than SPECT for populations with an intermediate (30%–50%) prevalence of CAD.[11] A 2013 decision analysis performed on a prospective cohort of 471 outpatients with stable chest pain concluded that a CT-based diagnostic strategy is equally effective and less expensive than a stress-ECG–based strategy in all women and in men with low to intermediate (<70%) pretest probability.[12] A systematic review on this topic concluded that coronary CTA for the initial diagnostic evaluation of patients with stable chest pain has superior cost-effectiveness compared with alternative strategies in patients with a low to intermediate likelihood of CAD without adverse effects on clinical outcomes.[13]

Appropriate Use

Current Appropriate Use Criteria rate CCTA as an appropriate test for the initial evaluation of patients with stable symptoms and an intermediate CAD likelihood, especially in the setting of an uninterpretable ECG or inability to exercise.[14] In symptomatic patients with a high pretest probability of CAD, CCTA may be an appropriate initial test as an alternative to invasive coronary angiography and/or functional testing.[14] In patients with a low pretest probability of CAD, CCTA may be appropriate only in the setting of an uninterpretable ECG or inability to exercise.[14] Patients with prior testing with abnormal results represent a different clinical scenario. Here, CCTA is an appropriate imaging test to evaluate patients with abnormal or equivocal findings at stress imaging or exercise ECG and may be appropriate in evaluating patients with abnormal, potentially ischemic findings at rest ECG.[14] Several large prospective trials incorporating CCTA into the diagnostic algorithm for patients with stable angina are ongoing and will further refine the role of CCTA for clinical decision making in these patients.[15]

ACUTE CHEST PAIN SYNDROME
Effectiveness

The use of CCTA in the setting of acute chest pain has been investigated in 3 multicenter randomized trials, which consistently demonstrated that CCTA-based strategies for ruling out acute coronary syndrome allow for an expedited discharge of patients compared with standard-of-care algorithms.[16–18]

Safety

In 2 of the multicenter randomized trials, the safety end point for the use of CCTA in patients presenting to the emergency department (ED) for acute chest pain was the rate of MACE occurring within 28 to 30 days in patients with a CCTA demonstrating no significant CAD. No such events were recorded in both trials.[16,17] The CT-STAT (Coronary Computed Tomographic Angiography for Systematic Triage of Acute Chest Pain Patients to Treatment) trial performed 6-month follow-up and found MACE in 0.8% of patients with normal or near-normal CCTA. Thus, the available data suggest that a normal or near-normal CCTA safely excludes acute coronary syndrome in patients with acute chest pain.

Cost-Effectiveness

Cost-effectiveness analyses on the use of CCTA in acute chest pain have indicated that CTA-based strategies are more cost-effective than radionucleotide myocardial perfusion imaging–based strategies.[19] The CT-STAT trial demonstrated that a CCTA-based diagnostic strategy in patients with acute chest pain resulted in a substantially shorter time to diagnosis and thus significantly reduced the total cost of the ED visit.[18] However, the longer-term cost-effectiveness of CCTA in acute chest pain remains controversial. The ROMICAT-II (Rule Out Myocardial Infarction using Computer Assisted Tomography II) trial found that an evaluation of patients with acute chest pain with CCTA resulted in an increase in downstream testing with no decrease in the overall cost of care compared with standard evaluation.[17] In

contrast, Poon and colleagues[20] reported reduced downstream health care resource utilization with the routine use of CCTA in the ED evaluation of acute chest pain.

Appropriate Use

CCTA is considered an appropriate test in patients with acute chest pain, low to intermediate CAD risk, normal or nondiagnostic ECG, and negative or equivocal cardiac biomarkers.[21] In this setting, the role of CCTA allows for fast and safe triage of patients. A substantial percentage of patients demonstrate no evidence of CAD or minimal atherosclerotic changes and can be recommended for immediate discharge. Individuals demonstrating severe coronary stenosis are often directly referred to invasive catheter angiography, whereas patients with intermediate stenosis, high overall plaque burden, or equivocal findings typically undergo functional testing.

ASYMPTOMATIC INDIVIDUALS
Prevalence of Coronary Artery Disease

A high prevalence of advanced CAD has been found in specific high-risk subgroups of asymptomatic individuals such as patients with diabetes,[22,23] patients with extracardiac arterial disease,[24] patients after mediastinal irradiation for Hodgkin lymphoma,[25] and patients with a family history of early-onset ischemic heart disease.[26]

Prognostic Value

There are limited data on the utility of CCTA for risk stratification in asymptomatic individuals. The initial study in the field by Choi and colleagues[27] investigated 1000 asymptomatic subjects and found more adverse events during follow-up in patients with CAD detected by CCTA. However, the study design was flawed as CCTA results were not blinded and most events were early revascularizations triggered by CCTA results. Publications with a more robust study design have resulted from the CONFIRM registry. Based on the data of this multicenter registry, an incremental prognostic value of CCTA over calcium scoring has been described in the subgroup of 400 asymptomatic diabetic patients.[22] In contrast, in a more general population of 7590 asymptomatic patients, no clinically meaningful improvement of risk prediction was seen with CCTA compared with calcium scoring.[28]

Appropriate Use

Outside of prospective clinical trials, there is currently no established indication to perform

CCTA in asymptomatic individuals because of the lack of a clear benefit/risk advantage.[29] Accordingly, the most recent multisociety appropriate use guidelines rate CCTA as "rarely appropriate" in asymptomatic patients with low to intermediate risk for CAD.[14] In view of the most recent evidence, the guidelines suggest that CCTA "may be appropriate" in asymptomatic patients with a high risk for CAD (>20% 10-year CAD risk or CAD equivalent such as diabetes or peripheral artery disease). A clearly inappropriate use of CCTA is the nonselective screening of asymptomatic patients as part of health checkup examinations, a growing trend particularly in Asian countries.[27,30–33]

OTHER CLINICAL APPLICATIONS
Evaluation of Arrhythmias

CCTA is useful to exclude an ischemic cause in patients with arrhythmias and no known CAD. On the other hand, arrhythmias may also pose a challenge to CCTA acquisition. In patients with arrhythmias during image acquisition, CCTA typically requires high radiation doses and may nevertheless be nondiagnostic in a substantial percentage of patients. According to the most recent appropriateness criteria, CCTA "may be appropriate" as an alternative to invasive coronary angiography and/or functional testing in patients with ventricular tachycardia, ventricular fibrillation, or frequent premature ventricular contractions.[14]

New-onset atrial fibrillation in patients without previous heart disease is a frequent clinical scenario, and ischemic cause is always a consideration. A meta-analysis published in 2013 found high diagnostic accuracy and high radiation dose for CCTA in patients with atrial fibrillation.[34] However, the results of this meta-analysis may be biased by the exclusion of nondiagnostic studies in some of the included studies and thus overestimate the performance of CCTA in clinical routine whereby nondiagnostic examinations are frequent in the setting of atrial fibrillation.[35] Thus, CCTA is currently considered "rarely appropriate" in the diagnostic evaluation of patients with new-onset atrial fibrillation.[14]

Surveillance of Heart Transplant Recipients for Allograft Vasculopathy

Following heart transplant, annual cardiac catheterizations are indicated to detect cardiac allograft vasculopathy, although the surveillance intervals may be increased in patients with normal findings.[36] A 2014 meta-analysis reported that CCTA has high sensitivity and negative predictive value for excluding allograft vasculopathy in this patient population.[37] Thus, CCTA may be a reasonable alternative to catheterization in the surveillance of stable heart transplant patients.[36]

Previous Coronary Revascularization

The evaluation of patients with previous coronary stents or bypass grafts remains a limitation for CCTA. Owing to blooming artifacts from the metal strut, the assessment of the in-stent lumen is typically only possible with larger stent sizes (>3 mm). For bypass grafts, CCTA has excellent accuracy in assessing the patency of grafts but the assessment of the distal anastomosis and the downstream native vessels is frequently challenging because of small vessel diameters and extensive calcifications.[38] CCTA is therefore rarely appropriate in asymptomatic patients after bypass grafting or coronary stent placement with the possible exception of prior left main coronary stent.[14] CCTA may be an option in the evaluation of symptomatic patients with prior revascularization, although invasive coronary angiography and/or functional tests are typically more appropriate in this setting.[14] A specific scenario is the preoperative evaluation of patients with bypass grafts who are scheduled for redo sternotomy. CCTA is useful to depict the exact anatomic relationship between sternum and bypass grafts in these patients.[39]

Newly Diagnosed Heart Failure

In patients with newly diagnosed heart failure, in particular those with systolic heart failure and no prior diagnosis of CAD, CCTA is an appropriate option to rule out ischemic heart disease.[14]

Evaluation of Syncope

Syncope is common but rare as an initial presentation of CAD. Thus, CCTA does not currently have an established role in the routine evaluation of patients presenting with syncope. However, it may be appropriate in patients with an intermediate to high global CAD risk.[14]

Pediatric Coronary Computed Tomographic Angiography for Known or Suspected Cardiovascular Anomalies

Clinical indications for CCTA in pediatric patients with known or suspected cardiovascular pathologies include the evaluation of coronary artery anomalies and pathologies, as well as the evaluation of the aortic root and intracardiac anatomy. Dose-reduction techniques are of particular importance because of children's greater susceptibility to radiation.[40,41] The stringent application of all available dose-reduction strategies and CTA protocols tailored to the individual body size allow performing pediatric CCTA with age-specific radiation doses on the order of 1 mSv.[42] Pediatric CCTA requires substantial expertise and should be performed by a dedicated team in specialized centers.

RISKS AND BENEFITS
Risks from Contrast Material Administration

For CCTA examinations, typically 50 to 100 mL of iodinated contrast material is administered intravenously with a small risk of hypersensitivity reactions. The frequencies of mild and severe general acute reactions have been estimated as 0.4% and 0.04%, respectively.[43] The acute mortality risk from hypersensitivity reactions to contrast material is exceedingly low (on the order of 6 in 1,000,000).[43] In addition, there is a small risk of delayed reactions to contrast material.[44] Traditionally, the most feared risk of intravenous contrast material administration was contrast-induced kidney injury. The results of more recent controlled studies have been partly conflicting but overall suggest that there is no risk for acute kidney injury from intravenously administered contrast material in patients with normal renal function, whereas there may be a risk in patients with preexisting renal impairment. However, even in this patient population, the risk, if any, is probably smaller than traditionally assumed.[45]

Radiation Risks

The radiation dose associated with CCTA varies widely with the acquisition technique used. Typical estimates of average dose are 12 mSv for retrospectively ECG-gated spiral acquisition and 3.5 mSv for a prospectively ECG-triggered sequential acquisition mode.[1,2] In suitable patients, that is, normal weight individuals with slow and regular rhythm, novel acquisition techniques such as high-pitch, dual-source acquisition allow to perform CCTA with less than 1.5 mSv.[46] Risk estimates for developing fatal cancer from diagnostic imaging examinations are fraught with considerable uncertainty.[47] Assuming a linear no-threshold relationship of radiation dose and risk, the average excess lifetime risk of fatal cancer has been estimated to be on the order of 1 in 2000 for an effective dose of 10 mSv. The risk estimate for an individual patient greatly depends on age, gender, and life expectancy, with a higher risk for women and younger and healthier patients and a lower risk for men, the elderly, and patients with life-limiting morbidities.[47]

WHAT THE REFERRING PHYSICIAN NEEDS TO KNOW

If a patient is referred to CCTA for suspected CAD, foremost the clinician needs to know if significant CAD that might explain the patient's complaints is present (Box 1). Stenosis severity, location, and extent of possible myocardium at risk have important clinical implications and determine whether further testing or mechanical intervention is required. When reporting the degree of coronary artery stenosis, it is recommended to add a quantitative range estimate and thus characterize the degree of diameter stenosis, if present, as minimal (<25% stenosis), mild (25%–49%), moderate (50%–69%), or severe (70%–99%).[48] Although less than 25% stenosis is typically regarded as nonobstructive and greater than 70% stenosis as obstructive, lesions in the mild to moderate range may require further testing to determine the extent of coronary flow limitation if the clinical presentation suggests a cardiac cause for the patient's complaints.

Although the focus of any CCTA is directed at the presence and severity of coronary atherosclerosis, other structural and functional findings may have relevance and need to be conveyed to the referring physician, including features such as wall motion, systolic function, and myocardial wall morphology (focal thinning).[49,50] These findings can function to augment the angiographic

---

Box 1
What the referring physician needs to know

Coronary artery disease

Presence and distribution of plaque (calcified, noncalcified, or mixed)

Stenosis severity, location, and extent of possible myocardium at risk

Other findings

Anatomic abnormalities and variants

Wall motion, systolic function (if functional data obtained)

Myocardial wall morphology

Size of cardiac chambers (and volumes, if functional data obtained)

Pericardial disease (effusion, calcification)

Intracardiac thrombus or masses

Valvular pathology

Significant extracardiac findings

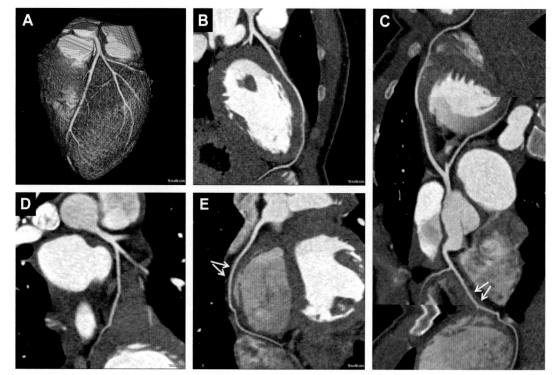

Fig. 1. Coronary CT angiography in a 42-year-old man with recurrent chest pain. Volume-rendered image (*A*) as well as multiplanar curved reformats of the left anterior descending artery (*B*), the left circumflex artery (*D*), the right coronary artery (*E*), and the coronary tree (*C*) demonstrate no evidence of coronary artery disease. There is a short intramyocardial segment of the right coronary artery (myocardial bridging, *arrows* in *C* and *E*).

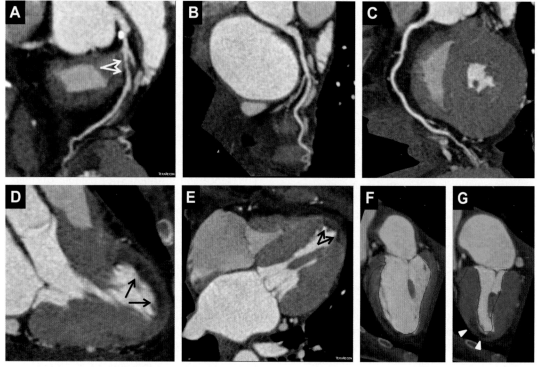

Fig. 2. Coronary CT angiography in a 49-year-old woman with acute chest pain. The multiplanar curved reformatted view of the left anterior descending artery (*A*) demonstrates critical stenosis of the proximal segment due to noncalcified plaque (*white arrows*). The left circumflex artery (*B*) and the right coronary artery (*C*) demonstrate luminal irregularities without significant stenosis. Long-axis (*D*) and four-chamber views (*E*) demonstrate subendocardial hypodensity of the anterior and apical myocardium (*black arrows*) consistent with acute infarction. On functional analysis (*F, G*), regional hypokinesis of the apical myocardium (*white arrowheads*) is noted. End-diastolic (*F*) and end-systolic (*G*) images are shown.

information and assist in clinical decision making. For example, an intermediate stenosis would be more likely to be considered clinically relevant if associated with a hypokinetic and thinned myocardial segment. Other structural heart features, such as pericardial disease (effusion, calcification), intracardiac thrombus or masses, and any valvular pathology, as well as significant extracardiac findings, need to be clearly conveyed to the referring physician.

FUTURE DIRECTIONS

CCTA offers the unique potential to noninvasively visualize, characterize, and quantify atherosclerotic plaque.[51] The notion of vulnerable plaques is still a vague concept and will likely be refined with the identification of new adverse plaque features. The identification of such high-risk plaques may thus improve risk estimates for the individual patient and may be of use in the selection of patients who benefit from revascularization. Several adverse features associated with vulnerable plaques have already been identified and include the presence of positive remodeling, low-attenuation plaque, spotty calcifications, and the napkin ring sign.[52–55] CCTA can further quantify the global burden of atherosclerotic plaque, which may evolve as a biomarker for risk prediction or therapy response monitoring.[56]

Overall, the assessment of a stenotic coronary lesion at CCTA will likely move away from the unidimensional method of assessing the degree of luminal diameter narrowing. Markers such as the local aggregate plaque volume and the morphologic index (lesion length divided by the fourth power of the minimal luminal diameter ratio) have been shown to correlate more strongly with the hemodynamic significance of a lesion.[57,58] Using complex computational fluid dynamics, fractional flow reserve can be calculated from anatomic CTA data sets. This approach for assessing the hemodynamic significance of coronary lesions has been assessed in large multicenter trials with promising results.[59,60]

Stress CT myocardial perfusion imaging has been developed as a strategy to directly visualize the hemodynamic consequences of CAD.[61] As an add-on to CCTA, CT myocardial perfusion imaging offers a comprehensive assessment of anatomically defined

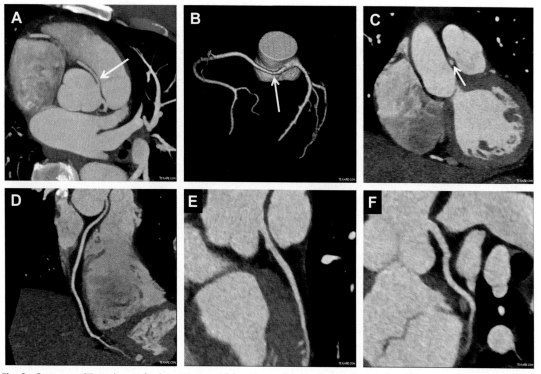

Fig. 3. Coronary CT angiography in a 73–year-old patient with recurrent chest pain. Thin maximum-intensity projection (*A*) and volume-rendered (*B*) images demonstrate anomalous origin of the right coronary artery (*arrow*) from the left sinus of Valsalva. The coronal oblique view (*C*) demonstrates the elliptical cross-sectional shape of the right coronary artery (*arrow*) as it courses between the ascending aorta and the right ventricular outflow tract. There is no evidence of coronary atherosclerosis on curved multiplanar reformats of the right coronary artery (*D*), left anterior descending coronary artery (*E*), and left circumflex coronary artery (*F*).

CAD and myocardial perfusion in a single modality. The results of the first multicenter study on CT myocardial perfusion imaging have been reported,[62] and multicenter registry data have become available.[63] Nevertheless, CT myocardial perfusion imaging is still in an early phase of development with only preliminary data on its diagnostic accuracy and clinical utility available.

SUMMARY

In state-of-the art clinical practice, CCTA is a valuable tool to guide patient management by noninvasive assessment of CAD and other cardiac pathologies (**Figs. 1–3**). A spectrum of appropriate indications for CCTA has been identified beyond stable and acute chest pain as the most common indications. Several novel techniques that may extend the ability of CCTA to characterize and quantify coronary artery plaque and assess the hemodynamic significance of stenosis are being investigated.

REFERENCES

1. De Cecco CN, Meinel FG, Chiaramida SA, et al. Coronary artery computed tomography scanning. Circulation 2014;129(12):1341–5.
2. Menke J, Unterberg-Buchwald C, Staab W, et al. Head-to-head comparison of prospectively triggered vs retrospectively gated coronary computed tomography angiography: meta-analysis of diagnostic accuracy, image quality, and radiation dose. Am Heart J 2013;165(2):154–63.e3.
3. von Ballmoos MW, Haring B, Juillerat P, et al. Meta-analysis: diagnostic performance of low-radiation-dose coronary computed tomography angiography. Ann Intern Med 2011;154(6):413–20.
4. Li S, Ni Q, Wu H, et al. Diagnostic accuracy of 320-slice computed tomography angiography for detection of coronary artery stenosis: meta-analysis. Int J Cardiol 2013;168(3):2699–705.
5. Salavati A, Radmanesh F, Heidari K, et al. Dual-source computed tomography angiography for diagnosis and assessment of coronary artery disease: systematic review and meta-analysis. J Cardiovasc Comput Tomogr 2012;6(2):78–90.
6. Li M, Zhang GM, Zhao JS, et al. Diagnostic performance of dual-source CT coronary angiography with and without heart rate control: systematic review and meta-analysis. Clin Radiol 2014;69(2):163–71.
7. Bamberg F, Sommer WH, Hoffmann V, et al. Meta-analysis and systematic review of the long-term predictive value of assessment of coronary atherosclerosis by contrast-enhanced coronary computed tomography angiography. J Am Coll Cardiol 2011;57(24):2426–36.
8. Hadamitzky M, Achenbach S, Al-Mallah M, et al. Optimized prognostic score for coronary computed tomographic angiography: results from the CONFIRM registry (COronary CT Angiography EvaluatioN For Clinical Outcomes: An InteRnational Multicenter Registry). J Am Coll Cardiol 2013;62(5):468–76.
9. Hadamitzky M, Taubert S, Deseive S, et al. Prognostic value of coronary computed tomography angiography during 5 years of follow-up in patients with suspected coronary artery disease. Eur Heart J 2013;34(42):3277–85.
10. Dougoud S, Fuchs TA, Stehli J, et al. Prognostic value of coronary CT angiography on long-term follow-up of 6.9 years. Int J Cardiovasc Imaging 2014;30(5):969–76.
11. Min JK, Gilmore A, Budoff MJ, et al. Cost-effectiveness of coronary CT angiography versus myocardial perfusion SPECT for evaluation of patients with chest pain and no known coronary artery disease. Radiology 2010;254(3):801–8.
12. Genders TS, Ferket BS, Dedic A, et al. Coronary computed tomography versus exercise testing in patients with stable chest pain: comparative effectiveness and costs. Int J Cardiol 2013;167(4):1268–75.
13. Nance JW Jr, Bamberg F, Schoepf UJ. Coronary computed tomography angiography in patients with chronic chest pain: systematic review of evidence base and cost-effectiveness. J Thorac Imaging 2012;27(5):277–88.
14. Wolk MJ, Bailey SR, Doherty JU, et al. ACCF/AHA/ASE/ASNC/HFSA/HRS/SCAI/SCCT/SCMR/STS 2013 multimodality appropriate use criteria for the detection and risk assessment of stable ischemic heart disease: a report of the American College of Cardiology Foundation Appropriate Use Criteria Task Force, American Heart Association, American Society of Echocardiography, American Society of Nuclear Cardiology, Heart Failure Society of America, Heart Rhythm Society, Society for Cardiovascular Angiography and Interventions, Society of Cardiovascular Computed Tomography, Society for Cardiovascular Magnetic Resonance, and Society of Thoracic Surgeons. J Am Coll Cardiol 2014;63(4):380–406.
15. Prospective Multicenter Imaging Study for Evaluation of Chest Pain (PROMISE). Identifier NCT01174550; International Study of Comparative Health Effectiveness with Medical and Invasive Approaches (ISCHEMIA), Identifier NCT01471522; Randomized Evaluation of Patients with Stable Angina Comparing Diagnostic Examination (RESCUE), Identifier NCT01262625. Available at: http://www.clinicaltrials.gov. Accessed June 17, 2013.
16. Litt HI, Gatsonis C, Snyder B, et al. CT angiography for safe discharge of patients with possible acute coronary syndromes. N Engl J Med 2012;366(15):1393–403.

17. Hoffmann U, Truong QA, Schoenfeld DA, et al. Coronary CT angiography versus standard evaluation in acute chest pain. N Engl J Med 2012;367(4):299–308.

18. Goldstein JA, Chinnaiyan KM, Abidov A, et al. The CT-STAT (Coronary Computed Tomographic Angiography for Systematic Triage of Acute Chest Pain Patients to Treatment) trial. J Am Coll Cardiol 2011; 58(14):1414–22.

19. Bamberg F, Marcus RP, Schlett CL, et al. Imaging evaluation of acute chest pain: systematic review of evidence base and cost-effectiveness. J Thorac Imaging 2012;27(5):289–95.

20. Poon M, Cortegiano M, Abramowicz AJ, et al. Associations between routine coronary computed tomographic angiography and reduced unnecessary hospital admissions, length of stay, recidivism rates, and invasive coronary angiography in the emergency department triage of chest pain. J Am Coll Cardiol 2013;62(6):543–52.

21. Taylor AJ, Cerqueira M, Hodgson JM, et al. ACCF/SCCT/ACR/AHA/ASE/ASNC/NASCI/SCAI/SCMR 2010 appropriate use criteria for cardiac computed tomography. Circulation 2010;122(21):e525–55.

22. Min JK, Labounty TM, Gomez MJ, et al. Incremental prognostic value of coronary computed tomographic angiography over coronary artery calcium score for risk prediction of major adverse cardiac events in asymptomatic diabetic individuals. Atherosclerosis 2014;232(2):298–304.

23. Kamimura M, Moroi M, Isobe M, et al. Role of coronary CT angiography in asymptomatic patients with type 2 diabetes mellitus. Int Heart J 2012;53(1):23–8.

24. den Dekker MA, van den Dungen JJ, Tielliu IF, et al. Prevalence of severe subclinical coronary artery disease on cardiac CT and MRI in patients with extracardiac arterial disease. Eur J Vasc Endovasc Surg 2013;46(6):680–9.

25. Daniels LA, Krol AD, de Graaf MA, et al. Screening for coronary artery disease after mediastinal irradiation in Hodgkin lymphoma survivors: phase II study of indication and acceptance. Ann Oncol 2014; 25(6):1198–203.

26. Kral BG, Becker LC, Vaidya D, et al. Noncalcified coronary plaque volumes in healthy people with a family history of early-onset coronary artery disease. Circ Cardiovasc Imaging 2014;7(3):446–53.

27. Choi EK, Choi SI, Rivera JJ, et al. Coronary computed tomography angiography as a screening tool for the detection of occult coronary artery disease in asymptomatic individuals. J Am Coll Cardiol 2008;52(5):357–65.

28. Cho I, Chang HJ, Sung JM, et al. Coronary computed tomographic angiography and risk of all-cause mortality and nonfatal myocardial infarction in subjects without chest pain syndrome from the CONFIRM registry (coronary CT angiography evaluation for clinical outcomes: an international multicenter registry). Circulation 2012;126(3):304–13.

29. Earls JP, Woodard PK, Abbara S, et al. ACR appropriateness criteria asymptomatic patient at risk for coronary artery disease. J Am Coll Radiol 2014; 11(1):12–9.

30. Yang DH, Kang JW, Kim HK, et al. Association between C-reactive protein and type of coronary arterial plaque in asymptomatic patients: assessment with coronary CT angiography. Radiology 2014;272(3):665–73. http://dx.doi.org/10.1148/radiol.14130772.

31. Jin KN, Chun EJ, Lee CH, et al. Subclinical coronary atherosclerosis in young adults: prevalence, characteristics, predictors with coronary computed tomography angiography. Int J Cardiovasc Imaging 2012; 28(Suppl 2):93–100.

32. Lee BC, Lee WJ, Hsu HC, et al. Using clinical cardiovascular risk scores to predict coronary artery plaque severity and stenosis detected by CT coronary angiography in asymptomatic Chinese subjects. Int J Cardiovasc Imaging 2011;27(5):669–78.

33. Ha EJ, Kim Y, Cheung JY, et al. Coronary artery disease in asymptomatic young adults: its prevalence according to coronary artery disease risk stratification and the CT characteristics. Korean J Radiol 2010;11(4):425–32.

34. Vorre MM, Abdulla J. Diagnostic accuracy and radiation dose of CT coronary angiography in atrial fibrillation: systematic review and meta-analysis. Radiology 2013;267(2):376–86.

35. Schuetz GM, Schlattmann P, Dewey M. Coronary CT angiography cannot be recommended in patients with atrial fibrillation. Radiology 2013;269(3): 947–8.

36. Kobashigawa J. Coronary computed tomography angiography: Is it time to replace the conventional coronary angiogram in heart transplant patients? J Am Coll Cardiol 2014;63(19):2005–6.

37. Wever-Pinzon O, Romero J, Kelesidis I, et al. Coronary computed tomography angiography for the detection of cardiac allograft vasculopathy: a meta-analysis of prospective trials. J Am Coll Cardiol 2014;63(19):1992–2004.

38. Bischoff B, Hausleiter J. Rational CT imaging in cardiology. Internist (Berl) 2013;54(7):810–7 [in German].

39. Gasparovic H, Rybicki FJ, Millstine J, et al. Three dimensional computed tomographic imaging in planning the surgical approach for redo cardiac surgery after coronary revascularization. Eur J Cardiothorac Surg 2005;28(2):244–9.

40. Miglioretti DL, Johnson E, Williams A, et al. The use of computed tomography in pediatrics and the associated radiation exposure and estimated cancer risk. JAMA Pediatr 2013;167(8):700–7.

41. Mathews JD, Forsythe AV, Brady Z, et al. Cancer risk in 680 000 people exposed to computed tomography

scans in childhood or adolescence: data linkage study of 11 million Australians. BMJ 2013;346:f2360.

42. Meinel FG, Henzler T, Schoepf UJ, et al. ECG-synchronized CT angiography in 324 consecutive pediatric patients: Spectrum of indications and trends in radiation dose. Pediatr Cardiol 2014. [Epub ahead of print].

43. Knuuti J, Bengel F, Bax JJ, et al. Risks and benefits of cardiac imaging: an analysis of risks related to imaging for coronary artery disease. Eur Heart J 2014; 35(10):633–8.

44. Egbert RE, De Cecco CN, Schoepf UJ, et al. Delayed adverse reactions to the parenteral administration of iodinated contrast media. AJR Am J Roentgenol 2014;203(6):1163–70.

45. Meinel FG, De Cecco CN, Schoepf UJ, et al. Contrast-induced acute kidney injury: definition, epidemiology, and outcome. Biomed Res Int 2014; 2014:859328.

46. Yin WH, Lu B, Hou ZH, et al. Detection of coronary artery stenosis with sub-milliSievert radiation dose by prospectively ECG-triggered high-pitch spiral CT angiography and iterative reconstruction. Eur Radiol 2013;23(11):2927–33.

47. Meinel FG, Nance JW Jr, Harris BS, et al. Radiation risks from cardiovascular imaging tests. Circulation 2014;130(5):442–5.

48. Raff GL, Abidov A, Achenbach S, et al. SCCT guidelines for the interpretation and reporting of coronary computed tomographic angiography. J Cardiovasc Comput Tomogr 2009;3(2):122–36.

49. Sharma A, Einstein AJ, Vallakati A, et al. Meta-analysis of global left ventricular function comparing multidetector computed tomography with cardiac magnetic resonance imaging. Am J Cardiol 2014; 113(4):731–8.

50. Sheth T, Amlani S, Ellins ML, et al. Computed tomographic coronary angiographic assessment of high-risk coronary anatomy in patients with suspected coronary artery disease and intermediate pretest probability. Am Heart J 2008;155(5):918–23.

51. Nance JW Jr, Bamberg F, Schoepf UJ, et al. Coronary atherosclerosis in African American and white patients with acute chest pain: characterization with coronary CT angiography. Radiology 2011; 260(2):373–80.

52. Motoyama S, Kondo T, Sarai M, et al. Multislice computed tomographic characteristics of coronary lesions in acute coronary syndromes. J Am Coll Cardiol 2007;50(4):319–26.

53. Maurovich-Horvat P, Schlett CL, Alkadhi H, et al. The napkin-ring sign indicates advanced atherosclerotic lesions in coronary CT angiography. JACC Cardiovasc Imaging 2012;5(12):1243–52.

54. Otsuka K, Fukuda S, Tanaka A, et al. Napkin-ring sign on coronary CT angiography for the prediction of acute coronary syndrome. JACC Cardiovasc Imaging 2013;6(4):448–57.

55. Motoyama S, Sarai M, Harigaya H, et al. Computed tomographic angiography characteristics of atherosclerotic plaques subsequently resulting in acute coronary syndrome. J Am Coll Cardiol 2009;54(1):49–57.

56. Versteylen MO, Kietselaer BL, Dagnelie PC, et al. Additive value of semiautomated quantification of coronary artery disease using cardiac computed tomographic angiography to predict future acute coronary syndrome. J Am Coll Cardiol 2013; 61(22):2296–305.

57. Nakazato R, Shalev A, Doh JH, et al. Aggregate plaque volume by coronary computed tomography angiography is superior and incremental to luminal narrowing for diagnosis of ischemic lesions of intermediate stenosis severity. J Am Coll Cardiol 2013; 62(5):460–7.

58. Li M, Zhang J, Pan J, et al. Coronary stenosis: morphologic index characterized by using CT angiography correlates with fractional flow reserve and is associated with hemodynamic status. Radiology 2013;269(3):713–21.

59. Min JK, Leipsic J, Pencina MJ, et al. Diagnostic accuracy of fractional flow reserve from anatomic CT angiography. JAMA 2012;308(12):1237–45.

60. Nakazato R, Park HB, Berman DS, et al. Noninvasive fractional flow reserve derived from computed tomography angiography for coronary lesions of intermediate stenosis severity: results from the DeFACTO study. Circ Cardiovasc Imaging 2013;6(6):881–9.

61. Rossi A, Merkus D, Klotz E, et al. Stress myocardial perfusion: imaging with multidetector CT. Radiology 2014;270(1):25–46.

62. Rochitte CE, George RT, Chen MY, et al. Computed tomography angiography and perfusion to assess coronary artery stenosis causing perfusion defects by single photon emission computed tomography: the CORE320 study. Eur Heart J 2014;35(17):1120–30.

63. Meinel FG, Ebersberger U, Schoepf UJ, et al. Global quantification of left ventricular myocardial perfusion at dynamic CT: feasibility in a multicenter patient population. AJR Am J Roentgenol 2014;203(2): W174–80.

Cardiac Computed Tomography for the Evaluation of the Acute Chest Pain Syndrome: State of the Art

Christopher L. Schlett, MD, MPH[a,b],
Udo Hoffmann, MD, MPH[b], Tobias Geisler, MD[c],
Konstantin Nikolaou, MD[d], Fabian Bamberg, MD, MPH[b,d],*

KEYWORDS

- Acute chest pain syndrome • Acute coronary syndrome • Cardiac computed tomography • CCTA

KEY POINTS

- Coronary computed tomography angiography (CCTA) is considered appropriate for the triage of acute chest pain in patients with a low-to-intermediate likelihood for acute coronary syndrome.
- Absence of any coronary artery disease (CAD) confirmed by CCTA allows rapid emergency department discharge.
- This article reviews the current scientific evidence and controversies on CCTA-based triage as a modality that is as safe as traditional triage, reduces the hospital length of stay, and may provide cost-effective or even cost-saving care.

PATHOPHYSIOLOGY AND CLINICAL PRESENTATION OF ACUTE CORONARY SYNDROME

The acute coronary syndrome (ACS) is mainly caused by underlying coronary atherosclerosis. Other, but extremely rarer pathophysiologic mechanisms are microvascular dysfunction or coronary vasospasm.[1] Today coronary atherosclerosis is known as a chronic inflammatory process within the tunica intima, forming a vessel wall thickening, which is called plaque if it reaches specific morphologic characteristics.

High-Risk Plaques and Significant Stenosis

There are two main concepts of how coronary, arteriosclerotic plaque can lead to ACS. In the first concept, ACS occurs after development of a superficial thrombus and subsequent obstruction of blood flow to downstream coronary segments. The formation of a thrombus is typically due to

Financial Disclosures and Conflicts of Interest: Dr F. Bamberg received unrestricted research grants from Bayer Healthcare and Siemens Healthcare. He serves on the speakers' bureau of Bayer Healthcare and Siemens Healthcare. Dr K. Nikolaou has served on a scientific advisory board for Bayer Schering Pharma and on speakers' bureaus for and has received speaker honoraria from Bayer Schering Pharma, Bracco, and Siemens Medical Solutions.
The authors have nothing to disclose.
[a] Department of Diagnostic and Interventional Radiology, University Hospital Heidelberg, Im Neuenheimer Feld 110, Heidelberg 69120, Germany; [b] Cardiac MR PET CT Program, Massachusetts General Hospital, Harvard Medical School, 165 Cambridge St, Suite 400, Boston, MA 02114, USA; [c] Department of Cardiology and Cardiovascular Medicine University Hospital of Tübingen, Hoppe-Seyler-Straße 3, Tübingen 72076, Germany; [d] Department of Diagnostic and Interventional Radiology, University Hospital of Tübingen, Hoppe-Seyler-Straße 3, Tübingen 72076, Germany
* Corresponding author. Department of Diagnostic and Interventional Radiology, University Hospital Tübingen, Hoppe-Seyler-Straße 3, Tübingen 72076, Germany.
E-mail address: fabian.bamberg@med.uni-tuebingen.de

0033-8389/15/$ – see front matter © 2015 Elsevier Inc. All rights reserved.

radiologic.theclinics.com

rupture ($\sim$60%) or erosion ($\sim$40%) of an underlying atherosclerotic plaque.[2,3] Particular morphologically features have been observed at the site of plaque rupture or erosion, including a large lipid/necrotic core, a thin fibrous cap, and small calcified embedded nodules. These form the concept of vulnerable plaque, which are at high risk for developing ACS (also called "high-risk plaque").[2] Also, a high inflammatory activity is discussed as a vulnerability factor following the observed increased density of macrophages in ruptured plaques.[2] Although factors such a large necrotic core favor that high-risk plaques are located in areas of high plaque burden, it is not necessarily associated with severe luminal stenosis. In approximately 5% to 20% of all ACS events, no significant stenosis is captured by standard invasive angiogram corresponding to the event location.[2,4]

The second concept is based on increasing luminal narrowing to due atherosclerotic plaque progression, in which a significant stenosis causes an imbalance between downstream blood-flow or oxygen supply and oxygen myocardial demand. Depending on the literature, a significant (possible flow-limiting) stenosis is considered equal to or greater than 50% luminal (diameter) narrowing and severe (probable flow-limiting) stenosis to be equal to or greater than 70% luminal (diameter) narrowing.[5] However, it is known from invasive fractional flow reserve measurements in combination with outcome trials that the decreased oxygen supply (and the survival of the patient) is not only influenced by the stenotic degree of a lesion.[6] These pathophysiologic concepts for developing ACS are not exclusively and often clinically not discriminable.

Unstable Angina Pectoris, Non–ST-Elevation Myocardial Infarction, and ST-Elevation Myocardial Infarction

Acute onset of chest pain with a burning sensation, pressure, or tightness is the typical symptom of ACS. However, chest pain can have other differential diagnoses, such as gastroesophageal reflux disease or musculoskeletal problems. On the other hand, many symptoms, including dyspnea or diaphoresis, may be clinical manifestations of ACS that complicate the diagnosis based on just clinical presentation. Furthermore, ACS consists of 3 subdiagnoses: ST-elevation myocardial infarction (STEMI), non-STEMI (NSTEMI), and unstable angina pectoris (UAP).[7,8] Whereas STEMI and NSTEMI are defined by the presence of myocardial necrosis (manifested by troponin elevation), UAP is defined as chest pain due to ischemia without the presence of myocardial necrosis.[8,9]

Traditional Triage of Patients with Acute Chest Pain

The traditional diagnostic workup of patients with acute chest pain for presence of ACS includes patient's history, physical examination, 12-lead electrocardiogram (ECG), and initial measurement of cardiac biomarkers.[8] Patients with high likelihood for ACS can be directly referred for further invasive diagnosis and treatment. Extreme low-risk patients can be readily discharged for outpatient follow-up. Patients with low-to-moderate likelihood for ACS after the initial evaluation remain for further observation and examination, including serial cardiac biomarker and ECG testing over the next 24 hours. These are frequently followed by a stress test for risk stratification, if subsequent ECG and biomarkers tests are inconclusive.

However, this traditional work-up of patients with acute chest pain, particularly in the triage in the emergency department (ED) has encountered several issues. Each year, more than 7 million patients are admitted to the ED in the United States with acute chest pain as their chief complaint, making it one of the most frequent causes of ED visits.[10] However, only 2% to 8% are diagnosed with ACS, most have chest pain of noncardiac origin.[11] Furthermore, a single troponin measurement is not sufficient to safely rule-out ACS because plasma troponin values have a delay function between the coronary event and the observed elevation at which serial cardiac biomarker measurements are recommended. With the introduction of high-sensitivity troponin (hsTn) measurements, this issue has been partially overcome, but a significant decrease in specificity was observed because hsTn is also associated with structural heart disease.[12] These issues lead to increased test burden and prolonged stay in the ED or chest pain unit. Despite that, about 2% to 3% of all patients suffering from ACS within 72 hours of ED presentation are erroneously discharged, contributing to missed ACS as the number-one cause for ED malpractice costs in the United States.[13,14] Accordingly, a great need for novel and improved triage strategies exists and coronary computed tomography angiography (CCTA) has been suggested as a safe, fast, and cost-effective modality to overcome these challenges.

EVIDENCE FOR USING COMPUTED TOMOGRAPHY ANGIOGRAPHY FOR THE EVALUATION FOR ACUTE CORONARY SYNDROME

Recently, several observational and interventional trials have been conducted to prove the accuracy, efficacy, and effectiveness of CCTA in the triage of patients with acute chest pain.

Diagnostic Accuracy of Computed Tomography Angiography for the Evaluation for Acute Coronary Syndrome

The diagnostic accuracy of CCTA for the presence of coronary arteriosclerosis, and for the clinical diagnosis of ACS, has been investigated in several studies that included more than 3000 patients presenting with acute chest pain to the ED. With current scanner technology, the temporal and spatial resolutions reach a sufficient level to reliably evaluate coronary arteriosclerosis, although assessment of noncalcified plaque remains most challenging. The probability in detecting any coronary arteriosclerosis by CCTA reached equal to or greater than 90% if the plaque's maximal intimal thickness was greater than 1 mm, as determined by intravascular ultrasound.[15] A good diagnostic accuracy for detecting significant stenosis was determined with a mean sensitivity of 99% and specificity of 89% in a meta-analysis that included 18 studies that compared 64-slice CCTA with invasive angiography.[16]

The hemodynamic relevance and, thus, the occurrence of ACS may not necessarily be directly linked to the stenotic degree of a coronary lesion (see previous discussion). Therefore, several major trails (eg, Rule Out Myocardial Infarction using Computer Assisted Tomography [ROMICAT I]) have been performed to assess the diagnostic accuracy of CCTA for presence of ACS in patients with acute chest pain presenting to the ED and with an initial inconclusive evaluation.[17–19] In summary, all trials demonstrated that absence of any coronary atherosclerosis by CCTA, which was observed in roughly half of the population, has an excellent negative predictive value (NPV) for presence of ACS. In contrast, presence of significant stenosis by CCTA was observed in about one-fifth of the population and showed only moderate diagnostic for ACS (ROMICAT I: significant stenosis (>50% luminal narrowing) leading to 77% sensitivity and 87% specificity for ACS).[18] In combination with the low prevalence of ACS in the acute chest pain population in the ED (2%–8%),[11] CCTA reveals a low positive predictive value (PPV) for ACS (~35–50%).

To improve the PPV of CCTA for ACS, different strategies have been followed:

1. Assessment of plaque morphology. Following the high-risk plaque concept (see previous discussion), CCTA has the potential to visualize some of the vulnerability factors. Low-attenuation plaque correlates with a high lipid-rich content in the plaque and the napkin-ring sign, a morphologic plaque pattern, is highly specific for fibroatheroma with a large necrotic core.[20,21] To diagnose ACS, a plaque morphology based score was developed, which resulted in a PPV of 100% for ACS in subjects with stenotic lesions.[22] However, the assessment of plaque morphology is not routinely performed in clinical practice and further data are needed to support these findings.

2. Assessment of left ventricular (LV) function. It has been demonstrated that the presence of regional LV dysfunction incrementally improves the diagnostic accuracy for ACS beyond assessment of the coronary arteries regarding stenosis.[23] However, the assessment of LV function comes with the expense of radiation and excludes the application of some novel computed tomography (CT) acquisition protocols.

3. Assessment of myocardial perfusion. Functional testing including rest and stress myocardial perfusion is possible using CT, but stress testing is not recommended in the acute setting considering the potential adverse effects of stressing a patient with NSTEMI. Similar to the nuclear literature,[24] an incremental value of assessing rest myocardial perfusion by CT was observed, particularly in improving PPV.[25,26]

In summary, the absence of coronary atherosclerosis as determined by CCTA is observed in 50% of acute chest pain population presented in the ED and, for ACS, provides a NPV of close to 100%. In contrast, significant stenosis has moderate diagnostic accuracy for ACS, although it remains superior to clinical risk scores such as Thrombolysis in Myocardial Infarction (TIMI) or Goldmann.[27] The low PPV can be improved by assessing either plaque morphology, LV function, or myocardial perfusion; however, such strategies warrant further investigation before applied clinically. Based on the current evidence, CCTA has a Class IIa, Level of Evidence B recommendation for the evaluation of patients with acute chest pain with a low-intermediate pretest probability of ACS and inconclusive initial ECG and biomarkers.[28,29]

Effectiveness of Coronary Computed Tomography Angiography in Patients with Acute Chest Pain in the Emergency Department

Based on the known clinical limitations, the following are considered major effectiveness criteria in patients presenting with acute chest pain to the ED: (1) safety and (2) length of hospital stay. Based on the hypothesis that cardiac CT allows for a more rapid discharge while maintaining similar safety (with no missed ACS cases), large clinical trials have recently been conducted.

The largest dedicated trial regarding safety of CCTA in the triage of patients with acute chest pain in the ED was conducted by Litt and colleagues.[30] A total of 1370 patients were enrolled and, in a ratio of 2:1, randomized into the CCTA versus standard-of-care (SOC) group (N = 908 vs 462, respectively). The primary endpoint was defined as an upper 95% CI below 1% for missed ACS or death during the 30-day follow-up in the CCTA group. In the CCTA group, 640 patients had a negative examination and none experienced an event with respect to the primary endpoint; thus, the results met the prespecified safety threshold (95% CI: 0%–0.57%). Other studies provided supporting evidence that CCTA is a safe method for triage of subjects with acute chest pain in the ED.[31,32]

With respect to clinical effectiveness defined as time to discharge, two major prospective trials have been published. In the Coronary Computed Tomographic Angiography for Systematic Triage of Acute Chest Pain Patients to Treatment (CT-STAT) trial by Goldstein and colleagues,[32] 749 patients with acute chest pain but negative ECG and initial biomarkers were enrolled. Patients were randomized to either early CCTA or to rest-stress single-photon emission computed tomography myocardial perfusion imaging (MPI). In contrast, the ROMICAT II trial by Hoffmann and colleagues[31] randomized 1000 low-to-intermediate risk patients with acute chest pain in the intervention groups with early CCTA as the first diagnostic test versus the control group. The control group received SOC ED evaluation, which included all options of stress testing or no testing at all, **Table 1**. Both trials demonstrated that the CCTA-based strategy resulted in a shorter length of stay without lower safety (2.9 vs 6.2 hours for time to diagnosis [CT-STAT] and 23 vs 31 hours for time to hospital discharge [ROMICAT II] for CCTA vs control strategy). These findings were supported by other studies, indicating that the rate of direct discharge from the ED increased to about 50% by using a CCTA strategy while a typical rate of 15% to 25% is observed for SOC.[30,31,33] In subanalysis, a higher effectiveness of the CCTA strategy was observed for women than for men (about 6 times higher reduction in length of stay by implementing CCTA strategy), mainly driven by the lower rate of obstructive coronary disease.[34]

As a consequence of these effectiveness trials, major concerns about downstream use and costs were raised, particularly because increased rates of cardiac catheterization were observed. In a meta-analysis by Hulten and colleagues,[35] an increase in invasive angiography after CCTA of 21

(95% CI: 2–45), as well as coronary revascularizations of 20 (95% CI: 5–41) per 1000 CCTA scans, were estimated. It remains unclear whether this observation can be interpreted as a positive effect with appropriate aggressive treatment per high-risk individual or as overtreatment of patients due to anatomic imaging testing such as CCTA.

In summary, use of CCTA in the early phase of managing patients with acute chest pain with a low-intermediate risk is safe and demonstrated strong evidence of effectiveness with shortened total length of stay. Whether increased percutaneous coronary intervention rates after CCTA may result in unnecessary downstream testing or improved long-term health outcomes remains unknown. Also, it remains unclear how CCTA compares with other novel biomarker-based approaches such as hsTn or if these strategies can serve as better gatekeepers for CCTA. However, despite these shortcomings, CCTA has been established as a viable method for the triage in patients with acute chest pain syndrome presenting to the ED.

Costs and Cost-Effectiveness of Using Coronary Computed Tomography Angiography for Acute Chest Pain Triage

In an optimal setting, CCTA would reduce costs and provide more cost-effective care in the triage of patients with acute chest pain, which may seem intuitive because it reduces the hospital length of stay. Estimations from the ROMICAT I trial suggested that CCTA could reduce total hospital costs by up to 23% if patients with no coronary artery disease (CAD) were discharged. However, this conclusion remained valid only for scenarios in which prevalence of obstructive CAD was less than 30%.[36] Similar results were found by Khare and colleagues.[37] They observed that a CCTA-based triage strategy dominates other strategies, such as stress echocardiography or ECG, regarding their cost-effectiveness.[37] When comparing CCTA with SOC (eg, stress ECG), CCTA was more expensive for men compared with women ($10190 vs $6630, respectively); however, CCTA remained the favorable strategy and resulted in an incremental cost-effectiveness ratio of $6400 per quality-adjusted life year for men and cost-savings for women.[38]

These large randomized control trials are inconclusive about whether the use of CCTA provides more cost-effective care overall. Both trials demonstrated a reduction of ED cost between 18% and 38%.[31,32] However, this was partially compensated by increased costs during hospitalization, which were mainly influenced by a higher number of revascularizations due to the increased

Table 1
Randomized controlled trials with coronary computed tomography angiography as a diagnostic intervention in subjects with acute chest pain

	Subjects	Number of Subjects and Centers	Intervention	Control	Outcome of Interest	Observed Difference (CCTA vs Control)
Goldstein et al,[32] 2011 (CT-STAT)	Negative troponin Normal ECG Age: 50 ± 10 y Female: 54%	749/16	CCTA	MPI	Prevalence of AMI MACE during follow-up direct Direct ED discharges Time to diagnosis[a] Invasive catheterization ED Cost[a] Radiation Dose[a]	0.3% vs 1.5% 0.8% vs 0.4% NA 2.9 h vs 6.2 h 7% vs 6% $2137 vs $3458 12 mSv vs 13 mSv
Litt et al,[30] 2012	Negative troponin Normal ECG Age: 49 ± 10 y Female: 53%	1370/5	CCTA	SOC	Prevalence of AMI MACE during Follow-up[a] Direct ED discharges[a] Time to diagnosis[a] Invasive catheterization ED Cost Radiation Dose	1% vs 1% 3% vs 1% 50% vs 23% 18.0 h vs 24.8 h 4% vs 4% NA NA
Hoffmann et al,[31] 2012 (ROMICAT II)	Negative troponin Normal ECG Age: 54 ± 8 y Female: 47%	1000/7	CCTA	SOC	Prevalence of AMI MACE during follow-up Direct ED discharges[a] Time to diagnosis[a] Invasive catheterization ED Cost Radiation Dose[a]	2% vs 3% 0.4% vs 1.2% 47% vs 12% 5.8 h vs 21.0 h 11% vs 7% $2101 vs $2566 14 mSv vs 5 mSv

The work-up in the ED using CCTA was compared either with a work-up strategy requiring nuclear MPI or to a traditional SOC work-up strategy. Normal ECG was defined as non-conclusive for myocardial ischemia.

Abbreviations: AMI, acute myocardial infarction; MACE, major adverse coronary event; NA, not available.

[a] Significant difference ($P<.05$).

sensitivity of CCTA in detecting obstructive CAD.[31] It remains unclear whether this shift of care to patients with obstructive CAD translates into improvement in quality of life or health outcomes.

Long-term Prognostic Value of Coronary Computed Tomography Angiography

In general, the subclinical CAD burden is recognized as the strongest predictor of future cardiac events.[39] Accordingly, this information can be obtained from the CCTA scan and may have prognostic value in patients with acute chest pain. However, the true value can only be explored in observational studies such as ROMICAT I, in which the CCTA result was neither disclosed to the patient nor to the caregivers, otherwise the disclosed CCTA results may have influenced treatment decision and therefore altered the "natural history" of the disease.

Overall, the cardiac event rate in patients initially ruled-out for ACS is low during follow-up, but it increased with increasing CAD burden (annual event rate of 0% for none, about 1% for nonobstructive, and 4% for obstructive CAD).[40,41] Information about plaque morphology (high-risk plaque concept; see previous discussion)[42,43] and about LV dysfunction in cardiac CT provided incremental value for the long-term prognosis (eg, estimated 2-year event rate for late major adverse coronary event for subjects with obstructive CAD and regional LV dysfunction was 18.5%).[40]

However, more importantly, patients with acute chest pain without CAD in CCTA remained event-free over a long period[40,41,44,45] and a 2-year event-free warranty period is accepted for patients with acute chest pain but without any plaque as defined by CCTA.[40] Using the prognostic power of CCTA is a key to increase the risk-benefit ratio, and the effectiveness of CCTA in the acute chest pains setting.

CORONARY COMPUTED TOMOGRAPHY ANGIOGRAPHY–BASED TRIAGE OF PATIENTS WITH ACUTE CHEST PAIN IN THE EMERGENCY DEPARTMENT
Scan Protocol

The scan protocol in patients with acute chest pain does not differ from standard clinical CCTA protocols (see the article by Meinel and colleagues elsewhere in this issue for further exploration of this topic). Although the assessment of LV function provides incremental value compared with a coronary assessment for diagnosis and prognosis,[23,40] it is unclear whether the incremental value outweighs the additional radiation exposure. In general, more recent technology should be applied to reduce radiation dose and administrated contrast agent.

Patient Selection

The appropriate patient selection is a crucial point for a safe and effective triage in the setting of acute chest pain. A low-to-intermediate risk of ACS is considered the correct pretest probability, which can be defined using different scores (eg, TIMI risk score ≤ 2 or clinical presentation, typical angina less than 30 minutes plus normal ECG findings or atypical symptoms, or normal or nondiagnostic ECG findings plus negative cardiac enzyme results). Furthermore, gender is an important risk modifier and should be included in the risk evaluation. A commonly used algorithm for assessing risk for ACS, modified based on the work of Diamond and Forrester,[46] is shown in Table 2.[28]

Table 2
Pretest probability for ACS in relation to gender, age, and clinical presentation, modified after Diamond-Forrester method

Age (y)	Typical Angina	Atypical Angina	Noncardiac Chest Pain	Asymptomatic
Women				
<40	Intermediate	Very low	Very low	Very low
40–49	Intermediate	Low	Very low	Very low
50–59	Intermediate	Intermediate	Very low	Very low
$\geq$60	High	Intermediate	Intermediate	Low
Men				
<40	Intermediate	Intermediate	Low	Very low
40–49	High	Intermediate	Intermediate	Low
50–59	High	Intermediate	Intermediate	Low
$\geq$60	High	Intermediate	Intermediate	Low

Triage of acute chest patients using only recommended for patients with low-to-intermediate risk (shadows in light gray).

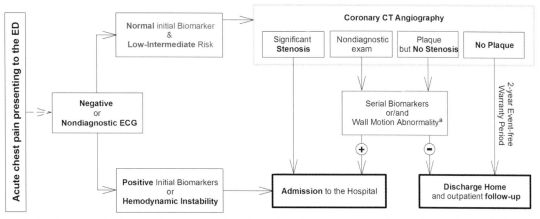

Fig. 1. Clinical flow-chart, including CCTA in the triage of patients with acute chest pain. [a] Left ventricular wall motion abnormalities are not available for all CT scan protocols (eg, prospective ECG-triggering).

CCTA in patients with high pretest probability is not recommended.

Further exclusion criteria apply, mainly linked to the CCTA technology and the needed administration of iodine contrast agent, including impaired renal function and large body size. Depending on the available scanner technology, high heart rate or inability to hold breath for at least 10 seconds can be additional exclusion criteria.

Clinical Flow-Chart

The diagnostic workup of acute chest pain (**Fig. 1**) includes an initial clinical assessment, including patient history, physical examination, 12-lead ECG, and laboratory findings, such as cardiac biomarkers.[8] If the patient is at low-to-intermediate risk for ACS, the initial cardiac biomarker is negative, and there are no other contraindications, she or he can be referred to CCTA imaging (see **Fig. 1**). The results can be stratified into four major categories: (1) no plaque, (2) presence of plaque but no significant stenosis, (3) presence of significant stenosis, and (4) nondiagnostic examination. In the case of absence of any coronary plaque, a cardiac reason for the acute chest pain can be excluded and if the patients does not have any other relevant comorbidities (eg, pneumothorax), she or he can be safely discharged from the ED. Also, a 2-year event-free warranty period can be considered and downstream testing in outpatient services can be modified accordingly.

In the case of presence of plaque but no significant stenosis or a nondiagnostic examination, further ED evaluation must be considered, including serial biomarkers and, potentially, stress testing.

In the case of presence of a significant stenosis, the likelihood is high enough that the patient should be admitted to the hospital and followed

with serial biomarkers and, potentially, stress testing or invasive angiography, depending on clinical presentation. However, it is important to remember that a significant stenosis has a PPV of only about 35-50%, implying that not everyone with significant CAD should undergo urgent invasive angiography and revascularization.

REFERENCES

1. Antman E. ST-segment elevation myocardial infarction: pathology, pathophysiology, and clinical features. 9th edition. Philadelphia: Elsevier; 2010.
2. Finn AV, Nakano M, Narula J, et al. Concept of vulnerable/unstable plaque. Arterioscler Thromb Vasc Biol 2010;30(7):1282–92.
3. Kolodgie FD, Virmani R, Burke AP, et al. Pathologic assessment of the vulnerable human coronary plaque. Heart 2004;90(12):1385–91.
4. Davies MJ. The pathophysiology of acute coronary syndromes. Heart 2000;83(3):361–6.
5. Raff GL, Abidov A, Achenbach S, et al. SCCT guidelines for the interpretation and reporting of coronary computed tomographic angiography. J Cardiovasc Comput Tomogr 2009;3(2):122–36.
6. Bartunek J, Sys SU, Heyndrickx GR, et al. Quantitative coronary angiography in predicting functional significance of stenoses in an unselected patient cohort. J Am Coll Cardiol 1995;26(2):328–34.
7. Braunwald E, Antman EM, Beasley JW, et al. ACC/AHA guideline update for the management of patients with unstable angina and non-ST-segment elevation myocardial infarction—2002: summary article: a report of the American College of Cardiology/American Heart Association Task Force on Practice Guidelines (Committee on the Management of Patients With Unstable Angina). Circulation 2002; 106(14):1893–900.

8. Anderson JL, Adams CD, Antman EM, et al. ACC/AHA 2007 guidelines for the management of patients with unstable angina/non ST-elevation myocardial infarction: a report of the American College of Cardiology/American Heart Association Task Force on Practice Guidelines (Writing Committee to Revise the 2002 Guidelines for the Management of Patients With Unstable Angina/Non ST-Elevation Myocardial Infarction): developed in collaboration with the American College of Emergency Physicians, the Society for Cardiovascular Angiography and Interventions, and the Society of Thoracic Surgeons: endorsed by the American Association of Cardiovascular and Pulmonary Rehabilitation and the Society for Academic Emergency Medicine. Circulation 2007;116(7):e148–304.

9. Braunwald E. Unstable angina: an etiologic approach to management. Circulation 1998;98(21):2219–22.

10. Niska R, Bhuiya F, Xu J. National hospital ambulatory medical care survey: 2007 emergency department summary. Natl Health Stat Report 2010;(26):1–31.

11. Roger VL, Go AS, Lloyd-Jones DM, et al. Heart disease and stroke statistics—2012 update: a report from the American Heart Association. Circulation 2012;125(1):e2–220.

12. Januzzi JL Jr, Bamberg F, Lee H, et al. High-sensitivity troponin T concentrations in acute chest pain patients evaluated with cardiac computed tomography. Circulation 2010;121(10):1227–34.

13. Pope JH, Aufderheide TP, Ruthazer R, et al. Missed diagnoses of acute cardiac ischemia in the emergency department. N Engl J Med 2000;342(16):1163–70.

14. Suter RE. The risk of missed diagnosis of acute myocardial infarction associated with emergency department volume. Ann Emerg Med 2007;50(2):203 [author reply: 203–4].

15. van der Giessen AG, Toepker MH, Donelly PM, et al. Reproducibility, accuracy, and predictors of accuracy for the detection of coronary atherosclerotic plaque composition by computed tomography: an ex vivo comparison to intravascular ultrasound. Invest Radiol 2010;45(11):693–701.

16. Mowatt G, Cook JA, Hillis GS, et al. 64-Slice computed tomography angiography in the diagnosis and assessment of coronary artery disease: systematic review and meta-analysis. Heart 2008;94(11):1386–93.

17. Rubinshtein R, Halon DA, Gaspar T, et al. Usefulness of 64-slice cardiac computed tomographic angiography for diagnosing acute coronary syndromes and predicting clinical outcome in emergency department patients with chest pain of uncertain origin. Circulation 2007;115(13):1762–8.

18. Hoffmann U, Bamberg F, Chae CU, et al. Coronary computed tomography angiography for early triage of patients with acute chest pain: the ROMICAT (Rule Out Myocardial Infarction using Computer Assisted Tomography) trial. J Am Coll Cardiol 2009;53(18):1642–50.

19. Hollander JE, Chang AM, Shofer FS, et al. Coronary computed tomographic angiography for rapid discharge of low-risk patients with potential acute coronary syndromes. Ann Emerg Med 2009;53(3):295–304.

20. Seifarth H, Schlett CL, Nakano M, et al. Histopathological correlates of the napkin-ring sign plaque in coronary CT angiography. Atherosclerosis 2012;224(1):90–6.

21. Maurovich-Horvat P, Hoffmann U, Vorpahl M, et al. The napkin-ring sign: CT signature of high-risk coronary plaques? JACC Cardiovasc Imaging 2010;3(4):440–4.

22. Motoyama S, Sarai M, Harigaya H, et al. Computed tomographic angiography characteristics of atherosclerotic plaques subsequently resulting in acute coronary syndrome. J Am Coll Cardiol 2009;54(1):49–57.

23. Seneviratne SK, Truong QA, Bamberg F, et al. Incremental diagnostic value of regional left ventricular function over coronary assessment by cardiac computed tomography for the detection of acute coronary syndrome in patients with acute chest pain: from the ROMICAT trial. Circ Cardiovasc Imaging 2010;3(4):375–83.

24. Wackers FJ, Brown KA, Heller GV, et al. American Society of Nuclear Cardiology position statement on radionuclide imaging in patients with suspected acute ischemic syndromes in the emergency department or chest pain center. J Nucl Cardiol 2002;9(2):246–50.

25. Feuchtner GM, Plank F, Pena C, et al. Evaluation of myocardial CT perfusion in patients presenting with acute chest pain to the emergency department: comparison with SPECT-myocardial perfusion imaging. Heart 2012;98(20):1510–7.

26. Bezerra HG, Loureiro R, Irlbeck T, et al. Incremental value of myocardial perfusion over regional left ventricular function and coronary stenosis by cardiac CT for the detection of acute coronary syndromes in high-risk patients: a subgroup analysis of the ROMICAT trial. J Cardiovasc Comput Tomogr 2011;5(6):382–91.

27. Ferencik M, Schlett CL, Bamberg F, et al. Comparison of traditional cardiovascular risk models and coronary atherosclerotic plaque as detected by computed tomography for prediction of acute coronary syndrome in patients with acute chest pain. Acad Emerg Med 2012;19(8):934–42.

28. Taylor AJ, Cerqueira M, Hodgson JM, et al. ACCF/SCCT/ACR/AHA/ASE/ASNC/NASCI/SCAI/SCMR 2010 appropriate use criteria for cardiac computed tomography. A report of the American College of Cardiology

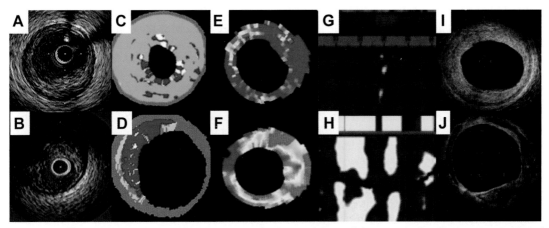

Fig. 1. Examples of stable and unstable plaque by invasive modalities. (*A*) Intravascular ultrasonography (IVUS) example of stable, fibrotic plaque. (*B*) IVUS example of attenuated plaque. (*C*) IVUS with virtual histology (IVUS-VH) example of concentric, fibrotic plaque. (*D*) IVUS-VH example of large necrotic core (*red*) abutting vessel lumen. (*E*) Elastography example of stable plaque. (*F*) Elastography example of unstable plaque. (*G*) Near-infrared spectroscopy (NIRS) showing no significant lipid pool. (*H*) Significant lipid pool (*yellow*) shown by NIRS. (*I*) Optical coherence tomography (OCT) showing concentric, stable plaque. (*J*) OCT image of a thin fibrous cap and significant lipid pool.

sensitivity than IVUS alone.[14] NIRS uses the principle that different organic compounds absorb unique wavelengths of near-infrared light (750–2500 nm wavelength). By analyzing the shift in the spectra, it is possible to identify lipid pools within coronary plaques.[15] Whereas the original NIRS catheter only provided information regarding lipid content, subsequent iterations use adjunctive IVUS to coregister NIRS and ultrasound data, with improvement in plaque characterization.[16]

Optical coherence tomography (OCT) is another intravascular imaging technique that uses reflected light waves to generate images at a substantially higher resolution than IVUS (axial resolution 12–18 μm, lateral resolution 20–90 μm).[17] These high-resolution images allow for precise visualization and depiction of calcium and TCFA (see **Fig. 1I**, J).[18] However, OCT is limited somewhat by a 3-mm depth of penetration, thus limiting its ability to detect large lipid cores and other deeper vessel structures.

Collectively, these technologies have demonstrated the ability to characterize intracoronary plaque and identify high-risk features consistent with vulnerable plaque. The unifying features of these plaques include positive vessel remodeling, a large plaque burden with variable luminal compromise, lipid-rich necrotic plaque, a thin fibrous cap, and spotty calcification. A shared disadvantage of each of these technologies is that they are inherently invasive, and require direct instrumentation and visualization of the intended coronary segments. As vulnerable plaque may be diffusely located and is often asymptomatic, identification

would ideally occur by noninvasive means. Given rapid, noninvasive, and comprehensive imaging of the entire coronary anatomy, coronary CT angiography (cCTA) is inherently attractive.

COMPUTED TOMOGRAPHY FOR PLAQUE CHARACTERIZATION

The first use of CT for plaque characterization took place in 1985 by Leeson and colleagues[19], who showed that focal mural thickening noted on CT scans proved to be primarily fibrotic atheromatous plaque on pathologic examination. In 1998, Estes and colleagues[20] sought to characterize plaque morphology through attenuation measurements with a single-slice scanner. This technique allowed a rough evaluation of plaque morphology in different stages of atherosclerosis. Unfortunately, poor image quality and resolution of the early scanners prevented precise evaluation of plaque composition, and concerns about radiation exposure tempered widespread enthusiasm for the technology.

Over time, innovations in scanner technology and acquisition protocols have substantially lowered radiation, and the introduction of the 64-slice platform markedly increased spatial and temporal resolution while further decreasing the radiation dose. Prospective electrocardiographic triggering has reduced the typical effective dose of cCTA to 3.5 mSv.[21] The latest generation of CT systems holds the promise of further reducing radiation exposure to less than 1 mSv in selected patients.[22]

At cCTA, plaque characterization is achieved by assessing the plaque density measured in Hounsfield units (HU). The density of intraluminal contrast media is generally around 300 HU. Calcified plaque commonly has a density of greater than 400 HU,[23] and can thus be easily differentiated from noncalcified plaque with a density in the range of 0 to 150 HU. Noncalcified plaque can further be subcategorized into denser fibrous and less dense lipid-rich (low-attenuation) plaque components.[24] Ex vivo studies have suggested that a CT density cutoff of less than 60 HU can identify lipid-rich plaque.[25,26] Others, however, have found that there is significant overlap in CT density between fibrous and lipid-rich plaque, and that the optimal cutoff value may depend on the CT systems, acquisition parameters, and the vessel of interest.[27]

COMPUTED TOMOGRAPHIC IDENTIFICATION AND CHARACTERIZATION OF INTRACORONARY PLAQUE

Over the past decade, several studies with various generations of CT systems comparing cCTA with IVUS have been published, demonstrating excellent correlations for the detection of intracoronary plaque (**Fig. 2, Table 2**).[23,28–36] More recently, Voros and colleagues[37] evaluated 50 lesions in 50 patients in a single center by cCTA and IVUS-VH among other modalities. The investigators demonstrated significant correlations between cCTA and IVUS-VH with regard to plaque geometry and composition on a slice-by-slice basis (r = 0.41–0.84, P<.001), but cCTA tended to overestimate lumen, vessel, and both calcified and noncalcified plaque. A recently published meta-analysis of 17 studies comparing cCTA with IVUS demonstrated

a pooled sensitivity and specificity to detect any coronary plaque of 93% and 92%, respectively with higher sensitivity and specificity for calcified plaque (93% and 98%) than for noncalcified plaque (88% and 92%).[38] In addition, in a study of 108 plaques in 57 patients with a subsequent validation cohort of 47 patients, Obaid and colleagues[39] investigated cCTA-derived "plaque maps" (**Fig. 3**) constructed from plaque/contrast attenuation ratios for the assessment of individual plaque components, in a comparison with IVUS-VH. There was favorable diagnostic accuracy in calcified (83% vs 92%), necrotic (80% vs 65%), and fibrolipidic plaques (80% vs 79%), but IVUS-VH–defined TCFA (necrotic core in contact with the vessel lumen) could not be demonstrated by cCTA, owing to limitations in spatial resolution.

COMPUTED TOMOGRAPHIC FEATURES OF PLAQUE VULNERABILITY

Of the many plaque characteristics detected by cCTA, a few have been shown to correlate with previously established high-risk features of plaque vulnerability and TCFA.[40,41] These features include positive remodeling, low-attenuation plaque (30–60 HU),[42] spotty calcification, and the napkin-ring lesion (**Fig. 4**). By definition, remodeling and spotty calcification is based on prior IVUS studies, and low-attenuation plaque is based on correlations with noncalcified plaque consistent with fibrolipidic plaque and necrotic core. The napkin-ring lesion is defined as a region of low attenuation surrounded by a higher-attenuation ring, and is thought to represent necrotic core surrounded by a fibrous cap.[43,44]

Several studies have demonstrated agreement between cCTA assessment of high-risk plaque

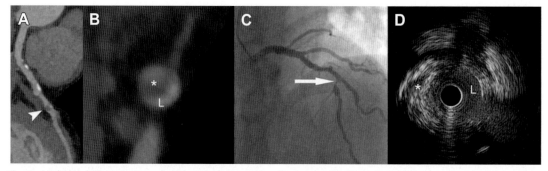

Fig. 2. Multimodality imaging of obstructive coronary soft plaque. (*A*) Curved multiplanar reconstruction of coronary CT angiography (cCTA) shows high-grade stenosis in the distal part of the left anterior descending coronary artery (LAD) (*arrowhead*). (*B*) Axial reconstruction shows severe lumen (L) restriction by an inhomogeneous soft plaque (*asterisk*). (*C*) Invasive coronary angiography confirms high-grade stenosis (*arrow*). (*D*) IVUS shows distinct luminal (L) stenosis caused by the obstructive soft plaque (*asterisk*). The patient underwent stenting with restored antegrade flow in the distal LAD.

Table 2
Sensitivity and specificity of cCTA compared with IVUS

Authors,[Ref.] Year	No. of Patients	Scanner	Sensitivity (95% CI)	Specificity (95% CI)
Achenbach et al,[28] 2004	22 (83 segments)	16-slice	0.82 (0.69–0.91)	0.88 (0.72–0.97)
Moselewski et al,[30] 2004	26 (100 lesions)	16-slice	0.91 (0.81–0.97)	0.94 (0.81–0.99)
Leber et al,[29] 2004	37 (68 vessels)	16-slice	0.85 (0.81–0.89)	0.92 (0.90–0.94)
Leber et al,[58] 2006	19 (36 vessels)	64-slice	0.90 (0.84–0.94)	0.94 (0.90–0.97)
Rasouli et al,[23] 2006	12 (59 segments)	60-slice	1.00 (0.93–1.00)	0.90 (0.55–1.00)
Iriart et al,[31] 2007	20 (169 segments)	16-slice	0.79 (0.69–0.87)	0.99 (0.93–1.00)
Sun et al,[59] 2008	26 (263 segments)	64-slice	0.97 (0.93–0.99)	0.90 (0.84–0.95)
Petranovic et al,[33] 2009	11 (17 segments)	64-slice	0.96 (0.87–0.99)	0.89 (0.78–0.95)
Schepis et al,[34] 2010	70 (100 plaques)	64-slice	0.85 (0.71–0.99)	0.89 (0.78–0.95)

Abbreviation: CI, confidence interval.

and those of the invasive modalities. In a study of 30 individual plaques evaluated with both cCTA and IVUS, Nakazato and colleagues[45] demonstrated excellent correlation between the 2 modalities for plaque volume and similar frequencies of adverse plaque characteristics, including low-attenuation plaque (10% cCTA vs 17% IVUS), positive remodeling (7% vs 10%), and spotty calcification (27% vs 33%). In addition, low-attenuation plaque and positive remodeling have been associated with hemodynamic significance as assessed by myocardial perfusion imaging.[46]

COMPUTED TOMOGRAPHIC ASSESSMENT OF PLAQUE AND OUTCOMES

Multiple studies have illustrated that normal cCTA confers an excellent prognosis, whereas abnormal

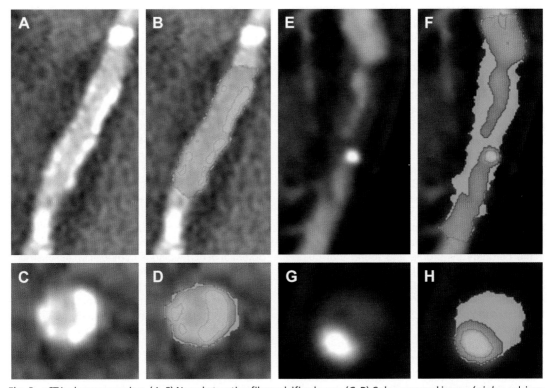

Fig. 3. cCTA plaque mapping. (*A, B*) Nonobstructive fibrocalcific plaque. (*C, D*) Color-mapped image (*pink* = calcium, *green* = soft plaque, *brown* = lumen). (*E, F*) Obstructive plaque. (*G, H*) Corresponding color-mapped image.

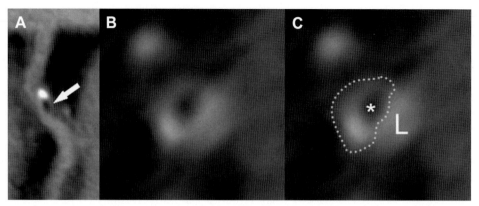

Fig. 4. cCTA images of a coronary lesion with Napkin-Ring sign. (*A*) Curved multiplanar reformation demonstrates the lesion (*arrow*) with partial obstruction of the lumen (*L*) and partial calcification. (*B, C*) The circumferential outer rim (*dotted line*) of the plaque has a higher CT attenuation than the central necrotic core (*asterisk*).

findings are associated with adverse events.[47–50] A meta-analysis of 11 studies evaluating 7335 patients demonstrated that the presence of coronary artery disease (CAD), an increase in the number of coronary segments with detectable plaque, the number of involved vessel segments with mixed plaques, and the presence of obstructive plaques were all associated with increased major adverse cardiac events (MACE).[51] Furthermore, the CONFIRM Investigators reported that the number of proximal segments with greater than 50% stenosis and with either calcified or mixed plaques increased clinical risk scores, and added further information to that of existing conventional clinical risk models. Of interest, 32% of the patients in the test sample could be reclassified into different risk profiles, with 22% of the patients reassigned to a lower cardiovascular risk and 10% reassigned to a higher cardiovascular risk.[52]

Regarding high-risk plaques, He and colleagues[53] performed cCTA plaque analysis in 1055 patients and demonstrated that calcification, erosion, and severe stenosis were strong predictors for MACE ($P<.05$). Benedek and colleagues[54] evaluated 118 coronary plaques in 45 patients with acute coronary syndrome and found that culprit lesions not only had larger plaque volumes (111 mm^3 vs 62 mm^3, $P<.0001$), higher remodeling index (1.27 vs 1.01, $P<.0001$), and lower attenuation at thresholds of both 30 and 60 HU compared with nonculprit lesions, but also had a higher frequency of all 3 markers (low attenuation, positive remodeling, and spotty calcification). Regarding the napkin-ring sign, Otsuka and colleagues[55] reported that the presence of this sign on cCTA, independent of positive remodeling

and low-attenuation plaque, had a high predictive value ($P<.0001$) for MACE during the follow-up period of 2.3 ± 0.8 years. In another study of 4425 patients, while cCTA and coronary artery calcium score added additional prognostic value for predicting MACE there was a significantly higher risk from noncalcified and mixed plaques than from calcified plaques.[56] These findings reaffirm the notion that soft, lipid-rich plaques are higher-risk plaques that can lead to subsequent MACE.[57]

FUTURE DIRECTIONS IN TECHNOLOGIES AND RESEARCH

The main focus of current research and development is to further reduce applied radiation dose and improve spatial resolution. Plaque characterization with cCTA continues to be an evolving application and the subject of multiple research efforts. Particular interest lies in the ability of cCTA to predict lesion-associated hemodynamic and physiologic relevance. To date, techniques combining cCTA with physiologic measures to identify ischemia-causing stenoses have yet to incorporate the potential of cCTA plaque composition assessment. Emerging data could potentially use CT-derived plaque characteristics as a predictor of hemodynamic significance to improve the correlation of cCTA with fractional flow reserve. Eventually cCTA could serve to identify only those patients with functionally significant lesions that should proceed to invasive angiography. An additional target is the further development of software solutions to enable reproducible plaque assessments across different CT vendors.[22]

SUMMARY

cCTA is well established as a tool to exclude CAD in patients with low to intermediate cardiovascular risk and acute chest pain. It is highly sensitive for the detection of CAD and is accurate for the quantification of coronary artery luminal area, atherosclerotic plaque area, plaque volume, and percentage stenosis. It has also demonstrated good correlation with invasive methods in terms of plaque characterization, with specific features being found to correlate with vulnerable plaque and subsequent events. Thus, cCTA has the ability to provide incremental diagnostic and prognostic value above traditional clinical risk factor models. Continued technological improvements will likely help further define the role of cCTA in coronary plaque assessment.

REFERENCES

1. Little WC. Angiographic assessment of the culprit coronary artery lesion before acute myocardial infarction. Am J Cardiol 1990;66(16):44G–7G.
2. Little WC, Constantinescu M, Applegate RJ, et al. Can coronary angiography predict the site of a subsequent myocardial infarction in patients with mild-to-moderate coronary artery disease? Circulation 1988;78(5 Pt 1):1157–66.
3. Mintz GS. Clinical utility of intravascular imaging and physiology in coronary artery disease. J Am Coll Cardiol 2014;64:207–22.
4. Hilty KC, Steinberg DH. Vulnerable plaque imaging-current techniques. J Cardiovasc Transl Res 2009;2(1):9–18.
5. Flohr TG, Schoepf UJ, Ohnesorge BM. Chasing the heart: new developments for cardiac CT. J Thorac Imaging 2007;22(1):4–16.
6. Burke AP, Kolodgie FD, Farb A, et al. Morphological predictors of arterial remodeling in coronary atherosclerosis. Circulation 2002;105(3):297–303.
7. Ehara S, Kobayashi Y, Yoshiyama M, et al. Spotty calcification typifies the culprit plaque in patients with acute myocardial infarction: an intravascular ultrasound study. Circulation 2004;110(22):3424–9.
8. Virmani R, Burke AP, Farb A, et al. Pathology of the vulnerable plaque. J Am Coll Cardiol 2006;47(8 Suppl):C13–8.
9. Mehta SK, McCrary JR, Frutkin AD, et al. Intravascular ultrasound radiofrequency analysis of coronary atherosclerosis: an emerging technology for the assessment of vulnerable plaque. Eur Heart J 2007;28(11):1283–8.
10. Yamagishi M, Terashima M, Awano K, et al. Morphology of vulnerable coronary plaque: insights from follow-up of patients examined by intravascular ultrasound

11. Potkin BN, Bartorelli AL, Gessert JM, et al. Coronary artery imaging with intravascular high-frequency ultrasound. Circulation 1990;81(5):1575–85.
12. Stone GW, Maehara A, Lansky AJ, et al. A prospective natural-history study of coronary atherosclerosis. N Engl J Med 2011;364(3):226–35.
13. de Korte CL, Pasterkamp G, van der Steen AF, et al. Characterization of plaque components with intravascular ultrasound elastography in human femoral and coronary arteries in vitro. Circulation 2000;102(6):617–23.
14. Schaar JA, De Korte CL, Mastik F, et al. Characterizing vulnerable plaque features with intravascular elastography. Circulation 2003;108(21):2636–41.
15. Moreno PR, Lodder RA, Purushothaman KR, et al. Detection of lipid pool, thin fibrous cap, and inflammatory cells in human aortic atherosclerotic plaques by near-infrared spectroscopy. Circulation 2002;105(8):923–7.
16. Pu J, Mintz GS, Brilakis ES, et al. In vivo characterization of coronary plaques: novel findings from comparing greyscale and virtual histology intravascular ultrasound and near-infrared spectroscopy. Eur Heart J 2012;33(3):372–83.
17. Bezerra HG, Costa MA, Guagliumi G, et al. Intracoronary optical coherence tomography: a comprehensive review clinical and research applications. JACC Cardiovasc Interv 2009;2(11):1035–46.
18. Kubo T, Imanishi T, Takarada S, et al. Assessment of culprit lesion morphology in acute myocardial infarction: ability of optical coherence tomography compared with intravascular ultrasound and coronary angioscopy. J Am Coll Cardiol 2007;50(10):933–9.
19. Leeson MD, Cacayorin ED, Iliya AR, et al. Atheromatous extracranial carotid arteries: CT evaluation correlated with arteriography and pathologic examination. Radiology 1985;156(2):397–402.
20. Estes JM, Quist WC, Lo Gerfo FW, et al. Noninvasive characterization of plaque morphology using helical computed tomography. J Cardiovasc Surg 1998;39(5):527–34.
21. Menke J, Unterberg-Buchwald C, Staab W, et al. Head-to-head comparison of prospectively triggered vs retrospectively gated coronary computed tomography angiography: meta-analysis of diagnostic accuracy, image quality, and radiation dose. Am Heart J 2013;165(2):154–63.e3.
22. Oberoi S, Meinel FG, Schoepf UJ, et al. Reproducibility of noncalcified coronary artery plaque burden quantification from coronary CT angiography across different image analysis platforms. AJR Am J Roentgenol 2014;202(1):W43–9.
23. Rasouli ML, Shavelle DM, French WJ, et al. Assessment of coronary plaque morphology by contrast-enhanced computed tomographic angiography:

comparison with intravascular ultrasound. Coron Artery Dis 2006;17(4):359–64.

24. Nance JW Jr, Schlett CL, Schoepf UJ, et al. Incremental prognostic value of different components of coronary atherosclerotic plaque at cardiac CT angiography beyond coronary calcification in patients with acute chest pain. Radiology 2012; 264(3):679–90.

25. Schlett CL, Maurovich-Horvat P, Ferencik M, et al. Histogram analysis of lipid-core plaques in coronary computed tomographic angiography: ex vivo validation against histology. Invest Radiol 2013; 48(9):646–53.

26. Becker CR, Nikolaou K, Muders M, et al. Ex vivo coronary atherosclerotic plaque characterization with multi-detector-row CT. Eur Radiol 2003;13(9): 2094–8.

27. Kristanto W, van Ooijen PM, Jansen-van der Weide MC, et al. A meta analysis and hierarchical classification of HU-based atherosclerotic plaque characterization criteria. PLoS One 2013;8(9):e73460.

28. Achenbach S, Moselewski F, Ropers D, et al. Detection of calcified and noncalcified coronary atherosclerotic plaque by contrast-enhanced, submillimeter multidetector spiral computed tomography: a segment-based comparison with intravascular ultrasound. Circulation 2004;109(1):14–7.

29. Leber AW, Knez A, Becker A, et al. Accuracy of multidetector spiral computed tomography in identifying and differentiating the composition of coronary atherosclerotic plaques: a comparative study with intracoronary ultrasound. J Am Coll Cardiol 2004; 43(7):1241–7.

30. Moselewski F, Ropers D, Pohle K, et al. Comparison of measurement of cross-sectional coronary atherosclerotic plaque and vessel areas by 16-slice multidetector computed tomography versus intravascular ultrasound. Am J Cardiol 2004;94(10):1294–7.

31. Iriart X, Brunot S, Coste P, et al. Early characterization of atherosclerotic coronary plaques with multidetector computed tomography in patients with acute coronary syndrome: a comparative study with intravascular ultrasound. Eur Radiol 2007; 17(10):2581–8.

32. Sun J, Sukhova GK, Wolters PJ, et al. Mast cells promote atherosclerosis by releasing proinflammatory cytokines. Nat Med 2007;13(6):719–24.

33. Petranovic M, Soni A, Bezzera H, et al. Assessment of nonstenotic coronary lesions by 64-slice multidetector computed tomography in comparison to intravascular ultrasound: evaluation of nonculprit coronary lesions. J Cardiovasc Comput Tomogr 2009;3(1):24–31.

34. Schepis T, Marwan M, Pflederer T, et al. Quantification of non-calcified coronary atherosclerotic plaques with dual-source computed tomography: comparison with intravascular ultrasound. Heart 2010;96(8):610–5.

35. Enrico B, Suranyi P, Thilo C, et al. Coronary artery plaque formation at coronary CT angiography: morphological analysis and relationship to hemodynamics. Eur Radiol 2009;19(4):837–44.

36. Henzler T, Porubsky S, Kayed H, et al. Attenuation-based characterization of coronary atherosclerotic plaque: comparison of dual source and dual energy CT with single-source CT and histopathology. Eur J Radiol 2011;80(1):54–9.

37. Voros S, Rinehart S, Qian Z, et al. Prospective validation of standardized, 3-dimensional, quantitative coronary computed tomographic plaque measurements using radiofrequency backscatter intravascular ultrasound as reference standard in intermediate coronary arterial lesions: results from the ATLANTA (assessment of tissue characteristics, lesion morphology, and hemodynamics by angiography with fractional flow reserve, intravascular ultrasound and virtual histology, and noninvasive computed tomography in atherosclerotic plaques) I study. JACC Cardiovasc Interv 2011;4(2):198–208.

38. Gao D, Ning N, Guo Y, et al. Computed tomography for detecting coronary artery plaques: a meta-analysis. Atherosclerosis 2011;219(2):603–9.

39. Obaid DR, Calvert PA, Gopalan D, et al. Atherosclerotic plaque composition and classification identified by coronary computed tomography: assessment of computed tomography-generated plaque maps compared with virtual histology intravascular ultrasound and histology. Circ Cardiovasc Imaging 2013;6(5):655–64.

40. Bauer RW, Thilo C, Chiaramida SA, et al. Noncalcified atherosclerotic plaque burden at coronary CT angiography: a better predictor of ischemia at stress myocardial perfusion imaging than calcium score and stenosis severity. AJR Am J Roentgenol 2009; 193(2):410–8.

41. Thilo C, Gebregziabher M, Mayer FB, et al. Correlation of regional distribution and morphological pattern of calcification at CT coronary artery calcium scoring with non-calcified plaque formation and stenosis. Eur Radiol 2010;20(4):855–61.

42. Motoyama S, Kondo T, Sarai M, et al. Multislice computed tomographic characteristics of coronary lesions in acute coronary syndromes. J Am Coll Cardiol 2007;50(4):319–26.

43. Maurovich-Horvat P, Hoffmann U, Vorpahl M, et al. The napkin-ring sign: CT signature of high-risk coronary plaques? JACC Cardiovasc Imaging 2010;3(4):440–4.

44. Narula J, Achenbach S. Napkin-ring necrotic cores: defining circumferential extent of necrotic cores in unstable plaques. JACC Cardiovasc Imaging 2009;2(12):1436–8.

45. Nakazato R, Shalev A, Doh JH, et al. Quantification and characterisation of coronary artery plaque volume and adverse plaque features by coronary computed tomographic angiography: a direct

comparison to intravascular ultrasound. Eur Radiol 2013;23(8):2109–17.

46. Shmilovich H, Cheng VY, Tamarappoo BK, et al. Vulnerable plaque features on coronary CT angiography as markers of inducible regional myocardial hypoperfusion from severe coronary artery stenoses. Atherosclerosis 2011;219(2):588–95.

47. Min JK, Shaw LJ, Devereux RB, et al. Prognostic value of multidetector coronary computed tomographic angiography for prediction of all-cause mortality. J Am Coll Cardiol 2007;50(12):1161–70.

48. Pundziute G, Schuijf JD, Jukema JW, et al. Prognostic value of multislice computed tomography coronary angiography in patients with known or suspected coronary artery disease. J Am Coll Cardiol 2007;49(1):62–70.

49. Ostrom MP, Gopal A, Ahmadi N, et al. Mortality incidence and the severity of coronary atherosclerosis assessed by computed tomography angiography. J Am Coll Cardiol 2008;52(16):1335–43.

50. Moscariello A, Vliegenthart R, Schoepf UJ, et al. Coronary CT angiography versus conventional cardiac angiography for therapeutic decision making in patients with high likelihood of coronary artery disease. Radiology 2012;265(2):385–92.

51. Bamberg F, Sommer WH, Hoffmann V, et al. Meta-analysis and systematic review of the long-term predictive value of assessment of coronary atherosclerosis by contrast-enhanced coronary computed tomography angiography. J Am Coll Cardiol 2011;57(24):2426–36.

52. Hadamitzky M, Achenbach S, Al-Mallah M, et al. Optimized prognostic score for coronary computed tomographic angiography: results from the CONFIRM registry (COronary CT Angiography EvaluatioN For Clinical Outcomes: An InteRnational Multicenter Registry). J Am Coll Cardiol 2013;62(5):468–76.

53. He B, Gai L, Gai J, et al. Correlation between major adverse cardiac events and coronary plaque characteristics. Exp Clin Cardiol 2013;18(2):e71–6.

54. Benedek T, Gyongyosi M, Benedek I. Multislice computed tomographic coronary angiography for quantitative assessment of culprit lesions in acute coronary syndromes. Can J Cardiol 2013;29(3):364–71.

55. Otsuka K, Fukuda S, Tanaka A, et al. Napkin-ring sign on coronary CT angiography for the prediction of acute coronary syndrome. JACC Cardiovasc Imaging 2013;6(4):448–57.

56. Hou ZH, Lu B, Gao Y, et al. Prognostic value of coronary CT angiography and calcium score for major adverse cardiac events in outpatients. JACC Cardiovasc Imaging 2012;5(10):990–9.

57. Shah PK. Pathophysiology of coronary thrombosis: role of plaque rupture and plaque erosion. Prog Cardiovasc Dis 2002;44(5):357–68.

58. Leber AW, Becker A, Knez A, et al. Accuracy of 64-slice computed tomography to classify and quantify plaque volumes in the proximal coronary system: a comparative study using intravascular ultrasound. J Am Coll Cardiol 2006;47(3):672–7.

59. Sun J, Zhang Z, Lu B, et al. Identification and quantification of coronary atherosclerotic plaques: a comparison of 64-MDCT and intravascular ultrasound. AJR Am J Roentgenol 2008;190(3):748–54.

Beyond Stenosis Detection
Computed Tomography Approaches for Determining the Functional Relevance of Coronary Artery Disease

Carlo Nicola De Cecco, MD[a,b],*,
Akos Varga-Szemes, MD, PhD[a], Felix G. Meinel, MD[a,c],
Matthias Renker, MD[a,d], U. Joseph Schoepf, MD[a,e]

KEYWORDS

- Coronary CT angiography • Coronary artery disease • Myocardial perfusion imaging
- Dual-energy CT • Fractional flow reserve • Transluminal attenuation gradient

KEY POINTS

- Pure anatomic assessment of coronary stenosis with coronary computed tomography (CT) angiography does not adequately predict hemodynamic relevance.
- Different CT techniques for the functional assessment of coronary stenosis are under investigation in clinical trials.
- These techniques can directly assess the presence of myocardial ischemia (CT myocardial perfusion imaging) or the hemodynamic significance of a specific coronary stenosis (CT-based fractional flow reserve or transluminal attenuation gradient).
- The combined acquisition of morphologic and functional data with a single imaging modality can allow a fast and comprehensive appraisal of coronary artery disease.

INTRODUCTION

In the past decade, coronary computed tomography angiography (CCTA) has developed into a robust imaging technique for the noninvasive assessment of coronary arteries. Systematic analysis of studies using regular-dose and low-radiation-dose CCTA revealed a pooled sensitivity and specificity of CCTA of 98% and 89%, respectively.[1] These results compare favorably with alternative noninvasive coronary artery disease (CAD) imaging tests, in which single-photon emission computed tomography (SPECT) reaches sensitivities and specificities of 88% and 61%, PET of 84% and 81%, and cardiac magnetic resonance imaging of 89% and 76%, respectively.[2]

Disclosures: Dr U.J. Schoepf is a consultant for and/or receives research support from Bayer, Bracco, GE and Siemens. The other authors have no conflicts of interest to disclose.

[a] Department of Radiology and Radiological Science, Medical University of South Carolina, 25 Courtenay Drive, Charleston, SC 29425, USA; [b] Department of Radiological Sciences, Oncology and Pathology, University of Rome "Sapienza" – Polo Pontino, Via Franco Faggiana 34, Latina 04100, Italy; [c] Institute for Clinical Radiology, Ludwig-Maximilians-University Hospital, Marchioninistraße 15, Munich 81377, Germany; [d] Department of Cardiology, Kerckhoff Heart and Thorax Center, Benekestraße 2-8, Bad Nauheim 61231, Germany; [e] Division of Cardiology, Department of Medicine, Medical University of South Carolina, 25 Courtenay Drive, Charleston, SC 29425, USA

* Corresponding author. Department of Radiology & Radiological Sciences, Medical University of South Carolina, 25 Courtenay Drive, Charleston, SC 29425.
E-mail address: dececco@musc.edu

0033-8389/15/$ – see front matter © 2015 Elsevier Inc. All rights reserved.

radiologic.theclinics.com

Although CCTA remains a morphologic technique that can accurately depict coronary anatomy and the atherosclerotic plaque burden, it still has the same limitations as invasive coronary angiography (ICA) in evaluating the hemodynamic significance of flow-limiting stenosis. A growing body of evidence has shown that the pure anatomic evaluation of coronary stenosis does not adequately predict the hemodynamic relevance,[3] as shown by the results of the FAME (Fractional Flow Reserve Versus Angiography for Multivessel Evaluation) trial,[4] in which patients who underwent coronary revascularization guided by a functional test showed an improved outcome. Likewise, a substudy of the COURAGE (Clinical Outcomes Utilizing Revascularization and Aggressive Drug Evaluation) trial showed an increased reduction of ischemia by percutaneous coronary intervention[5] when patients selected through a functional test. Moreover, without functional data, ICA and CCTA can only provide limited correlation with myocardial perfusion defects.[6,7] Because revascularization should be guided by information on the state of myocardial perfusion, increasing efforts are being made to determine the functional relevance of lesions by CCTA.

Thanks to recent technological advancements, new computed tomography (CT) techniques are emerging that hold promise for achieving a comprehensive appraisal of anatomic and functional aspects of coronary heart disease with a single modality.

In this regard the existing CT functional analysis techniques for coronary physiology evaluation can be classified as follows:

1. Techniques for the direct assessment of myocardial ischemia:
   - Dynamic CT myocardial perfusion imaging (dCTMPI)
   - Static CT myocardial perfusion imaging (sCTMPI).
2. Techniques for the direct assessment of coronary stenosis significance:
   - CT-based fractional flow reserve (FFR)
   - Transluminal attenuation gradient (TAG)

The first group includes those techniques in which a dedicated stress/rest examination is performed to directly detect the presence of perfusion defects in the myocardium. They usually require state-of-the-art CT technology with the acquisition of specific protocols and the administration of pharmacologic stress. The second group involves those techniques in which direct assessment of the hemodynamic significance of a flow-limiting stenosis is performed during the postprocessing

of a standard CCTA data set, without the need for a dedicated acquisition protocol, pharmacologic stress, or state-of-the-art CT technology. The advantages and disadvantages of each of these techniques are summarized in **Table 1**.

Thus, this article provides a systematic overview of the available CT techniques for the functional analysis of flow-limiting stenosis of the coronary arteries.

TECHNIQUES FOR THE DIRECT ASSESSMENT OF MYOCARDIAL ISCHEMIA

CT assessment of myocardial perfusion is based on the distribution of the iodinated contrast material during its first pass through the myocardium as an indicator of myocardial blood flow. Because the contrast distribution is determined by the arterial blood supply, myocardial perfusion defects can be identified as hypoattenuating areas containing reduced amounts of contrast material.[8] In static myocardial perfusion imaging, a static image of myocardial attenuation during first-pass perfusion gives a snapshot of iodine distribution, whereas attenuation followed over several consecutive time points provides dynamic myocardial perfusion imaging.

DYNAMIC COMPUTED TOMOGRAPHY MYOCARDIAL PERFUSION IMAGING
Acquisition Technique and Data Analysis

Dynamic CT myocardial perfusion imaging is the only CT-based technology capable of directly measuring absolute myocardial perfusion. Through electrocardiogram (ECG)-synchronized, repetitive scanning of the myocardium and cardiac blood pool, time attenuation curves (TACs) are generated while the contrast bolus is undergoing first pass, arterial phase, and microcirculation.

The acquisition is usually performed in the systolic phase of the cardiac cycle because this provides several advantages, such as the constant length of the systolic phase regardless of heart frequency, less susceptibility to beam-hardening artifacts, and a shorter apicobasal length with a thicker myocardial wall.[9]

At present, there are 2 major approaches available for dynamic imaging. Multidetector CT (with 256 or 320 detectors) has the necessary detector width to cover the whole heart while the table is stationary.[10] Dual-source CT (DSCT) scanners are also able to perform dynamic myocardial perfusion by using a shuttle table mode.[11–13] Because the detector coverage of the DSCT is limited to 38 mm, the whole heart coverage can only be obtained by applying the shuttle mode, in

Table 1
Cardiac CT functional analysis techniques

	Direct Techniques for Myocardial Ischemia Assessment		Indirect Techniques for Coronary Flow Assessment	
	Dynamic	**Static First Pass**	**CT-based FFR**	**TAG**
Advantages	Absolute perfusion quantification	CCTA acquisition can be used as rest phase Dual energy improves iodine detection	No need for state-of-the-art CT technology No need for dedicated acquisition protocols Same radiation dose of CCTA	No need for state-of-the-art CT technology or dedicated postprocessing algorithms No need for dedicated acquisition protocols Same radiation dose of CCTA
Limitations	State-of-the-art CT technology High radiation dose Cannot used for the assessment of coronary artery morphology	No absolute perfusion quantification High radiation dose with rest/stress protocol State-of-the-art technology needed for dual-energy acquisition	Dedicated software and high computational power Long postprocessing time Calcification or low-quality data sets can limit the analysis	Indirect assessment of FFR Dependent on several parameters that can hamper the evaluation

which the table moves back and forth between the 2 scanning positions, resulting in a total coverage of 73 mm.

Both semiquantitative and quantitative analysis methods are available for the assessment of dynamic myocardial perfusion. The upslope analysis is the most common semiquantitative method used to evaluate TACs. With this method, semiquantitative measurements from the upslope portion of the TACs are produced, deriving blood flow–related parameters in the form of time to peak, peak enhancement, attenuation upslope, and area under the TAC. Ischemic myocardial regions correspond with decreased upslope values and peak enhancement with an increased time-to-peak value (**Fig. 1**).

Quantitative measurements of myocardial perfusion are based on the recognition of input and output functions of blood flow and extraction rate of the contrast agent from the intravascular space, in order to allow the extraction of absolute perfusion parameters through mathematical model fitting (**Fig. 2**). In this case, the most commonly used methods are the deconvolution methods and derivatives of the deconvolution methods. Deconvolution methods have previously been used in cardiac magnetic resonance (CMR) perfusion[14]

and rely on the entirety of the first-pass data set in order to derive a perfusion estimate. Based on a 2-compartment model, blood-attenuation and tissue-attenuation curves are created. In dual-source CT systems, a modified deconvolution method compatible with the slower sampling rate of shuttle mode has been the most frequently used in available studies to date.[11,15,16]

Limitations

The major limitation of dynamic CT perfusion technology is the comparably high radiation exposure. Combined rest and stress CT perfusion studies can require a mean radiation dose of 18 mSv.[12] Furthermore, dynamic CT perfusion acquisition cannot be used for the assessment of coronary artery morphology; thus, it has to be performed in addition to the regular CCTA. Other challenges specific to dynamic perfusion include the requirement for breath holding over 30 to 40 seconds. Moreover, the shuttle mode data from 2 separate table positions are combined, thereby increasing the risk of spatial misalignment resulting from table movements or extrasystole and arrhythmia.

Several solutions have been developed to address these problems. Motion correction and

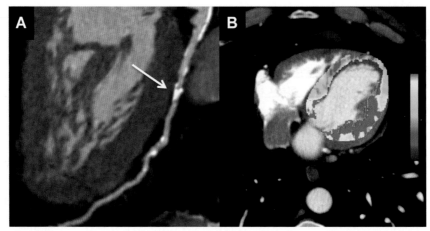

Fig. 1. Dynamic CT myocardial perfusion imaging. This 72-year-old man presented with recurrent chest pain. CCTA showed a calcified stenosis in the left descending artery (*A, arrow*). The parametric map of myocardial blood flow (*B*) derived from stress dynamic CT myocardial perfusion imaging shows an area of decreased myocardial blood flow to the anteroseptal wall of the left ventricle. The scale shows myocardial blood flow in milliliters per 100 mL per minute.

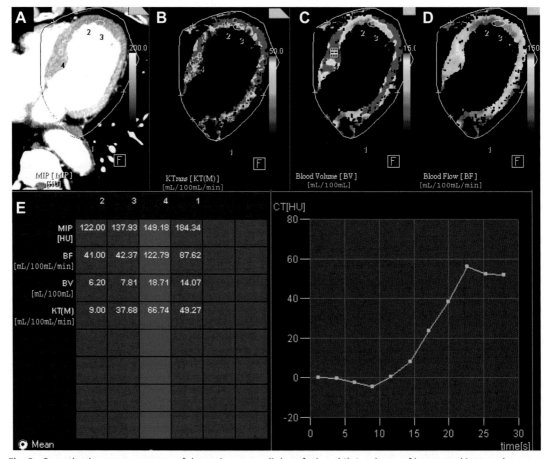

Fig. 2. Quantitative measurements of dynamic myocardial perfusion. (*A*) A volume of interested is traced, encompassing the left ventricle, and the ascending aorta and descending aorta are designated as the input and output functions. From these parameters, the volume transfer coefficient (K-trans) (*B*), blood volume (*C*), and blood flow (*D*) of the entire myocardium are derived, obtaining a quantitative evaluation of myocardial perfusion (*E*).

beam-hardening correction algorithms can increase spatial alignment, improving myocardial evaluation.[17,18] Semiautomated three-dimensional software has been developed for perfusion data analysis and can substantially reduce processing time, improving the consistency of the acquired data and thus sustaining the integration of dynamic perfusion in clinical workflow.[19]

In addition, the reduction of the tube kilovoltage, along with the application of iterative reconstruction techniques,[20–22] can be beneficial in reducing radiation dosage and keeping it at an acceptable level, especially compared with nuclear imaging.[23] With the application of these recent technological advancements, a comprehensive stress/rest static CT myocardial perfusion protocol can deliver a radiation dosage as low as 2.5 mSv.[24]

Clinical Results

Diagnostic accuracy of dynamic CT perfusion has been validated in comparison with CMR, SPECT, ICA, and FFR,[11–13,25–30] showing a sensitivity, specificity, positive predictive value (PPV), and negative predictive value (NPV) in the range of 76% to 100%, 74% to 100%, 48% to 100%, and 82% to 100%, respectively (Table 2).

In particular, compared with the gold standard of invasive FFR, a cutoff of 75 mL/100 mL/min for the differentiation of hemodynamically significant and nonsignificant stenosis was reported by Bamberg and colleagues.[25] Rossi and colleagues[29] found a similar cutoff of 78 mL/100 mL/min in a study of 80 patients. The investigators further showed improvement of specificity compared with visual and quantitative ICA for patients with intermediate coronary stenosis (30%–70% by ICA), compared with the reference standard of FFR.[15]

A recent multicenter study on 146 patients[31] showed the utility of dynamic CT myocardial perfusion in the global quantitative assessment of left ventricular perfusion. A cutoff value of 92 mL/100 mL/min seems to be able to distinguish between global myocardial hypoperfusion in the presence of 3-vessel disease. This result could be clinically useful for differentiating normal from globally reduced myocardial perfusion in the presence of balanced ischemia.

STATIC COMPUTED TOMOGRAPHY MYOCARDIAL PERFUSION IMAGING
Acquisition Technique and Data Analysis

Static CT myocardial perfusion imaging can be further categorized into single-energy and dual-energy techniques.

Single-energy First-pass Computed Tomography

Static CT perfusion imaging uses static distribution of contrast material during early arterial attenuation to detect myocardial blood perfusion abnormalities during the early arterial phase of the first-pass contrast enhancement[32] and provide a qualitative visual assessment of a single snapshot of myocardial iodine contrast attenuation. Image acquisition is performed at peak coronary contrast and thus the scan times, together with the acquisition parameters and radiation dose, are identical to those for CCTA. For this reason, the rest acquisition can serve as the morphologic assessment of the coronary arteries,[33] without any additional acquisition time and radiation dose, as should otherwise be done for dynamic perfusion imaging. Furthermore, CT static perfusion can be performed using any CT scanner that is capable of acquiring diagnostic-quality CCTA.[34]

On static CT myocardial perfusion imaging, myocardial blood pool defects have mostly been qualitatively assessed by visual evaluation of left ventricular myocardial contrast enhancement (Fig. 3). Reconstruction at several phases of the cardiac cycle, if corresponding data are available, can help in distinguishing suspected defects from artifacts. A real perfusion defect should persist as hypoattenuation throughout the cardiac cycle.[34]

As a comparable quantifiable measure, the transmural perfusion ratio, which is the ratio between mean subendocardial and mean subepicardial attenuation, has shown good predictive value compared with SPECT and invasive angiography.[35,36] The attenuation of the ischemic myocardium is usually compared either with the remote myocardium or with the left ventricular cavity. Indices for transmural, subendocardial, and myocardial perfusion provided incremental diagnostic accuracy when using control group measurements as a standard.[37]

Compared with dynamic CT perfusion, static CT perfusion imaging is a favorable choice in terms of radiation dose. A comprehensive static CT perfusion study including rest and stress acquisitions delivers an average dose of 12 mSv (see Table 1). This value is supposedly decreased with the application of the latest technology in terms of iterative reconstruction and low-kilovolt acquisition.

Dual-energy First-pass Computed Tomography

Similar to the single-energy static technique, single-shot dual-energy CT generates a snapshot of the myocardial iodine distribution at a single

Table 2
Static and dynamic CT myocardial perfusion studies

Author	Patient Population	CT Technology	CT Perfusion Protocol	Sensitivity	Specificity	PPV	NPV	Average CT Dose (mSv)
Dynamic CT Myocardial Perfusion Studies								
Bastarrika et al,[11] 2010	10	Second DSCT	Stress	86	98	94	96	18.8[a]
Ho et al,[12] 2010	35	Second DSCT	Stress/Rest	83	78	79	82	18.2
Bamberg et al,[25] 2011	33	Second DSCT	Stress	93	87	75	97	10
Wang et al,[30] 2012	30	Second DSCT	Stress	85	92	55	98	9.5
	—	—	—	90	81	58	96	—
Weininger et al,[13] 2012	20	Second DSCT	Stress	86	98	94	96	12.8[b]
	—	—	—	84	92	88	92	—
Greif et al,[27] 2013	65	Second DSCT	Stress	95	74	48	98	9.7
Huber et al,[28] 2013	32	256-MDCT	Stress	76	100	100	90	9.5
Rossi et al,[29] 2014	80	Second DSCT	Stress	88	90	77	95	9.4
Bamberg et al,[26] 2014	31	Second DSCT	Stress	78	75	51	91	11.1
	—	—	—	100	75	92	100	—
Static Single-energy CT Myocardial Perfusion Studies								
Kachenoura et al,[37] 2009	64	64-MDCT	Rest	96	68	88	87	7–15
George et al,[51] 2009	24	64-MDCT	Rest	86	92	92	85	16.8
	16	256-MDCT	Stress/rest	75	87	60	93	21.6
Blankstein et al,[42] 2009	34	First DSCT	Stress/rest	84	80	71	90	11.1
Cury et al,[50] 2010	36	64-MDCT	Stress/rest	88	79	67	93	14.7

Rocha-Filho et al,[55] 2010	35	First DSCT	Stress/rest	91	91	86	93	11.8
Feuchtner et al,[24] 2011	30	Second DSCT	Stress/rest	96	88	93	94	2.5
Cury et al,[35] 2011	26	64-MDCT	Stress/rest	94	78	89	87	14.4
Ko et al,[52] 2012	42	320-MDCT	Stress/rest	76	84	82	79	11.1
George et al,[36] 2012	50	320-MDCT	Rest/stress	50	89	55	87	11.5
Nasis et al,[53] 2013	20	320-MDCT	Rest/stress	94	98	94	98	9.2
Rochitte et al,[56] 2014	381	320-MDCT	Rest/stress	80	74	65	86	9.3
				52	88	57	86	—
Osawa et al,[54] 2014	145	Second DSCT	Rest	85	94	79	96	14.8
Static Dual-energy CT Myocardial Perfusion Studies								
Ruzsics et al,[38] 2009	36	First DSCT	Rest	92	93	83	97	14
Ko et al,[44] 2011	50	First DSCT	Stress	89	78	74	91	8.6
Wang et al,[60] 2011	31	First DSCT	Rest	89	98	87	98	10.5
				82	91	91	81	—
Ko et al,[58] 2012	45	First DSCT	Rest/stress	89	74	80	85	16.5
Ko et al,[59] 2014	40	First DSCT	Rest	42	83	59	70	4.2
			Stress	87	79	71	91	4.6
Kim et al,[57] 2014	50	Second DSCT	Stress/rest	77	94	53	98	12.5
				94	71	60	96	—
De Cecco et al,[61] 2014	29	Second DSCT	Stress/rest	86	75	—	—	16.9

Abbreviations: DSCT, dual-source computed tomography; MDCT, multidetector computed tomography.
[a] Including calcium scoring, rest CT angiography, and delayed enhancement.
[b] Including rest CT angiography, and delayed enhancement.

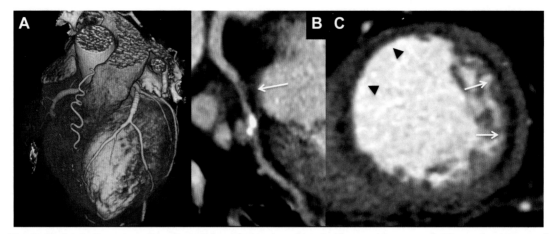

Fig. 3. Static single-energy CT myocardial perfusion imaging. A 68-year-old woman with a prior history of myocardial infarction and stent insertion in the left anterior descending artery (*A*), presented with recurrent chest pain. CCTA showed the presence of a soft plaque in the circumflex artery causing stenosis (*B, arrow*). Contrast-enhanced, retrospectively ECG-gated, first-pass, arterial-phase CT study showed the presence of a subendocardial dark rim of hypoattenuation in the lateral wall (*C, white arrows*) suggesting myocardial ischemia or infarction. Likewise, a second myocardial dark rim consistent with previous myocardial infarction was observed in the territory of vascularization of the left anterior descending artery (*black arrowheads*).

time point using 2 different kilovolt acquisitions of the same body region. Myocardial perfusion dual-energy CT (DECT) can be performed using dual-source CT[38] or single-source CT with rapid kilovolt switching.[39] A reduction in beam-hardening artifacts and direct visualization of myocardial iodine content give DECT multiple advantages compared with single-energy acquisition. For these reasons, perfusion defects and late enhancement are often more easily recognized on DECT.[34]

Different vendor-specific CT technologies have been developed to perform dual-energy acquisitions. Dual-source scanners make use of independent tubes paired with 2 detectors, which simultaneously operate with low (80–90–100 kV) and high (140–150 kV) tube voltages,[38,40–45] whereas single-source CT scanners can produce dual-energy images through rapid tube current switching between 80 and 140 kV.[39,46] Both prospective ECG-triggered and retrospectively ECG-gated protocols are available for DECT acquisition. Previous challenges in temporal resolution have been overcome with second-generation dual-source scanners (75 milliseconds)[40] and third-generation scanners are promising to further decrease temporal resolution.[21]

Independent from the technology used, an iodine distribution map is generated by merging the low and high kilovolt data sets. Because iodine concentration is a surrogate for myocardial perfusion, the myocardial blood pool can be quantified based on the per-voxel amount of iodine.[47] Dedicated software typically generates a color-coded iodine distribution map overlay on top of a virtual noncontrasted image (**Fig. 4**). The iodine concentrations are normalized to the myocardial areas with normal perfusion.[43]

Areas with reduced myocardial iodine content at DECT perfusion studies are mainly evaluated with a qualitative approach in the literature, which can introduce bias, given that myocardial blood pool defect interpretation is often highly user dependent compared with the absolute quantitative assessment obtained with dynamic perfusion. Quantitative evaluation was recently performed on a phantom study showing high accuracy for myocardial iodine quantification.[47]

Radiation doses for prospective ECG-triggered or retrospectively ECG-triggered acquisition are equivalent to those of single-energy cardiac CT acquisition.[34]

Limitations

As previously mentioned, the main limitation of static single-energy and dual-energy CT myocardial perfusion techniques was their reliance on the acquisition timing, which can significantly influence the diagnostic accuracy. Because single-shot techniques only acquire a single data set, the peak of the contrast attenuation may be missed.[32] Furthermore, the data collection from consecutive parts of the heart may be performed during different cardiac cycles depending on the CT system and acquisition technique, resulting in heterogeneous apicobasal attenuation. In addition, several types of artifacts may be associated

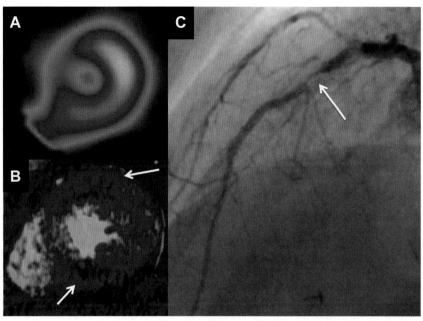

Fig. 4. Static dual-energy CT myocardial perfusion imaging. A 65-year-old man presented with recurrent chest pain. Stress SPECT imaging showed the presence of an inducible myocardial perfusion defect in the anteroseptal wall (*A*) suggesting myocardial ischemia. Contrast-enhanced, retrospectively ECG-gated, first-pass, arterial-phase, dual-energy CT technique showed an anteroseptal and inferior wall contrast uptake defect in the iodine map (*B*, *arrows*). Coronary angiography confirmed the presence of a tight coronary stenosis in the left anterior descending artery (*C*, *arrow*).

with single-shot image acquisitions, such as beam-hardening, motion, and partial scan artifacts.[18,48,49]

Clinical Results

Static single-energy studies showed high specificity and sensitivity for the detection of hemodynamically significant CAD compared with SPECT, SPECT/ICA,[35–37,42,50–56] or CMR.[24] Vessel-based sensitivity and specificity range from 50% to 96% and 68% to 98%, respectively, whereas the PPV and NPV are from 55% to 94% and 79% to 98%, respectively (see **Table 2**).

The accuracy of CCTA is significantly improved by the addition of CT perfusion imaging, and the combined protocol has the ability to identify patients with hemodynamically significant CAD. Initial evidence showed that the addition of the rest-only static single-energy study to CCTA significantly improved diagnostic performance compared with CCTA alone with a sensitivity and specificity of 85% and 94%, respectively.[54]

Rocha-Filoh and colleagues[55] showed considerable improvements in sensitivity (91% from 83%), specificity (91% from 71%), PPV (86% from 66%), and NPV (87% from 93%) by adding a stress phase to CCTA for detection of stenosis

greater than 50% against a standard of invasive angiography in 35 patients with a high risk of CAD.

In addition, the first single-vendor multicenter trial[56] evaluating 381 patients compared with combined ICA and SPECT showed that the accuracy of CCTA in identifying patients with hemodynamically significant CAD is significantly improved by the addition of CT perfusion imaging. The sensitivity, specificity, PPV, and NPV of the combined method in the patient-based analysis were 80%, 74%, 65%, and 86%, respectively. The patient-based diagnostic accuracy of combined CCTA and CT perfusion imaging in patients without prior myocardial infarction or prior CAD accuracy was 90% and 93%, respectively, and 87% in the whole patient population.

Dual-energy CT myocardial perfusion studies performed during rest or stress protocol showed good accuracy compared with different reference modalities.[38,44,57–60] Vessel-based sensitivity and specificity for the stress/rest approach range from 77% to 94% and 74% to 94%, respectively, whereas the PPV and NPV are from 53% to 91% and 85% to 98%, respectively.

Compared with single-energy CT myocardial perfusion, the dual-energy technique showed superior diagnostic performance because of the use of dual-energy iodine maps for the detection of perfusion defects with SPECT as the reference standard.[41]

Recent studies have shown that the combined analysis of CCTA and DECT myocardial perfusion reduces the number of false-positives in a population at high risk for coronary artery disease (with a 17% higher specificity than that of either test separately), and outperforms the anatomic test of CCTA alone for detection of hemodynamically significant coronary artery stenosis.[61]

Ko and colleagues[59] found fair agreement between rest and stress dual-energy CT iodine maps, and described a significant improvement in the accuracy using the stress protocol (0.83) compared with rest protocol (0.62) for the detection of hemodynamically significant CAD. However, Meinel and colleagues[62] recently showed that the addition of a delayed-phase acquisition

for late iodine enhancement does not improve diagnostic accuracy and can thus safely be omitted. Furthermore, they showed that almost one-half of reversible perfusion defects at SPECT are classified as fixed with DECT.

Pharmacologic Stress Agents

The sensitivity for the detection of reversible perfusion defects significantly improves under pharmacologic stress.[63] Such stress is induced by the vasodilative substances adenosine, regadenoson, dobutamine, or dipyridamole (**Table 3**).[64] In healthy subjects, the response from coronary vessels to pharmacologic stress induces hyperemic myocardium. A hypoattenuated myocardium during pharmacologic stress is classified by comparison with images in rest conditions.

Table 3
Common pharmacologic agents used for stress perfusion

	Adenosine	Regadenoson	Dobutamine	Dipyridamole
Mechanism	Adenosine receptor agonist	A_{2A} selective adenosine receptor agonist	Stimulation of beta-1 receptors	Increase endogenous levels of adenosine blocking cellular uptake
Effects	Vasodilator	Vasodilator	Increases heart rate and myocardial contractility	Indirect vasodilator
Half-life	<10 s	2 min	2 min	30 min
Dosage	140 μg/kg/min for 3–6 min	0.4 mg at 5 mL/s	High-dose protocol: IV dobutamine infusion at 3-min stages (10, 20, 30, 40 μg/kg/min) Low-dose protocol: 5–10 μg/kg/min	0.56 mg/kg IV over 4 min
Contraindications	(1) High-grade AV block; (2) asthma or COPD; (3) sinus bradycardia; (4) systemic hypotension (BP <90 mm Hg); (5) severe carotid stenosis	(1) High-grade AV block; (2) sinus bradycardia; (3) systemic hypotension (BP <90 mm Hg); (4) severe carotid stenosis	(1) Severe hypertension (>220/120 mm Hg); (2) congestive heart failure; (3) unstable angina; (4) aortic valve stenosis (peak gradient >50 mm Hg); (5) HCM; (6) complex arrhythmias; (7) myocarditis; (8) pericarditis	(1) High-grade AV block; (2) asthma or COPD; (3) sinus bradycardia; (4) systemic hypotension (BP <90 mm Hg); (5) severe carotid stenosis

Abbreviations: AV, atrioventricular; BP, blood pressure; COPD, chronic obstructive pulmonary disease; HCM, hypertrophic cardiomyopathy; IV, intravenous.

Because of a safety profile, the 2 most commonly used agents in CT perfusion are adenosine and regadenoson. Adenosine is administered in continuous infusion with a dose of 140 μg/kg/min for at least 2 minutes to induce an increase of 10 to 20 beats per minute compared with the resting heart rate. Regadenoson is a selective A2A receptor agonist (whereas adenosine acts on A1 receptors), thus allowing regadenoson to cause fewer systemic side effects, which is beneficial for patients with asthma or chronic obstructive pulmonary disease.[65,66] Furthermore, because regadenoson can be administered in a single dose, CT studies are more time efficient.[64] Both stress agents may cause moderate to severe complications.[67,68] Ventricular tachycardia and transient, asymptomatic atrioventricular block occur in 0.14% of patients, and recent case reports indicate that adenosine and regadenoson may cause acute myocardial infarction and death.[68–70]

Clinical protocols describing the appropriate rest, stress, and delayed enhancement acquisition timing both for static and dynamic myocardial perfusion studies are presented in **Fig. 5**.

TECHNIQUES FOR THE DIRECT ASSESSMENT OF CORONARY STENOSIS SIGNIFICANCE

These techniques are based on the postprocessing analysis of the standard CCTA data set without the need of stress agents, additional acquisition protocols, radiation dose administration, or contrast medium injections. CT-based FFR (FFR-CT) requires the used of dedicated off-site postprocessing or in-house dedicated software. Otherwise, the TAG can be calculated directly from the in-lumen contrast medium density without the need for any dedicated software.

COMPUTED TOMOGRAPHY–BASED FRACTIONAL FLOW RESERVE
Technique and Data Analysis

FFR was developed to evaluate lesion-specific hemodynamic relevance. FFR expresses the ratio between the maximum coronary flow in the presence of a stenosis and the maximum coronary flow in the hypothetical absence of a stenosis. In routine clinical practice, hyperemia is induced by pharmacologic stress agents and FFR is measured as the coronary pressure distal to the stenosis of interest divided by the proximal pressure within the ascending aorta. FFR values less than 0.80 or less than 0.75 have been shown to cause ischemia and indicate the necessity for revascularization.[4,71] Therefore, FFR was established as the reference standard for assessing the functional impact of a stenotic lesion on myocardial perfusion.

Recent technological advancements enable the noninvasive evaluation of FFR based on standard

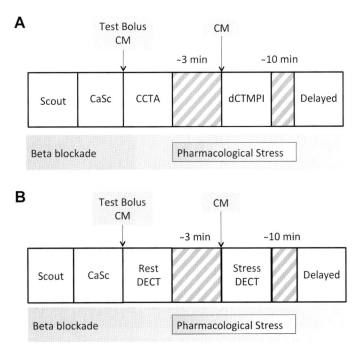

Fig. 5. Clinical protocols describing the appropriate rest, stress and delayed enhancement acquisition timing both for dynamic (A) and static (B) myocardial perfusion studies. CaSc, calcium score; CM, contrast medium.

CCTA acquisitions.[72] Noninvasive FFR-CT is computed from CT angiography images that apply computational fluid dynamic techniques.[73]

FFR-CT builds on the principles of computational fluid dynamics, a branch of fluid mechanics used to model fluid flows, originally developed for nonmedical fields such as airplane design. FFR-CT was initially introduced in CCTA imaging by HeartFlow, Inc (FFR$_{CT}$, HeartFlow, Inc, Redwood City, CA) as an off-site service that can take advantage of parallel supercomputers at core laboratories to solve complex Reynolds-averaged Navier-Stokes equations. A newly developed algorithm (cFFR, Siemens Healthcare, Forchheim, Germany) enables the on-site assessment of FFR-CT without the need for outsourcing analysis, thus promising time-efficient, in-hospital evaluation of FFR from CCTA (**Fig. 6**).[74]

Compared with myocardial perfusion techniques, FFR-CT requires neither dedicated acquisition nor the administration of stress agents, which makes it possible to apply this technique to any CCTA acquisition, regardless of the scanner generation, without any additional risk for the patients that may stem from higher radiation dose or drug administration.

Limitations

The main limitations of FFR-CT are in the prolonged need for the analysis and the necessity to outsource the analysis to a site with sufficient computational power. The development of a new algorithm that facilitates a fast in-house analysis could allow the application of FFR-CT in clinical practice.

Clinical Results

Compared with morphologic CCTA evaluation alone, the combination of CCTA and FFR-CT provides significantly improved diagnostic accuracy for the diagnosis of hemodynamically significant CAD (**Table 4**).[72,75]

Three prospective clinical trials have shown that the FFR-CT approach by HeartFlow, Inc compares favorably with the invasively derived reference standard FFR.[75–77] Within the single-center DISCOVER-FLOW (Diagnosis of Ischemia-causing Stenoses Obtained Via Noninvasive Fractional Flow Reserve) trial,[76] FFR-CT, compared with invasive FFR, showed an accuracy of 81%, a sensitivity of 93%, a specificity of 82%, a PPV of 85%, and a NPV of 91% on a per-patient basis.

In the international multicenter trial DeFACTO (Determination of Fractional Flow Reserve by Anatomic Computed Tomographic Angiography),[77] FFR-CT yielded higher diagnostic performance than anatomic CCTA for the identification of functionally relevant stenoses (accuracy, 73% vs 64%; sensitivity, 90% vs 84%; specificity, 54% vs 42%; PPV, 67% vs 61%; NPV, 84% vs 72%).[77] The sensitivity in patients with intermediate-grade stenosis showed an increase greater than 2-fold in FFR-CT compared with CCTA alone (82% vs 37%), without any decrease in specificity (66% vs 66%).[77]

In addition, the NXT (Analysis of Coronary Blood Flow Using CT Angiography: Next Steps) trial[75] showed superior diagnostic accuracy of FFR-CT compared with anatomic CCTA on both a per-patient (area under the curve [AUC], 0.90 vs 0.81) and per-vessel basis (AUC, 0.93 vs 0.79). Compared with CCTA alone, FFR-CT correctly

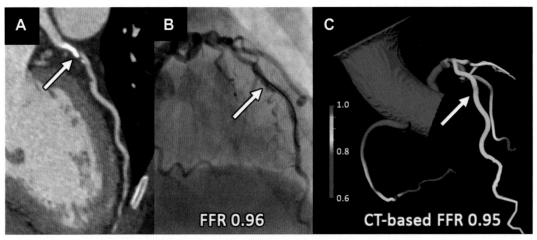

Fig. 6. FFR-CT. A 62 year-old man with a CCTA finding of calcified stenosis in the proximal left descending artery (*A, arrow*) with a coronary angiography FFR confirming the flow-limiting nature (*B, arrow*). Using FFR-CT analysis, a similar FFR value was obtained at the level of the corresponding stenosis (*C, arrow*).

Table 4
FFR-CT and TAG studies

Author	Patient Population	Sensitivity	Specificity	PPV	NPV
FFR-CT Studies					
DISCOVER-FLOW[76] 2011	103	93	82	85	91
DeFACTO[77] 2011	252	90	52	67	84
NXT[75] 2014	251	86	79	65	93
Renker et al,[78] 2014	53	84	94	71	97
TAG Studies					
Choi et al,[82] 2011	126	83	94	96	75
Yoon et al,[85] 2012	53	37	88	67	69
Wong et al,[81] 2013	54	77	74	67	86
Stuijfzand et al,[80] TAG 2014	85	95	76	98	54
TAG-ExC	—	95	77	98	56
TAG-CCO	—	95	76	98	54
Wong et al,[86] 2014	75	73	97	92	87
CCTA + TAG + CTP	—	88	83	74	93

Abbreviations: CCO, coronary density to corresponding descending aortic opacification; CTP, CT perfusion; DeFACTO, Determination of Fractional Flow Reserve by Anatomic Computed Tomographic Angiography; DISCOVER-FLOW, Diagnosis of Ischemia-causing Stenoses Obtained Via Noninvasive Fractional Flow Reserve; NXT, Analysis of Coronary Blood Flow Using CT Angiography: Next Steps; TAG-ExC, TAG excluding calcified coronary segments.

reclassified 68% of false-positive patient results as confirmed by invasive FFR.[75]

A recent study performed using the experimental cFFR software showed the possibility of obtaining similar results with an in-house analysis. On a per-lesion and per-patient basis, FFR-CT resulted in a sensitivity of 85% and 94%, a specificity of 85% and 84%, a PPV of 71% and 71%, and an NPV of 93% and 97%, respectively.[78]

In addition, a novel field for computational fluid dynamics is the possibility of virtual stent placement, which would allow the assessment and comparison of different stenting strategies and the prediction of outcomes based on changes in the functional assessment of FFR.[79]

TRANSLUMINAL ATTENUATION GRADIENT
Technique and Data Analysis

TAG is a recently introduced image postprocessing method providing functional assessment of CAD. TAG is defined as the contrast opacification gradient along the length of a coronary artery on CCTA images.[80] As with FFR-CT, TGA is based on the conventional CCTA dataset and does not require additional radiation or contrast material exposure.[81] Preliminary data suggest that TAG provides additional functional information compared with CCTA, improving the accuracy in detecting hemodynamically significant CAD.[81]

Limitations

TAG interpretation can be hampered by the temporal uniformity that is disrupted by multiple heartbeat acquisitions. Furthermore, distortions from highly calcified coronary plaques may influence results. In order to avoid these limitations, 2 correction models have been proposed based on either dephasing of contrast delivery by relating coronary density to corresponding descending aortic opacification (CCO) in the same axial plain[82] (CCO is then defined as the quotient of this value obtained proximal and distal of a coronary lesion; **Fig. 7**), or by excluding calcified coronary segments (TAG-ExC).[83]

Clinical Results

TGA, CCO, or TAG-ExC used alone or in combination with CCTA, FFR-CT, or CTMPI showed wide variation in accuracy for the detection of flow-limiting stenosis. Compared with ICA and FFR, vessel-based sensitivity and specificity ranged from 37% to 95% and 76% to 97%, respectively, whereas the PPV and NPV were from 67% to 98% and 54% to 93%, respectively (see **Table 4**).

Choi and colleagues[84] showed that TAG compared with ICA decreased maximum stenosis severity and that the addition of TAG to the interpretation of CCTA improved diagnostic accuracy, especially in vessels with calcified lesions.

In comparing TAG with FFR-CT, Yoon and colleagues[85] found that the diagnostic accuracy of

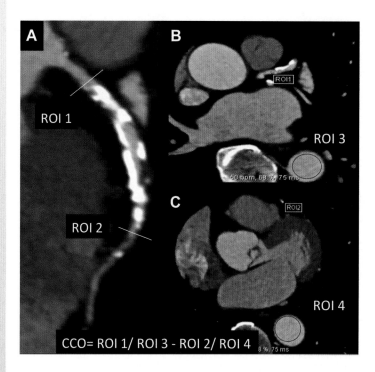

CCO= ROI 1/ ROI 3 - ROI 2/ ROI 4

Fig. 7. CCO technique. Intravessel density is measured before and after the coronary stenosis (*A*); the obtained values are then corrected for the corresponding density of the descending aorta measured at the same level (*B, C*). In this case, a CCO value of 0.243 was calculated, indicating a nonsignificant stenosis. Coronary angiography FFR confirmed the finding with a value of 0.85. ROI, region of interest.

FFR-CT was superior to TAG for the diagnosis of ischemia-causing lesions as determined by an invasive FFR.

Using 320-detector-row CT, Wong and colleagues[81] found that TAG provides acceptable prediction of invasive FFR. The combination of TAG and CCTA assessment may have incremental predictive value compared with CCTA alone for detecting functionally significant coronary arterial stenosis.

In contrast, Stuijfzand and colleagues[80] showed in 85 patients that TAG and TAG-ExC, compared with FFR, did not discriminate between vessels with or without hemodynamically significant lesions. Only CCO was significantly lower in vessels with impaired resting flow, but it was not possible to distinguish significant stenosis from low-grade stenosis.

In addition, in a recent study comparing TAG plus CCTA and CT perfusion (CTP) plus CCTA, Wong and colleagues[86] found that each method provides similar diagnostic accuracy for the functional assessment of coronary stenosis, with the best results provide by a combined protocol CCTA plus CTP plus TAG (sensitivity, 73% vs 88%; specificity, 97% vs 83%; PPV, 92% vs 74%; NPV, 87% vs 93%).

SUMMARY

In an environment in which CCTA has been established as the imaging technique of choice for morphologic noninvasive assessment of CAD,

recent technological improvements are producing valuable information on coronary flow and myocardium blood supply in clinical CCTA studies. Based on a growing body of evidence, the combination of morphologic and functional assessment can enhance the accuracy of CCTA in detecting hemodynamically relevant CAD. Larger multicenter trials are needed in order to confirm these positive initial results and to define the most effective functional technique, its cost-effectiveness, and the impact on patient management and outcome.

REFERENCES

1. von Ballmoos MW, Haring B, Juillerat P, et al. Meta-analysis: diagnostic performance of low-radiation-dose coronary computed tomography angiography. Ann Intern Med 2011;154:413–20.
2. Jaarsma C, Leiner T, Bekkers SC, et al. Diagnostic performance of noninvasive myocardial perfusion imaging using single-photon emission computed tomography, cardiac magnetic resonance, and positron emission tomography imaging for the detection of obstructive coronary artery disease: a meta-analysis. J Am Coll Cardiol 2012;59:1719–28.
3. Sarno G, Decraemer I, Vanhoenacker PK, et al. On the inappropriateness of noninvasive multidetector computed tomography coronary angiography to trigger coronary revascularization: a comparison with invasive angiography. JACC Cardiovasc Interv 2009;2:550–7.

4. Pijls NH, Fearon WF, Tonino PA, et al. Fractional flow reserve versus angiography for guiding percutaneous coronary intervention in patients with multivessel coronary artery disease: 2-year follow-up of the FAME (Fractional Flow Reserve Versus Angiography for Multivessel Evaluation) study. J Am Coll Cardiol 2010;56:177–84.

5. Shaw LJ, Berman DS, Maron DJ, et al. Optimal medical therapy with or without percutaneous coronary intervention to reduce ischemic burden: results from the Clinical Outcomes Utilizing Revascularization and Aggressive Drug Evaluation (COURAGE) trial nuclear substudy. Circulation 2008;117:1283–91.

6. Kern MJ, Samady H. Current concepts of integrated coronary physiology in the catheterization laboratory. J Am Coll Cardiol 2010;55:173–85.

7. Meijboom WB, Van Mieghem CA, van Pelt N, et al. Comprehensive assessment of coronary artery stenoses: computed tomography coronary angiography versus conventional coronary angiography and correlation with fractional flow reserve in patients with stable angina. J Am Coll Cardiol 2008; 52:636–43.

8. George RT, Silva C, Cordeiro MA, et al. Multidetector computed tomography myocardial perfusion imaging during adenosine stress. J Am Coll Cardiol 2006;48:153–60.

9. Mahnken AH, Klotz E, Pietsch H, et al. Quantitative whole heart stress perfusion CT imaging as noninvasive assessment of hemodynamics in coronary artery stenosis: preliminary animal experience. Invest Radiol 2010;45:298–305.

10. Hsiao EM, Rybicki FJ, Steigner M. CT coronary angiography: 256-slice and 320-detector row scanners. Curr Cardiol Rep 2010;12:68–75.

11. Bastarrika G, Ramos-Duran L, Rosenblum MA, et al. Adenosine-stress dynamic myocardial CT perfusion imaging: initial clinical experience. Invest Radiol 2010;45:306–13.

12. Ho KT, Chua KC, Klotz E, et al. Stress and rest dynamic myocardial perfusion imaging by evaluation of complete time-attenuation curves with dual-source CT. JACC Cardiovasc Imaging 2010;3: 811–20.

13. Weininger M, Schoepf UJ, Ramachandra A, et al. Adenosine-stress dynamic real-time myocardial perfusion CT and adenosine-stress first-pass dual-energy myocardial perfusion CT for the assessment of acute chest pain: initial results. Eur J Radiol 2012; 81:3703–10.

14. Futamatsu H, Wilke N, Klassen C, et al. Usefulness of cardiac magnetic resonance imaging for coronary artery disease detection. Minerva Cardioangiol 2007;55:105–14.

15. Rossi A, Merkus D, Klotz E, et al. Stress myocardial perfusion: imaging with multidetector CT. Radiology 2014;270:25–46.

16. So A, Wisenberg G, Islam A, et al. Non-invasive assessment of functionally relevant coronary artery stenoses with quantitative CT perfusion: preliminary clinical experiences. Eur Radiol 2012;22:39–50.

17. Muenzel D, Kabus S, Gramer B, et al. Dynamic CT perfusion imaging of the myocardium: a technical note on improvement of image quality. PLoS One 2013;8:e75263.

18. Stenner P, Schmidt B, Bruder H, et al. Partial scan artifact reduction (PSAR) for the assessment of cardiac perfusion in dynamic phase-correlated CT. Med Phys 2009;36:5683–94.

19. Ebersberger U, Marcus RP, Schoepf UJ, et al. Dynamic CT myocardial perfusion imaging: performance of 3D semi-automated evaluation software. Eur Radiol 2014;24:191–9.

20. Zhang LJ, Qi L, Wang J, et al. Feasibility of prospectively ECG-triggered high-pitch coronary CT angiography with 30 mL iodinated contrast agent at 70 kVp: initial experience. Eur Radiol 2014;24:1537–46.

21. Meinel FG, Canstein C, Schoepf UJ, et al. Image quality and radiation dose of low tube voltage 3rd generation dual-source coronary CT angiography in obese patients: a phantom study. Eur Radiol 2014;24:1643–50.

22. Yin WH, Lu B, Hou ZH, et al. Detection of coronary artery stenosis with sub-milliSievert radiation dose by prospectively ECG-triggered high-pitch spiral CT angiography and iterative reconstruction. Eur Radiol 2013;23:2927–33.

23. De Cecco CN, Meinal FG, Chiaramida SA, et al. Coronary artery computed tomography scanning. Circulation 2014;129:1341–5.

24. Feuchtner G, Goetti R, Plass A, et al. Adenosine stress high-pitch 128-slice dual-source myocardial computed tomography perfusion for imaging of reversible myocardial ischemia: comparison with magnetic resonance imaging. Circ Cardiovasc Imaging 2011;4:540–9.

25. Bamberg F, Becker A, Schwarz F, et al. Detection of hemodynamically significant coronary artery stenosis: incremental diagnostic value of dynamic CT-based myocardial perfusion imaging. Radiology 2011;260:689–98.

26. Bamberg F, Marcus RP, Becker A, et al. Dynamic myocardial CT perfusion imaging for evaluation of myocardial ischemia as determined by MR imaging. JACC Cardiovasc Imaging 2014;7:267–77.

27. Greif M, von Ziegler F, Bamberg F, et al. CT stress perfusion imaging for detection of haemodynamically relevant coronary stenosis as defined by FFR. Heart 2013;99:1004–11.

28. Huber AM, Leber V, Gramer BM, et al. Myocardium: dynamic versus single-shot CT perfusion imaging. Radiology 2013;269:378–86.

29. Rossi A, Dharampal A, Wragg A, et al. Diagnostic performance of hyperaemic myocardial blood flow

index obtained by dynamic computed tomography: does it predict functionally significant coronary lesions? Eur Heart J Cardiovasc Imaging 2014;15: 85–94.

30. Wang Y, Qin L, Shi X, et al. Adenosine-stress dynamic myocardial perfusion imaging with second-generation dual-source CT: comparison with conventional catheter coronary angiography and SPECT nuclear myocardial perfusion imaging. AJR Am J Roentgenol 2012;198:521–9.

31. Meinel FG, Ebersberger U, Schoepf UJ, et al. Global quantification of left ventricular myocardial perfusion at dynamic CT: feasibility in a multicenter patient population. AJR Am J Roentgenol 2014; 203:W174–80.

32. Bischoff B, Bamberg F, Marcus R, et al. Optimal timing for first-pass stress CT myocardial perfusion imaging. Int J Cardiovasc Imaging 2013;29:435–42.

33. Nagao M, Matsuoka H, Kawakami H, et al. Quantification of myocardial perfusion by contrast-enhanced 64-MDCT: characterization of ischemic myocardium. AJR Am J Roentgenol 2008;191: 19–25.

34. Vliegenthart R, Pelgrim GJ, Ebersberger U, et al. Dual-energy CT of the heart. AJR Am J Roentgenol 2012;199:S54–63.

35. Cury RC, Magalhaes TA, Paladino AT, et al. Dipyridamole stress and rest transmural myocardial perfusion ratio evaluation by 64 detector-row computed tomography. J Cardiovasc Comput Tomogr 2011;5: 443–8.

36. George RT, Arbab-Zadeh A, Miller JM, et al. Computed tomography myocardial perfusion imaging with 320-row detector computed tomography accurately detects myocardial ischemia in patients with obstructive coronary artery disease. Circ Cardiovasc Imaging 2012;5:333–40.

37. Kachenoura N, Gaspar T, Lodato JA, et al. Combined assessment of coronary anatomy and myocardial perfusion using multidetector computed tomography for the evaluation of coronary artery disease. Am J Cardiol 2009;103:1487–94.

38. Ruzsics B, Schwarz F, Schoepf UJ, et al. Comparison of dual-energy computed tomography of the heart with single photon emission computed tomography for assessment of coronary artery stenosis and of the myocardial blood supply. Am J Cardiol 2009;104:318–26.

39. So A, Hsieh J, Imai Y, et al. Prospectively ECG-triggered rapid kV-switching dual-energy CT for quantitative imaging of myocardial perfusion. JACC Cardiovasc Imaging 2012;5:829–36.

40. Nance JW Jr, Bastarrika G, Kang DK, et al. High-temporal resolution dual-energy computed tomography of the heart using a novel hybrid image reconstruction algorithm: initial experience. J Comput Assist Tomogr 2011;35:119–25.

41. Arnoldi E, Lee YS, Ruzsics B, et al. CT detection of myocardial blood volume deficits: dual-energy CT compared with single-energy CT spectra. J Cardiovasc Comput Tomogr 2011;5:421–9.

42. Blankstein R, Shturman LD, Rogers IS, et al. Adenosine-induced stress myocardial perfusion imaging using dual-source cardiac computed tomography. J Am Coll Cardiol 2009;54:1072–84.

43. Kang DK, Schoepf UJ, Bastarrika G, et al. Dual-energy computed tomography for integrative imaging of coronary artery disease: principles and clinical applications. Semin Ultrasound CT MR 2010;31: 276–91.

44. Ko SM, Choi JW, Song MG, et al. Myocardial perfusion imaging using adenosine-induced stress dual-energy computed tomography of the heart: comparison with cardiac magnetic resonance imaging and conventional coronary angiography. Eur Radiol 2011;21:26–35.

45. Meyer M, Nance JW Jr, Schoepf UJ, et al. Cost-effectiveness of substituting dual-energy CT for SPECT in the assessment of myocardial perfusion for the workup of coronary artery disease. Eur J Radiol 2012;81:3719–25.

46. Matsumoto K, Jinzaki M, Tanami Y, et al. Virtual monochromatic spectral imaging with fast kilovoltage switching: improved image quality as compared with that obtained with conventional 120-kVp CT. Radiology 2011;259:257–62.

47. Koonce JD, Vliegenthart R, Schoepf UJ, et al. Accuracy of dual-energy computed tomography for the measurement of iodine concentration using cardiac CT protocols: validation in a phantom model. Eur Radiol 2014;24:512–8.

48. Nagao M, Matsuoka H, Kawakami H, et al. Detection of myocardial ischemia using 64-slice MDCT. Circ J 2009;73:905–11.

49. Busch JL, Alessio AM, Caldwell JH, et al. Myocardial hypo-enhancement on resting computed tomography angiography images accurately identifies myocardial hypoperfusion. J Cardiovasc Comput Tomogr 2011;5:412–20.

50. Cury RC, Magalhaes TA, Borges AC, et al. Dipyridamole stress and rest myocardial perfusion by 64-detector row computed tomography in patients with suspected coronary artery disease. Am J Cardiol 2010;106:310–5.

51. George RT, Arbab-Zadeh A, Miller JM, et al. Adenosine stress 64- and 256-row detector computed tomography angiography and perfusion imaging: a pilot study evaluating the transmural extent of perfusion abnormalities to predict atherosclerosis causing myocardial ischemia. Circ Cardiovasc Imaging 2009;2:174–82.

52. Ko BS, Cameron JD, Meredith IT, et al. Computed tomography stress myocardial perfusion imaging in patients considered for revascularization: a

comparison with fractional flow reserve. Eur Heart J 2012;33:67–77.

53. Nasis A, Ko BS, Leung MC, et al. Diagnostic accuracy of combined coronary angiography and adenosine stress myocardial perfusion imaging using 320-detector computed tomography: pilot study. Eur Radiol 2013;23:1812–21.

54. Osawa K, Miyoshi T, Koyama Y, et al. Additional diagnostic value of first-pass myocardial perfusion imaging without stress when combined with 64-row detector coronary CT angiography in patients with coronary artery disease. Heart 2014;100:1008–15.

55. Rocha-Filho JA, Blankstein R, Shturman LD, et al. Incremental value of adenosine-induced stress myocardial perfusion imaging with dual-source CT at cardiac CT angiography. Radiology 2010;254:410–9.

56. Rochitte CE, George RT, Chen MY, et al. Computed tomography angiography and perfusion to assess coronary artery stenosis causing perfusion defects by single photon emission computed tomography: the CORE320 study. Eur Heart J 2014;35:1120–30.

57. Kim SM, Chang SA, Shin W, et al. Dual-energy CT perfusion during pharmacologic stress for the assessment of myocardial perfusion defects using a second-generation dual-source CT: a comparison with cardiac magnetic resonance imaging. J Comput Assist Tomogr 2014;38:44–52.

58. Ko SM, Choi JW, Hwang HK, et al. Diagnostic performance of combined noninvasive anatomic and functional assessment with dual-source CT and adenosine-induced stress dual-energy CT for detection of significant coronary stenosis. AJR Am J Roentgenol 2012;198:512–20.

59. Ko SM, Park JH, Hwang HK, et al. Direct comparison of stress- and rest-dual-energy computed tomography for detection of myocardial perfusion defect. Int J Cardiovasc Imaging 2014;30(Suppl 1):41–53.

60. Wang R, Yu W, Wang Y, et al. Incremental value of dual-energy CT to coronary CT angiography for the detection of significant coronary stenosis: comparison with quantitative coronary angiography and single photon emission computed tomography. Int J Cardiovasc Imaging 2011;27:647–56.

61. De Cecco CN, Schoepf UJ, Silverman JR, et al. Incremental value of pharmacological stress dual-energy cardiac CT over coronary CT angiography alone for the assessment of coronary artery disease in a high-risk population. AJR Am J Roentgenol 2014;203:W70–7.

62. Meinel FG, De Cecco CN, Schoepf UJ, et al. First-arterial-pass dual-energy CT for assessment of myocardial blood supply: do we need rest, stress, and delayed acquisition? Comparison with SPECT. Radiology 2014;270:708–16.

63. Gould KL, Lipscomb K. Effects of coronary stenoses on coronary flow reserve and resistance. Am J Cardiol 1974;34:48–55.

64. Kurata A, Mochizuki T, Koyama Y, et al. Myocardial perfusion imaging using adenosine triphosphate stress multi-slice spiral computed tomography: alternative to stress myocardial perfusion scintigraphy. Circ J 2005;69:550–7.

65. Mahmarian JJ, Cerqueira MD, Iskandrian AE, et al. Regadenoson induces comparable left ventricular perfusion defects as adenosine: a quantitative analysis from the ADVANCE MPI 2 trial. JACC Cardiovasc Imaging 2009;2:959–68.

66. Salgado Garcia C, Jimenez Heffernan A, Sanchez de Mora E, et al. Comparative study of the safety of regadenoson between patients with mild/moderate chronic obstructive pulmonary disease and asthma. Eur J Nucl Med Mol Imaging 2014;41:119–25.

67. Iskandrian AE, Bateman TM, Belardinelli L, et al. Adenosine versus regadenoson comparative evaluation in myocardial perfusion imaging: results of the ADVANCE phase 3 multicenter international trial. J Nucl Cardiol 2007;14:645–58.

68. Luu JM, Filipchuk NG, Friedrich MG. Indications, safety and image quality of cardiovascular magnetic resonance: experience in >5,000 North American patients. Int J Cardiol 2013;168:3807–11.

69. Shah S, Parra D, Rosenstein RS. Acute myocardial infarction during regadenoson myocardial perfusion imaging. Pharmacotherapy 2013;33:e90–5.

70. Hsi DH, Marreddy R, Moshiyakhov M, et al. Regadenoson induced acute ST-segment elevation myocardial infarction and multivessel coronary thrombosis. J Nucl Cardiol 2013;20:481–4.

71. Tonino PA, De Bruyne B, Pijls NH, et al. Fractional flow reserve versus angiography for guiding percutaneous coronary intervention. N Engl J Med 2009;360:213–24.

72. Leipsic J, Yang TH, Thompson A, et al. CT angiography (CTA) and diagnostic performance of noninvasive fractional flow reserve: results from the Determination of Fractional Flow Reserve by Anatomic CTA (DeFACTO) study. AJR Am J Roentgenol 2014;202:989–94.

73. Min JK, Berman DS, Budoff MJ, et al. Rationale and design of the DeFACTO (Determination of Fractional Flow Reserve by Anatomic Computed Tomographic AngiOgraphy) study. J Cardiovasc Comput Tomogr 2011;5:301–9.

74. Baumann S, Wang R, Schoepf UJ, et al. Coronary CT angiography-derived fractional flow reserve correlated with invasive fractional flow reserve measurements – initial experience with a novel physician-driven algorithm. Eur Radiol 2014. [Epub ahead of print].

75. Norgaard BL, Leipsic J, Gaur S, et al. Diagnostic performance of noninvasive fractional flow reserve derived from coronary computed tomography angiography in suspected coronary artery disease: the

NXT trial (Analysis of Coronary Blood Flow Using CT Angiography: Next Steps). J Am Coll Cardiol 2014; 63:1145–55.

76. Koo BK, Erglis A, Doh JH, et al. Diagnosis of ischemia-causing coronary stenoses by noninvasive fractional flow reserve computed from coronary computed tomographic angiograms. Results from the prospective multicenter DISCOVER-FLOW (Diagnosis of Ischemia-Causing Stenoses Obtained Via Noninvasive Fractional Flow Reserve) study. J Am Coll Cardiol 2011;58:1989–97.

77. Min JK, Leipsic J, Pencina MJ, et al. Diagnostic accuracy of fractional flow reserve from anatomic CT angiography. JAMA 2012;308:1237–45.

78. Renker M, Schoepf UJ, Wang R, et al. Diagnostic value of a novel coronary computed tomography angiography-based approach for assessing fractional flow reserve: comparison with invasive measurement. Am J Cardiol 2014;114(9):1303–8.

79. Kim KH, Doh JH, Koo BK, et al. A novel noninvasive technology for treatment planning using virtual coronary stenting and computed tomography-derived computed fractional flow reserve. JACC Cardiovasc Interv 2014;7:72–8.

80. Stuijfzand WJ, Danad I, Raijmakers PG, et al. Additional value of transluminal attenuation gradient in CT angiography to predict hemodynamic significance of coronary artery stenosis. JACC Cardiovasc Imaging 2014;7:374–86.

81. Wong DT, Ko BS, Cameron JD, et al. Transluminal attenuation gradient in coronary computed tomography angiography is a novel noninvasive approach to the identification of functionally significant coronary artery stenosis: a comparison with fractional flow reserve. J Am Coll Cardiol 2013;61:1271–9.

82. Choi JH, Min JK, Labounty TM, et al. Intracoronary transluminal attenuation gradient in coronary CT angiography for determining coronary artery stenosis. JACC Cardiovasc Imaging 2011;4:1149–57.

83. Chow BJ, Kass M, Gagné O, et al. Can differences in corrected coronary opacification measured with computed tomography predict resting coronary artery flow? J Am Coll Cardiol 2011;57:1280–8.

84. Choi JH, Koo BK, Yoon YE, et al. Diagnostic performance of intracoronary gradient-based methods by coronary computed tomography angiography for the evaluation of physiologically significant coronary artery stenoses: a validation study with fractional flow reserve. Eur Heart J Cardiovasc Imaging 2012;13:1001–7.

85. Yoon YE, Choi JH, Kim JH, et al. Noninvasive diagnosis of ischemia-causing coronary stenosis using CT angiography: diagnostic value of transluminal attenuation gradient and fractional flow reserve computed from coronary CT angiography compared to invasively measured fractional flow reserve. JACC Cardiovasc Imaging 2012;5:1088–96.

86. Wong DT, Ko BS, Cameron JD, et al. Comparison of diagnostic accuracy of combined assessment using adenosine stress computed tomography perfusion + computed tomography angiography with transluminal attenuation gradient + computed tomography angiography against invasive fractional flow reserve. J Am Coll Cardiol 2014;63:1904–12.

Current State of the Art Cardiovascular MR Imaging Techniques for Assessment of Ischemic Heart Disease

Christopher J. François, MD

KEYWORDS

- Cardiac magnetic resonance imaging • Ischemic heart disease • Myocardial perfusion
- Myocardial infarction

KEY POINTS

- CMR can be used to image nearly all aspects of the ischemic cascade, from decreased perfusion through wall motion abnormalities to infarction.
- Stress-rest perfusion CMR has been shown to be more accurate than single-photon emission computed tomography for detection of coronary artery disease in recent, large studies and new perfusion techniques should enable whole-heart, high-resolution quantitative perfusion.
- CMR is the reference standard to assessing ventricular size and systolic function using cine balanced SSFP imaging and new sequences enable whole-heart acquisition in a single breath hold or during exercise stress.
- CMR is the clinical standard of reference for viability imaging with the use of inversion recovery prepared sequences with newer sequences enabling whole-heart coverage in a single breath hold or during free breathing.
- Quantitative T1 and T2 mapping methods are promising methods for objectively differentiating between normal, ischemic, and at-risk and infarcted myocardium.

INTRODUCTION

Cardiac magnetic resonance (CMR) imaging is increasingly being used to evaluate patients with known or suspected ischemic heart disease. This is because of the ability to acquire images in any orientation and the wide variety of sequences available to characterize normal and abnormal structure and function. In the last two decades, substantial improvements have been made in the hardware and software used to perform CMR, resulting in better and more consistent image quality. Furthermore, there has been a greater emphasis in developing and validating quantitative CMR techniques. This article reviews recent advances in CMR techniques for assessing cardiac function, myocardial perfusion, late gadolinium enhancement (LGE), and tissue characterization with T1 and T2 mapping sequences (topics discussed in greater detail elsewhere in this issue).

The changes observed with CMR in patients with ischemic heart disease are directly linked to the pathologic changes that occur during the myocardial ischemic cascade. Specifically, decreased perfusion can be characterized by delayed enhancement of the myocardium during first-pass myocardial perfusion imaging. As myocardial perfusion deficits become more severe or prolonged, myocardial metabolism becomes

University of Wisconsin – Madison, 600 Highland Avenue, CSC/3252, Madison, WI 53562–3252, USA
E-mail address: cjfrancois@wisc.edu

Radiol Clin N Am 53 (2015) 335–344
http://dx.doi.org/10.1016/j.rcl.2014.11.002
0033-8389/15/$ – see front matter © 2015 Elsevier Inc. All rights reserved.

radiologic.theclinics.com

altered, which can be detected using magnetic resonance spectroscopy. With prolonged derangements in myocardial metabolism, myocardial dysfunction begins to occur, which can be detected using cine imaging to assess regional and global wall motion abnormalities. Finally, following myocardial infarction (MI), the presence of myocardial damage, including microvascular injury, can be characterized using LGE and T1/T2 mapping sequences.

MYOCARDIAL PERFUSION

In the myocardial ischemic cascade, decreased myocardial perfusion is the earliest physiologic abnormality that is observed. The resistance to coronary blood flow under normal, resting conditions is determined primarily by the myocardial microcirculation. Autoregulation of flow through the coronary circulation is tightly regulated to maintain adequate supply of oxygen to meet the demands of the myocardium. When flow through the epicardial coronary arteries becomes severely restricted, the myocardial microcirculation becomes maximally dilated at rest and can no longer accommodate further increases in demand. Noninvasive myocardial perfusion imaging methods take advantage of these alterations in capacity to increase flow with exercise or pharmacologic stress to detect areas of decreased perfusion distal to a hemodynamically significant coronary artery stenosis.

Nuclear scintigraphy remains the most widely used modality for noninvasively evaluating myocardial perfusion because it has been shown in large trials to be strongly predictive of cardiac death and MI.[1] CMR has increasingly been investigated as an alternative to nuclear scintigraphy for myocardial perfusion imaging because of its higher spatial resolution and its potential to provide additional information on cardiac structure and function within the same examination. In fact, recent trials have shown stress-rest perfusion CMR to be a safe alternative with higher sensitivity than nuclear scintigraphy for detecting coronary artery disease (CAD) based on x-ray coronary angiography.[2,3] Furthermore, a recent meta-analysis of the prognostic value of stress-rest perfusion CMR reported that a negative stress CMR has excellent prognostic value in predicting a very low risk of cardiovascular death.[4]

CMR of myocardial perfusion is predominantly based on contrast-enhanced T1-sensitive sequences, although T2*-weighted sequences have also been used. Magnetization-prepared fast gradient-recalled echo (GRE) sequences have been extensively used for clinical and research studies. The magnetization preparation can be performed with either a nonselective inversion recovery (IR; 180 degrees) preparation pulse[5] or a nonselective saturation recovery (90 degrees) preparation pulse.[6] With the saturation recovery preparation, multiple slices through the left ventricle are acquired during each cardiac cycle throughout the first pass of contrast through the myocardium (**Fig. 1**). Other techniques for performing perfusion CMR include echo-planar imaging[7] and magnetization-prepared balanced steady-state free precession (bSSFP) imaging.[8] Although most clinical and research studies are conducted at 1.5 T, there are data to suggest that myocardial perfusion imaging at 3.0 T is superior to that at 1.5 T[9] because of increased signal-to-noise ratio (SNR) and contrast enhancement.[10,11]

More recently, accelerated two- and three-dimensional perfusion imaging has been introduced to increase coverage and spatial resolution with stress perfusion MRI. Accelerated image acquisition takes advantage of the fact that much of the information within the images remains the same throughout the time of data acquisition, so that there are substantial correlations across

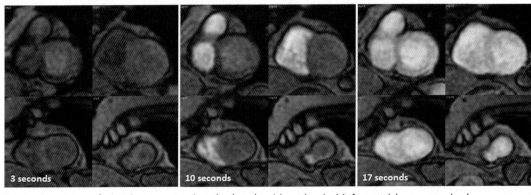

Fig. 1. First-pass perfusion images covering the basal, mid, and apical left ventricle are acquired over approximately 40 to 50 seconds as the administered contrast agent passes through the circulation.

k-space and time (k-t).[12,13] This, then, enables the acquisition of perfusion images with higher in-plane spatial resolution.[14,15] Performing accelerated perfusion imaging at 3.0 T can take advantage of the inherently higher SNR to obtain images with similar image quality as standard, unaccelerated perfusion techniques at 1.5 T.[16] Accelerated image acquisition methods have also been used to successfully implement three-dimensional perfusion sequences that provide full heart coverage.[17,18] As with earlier studies validating the accuracy of two-dimensional perfusion for the detection of CAD, three-dimensional perfusion imaging has also been shown to be very accurate using fractional flow reserve as a reference standard.[19,20]

Protocols for performing perfusion CMR vary. Ideally, stress CMR would be performed with exercise[21]; however, these approaches are still investigational and not widely used. As a result, most stress CMR studies are conducted using pharmacologic vasodilator stress. Dipyridamole, adenosine, and regadenoson are all Food and Drug Administration–approved vasodilators for noninvasive detection of CAD. Dipyridamole is an indirect vasodilator through its inhibition of adenosine reuptake, which increases endogenous adenosine. Adenosine is a nonselective vasodilator that activates adenosine A1 receptors. However, adenosine also activates adenosine A3 receptors, which causes bronchospasm and mast cell degranulation. Regadenoson is a newly approved vasodilator that selectively activates the adenosine 2A receptors present primarily in the coronary circulation. Any of these agents can be used reliably to perform stress perfusion CMR; however, because of its selectivity and ease of use, regadenoson is increasingly being used.[22,23] Although adenosine is attractive because it has a very short half-life, it is more difficult to administer and has a slightly higher rate of intolerance than regadenoson.[23]

With respect to stress-rest perfusion CMR protocols,[24] the stress and rest perfusion imaging acquisitions are separated by a delay to allow for the washout of the gadolinium-based contrast agent (GBCA) from the first perfusion acquisition. Images are acquired over a period of 40 to 50 seconds with GBCA injected with a power injector at a rate of 3 to 7 mL/s. The total GBCA dose is divided in two, with half administered during stress and half administered at rest. Normal saline (20–30 mL injected at same rate as GBCA) is administered following the injection of the GBCA. Either the stress or rest perfusion can be performed initially. If the pharmacologic stress perfusion is performed first, the delay also allows for the effects of the vasodilator to wear off before the acquisition of the resting perfusion images. LGE images are then acquired following an appropriate delay after the second perfusion imaging is performed.

Qualitative and quantitative assessment of the perfusion images is feasible. Because of the relatively high spatial resolution of CMR, it is possible to detect small subendocardial perfusion defects (Fig. 2) that can be missed with scintigraphic approaches. The interpretation of the perfusion images is conducted in conjunction with the LGE images. Areas with subendocardial LGE caused by prior infarct indicate the presence of CAD.[25] In areas without subendocardial LGE, the stress perfusion images are evaluated first followed by review of the resting perfusion images. The absence of a perfusion deficit on the stress perfusion images indicates that the patient does not have CAD. In patients with a stress perfusion defect without a corresponding area of LGE, the

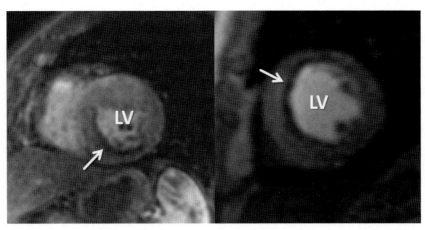

Fig. 2. Stress-induced decreased myocardial perfusion (arrows) in two patients, one with right coronary artery stenosis (left) and one with left anterior descending coronary artery stenosis (right). LV, left ventricle.

resting perfusion images are normal in patients with CAD.[25] If, however, there is a matched stress-rest perfusion deficit without LGE, this is presumed to be caused by artifact.[25]

CARDIAC STRUCTURE AND FUNCTION

Following decreased myocardial perfusion, cardiac contractility becomes dysfunctional. Initially, alterations in myocardial metabolism affect diastolic dysfunction. This is followed rather quickly by decreased systolic function. In the setting of acute ischemia, systolic dysfunction is observed on cine imaging as decreased myocardial thickening. This is distinct from the myocardial thinning observed in the setting of chronic myocardial ischemia or infarction (Fig. 3). Furthermore, the decreased contractility can be observed in the absence of complete MI. With chronic myocardial ischemia and infarction, the myocardium is thinned and contractility is abnormal. Wall motion abnormalities in the ischemic and infarcted areas can range from mild hypokinesis to akinesis to dyskinesis. In addition, these wall motion abnormalities can be regional or global. Accurate quantification of left ventricular size and function following acute MI is critical in assessing prognosis because of the relationship between poor left ventricular ejection fraction and incidence of arrhythmias and sudden cardiac death.[26,27]

CMR has become the gold standard for imaging cardiac function because of the combination of (1) high spatial and temporal resolution, (2) contrast between blood pool and myocardium, and (3) true three-dimensional coverage of the heart.[28] Studies have shown CMR-derived values for right and left ventricular volumes and ejection fraction to be very reproducible with minimal intraobserver and interobserver variability.[29,30] Cine imaging can be done using GRE or bSSFP sequences. The fast

GRE sequences use radiofrequency and gradient spoiling to achieve steady-state conditions for longitudinal magnetization. The TR and flip angle in GRE sequences are limited by the T1 relaxation times of tissue being imaged and must be optimized to maximize differences in signal intensity between myocardium and blood pool. In addition, the signal of blood pool in GRE sequences is flow-dependent, with blood flowing into the imaging plane having fully recovered signal relative to those that remain within the imaging plane. Therefore, cine GRE sequences are typically suboptimal in areas with slow flow, which can be present in areas of severe hypokinesis or akinesis especially when acquiring long-axis images.

Cine bSSFP imaging overcomes some of the limitations inherent in the GRE sequences. Cine bSSFP sequences completely refocus the magnetization during each TR and alternate the direction of the radiofrequency excitation phase. In addition, bSSFP sequences do not require spoiling and both transverse and longitudinal magnetizations are in the steady state and contribute to the signal. This contributes to the overall increased SNR and contrast-to-noise ratio (CNR) with bSSFP relative to GRE CMR sequences.[31–33] Although the contrast between myocardium and blood pool with GRE sequences is based on the T1 characteristics of the tissues and flow-effects, the blood pool signal with bSSFP imaging is inherently high because of its high T2/T1 ratio. As a result, cine bSSFP imaging has become the reference standard for cardiac morphology and function assessment with CMR.

Traditionally, cine bSSFP has been performed using a stack of contiguous two-dimensional slices through the heart in multiple orientations. However, this approach requires multiple breath holds and is time-consuming. Accelerated image acquisition methods, such as radial

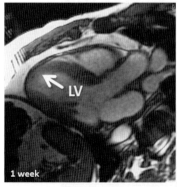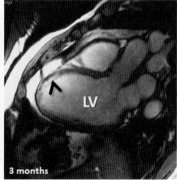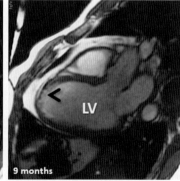

Fig. 3. Cine bSSFP images acquired 1 week, 3 months, and 9 months following acute ST-elevation myocardial infarction caused by left anterior descending coronary artery stenosis. Acutely, left ventricular (LV) wall thickness is normal (*arrow*). Over time, the apical LV remodels and becomes thinned (*arrowheads*).

undersampling[34,35] and k-t undersampling,[12,13] have been used to decrease scan time dramatically such that it is now possible to acquire a full three-dimensional cine bSSFP dataset in a single breath hold. A limitation of three-dimensional cine bSSFP is the increased susceptibility to banding artifacts, requiring precise shimming over the entire heart.

As indicated previously, myocardial thinning occurs with chronic ischemia and infarction. Clinically, it is important to distinguish between chronically ischemic, but still viable ("hibernating"), myocardium and infarcted, and not viable, myocardium. This cannot be done with resting functional imaging alone. Assessment of myocardial function with exercise or dobutamine stress can identify ischemia-induced wall motion abnormalities. Clinically, this is routinely done with echocardiography. However, these studies can be limited by body habitus, diffuse lung disease, excessive cardiac motion, and hyperventilation in 15% to 30% of cases.[36,37] As a result, there is growing interest in using dobutamine stress CMR to detect CAD[38–40] and provide prognostic information on future risk of adverse cardiovascular events.[41,42] True exercise stress CMR protocols using treadmill[21] or recumbent cycle[43] are also under development because of the increased prognostic value of exercise stress testing.[44]

With dobutamine stress CMR, the cine bSSFP images are acquired at rest and during the administration of dobutamine. Both low- and high-dose dobutamine administration protocols have been investigated. Low-dose protocols administer dobutamine at a rate of 10 μg/kg/min for 5 to 10 minutes. High-dose protocols administer dobutamine at an initial rate of 10 μg/kg/min for 3 minutes, followed by incremental increases of 10 μg/kg/min every 3 minutes until a target of 85% of maximum predicted heart rate is achieved. Atropine can be given in small incremental doses if the initial response to dobutamine is less than expected. A minimum of three short axis and three long axis cine views is recommended at each level of stress.

MYOCARDIAL INFARCTION

The final stage in the ischemic cascade, MI, occurs with severe and prolonged perfusion deficits. The myocardial injury with MI begins with myocyte cell death along the subendocardium and then, with time, extends to involve the entire wall thickness. If normal perfusion is not restored, necrosis of the endothelial cell lining and surrounding the capillaries also occurs. During and in the initial period following acute MI, the area of myocardium affected is thickened and edematous. If normal myocardial perfusion is not restored, the infarcted myocardium remodels and becomes thinned and fibrotic.

Distinguishing between viable and nonviable myocardium is important in the setting of acute MI because early restoration of coronary blood flow improves the likelihood of restoring left ventricular systolic function and survival.[45,46] Assessment of myocardial viability in chronic ischemic heart disease is also valuable to determine whether or not the affected territory will improve following revascularization. Myocardial viability can be assessed with several noninvasive imaging modalities, including PET, thallium 201 or technetium 99m single-photon emission computed tomography, stress echocardiography, and CMR.[47] Local expertise influences the predicted accuracy of these various methods and it is still not clear if there are differences in utility in different patient groups. As a result, a combination of these studies is typically used to identify areas of viable and nonviable myocardium. Of all of these modalities, CMR has the highest sensitivity for detecting subendocardial infarctions and offers the greatest flexibility in terms of tissue characterization.

Late Gadolinium Enhancement

The detection of infarcted myocardium with CMR is based on the differences in contrast enhancement between infarcted and noninfarcted myocardium.[48] Most GBCAs used in CMR do not remain in the intravascular space. As GBCAs pass through the circulation, a portion of the administered dose washes in and out of the extracellular space. CMR techniques used to identify infarcted myocardium take advantage of the differences in extracellular volume between noninfarcted and infarcted myocardium. Noninfarcted myocardium has very minimal extracellular space and GBCAs wash in and out fairly quickly. Acutely infarcted myocardium has a much larger extracellular volume because of edema, allowing for a greater concentration of GBCA and decreasing the wash-out kinetics (Fig. 4). In addition, the myocyte cell walls are damaged and permeable, allowing for GBCA to become intracellular. Chronic infarctions are characterized by the presence of a dense collagenous matrix. Animal studies in acute and chronic MI have shown that the areas of LGE correspond almost perfectly to the areas of infarction at histology.[49,50]

The sequences used to identify areas of infarcted myocardium with CMR are based on T1-weighted IR fast GRE or bSSFP sequences.

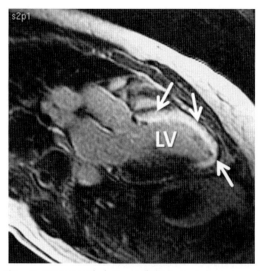

Fig. 4. Transmural late gadolinium enhancement (*arrows*) following acute ST-elevation myocardial infarction caused by severe left anterior descending coronary artery stenosis. Wall motion in this area did not recover despite revascularization. LV, left ventricle.

T1 weighting is achieved by using a nonselective 180-degree IR preparation pulse followed by a delay (or inversion time [TI]) such that normal myocardium has zero longitudinal magnetization. Following the TI, a rapid segmented GRE or bSSFP readout is acquired over several heartbeats. The optimum TI to achieve complete nulling of the signal from normal myocardium depends on the amount and type of GBCA administered, the magnetic field strength, and time delay between GBCA injection and image acquisition.[51] Because of the potential variation in TI time required, an initial, very rapid, low spatial resolution scout IR-prepared acquisition is performed with a variety of TIs. The greater GBCA concentration in infarcted myocardium results in quicker T1 recovery in these areas than in areas of noninfarcted myocardium.

The conspicuity of the abnormal areas of LGE is accentuated at 3.0 T because of increases in SNR and CNR, in addition to the inherent increase in T1 recovery time of normal myocardium at 3.0 T, relative to 1.5 T.[52] The increased SNR and CNR at 3.0 T can be taken advantage of to improve spatial resolution or shorten scan time through the use of single-shot[53,54] and parallel imaging techniques. Higher spatial resolution LGE imaging has also been achieved with the implementation of free-breathing techniques.[55–58] Free-breathing LGE techniques may be particularly useful in detecting areas of fibrosis in patients with ischemic heart disease because they are frequently

dyspneic and cannot hold their breath uniformly throughout the standard two-dimensional LGE acquisitions.[59]

Very early on following the implementation of the IR-GRE sequence for imaging MI, studies demonstrated an inverse relationship between the transmural extent of LGE and functional recovery following revascularization (see **Fig. 4**; **Fig. 5**).[60] In fact, the size of the area of abnormal LGE is more predictive of future adverse cardiovascular events than left ventricular volume or ejection fraction.[61]

T1 and T2 Mapping

After acute MI there is usually edema in and around the area of infarction. The increased myocardial tissue water content leads to longer myocardial T1 and T2 times.[62–64] Myocardial edema can be observed with T2-weighted CMR within 30 minutes of the ischemic injury (**Fig. 6**).[65] The myocardial edema observed on T2-weighted CMR persists for approximately 2 to 3 weeks following acute MI[66] and can therefore be used to distinguish between acute and chronic MI. Areas of myocardium that are hyperintense on T2-weighted images that do not have abnormal LGE correspond to regions of reversible myocardial injury.[65,67] T2-weighted imaging is typically performed using a short-tau IR sequence at 1.5T.[68] T2-weighted imaging is, however, limited by variation in the regional myocardial signal intensity caused by phased-array coils, high signal

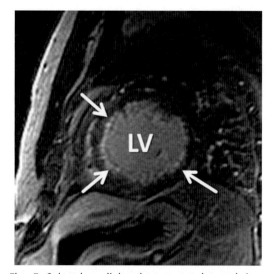

Fig. 5. Subendocardial enhancement (*arrows*) in a patient with chronic, severe three-vessel coronary artery disease. Left ventricular (LV) systolic function improved following three-vessel coronary artery bypass surgery.

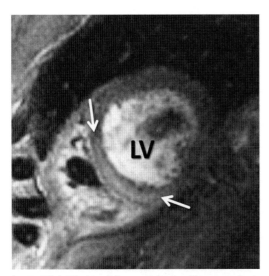

Fig. 6. High T2 signal (*arrows*) in the interventricular septum following acute ST-elevation myocardial infarction in the right coronary artery distribution. LV, left ventricle.

adjacent to the subendocardium caused by slow flow, through-plane motion signal loss, and differences induced by subtle changes in sequence parameters.

Recently, rapid and reproducible methods for quantifying T1[69,70] and T2[71] have been developed. These are based on the acquisition of multiple images in the same location with varying T1 or T2 recovery times to generate "maps" of the corresponding recovery times. Because these techniques directly measure physical properties of normal and abnormal tissue, they are less subjective than LGE methods. The most widely used methods of T1 mapping are based on a modified look-locker IR technique.[72] New and faster methods of T1 mapping have been developed using IR, saturation recovery, or hybrid approaches.[73,74]

Rapid T2 mapping has been performed using a T2 preparation bSSFP sequence.[71,75] T2 mapping is currently less widely used because of greater variation in measured T2 values secondary to artifacts induced by the sensitivity of these methods to flip angle, T1 effects on the bSSFP signal, and heart rate.[71,76–78]

SUMMARY

The role of cardiac MR in the management of patients with ischemic heart disease continues to grow with improvements in MRI hardware and software. New techniques have been and are being developed to decrease overall scan time through the use of parallel imaging, to improve the ease of image acquisition with free-breathing sequences, and for greater use of quantitative methods of detecting myocardial ischemia and infarction. With the breadth of sequences available, the use of CMR spans the entire ischemic cascade, from decreased perfusion through infarction.

REFERENCES

1. Iskander S, Iskandrian AE. Risk assessment using single-photon emission computed tomographic technetium-99m sestamibi imaging. J Am Coll Cardiol 1998;32(1):57–62.
2. Greenwood JP, Maredia N, Younger JF, et al. Cardiovascular magnetic resonance and single-photon emission computed tomography for diagnosis of coronary heart disease (CE-MARC): a prospective trial. Lancet 2012;379(9814):453–60.
3. Schwitter J, Wacker CM, Wilke N, et al. MR-IMPACT II: Magnetic Resonance Imaging for Myocardial Perfusion Assessment in Coronary Artery Disease Trial: perfusion-cardiac magnetic resonance vs. single-photon emission computed tomography for the detection of coronary artery disease: a comparative multicentre, multivendor trial. Eur Heart J 2013; 34(10):775–81.
4. Lipinski MJ, McVey CM, Berger JS, et al. Prognostic value of stress cardiac magnetic resonance imaging in patients with known or suspected coronary artery disease: a systematic review and meta-analysis. J Am Coll Cardiol 2013;62(9):826–38.
5. Fritz-Hansen T, Rostrup E, Ring PB, et al. Quantification of gadolinium-DTPA concentrations for different inversion times using an IR-turbo flash pulse sequence: a study on optimizing multislice perfusion imaging. Magn Reson Imaging 1998;16(8):893–9.
6. Tsekos NV, Zhang Y, Merkle H, et al. Fast anatomical imaging of the heart and assessment of myocardial perfusion with arrhythmia insensitive magnetization preparation. Magn Reson Med 1995;34(4):530–6.
7. Epstein FH, London JF, Peters DC, et al. Multislice first-pass cardiac perfusion MRI: validation in a model of myocardial infarction. Magn Reson Med 2002;47(3):482–91.
8. Hunold P, Maderwald S, Eggebrecht H, et al. Steady-state free precession sequences in myocardial first-pass perfusion MR imaging: comparison with TurboFLASH imaging. Eur Radiol 2004;14(3): 409–16.
9. Cheng AS, Pegg TJ, Karamitsos TD, et al. Cardiovascular magnetic resonance perfusion imaging at 3-tesla for the detection of coronary artery disease: a comparison with 1.5-tesla. J Am Coll Cardiol 2007;49(25):2440–9.
10. Gutberlet M, Noeske R, Schwinge K, et al. Comprehensive cardiac magnetic resonance imaging

at 3.0 tesla: feasibility and implications for clinical applications. Invest Radiol 2006;41(2):154–67.

11. Araoz PA, Glockner JF, McGee KP, et al. 3 tesla MR imaging provides improved contrast in first-pass myocardial perfusion imaging over a range of gadolinium doses. J Cardiovasc Magn Reson 2005;7(3):559–64.

12. Tsao J, Boesiger P, Pruessmann KP. k-t BLAST and k-t SENSE: dynamic MRI with high frame rate exploiting spatiotemporal correlations. Magn Reson Med 2003;50(5):1031–42.

13. Tsao J, Kozerke S, Boesiger P, et al. Optimizing spatiotemporal sampling for k-t BLAST and k-t SENSE: application to high-resolution real-time cardiac steady-state free precession. Magn Reson Med 2005;53(6):1372–82.

14. Plein S, Kozerke S, Suerder D, et al. High spatial resolution myocardial perfusion cardiac magnetic resonance for the detection of coronary artery disease. Eur Heart J 2008;29(17):2148–55.

15. Plein S, Ryf S, Schwitter J, et al. Dynamic contrast-enhanced myocardial perfusion MRI accelerated with k-t sense. Magn Reson Med 2007;58(4):777–85.

16. Plein S, Schwitter J, Suerder D, et al. k-Space and time sensitivity encoding-accelerated myocardial perfusion MR imaging at 3.0 T: comparison with 1.5 T. Radiology 2008;249(2):493–500.

17. Manka R, Jahnke C, Kozerke S, et al. Dynamic 3-dimensional stress cardiac magnetic resonance perfusion imaging: detection of coronary artery disease and volumetry of myocardial hypoenhancement before and after coronary stenting. J Am Coll Cardiol 2011;57(4):437–44.

18. Vitanis V, Manka R, Giese D, et al. High resolution three-dimensional cardiac perfusion imaging using compartment-based k-t principal component analysis. Magn Reson Med 2011;65(2):575–87.

19. Jogiya R, Kozerke S, Morton G, et al. Validation of dynamic 3-dimensional whole heart magnetic resonance myocardial perfusion imaging against fractional flow reserve for the detection of significant coronary artery disease. J Am Coll Cardiol 2012;60(8):756–65.

20. Manka R, Paetsch I, Kozerke S, et al. Whole-heart dynamic three-dimensional magnetic resonance perfusion imaging for the detection of coronary artery disease defined by fractional flow reserve: determination of volumetric myocardial ischaemic burden and coronary lesion location. Eur Heart J 2012;33(16):2016–24.

21. Thavendiranathan P, Dickerson JA, Scandling D, et al. Comparison of treadmill exercise stress cardiac MRI to stress echocardiography in healthy volunteers for adequacy of left ventricular endocardial wall visualization: a pilot study. J Magn Reson Imaging 2014;39(5):1146–52.

22. DiBella EV, Fluckiger JU, Chen L, et al. The effect of obesity on regadenoson-induced myocardial hyperemia: a quantitative magnetic resonance imaging study. Int J Cardiovasc Imaging 2012;28(6):1435–44.

23. Vasu S, Bandettini WP, Hsu LY, et al. Regadenoson and adenosine are equivalent vasodilators and are superior than dipyridamole: a study of first pass quantitative perfusion cardiovascular magnetic resonance. J Cardiovasc Magn Reson 2013;15:85.

24. Kramer CM, Barkhausen J, Flamm SD, et al, Society for Cardiovascular Magnetic Resonance Board of Trustees Task Force on Standardized Protocols. Standardized cardiovascular magnetic resonance imaging (CMR) protocols, society for cardiovascular magnetic resonance: board of trustees task force on standardized protocols. J Cardiovasc Magn Reson 2008;10:35.

25. Klem I, Heitner JF, Shah DJ, et al. Improved detection of coronary artery disease by stress perfusion cardiovascular magnetic resonance with the use of delayed enhancement infarction imaging. J Am Coll Cardiol 2006;47(8):1630–8.

26. Greenberg H, Case RB, Moss AJ, et al. Analysis of mortality events in the Multicenter Automatic Defibrillator Implantation Trial (MADIT-II). J Am Coll Cardiol 2004;43(8):1459–65.

27. Solomon SD, Zelenkofske S, McMurray JJ, et al. Sudden death in patients with myocardial infarction and left ventricular dysfunction, heart failure, or both. N Engl J Med 2005;352(25):2581–8.

28. Bellenger NG, Burgess MI, Ray SG, et al. Comparison of left ventricular ejection fraction and volumes in heart failure by echocardiography, radionuclide ventriculography and cardiovascular magnetic resonance; are they interchangeable? Eur Heart J 2000;21(16):1387–96.

29. Grothues F, Moon JC, Bellenger NG, et al. Interstudy reproducibility of right ventricular volumes, function, and mass with cardiovascular magnetic resonance. Am Heart J 2004;147(2):218–23.

30. Hudsmith LE, Petersen SE, Francis JM, et al. Normal human left and right ventricular and left atrial dimensions using steady state free precession magnetic resonance imaging. J Cardiovasc Magn Reson 2005;7(5):775–82.

31. Hudsmith LE, Petersen SE, Tyler DJ, et al. Determination of cardiac volumes and mass with FLASH and SSFP cine sequences at 1.5 vs. 3 tesla: a validation study. J Magn Reson Imaging 2006;24(2):312–8.

32. Alfakih K, Plein S, Thiele H, et al. Normal human left and right ventricular dimensions for MRI as assessed by turbo gradient echo and steady-state free precession imaging sequences. J Magn Reson Imaging 2003;17(3):323–9.

33. Tyler DJ, Hudsmith LE, Petersen SE, et al. Cardiac cine MR-imaging at 3T: FLASH vs SSFP. J Cardiovasc Magn Reson 2006;8(5):709–15.

34. Liu J, Wieben O, Jung Y, et al. Single breathhold cardiac CINE imaging with multi-echo three-dimensional hybrid radial SSFP acquisition. J Magn Reson Imaging 2010;32(2):434–40.

35. Peters DC, Ennis DB, Rohatgi P, et al. 3D breath-held cardiac function with projection reconstruction in steady state free precession validated using 2D cine MRI. J Magn Reson Imaging 2004;20(3):411–6.

36. Marwick TH, Nemec JJ, Pashkow FJ, et al. Accuracy and limitations of exercise echocardiography in a routine clinical setting. J Am Coll Cardiol 1992; 19(1):74–81.

37. Mulvagh SL, Rakowski H, Vannan MA, et al. American Society of Echocardiography consensus statement on the clinical applications of ultrasonic contrast agents in echocardiography. J Am Soc Echocardiogr 2008;21(11):1179–201 [quiz: 281].

38. Hundley WG, Hamilton CA, Thomas MS, et al. Utility of fast cine magnetic resonance imaging and display for the detection of myocardial ischemia in patients not well suited for second harmonic stress echocardiography. Circulation 1999;100(16):1697–702.

39. Nagel E, Lehmkuhl HB, Bocksch W, et al. Noninvasive diagnosis of ischemia-induced wall motion abnormalities with the use of high-dose dobutamine stress MRI: comparison with dobutamine stress echocardiography. Circulation 1999;99(6):763–70.

40. Wahl A, Paetsch I, Gollesch A, et al. Safety and feasibility of high-dose dobutamine-atropine stress cardiovascular magnetic resonance for diagnosis of myocardial ischaemia: experience in 1000 consecutive cases. Eur Heart J 2004;25(14): 1230–6.

41. Gebker R, Jahnke C, Manka R, et al. The role of dobutamine stress cardiovascular magnetic resonance in the clinical management of patients with suspected and known coronary artery disease. J Cardiovasc Magn Reson 2011;13:46.

42. Kelle S, Chiribiri A, Vierecke J, et al. Long-term prognostic value of dobutamine stress CMR. JACC Cardiovasc Imaging 2011;4(2):161–72.

43. Gusso S, Salvador C, Hofman P, et al. Design and testing of an MRI-compatible cycle ergometer for non-invasive cardiac assessments during exercise. Biomed Eng Online 2012;11:13.

44. Roger VL, Jacobsen SJ, Pellikka PA, et al. Prognostic value of treadmill exercise testing: a population-based study in Olmsted County, Minnesota. Circulation 1998;98(25):2836–41.

45. Grines CL, Browne KF, Marco J, et al. A comparison of immediate angioplasty with thrombolytic therapy for acute myocardial infarction. The Primary Angioplasty in Myocardial Infarction Study Group. N Engl J Med 1993;328(10):673–9.

46. Zijlstra F, de Boer MJ, Hoorntje JC, et al. A comparison of immediate coronary angioplasty with intravenous streptokinase in acute myocardial infarction. N Engl J Med 1993;328(10):680–4.

47. Buckley O, Di Carli M. Predicting benefit from revascularization in patients with ischemic heart failure: imaging of myocardial ischemia and viability. Circulation 2011;123(4):444–50.

48. Wesbey GE, Higgins CB, McNamara MT, et al. Effect of gadolinium-DTPA on the magnetic relaxation times of normal and infarcted myocardium. Radiology 1984;153(1):165–9.

49. Kim RJ, Fieno DS, Parrish TB, et al. Relationship of MRI delayed contrast enhancement to irreversible injury, infarct age, and contractile function. Circulation 1999;100(19):1992–2002.

50. Fieno DS, Kim RJ, Chen EL, et al. Contrast-enhanced magnetic resonance imaging of myocardium at risk: distinction between reversible and irreversible injury throughout infarct healing. J Am Coll Cardiol 2000; 36(6):1985–91.

51. Petersen SE, Mohrs OK, Horstick G, et al. Influence of contrast agent dose and image acquisition timing on the quantitative determination of nonviable myocardial tissue using delayed contrast-enhanced magnetic resonance imaging. J Cardiovasc Magn Reson 2004;6(2):541–8.

52. Klumpp B, Fenchel M, Hoevelborn T, et al. Assessment of myocardial viability using delayed enhancement magnetic resonance imaging at 3.0 tesla. Invest Radiol 2006;41(9):661–7.

53. Bauner KU, Muehling O, Wintersperger BJ, et al. Inversion recovery single-shot TurboFLASH for assessment of myocardial infarction at 3 tesla. Invest Radiol 2007;42(6):361–71.

54. Huber A, Schoenberg SO, Spannagl B, et al. Single-shot inversion recovery TrueFISP for assessment of myocardial infarction. AJR Am J Roentgenol 2006; 186(3):627–33.

55. Amano Y, Matsumura Y, Kumita S. Free-breathing high-spatial-resolution delayed contrast-enhanced three-dimensional viability MR imaging of the myocardium at 3.0 T: a feasibility study. J Magn Reson Imaging 2008;28(6):1361–7.

56. Goldfarb JW, Shinnar M. Free-breathing delayed hyperenhanced imaging of the myocardium: a clinical application of real-time navigator echo imaging. J Magn Reson Imaging 2006;24(1):66–71.

57. Kecskemeti S, Johnson K, Francois CJ, et al. Volumetric late gadolinium-enhanced myocardial imaging with retrospective inversion time selection. J Magn Reson Imaging 2013;38(5):1276–82.

58. Nguyen TD, Spincemaille P, Cham MD, et al. Free-breathing 3D steady-state free precession coronary magnetic resonance angiography: comparison of diaphragm and cardiac fat navigators. J Magn Reson Imaging 2008;28(2):509–14.

59. Yin G, Zhao S, Lu M, et al. Assessment of left ventricular myocardial scar in coronary artery disease by a three-dimensional MR imaging technique. J Magn Reson Imaging 2013;38(1):72–9.

60. Kim RJ, Wu E, Rafael A, et al. The use of contrast-enhanced magnetic resonance imaging to identify reversible myocardial dysfunction. N Engl J Med 2000;343(20):1445–53.

61. Wu E, Ortiz JT, Tejedor P, et al. Infarct size by contrast enhanced cardiac magnetic resonance is a stronger predictor of outcomes than left ventricular ejection fraction or end-systolic volume index: prospective cohort study. Heart 2008;94(6):730–6.

62. Higgins CB, Herfkens R, Lipton MJ, et al. Nuclear magnetic resonance imaging of acute myocardial infarction in dogs: alterations in magnetic relaxation times. Am J Cardiol 1983;52(1):184–8.

63. Brown JJ, Peck WW, Gerber KH, et al. Nuclear magnetic resonance analysis of acute and chronic myocardial infarction in dogs: alterations in spin-lattice relaxation times. Am Heart J 1984;108(5):1292–7.

64. McNamara MT, Higgins CB, Schechtmann N, et al. Detection and characterization of acute myocardial infarction in man with use of gated magnetic resonance. Circulation 1985;71(4):717–24.

65. Abdel-Aty H, Cocker M, Meek C, et al. Edema as a very early marker for acute myocardial ischemia: a cardiovascular magnetic resonance study. J Am Coll Cardiol 2009;53(14):1194–201.

66. Abdel-Aty H, Simonetti O, Friedrich MG. T2-weighted cardiovascular magnetic resonance imaging. J Magn Reson Imaging 2007;26(3):452–9.

67. Abdel-Aty H. Myocardial edema imaging of the area at risk in acute myocardial infarction: seeing through water. JACC Cardiovasc Imaging 2009;2(7):832–4.

68. Simonetti OP, Finn JP, White RD, et al. "Black blood" T2-weighted inversion-recovery MR imaging of the heart. Radiology 1996;199(1):49–57.

69. Messroghli DR, Greiser A, Frohlich M, et al. Optimization and validation of a fully-integrated pulse sequence for modified look-locker inversion-recovery (MOLLI) T1 mapping of the heart. J Magn Reson Imaging 2007;26(4):1081–6.

70. Messroghli DR, Walters K, Plein S, et al. Myocardial T1 mapping: application to patients with acute and chronic myocardial infarction. Magn Reson Med 2007;58(1):34–40.

71. Giri S, Chung YC, Merchant A, et al. T2 quantification for improved detection of myocardial edema. J Cardiovasc Magn Reson 2009;11:56.

72. Messroghli DR, Radjenovic A, Kozerke S, et al. Modified look-locker inversion recovery (MOLLI) for high-resolution T1 mapping of the heart. Magn Reson Med 2004;52(1):141–6.

73. Chow K, Flewitt JA, Green JD, et al. Saturation recovery single-shot acquisition (SASHA) for myocardial T(1) mapping. Magn Reson Med 2014;71(6):2082–95.

74. Piechnik SK, Ferreira VM, Dall'Armellina E, et al. Shortened modified look-locker inversion recovery (ShMOLLI) for clinical myocardial T1-mapping at 1.5 and 3 T within a 9 heartbeat breathhold. J Cardiovasc Magn Reson 2010;12:69.

75. Huang TY, Liu YJ, Stemmer A, et al. T2 measurement of the human myocardium using a T2-prepared transient-state TrueFISP sequence. Magn Reson Med 2007;57(5):960–6.

76. Thavendiranathan P, Walls M, Giri S, et al. Improved detection of myocardial involvement in acute inflammatory cardiomyopathies using T2 mapping. Circ Cardiovasc Imaging 2012;5(1):102–10.

77. von Knobelsdorff-Brenkenhoff F, Prothmann M, Dieringer MA, et al. Myocardial T1 and T2 mapping at 3 T: reference values, influencing factors and implications. J Cardiovasc Magn Reson 2013;15(1):53.

78. Wassmuth R, Prothmann M, Utz W, et al. Variability and homogeneity of cardiovascular magnetic resonance myocardial T2-mapping in volunteers compared to patients with edema. J Cardiovasc Magn Reson 2013;15:27.

MR Imaging of the Coronary Vasculature
Imaging the Lumen, Wall, and Beyond

Kai Lin, MD*, James C. Carr, MD

KEYWORDS

• Coronary artery disease • Magnetic resonance imaging • Noninvasive

KEY POINTS

• Magnetic resonance (MR) imaging is a useful noninvasive tool for the detection of coronary stenosis.
• MR imaging can detect morphologic and functional changes of remodeled coronary artery.
• Many technical advances have been adopted to improve the performance of coronary MR imaging/ MR angiography for cardiovascular risk estimation.

INTRODUCTION

Coronary artery disease (CAD) is the leading cause of death worldwide. The characteristics of CAD are gradual thickening of the coronary walls and narrowing of the vascular lumen caused by the buildup of atherosclerosis plaques. Subclinical CAD may silently progress over a long time period until coronary events (a group of symptoms attributed to myocardial ischemia) affect patients.[1,2] Therefore, the detection of CAD in its early stage is clinically significant. However, the morphologic and functional features of the remodeled coronary artery, which may convey risk of subclinical CAD, have not been comprehensively investigated in asymptomatic individuals who do not have documented or suspected structural cardiovascular disease. This knowledge gap exists mainly because clinical examinations for detecting coronary wall are either invasive or require x-ray exposure. Therefore, noninvasive imaging methods for the evaluation of coronary artery are highly desired for optimal cardiovascular prevention.

Over the past decade, magnetic resonance (MR) imaging/MR angiography (MRA) has emerged as a promising noninvasive method for observing both morphologic and functional changes on coronary walls.[3,4] This article summarizes state-of art coronary MR imaging/MRA techniques for detecting CAD from various aspects, including luminal stenosis, coronary wall plaques, and coronary functional changes. In addition, clinical applications and limitations of current coronary MR imaging techniques in clinical practice are also discussed.

IMAGING OF CORONARY LUMEN USING MAGNETIC RESONANCE IMAGING

In the past, stenosis of the coronary lumen was considered to be an indicator of obstructive CAD, and subsequent treatments, such as coronary artery bypass graft surgery and percutaneous transluminal coronary angioplasty were based on extent and severity of disease. Multiple bright-blood MR imaging pulse sequences can be used

Conflicts of interest: The authors have nothing to disclosure.
Department of Radiology, Northwestern University Feinberg School of Medicine, 737 North Michigan Avenue, Suite 1600, Chicago, IL 60611, USA
* Corresponding author.
E-mail address: kai-lin@northwestern.edu

Radiol Clin N Am 53 (2015) 345–353
http://dx.doi.org/10.1016/j.rcl.2014.11.003

0033-8389/15/$ – see front matter © 2015 Elsevier Inc. All rights reserved.

to rapidly image the coronary lumen and detect coronary stenosis, such as spoiled gradient echo and steady-state free precession (SSFP) (Table 1).[5]

Regenfus and colleagues[6] evaluated 50 patients with suspected CAD using a turbo fast low-angle shot MR imaging (FLASH) sequence within a single breath-hold. Of 350 coronary segments, 268 (76.6%) could be evaluated. In those coronary segments, 48 of 56 luminal stenoses could be detected by MR imaging. With T1-shortening contrast agents, such as gadolinium, spoiled gradient echo sequences can be used to depict contours of the coronary lumen. In a study with 9 healthy volunteers, Bi and colleagues[7] showed that gadolinium may significantly increase the image quality of coronary MRA. However, spatial resolution and coverage of coronary MRA may be limited by the length of breath hold and the duration of sustainable blood pool enhancement generated by contrast agents.[8] Using a free-breathing technique and a scheme of slow infusion (0.3 mL/s) of the contrast agent (for prolonged T1 contrast between vessel wall and the blood pool), Bi and colleagues[9] showed that coronary MRA (FLASH sequence) is capable of imaging the whole coronary tree within a short period (4.5 ± 0.6 minutes) for 8 volunteers. In a single-center study, Yang and colleagues[10] performed contrast-enhanced whole-heart MRA in 69 consecutive patients with suspected CAD. Whole-heart MRA identified clinically significant coronary stenosis in 32 patients and ruled out CAD in 23 patients. On a per-segment basis, MRA had high sensitivity (91.6%), specificity (83.1%), and accuracy (84.1%) for the detection of CAD (using x-ray angiography as the gold standard). On a per-patient basis, these values for accurate CAD diagnosis were 94.1%, 82.1%, and 88.7%, respectively. The same group recently showed a comparable diagnostic accuracy for the detection of CAD (significant coronary luminal stenosis) in 110 patients using similar imaging techniques with a 32-channel coil.[11]

Patients with CAD have varying degrees of coexisting kidney dysfunction.[12] Therefore, noncontrast coronary MRA techniques may provide added benefits in this patient population by avoiding nephrotoxic contrast agents and the risk of nephrogenic systemic fibrosis. The high T2/T1 ratio of the blood provides strong blood signal and may serve as an intrinsic contrast agent for the SSFP technique in coronary MRA.[13,14] Using noncontrast whole-heart coronary MRA, Kato and colleagues[15] detected significant CAD in 138 patients with suspected CAD with high sensitivity and high negative predictive value (88%). Using quantitative analysis of coronary MRA, Yonezawa and colleagues[16] found that receiver operating characteristic (ROC) curve analysis in a segment-based analysis for identifying significant coronary stenosis was 0.96. In a multicenter study, coronary MRA provided an accuracy of 72% (95% confidence interval, 63%–81%) in diagnosing CAD.[17] Stuber and colleagues[18] showed good agreement of anatomy and disorder between coronary MRA and x-ray angiography in depicting the coronary tree in 7 patients with CAD confirmed by x-ray angiography and 15 healthy adult volunteers. Indicated by higher sensitivity, specificity, and area under the ROC curve (AUC), Liu and colleagues[19] found that noncontrast coronary MRA is superior to coronary CT angiography (CTA) for delineating luminal narrowing of the coronary artery in the segments with heavy calcification. Yoon and colleagues[20] studied 207 patients with suspected CAD using noncontrast whole-heart coronary MRA. The investigators observed 10 coronary events (half of them were deadly events) in 84 patients with significant coronary stenosis identified with MRA during a follow-up of 25 months. However, only 1 coronary event happened in 123 patients without CAD (also defined using MRA findings). Cox regression showed that a coronary stenosis on MRA is an independent risk factor associated with significant increase for all cardiac events (risk ratio = 20.78; P = .001). Figs. 1 and 2 show that coronary MRA (with and without contrast enhancement) is able to show coronary stenosis.

Table 1
MR imaging sequences used in the evaluation of coronary luminal stenosis (bright blood)

Sequences				Need Contrast Agent?
Spoiled gradient echo	FLASH	SPGR	T1 FFE	Yes
SSFP	FISP	GRASS	FFE	No

Names vary between different MR imaging scanner manufacturers.
Abbreviations: FFE, fast field echo; FISP, fast imaging with steady-state precession; FLASH, fast low-angle shot MR imaging; GRASS, gradient recall acquisition using steady states; SPGR, spoiled gradient recall acquisition using steady states.

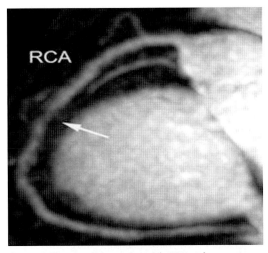

Fig. 1. A 54-year-old woman with CAD. A lumen stenosis on the right coronary artery (RCA) was identified by contrast-enhanced MRA. (*From* Yang Q, Li K, Liu X, et al. Contrast-enhanced whole-heart coronary magnetic resonance angiography at 3.0-T: a comparative study with X-ray angiography in a single center. J Am Coll Cardiol 2009;54(1):74; with permission.)

IMAGING CORONARY DILATATION AND FLOW USING MAGNETIC RESONANCE IMAGING

Coronary MRA may also be used to evaluate coronary dilatation or stiffness (indicated by changes in lumen area). Terashima and colleagues[21] studied 12 patients with CAD and 20 healthy controls

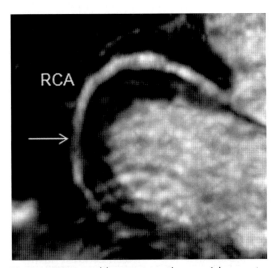

Fig. 2. A 74-year-old asymptomatic man. A lumen stenosis on the RCA could be identified by noncontrast MRA (confirmed by coronary angiogram). LAD, left anterior descending artery. (Image of unpublished data from Lin & Carr, 2011.)

before and after the administration of vasodilator (sublingual nitroglycerin). In 20 healthy adults and 17 patients with CAD, Hays and colleagues[22] observed impaired coronary endothelial function associated with CAD (indicated by less cross-sectional coronary dilatation after the administration of vasoactive medication). Similar impaired endothelial function was also found in patients with CAD before and after isometric handgrip exercise (another endothelial-dependent stressor) by the same group.[23] Using three-dimensional (3D) coronary MRA pictures acquired at diastole and systole, Lin and colleagues[24] calculated coronary dispensability index (CDI), an index of coronary stiffness, within cardiac cycles based on the differences of cross-sectional coronary lumen areas. The investigators found that older patients with type 2 diabetes mellitus (T2DM) without documented cardiovascular disease have lower CDIs in all coronary branches than healthy elderly individuals. **Fig. 3** shows the measurement of coronary distensibility.

Coronary flow is another important index for evaluating coronary atherosclerosis and endothelial function of the coronary wall. Altered blood flow usually accompanies luminal narrowing. Phase contrast MR imaging is a traditional technique for quantifying two-dimensional (2D) blood flow in the vessel. Shibata and colleagues[25] showed good agreement between MR imaging–derived coronary flow velocity reserve (calculated using flow difference before and after the administration of dipyridamole) and that measured using Doppler guidewire in 19 patients with heart disease ($r = 0.91$). Insufficient coronary flow reserve (calculated on measurements before and after stress) was identified in patients diagnosed with CAD (with flow-limiting luminal stenosis) compared with healthy volunteers.[22,23]

IMAGING CORONARY WALL USING MAGNETIC RESONANCE IMAGING

As a major manifestation of CAD, coronary remodeling involves the long-term, active modification of the vessel structure in response to pathologic changes in its milieu, such as the development of atherosclerotic plaques. Because remodeled coronary wall (positive or negative) is the underlying source of myocardial ischemia, coronary remodeling is a reliable indicator of CAD and serves as a strong predictor of near-term coronary events.[26] Coronary culprit plaque is the immediate source of cardiovascular events.[26,27] Therefore, imaging of the coronary artery is of great clinical significance because it proves the existence of coronary plaques. The

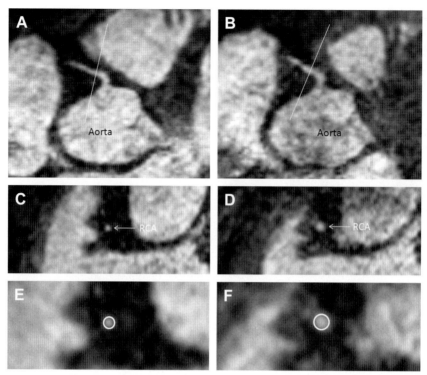

Fig. 3. A 73-year-old healthy man. His peripheral blood pressure was 130/70 mm Hg (Pulse pressure = 60 mm Hg). (*A*) Longitudinal view of the RCA in mid-diastole (*B*) Longitudinal view of the RCA in end-systole. (*C*) Transverse view of lumen in mid-diastole. (*D*) Transverse view of lumen in end-systole. (*E*) Zoomed diastolic lumen with contour shows that the area is 7.61 mm². (*F*) Zoomed systolic lumen with contour shows that the area is 15.05 mm². CDI = (15.05−7.61)/7.61/60 × 1000 = 16.29 (mm Hg⁻¹). (*From* Lin K, Lloyd-Jones DM, Liu Y, et al. Noninvasive evaluation of coronary distensibility in older adults: a feasibility study with MR angiography. Radiology 2011;261(3):771–8.)

patterns of coronary remodeling have been found to be associated with clinical presentations of CAD. At present, x-ray angiography is the standard clinical examination for the diagnosis of CAD. With x-ray angiography, Nahser and colleagues[28] observed a reduction in coronary vasodilatation and impaired regulation of coronary flow in patients with T2DM. However, angiography shows only the coronary lumen, whereas CAD is a disease that originates in the vessel wall. Many acute coronary events are triggered by superficial plaque erosion or rupture without obstructive lesions.[29,30] Coronary artery plaques with positive remodeling (a nearly normal lumen gauge with compensatory vessel enlargement) have higher plaque vulnerability, indicated by a higher macrophage count and lipid content,[31] which means that a substantial burden of atherosclerosis can exist without producing stenosis.[32] Individuals with increasing cardiovascular risk may have low-grade narrowing in coronary arteries, which may be ignored by x-ray angiography. Existing studies have shown the relationships between morphologic changes of coronary plaques and

risk of coronary events. However, current clinical methods for coronary wall examination, such as intravascular ultrasonography (IVUS), are limited by invasiveness. As a noninvasive imaging method, MR imaging may address this unmet clinical need by detecting risky coronary plaques without significant lumen stenosis. Over the past decade, MR imaging has emerged as a radiation-free, noninvasive method for the accurate detection of in situ atherosclerotic lesions on the coronary wall (**Table 2**).[33,34]

Botnar and colleagues acquired coronary wall images in 5 healthy volunteers and 5 patients

Table 2		
MR imaging sequences used in the evaluation of coronary wall		
Sequences		**Need Contrast Agent?**
FSE	TSE	No

Names vary between different MR imaging scanner manufacturers.
Abbreviations: FSE, fast spin echo; TSE, turbo spin echo.

with CAD (confirmed by x-ray angiography).[35] Fayad and colleagues[4] also detected a significant difference in the maximal coronary wall thickness between subjects with and without CAD (4.38 ± 0.71 mm vs 0.75 ± 0.17 mm) using a 2D fast spin echo (FSE) sequence. In a cross-sectional study, Kim and colleagues[36] found that subjects with type 1 diabetes mellitus (T1DM) and diabetic nephropathy had thicker coronary walls than T1DM patients free of kidney involvements using a 3D turbo spin echo (TSE) sequence. Coronary wall MR imaging has also been adopted as a quantitative tool for cardiovascular risk estimation in epidemiologic studies. In the Multi-Ethnic Study of Atherosclerosis (MESA) study, Miao and colleagues[37] detected positive coronary remodeling, a predictor for future cardiovascular events, in asymptomatic older adults using MR imaging (n = 179).[38] Pericardial fat volume, an index of cardiovascular vulnerability, was also found to relate strongly to coronary plaque eccentricity (detected with MR imaging) in healthy older adults. Lin and colleagues[39] showed the differences of coronary wall thickness and stiffness between subjects with primary hypertension and healthy controls. Those results suggest that coronary wall features have the potential to serve as quantitative imaging biomarkers in evaluating cardiovascular risks. **Fig. 4** shows positive remodeling of the coronary wall in an asymptomatic subject with T2DM.

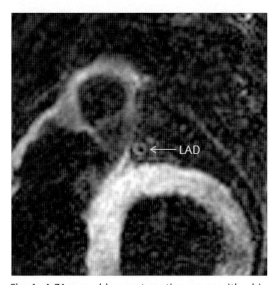

Fig. 4. A 71-year-old asymptomatic woman with a history of T2DM for 10 years. An eccentrically remodeled coronary segment on the left anterior descending artery (LAD) (without significant lumen stenosis) could be identified by MR imaging. (Image of unpublished data from Lin & Carr, 2011.)

APPLICATION AND LIMITATIONS OF MAGNETIC RESONANCE IMAGING/ MAGNETIC RESONANCE ANGIOGRAPHY FOR CORONARY ARTERY DISEASE MANAGEMENT IN CLINICAL PRACTICE

At present, coronary MR imaging/MRA has not been widely accepted as a regular examination in clinical practice. Many factors may affect image quality of coronary arteries, which may compromise clinical diagnosis. Such a situation is caused by several technical limitations of this technique. However, many novel technical innovations have been developed to solve those problems (**Table 3**).

When an acute coronary syndrome develops, it has been said that "time is myocardium and time is outcome."[40] Therefore, MR imaging is not suitable for CAD diagnosis under acute situations because of long scan times. Although MR imaging can be a useful tool for screening subclinical CAD, MR imaging may need more time than other noninvasive imaging tools, such as coronary CTA, for the detection of CAD. In addition, a long scan may adversely affect the image quality of coronary MR imaging/MRA because of unexpected motion artifacts and potentially reduces the clinical value of coronary MR imaging. During the last few decades, many technical advances have been applied to shorten coronary MR imaging scan times. Parallel imaging takes advantage of spatial encoding from multiple parts of phase-array receive coils to shorten the MR imaging acquisition time.[41] Huber and colleagues[42] reported the implementation and evaluation of sensitivity-encoding (SENSE) free-breathing navigator-gated 3D coronary MRA at 3 T. SENSE significantly reduced MR imaging scan times for the coronary tree in 11 healthy volunteers. However, there is

Table 3 Major challenges for current coronary MR imaging/MRA techniques	
Challenges	**Possible Solutions**
Long scan time	Developing fast imaging techniques
Low spatial resolution and SNR	Using high magnetic field and administrating of contrast agents
Adverse physiologic conditions, such as fast heart rate and irregular breath modes	Developing novel imaging techniques, suppressing adverse pathophysiologic conditions

Abbreviation: SNR, signal/noise ratio.

usually a trade-off between short acquisition time and lower signal/noise ratio (representing inferior visualization of coronary branches).[43] Using a 32-channel coil, Nehrke and colleagues[44] acquired free-breathing whole-heart coronary MRA in 4 minutes with the use of SENSE and partial Fourier encoding for k-space acceleration. In a recent study, Nam and colleagues[45] applied a novel B(1)-weighted compressed sensing (CS) technique in 3D whole-heart coronary MRA. With a CS-based acquisition and reconstruction strategy (low-dimensional-structure self-learning and thresholding [LOST]), the investigators acquired high-resolution coronary MRA in 7 healthy volunteers with a shorter acquisition time than that of the traditional SENSE technique.[45]

Administration of contrast agents is a common way to improve image quality. Paetsch and colleagues[46] successfully used an intravascular contrast agent, B-22956, to significantly improve the image quality of 3D coronary MRA. Yu and colleagues[47] performed contrast-enhanced whole-heart coronary MRA (with SENSE) in 11 healthy volunteers. A longer left anterior descending artery could be depicted compared with that presented by noncontrast coronary MRA. Many solutions could be applied to jointly improve the performance of coronary MR imaging/MRA.

Compared with imaging other solid organs, continuous motion of the coronary tree in the 3D space is a specific challenge for coronary imaging. Heartbeat and breathing are major sources of coronary motion. In order to minimize the adverse effects of motion on coronary image quality, segmented acquisition schemes were designed to collect imaging data over multiple heartbeat and respiration cycles. Only the signal received within a highly selected acquisition window for minimal coronary motion is accepted for filling k-space. An ideal acquisition window should be both cardiac motion free (a rest period of regional cardiac motion chosen with electrocardiography) and respiratory freezing (identified with 2D motion-adapted navigator [NAV] echo).[48–50] However, current motion correction/suppression strategies are still unable to eliminate the adverse effects of motion on cardiovascular MR scans. Severe cardiac motion, associated with faster heart rates and shortened rest periods in cardiac cycles, has already been proved to be a prominent determinant of poor image quality in coronary wall MR imaging.[51] β-Blockers can significantly reduce heart rate and increase rest duration in the cardiac cycle.[52] SSFP is a fast MR imaging pulse sequence. With spatial resolution and gross imaging time identical to that used for TSE (FSE), SSFP can therefore acquire data in a shorter time

window in a single cardiac cycle. Such a physical characteristic can particularly be used in cardiac imaging, which is affected by severe cardiac motion. Using a black-blood SSFP sequence, Lin and colleagues[53] significantly increased image quality of the coronary wall under conditions of fast heart rate (>80 beats/min) in healthy subjects. Compared with traditional TSE (FSE) sequences for coronary wall imaging, SSFP also had better performance in directly observing the coronary wall for the detection of potential cardiac allograft vasculopathy in heart transplant (HTx) recipients, who usually have extremely fast heart rates caused by denervation of transplanted hearts.[54] **Fig. 5** shows a coronary wall image in an HTx recipient.

Limited by the length and stability of breath holding, breath-hold MR imaging is not suitable for all coronary examinations. Free-breathing coronary MR imaging/MRA has become the preferred choice in most large-scale clinical/epidemiologic studies for guiding cardiovascular prevention, such as the MESA study.[37] However, changes of breathing patterns (indicated by changes in the location of the diaphragm during the scan) may significantly affect image quality.[48,50,55] Irregular breathing modes may widely exist in healthy populations. Older subjects are more likely to have inconsistent breathing modes.[56] Advanced respiratory motion compensation has been used to suppress such adverse effects caused by

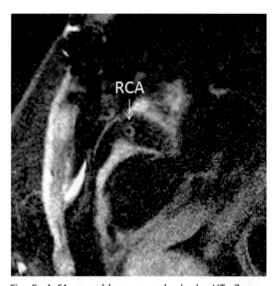

Fig. 5. A 61-year-old woman who had a HTx 7 years ago. Her heart rate is 108 beats/min. The RCA can clearly be seen using the black-blood SSFP MR imaging technique. (*From* Lin K, Bi X, Liu Y, et al. Black-blood steady-state free precession (SSFP) coronary wall MRI for cardiac allografts: a feasibility study. J Magn Reson Imaging 2012;35(5):1210–5; with permission.)

motion.[57] Using 3D-NAV and 3D affine correction, Henningsson and colleagues[58] showed 100% scan efficiency in performing high-resolution whole-heart 3D coronary MRA with high image quality in a recent study. Pang and colleagues[59] developed a whole-heart coronary MRA technique using motion-corrected sensitivity encoding with 3D projection reconstruction. Such a sequence can be used to image the whole coronary tree in 5 minutes with good image quality despite the adverse effects of respiratory motion. In addition, some adjuncts, such as abdominal belts, have been applied to stabilize respiratory motion during coronary MR imaging/MRA. Ishida and colleagues[60] used a dedicated abdominal belt to regulate respiratory motion during coronary scans and therefore achieved a higher scan efficiency, shorter scan time, and better image quality.[15,61]

FUTURE DIRECTIONS

Because coronary MR imaging/MRA may provide a cluster of quantitative measurements to evaluate the progression of coronary atherosclerosis, it will become increasingly important in cardiovascular disease diagnosis and management. In addition, CAD may also be considered as a secondary target-organ involvement of nephrology, endocrinology, and rheumatology disorders, including chronic kidney disease, T2DM, and systemic lupus erythematosus.[62–64] A noninvasive, standardized approach to measure subclinical CAD and related cardiac changes from multiple aspects is important for guiding CAD management and improving patient survival by measuring individual responses to comprehensive target-organ protection. In a recent study, Pang and colleagues[65] developed a self-gated four-dimensional whole-heart imaging technique to detect coronary anatomy and cardiac function simultaneously. However, although coronary MR imaging/MRA has been used for CAD estimation for more than 10 years, many technical and physiologic conditions still significantly affect its performance in clinical practice. Further work is needed to optimize the technique and extend its clinical application for patient care.

REFERENCES

1. Wingard DL, Barrett-Connor EL, Scheidt-Nave C, et al. Prevalence of cardiovascular and renal complications in older adults with normal or impaired glucose tolerance or NIDDM. A population-based study. Diabetes Care 1993;16(7):1022–5.
2. Grundy SM, Benjamin IJ, Burke GL, et al. Diabetes and cardiovascular disease: a statement for healthcare professionals from the American Heart Association. Circulation 1999;100(10):1134–46.
3. Worthley SG, Helft G, Fuster V, et al. Noninvasive in vivo magnetic resonance imaging of experimental coronary artery lesions in a porcine model. Circulation 2000;101(25):2956–61.
4. Fayad ZA, Nahar T, Fallon JT, et al. In vivo magnetic resonance evaluation of atherosclerotic plaques in the human thoracic aorta: a comparison with transesophageal echocardiography. Circulation 2000; 101(21):2503–9.
5. Ishida M, Sakuma H. Magnetic resonance of coronary arteries: assessment of luminal narrowing and blood flow in the coronary arteries. J Thorac Imaging 2014;29(3):155–62.
6. Regenfus M, Ropers D, Achenbach S, et al. Noninvasive detection of coronary artery stenosis using contrast-enhanced three-dimensional breath-hold magnetic resonance coronary angiography. J Am Coll Cardiol 2000;36(1):44–50.
7. Bi X, Li D. Coronary arteries at 3.0 T: Contrast-enhanced magnetization-prepared three-dimensional breathhold MR angiography. J Magn Reson Imaging 2005;21(2):133–9.
8. Lin K, Lloyd-Jones DM, Spottiswoode B, et al. T1 contrast in the myocardium and blood pool: a quantitative assessment of gadopentetate dimeglumine and gadofosveset trisodium at 1.5 and 3 T. Invest Radiol 2014;49(4):243–8.
9. Bi X, Carr JC, Li D. Whole-heart coronary magnetic resonance angiography at 3 Tesla in 5 minutes with slow infusion of Gd-BOPTA, a high-relaxivity clinical contrast agent. Magn Reson Med 2007; 58(1):1–7.
10. Yang Q, Li K, Liu X, et al. Contrast-enhanced whole-heart coronary magnetic resonance angiography at 3.0-T: a comparative study with X-ray angiography in a single center. J Am Coll Cardiol 2009;54(1):69–76.
11. Yang Q, Li K, Liu X, et al. 3.0T whole-heart coronary magnetic resonance angiography performed with 32-channel cardiac coils: a single-center experience. Circ Cardiovasc Imaging 2012;5(5):573–9.
12. Notaro LA, Usman MH, Burke JF, et al. Secondary prevention in concurrent coronary artery, cerebrovascular, and chronic kidney disease: focus on pharmacological therapy. Cardiovasc Ther 2009; 27(3):199–215.
13. McCarthy RM, Shea SM, Deshpande VS, et al. Coronary MR angiography: true FISP imaging improved by prolonging breath holds with preoxygenation in healthy volunteers. Radiology 2003;227(1):283–8.
14. Spuentrup E, Katoh M, Buecker A, et al. Free-breathing 3D steady-state free precession coronary MR angiography with radial k-space sampling: comparison with cartesian k-space sampling and cartesian gradient-echo coronary MR angiography–pilot study. Radiology 2004;231(2):581–6.

15. Kato S, Kitagawa K, Ishida N, et al. Assessment of coronary artery disease using magnetic resonance coronary angiography: a national multicenter trial. J Am Coll Cardiol 2010;56(12):983–91.

16. Yonezawa M, Nagata M, Kitagawa K, et al. Quantitative analysis of 1.5-T whole-heart coronary MR angiograms obtained with 32-channel cardiac coils: a comparison with conventional quantitative coronary angiography. Radiology 2014;271(2):356–64.

17. Kim WY, Danias PG, Stuber M, et al. Coronary magnetic resonance angiography for the detection of coronary stenoses. N Engl J Med 2001;345(26): 1863–9.

18. Stuber M, Botnar RM, Danias PG, et al. Double-oblique free-breathing high resolution three-dimensional coronary magnetic resonance angiography. J Am Coll Cardiol 1999;34(2):524–31.

19. Liu X, Zhao X, Huang J, et al. Comparison of 3D free-breathing coronary MR angiography and 64-MDCT angiography for detection of coronary stenosis in patients with high calcium scores. AJR Am J Roentgenol 2007;189(6):1326–32.

20. Yoon YE, Kitagawa K, Kato S, et al. Prognostic value of coronary magnetic resonance angiography for prediction of cardiac events in patients with suspected coronary artery disease. J Am Coll Cardiol 2012;60(22):2316–22.

21. Terashima M, Meyer CH, Keeffe BG, et al. Noninvasive assessment of coronary vasodilation using magnetic resonance angiography. J Am Coll Cardiol 2005;45(1):104–10.

22. Hays AG, Hirsch GA, Kelle S, et al. Noninvasive visualization of coronary artery endothelial function in healthy subjects and in patients with coronary artery disease. J Am Coll Cardiol 2010;56(20): 1657–65.

23. Hays AG, Kelle S, Hirsch GA, et al. Regional coronary endothelial function is closely related to local early coronary atherosclerosis in patients with mild coronary artery disease: pilot study. Circ Cardiovasc Imaging 2012;5(3):341–8.

24. Lin K, Lloyd-Jones DM, Liu Y, et al. Noninvasive evaluation of coronary distensibility in older adults: a feasibility study with MR angiography. Radiology 2011;261(3):771–8.

25. Shibata M, Sakuma H, Isaka N, et al. Assessment of coronary flow reserve with fast cine phase contrast magnetic resonance imaging: comparison with measurement by Doppler guide wire. J Magn Reson Imaging 1999;10(4):563–8.

26. Virmani R, Kolodgie FD, Burke AP, et al. Lessons from sudden coronary death: a comprehensive morphological classification scheme for atherosclerotic lesions. Arterioscler Thromb Vasc Biol 2000; 20(5):1262–75.

27. Waxman S, Ishibashi F, Muller JE. Detection and treatment of vulnerable plaques and vulnerable patients: novel approaches to prevention of coronary events. Circulation 2006;114(22):2390–411.

28. Nahser PJ Jr, Brown RE, Oskarsson H, et al. Maximal coronary flow reserve and metabolic coronary vasodilation in patients with diabetes mellitus. Circulation 1995;91(3):635–40.

29. Burke AP, Farb A, Malcom GT, et al. Coronary risk factors and plaque morphology in men with coronary disease who died suddenly. N Engl J Med 1997;336(18):1276–82.

30. Falk E, Shah PK, Fuster V. Coronary plaque disruption. Circulation 1995;92(3):657–71.

31. Varnava AM, Mills PG, Davies MJ. Relationship between coronary artery remodeling and plaque vulnerability. Circulation 2002;105(8):939–43.

32. Arnett EN, Isner JM, Redwood DR, et al. Coronary artery narrowing in coronary heart disease: comparison of cineangiographic and necropsy findings. Ann Intern Med 1979;91(3):350–6.

33. Nagata M, Kato S, Kitagawa K, et al. Diagnostic accuracy of 1.5-T unenhanced whole-heart coronary MR angiography performed with 32-channel cardiac coils: initial single-center experience. Radiology 2011;259(2):384–92.

34. He Y, Zhang Z, Dai Q, et al. Accuracy of MRI to identify the coronary artery plaque: a comparative study with intravascular ultrasound. J Magn Reson Imaging 2012;35(1):72–8.

35. Botnar RM, Stuber M, Kissinger KV, et al. Noninvasive coronary vessel wall and plaque imaging with magnetic resonance imaging. Circulation 2000; 102(21):2582–7.

36. Kim WY, Astrup AS, Stuber M, et al. Subclinical coronary and aortic atherosclerosis detected by magnetic resonance imaging in type 1 diabetes with and without diabetic nephropathy. Circulation 2007;115(2):228–35.

37. Miao C, Chen S, Macedo R, et al. Positive remodeling of the coronary arteries detected by magnetic resonance imaging in an asymptomatic population: MESA (Multi-Ethnic Study of Atherosclerosis). J Am Coll Cardiol 2009;53(18):1708–15.

38. Miao C, Chen S, Ding J, et al. The association of pericardial fat with coronary artery plaque index at MR imaging: the Multi-Ethnic Study of Atherosclerosis (MESA). Radiology 2011;261(1):109–15.

39. Lin K, Lloyd-Jones DM, Liu Y, et al. Potential quantitative magnetic resonance imaging biomarkers of coronary remodeling in older hypertensive patients. Arterioscler Thromb Vasc Biol 2012;32(7):1742–7.

40. Gibson CM. Time is myocardium and time is outcomes. Circulation 2001;104(22):2632–4.

41. Sodickson DK, McKenzie CA. A generalized approach to parallel magnetic resonance imaging. Med Phys 2001;28(8):1629–43.

42. Huber ME, Kozerke S, Pruessmann KP, et al. Sensitivity-encoded coronary MRA at 3T. Magn Reson Med 2004;52(2):221–7.

43. Bluemke DA, Achenbach S, Budoff M, et al. Noninvasive coronary artery imaging: magnetic resonance angiography and multidetector computed tomography angiography: a scientific statement from the American Heart Association Committee on Cardiovascular Imaging and Intervention of the Council on Cardiovascular Radiology and Intervention, and the Councils on Clinical Cardiology and Cardiovascular Disease in the Young. Circulation 2008;118(5):586–606.

44. Nehrke K, Bornert P, Mazurkewitz P, et al. Free-breathing whole-heart coronary MR angiography on a clinical scanner in four minutes. J Magn Reson Imaging 2006;23(5):752–6.

45. Nam S, Hong SN, Akcakaya M, et al. Compressed sensing reconstruction for undersampled breath-hold radial cine imaging with auxiliary free-breathing data. J Magn Reson Imaging 2014;39(1):179–88.

46. Paetsch I, Huber ME, Bornstedt A, et al. Improved three-dimensional free-breathing coronary magnetic resonance angiography using gadocoletic acid (B-22956) for intravascular contrast enhancement. J Magn Reson Imaging 2004;20(2):288–93.

47. Yu J, Paetsch I, Schnackenburg B, et al. Use of 2D sensitivity encoding for slow-infusion contrast-enhanced isotropic 3-T whole-heart coronary MR angiography. AJR Am J Roentgenol 2011;197(2):374–82.

48. Lin K, Lloyd-Jones DM, Bi X, et al. Effects of respiratory motion on coronary wall MR imaging: a quantitative study of older adults. Int J Cardiovasc Imaging 2013;29(5):1069–76.

49. Taylor AM, Jhooti P, Firmin DN, et al. Automated monitoring of diaphragm end-expiratory position for real-time navigator echo MR coronary angiography. J Magn Reson Imaging 1999;9(3):395–401.

50. Taylor AM, Jhooti P, Wiesmann F, et al. MR navigator-echo monitoring of temporal changes in diaphragm position: implications for MR coronary angiography. J Magn Reson Imaging 1997;7(4):629–36.

51. Malayeri AA, Macedo R, Li D, et al. Coronary vessel wall evaluation by magnetic resonance imaging in the multi-ethnic study of atherosclerosis: determinants of image quality. J Comput Assist Tomogr 2009;33(1):1–7.

52. Jahnke C, Paetsch I, Achenbach S, et al. Coronary MR imaging: breath-hold capability and patterns, coronary artery rest periods, and beta-blocker use. Radiology 2006;239(1):71–8.

53. Lin K, Bi X, Taimen K, et al. Coronary wall MR imaging in patients with rapid heart rates: a feasibility study of black-blood steady-state free precession (SSFP). Int J Cardiovasc Imaging 2012;28(3):567–75.

54. Lin K, Bi X, Liu Y, et al. Black-blood steady-state free precession (SSFP) coronary wall MRI for cardiac allografts: a feasibility study. J Magn Reson Imaging 2012;35(5):1210–5.

55. Danias PG, Stuber M, Botnar RM, et al. Relationship between motion of coronary arteries and diaphragm during free breathing: lessons from real-time MR imaging. AJR Am J Roentgenol 1999;172(4):1061–5.

56. Tobin MJ, Chadha TS, Jenouri G, et al. Breathing patterns. 1. Normal subjects. Chest 1983;84(2):202–5.

57. Henningsson M, Botnar RM. Advanced respiratory motion compensation for coronary MR angiography. Sensors (Basel) 2013;13(6):6882–99.

58. Henningsson M, Prieto C, Chiribiri A, et al. Whole-heart coronary MRA with 3D affine motion correction using 3D image-based navigation. Magn Reson Med 2014;71(1):173–81.

59. Pang J, Sharif B, Arsanjani R, et al. Accelerated whole-heart coronary MRA using motion-corrected sensitivity encoding with three-dimensional projection reconstruction. Magn Reson Med 2014. [Epub ahead of print].

60. Ishida M, Schuster A, Takase S, et al. Impact of an abdominal belt on breathing patterns and scan efficiency in whole-heart coronary magnetic resonance angiography: comparison between the UK and Japan. J Cardiovasc Magn Reson 2011;13:71.

61. McConnell MV, Khasgiwala VC, Savord BJ, et al. Comparison of respiratory suppression methods and navigator locations for MR coronary angiography. AJR Am J Roentgenol 1997;168(5):1369–75.

62. Lin K, Lloyd-Jones DM, Li D, et al. Quantitative imaging biomarkers for the evaluation of cardiovascular complications in type 2 diabetes mellitus. J Diabetes Complications 2014;28(2):234–42.

63. Briasoulis A, Bakris GL. Chronic kidney disease as a coronary artery disease risk equivalent. Curr Cardiol Rep 2013;15(3):340.

64. Roman MJ, Shanker BA, Davis A, et al. Prevalence and correlates of accelerated atherosclerosis in systemic lupus erythematosus. N Engl J Med 2003;349(25):2399–406.

65. Pang J, Sharif B, Fan Z, et al. ECG and navigator-free four-dimensional whole-heart coronary MRA for simultaneous visualization of cardiac anatomy and function. Magn Reson Med 2014;72(5):1208–17.

Stress Cardiac MR Imaging
The Role of Stress Functional Assessment and Perfusion Imaging in the Evaluation of Ischemic Heart Disease

Dr. Saeed Al Sayari, MBBS, German Board of Radiology,
European Board of Cardiac Radiology (EBCR)[a,b],
Dr. Sebastien Kopp, MD, Swiss Board of Radiology[a],
Prof. Dr. Jens Bremerich, MD, Swiss Board of Radiology,
European Board of Cardiac Radiology (EBCR)[a,*]

KEYWORDS

- Imaging of myocardial ischemia • Non-ischemic heart failure • Left ventricular dysfunction
- Coronary artery disease • Myocarditis • Adenosine stress CMR • Dobutamine stress CMR
- Myocardial ischemia

KEY POINTS

- Stress cardiac magnetic resonance (CMR) imaging plays an important role in the diagnosis and management of ischemic heart disease (IHD).
- It can be used for initial diagnosis of significant coronary artery disease (CAD).
- It can help diagnose complications post–myocardial infarction (MI) or postinterventions.
- It can predict myocardial recovery.
- It can also help differentiate ischemic from nonischemic causes of heart failure.

According to the World Health Organization, IHD is the leading cause of death worldwide, with more than 7 million deaths in 2008. Although it remains a major problem in the Western world, the burden of IHD mortality has shifted away from high-income countries to other parts of the world.[1]

With the emergence of CMR stress imaging as a valuable tool in the diagnosis of stress-inducible cardiac ischemia, it became of utmost importance to master the different techniques of CMR stress imaging. The advantage of this modality is that it is a noninvasive examination that does not expose the patient to any radiation compared with other modalities such as single-photon emission computed tomography (SPECT), positron emission tomography, or conventional catheter angiography. At the same time, CMR imaging is capable of providing a large volume of information that is superior or comparable to well-established modalities like SPECT.[2]

CMR imaging offers the ability to study cardiac morphology, function, myocardial perfusion, detection of scar tissue, and additional information such as thrombus formation or no-reflow phenomenon that are usually not detected by other imaging modalities.

This review focuses on the role of CMR stress examination in regard to evaluation of IHD

[a] Cardiothoracic Section, Department of Radiology and Nuclear Medicine, University of Basel Hospital, Petersgraben 4, Basel 4031, Switzerland; [b] Department of Radiology, Mafraq Hospital, Al Mafraq Area, P.O.Box 2951, Abu Dhabi, UAE
* Corresponding author. Department of Cardiothoracic Imaging, Petersgraben 4, Basel 4031, Switzerland.
E-mail address: Jens.bremerich@usb.ch

Radiol Clin N Am 53 (2015) 355–367
http://dx.doi.org/10.1016/j.rcl.2014.11.006
0033-8389/15/$ – see front matter © 2015 Elsevier Inc. All rights reserved.

radiologic.theclinics.com

Societies and Organizations	
AACF	American College of Cardiology Foundation
AATS	American Association for Thoracic Surgery
ACP	American College of Physicians
ACR	American College of Radiology
AHA	American Heart Association
NASCI	North American Society for Cardiovascular Imaging
PCNA	Preventive Cardiovascular Nurses Association
SCAI	Society for Cardiovascular Angiography and Interventions
SCMR	Society for Cardiovascular Magnetic Resonance
SPR	Society of Pediatric Radiology
STS	Society of Thoracic Surgeons

including the diagnostic performance and prognostic value. It does not cover the technical or practical aspects of the examination nor the pathologic or pharmacologic details. The use of stress CMR imaging in different clinical scenarios is explored, including roles

- In the emergency department (ED)
- In differential diagnosis of chest pain
- In diagnosing complications post–MI
- In the assessment of the right ventricle after left ventricle infarction
- In detecting complications due to or after interventions

- In prediction of myocardial recovery
- In detecting inducible ischemia in patients with known IHD.
- In differentiating ischemic from nonischemic heart failure.
- In risk stratification

DIFFERENT GUIDELINES AND INDICATIONS OF STRESS CARDIAC MAGNETIC RESONANCE IN ISCHEMIC HEART DISEASE

At present, both North American and European guidelines concerning the diagnosis and

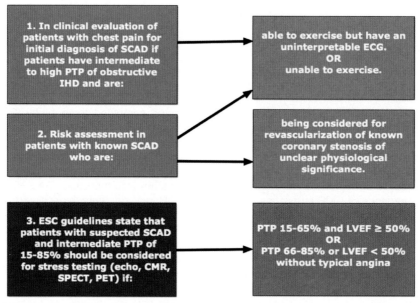

Fig. 1. (1, 2) Based on the 2012 ACCF/AHA/ACP/AATS/PCNA/SCAI/STS Guidelines for the Diagnosis and Management of Patients with Stable Ischemic Heart Disease (SIDH).[3] (3) Based on the 2013 ESC guidelines on the management of stable coronary artery disease (SCAD).[4] LVEF, left ventricular ejection fraction; PET, positron emission tomography; PTP, pretest probability. (Data from [1, 2] Fihn SD, Gardin JM, Abrams J, et al. 2012 ACCF/AHA/ACP/AATS/PCNA/SCAI/STS guideline for the diagnosis and management of patients with stable ischemic heart disease: executive summary. Circulation 2012;126(25):3097–137; and [3] Montalescot G, Sechtem U, Achenbach S, et al. 2013 ESC guidelines on the management of stable coronary artery disease: the Task Force on the management of stable coronary artery disease of the European Society of Cardiology. Eur Heart J 2013;34(38):2949–3003.)

management of IHD incorporate different types of stress tests including CMR imaging. In both guidelines, stress CMR imaging plays a role in multiple scenarios. It is useful in the clinical evaluation of patients with chest pain in the initial diagnosis of stable coronary artery disease (SCAD), and it is also recommended as one of the examination modalities (along with nuclear myocardial perfusion imaging (MPI) and echocardiography) for risk assessment in patients before revascularization of a known coronary stenosis, especially if the physiologic significance of this stenosis was unclear.[3]

In 2012, practice guidelines were published by ACCF/AHA/ACP/AATS/PCNA/SCAI/STS Task Force for the diagnosis and management of patients with stable IHD. The most recent European Society of Cardiology guidelines on the management of SCAD were published in 2013. **Fig. 1** explores the possible uses of stress MRI according to these guidelines.[3,4]

In addition to the above-mentioned guidelines, other societies and medical bodies came up with similar potential indications. The American College of Radiology (ACR), the North American Society for Cardiovascular Imaging (NASCI), and the Society for Pediatric Radiology (SPR) published a list of primary indications in 2011, which include guidelines for CMR use in IHD among others.[5] **Box 1** summarizes the ACR-NASCI-SPR guidelines in addition to the indications mentioned in the ACCF/ACR/AHA/NASCI/SCMR 2010 Expert Consensus Document on CMR.[6]

One study listed the referral patterns of stress CMR imaging in routine clinical practice. A total of 654 patients were scanned, of which 7 (1%) were referred as a part of research study. The other indications for referral were chest pain (129 patients; 20%), left ventricular (LV) dysfunction (112 patients; 17%), left bundle branch block (LBBB) (45 patients; 7%), and known CAD (361 patients; 55%); the clinical question being "evidence of reversible perfusion defect?" The first 3 groups (286 patients; 44%) did not have a previously known CAD.[7]

STRESS CARDIAC MAGNETIC RESONANCE IMAGING PROTOCOL

A basic stress CMR imaging protocol consists of multiple modules. It starts with a functional assessment, followed by pharmacologic stress (either a perfusion stress with a vasodilator or a wall motion abnormality assessment with dobutamine). If a vasodilator is used, then perfusion at rest is also considered. The examination ends with late gadolinium enhancement (LGE) module to detect scars.[8] Because all these modules are

---

Box 1
Summary of potential uses of CMR imaging in patients with IHD

CMR is more accurate and reproducible in ventricular function assessment.

Appropriate qualitative assessment of regional wall-motion abnormalities (WMAs) and quantitative assessment of LV function is possible.

Useful for follow-up and assessment of ventricular remodeling post-MI.

MRI is able to distinguish ischemic scar from other causes of myocardial scarring and to identify the extent and location of myocardial necrosis.

May be used to evaluate the likelihood of recovery after revascularization in chronic IHD.

CMR imaging is helpful in identification of ventricular thrombus in association with ischemic scar.

MRI perfusion can be used to detect areas of perfusion abnormality at rest or during pharmacologically induced stress.

CMR imaging can help differentiate between normal, ischemic but viable, and nonviable myocardium.

Inducible WMAs can be detected with high-dose dobutamine stress indicating inducible ischemia.

CMR imaging can be used to diagnose IHD in patients with resting ECG abnormalities or inability to exercise.

Functional MRI, late-enhancement module, and perfusion at rest may be helpful to diagnose segments with regional ischemia and acute myocardial infarction in acute coronary syndrome, especially if ECG and enzymes are indeterminate.

Based on the ACR-NASCI-SPR guidelines (2011 revision) and the ACCF/ACR/AHA/NASCI/SCMR 2010 expert consensus document on CMR.

---

used to reach a diagnosis, their role, in addition to the role of stress module itself, is discussed in different clinical scenarios.

ROLE IN THE EMERGENCY DEPARTMENT

A multicenter study in the United States with 10,689 patients presenting to the ED with chest discomfort or symptoms consistent with acute cardiac ischemia (ACI) revealed that only 23% of these patients had true ACI. Of those, 94% were hospitalized and 6% were sent home. Acute myocardial infarction (AMI) was present in 36%; 64% had unstable angina. Of the 77% who did not have an ACI, 59% were hospitalized and 41% were sent home. The diagnosis of AMI was made based on clinical course, electrocardiographic (ECG) findings, and enzyme elevation. Initially 20% of patients with AMI and 37% of patients with unstable angina showed normal ECG findings.[9] The figures reveal that there are many unnecessary hospital admissions with huge financial burdens to health care systems. At the same time, some patients with true ACI are sent home with potential dire consequences. At this rate of discharge, one study estimated the number of missed diagnoses of MI in the United States to be at least 11,000 per year.[10]

CMR imaging allows for detection of both myocardial edema and myocardial scar, indicating a significant value in the triage of patients with suspected ACI. Kwong and colleagues[11] evaluated 161 consecutive patients who presented to the ED with chest pain but no signs of ST-elevation on ECG and concluded that resting CMR imaging is suitable for triage of patients with chest pain in the ED, especially those with enzyme-negative unstable angina.

Many studies and reviews discussed the feasibility and practicability of detecting acute coronary syndrome (ACS) by CMR imaging in the ED. CMR imaging can provide valuable information to confirm the diagnosis or to aid in risk stratification after resolution of chest pain and stabilization of the patient in the ED.[12]

The imaging protocol may include LV function module, myocardial edema module (T2W), first-pass myocardial perfusion (rest, and in some cases stress), and early/late gadolinium enhancement. This protocol can effectively evaluate the heart for the LV function, ischemia, viability, MI and its size, microvascular obstruction, and presence or absence of a thrombus.[13]

With T2W imaging, one can measure the area at risk (AAR) as indicated by myocardial edema, which denotes the ischemic AAR and myocardial hemorrhage. This AAR includes both reversible and irreversible myocardial injury. With LGE the infarct size and extent is measured, in addition to the myocardial salvage estimation (AAR-LGE).[14]

Gadolinium enters the intracellular space in the affected zone as a result of the damage to the cell membrane in the acute stage of MI. It is retained there with a slow wash out compared with areas of healthy myocardium, which show a rapid contrast wash out. With a correct inversion time (TI) value and nulling of the myocardium, the retained gadolinium shortens the T1 relaxation time, resulting in hyperenhancement of the infarcted zone. Areas that show tissue edema but no LGE are considered to represent viable but stunned myocardium.[14]

A CMR imaging protocol with T2W imaging and LV wall thickness assessment has an increased specificity, positive predictive value, and overall accuracy from 84% to 96%, 55% to 85%, and 84% to 93%, respectively, compared with a conventional CMR imaging protocol (LV function, perfusion, LGE).[15] Another study evaluated the prognostic value of negative adenosine stress CMR imaging in 135 patients presented to the ED with chest pain but with negative troponin and nondiagnostic ECG. Adenosine stress CMR imaging was performed at initial presentation, and patients were contacted a year later to determine the incidence of significant CAD (coronary artery stenosis >50%, abnormal stress test, new MI, or death). Adenosine perfusion abnormalities were shown to have 100% sensitivity and 93% specificity, with abnormal CMR findings adding significant prognostic value in predicting future events.[16] A study comparing stress CMR imaging with stress echocardiography showed stress CMR imaging to be the strongest independent predictor of significant CAD in patients presenting to the ED with intermediate-risk chest pain, if the examination is performed within 12 hours of presentation.[17]

It is important to understand that in patients with acute ST elevation myocardial infarction (STEMI), an immediate reperfusion therapy is indicated with a door-to-balloon time of less than 90 minutes. A further reduction in this period might reduce mortality as suggested by one study.[18]

ROLE IN DIFFERENTIAL DIAGNOSIS OF CHEST PAIN

CMR imaging can also play a role in the differential diagnosis of acute chest pain in patients with normal or elevated cardiac enzymes. The most important causes of chest pain that are of importance from CMR point of view are listed in **Box 2**.

Acute myocarditis may present with acute chest pain and increased levels of creatine-kinase (CK),

---

Box 2
Most important causes of chest pain from CMR point of view

Acute myocarditis

Acute myocardial infarction

Takotsubo cardiomyopathy

Dilated cardiomyopathy

Acute pericarditis

Hypertrophic cardiomyopathy

Pulmonary embolism

Aortic dissection

creatine-kinase-MB (CK-MB), and troponin, mimicking a small to medium-sized MI.[19] A small focal myocarditis may also present with ECG and enzyme findings indistinguishable from an acute STEMI.[20] Although endomyocardial biopsy might be the most widely accepted method for diagnosis of myocarditis, owing to the patchy nature of the disease, a biopsy does not necessarily sample the affected tissue.[21] Taking this sampling error and possible complications (perforation, tamponade) into consideration, it became apparent that another modality of examination is needed to confirm the diagnosis of myocarditis. Friedrich and colleagues[22] were the first to conclude that contrast media–enhanced CMR imaging could determine the localization, activity, and extent of inflammation in myocarditis. T2W imaging with early and late gadolinium enhancement has been shown to provide a high diagnostic accuracy in patients with suspected acute myocarditis.[23] Findings in acute myocarditis include myocardial edema (regional or global) in T2W images, early gadolinium enhancement due to hyperemia or capillary leakage, and LGE due to necrosis and fibrosis.[19] The classic pattern of enhancement in myocarditis is subepicardial LGE (**Fig. 2**).

In case of pericarditis, CMR imaging may detect pericardial thickening, inflammatory changes of the pericardium and/or epicardial fat. It also has the ability to detect small pericardial effusions and show pericardial enhancement after contrast media injection.[24]

Dilated cardiomyopathy (DCM), Takotsubo cardiomyopathy (**Fig. 3**), and hypertrophic cardiomyopathy have all been reported to present with acute chest pain and positive biomarkers.[25] CMR imaging features for these entities are well documented and out of the scope of this review.

A study concluded that compared with other imaging modalities, CMR imaging is considered to be a valuable tool in the management of patients with chest pain and elevated troponin levels but with unobstructed coronary arteries.[26]

ROLE IN DIAGNOSIS OF COMPLICATIONS POST-MYOCARDIAL INFARCTION

The most common complications seen after MI include ventricular aneurysm, ventricular free wall rupture, rupture of the interventricular septum or the papillary muscle, and formation of an LV mural thrombus.[27] CMR imaging plays a pivotal role in the diagnosis of those complications, especially in the case of an LV mural thrombus (**Fig. 4**), whereby further serious complications may occur due to systemic embolization. In one study, LGE was able to detect thrombus in 7% of patients with MI, whereas cine-CMR imaging was able to do so in 4.7% only.[28]

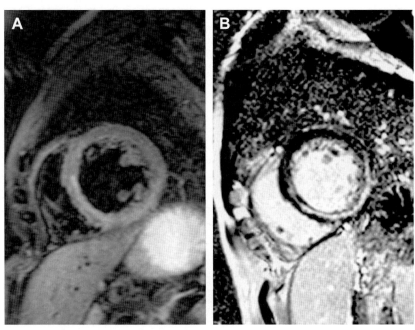

Fig. 2. A 48-year-old man presented to the ED with chest pain. Laboratory tests showed high troponin levels. A myocardial infarction was suspected, and the patient underwent an invasive coronary angiography, which was normal. A subsequent CMR examination showed myocardial edema inferior and inferoseptal (*A*) with subepicardial and mesocardial LGE (*B*).

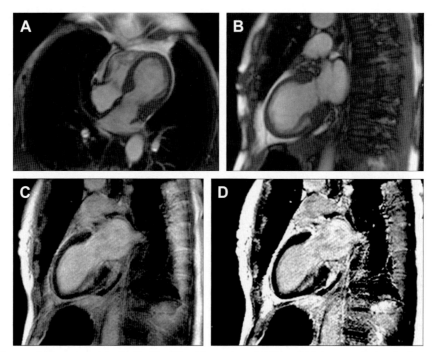

Fig. 3. A 53-year-old woman presented to the ED with suspected ACS and high troponin levels. A coronary angiography was performed, but was normal. Regional wall-motion abnormalities were noticed posteriorly and anterolaterally. Myocarditis was suspected. CMR imaging revealed Takotsubo cardiomyopathy with typical appearance in the SSFP images (*A, B*) and no LGE (*C, D*).

ROLE IN THE ASSESSMENT OF THE RIGHT VENTRICLE AFTER LEFT VENTRICULAR INFARCTION

Right ventricular failure after an acute MI increases the risk of in-hospital mortality to more than 4-fold.[29] Right ventricular involvement was diagnosed in 54% of patients presenting with AMI in several studies; this was detected with contrast-enhanced CMR imaging and was shown to be an independent prognostic indicator. CMR imaging was able to detect those cases more frequently compared with other modalities (eg, ECG or echocardiography).[30,31] Another study concluded that

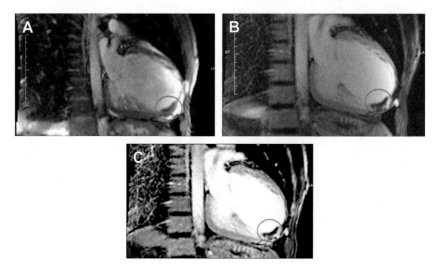

Fig. 4. A patient with known myocardial infarction and triple artery disease, admitted to the hospital because of deterioration of his condition. The cine SSFP showed a small area of suspected thrombus (*red circle*) (*A*). Late gadolinium enhancement with a long TI of 600 ms confirmed the diagnosis on source (*B*) and phase sensitive inversion recovery images (*C*).

evaluation of right ventricular ejection fraction using CMR imaging late after MI may improve risk stratification and patient management.[29]

ROLE IN DETECTING COMPLICATIONS DUE TO OR AFTER INTERVENTIONS

With the increase in myocardial revascularization procedures in recent years, there has been an increase in the so-called procedural myocardial injuries. These injuries are defined as irreversible myocardial injuries during percutaneous coronary intervention (PCI) or coronary artery bypass graft (CABG) and may include coronary dissection, side-branch occlusion, and plaque embolization. Several studies found a strong correlation between the increase in troponin levels at 24 hours after PCI and areas of new myocardial hyperenhancement on LGE module.[32] One study evaluated the prognostic value of such injuries using LGE and concluded that they adversely affect clinical outcome.[32,33]

ROLE IN PREDICTION OF MYOCARDIAL RECOVERY

Larose and colleagues[34] examined 103 patients with acute STEMI with contrast-enhanced CMR imaging within 12 hours of primary angioplasty and at 6 months and followed them for more than 2 years, with the primary end point being LV dysfunction and the secondary end point being poor outcomes. They compared traditional risk factors such as infarct territory, maximum biomarkers elevation, pain-to-balloon time, presence of Q waves, and LV ejection fraction during STEMI as predictors of late LV dysfunction with LGE. A myocardial segment was considered to have a transmural LGE if at least 50% or more of the wall showed transmural LGE in greater than 50% of the segment's total extension. Salvaged myocardium was defined as the edematous myocardium that did not show LGE. It has been shown that LGE quantification very early during STEMI was better at predicting late heart failure and poor outcomes compared with traditional risk factors.

In patients with chronic IHD, CMR imaging can aid in decision making on revascularization. A combination of perfusion imaging at stress and rest followed by a delayed enhancement can detect stress-induced ischemia and the presence (or absence) of viable myocardium. Pegg and colleagues[35] found that based on 50% transmural viability cutoff, patients with 10 or more viable and normal segments show an improvement in global LV function postrevascularization. Patients with fewer such segments do not show functional recovery. Other studies revealed similar findings with the conclusion that it is possible to identify reversible myocardial dysfunction by contrast-enhanced CMR imaging before coronary revascularization (**Fig. 5**).[36,37]

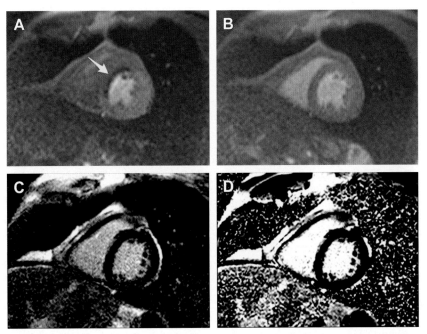

Fig. 5. A zone of subendocardial perfusion defect (*arrow* in image A) in adenosine stress CMR image (first-pass perfusion). No perfusion defect at rest (*B*) or LGE (*C, D*) indicating viable myocardium.

Segments that do not show transmural infarction with LGE were studied using low-dose dobutamine CMR imaging as a predictor of improvement of wall motion after revascularization. It was concluded that low-dose dobutamine CMR imaging was superior at identifying segments that maintain contractile reserve and show functional improvement after revascularization.[38,39]

Along with LGE module and low-dose dobutamine CMR imaging, stress CMR imaging plays an important role in identifying "hibernating myocardium." This term refers to myocardium that shows progressive and chronic abnormal contraction, with improved function after revascularization. This dysfunction is revealed during stress (unlike the studies mentioned earlier). After revascularization, patients with hibernating myocardium have a significant survival advantage compared with patients on medical therapy alone. High-dose dobutamine CMR imaging in combination with LGE provides accurate information on ischemia and hibernating myocardium.[40]

ROLE IN DETECTING INDUCIBLE ISCHEMIA IN PATIENTS WITH KNOWN ISCHEMIC HEART DISEASE

Inducible ischemia is detected either by dobutamine/atropine or by vasodilator first-pass perfusion stress CMR imaging. Dobutamine stress CMR imaging starts typically with the LV structure and function module followed by dobutamine stimulation and atropine is added if needed. Three short-axis slices (basal, mid-ventricular, and apical) and 3 long-axis slices (horizontal, vertical, and LV outflow tract) are selected for examination in rest and stress. Using cine steady-state free precession (SSFP) sequences with parallel imaging techniques sensitivity encoding (SENSE), images are acquired in breath-hold during each dobutamine increment.[41]

Nagel and colleagues[42] compared the diagnostic performance of dobutamine stress MRI (DS-CMR) with dobutamine stress echocardiography (DSE) in about 200 consecutive patients with suspected CAD. Both examinations were performed on all patients before cardiac catheterization. DS-CMR showed a significantly higher diagnostic accuracy compared with DSE, with a sensitivity of 86.2% versus 74.3% and a specificity of 85.7% versus 69.8%. Dobutamine stress CMR imaging is particularly useful in patients who are not well suited for stress echocardiography because of poor acoustic window.[43]

Although dobutamine is mainly used to detect wall motion abnormalities, Manka and colleagues[44] conducted a direct comparison between adenosine and dobutamine/atropine using first-pass myocardial perfusion CMR imaging. They concluded that both agents were equally capable of identifying stress-inducible perfusion defect. Another study identified the high value of first-pass myocardial perfusion during peak-dose dobutamine stress CMR imaging in differentiating a true new induced wall motion abnormality due to ischemia from an abnormality due to an inducible LBBB.[45]

The principle of first-pass perfusion imaging is to inject an intravenous bolus of gadolinium-based contrast agent during stress, trying to visually detect areas of hypointensity during first pass, indicating hypoperfusion and possibly stress-inducible ischemia. Adenosine or regadenoson stress CMR imaging starts with a LV structure and function module, followed by a 3-minute infusion of adenosine or an injection of regadenoson. Gadolinium is injected during stress, and at least 3 preselected 8-mm-thick short-axis slices representing basal, mid-ventricular, and apical regions are imaged with a T1-weighted sequence for 40 to 50 heart beats with the patient holding his or her breath as long as possible (see **Fig. 5A**).

Parallel imaging techniques are used to accelerate acquisition.[45] Perfusion at rest (without adenosine or regadenoson) is done followed by LGE module at least 5 minutes later.[46] If the perfusion images at stress show no perfusion defects, perfusion at rest could be omitted.

A meta-analysis of 35 studies done between 2000 and 2008 evaluated the diagnostic performance of stress CMR imaging and demonstrated a sensitivity of 89% and a specificity of 80%.[47] A more recent comparison between CMR imaging and SPECT was done in a large prospective trial with 752 patients clinical evaluation of magnetic resonance imaging in coronary heart disease (CE-MARC). It showed the sensitivity, specificity, positive predictive value, and negative predictive value of a multiparametric perfusion stress CMR imaging to be 86.5%, 83.4%, 77.2%, and 90.5%, respectively, compared with 66.5%, 82.6%, 71.4%, and 79.1% for SPECT. This trial established the high diagnostic accuracy of CMR imaging in IHD and its superiority over SPECT.[48] The accuracy of CMR imaging can be improved further with the use of 3 T scanners for stress perfusion imaging as concluded in several studies.[49] Moreover, first-pass perfusion with adenosine stress CMR imaging combined with LGE was shown to be highly accurate in detecting inducible ischemia in patients post-PCI and to a lesser extent following a coronary bypass graft.[50]

ROLE IN DIFFERENTIATING ISCHEMIC FROM NONISCHEMIC HEART FAILURE

Both ischemic and nonischemic cardiomyopathy can cause LV dysfunction, dilatation, and heart failure. Unlike patients with IHD who may require a revascularization procedure, patients with nonischemic DCM need a different therapeutic approach, usually have a better prognosis, and require further evaluation to identify secondary causes of DCM (eg, myocarditis, drug toxicity, alcohol abuse).[51]

The pattern of LGE plays a major role in distinguishing ischemic from nonischemic cardiomyopathy. The most common pattern of LGE in IHD is a subendocardial or a transmural enhancement with a distribution correlating to the segments supplied by the affected coronary artery (Fig. 6).

Patients with nonischemic DCM present with a progressive congestive heart failure, LV enlargement, and decreased ejection fraction. Late enhancement is found most commonly in the mid-interventricular septum (Fig. 7).[52] However, one study revealed that 59% of patients with DCM did not have LGE, 13% had LGE pattern similar to patients with CAD, and 28% had patchy or linear mid-wall enhancement with a distribution pattern different from CAD patients. In patients with subendocardial and transmural late enhancement, coronary angiography did not detect any luminal narrowing or obstruction. It was suggested that these patients might have had a prior infarction with recanalization or embolization from a small plaque.[53]

PROGNOSTIC VALUE AND ROLE IN RISK STRATIFICATION

Role in risk stratification might be one of the most important roles of stress CMR imaging in the management of patients with IHD. Steel and colleagues[54] evaluated the prognostic value of adenosine stress myocardial perfusion and LGE in 254 patients referred with suspected myocardial ischemia. Patients who had both reversible perfusion defect and LGE showed a greater than 3-fold association with cardiac death or acute MI. Patients without a perfusion defect or LGE had a 98.1% negative annual event rate for death or MI. It was concluded that stress CMR imaging provides a solid risk stratification method for patients presenting with symptoms of IHD.

Jahnke and colleagues[55] performed both adenosine stress and dobutamine stress CMR imaging on 513 patients in a combined single-session examination. For patients who did not show any abnormalities on both studies, the 3-year event-free survival was 99.2%.

A recent study evaluated the prognostic value of adenosine stress CMR imaging in patients presenting to the ED with chest pain. Patients

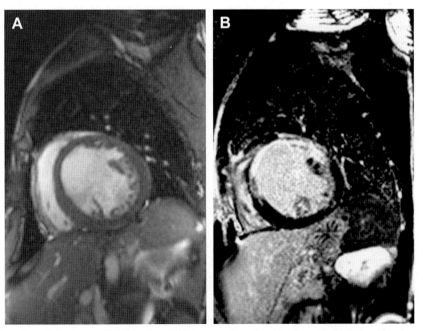

Fig. 6. LV dilatation with myocardial thinning (A) transmural and subendocardial LGE on phase sensitive inversion recovery image (B) in the left anterior descending artery territory indicating an ischemic cause for LV dilatation.

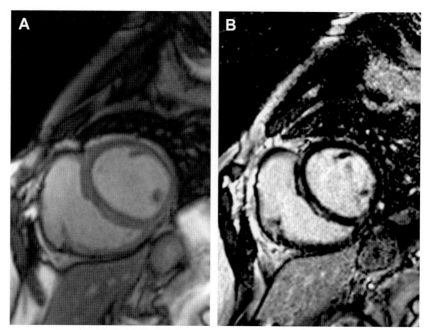

Fig. 7. SSFP image of a patient presented with dilatation of both ventricles (*A*). The PSIR-LGE image shows a mid-interventricular linear enhancement typical of a dilated cardiomyopathy (*B*).

with normal findings showed a low risk (<15) of a major adverse cardiac event (MACE) over a median follow-up period of 51 months. The findings of ischemia or scar were significant and independent predictors of MACE.[56] Similar data were obtained with regadenoson stress perfusion.[57]

First-pass perfusion CMR imaging might also be helpful in risk stratification in patients presenting with stable angina pectoris. In a recent study, Buckert and colleagues[58] examined 1229 patients with adenosine stress CMR imaging with a mean follow-up period of 4.2 ± 2.1 years. Patients with reversible perfusion defect had significantly increased major events.

Several studies evaluated the prognostic value of dobutamine stress wall motion abnormality assessment. The presence of inducible ischemia or an LV ejection fraction less than 40% was identified as independent predictors of future MI or cardiac death by Hundley and colleagues.[59]

A large study by Korosoglou and colleagues[60] performed dobutamine stress CMR imaging on 1493 patients with a follow-up of 2 ± 1 year. It was revealed that wall motion abnormalities during stress presented a strong independent prognostic value for hard events and late revascularization. Patients with normal wall motion at stress had a very low risk for future cardiac events.

SUMMARY

With recent advances in cardiac MRI, both dobutamine and adenosine stress CMR imaging are becoming the modality of choice for noninvasive imaging in IHD. The excellent diagnostic and prognostic values of stress CMR imaging have contributed largely to its acceptance in the diagnosis and management of IHD. It can provide valuable information and play a major role in the initial diagnosis in patients with acute chest pain, in the diagnosis of complications post-MI, in the assessment of the right ventricle after an acute MI, to detect complications due to or after interventions (PCI or CABG), in prediction of myocardial recovery, to detect inducible ischemia in patients with known IHD, in differentiating ischemic from nonischemic heart failure, and in risk stratification.

REFERENCES

1. Finegold JA, Asaria P, Francis DP. Mortality from ischaemic heart disease by country, region, and age: statistics from World Health Organisation and United Nations. Int J Cardiol 2013;168(2):934–45. http://dx.doi.org/10.1016/j.ijcard.2012.10.046.
2. Schwitter J, Wacker CM, Wilke N, et al. MR-IMPACT II: magnetic resonance imaging for myocardial perfusion assessment in coronary artery disease trial: perfusion-cardiac magnetic resonance vs.

single-photon emission computed tomography for the detection of coronary artery disease: a comparative multicentre, multivendor trial. Eur Heart J 2013; 34(10):775–81. http://dx.doi.org/10.1093/eurheartj/ehs022.

3. Fihn SD, Gardin JM, Abrams J, et al. 2012 ACCF/AHA/ACP/AATS/PCNA/SCAI/STS guideline for the diagnosis and management of patients with stable ischemic heart disease: executive summary. Circulation 2012. http://dx.doi.org/10.1161/CIR.0b013e3182776f83.

4. Montalescot G, Sechtem U, Achenbach S, et al. 2013 ESC guidelines on the management of stable coronary artery disease: the Task Force on the management of stable coronary artery disease of the European Society of Cardiology. Eur Heart J 2013;34(38):2949–3003. http://dx.doi.org/10.1093/eurheartj/eht296.

5. ACR–NASCI–SPR practice guideline for the performance and interpretation of cardiac magnetic resonance imaging (MR). Revised 2011 (Resolution 25).

6. Hundley WG, Bluemke DA, Finn JP, et al. ACCF/ACR/AHA/NASCI/SCMR 2010 expert consensus document on cardiovascular magnetic resonance: a report of the American College of Cardiology Foundation Task Force on expert consensus documents. Circulation 2010;121:2462–508. http://dx.doi.org/10.1161/CIR.0b013e3181d44a8f.

7. Khoo JP, Grundy BJ, Steadman CD, et al. Stress cardiovascular MR in routine clinical practice: referral patterns, accuracy, tolerance, safety and incidental findings. Br J Radiol 2012;85(1018): e851–7. http://dx.doi.org/10.1259/bjr/14829242.

8. Kawel-Boehm N, Bremerich J. Magnetic resonance stress imaging of myocardial perfusion and wall motion. J Thorac Imaging 2014;29(1):30–7. http://dx.doi.org/10.1097/RTI.0000000000000045.

9. Pope J, Ruthazer R, Beshansky J, et al. Clinical features of emergency department patients presenting with symptoms suggestive of acute cardiac ischemia: a multicenter study. J Thromb Thrombolysis 1998;6(1):63–74. http://dx.doi.org/10.1023/A:1008876322599.

10. Pope JH, Aufderheide TP, Ruthazer R, et al. Missed diagnoses of acute cardiac ischemia in the emergency department. N Engl J Med 2000;342(16): 1163–70. http://dx.doi.org/10.1056/NEJM200004203421603.

11. Kwong RY, Schussheim AE, Rekhraj S, et al. Detecting acute coronary syndrome in the emergency department with cardiac magnetic resonance imaging. Circulation 2003. http://dx.doi.org/10.1161/01.CIR.0000047527.11221.29.

12. Sechtem U, Achenbach S. Non-invasive imaging in acute chest pain syndromes. Eur Heart J Cardiovasc Imaging 2012;13:69–78. http://dx.doi.org/10.1093/ehjci/jer250.

13. Lockie T, Nagel E, Redwood S, et al. Use of cardiovascular magnetic resonance imaging in acute coronary syndromes. Circulation 2009;119(12):1671–81. http://dx.doi.org/10.1161/CIRCULATIONAHA.108.816512.

14. Ahmed N, Carrick D, Layland J, et al. The role of cardiac magnetic resonance imaging (MRI) in acute myocardial infarction (AMI). Heart Lung Circ 2013;22(4): 243–55. http://dx.doi.org/10.1016/j.hlc.2012.11.016.

15. Cury RC, Shash K, Nagurney JT, et al. Cardiac magnetic resonance with T2-weighted imaging improves detection of patients with acute coronary syndrome in the emergency department. Circulation 2008;118(8):837–44. http://dx.doi.org/10.1161/CIRCULATIONAHA.107.740597.

16. Ingkanisorn WP, Kwong RY, Bohme NS, et al. Prognosis of negative adenosine stress magnetic resonance in patients presenting to an emergency department with chest pain. J Am Coll Cardiol 2006;47(7):1427–32. http://dx.doi.org/10.1016/j.jacc.2005.11.059.

17. Heitner JF, Klem I, Rasheed D, et al. Stress cardiac MR imaging compared with stress echocardiography in the early evaluation of patients who present to the emergency department with intermediate-risk chest pain. Radiology 2014; 271(1):56–64. http://dx.doi.org/10.1148/radiol.13130557.

18. Rathore SS, Curtis JP, Chen J, et al. Association of door-to-balloon time and mortality in patients admitted to hospital with ST elevation myocardial infarction: national cohort study. BMJ 2009;338: b1807. http://dx.doi.org/10.1136/bmj.b1807.

19. Friedrich MG, Sechtem U, Schulz-Menger J, et al. Cardiovascular magnetic resonance in myocarditis: a JACC white paper. J Am Coll Cardiol 2009; 53(17):1475–87. http://dx.doi.org/10.1016/j.jacc.2009.02.007.

20. Testani JM, Kolansky DM, Litt H, et al. Focal myocarditis mimicking acute ST-elevation myocardial infarction: diagnosis using cardiac magnetic resonance imaging. Tex Heart Inst J 2006;33(2):256–9.

21. Karamitsos TD, Francis JM, Myerson S, et al. The role of cardiovascular magnetic resonance imaging in heart failure. J Am Coll Cardiol 2009;54(15):1407–24. http://dx.doi.org/10.1016/j.jacc.2009.04.094.

22. Friedrich MG, Strohm O, Schulz-Menger J. Contrast media–enhanced magnetic resonance imaging visualizes myocardial changes in the course of viral myocarditis. Circulation 1998. http://dx.doi.org/10.1161/01.CIR.97.18.1802.

23. Abdel-Aty H, Boyé P, Zagrosek A, et al. Diagnostic performance of cardiovascular magnetic resonance in patients with suspected acute myocarditis comparison of different approaches. J Am Coll Cardiol 2005;45(11):1815–22. http://dx.doi.org/10.1016/j.jacc.2004.11.069.

24. Verhaert D, Gabriel RS, Johnston D, et al. The role of multimodality imaging in the management of pericardial disease. Circulation 2010;3(3):333–43. http://dx.doi.org/10.1161/CIRCIMAGING.109.921791.

25. Mather AN, Fairbairn TA, Artis NJ, et al. Diagnostic value of CMR in patients with biomarker-positive acute chest pain and unobstructed coronary arteries. JACC Cardiovasc Imaging 2010;3(6):661–4. http://dx.doi.org/10.1016/j.jcmg.2010.03.006.

26. Assomull RG, Lyne JC, Keenan N, et al. The role of cardiovascular magnetic resonance in patients presenting with chest pain, raised troponin, and unobstructed coronary arteries. Eur Heart J 2007;28(10):1242–9. http://dx.doi.org/10.1093/eurheartj/ehm113.

27. Wong DT, Richardson JD, Puri R, et al. The role of cardiac magnetic resonance imaging following acute myocardial infarction. Eur Radiol 2012;22(8):1757–68. http://dx.doi.org/10.1007/s00330-012-2420-7.

28. Weinsaft JW, Kim HW, Shah DJ, et al. Detection of left ventricular thrombus by delayed-enhancement cardiovascular magnetic resonance. J Am Coll Cardiol 2008;52(2):148–57. http://dx.doi.org/10.1016/j.jacc.2008.03.041.

29. Larose E, Ganz P, Reynolds HG, et al. Right ventricular dysfunction assessed by cardiovascular magnetic resonance imaging predicts poor prognosis late after myocardial infarction. J Am Coll Cardiol 2007;49(8):855–62. http://dx.doi.org/10.1016/j.jacc.2006.10.056.

30. Kumar A, Abdel-Aty H, Kriedemann I, et al. Contrast-enhanced cardiovascular magnetic resonance imaging of right ventricular infarction. J Am Coll Cardiol 2006;48(10):1969–76. http://dx.doi.org/10.1016/j.jacc.2006.05.078.

31. Jensen CJ, Jochims M, Hunold P, et al. Right ventricular involvement in acute left ventricular myocardial infarction: prognostic implications of MRI findings. Am J Roentgenol 2010;194(3):592–8. http://dx.doi.org/10.2214/AJR.09.2829.

32. Selvanayagam JB. Troponin elevation after percutaneous coronary intervention directly represents the extent of irreversible myocardial injury: insights from cardiovascular magnetic resonance imaging. Circulation 2005;111(8):1027–32. http://dx.doi.org/10.1161/01.CIR.0000156328.28485.AD.

33. Rahimi K, Banning AP, Cheng AS, et al. Prognostic value of coronary revascularisation-related myocardial injury: a cardiac magnetic resonance imaging study. Heart 2009;95(23):1937–43. http://dx.doi.org/10.1136/hrt.2009.173302.

34. Larose E, Rodés-Cabau J, Pibarot P, et al. Predicting late myocardial recovery and outcomes in the early hours of ST-segment elevation myocardial infarction. J Am Coll Cardiol 2010;55(22):2459–69. http://dx.doi.org/10.1016/j.jacc.2010.02.033.

35. Pegg TJ, Selvanayagam JB, Jennifer J, et al. Prediction of global left ventricular functional recovery in patients with heart failure undergoing surgical revascularisation, based on late gadolinium enhancement cardiovascular magnetic resonance. J Cardiovasc Magn Reson 2010;12(1):56. http://dx.doi.org/10.1186/1532-429X-12-56.

36. Kim RJ, Wu E, Rafael A, et al. The use of contrast-enhanced magnetic resonance imaging to identify reversible myocardial dysfunction. N Engl J Med 2000;343(20):1445–53. http://dx.doi.org/10.1056/NEJM200011163432003.

37. Selvanayagam JB. Value of delayed-enhancement cardiovascular magnetic resonance imaging in predicting myocardial viability after surgical revascularization. Circulation 2004;110(12):1535–41. http://dx.doi.org/10.1161/01.CIR.0000142045.22628.74.

38. Wellnhofer E. Magnetic resonance low-dose dobutamine test is superior to SCAR quantification for the prediction of functional recovery. Circulation 2004;109(18):2172–4. http://dx.doi.org/10.1161/01.CIR.0000128862.34201.74.

39. Kirschbaum SW, Rossi A, van Domburg RT, et al. Contractile reserve in segments with nontransmural infarction in chronic dysfunctional myocardium using low-dose dobutamine CMR. JACC Cardiovasc Imaging 2010;3(6):614–22. http://dx.doi.org/10.1016/j.jcmg.2010.03.007.

40. Schuster A, Morton G, Chiribiri A, et al. Imaging in the management of ischemic cardiomyopathy. J Am Coll Cardiol 2012;59(4):359–70. http://dx.doi.org/10.1016/j.jacc.2011.08.076.

41. Charoenpanichkit C, Hundley WG. The 20 year evolution of dobutamine stress cardiovascular magnetic resonance. J Cardiovasc Magn Reson 2010;12(1):59. http://dx.doi.org/10.1186/1532-429X-12-59.

42. Nagel E, Lehmkuhl HB, Bocksch W, et al. Noninvasive diagnosis of ischemia-induced wall motion abnormalities with the use of high-dose dobutamine stress MRI: comparison with dobutamine stress echocardiography. Circulation 1999. http://dx.doi.org/10.1161/01.CIR.99.6.763.

43. Hundley WG, Hamilton CA, Thomas MS. Utility of fast cine magnetic resonance imaging and display for the detection of myocardial ischemia in patients not well suited for second harmonic stress echocardiography. Circulation 1999. http://dx.doi.org/10.1161/01.CIR.100.16.1697.

44. Manka R, Jahnke C, Gebker R, et al. Head-to-head comparison of first-pass MR perfusion imaging during adenosine and high-dose dobutamine/atropine stress. Int J Cardiovasc Imaging 2010;27(7):995–1002. http://dx.doi.org/10.1007/s10554-010-9748-3.

45. Lubbers DD, Janssen CH, Kuijpers D, et al. The additional value of first pass myocardial perfusion

imaging during peak dose of dobutamine stress cardiac MRI for the detection of myocardial ischemia. Int J Cardiovasc Imaging 2007; 24(1):69–76. http://dx.doi.org/10.1007/s10554-006-9205-5.

46. Kramer CM, Barkhausen JR, Flamm SD, et al. Standardized cardiovascular magnetic resonance (CMR) protocols 2013 update. J Cardiovasc Magn Reson 2013;15(1):91. http://dx.doi.org/10.1186/1532-429X-15-91.

47. Hamon M, Fau G, Née G, et al. Meta-analysis of the diagnostic performance of stress perfusion cardiovascular magnetic resonance for detection of coronary artery disease. J Cardiovasc Magn Reson 2010; 12(1):29. http://dx.doi.org/10.1186/1532-429X-12-29.

48. Greenwood JP, Maredia N, Younger JF, et al. Cardiovascular magnetic resonance and single-photon emission computed tomography for diagnosis of coronary heart disease (CE-MARC): a prospective trial. Lancet 2012;379(9814):453–60. http://dx.doi.org/10.1016/S0140-6736(11)61335-4.

49. Cheng AS, Pegg TJ, Karamitsos TD, et al. Cardiovascular magnetic resonance perfusion imaging at 3-tesla for the detection of coronary artery disease. J Am Coll Cardiol 2007;49(25):2440–9. http://dx.doi.org/10.1016/j.jacc.2007.03.028.

50. Bernhardt P, Spiess J, Levenson B, et al. Combined assessment of myocardial perfusion and late gadolinium enhancement in patients after percutaneous coronary interventionor bypass grafts. JACC Cardiovasc Imaging 2009;2(11):1292–300. http://dx.doi.org/10.1016/j.jcmg.2009.05.011.

51. Casolo G, Minneci S, Manta R, et al. Identification of the ischemic etiology of heart failure by cardiovascular magnetic resonance imaging: diagnostic accuracy of late gadolinium enhancement. Am Heart J 2006;151(1):101–8. http://dx.doi.org/10.1016/j.ahj.2005.03.068.

52. Cummings KW, Bhalla S, Javidan-Nejad C, et al. A pattern-based approach to assessment of delayed enhancement in nonischemic cardiomyopathy at MR imaging. Radiographics 2009;29(1):89–103. http://dx.doi.org/10.1148/rg.291085052.

53. McCrohon JA. Differentiation of heart failure related to dilated cardiomyopathy and coronary artery disease using gadolinium-enhanced cardiovascular magnetic resonance. Circulation 2003;108(1):54–9. http://dx.doi.org/10.1161/01.CIR.0000078641.19365.4C.

54. Steel K, Broderick R, Gandla V, et al. Complementary prognostic values of stress myocardial perfusion and late gadolinium enhancement imaging by cardiac magnetic resonance in patients with known or suspected coronary artery disease. Circulation 2009;120(14):1390–400. http://dx.doi.org/10.1161/CIRCULATIONAHA.108.812503.

55. Jahnke C, Nagel E, Gebker R, et al. Prognostic value of cardiac magnetic resonance stress tests: adenosine stress perfusion and dobutamine stress wall motion imaging. Circulation 2007;115(13):1769–76. http://dx.doi.org/10.1161/CIRCULATIONAHA.106.652016.

56. Rachid R, Macwar MD, Brent A, et al. Prognostic value of adenosine cardiac magnetic resonance imaging in patients presenting with chest pain. Am J Cardiol 2013;112(1):46–50. http://dx.doi.org/10.1016/j.amjcard.2013.02.054.

57. Freed BH, Narang A, Bhave NM, et al. Prognostic value of normal regadenoson stress perfusion cardiovascular magnetic resonance. J Cardiovasc Magn Reson 2013;15(1):108. http://dx.doi.org/10.1186/1532-429X-15-108.

58. Buckert D, Dewes P, Walcher T, et al. Intermediate-term prognostic value of reversible perfusion deficit diagnosed by adenosine CMR. JACC Cardiovasc Imaging 2013;6(1):56–63. http://dx.doi.org/10.1016/j.jcmg.2012.08.011.

59. Hundley WG, Morgan TM, Neagle CM, et al. Magnetic resonance imaging determination of cardiac prognosis. Circulation 2002. http://dx.doi.org/10.1161/01.CIR.0000036017.46437.02.

60. Korosoglou G, Elhmidi Y, Steen H, et al. Prognostic value of high-dose dobutamine stress magnetic resonance imaging in 1,493 consecutive patients. J Am Coll Cardiol 2010;56(15):1225–34. http://dx.doi.org/10.1016/j.jacc.2010.06.020.

Global and Regional Functional Assessment of Ischemic Heart Disease with Cardiac MR Imaging

Jeremy D. Collins, MD

KEYWORDS

- Cardiac MR imaging • Myocardial strain • Myocardial velocities • Ischemic heart disease
- Myocardial systolic function • Myocardial motion

KEY POINTS

- Cardiac MR imaging (CMR) is the reference standard for the assessment of global left ventricular systolic function.
- A substantial body of literature supports risk prognostication and assessment of response to medical therapy and percutaneous coronary interventions based on changes in the left ventricular ejection fraction (LVEF) in patients with ischemic heart disease.
- Accurate assessment of the LVEF is vital in patients with ischemic heart disease who are being evaluated for an implantable cardiac defibrillator for primary prophylaxis against sudden cardiac death.
- Changes in regional left ventricular myocardial function may be apparent without alterations in global systolic function parameters.
- Multiple CMR techniques enable assessment of regional function, through calculation of myocardial strain, myocardial velocities, or quantification of regional myocardial thickening.

INTRODUCTION

Ischemic heart disease (IHD) is highly prevalent in the United States, affecting 15.4 million people, and is the leading cause of death.[1] The hallmark of IHD at cardiac MR imaging (CMR) includes wall-motion abnormalities with or without reduced systolic function, diastolic dysfunction, progressive chamber enlargement, wall thinning, perfusion defects at pharmacologic stress, and myocardial scar contacting the subendocardium within a coronary territory. In addition, as the left ventricular (LV) chamber progressively dilates, patients may experience ischemic mitral insufficiency, which has been linked to symptoms of heart failure and to mortality. However, it is increasingly recognized that global measures of LV systolic dysfunction are insensitive to early changes associated with IHD. Quantitative contractile parameters including myocardial velocities and strain show promise for the detection of early, possibly subclinical, manifestations of IHD.

STRATEGIES FOR GLOBAL MYOCARDIAL FUNCTION ASSESSMENT AT CARDIAC MR IMAGING

Myocardial function is subdivided into 2 energy-requiring processes: systolic contraction and diastolic relaxation. Patients with IHD often have abnormalities of both systolic and diastolic function; however, in this patient population abnormalities of

Disclosure: The author does not have a conflict of interest.
Department of Radiology, Feinberg School of Medicine, Northwestern University, 737 North Michigan Avenue, Suite 1600, Chicago, IL 60611, USA
E-mail address: collins@fsm.northwestern.edu

Radiol Clin N Am 53 (2015) 369–395
http://dx.doi.org/10.1016/j.rcl.2014.11.001
0033-8389/15/$ – see front matter © 2015 Elsevier Inc. All rights reserved.

systolic function supersede and often lead to clinical symptoms. In this context, this article focuses on assessment of LV systolic function.

Assessment of Systolic Function

Systolic function is primarily determined through quantitation of the LV ejection fraction (EF). Although this measure has been postulated as insensitive to subtle changes in myocardial contractile reserve, most published data support the utility of quantitation of LV systolic function including the LVEF. Data are accumulating regarding the potential utility of alternative strategies to evaluate myocardial systolic function, including myocardial velocities and strain in the assessment of global and regional myocardial function, as discussed in detail later.

Left ventricular ejection fraction and volumes

Assessment of global myocardial systolic function at CMR primarily relies on quantification of systolic function on electrocardiogram (ECG)-gated segmented balanced steady-state free precession (bSSFP) cinegraphic (cine) imaging.[2–5] bSSFP techniques are preferred, as these benefit from inherently bright blood signal, with excellent contrast between the blood pool and myocardium without contrast. State-of-the-art scanners now routinely use multichannel cardiac coil elements combined with parallel imaging to accelerate bSSFP cine sequences to acquire a single slice in a short (4–8 seconds) breath-hold. LV systolic function quantification is performed on a stack of short-axis cine images acquired with a slice thickness of 6 to 8 mm and a 20% to 50% gap between slices to achieve complete ventricular coverage with 8 to 12 slices (**Fig. 1**). Acquisition of imaging at end-expiration results in a more consistent cardiac location from slice to slice, and is preferable to end-inspiration instructions if tolerable by the patient. Retrospective ECG gating is preferred, as the entirety of the cardiac cycle is sampled; prospective approaches can be performed, but necessarily exclude a portion of diastole to detect the subsequent R wave.

Image quality for segmented bSSFP cine imaging may be limited in patients with dyspnea or arrhythmias. Arrhythmia rejection can be used in patients with intermittent arrhythmias, such as ventricular ectopy. This ECG-dependent strategy uses retrospective gating and eliminates data from R-R intervals that fall outside of a prespecified range. As data are rejected from the cine acquisition, this approach necessarily prolongs acquisition of complete k-space data and may exceed breath-holding capabilities of patients with dyspnea or more frequent ectopy. ECG-triggered real-time cine imaging is an alternative strategy to segmented cine sequences in patients with intermittent arrhythmias and dyspnea (**Fig. 2**).[6] Quantification of systolic function on ECG-triggered real-time sequences is similar to that of segmented sequences, with the noted exception of trade-offs in spatial resolution necessitated to achieve a single-shot acquisition time of 50 to 80 milliseconds. Despite these solutions, quantification of systolic function is limited in frequent ectopy or atrial fibrillation, owing to the inconsistent myocardial positioning from beat to beat resulting in spatial and temporal blurring. The utility of real-time sequences for quantitation of systolic function is also limited in patients with irregular arrhythmias, as inconsistent R-R intervals preclude accurate quantitation of the systolic function over multiple short-axis slices.

The LVEF is the most commonly reported metric when considering global measures of LV systolic function. However, absolute and indexed chamber volumes, and absolute and indexed LV myocardial mass are important quantitative indices to be considered when evaluating global LV function. LV systolic function parameters are defined in **Table 1**.

Systolic function assessment on bSSFP cine images requires segmentation of the myocardium (**Fig. 3**). Several different strategies for myocardial contouring have been studied and integrated into clinical workflows. Traditionally, endocardial contours are drawn or detected semiautomatically, including the myocardial trabecula and papillary muscles within the blood pool on short-axis cine images at end-diastole and end-systole. Some investigators exclude the papillary muscles from the blood pool, and some software vendors have separate contours that can be used to delineate the papillary muscles separate from the remainder of the subendocardium. Epicardial contours are drawn to separate the myocardium from the epicardial fat along the free wall and the right ventricular (RV) blood pool along the interventricular septum, excluding visible RV trabecula from the LV epicardial contour. An alternative approach involves thresholding bSSFP cine sequences to capture voxels with myocardial signal intensity within the epicardial contour. This approach warrants additional study, but may offer a more efficient solution to LV systolic function analysis, as users only need to define the epicardial contours and set the myocardial thresholding appropriately. Defining the LV base plane is important in both approaches, and is facilitated by cross-referencing the short-axis cine sequences with long-axis bSSFP cine imaging to fully define the location of the mitral annulus in at least 2 dimensions.

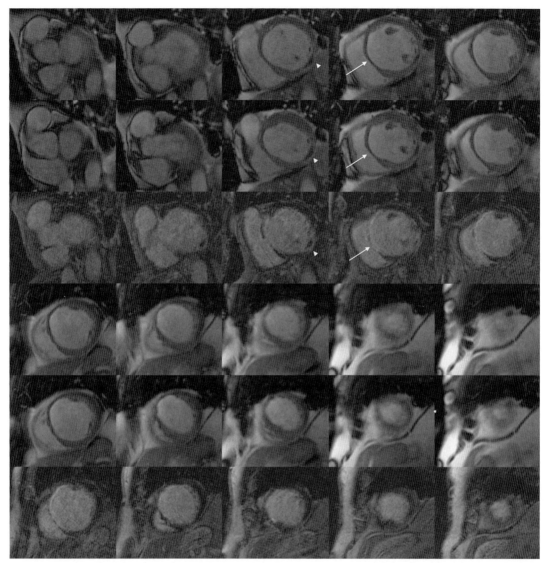

Fig. 1. A 74-year-old man with ischemic cardiomyopathy. Short-axis cine frames from end-diastole (*top row, 4th row*) and end-systole (*2nd row, 5th row*) are matched with delayed-enhancement images (*3rd row, 6th row*). A chronic nonviable left anterior descending infarction (*arrow*) is present with a nonviable acute left circumflex infarct (*arrowhead*), with associated regional akinesia.

Key Points

- Global systolic function parameters include EF, stroke volume, end-diastolic volume, and end-systolic volume.

- Indexing systolic function parameters is important for comparisons between patients.

- Quantitation of global systolic function at CMR is limited in patients with frequent, irregular arrhythmias.

- Real-time or highly accelerated acquisition strategies can be useful in dyspneic patients in sinus rhythm.

Accuracy and reproducibility of left ventricular ejection fraction and volumes at cardiac MR imaging

Multiple studies have evaluated the accuracy and reproducibility of segmented bSSFP cine imaging at CMR for the quantification of LV systolic function both within and between CMR examinations.[3,7,8] Chuang and colleagues[7] performed a subgroup analysis in 10 patients to assess the within-study interobserver and intraobserver variance of CMR-determined LVEF, LV end-diastolic volume (EDV), and LV end-systolic volume (ESV) (**Table 2**). The subgroup comprised 8 patients

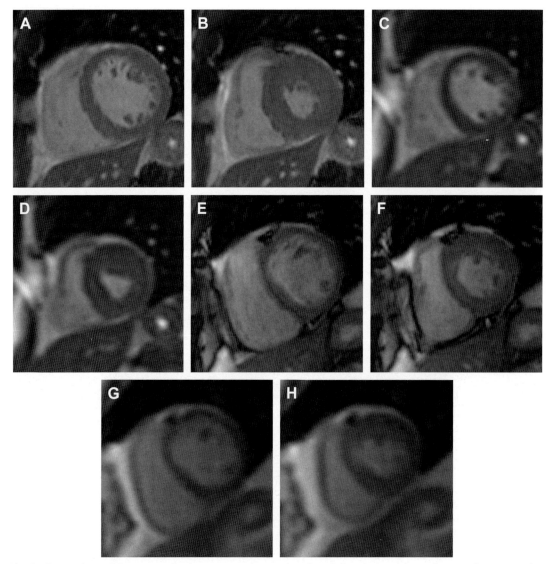

Fig. 2. Comparison of image quality between segmented and real-time balanced steady-state free precession (bSSFP) cine acquisitions in patients without arrhythmia (*A-B, C-D*) and with (*E-F, G-H*) arrhythmia, respectively, with end-diastolic and end-systolic phase images depicted. Segmented and real-time acquisitions were performed with GRAPPA factor 2 and 3 acceleration, respectively.

and 2 healthy volunteers, with excellent intraobserver and interobserver within-study agreement. Blalock and colleagues[8] performed an evaluation of within-study interobserver agreement in a cohort of 30 patients with repaired tetralogy of Fallot investigating CMR-determined LVEF, LVEDV, and LVESV (see **Table 2**). Similar agreement was found both within and between observers in both studies. Interstudy agreement was evaluated both in this study by Blalock and colleagues and in a separate study of 60 subjects by Grothues and colleagues.[3] In both studies, CMR examinations were performed between 15 and 60 minutes

apart; a different technologist performed the second CMR examination in the study by Blalock and colleagues.[8] Across both studies, interstudy intraobserver and interobserver agreement was good for LVEF, LVEDV, and LVESV, with coefficients of variability that compared favorably with within-study interobserver values (see **Table 2**).

Intermodality agreement
A discussion of the accuracy of the assessment of global LV systolic function at CMR would be incomplete without considering agreement with

Table 1
Ventricular systolic function parameters from balanced steady-state free precession cine imaging

Parameter	Abbreviation	Definition	Unit
End-diastolic volume	EDV	Chamber volume at end-diastole	mL
End-diastolic volume index	EDV_i	Chamber volume at end-diastole per m^2 body surface area	mL/m^2
End-systolic volume	ESV	Chamber volume at end-systole	mL
End-systolic volume index	ESV_i	Chamber volume at end-systole per m^2 body surface area	mL/m^2
Stroke volume	SV	Volume of blood ejected during systole	mL
Ejection fraction	EF	Stroke volume divided by the end-diastolic volume	%
Mass		Quantified myocardial mass at end-diastole	g
Mass index		Myocardial mass per m^2 body surface area	g/m^2
Cardiac output	CO	Heart rate × stroke volume	L/min
Cardiac index	CI	Cardiac output divided by m^2 body surface area	$L/min/m^2$

other modalities. Many clinical trials have been performed using 2-dimensional (2D) transthoracic echocardiography (TTE) for the assessment of global LV systolic function. Studies have demonstrated systematic differences in quantitation of LV systolic function between CMR and TTE. A study by Bellenger and colleagues[9] investigated 50 patients with chronic IHD and systolic heart failure, demonstrating the best agreement between TTE using Simpson's technique and CMR. Data from this study and others in patients with IHD demonstrated a wide range of agreement between LVEF calculations using TTE and CMR, with correlation values ranging from 0.41 to 0.9 and the standard deviation of the difference ranging from 11% to 17%.[9–12] Gardner and colleagues[13] analyzed a cohort of 47 patients with a recent myocardial infarction, evaluating LV volumes and LVEF at CMR and TTE performed 60 minutes apart. Although modest correlations from 0.70 to 0.75 (P<.0001) were found for LV volumes, large and significant differences were found in absolute volumes (P<.0001) and LVEF (P = .02) between modalities (Table 3). Similar results were noted in a cohort of 67 patients with ischemic heart failure reported by Gruszczynska and colleagues[14] analyzing TTE and CMR. Despite correlations between LVEDV and LVESV indices (0.85 and 0.83, P<.0001), significant absolute differences were noted between modalities, with LV volumes underestimated at TTE. Poor correlations were noted for LVEF (0.46, P = .001), which was overestimated at TTE. Hence, apparent changes in LV systolic function parameters between CMR and 2D TTE

should be interpreted cautiously. More recent data using 3-dimensional (3D) echocardiography has demonstrated improved agreement with CMR for quantitation of the LVEF, yielding a correlation of 0.94 with similar LVEF values between modalities (50% ± 14% vs 50% ± 16%, P = .23).[15]

Clinical trials have been performed using planar radionuclide ventriculography and gated single-photon emission computed tomography (gSPECT) for the assessment of global LV systolic function. As in the case of TTE, studies have demonstrated systematic differences between quantitation of LV systolic function at radionuclide ventriculography and gSPECT with CMR. Comparatively, agreement between radionuclide ventriculography and CMR is better than that with TTE. Studies have reported better correlations between CMR and planar radionuclide ventriculography, with correlation values ranging from 0.67 to 0.91 and a standard deviation of the difference between modalities ranging from 7.5% to 8%.[9,10,12,16] Xie and colleagues[17] evaluated blood pool gSPECT in a cohort of 32 patients with systolic dysfunction, and found good to excellent correlation between LV volumes and LVEF; however, they found that gSPECT significantly underestimated absolute LV volumes in comparison with CMR (Table 4). Of note, LVEF was similar at gSPECT and CMR, without bias (1% ± 4%, P = .24). These data suggest that LVEF assessment is similar in planar radionuclide ventriculography and gSPECT; however, caution is warranted when comparing absolute changes in LV volumes.

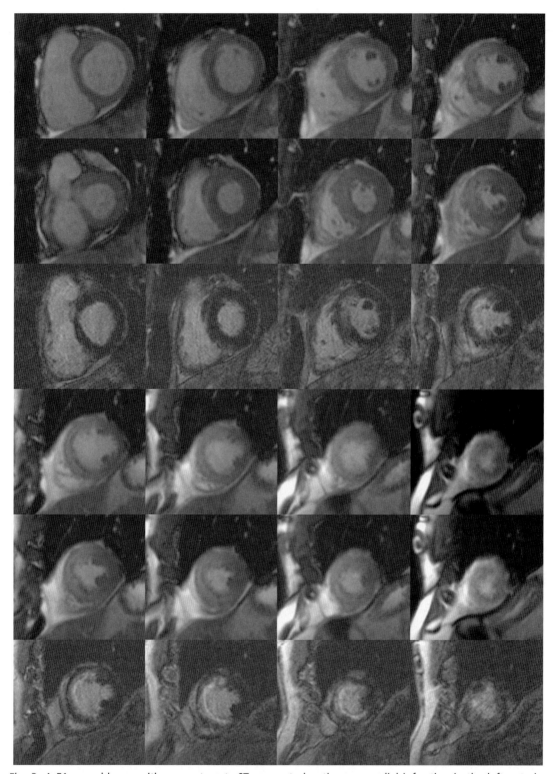

Fig. 3. A 51-year-old man with a recent acute ST-segment elevation myocardial infarction in the left anterior descending coronary artery territory. Cardiac MR imaging (CMR) demonstrates moderate hypokinesia in the infarct-related artery territory (*rows 1, 4*: Cine end-diastolic frame; *rows 2, 5*: cine end-systolic frame; *rows 3, 6*: delayed-enhancement sequences). Note the subendocardial scar (25% wall thickness) with extensive intermediate signal in the region of wall motion abnormality corresponding to myocardial edema on T2-weighted sequences (not shown). Left ventricular (LV) systolic function was preserved with a calculated ejection fraction (EF) of 60%.

Table 2
Intraobserver and interobserver within- and between-study agreement for CMR-derived LVEF, LVEDV, and LVESV parameters

Within Study	LVEF		LVEDV		LVESV	
	Chuang et al[7]	Blalock et al[8]	Chuang et al[7]	Blalock et al[8]	Chuang et al[7]	Blalock et al[8]
Intraobserver						
Variability (%)	3.6		2.6		3.5	
Mean ± SD (%)	0.5 ± 1.5					
Correlation	0.99					
ICC						
Interobserver						
Variability (%)	5.1	6.3	3.5	3.9	4.8	10.7
Mean ± SD (%)	−1.1 ± 2.1	1.0 ± 3.7		−8.5 ± 6.1		−5.8 ± 7.4
Correlation	0.99					
ICC		0.71		0.98		0.94

Between Study	LVEF		LVEDV		LVESV	
	Grothues et al[3]	Blalock et al[8]	Grothues et al[3]	Blalock et al[8]	Grothues et al[3]	Blalock et al[8]
Intraobserver						
Variability (%)	3.7	5.7	3.7	5.7	6.2	8.8
Mean ± SD (%)	0.1 ± 2.1	1.1 ± 3.3	0.1 ± 6.7	−0.6 ± 9.0	−0.3 ± 5.4	−2.3 ± 6.1
ICC		0.84		0.98		0.98
Interobserver						
Variability (%)		6.3		7.6		14.2
Mean ± SD (%)		−1.7 ± 3.6		6.4 ± 12.0		6.0 ± 9.8
ICC		0.80		0.97		0.95

Abbreviations: CMR, cardiac MR imaging; ICC, intraclass correlation coefficient; LVEDV, left ventricular end-diastolic volume; LVEF, left ventricular ejection fraction; LVESV, left ventricular end-systolic volume.
  Data from Refs.[3,7,8]

Key Points

- Interobserver, intraobserver, and interstudy agreement for global LV systolic function assessment at CMR is superior to that achieved by alternative techniques.
- Significant differences are noted in LV volumes between modalities in multiple studies.
- Gated blood pool SPECT and 3D echocardiography demonstrate better agreement with CMR than 2D echocardiography and planar radionuclide ventriculography.

Clinical Utility of Left Ventricular Ejection Fraction and Left Ventricular Volume Assessment by Cardiac MR Imaging in Ischemic Heart Disease

Patients with IHD and reduced LV systolic function are classified as having an ischemic

Table 3
Summary of left ventricular volumes and function by CMR versus TTE in patients with recent myocardial infarction

Parameter (Unit)	CMR	TTE	Correlation
LVEDV (mL)	171 ± 62[a]	102 ± 42	0.701
LVESV (mL)	88 ± 47[a]	53 ± 28	0.746
LVEF (%)	51 ± 11[b]	49 ± 22	0.672

Data presented as value ± standard deviation.
  Abbreviation: TTE, transthoracic echocardiography.
  [a] Significant difference (P<.0001).
  [b] Significant difference (P = .02).
  Data from Gardner BI, Bingham SE, Allen MR, et al. Cardiac magnetic resonance versus transthoracic echocardiography for the assessment of cardiac volumes and regional function after myocardial infarction: an intrasubject comparison using simultaneous intrasubject recordings. Cardiovasc Ultrasound 2009;7:38.

Table 4
Left ventricular volumes and function by CMR versus gSPECT in patients with systolic dysfunction

Parameter (Unit)	CMR	gSPECT	Limits of Agreement	Correlation
LVEDV (mL)	261.3 ± 68.9[a]	229.0 ± 68.5	−109.8 to 45.1	0.83
LVESV (mL)	215.6 ± 69.6[a]	187.5 ± 67.0	−94.7 to 38.6	0.88
LVEF (%)	18.5 ± 7.34	19.25 ± 7.33	−6.1 to 7.6	0.89

Abbreviation: gSPECT, gated single-photon emission computed tomography.
[a] Significant difference ($P<.001$).
Data from Xie BQ, Tian YQ, Zhang J, et al. Evaluation of left and right ventricular ejection fraction and volumes from gated blood-pool SPECT in patients with dilated cardiomyopathy: comparison with cardiac MRI. J Nucl Med 2012;53(4):584–91.

cardiomyopathy (ICM). These individuals are at risk for sudden cardiac death (SCD) through several mechanisms including rhythm disturbances, which can be influenced by the extent and distribution of myocardial scar. It is increasingly clear from randomized clinical trial data, however, that global LV systolic function as determined by the LVEF is an important risk factor for SCD.

A substantial body of clinical trial data supports the use of implanted cardiac defibrillators (ICDs) for primary prevention of SCD in patients with chronic IHD. The 2012 American College of Cardiology Foundation/American Heart Association/Heart Rhythm Society (ACCF/AHA/HRS) clinical guidelines for device-based therapy for cardiac rhythm abnormalities provides a succinct summary of clinical trial data supporting primary prophylaxis for SCD with ICDs.[18] Several major clinical trials performed in patients with IHD demonstrated a statistically significant reduction in all-cause mortality with an absolute and relative risk reduction ranging from 5.6% to 22.8% and 18% to 54%, respectively, corresponding to a number needed to treat of between 4 and 18 (**Table 5**).[19–25] Of importance is that a reduced LVEF was a vital aspect of patient selection in identifying those likely to benefit from ICD placement in these trials. Based on these trial results, the 2012 ACCF/AHA/HRS clinical guidelines recommend primary prophylaxis with ICD placement in patients with clinical profiles similar to those in the clinical trials outlined in **Table 5**.[18] The Writing Committee noted differences between LVEF calculations across imaging modalities, and recommended that clinicians use the modality that they consider is most accurate and appropriate at their institution to assess LVEF in patients with IHD being considered for ICD placement for primary prophylaxis.

LV global systolic function has also been evaluated as a quantitative measure to assess response to medical therapy in patients with ischemic cardiomyopathy. Kaandorp and colleagues[26] evaluated 32 consecutive patients with a baseline LVEF less than 40% at gSPECT without recent infarction or unstable angina. Patients underwent CMR 8 ± 3 and 9 ± 4 months following the initiation of β-blocker therapy or successful revascularization, respectively. Baseline and follow-up LVEF and LV volumes are presented in **Table 6**. Although both β-blocker therapy and revascularization resulted in significant increases in LVEF, changes in LVESV were more pronounced in the β-blocker therapy group. There was no significant difference in LVEDV between groups.

Key Points

- Assessment of global systolic function is critical for patient selection for primary prevention of sudden cardiac death through implantable cardiac defibrillator placement in patients with IHD.

- CMR assessment of global LV systolic function is sensitive in detecting response to medical therapy and revascularization in patients with IHD.

- CMR-derived myocardial scar burden is not an evidence-based component in risk stratification of patients with IHD for SCD.

STRATEGIES FOR REGIONAL MYOCARDIAL FUNCTION ASSESSMENT AT CARDIAC MR IMAGING

Despite data regarding the clinical utility of global systolic function assessment with LVEF (see earlier discussion), it is recognized that LVEF is relatively insensitive to early manifestations of IHD. For example, nontransmural infarctions may not alter regional wall motion to an extent sufficient to reduce the LVEF (**Fig. 4**). Similarly, small transmural

Table 5
Summary of indications, inclusion criteria, and results from pivotal primary prophylaxis ICD studies in patients with IHD

Study	Patients (N)[a]	Comparison	Inclusion Criteria			Primary Outcomes			
			LVEF (%)	NYHA	Other	Primary End Point	ARR (%)	RRR (%)	NNT (n)
MADIT[22]	196	ICD vs placebo	≤35	I–III	Q wave MI >3 wk; If CABG >3 mo; NSVT; EPS	All-cause mortality	22.8	54	4
MUSTT[23]	704	ICD vs antiarrhythmics	≤40	I–III	MI >4 d; NSVT; EPS	All-cause mortality	23	51	4
MADIT II[21]	1232	ICD vs placebo	≤30	I–III	MI >30 d	All-cause mortality	5.6	28	18
SCD-HeFT[20]	1676 (1310)	ICD vs amiodarone or placebo	≤35	II or III	HF >3 mo; MI and medical tx >1 mo; PCI/CABG >1 mo	All-cause mortality	7.2	25	14
COMPANION[19]	903 (842)	Placebo vs CRT-P vs CRT-D	≤35	III or IV	QRS >120 ms; HF >6 mo; If MI or CABG >60 d	Time to death from, or hx for any cause	7.3	36	14
MADIT-CRT[25]	1820 (999)	CRT-D vs ICD	≤30	I or II	QRS ≥130 ms	All-cause mortality or HF event	8.1	32	12
RAFT[24]	1798 (1201)	CRT-D vs ICD	≤30	II or III	QRS ≥130 ms	All-cause mortality or HF event	7.1	18	14

Abbreviations: ARR, absolute risk reduction; CABG, coronary artery bypass graft placement; CRT-D, cardiac resynchronization therapy with defibrillator function; EPS, electrophysiology study; HF, heart failure; hx, hospitalization; ICD, implantable cardiac defibrillator; MI, myocardial infarction; NNT, number needed to treat; NSVT, nonsustained ventricular tachycardia; NYHA, New York Heart Association functional class; PCI, percutaneous coronary intervention; RRR, relative risk reduction; tx, treatment.

[a] Subgroup with ischemic heart disease, if study included nonischemic heart disease patients.

Adapted from Mountantonakis SE, Hutchinson MD. Indications for implantable cardioverter-defibrillator placement in ischemic cardiomyopathy and after myocardial infarction. Curr Heart Fail Rep 2011;8(4):252–9; with permission.

Table 6
Effect of β-blocker therapy and revascularization on global systolic function and left ventricular chamber volumes

	β-Blocker Group		Revascularization Group	
	Baseline	Follow-Up	Baseline	Follow-Up
LVEDV (mL)	271 ± 63	254 ± 55	238 ± 48	250 ± 59
LVESV (mL)	190 ± 63[a]	163 ± 54	152 ± 35[a]	140 ± 41
LVEF (%)	31 ± 7[a]	37 ± 9	36 ± 6[a]	44 ± 6

[a] $P<.05$ for baseline versus follow-up values.
  Data from Kaandorp TA, Bax JJ, Bleeker SE, et al. Relation between regional and global systolic function in patients with ischemic cardiomyopathy after beta-blocker therapy or revascularization. J Cardiovasc Magn Reson 2010;12:7.

infarctions may not adversely affect the LVEF, as regional function in myocardium remote from the infarction may compensate for hypokinetic segments (**Fig. 5**). Myocardial velocities and strain are alternative quantitative imaging parameters that have shown promise in quantifying regional myocardial function and in the detection of LV dysfunction in the presence of a normal LVEF.

Left Ventricular Myocardial Structure and Motion

A brief review of LV myocardial structure and motion is fitting to a discussion of regional myocardial function. The LV shape is a prolate ellipsoid, with the long axis oriented from base to apex and the inlet and outlet structures oriented 30° to each other.[27] Understanding muscle-fiber orientation is necessary to understand abnormalities in myocardial motion. The left ventricle has 3 different fiber orientations with longitudinal, circumferential, and oblique fibers. Several autopsy studies have shown that 2 helical fiber geometries are present in the left ventricle, with a right-handed helix in the subendocardium that gradually changes to a left-handed helix in the subepicardium, with circumferentially oriented fibers in the mid-wall.[28] The helix angle varies continuously across the myocardium, ranging from +60° in the subendocardium to −60° in the subepicardium (**Fig. 6**).[29]

Myocardial thickness follows the law of Laplace, explaining the gradation of LV thickness from base to apex.[30] Regions of the left ventricle with a small radius of curvature, such as the ventricular apex, are able to generate enough force without significant myocardial thickness. However, basal segments demonstrate larger radii of curvature; hence, the tension that must be generated is greater, requiring increased myocardial thickness to generate the same degree of force.

LV motion is best described in terms of radial displacement, longitudinal deformation, and circumferential deformation. Radial displacement is directed inward throughout the chamber with spatial variation, and is least in the apical septum and anterior segments and greatest in the apical inferior and lateral segments. Radial displacement increases moving from the base to the apex. Longitudinal shortening manifests as displacement of the base toward the apex, with greatest displacement occurring in the basal chamber. Circumferential deformation varies across the chamber from base to apex. Viewed from the apex, basal rotation is counterclockwise initially and then clockwise to peak systole. Circumferential deformation varies across the chamber, and is best described by the parameters torsion and twist.[31] Twist refers to the angle of rotation between the base and the apex across the chamber. Torsion is best described as the shear angle that results from twist (**Fig. 7**).[32] Considered from an apical frame of reference, the apical left ventricle rotates counterclockwise to a maximum of approximately 10° while the base achieves a net clockwise rotation of approximately 3°. Torsion is crucial to equalize systolic fiber strain across the myocardium, owing to the differing fiber orientations through the wall (**Fig. 8**).[33]

Myocardial fiber orientation is directly influenced by the shape of the left ventricle. Hence, changes in the LV shape adversely affect systolic function by reducing the efficiency of the contraction process. Salin[34] evaluated the effect of LV shape on the LVEF, assuming a constant myocardial fiber shortening of 15% (**Fig. 9**). As the left ventricle became progressively spherical, the LVEF declined to less than 40%. On the other hand, as the left ventricle elongated with a constant radius, becoming more conical, the LVEF approached 80%. Salin and others made the observation that a spherical chamber, commonly seen in the context of IHD, reorients the myocardial fiber angles, away from the optimal 60° to a more transverse orientation requiring greater fiber shortening to maintain the LVEF.

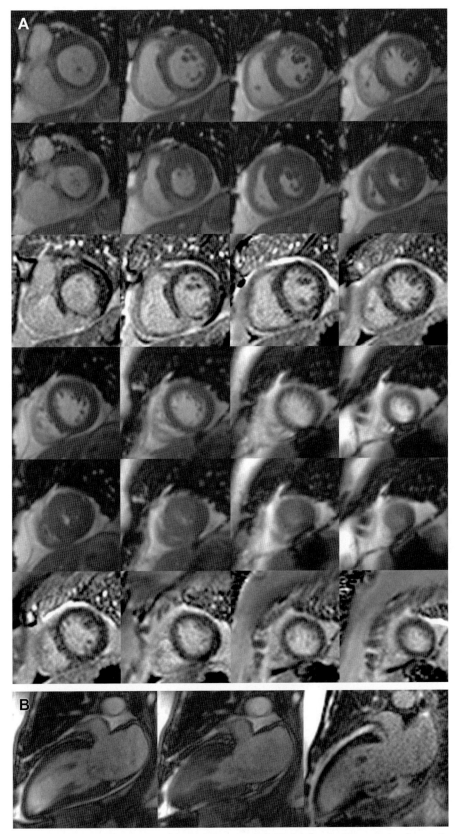

Fig. 4. A 65-year-old man with chest pain, with an acute myocardial infarction in the posterior descending coronary territory with greater than 50% thickness delayed enhancement and no reflow. (*A*) Short-axis orientation cine images at end-diastole (*rows 1, 4*) and end-systole (*rows 2, 5*) with corresponding delayed-enhancement images (*rows 3, 6*). (*B*) Corresponding 2-chamber orientation end-diastolic and end-systolic cine images with delayed-enhancement image. The basilar inferior wall is akinetic with preserved LV systolic function and a calculated EF of 57%.

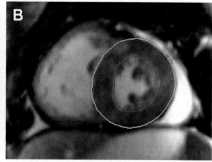

Fig. 5. Representative end-diastolic (*A*) and end-systolic (*B*) images with subendocardial (*red*) and subepicardial (*green*) contours for quantitative analysis of LV systolic function.

Key Points

- Changes in LV shape reorient myocardial fiber angles, reducing efficiency of contraction.
- LV myocardial fibers are oriented in a right-handed helix in the subendocardium, transitioning to a left-handed helix in the subepicardium.
- Myocardial torsion is crucial in equalizing strain across the LV wall at systole.

Myocardial Strain

Strain, a measure of an object's deformation, is defined as the change in object length relative to its original length, and is expressed as a percentage (**Fig. 10**). There are 2 frames of reference that can be used to define strain: Eularian and Lagrangian. Lagrangian strain displacements are calculated using the deforming myocardium itself as the reference, whereas Eularian strain uses a fixed frame of reference. These differences

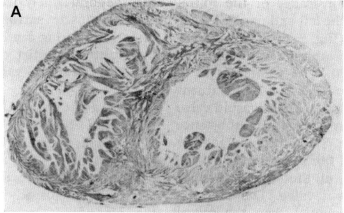

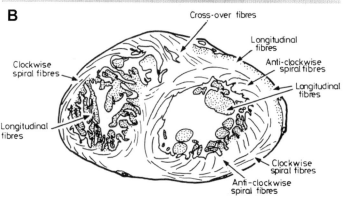

Fig. 6. Mid-chamber slice through heart at pathology (*A*) and schematically (*B*). Two sets of spiral fibers are present in the LV wall. Along the subendocardium, fibers follow a counterclockwise spiral, transitioning to a circumferential orientation in the mid-wall, and a clockwise spiral in the subepicardium. Longitudinally oriented fibers are present in the anterior and obtuse marginal regions of the subepicardial mid–left ventricle. (*From* Greenbaum RA, Ho SY, Gibson DG, et al. Left ventricular fibre architecture in man. Br Heart J 1981;45(3):257; with permission from BMJ publishing group.)

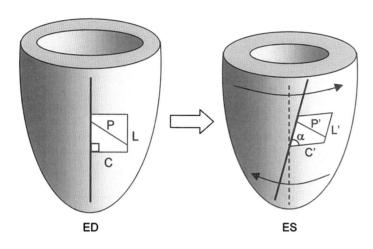

ED   ES

Fig. 7. Axial and shear strains in systole. At end-systole (ES), the left ventricle has shortened in both the longitudinal (L → L') and circumferential (C → C') directions. Torsional shear is also present, with basal clockwise and apical counterclockwise rotation (*arrows*). Torsional shear causes the greatest shortening obliquely oriented to axial strains (P → P'), approximating the orientation of the subepicardial fibers. ED, end-diastole. (*From* Fonseca CG, Dissanayake AM, Doughty RN, et al. Three-dimensional assessment of left ventricular systolic strain in patients with type 2 diabetes mellitus, diastolic dysfunction, and normal ejection fraction. Am J Cardiol 2004;94(11):1393; with permission from Elsevier.)

translate into a smaller positive and a larger negative Eularian strain for their positive and negative Lagrangian equivalents.[35]

Two coordinate systems are used for myocardial strain components: the radial-circumferential-longitudinal (RCL) and principal strains (**Fig. 11**). Orthogonal or normal strains in the RCL system are designated E_{RR}, E_{CC}, and E_{LL}. Similarly, in the principal system these are referred to as E_{11}, E_{22}, and E_{33}. As most of the available literature uses the RCL system and calculates Lagrangian strains, strain values in this article are reported in the RCL system using Lagrangian strain values.

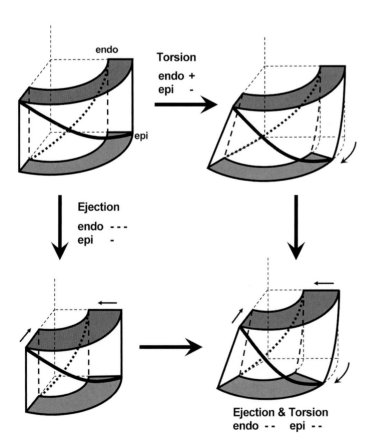

Fig. 8. Diagram of an LV midchamber segment illustrating the influence of ejection and torsion on myocardial fibers. With ejection alone (*lower left*), subendocardial fiber shortening is greater than subepicardial shortening. With torsion alone (*upper right*), subepicardial fibers shorten, with lengthening of the subendocardial fibers. Physiologically with appropriately balanced ejection and torsion (*lower right*), the homogeneity of fiber shortening is achieved across the left ventricular wall. (*From* Lumens J, Delhaas T, Arts T, et al. Impaired subendocardial contractile myofiber function in asymptomatic aged humans, as detected using MRI. Am J Physiol Heart Circ Physiol 2006;291(4):H1574; with permission from the American Physiological Society.)

Effect of Shape on Ejection

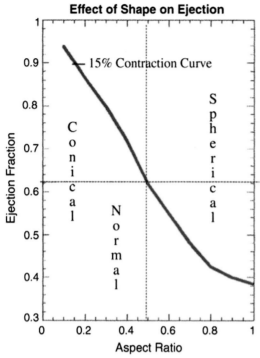

Fig. 9. Analysis of the relationship between ventricular shape and EF assuming a constant 15% fiber contraction. The aspect ratio is the length of the chamber divided by its diameter; spherical chambers have an aspect ratio of 1. As the chamber departs from an ellipsoid and becomes more spherical, the EF declines. Conversely, conical-shaped chambers demonstrate greater EFs than ellipsoid chambers at a constant rate of fiber shortening. (*From* Adhyapak SM, Parachuri VR. Architecture of the left ventricle: insights for optimal surgical ventricular restoration. Heart Fail Rev 2010;15(1):75; with permission from Springer.)

Normal values for myocardial strain have been reported in the literature using several techniques. Myocardial tagging is an accepted standard of reference for LV myocardial strain calculations. At tagging, normal end-systolic values for E_{RR}, E_{CC}, and E_{LL} are reported as 35%, −20%, and −15%, respectively.[36] In addition, end-systolic values of all 3 strain components vary across the myocardium, increasing (becoming more positive or negative) from the subepicardium to the subendocardium.[37]

Regional variations in myocardial strain are well recognized, with greater longitudinal and circumferential strains at the apex in comparison with the base.[38,39] Of interest is that strain variation has not been reliably reproduced between strain techniques in the basal and apical chamber. Normal heterogeneity in regional strain has also

been recognized for end-systolic longitudinal strain with more positive values in inferior rather than anterior regions in the basal and midchamber, with the reverse in the apical chamber.[38,39] Variation is also seen in end-systolic circumferential strains, with more negative values in anterior and lateral regions than in inferior regions throughout the chamber.[37,38] Radial strain values generally demonstrate less regional variation, with lower values reported in the septum at all levels.[38,39]

> **Key Points**
>
> - Strain is a measure of deformation, defined as the change in object's length divided by its original length.
> - Lagrangian strain is more commonly reported, and uses the deforming myocardium itself as the reference system.
> - Regional variations in longitudinal and circumferential strains are well recognized, with greater strains in apical than in basal segments.

Techniques to Evaluate Regional Myocardial Function

Regional myocardial function can be quantitated by multiple CMR techniques, including segmental myocardial thickening on segmented or real-time bSSFP cine sequences, myocardial tagging, tissue phase mapping (TPM), displacement encoding with stimulated echoes (DENSE), and strain encoding (SENC). Feature tracking on bSSFP cine sequences, a technique that resembles speckle-tracking echocardiography, is also a promising technique. Each of these techniques are briefly reviewed here along with the available validation data. Advantages and disadvantages of each are discussed, including necessary data processing, an important consideration for translation into clinical practice.

Regional myocardial thickening at balanced steady-state free precession cine imaging

Regional myocardial function can be assessed qualitatively or quantitatively through segmental analysis of wall motion on bSSFP cine sequences. Segmental wall-motion analysis is more sensitive than global systolic function parameters in the detection of IHD (see **Figs. 4** and **5**). Qualitatively, regional wall motion is graded on a 5- or 6-point scale as normal, hypokinetic (mild/moderate/severe vs mild/severe), akinetic, or dyskinetic.

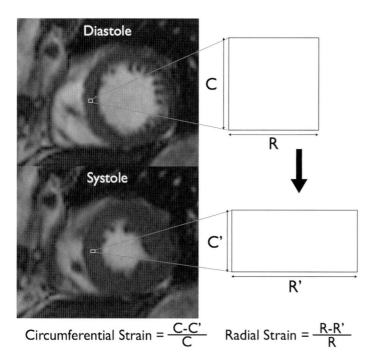

Fig. 10. Lagrangian circumferential and radial strains. For illustration purposes, a square region of myocardium is detailed at diastole deforming into a rectangle at systole, with circumferential shortening and radial lengthening. Hence circumferential strains are negative, whereas radial strains are positive.

$$\text{Circumferential Strain} = \frac{C-C'}{C} \quad \text{Radial Strain} = \frac{R-R'}{R}$$

For quantitative analysis, myocardial thickening is calculated by measuring the change in segmental myocardial thickness between diastole and systole from endocardial and epicardial contours. Segmented and real-time bSSFP cine imaging can be used for qualitative regional thickening analysis; real-time sequences are not well suited for quantitative analysis, as discussed previously in the context of LVEF and LV volumes (see **Fig. 2**). Postprocessing for quantitative analysis can be performed as part of the clinical routine, and is available on many software platforms.

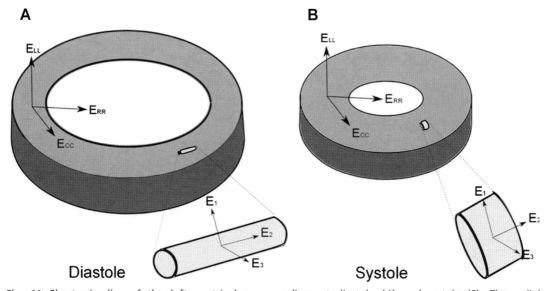

Fig. 11. Short-axis slice of the left ventricular myocardium at diastole (*A*) and systole (*B*). The radial-circumferential-longitudinal system uses the cardiac axes to define the 3 orthogonal strains (E_{RR}, E_{CC}, and E_{LL}) at each point in the myocardium. The principal strain coordinate system uses myocardial fiber geometry to define 3 orthogonal strains at each point. E_{11} is in the direction of the greatest length increase, E_{22} is in the direction of greatest shortening, and E_{33} is orthogonal to E_{11} and E_{22}. (*From* Simpson RM, Keegan J, Firmin DN. MR assessment of regional myocardial mechanics. J Magn Reson Imaging 2013;37(3):578; with permission from Wiley.)

Key Points

- Regional myocardial thickening assessment can be performed on routinely acquired conventional segmented ECG-gated bSSFP cine images.
- Both qualitative and quantitative analyses are easy to perform on segmented cine sequences.
- Qualitative analysis can be performed on real-time cine sequences.

Myocardial tagging

Tissue tagging is perhaps the most studied CMR technique for the analysis of regional myocardial function (Fig. 12). Tagging consists of a preparatory pulse that generates a grid on the myocardium starting at the R wave, with an imaging phase demonstrating the deformation of the grid throughout the cardiac cycle. Tagging is primarily accomplished by using 1 of 2 well-described imaging approaches: spatial modulation of magnetization (SPAMM)[40] or complementary SPAMM (C-SPAMM).[41] SPAMM uses an encoding gradient (G_{enc}), which determines the tag spacing and is usually set between 4 and 8 mm. Visualization of SPAMM tags is limited to the first two-thirds of the cardiac cycle, making assessment of diastolic motion difficult with this technique, although longer T1 times at higher field strengths increases tag persistence (Fig. 13).[42] C-SPAMM improves tag contrast by incrementing the flip angle through the cardiac cycle, and adding a second acquisition differing by the sign of the radiofrequency pulse from the original SPAMM acquisition. Subtraction of the 2 data sets removes nonmodulated T1 signal, greatly improving the tag contrast; however, this occurs at the expense of doubling the acquisition time. Typical parameters for SPAMM tagging include an in-plane resolution of 1.6 mm^2 with an effective temporal resolution of 32 milliseconds.[43] Parallel imaging can shorten the acquisition from 14 to as few as 5 heartbeats; free-breathing acquisitions with navigator gating have also been described to further improve the spatial and temporal resolution.

Although qualitative tag analysis is intuitive, quantitative analysis of tagged data is complex and time consuming. Tag following with manual or semiautomated segmentation of tag lines is clinically impractical. Optical flow techniques track individual pixels from time point to time point, applying a constant brightness constraint to identify and track pixels by searching for adjacent pixels with similar brightness in adjoining time frames. Optical flow techniques are more robust than tag following, as the approach is independent of tag spacing. Harmonic phase (HARP) analysis is a robust technique tracking pixels from time point to time point by a constant phase constraint.[44] HARP isolates the tag peaks through the use of a bandpass filter; an inverse Fourier transform generates a magnitude reconstruction with low-resolution anatomic data, and a phase reconstruction with varying signal intensities similar to the positions of the original myocardial tags (Fig. 14).

Tissue tagging has been validated against both phantoms and implanted gold fiducial markers in dogs. Myocardial motion has been described using myocardial tagging techniques (see earlier discussion). Assessment of E_{CC} has generally demonstrated higher precision than E_{RR} at myocardial tagging. Intraobserver and interobserver reproducibility for systolic strain analysis using HARP was good to excellent for E_{CC}, and good for E_{RR}.[45]

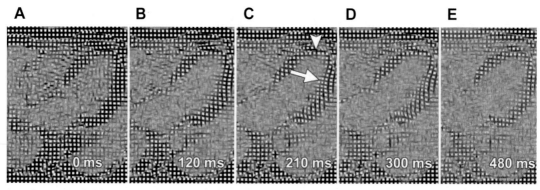

Fig. 12. Myocardial tagging in the 4-chamber orientation in a 52 year-old patient with an anterior myocardial infarct demonstrates tag deformation over the cardiac cycle. In the region of the infarction (*arrowhead*) there is little movement of tags, compared to the convex inward motion of tags in the lateral wall (*arrow*). Note the tag fading that occurs with time. (*From* Jeung M-Y, Germain P, Croisille P, et al. Myocardial Tagging with MR Imaging: Overview of Normal and Pathologic Findings. RadioGraphics 2012;32:1383; with permission.)

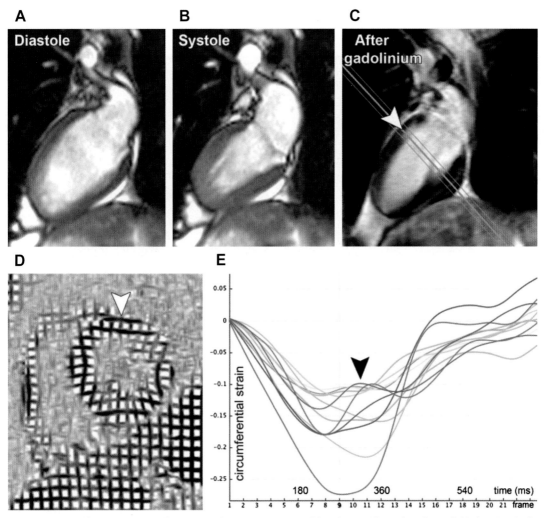

Fig. 13. Regional heterogeneity of myocardial tags in a 37-year-old patient with a subendocardial infarction in the basal anterior wall. bSSFP cine at (*A*) diastole and (*B*) peak systole demonstrate mild hypokinesia of the anterior basal segment, with subendocardial delayed enhancement (*C*). Myocardial tagging performed in the short axis orientation demonstrates reduced systolic tag deformation (*D, E, arrowhead*). (*From* Jeung M-Y, Germain P, Croisille P, et al. Myocardial Tagging with MR Imaging: Overview of Normal and Pathologic Findings. RadioGraphics 2012;32:1391; with permission.)

Key Points

- Myocardial tagging measures tissue displacement by tracking tags, generating Lagrangian strain values.

- A principal advantage of tagging over other techniques is the intuitive, visually appearing images.

- Disadvantages include lengthy processing times, tag fading throughout the cardiac cycle, and spatial resolution limited to tag spacing.

- HARP analysis enables both Lagrangian and Eularian strain analyses, but is limited by signal-to-noise ratio (SNR), with lower spatial resolution in comparison with conventionally analyzed tag images.

- HARP analysis is more efficient than conventional tag analysis, and is used clinically.

Tissue phase mapping

TPM uses a bipolar gradient to encode velocity information into the phase.[46] Hence, the phase shift is directly proportional to the velocity in the direction of the encoding gradient. As for other applications, velocities with phase shifts of greater than 180° result in aliasing. The largest velocity that can be measured without aliasing is referred to as the velocity-encoding gradient (V_{enc}). Typical values are 15 to 25 cm/s. TPM acquires a flow-compensated echo along with velocity encoding in-plane and through-plane, in a single acquisition combined with parallel imaging techniques, to achieve a temporal resolution of 37 to 87 milliseconds. Free-breathing techniques with navigator gating have also been used. Motion artifacts and phase distortion are important image-quality

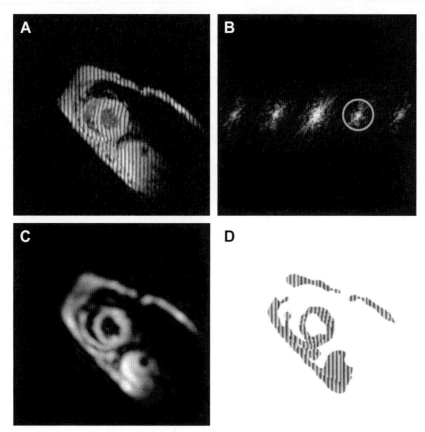

Fig. 14. (*A*) Generation of harmonic phase images from vertical spatial modulation of magnetization (SPAMM) tags. (*B*) The magnitude of the Fourier transform of image data, with 4 spectral frequency peaks outside the center of k-space. Isolating the spectral peak (*circle*) in *B* and performing an inverse Fourier transform generates magnitude (*C*) and phase images (*D*). Discontinuities in *D* are in proximity to vertical SPAMM tags seen in *A*. (*From* Osman NF, Kerwin WS, McVeigh ER, et al. Cardiac motion tracking using CINE harmonic phase (HARP) magnetic resonance imaging. Magn Reson Med 1999;42(6):1048–60; with permission from Wiley.)

limitations for TPM. TPM is performed with a black blood preparation to minimize ghosting in the phase-encoding direction.

TPM is available on many imaging platforms. Postprocessing requires segmentation of the myocardium and correction for background phase offset errors. Analysis yields voxelwise time-resolved myocardial velocities, which can be translated from the x-, y-, and z-coordinates into the cardiac axes of radial and longitudinal motion (**Fig. 15**). Although Eularian strain rate can be generated from TPM data, strain is not often generated because of the lengthy required analysis and amplification of errors in strain through time.

Myocardial velocities and time to peak velocities (a measure of dyssynchrony) at TPM have been validated against tissue Doppler imaging, with excellent agreement for both measures.[47]

> **Key Points**
>
> - TPM encodes myocardial velocities by directly measuring the phase shift for a given velocity-encoding gradient.
> - Regional function is measured using myocardial velocities or Eularian strain rate.
> - TPM can analyze the entire cardiac cycle and uses a vendor-neutral technique.
> - A primary disadvantage of TPM is proclivity to motion artifacts; black blood preparation pulses are necessary to reduce artifacts from motion.

Displacement encoding with stimulated echoes

DENSE encodes through-plane or in-plane tissue motion into the image phase. A stimulated echo

Tissue Phase Mapping

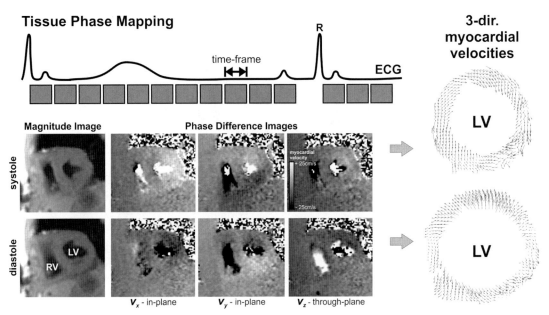

Fig. 15. Tissue phase mapping uses an accelerated phase-contrast sequence with tridirectional velocity encoding and a black blood preparation to generate time-resolved voxel-wise myocardial velocity data. V_x, V_y, and V_z can be converted into the cardiac axes of radial and longitudinal motion. ECG, electrocardiogram; LV, left ventricle; RV, right ventricle. (*Courtesy of* Michael Markl, PhD, Northwestern University, Chicago, IL, USA.)

is generated by 3 radiofrequency pulses while displacement is encoded into the image phase by encoding and decoding gradients (**Fig. 16**).[48] The encoding does not last for the entire cardiac cycle secondary to T1 recovery, limiting assessment of diastolic tissue displacement. DENSE has an intrinsically low SNR, as the encoding is related to the stimulated echo.[35] Original implementations acquired a single image at a preset point in the cardiac cycle with an unsegmented acquisition lasting longer than 4 minutes; a multi-shot segmented echo planar imaging (EPI) pulse sequence shortened the acquisition to 24 heartbeats. Cine-DENSE has been developed using both EPI and a spiral readout, achieving good spatial and temporal resolution with acquisition in a 19-heartbeat breath-hold. Further improvements to cine-DENSE made by Kim and Kellman[49] yielded fast cine-DENSE; based on a bSSFP pulse sequence, this technique improves SNR at 3 T with a breath-hold of 12 to 24 heartbeats.

DENSE, cine-DENSE, and fast cine-DENSE have been validated against HARP analysis and C-SPAMM tagging.[35] Fast cine-DENSE has low intraobserver and interobserver variability for E_{CC}. E_{CC} and E_{RR} at cine-DENSE in mice correlated well with HARP analysis, although cine-DENSE–derived strains were underestimated by 10%, and at lower strain values differences between modalities increased.[50]

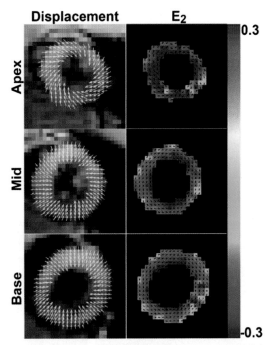

Fig. 16. Displacement (*left*) and E_2 strain maps (*right*) at systole at the base, mid-chamber, and apex using displacement encoding with stimulated echoes (DENSE). (*From* Kim D, Kellman P. Improved cine displacement-encoded MRI using balanced steady-state free precession and time-adaptive sensitivity encoding parallel imaging at 3 T. NMR Biomed 2007;20(6):599; with permission.)

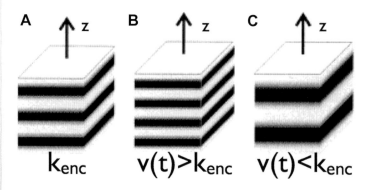

Fig. 17. Diagrammatic depiction of through-plane compression and stretching on strain encoding tagging parallel to the imaging plane on strain encoding (SENC) imaging. (*A*) Tissue is tagged at a frequency of k_{enc}. (*B*) Compressed tissue demonstrates a frequency greater than k_{enc}. (*C*) Frequency of stretched tissue is less than k_{enc}. (*From* Osman NF, Sampath S, Atalar E, et al. Imaging longitudinal cardiac strain on short-axis images using strain-encoded MRI. Magn Reson Med 2001;46(2):326; with permission from Wiley.)

Key Points

- DENSE encodes displacement on a pixel level, enabling both Eularian and Lagrangian strain analysis.
- Advantages include quick processing with generation of strain-time curves through tissue-tracking techniques.
- Disadvantages are intrinsic to the stimulated echo technique, with a low SNR and short tag duration.

Strain-encoded imaging

SENC shares some similarities with conventional tagging and DENSE, but differs in that the tag planes are oriented parallel to the imaging plane (**Fig. 17**).[51] As with other techniques, tags fade throughout the cardiac cycle, limiting assessment to systole and early diastole. Through-plane strain is directly encoded by an SPAMM tagging pulse applying a gradient to sinusoidally modulate the longitudinal magnetization in the through-plane direction; a demodulating gradient is then incorporated into the slice-rephasing gradient. Hence, through-plane strain is directly encoded by pixel intensity. Because of the tag orientations, E_{LL} and E_{CC} are measured on short-axis and long-axis images, respectively. SENC acquires low-tuning and high-tuning frequency images, with the tag frequency estimated as the approximate center of mass of the image intensities on the resulting images (**Fig. 18**).[35]

The original SENC implementation required two 16-heartbeat breath-holds. Subsequent iterations used an interleaved spiral trajectory acquiring both the low-tuning and high-tuning images in a single cardiac cycle, with an in-plane spatial resolution of 2 to 2.5 mm² in a single breath-hold. A lower-resolution iteration has been developed (fast SENC) enabling whole-heart coverage in a breath-hold or real-time strain imaging; however, fast SENC has not been widely used because of its low SNR.

Multiple studies have demonstrated interstudy and interrater reproducibility of peak systolic

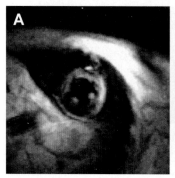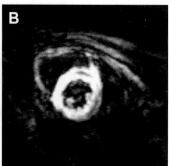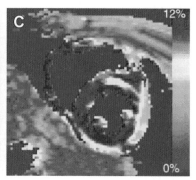

Fig. 18. SENC imaging in a healthy volunteer. (*A*) Low-tuning and (*B*) high-tuning images demonstrate low and high strain, respectively. (*C*) E_{LL} composite image with pixelwise SENC. (*From* Osman NF, Sampath S, Atalar E, et al. Imaging longitudinal cardiac strain on short-axis images using strain-encoded MRI. Magn Reson Med 2001;46(2):331, 332; with permission from Wiley.)

SENC-derived E_{CC} and E_{LL}. Good agreement has been demonstrated between SENC and fast SENC with tagging in healthy volunteers and patients, although there are relatively wide limits of agreement without bias between the techniques.[52]

Key Points

- SENC strain is encoded pixelwise, directly measuring through-plane Eularian strain.
- Advantages include efficient processing.
- Disadvantages include an intrinsically low SNR, inability to measure radial strain, and short duration of myocardial tags.

Feature-tracking cardiac MR imaging

Feature tracking is an optical flow technique whereby image features known at an instantaneous time point are tracked or followed over time. This technique is analogous to speckle-tracking echocardiography whereby velocities are used to quantify physiologic myocardial motion. Feature-tracking CMR (FT-CMR) is a recently developed technique that can be applied to bSSFP cine sequences to derive quantitative measures of myocardial motion including displacement, strain, strain rate, and tissue velocities.[53] Endocardial and epicardial borders are delineated on an arbitrary time frame. Each boundary point is tracked individually using a multiscale hierarchical algorithm. This process integrates 1-dimensional techniques with 2D tracking to facilitate identification of more complex, spatially protracted image features. This technique is not limited to tracking myocardial blood pool boundaries; midmyocardial features can be tracked as well.

The primary advantage of FT-CMR compared with other approaches to regional myocardial function assessment is the ability to extract these measures from sequences performed as part of the clinical routine (**Fig. 19**). In addition, image processing is less time consuming than with myocardial tagging and DENSE, and FT-CMR can assess strain throughout the cardiac cycle. Prototype analysis tools are being developed, leveraging myocardial border detection used for LV systolic function analysis with feature tracking to enable completely automated FT-CMR analysis.

FT-CMR has demonstrated good intrarater and interrater agreement for both control subjects and patients.[54] In the same study the per-slice average peak systolic E_{CC} at FT-CMR demonstrated excellent agreement with HARP analysis. Segmental agreement between peak E_{CC} and tagging was less promising, however, in a study

by Wu and colleagues.[55] The investigators suggest that caution should be exercised for segmental strain analysis. Unpublished data from the author's group (Collins JD, 2014) suggest that FT-CMR underestimates regional E_{CC}, E_{RR}, and E_{LL} in both healthy volunteers and patients in comparison with speckle-tracking echocardiography (STE), with significant within-slice segmental variability in peak E_{RR} and E_{CC} strains (see **Fig. 19**).

Key Points

- FT-CMR uses a hierarchical processing scheme to identify and track myocardial features throughout the cardiac cycle.
- Principal advantages include analysis of cine images acquired as part of the clinical routine, efficient processing, and diastolic strain assessment.
- Disadvantages include regional strain heterogeneity, limiting FT-CMR to segmental-level strain analysis with current techniques.

UTILITY OF REGIONAL MYOCARDIAL FUNCTION ASSESSMENT IN ISCHEMIC HEART DISEASE

Qualitative and quantitative approaches have been used in conjunction with dobutamine to assess myocardial thickening (contractile reserve) as a measure of myocardial viability.[26] Assessment of regional wall motion at CMR is considered the gold standard to assess response to revascularization therapy. This approach has also been used to assess response to medical therapy (see **Table 6**).[26] Segmental-level analysis is more sensitive to changes in regional wall thickening than are global measures such as the chamber size or LVEF.

Myocardial tagging was evaluated in several subgroups of patients from the multiethnic study of atherosclerosis (MESA). In this cohort, reduced peak systolic E_{CC} correlated with increased diastolic blood pressure in myocardium perfused by coronary arteries with coronary artery disease. Reduced peak systolic E_{CC} was also seen in MESA patients with coronary artery calcification and regional myocardial perfusion reserve. It is interesting that in the MESA cohort, tobacco use correlated negatively with peak systolic E_{CC}, suggesting the ability to detect subclinical myocardial dysfunction.

Patients with IHD demonstrate altered myocardial velocities and time to peak velocities at TPM. Compared with healthy controls, maximal long-axis velocities were reduced in a cohort of

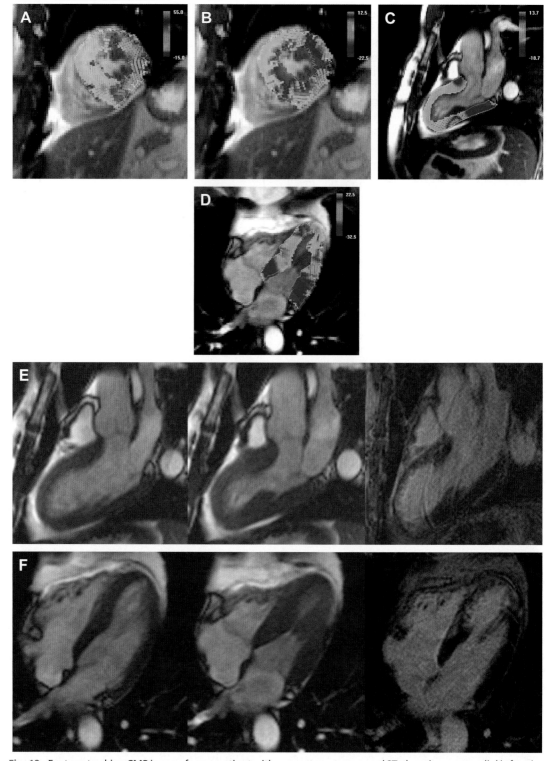

Fig. 19. Feature-tracking CMR images from a patient with a recent nontransmural ST-elevation myocardial infarction in left anterior descending coronary artery territory. Abnormal peak regional (*A*) radial, (*B*) circumferential, and longitudinal 3-chamber (*C*) and 4-chamber. (*D*) Lagrangian strain values are noted in the mid-chamber anterior wall, septum, and inferior wall. Corresponding 3-chamber and 4-chamber end-diastolic and end-systolic cine frames with delayed enhancement images are provided in *E* and *F*; short-axis images are shown in **Fig. 3**. Peak global strain-time curves are presented in *G*, with substantially reduced circumferential and longitudinal strains.

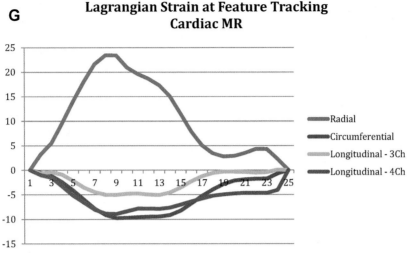

Fig. 19. (*continued*)

patients with IHD (99 vs 125 mm/s), and were further reduced in those with infarctions (80 mm/s).[56] Radial velocities were significantly reduced in patients with infarctions.[57] Patients with IHD also demonstrated reduced diastolic velocities.[46]

Although not widely used clinically, DENSE has been shown to be useful in the evaluation of patients with myocardial infarction and ventricular dyssynchrony.[48] DENSE has demonstrated good agreement for E_{CC} in comparison with STE in patients with IHD.[58]

SENC has been evaluated in patients with IHD. SENC-derived peak systolic and diastolic E_{CC} performed favorably in comparison with late-enhancement imaging in the prediction of viability in patients with acute myocardial infarction.[52] The ratio of peak E_{CC} at full dobutamine stress to that at rest (strain-rate reserve) was shown to predict the presence of significant coronary artery stenosis.[59] Similarly, strain-rate reserve at intermediate dobutamine stress had diagnostic accuracy for significant coronary artery disease similar to that achieved by assessment of regional wall-motion abnormalities at peak stress.[60] Peak systolic E_{CC} and E_{LL} at real-time fast SENC has shown usefulness in identifying chronic myocardial infarctions and determining the myocardial scar transmurality.[61]

Few studies have been performed to date assessing the clinical utility of FT-CMR in patients with IHD. FT-CMR applied to patients enrolled in the Amoricyte Phase I trial evaluating the influence of stem cell therapy infused into an infarct-related artery 5 to 11 days after primary coronary

intervention demonstrated modest improvement in peak segmental E_{CC} in a comparison with control subjects, suggesting the feasibility of this technique.[62] FT-CMR also showed promise in a study by Schuster and colleagues[63] as a strategy to quantify reversible myocardial dysfunction at low-dose dobutamine stress in patients with IHD (**Fig. 20**). Early work assessing the utility of FT-CMR suggested that a peak systolic E_{RR} threshold of 38.8% was accurate in the identification of regional dysfunction secondary to transmural myocardial infarction. These early results suggest that assessment of regional myocardial function using FT-CMR may be a useful adjunct in patients with IHD to assess viability and ischemia.

Key Points

- Numerous clinical studies support the utility of regional LV function analysis in IHD.

- Regional wall-motion analysis at segmented cine imaging, myocardial tagging, and TPM are well-established techniques for assessment of regional function.

- SENC strain analysis has been applied to low-dose dobutamine stress to predict myocardial viability.

- DENSE demonstrates good agreement with STE for strain measurement in IHD.

- Only segmental wall-motion analysis and FT-CMR can be applied to existing data or used clinically without lengthening the CMR examination time.

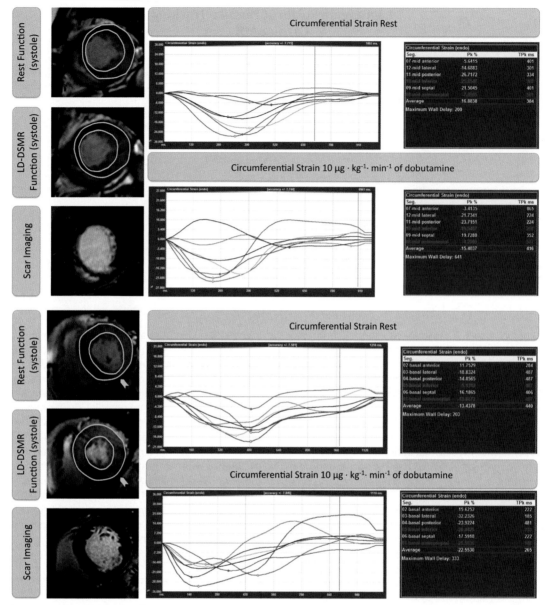

Fig. 20. Two examples of end-systolic cine images at rest and at low-dose dobutamine stress (LD-DSMR), with corresponding delayed-enhancement imaging and segmental circumferential strain curves. The top panel demonstrates a nonviable septal infarct, with akinesia that persists at low-dose dobutamine. The bottom panel demonstrates a subendocardial infarction in the inferolateral segment, with an associated reversible wall motion abnormality at low-dose dobutamine stress. (*From* Schuster A, Paul M, Bettencourt N, et al. Cardiovascular magnetic resonance myocardial feature tracking for quantitative viability assessment in ischemic cardiomyopathy. Int J Cardiol 2013;166(2):416; with permission.)

SUMMARY

CMR is considered the gold standard for global assessment of LV myocardial structure and function, with intraobserver and interobserver agreement superior to other modalities. A large body of evidence supports the use of global LV systolic function parameters for the management of patients with IHD. However, it is increasingly recognized that subtle changes in myocardial structure can occur without adversely affecting global measures of systolic function. A growing body of literature supports the assessment of regional myocardial function to improve the sensitivity of CMR early changes in myocardial structure, which adversely affect regional function. It is important to understand the quantitative imaging parameters that can be generated from each CMR technique, in addition to the trade-offs inherent with each approach. Cautious optimism is warranted for the clinical application of novel techniques such as FT-CMR. Additional research is warranted to establish age-specific and gender-specific normal ranges for regional function to enable broad clinical applications. Combining regional myocardial function with tissue characterization using quantitative T1-weighted and T2-weighted imaging techniques may further improve the utility of CMR in IHD, particularly in patients in whom gadolinium-based contrast medium is contraindicated.

REFERENCES

1. Go AS, Mozaffarian D, Roger VL, et al. Heart disease and stroke statistics—2014 update: a report from the American Heart Association. Circulation 2014;129(3):e28–292.

2. Carr JC, Simonetti O, Bundy J, et al. Cine MR angiography of the heart with segmented true fast imaging with steady-state precession. Radiology 2001; 219(3):828–34.

3. Grothues F, Smith GC, Moon JC, et al. Comparison of interstudy reproducibility of cardiovascular magnetic resonance with two-dimensional echocardiography in normal subjects and in patients with heart failure or left ventricular hypertrophy. Am J Cardiol 2002;90(1):29–34.

4. Scharf M, Brem MH, Wilhelm M, et al. Atrial and ventricular functional and structural adaptations of the heart in elite triathletes assessed with cardiac MR imaging. Radiology 2010;257(1):71–9.

5. Lanzer P, Botvinick EH, Schiller NB, et al. Cardiac imaging using gated magnetic resonance. Radiology 1984;150(1):121–7.

6. Kaji S, Yang PC, Kerr AB, et al. Rapid evaluation of left ventricular volume and mass without breath-holding using real-time interactive cardiac magnetic resonance imaging system. J Am Coll Cardiol 2001; 38(2):527–33.

7. Chuang ML, Hibberd MG, Salton CJ, et al. Importance of imaging method over imaging modality in noninvasive determination of left ventricular volumes and ejection fraction: assessment by two- and three-dimensional echocardiography and magnetic resonance imaging. J Am Coll Cardiol 2000;35(2): 477–84.

8. Blalock SE, Banka P, Geva T, et al. Interstudy variability in cardiac magnetic resonance imaging measurements of ventricular volume, mass, and ejection fraction in repaired tetralogy of Fallot: a prospective observational study. J Magn Reson Imaging 2013; 38(4):829–35.

9. Bellenger NG, Burgess MI, Ray SG, et al. Comparison of left ventricular ejection fraction and volumes in heart failure by echocardiography, radionuclide ventriculography and cardiovascular magnetic resonance; are they interchangeable? Eur Heart J 2000; 21(16):1387–96.

10. Mogelvang J, Stokholm KH, Saunamaki K, et al. Assessment of left ventricular volumes by magnetic resonance in comparison with radionuclide angiography, contrast angiography and echocardiography. Eur Heart J 1992;13(12):1677–83.

11. Bloomgarden DC, Fayad ZA, Ferrari VA, et al. Global cardiac function using fast breath-hold MRI: validation of new acquisition and analysis techniques. Magn Reson Med 1997;37(5):683–92.

12. Bellenger NG, Francis JM, Davies CL, et al. Establishment and performance of a magnetic resonance cardiac function clinic. J Cardiovasc Magn Reson 2000;2(1):15–22.

13. Gardner BI, Bingham SE, Allen MR, et al. Cardiac magnetic resonance versus transthoracic echocardiography for the assessment of cardiac volumes and regional function after myocardial infarction: an intrasubject comparison using simultaneous intrasubject recordings. Cardiovasc Ultrasound 2009;7:38.

14. Gruszczynska K, Krzych LJ, Golba KS, et al. Statistical agreement of left ventricle measurements using cardiac magnetic resonance and 2D echocardiography in ischemic heart failure. Med Sci Monit 2012;18(3):MT19–25.

15. Pouleur AC, le Polain de Waroux JB, Pasquet A, et al. Assessment of left ventricular mass and volumes by three-dimensional echocardiography in patients with or without wall motion abnormalities: comparison against cine magnetic resonance imaging. Heart 2008;94(8):1050–7.

16. Underwood SR, Klipstein RH, Firmin DN, et al. Magnetic resonance assessment of aortic and mitral regurgitation. Br Heart J 1986;56(5):455–62.

17. Xie BQ, Tian YQ, Zhang J, et al. Evaluation of left and right ventricular ejection fraction and volumes from gated blood-pool SPECT in patients with dilated cardiomyopathy: comparison with cardiac MRI. J Nucl Med 2012;53(4):584–91.

18. Epstein AE, DiMarco JP, Ellenbogen KA, et al. 2012 ACCF/AHA/HRS focused update incorporated into the ACCF/AHA/HRS 2008 guidelines for device-based therapy of cardiac rhythm abnormalities: a report of the American College of Cardiology Foundation/American Heart Association Task Force on Practice Guidelines and the Heart Rhythm Society. J Am Coll Cardiol 2013;61(3):e6–75.

19. Bristow MR, Saxon LA, Boehmer J, et al. Cardiac-resynchronization therapy with or without an implantable

defibrillator in advanced chronic heart failure. N Engl J Med 2004;350(21):2140–50.

20. Bardy GH, Lee KL, Mark DB, et al. Amiodarone or an implantable cardioverter-defibrillator for congestive heart failure. N Engl J Med 2005;352(3):225–37.

21. Moss AJ, Zareba W, Hall WJ, et al. Prophylactic implantation of a defibrillator in patients with myocardial infarction and reduced ejection fraction. N Engl J Med 2002;346(12):877–83.

22. Moss AJ, Hall WJ, Cannom DS, et al. Improved survival with an implanted defibrillator in patients with coronary disease at high risk for ventricular arrhythmia. N Engl J Med 1996;335(26):1933–40.

23. Buxton AE, Lee KL, Fisher JD, et al. A randomized study of the prevention of sudden death in patients with coronary artery disease. Multicenter Unsustained Tachycardia Trial Investigators. N Engl J Med 1999;341(25):1882–90.

24. Tang ASL, Wells GA, Talajic M, et al. Cardiac-resynchronization therapy for mild-to-moderate heart failure. N Engl J Med 2010;363(25):2385–95.

25. Moss AJ, Hall WJ, Cannom DS, et al. Cardiac-resynchronization therapy for the prevention of heart-failure events. N Engl J Med 2009;361(14):1329–38.

26. Kaandorp TA, Bax JJ, Bleeker SE, et al. Relation between regional and global systolic function in patients with ischemic cardiomyopathy after beta-blocker therapy or revascularization. J Cardiovasc Magn Reson 2010;12:7.

27. Adhyapak SM, Parachuri VR. Architecture of the left ventricle: insights for optimal surgical ventricular restoration. Heart Fail Rev 2010;15(1):73–83.

28. Chen JL, Liu W, Zhang H, et al. Regional ventricular wall thickening reflects changes in cardiac fiber and sheet structure during contraction: quantification with diffusion tensor MRI. Am J Physiol Heart Circ Physiol 2005;289(5):H1898–907.

29. Greenbaum RA, Ho SY, Gibson DG, et al. Left ventricular fibre architecture in man. Br Heart J 1981;45(3):248–63.

30. Wong AY, Rautaharju PM. Stress distribution within the left ventricular wall approximated as a thick ellipsoidal shell. Am Heart J 1968;75(5):649–62.

31. Young AA, Cowan BR. Evaluation of left ventricular torsion by cardiovascular magnetic resonance. J Cardiovasc Magn Reson 2012;14:49.

32. Fonseca CG, Dissanayake AM, Doughty RN, et al. Three-dimensional assessment of left ventricular systolic strain in patients with type 2 diabetes mellitus, diastolic dysfunction, and normal ejection fraction. Am J Cardiol 2004;94(11):1391–5.

33. Lumens J, Delhaas T, Arts T, et al. Impaired subendocardial contractile myofiber function in asymptomatic aged humans, as detected using MRI. Am J Physiol Heart Circ Physiol 2006;291(4):H1573–9.

34. Sallin EA. Fiber orientation and ejection fraction in the human left ventricle. Biophys J 1969;9(7):954–64.

35. Simpson RM, Keegan J, Firmin DN. MR assessment of regional myocardial mechanics. J Magn Reson Imaging 2013;37(3):576–99.

36. Epstein F. MRI of left ventricular function. J Nucl Cardiol 2007;14(5):729–44.

37. Shehata ML, Cheng S, Osman NF, et al. Myocardial tissue tagging with cardiovascular magnetic resonance. J Cardiovasc Magn Reson 2009;11:55.

38. Kuijer JP, Marcus JT, Gotte MJ, et al. Three-dimensional myocardial strains at end-systole and during diastole in the left ventricle of normal humans. J Cardiovasc Magn Reson 2002;4(3):341–51.

39. Moore CC, Lugo-Olivieri CH, McVeigh ER, et al. Three-dimensional systolic strain patterns in the normal human left ventricle: characterization with tagged MR imaging. Radiology 2000;214(2):453–66.

40. Axel L, Dougherty L. MR imaging of motion with spatial modulation of magnetization. Radiology 1989;171(3):841–5.

41. Fischer SE, McKinnon GC, Maier SE, et al. Improved myocardial tagging contrast. Magn Reson Med 1993;30(2):191–200.

42. Gutberlet M, Schwinge K, Freyhardt P, et al. Influence of high magnetic field strengths and parallel acquisition strategies on image quality in cardiac 2D CINE magnetic resonance imaging: comparison of 1.5 T vs. 3.0 T. Eur Radiol 2005;15(8):1586–97.

43. Rosen BD, Lima JA, Nasir K, et al. Lower myocardial perfusion reserve is associated with decreased regional left ventricular function in asymptomatic participants of the multi-ethnic study of atherosclerosis. Circulation 2006;114(4):289–97.

44. Osman NF, Kerwin WS, McVeigh ER, et al. Cardiac motion tracking using CINE harmonic phase (HARP) magnetic resonance imaging. Magn Reson Med 1999;42(6):1048–60.

45. Castillo E, Osman NF, Rosen BD, et al. Quantitative assessment of regional myocardial function with MR-tagging in a multi-center study: interobserver and intraobserver agreement of fast strain analysis with Harmonic Phase (HARP) MRI. J Cardiovasc Magn Reson 2005;7(5):783–91.

46. Markl M, Schneider B, Hennig J, et al. Cardiac phase contrast gradient echo MRI: measurement of myocardial wall motion in healthy volunteers and patients. Int J Cardiovasc Imaging 1999;15(6):441–52.

47. Jung B, Schneider B, Markl M, et al. Measurement of left ventricular velocities: phase contrast MRI velocity mapping versus tissue-Doppler-ultrasound in healthy volunteers. J Cardiovasc Magn Reson 2004;6(4):777–83.

48. Aletras AH, Ingkanisorn WP, Mancini C, et al. DENSE with SENSE. J Magn Reson 2005;176(1):99–106.

49. Kim D, Kellman P. Improved cine displacement-encoded MRI using balanced steady-state free precession and time-adaptive sensitivity encoding parallel imaging at 3 T. NMR Biomed 2007;20(6):591–601.

50. Zhong J, Yu X. Strain and torsion quantification in mouse hearts under dobutamine stimulation using 2D multiphase MR DENSE. Magn Reson Med 2010;64(5):1315–22.

51. Osman NF, Sampath S, Atalar E, et al. Imaging longitudinal cardiac strain on short-axis images using strain-encoded MRI. Magn Reson Med 2001; 46(2):324–34.

52. Neizel M, Lossnitzer D, Korosoglou G, et al. Strain-encoded (SENC) magnetic resonance imaging to evaluate regional heterogeneity of myocardial strain in healthy volunteers: comparison with conventional tagging. J Magn Reson Imaging 2009;29(1):99–105.

53. Hor KN, Baumann R, Pedrizzetti G, et al. Magnetic resonance derived myocardial strain assessment using feature tracking. J Vis Exp 2011;(48). pii:2356.

54. Hor KN, Gottliebson WM, Carson C, et al. Comparison of magnetic resonance feature tracking for strain calculation with harmonic phase imaging analysis. JACC Cardiovasc Imaging 2010;3(2):144–51.

55. Wu L, Germans T, Guclu A, et al. Feature tracking compared with tissue tagging measurements of segmental strain by cardiovascular magnetic resonance. JCMR 2014;16(1):10.

56. Karwatowski SP, Mohiaddin RH, Yang GZ, et al. Regional myocardial velocity imaged by magnetic resonance in patients with ischaemic heart disease. Br Heart J 1994;72(4):332–8.

57. Schneider B, Markl M, Geiges C, et al. Cardiac phase contrast gradient echo MRI: characterization of abnormal left ventricular wall motion in patients with ischemic heart disease. J Comput Assist Tomogr 2001;25(4):550–7.

58. Wen H, Marsolo KA, Bennett EE, et al. Adaptive postprocessing techniques for myocardial tissue tracking with displacement-encoded MR imaging. Radiology 2008;246(1):229–40.

59. Korosoglou G, Lossnitzer D, Schellberg D, et al. Strain-encoded cardiac MRI as an adjunct for dobutamine stress testing: incremental value to conventional wall motion analysis. Circulation 2009; 2(2):132–40.

60. Korosoglou G, Lehrke S, Wochele A, et al. Strain-encoded CMR for the detection of inducible ischemia during intermediate stress. JACC Cardiovasc Imaging 2010;3(4):361–71.

61. Oyama-Manabe N, Ishimori N, Sugimori H, et al. Identification and further differentiation of subendo-cardial and transmural myocardial infarction by fast strain-encoded (SENC) magnetic resonance imaging at 3.0 Tesla. Eur Radiol 2011;21(11):2362–8.

62. Bhatti S, Al-Khalidi H, Hor K, et al. Assessment of myocardial contractile function using global and segmental circumferential strain following intracoronary stem cell infusion after myocardial infarction: MRI feature tracking feasibility study. ISRN Radiol 2013;2013:371028.

63. Schuster A, Paul M, Bettencourt N, et al. Cardiovascular magnetic resonance myocardial feature tracking for quantitative viability assessment in ischemic cardiomyopathy. Int J Cardiol 2013; 166(2):413–20.

Late Gadolinium Enhancement Imaging in Assessment of Myocardial Viability

Techniques and Clinical Applications

Laura Jimenez Juan, MD[a,b], Andrew M. Crean, MD[a,c,d,e],
Bernd J. Wintersperger, MD[a,c],*

KEYWORDS

- Magnetic resonance imaging • Heart • Myocardial viability • Late gadolinium enhancement
- Delayed enhancement • Microvascular obstruction • Thrombus • Revascularization

KEY POINTS

- Magnetic resonance imaging allows reliable assessment of the extent of nonviable and viable myocardium after myocardial infarction.
- Late gadolinium enhancement imaging allows transmural differentiation of viable versus nonviable myocardium.
- Late gadolinium enhancement imaging allows prediction of functional recovery after revascularization in obstructive coronary artery disease.
- Besides assessment of myocardial viability, late gadolinium enhancement imaging provides additional insight in potential complications of myocardial infarction.

INTRODUCTION

Within just over a decade late gadolinium enhancement (LGE) imaging has become a mainstay of cardiac magnetic resonance (MR) imaging supported by extensive study data showing the precision with which the technique identifies nonsalvageable myocardium. It also now plays a key role in differential diagnosis of ischemic and nonischemic cardiomyopathies.[1–3]

Although the exact role of preoperative viability testing remains controversial, many physicians continue to think that clinical decision making in high-risk patients warrants assessment of myocardial viability and the probable myocardial response to revascularization.[4]

However, LGE imaging remains in competition with other established imaging modalities. This article focuses on technical aspects of LGE imaging as well as on the clinical use and impact of the technique in the light of the current multimodality cardiac imaging environment.

TECHNIQUES AND IMPLEMENTATION

Although postcontrast imaging methods for imaging of myocardial infarction using contrast-enhanced MR imaging date back to the early

a Department of Medical Imaging, University of Toronto, Toronto, Ontario, Canada; b Department of Medical Imaging, Sunnybrook Health Science Centre, Toronto, Ontario, Canada; c Department of Medical Imaging, Peter Munk Cardiac Center, Toronto General Hospital, 585 University Avenue, Toronto, Ontario M5G 2N2, Canada; d Department of Medicine, University of Toronto, Toronto, Ontario, Canada; e Division of Cardiology, Peter Munk Cardiac Center, Toronto General Hospital, Toronto, Ontario, Canada
* Corresponding author. Department of Medical Imaging, Toronto General Hospital, 585 University Avenue, Toronto, Ontario M5G 2N2, Canada.
E-mail address: bernd.wintersperger@uhn.ca

Radiol Clin N Am 53 (2015) 397–411
http://dx.doi.org/10.1016/j.rcl.2014.11.004
0033-8389/15/$ – see front matter © 2015 Elsevier Inc. All rights reserved.

1980s the underlying theoretic basis of differential enhancement patterns had already been studied in the late 1970s using computed tomography (CT) imaging.[5,6] Development of fast MR imaging techniques and groundbreaking investigations in the late 1990s and early 2000s pushed the boundaries of postcontrast imaging of myocardial infarction.[7,8]

Contrast Mechanism and Imaging Sequence Techniques

Underlying principles of contrast agent dynamics

Basic knowledge of the pharmacokinetics of extracellular gadolinium-based contrast agents (GBCAs) is important for a better understanding of LGE imaging techniques. After GBCA bolus injection, extravasation into the interstitial (extra-cellular-extravascular) space (including myocardium) occurs along a gradient (wash-in) and only reverses (wash-out) over time with continuous renal excretion of GBCA. These processes have been found to be altered in the setting of myocardial infarction.[9–11] Together with a markedly increased GBCA distribution volume based on cell membrane ruptures in acute myocardial infarction (AMI) and the large extracellular space of collagen matrices in chronic myocardial infarction (CMI), these changes result in GBCA accumulation in the infarct area.[12–16] Differences in GBCA concentrations between normal (viable) and infarcted (nonviable) myocardium result in proportional alterations of the relaxivity rate R1 ($1/T1$).[17,18]

Principles of imaging sequence techniques

Optimizing image contrast T1-weighted imaging techniques are used for assessment of R1 differences in infarct and viability assessment. After initial use of spin-echo techniques, the application of gradient echo sequences speeded up imaging and resulted in improved image quality of the contrast-enhanced imaging of myocardial infarction. The push toward the modern practice of LGE imaging dates back to the implementation of strong T1-weighted inversion recovery (IR) gradient recalled echo (GRE) techniques in the early 2000s.[19] With appropriate inversion time (TI) selection, such techniques enable a ~5-fold difference in signal intensity between viable and nonviable myocardium (**Fig. 1**). Although TI settings may be affected by various factors (**Table 1**) and were initially based on empirical knowledge and user expertise, T1 scouts improve accuracy and ensure adequate nulling of viable or remote myocardium, whereas infarcted/nonviable myocardium is typically displayed with prominent

hyperenhancement (**Fig. 2**).[20] Kellman and colleagues[21,22] implemented additional phase-sensitive image reconstruction techniques (PSIR) that have been shown to also permit quantification of infarct sizes with less dependency on optimized TI settings (**Fig. 3**).[21–23]

Data acquisition strategies Cardiac MR imaging now enables a variety of different acquisition strategies for LGE imaging that allow tailoring to the individual situation and patient. In most situations coverage of the ventricular myocardium in short-axis orientation with additional single-slice long-axis views in 4-chamber, 2-chamber, and 3-chamber orientation is sufficient. This coverage is commonly achieved with two-dimensional (2D) techniques using noncontiguous coverage and LGE slices matching cine steady-state free precession (SSFP) slice locations (**Table 2**).

Segmented data sampling strategies, which acquire a few k-space lines/heartbeat, are most commonly used but result in multiheartbeat breath-hold periods per single 2D LGE slice.[19] In combination with phase-sensitive IR, such strategies result in a prolonged acquisition time for ventricular coverage and multiorientation acquisition. In patients with breath-hold limitations or cardiac arrhythmia, those techniques are likely to fail.

As an alternative, single slices may be acquired within a single heartbeat using single-shot techniques. Those techniques can also be applied during shallow breathing and allow ventricular coverage in ~2 breath holds but at the cost of lower spatial and temporal resolution (**Fig. 4**, see **Table 2**). In order to maintain adequate signal/noise ratio (SNR) and contrast/noise ratio (CNR), these approaches typically use an SSFP data read-out.[24,25] In general, single-shot techniques showed excellent correlation of infarct extent compared with segmented techniques.[24–26] Respiratory gating using Navigator techniques may be used as alternatives in the setting of stable sinus rhythm.[27]

Despite the high image quality of 2D techniques, various three-dimensional (3D) techniques have become available covering the ventricles in a single volume either using respiratory-gated or breath-held approaches.[28,29] Three-dimensional IR GRE approaches showed superior SNR, CNR, and image quality with improved delineation of nontransmural hyperenhancement and subtle involvement of papillary muscles.[30,31] However, using 3D respiratory-gated LGE imaging, proper myocardial nulling remains challenging because data sampling continues for minutes and TI settings may not remain optimal throughout acquisition (**Fig. 5**, see **Table 2**).

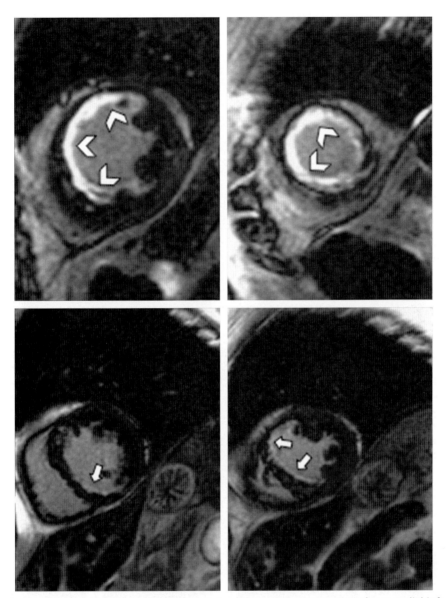

Fig. 1. Short-axis LGE data sets of 2 cases with (*upper row*) extensive near transmural myocardial infarction (*arrowheads*) and (*lower row*) subtle subendocardial infarction (*arrows*).

Contrast agents, dosing, and imaging timing

GBCA selection and contrast dosing may affect exact imaging parameters and timing in LGE imaging because various factors affect tissue T1 properties (see **Table 1**; **Table 3**).

In recent years, various extracellular GBCAs have become generally available for use in MR imaging. With respect to the use of a specific GBCA for cardiac MR, and especially LGE imaging, users need to refer to their respective authorities.

Extracellular GBCA can generally be classified using various criteria. The following have been identified as criteria potentially influencing LGE imaging:

- GBCA concentration
- Protein-binding capabilities

Together with other characteristics, these factors may result in differences of GBCA R1 and R2 properties, potentially affecting signal characteristics in LGE imaging.

Various comparative studies have shown differences between agents as a result of different R1,

Table 1
Influencing factors of postcontrast myocardial T1 and TI in LGE imaging

GBCA R1 relaxivity	Higher GBCA R1 relaxivity = ↓ TI[a]
GBCA volume	Higher GBCA volume = ↓ TI[b]
Time after GBCA application	Shorter wait time = ↓ TI[c]
Magnetic field strength (B_0)	Higher B_0 = ↑ TI

[a] Assumes otherwise identical GBCA.
[b] Assumes volume differences of the identical GBCA (with stable remaining factors).
[c] Also higher rate of T1 change early after injection potentially requiring repeated TI adjustment.

doses, or protein-binding capabilities but generally enable reliable identification and delineation of infarcted, nonviable tissue (see **Table 3**).[32–38]

LGE imaging is typically performed 8 to 20 minutes after contrast application with imaging at higher end dosages (0.15–0.2 mmol/kg body weight) potentially requiring TI adjustments over time to account for contrast agent concentration changes (see **Table 3**). The application of identical imaging techniques in the early stages postinjection (1–5 minutes) is referred to as early gadolinium enhancement (EGE) and may be used for the delineation of specific features in AMI without myocardial nulling (discussed later).

CLINICAL IMPACT AND OUTCOMES OF LATE GADOLINIUM ENHANCEMENT IMAGING
Clinical Importance of the Assessment of Myocardial Viability

Risk stratification of patients after AMI is crucial for effective treatment planning. The steady improvement of the outcome of patients with acute coronary syndrome has resulted in a higher incidence of patients with chronic left ventricular (LV) dysfunction. Therefore, there is increasing interest in identifying accurate predictors of outcome that may improve risk stratification and guide management.[39–41]

The differentiation of dysfunctional myocardium as viable or nonviable is an important predictor of outcome after myocardial infarction (**Table 4**).

A multitude of studies have supported the notion that patients with ischemic cardiomyopathy with dysfunctional but still viable myocardium derive prognostic benefit from revascularization and that, conversely, they do poorly if treated medically.[42] In contrast, there is a low likelihood that patients with nonviable myocardium benefit from coronary revascularization.[43,44]

The recent STICH (Surgical Treatment for Ischemic Heart Failure) trial controversially failed to show such an advantage of revascularization compared with optimum medical therapy in patients with ischemic cardiomyopathy.[45] Although the study has been subject to major criticism, including the lack of any viability testing in greater than 50% of patients, subsequent substudies only showed minimal benefit of revascularization in the

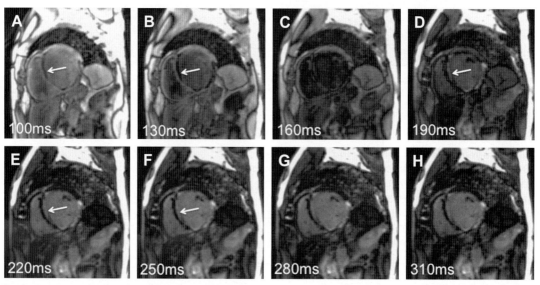

Fig. 2. TI scout series (*A–H*) ranging from 100 to 310 milliseconds TI. Note that the zero pass of blood pool (*C*) happens before normal myocardium and that at short TI times (100–160 milliseconds) nonviable infarcted myocardium (*arrows*) is predominantly dark and shows optimal nulling at 250 milliseconds (*F*).

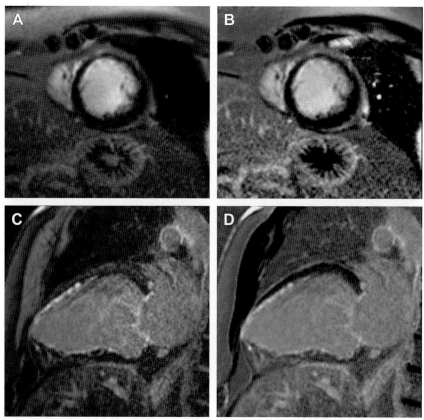

Fig. 3. Comparison of magnitude (*A, C*) and phase (*B, D*) reconstructions in PSIR GRE. Although optimal TI settings show optimized nulling (TI, 280 milliseconds; 3T) in the magnitude display (*A*) with no difference to phase display (*B*) on the short-axis slices, the long-axis example shows dark myocardium in phase reconstruction (*D*) despite nonoptimal (too short) TI (200 milliseconds; 1.5 T) in the magnitude display (*C*).

Table 2
LGE acquisition techniques: benefits and limitations

Technique	Benefits	Limitations
2D segmented IR GRE	High spatial resolution	Single slice/breath hold Breathing/motion artifacts Arrhythmia artifacts Possibly TI readjustment
2D segmented IR SSFP	High spatial resolution High SNR	Single slice/breath hold Breathing/motion artifacts Arrhythmia artifacts Possibly TI readjustment
2D single-shot IR SSFP	Multiple slices/breath hold or free breathing No arrhythmia artifacts No TI readjustment	Limited spatial resolution Possible image blurring
3D breath-hold IR GRE	Smaller voxel size Fast ventricular coverage Contiguous coverage	Breathing/motion artifacts Arrhythmia artifacts
3D respiratory-gated IR GRE	High spatial resolution Free breathing Higher CNR	Arrhythmia artifacts Nonoptimized nulling

Abbreviations: CNR, contrast/noise ratio; SNR, signal/noise ratio.

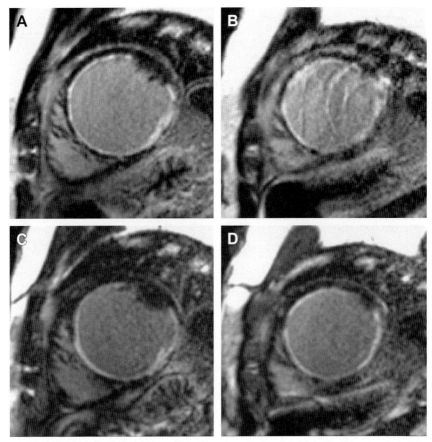

Fig. 4. Two-dimensional short-axis segmented IR GRE slices (*A, B*) and corresponding 2D single-shot SSFP slices (*C, D*) in the same patient. Although segmented IR GRE shows artifacts (*B*), the corresponding single-shot data are artifact free (*D*).

setting of significant viability.[46] The prospective PARR-2 (PET and Recovery Following Revascularization) trial, with the inclusion of viability assessment by means of PET, also failed to show a difference in primary outcome, whereas the local Ottawa-FIVE (18F-FDG PET Imaging of Myocardial Viability in an Experienced Center with Access to 18F-FDG and Integration with Clinical Management Teams) PARR-2 substudy confirmed a significant outcome benefit in the PET-guided group.[47]

Prognostic Value of Late Gadolinium Enhancement Imaging After Myocardial Infarction

Cardiac MR imaging has become a valuable noninvasive tool for the assessment and risk stratification of patients after myocardial infarction. In particular, the contribution of LGE imaging to viability imaging has produced a paradigm shift in the assessment of myocardial viability.[48]

Besides being an important diagnostic tool, LGE imaging is also able to provide prognostic information.[49] There is substantial evidence that the infarct extent assessed by LGE imaging correlates with the likelihood of functional recovery of dysfunctional myocardium after coronary revascularization.[8,50,51]

Furthermore, LGE imaging provides additional parameters related to AMI that may affect patient outcome, such as microvascular obstruction (MVO),[52] thrombus formation[53] and peri-infarct zone.[54] In addition, LGE imaging can easily be combined with stress MR perfusion imaging, allowing the combined evaluation of myocardial viability and ischemia.

Various studies have also shown the high sensitivity of LGE imaging in the identification of otherwise potentially unrecognized non–Q-wave myocardial infarctions.[55–57]

Infarct extent and viability

Using animal experiments with histopathologic validation, Kim and colleagues[7] validated the ability of LGE imaging to distinguish between

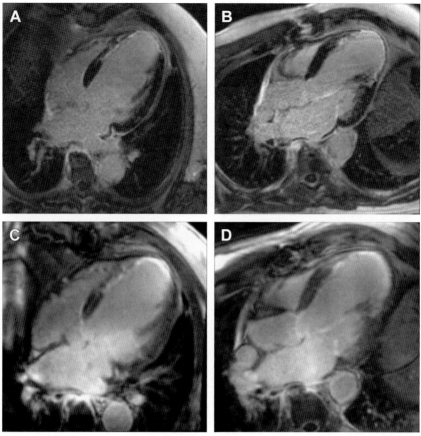

Fig. 5. Comparison of 2D LGE (*A, B*) and respiratory-gated 3D LGE (*C, D*) in a patient with extensive left anterior descending (LAD) infarction. Note the nonnulled viable myocardium in the 3D approach.

ischemic but viable myocardium, which showed no hyperenhancement, versus infarcted myocardium that showed hyperenhancement in AMI and CMI. A human pioneer study showed an inversely proportional relationship between the likelihood of improvement in regional contractility after revascularization and the transmural extent of hyperenhancement in LGE imaging before revascularization.[8]

Since then, multiple cardiac MR studies have been performed with the primary outcome of evaluating the recovery in contractility and LV systolic function after revascularization, based on the amount of viable myocardium.[58–60]

It has been shown that changes in LV ejection fraction after revascularization are linearly correlated with the number of viable segments and baseline amount of scar, resulting in a general

Table 3		
Contrast agent selection, dosing, and imaging timing for LGE		
		Remarks
Contrast agent	Extracellular GBCA	Agent with minor protein-binding applicable
Contrast volume/dose	0.1–0.2 mmol/kg BW	Lower dose with high R1 or 1M agents
Data acquisition	8–20 min postinjection[a]	≥10 min recommended for protein-binding agents[a]; less TI variation over time with later start

Abbreviation: BW, body weight.

[a] With the same contrast injection early gadolinium enhancement imaging may additionally performed 1 to 5 minutes postinjection (eg, thrombus assessment, microvascular obstruction assessment).

Table 4
Myocardial viability: definition of terms

Viable	
Hibernating myocardium	State of reversible contractile myocardial dysfunction with reduced myocardial perfusion
Stunned myocardium	State of reversible contractile myocardial dysfunction with restored myocardial perfusion
Nonviable	
Necrotic/scarred myocardium	Irreversible contractile myocardial dysfunction with tissue necrosis/ replacement scar

consensus about patient-based criteria for prediction of global LV improvement after revascularization.[60–62] Although no LGE or less than 25% transmurality is the best predictor of recovery, segments with less than 50% of transmural LGE extent are generally considered viable.[63] The latter threshold has also been implemented in current guidelines as an established predictor of significant LV function improvement after coronary revascularization (**Table 5**).[62]

Although it is not routinely part of myocardial viability assessment in cardiac MR,[62,64] several studies have shown the prognostic value of MR stress perfusion in the assessment of myocardial ischemia and an improved accuracy of LGE imaging in viability imaging.[51,65–67]

Microvascular obstruction

MVO or the no-reflow phenomenon is defined as an area of nonviable tissue within the infarct core mainly related to microvascular injury with endothelial swelling/blebs. As a result, there is substantial limitation of blood flow despite successful revascularization of the epicardial vasculature.[68]

MVO only occurs in acute infarcts and it is not typically seen in CMI. It therefore helps to determine the acuity of the myocardial infarction (see **Table 5**). Wu and colleagues[52] found that MVO persists for at least 9 days after the infarction and it resolves completely in 6 months.

LGE imaging, first-pass perfusion imaging, and EGE imaging are highly sensitive techniques in detecting the characteristic hypoenhanced areas of MVO within the infarcted myocardium, providing important information that is also related to the total infarct size (**Fig. 6**). However, the extent of MVO on these various imaging techniques varies because the contrast agent may gradually diffuse into hypoenhancing cores over time.

Although there are limited data on how MVO affects contractile recovery of the infarct zone,[69] the presence of MVO, in addition to myocardial infarction, is a strong predictor of LV remodeling,[70,71] adverse cardiovascular complications, and poor outcome.[72,73]

Thrombus

Myocardial infarction/scar is a major risk factor for mural thrombus formation which is most common in apical infarcts.[74,75] The detection of LV thrombus is important because of the related high risk of systemic embolization.[76] LGE imaging has 88% sensitivity and 99% specificity for detection of thrombus and it is especially useful in detecting small, apical, and layered thrombi that can easily be missed in echocardiography (**Fig. 7**, see **Table 5**).[53]

Table 5
Checklist for LGE imaging of myocardial infarction and viability

LGE Parameter	Description	Clinical Outcome
Infarct extension	Myocardial involvement of LGE: <50% myocardial thickness; ≥50% myocardial thickness	High likelihood of functional recovery if LGE involves <50% transmural myocardial thickness and >10 viable segments[a]
MVO	In acute infarcts, hypoenhanced areas within the infarct core	Predictor of adverse LV remodeling and major cardiovascular events
Thrombus	Hypoenhanced intracavitary masses, typically adjacent to myocardial scar	High risk of systemic embolization
Peri-infarct zone	Peripheral regions adjacent to the infarct core	Predictor of ventricular tachycardia and mortality

[a] Based on American Heart Association 16-segment model.

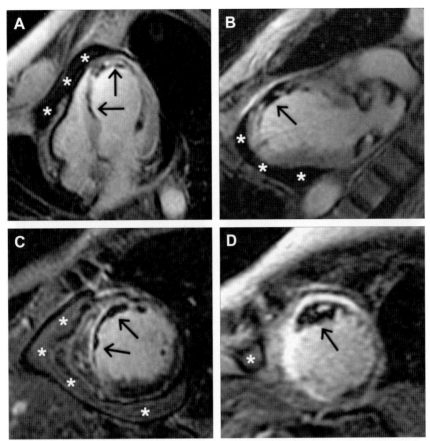

Fig. 6. Extensive coronary artery disease imaged before potential coronary revascularization. EGE imaging (*A, B*) and LGE imaging (*C, D*) show LV dilatation with a laminated thrombus (*arrows*) extending from the midcavity to the anterior apex, adjacent to a transmural LAD infarction. A small pericardial effusion was present (*asterisks*). Previous echocardiography failed to depict the thrombus.

Peri-infarct zone

There is increasing evidence that infarct border characterization may also have important prognostic implications. Although of limited use in clinical practice, LGE imaging has been introduced as a promising tool to differentiate the infarct core and peripheral regions (peri-infarct zone).

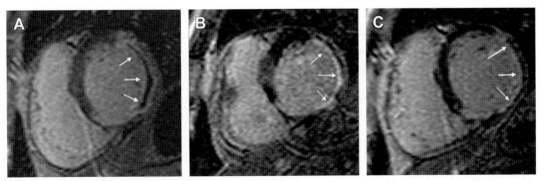

Fig. 7. ST-elevation myocardial infarction and ad hoc angioplasty of a totally occluded left circumflex coronary artery. (*A*) LGE imaging within 48 hours showing a large hypoenhanced area within the infarct core compatible with MVO (*arrows*). Follow-up imaging after 1 month (*B*) shows resolution of the MVO, LV wall thinning, and greater than 50% transmural LGE extent consistent with previous myocardial infarction. Further follow-up at 6 months (*C*) shows increased LV wall thinning of the ischemic scar and LV remodeling.

The heterogeneity and extent of the peri-infarct zone morphology is a good predictor of ventricular tachycardia inducibility[77] and has been associated with increased mortality after myocardial infarction,[54] independent of age and LV ejection fraction (see **Table 5**).[78]

MAGNETIC RESONANCE VIABILITY IMAGING IN THE CONTEXT OF MULTIMODALITY IMAGING: STRENGTHS AND WEAKNESSES
Competing and Complementing Modalities in Assessment of Myocardial Viability

At present, applicable modalities for assessment of myocardial viability may rely on the injection of a tracer/contrast agent or highlight the presence of viability based on functional recovery under pharmacologic challenges. Important aspects to consider when selecting an imaging technique for viability assessment are provided in **Table 6**.

In single-photon emission computed tomography (SPECT), cardiomyocytes retaining radioactive label are, by definition, viable. Thallium (thallium-201) imaging depends on the integrity of the cell membrane Na/K pumps, whereas technetium (Tc-99m) agents relate to mitochondrial integrity. Maximal thallium retention may not occur within the first 3 to 4 hours and therefore may require delayed imaging to assess uptake 24 hours after injection (rest-redistribution). Tc-99m agents relate to mitochondrial integrity and do not redistribute to any great extent but

require tracer reinjection for rest distribution imaging. Increased specificity may be achieved by nitrate-enhanced protocols.[79] Because the photon energy of both tracers is low, attenuation artifacts may consequently reduce accuracy. In addition, spatial resolution is limited and thus thinned but hibernating segments may appear as fixed defects. SPECT has also been shown to miss up to ~45% of subendocardial infarctions.[48]

The metabolic signature of viable but oxygen-deplete myocytes, with a switch from fatty acid metabolism to dominance of glucose metabolism, are exploited by PET. Segments with little or no blood flow tracer (eg, N-13 ammonia or Rb-82 Cl) uptake at rest but extensive uptake of [18F]fluorodeoxyglucose PET (18FDG-PET) show a perfusion/metabolism mismatch that is characteristic of hibernating myocardium. Matched defects in blood flow imaging and 18FDG-PET are characteristic of transmural scar/infarct extent. Although PET provides improved spatial resolution, identification of subendocardial infarcts is potentially still limited and again sensitivity is higher than specificity (**Fig. 8**).[80] LGE and 18FDG-PET imaging comparisons have shown general good agreement, with MR imaging showing hyperenhancement in 11% of segments classified as normal by PET.[81]

In echocardiography, residual viability is shown by the presence of a biphasic response to a dobutamine challenge in segments with resting dysfunction. Although hibernating myocardium responds

Table 6
Considerations for viability assessment modality selection

	SPECT	FDG-PET	Echocardiography	LGE MR Imaging
Underlying mechanism	Perfusion; cellular integrity	Metabolic integrity	Contractile reserve	Perfusion; passive tracer distribution
Spatial resolution	+	++	++	+++
Availability	+++	+	+++	++
Radiation	++	++	−	−
Cost	+	++	+	++
Potential for artifact	++	+	++	+/−
Safe in renal failure	Y	Y	Y	N
Safe with pacemaker/AICD	Y	Y	Y	N
Influence of body habitus	+++	++	+++	−
Time required	+++	++	+	+
Sensitivity	++	++	++	++
Specificity	+	+	+++	++
Supporting data	+++	++	++	++

Abbreviations: AICD, automatic implantable cardioverter-defibrillator; FDG, [18F]fluorodeoxyglucose; SPECT, single-photon emission computed tomography.

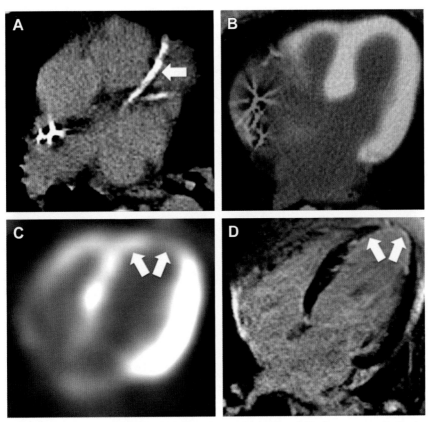

Fig. 8. (A) Male patient with severe global LV dysfunction and heavily calcified coronary arteries (arrow). 18FDG PET study shows normal metabolic activity throughout the left ventricle (B), suggesting myocardial viability. (C) Female patient with decreased tracer uptake in the distal septum and apex (arrows) at 18FDG PET with (D) matching hyperenhancing scar on LGE imaging.

with an appearance of improved contractility reserve at low doses of dobutamine (maximum 10 µg/kg/min), segmental function deteriorates again with further dose increase (−40 µg/kg/min). Such a response pattern predicts recovery after revascularization with pooled sensitivity and specificity of 79% and 87% respectively.[82] General echocardiography limitations apply, such as operator dependency and the subjective nature of wall motion interpretation. In addition, echocardiography does not directly visualize the extent of nonviable myocardium.

Low-dose dobutamine cardiac MR was reported to predict functional recovery in a similar way to echocardiography, albeit with improved diagnostic accuracy.[83,84] In addition, simple end-diastolic wall thickness assessment with a threshold of less than 5.5 to 6 mm was used to indicate nonviability in cardiac MR before the LGE era.[85] However, this technique ignores the significant thinning that may occur without scar in hibernating segments.

New Developments

In recent years, cardiac CT has been explored with regard to viability assessment but for now remains the least-explored technique.[86] As mentioned earlier, basic principles of iodinated contrast agent distribution patterns are similar to LGE MR, leading to the term late iodine enhancement to identify regions of infarcted myocardium.[5,6,87] Limitations to CT viability imaging include radiation dose, the poor CNR compared with LGE MR techniques, and the potential need for a large amount of iodinated contrast agent. The use of dual-energy CT has recently shown promise in animal and patient studies of myocardial infarction.[88–91]

In addition, the development of hybrid MR-PET imaging holds great promise in further improvement of viability assessment and even more precise prediction of functional recovery after revascularization.[92] However, installed bases may limit the use to dedicated research applications. Most importantly, the likely high costs of such hybrid examinations would demand a clear benefit with respect to the predictive value and specificity of viability assessment.

SUMMARY

Assessment of myocardial viability is of ever-evolving interest in cardiovascular imaging, with major societies having incorporated viability imaging as class I or class IIa indications in their guidelines to better guide patient management. As with LGE cardiac MR, assessment of residual myocardial viability or the extent of myocardial infarction is straightforward and this technique may easily be combined with other cardiac MR modules. In clinical routine, functional assessment and myocardial perfusion imaging if often used in conjunction allowing for a comprehensive assessment of ischemic heart disease.

REFERENCES

1. Mahrholdt H, Wagner A, Judd RM, et al. Delayed enhancement cardiovascular magnetic resonance assessment of non-ischaemic cardiomyopathies. Eur Heart J 2005;26(15):1461–74.
2. Cummings KW, Bhalla S, Javidan-Nejad C, et al. A pattern-based approach to assessment of delayed enhancement in nonischemic cardiomyopathy at MR imaging. Radiographics 2009;29(1):89–103.
3. Hunold P, Schlosser T, Vogt FM, et al. Myocardial late enhancement in contrast-enhanced cardiac MRI: distinction between infarction scar and non-infarction-related disease. AJR Am J Roentgenol 2005;184(5):1420–6.
4. Cortigiani L, Bigi R, Sicari R. Is viability still viable after the STICH trial? Eur Heart J Cardiovasc Imaging 2012;13(3):219–26.
5. Siemers PT, Higgins CB, Schmidt W, et al. Detection, quantitation and contrast enhancement of myocardial infarction utilizing computerized axial tomography: comparison with histochemical staining and 99mTc-pyrophosphate imaging. Invest Radiol 1978;13(2):103–9.
6. Higgins CB, Siemers PT, Schmidt W, et al. Evaluation of myocardial ischemic damage of various ages by computerized transmission tomography. Time-dependent effects of contrast material. Circulation 1979;60(2):284–91.
7. Kim RJ, Fieno DS, Parrish TB, et al. Relationship of MRI delayed contrast enhancement to irreversible injury, infarct age, and contractile function. Circulation 1999;100(19):1992–2002.
8. Kim RJ, Wu E, Rafael A, et al. The use of contrast-enhanced magnetic resonance imaging to identify reversible myocardial dysfunction. N Engl J Med 2000;343(20):1445–53.
9. Kim RJ, Chen EL, Lima JA, et al. Myocardial Gd-DTPA kinetics determine MRI contrast enhancement and reflect the extent and severity of myocardial injury after acute reperfused infarction. Circulation 1996;94(12):3318–26.
10. Klein C, Nekolla SG, Balbach T, et al. The influence of myocardial blood flow and volume of distribution on late Gd-DTPA kinetics in ischemic heart failure. J Magn Reson Imaging 2004;20(4):588–93.
11. Klein C, Schmal TR, Nekolla SG, et al. Mechanism of late gadolinium enhancement in patients with acute myocardial infarction. J Cardiovasc Magn Reson 2007;9(4):653–8.
12. Flacke SJ, Fischer SE, Lorenz CH. Measurement of the gadopentetate dimeglumine partition coefficient in human myocardium in vivo: normal distribution and elevation in acute and chronic infarction. Radiology 2001;218(3):703–10.
13. Wendland MF, Saeed M, Arheden H, et al. Toward necrotic cell fraction measurement by contrast-enhanced MRI of reperfused ischemically injured myocardium. Acad Radiol 1998;5(Suppl 1):S42–4 [discussion: S45–6].
14. Arheden H, Saeed M, Higgins CB, et al. Measurement of the distribution volume of gadopentetate dimeglumine at echo-planar MR imaging to quantify myocardial infarction: comparison with 99mTc-DTPA autoradiography in rats. Radiology 1999; 211(3):698–708.
15. Mahrholdt H, Wagner A, Judd RM, et al. Assessment of myocardial viability by cardiovascular magnetic resonance imaging. Eur Heart J 2002;23(8):602–19.
16. Mewton N, Liu CY, Croisille P, et al. Assessment of myocardial fibrosis with cardiovascular magnetic resonance. J Am Coll Cardiol 2011;57(8):891–903.
17. Burstein D, Taratuta E, Manning WJ. Factors in myocardial "perfusion" imaging with ultrafast MRI and Gd-DTPA administration. Magn Reson Med 1991;20(2):299–305.
18. Tweedle MF, Wedeking P, Telser J, et al. Dependence of MR signal intensity on Gd tissue concentration over a broad dose range. Magn Reson Med 1991;22(2):191–4 [discussion: 195–6].
19. Simonetti OP, Kim RJ, Fieno DS, et al. An improved MR imaging technique for the visualization of myocardial infarction. Radiology 2001; 218(1):215–23.
20. Gupta A, Lee VS, Chung YC, et al. Myocardial infarction: optimization of inversion times at delayed contrast-enhanced MR imaging. Radiology 2004; 233(3):921–6.
21. Kellman P, Arai AE, McVeigh ER, et al. Phase-sensitive inversion recovery for detecting myocardial infarction using gadolinium-delayed hyperenhancement. Magn Reson Med 2002;47(2):372–83.
22. Kellman P, Larson AC, Hsu LY, et al. Motion-corrected free-breathing delayed enhancement

imaging of myocardial infarction. Magn Reson Med 2005;53(1):194–200.

23. Huber AM, Schoenberg SO, Hayes C, et al. Phase-sensitive inversion-recovery MR imaging in the detection of myocardial infarction. Radiology 2005; 237(3):854–60.

24. Huber A, Bauner K, Wintersperger BJ, et al. Phase-sensitive inversion recovery (PSIR) single-shot True-FISP for assessment of myocardial infarction at 3 tesla. Invest Radiol 2006;41(2):148–53.

25. Huber A, Hayes C, Spannagl B, et al. Phase-sensitive inversion recovery single-shot balanced steady-state free precession for detection of myocardial infarction during a single breathhold. Acad Radiol 2007;14(12):1500–8.

26. Bauner KU, Muehling O, Wintersperger BJ, et al. Inversion recovery single-shot TurboFLASH for assessment of myocardial infarction at 3 Tesla. Invest Radiol 2007;42(6):361–71.

27. Matsumoto H, Matsuda T, Miyamoto K, et al. Feasibility of free-breathing late gadolinium-enhanced cardiovascular MRI for assessment of myocardial infarction: navigator-gated versus single-shot imaging. Int J Cardiol 2013;168(1):94–9.

28. Nguyen TD, Spincemaille P, Weinsaft JW, et al. A fast navigator-gated 3D sequence for delayed enhancement MRI of the myocardium: comparison with breathhold 2D imaging. J Magn Reson Imaging 2008;27(4):802–8.

29. Bauner KU, Muehling O, Theisen D, et al. Assessment of myocardial viability with 3D MRI at 3 T. AJR Am J Roentgenol 2009;192(6):1645–50.

30. Peters DC, Appelbaum EA, Nezafat R, et al. Left ventricular infarct size, peri-infarct zone, and papillary scar measurements: a comparison of high-resolution 3D and conventional 2D late gadolinium enhancement cardiac MR. J Magn Reson Imaging 2009;30(4):794–800.

31. Viallon M, Jacquier A, Rotaru C, et al. Head-to-head comparison of eight late gadolinium-enhanced cardiac MR (LGE CMR) sequences at 1.5 tesla: from bench to bedside. J Magn Reson Imaging 2011; 34(6):1374–87.

32. Schlosser T, Hunold P, Herborn CU, et al. Myocardial infarct: depiction with contrast-enhanced MR imaging–comparison of gadopentetate and gadobenate. Radiology 2005;236(3):1041–6.

33. Wildgruber M, Stadlbauer T, Rasper M, et al. Single-dose gadobutrol in comparison with single-dose gadobenate dimeglumine for magnetic resonance imaging of chronic myocardial infarction at 3 T. Invest Radiol 2014;49:728–34.

34. Bauner KU, Reiser MF, Huber AM. Low dose gadobenate dimeglumine for imaging of chronic myocardial infarction in comparison with standard dose gadopentetate dimeglumine. Invest Radiol 2009;44(2):95–104.

35. Tumkosit M, Puntawangkoon C, Morgan TM, et al. Left ventricular infarct size assessed with 0.1 mmol/kg of gadobenate dimeglumine correlates with that assessed with 0.2 mmol/kg of gadopentetate dimeglumine. J Comput Assist Tomogr 2009; 33(3):328–33.

36. Durmus T, Schilling R, Doeblin P, et al. Gadobutrol for magnetic resonance imaging of chronic myocardial infarction: intraindividual comparison with gadopentetate dimeglumine. Invest Radiol 2012;47(3): 183–8.

37. Wagner M, Schilling R, Doeblin P, et al. Macrocyclic contrast agents for magnetic resonance imaging of chronic myocardial infarction: intraindividual comparison of gadobutrol and gadoterate meglumine. Eur Radiol 2013;23(1):108–14.

38. Doltra A, Skorin A, Hamdan A, et al. Comparison of acquisition time and dose for late gadolinium enhancement imaging at 3.0 T in patients with chronic myocardial infarction using Gd-BOPTA. Eur Radiol 2014;24:2192–200.

39. Gheorghiade M, Bonow RO. Chronic heart failure in the United States: a manifestation of coronary artery disease. Circulation 1998;97(3):282–9.

40. Jessup M, Brozena S. Heart failure. N Engl J Med 2003;348(20):2007–18.

41. Hung J, Teng TH, Finn J, et al. Trends from 1996 to 2007 in incidence and mortality outcomes of heart failure after acute myocardial infarction: a population-based study of 20,812 patients with first acute myocardial infarction in Western Australia. J Am Heart Assoc 2013;2(5):e000172.

42. Camici PG, Prasad SK, Rimoldi OE. Stunning, hibernation, and assessment of myocardial viability. Circulation 2008;117(1):103–14.

43. Beller GA. Assessment of myocardial viability. Curr Opin Cardiol 1997;12(5):459–67.

44. Wijns W, Vatner SF, Camici PG. Hibernating myocardium. N Engl J Med 1998;339(3):173–81.

45. Velazquez EJ, Lee KL, Deja MA, et al. Coronary-artery bypass surgery in patients with left ventricular dysfunction. N Engl J Med 2011;364(17):1607–16.

46. Bonow RO, Maurer G, Lee KL, et al. Myocardial viability and survival in ischemic left ventricular dysfunction. N Engl J Med 2011;364(17):1617–25.

47. Abraham A, Nichol G, Williams KA, et al. 18F-FDG PET imaging of myocardial viability in an experienced center with access to 18F-FDG and integration with clinical management teams: the Ottawa-FIVE substudy of the PARR 2 trial. J Nucl Med 2010;51(4):567–74.

48. Wagner A, Mahrholdt H, Holly TA, et al. Contrast-enhanced MRI and routine single photon emission computed tomography (SPECT) perfusion imaging for detection of subendocardial myocardial infarcts: an imaging study. Lancet 2003;361(9355): 374–9.

49. El Aidi H, Adams A, Moons KG, et al. Cardiac magnetic resonance imaging findings and the risk of cardiovascular events in patients with recent myocardial infarction or suspected or known coronary artery disease: a systematic review of prognostic studies. J Am Coll Cardiol 2014;63(11): 1031–45.

50. Schvartzman PR, Srichai MB, Grimm RA, et al. Nonstress delayed-enhancement magnetic resonance imaging of the myocardium predicts improvement of function after revascularization for chronic ischemic heart disease with left ventricular dysfunction. Am Heart J 2003;146(3):535–41.

51. Kelle S, Roes SD, Klein C, et al. Prognostic value of myocardial infarct size and contractile reserve using magnetic resonance imaging. J Am Coll Cardiol 2009;54(19):1770–7.

52. Wu KC, Zerhouni EA, Judd RM, et al. Prognostic significance of microvascular obstruction by magnetic resonance imaging in patients with acute myocardial infarction. Circulation 1998;97(8):765–72.

53. Srichai MB, Junor C, Rodriguez LL, et al. Clinical, imaging, and pathological characteristics of left ventricular thrombus: a comparison of contrast-enhanced magnetic resonance imaging, transthoracic echocardiography, and transesophageal echocardiography with surgical or pathological validation. Am Heart J 2006;152(1):75–84.

54. Yan AT, Shayne AJ, Brown KA, et al. Characterization of the peri-infarct zone by contrast-enhanced cardiac magnetic resonance imaging is a powerful predictor of post-myocardial infarction mortality. Circulation 2006;114(1):32–9.

55. Kwong RY, Sattar H, Wu H, et al. Incidence and prognostic implication of unrecognized myocardial scar characterized by cardiac magnetic resonance in diabetic patients without clinical evidence of myocardial infarction. Circulation 2008;118(10): 1011–20.

56. Kim HW, Klem I, Shah DJ, et al. Unrecognized non-Q-wave myocardial infarction: prevalence and prognostic significance in patients with suspected coronary disease. PLoS Med 2009;6(4):e1000057.

57. Schelbert EB, Cao JJ, Sigurdsson S, et al. Prevalence and prognosis of unrecognized myocardial infarction determined by cardiac magnetic resonance in older adults. JAMA 2012;308(9):890–6.

58. Child NM, Das R. Is cardiac magnetic resonance imaging assessment of myocardial viability useful for predicting which patients with impaired ventricles might benefit from revascularization? Interact Cardiovasc Thorac Surg 2012;14(4):395–8.

59. Selvanayagam JB, Kardos A, Francis JM, et al. Value of delayed-enhancement cardiovascular magnetic resonance imaging in predicting myocardial viability after surgical revascularization. Circulation 2004;110(12):1535–41.

60. Pegg TJ, Selvanayagam JB, Jennifer J, et al. Prediction of global left ventricular functional recovery in patients with heart failure undergoing surgical revascularisation, based on late gadolinium enhancement cardiovascular magnetic resonance. J Cardiovasc Magn Reson 2010;12:56.

61. Bondarenko O, Beek AM, Twisk JW, et al. Time course of functional recovery after revascularization of hibernating myocardium: a contrast-enhanced cardiovascular magnetic resonance study. Eur Heart J 2008;29(16):2000–5.

62. Canadian Cardiovascular Society Heart Failure Management Primary Panel, Moe GW, Ezekowitz JA, et al. The 2013 Canadian Cardiovascular Society Heart Failure Management Guidelines Update: focus on rehabilitation and exercise and surgical coronary revascularization. Can J Cardiol 2014; 30(3):249–63.

63. Choi KM, Kim RJ, Gubernikoff G, et al. Transmural extent of acute myocardial infarction predicts long-term improvement in contractile function. Circulation 2001;104(10):1101–7.

64. Selvanayagam JB, Jerosch-Herold M, Porto I, et al. Resting myocardial blood flow is impaired in hibernating myocardium: a magnetic resonance study of quantitative perfusion assessment. Circulation 2005;112(21):3289–96.

65. Jahnke C, Nagel E, Gebker R, et al. Prognostic value of cardiac magnetic resonance stress tests: adenosine stress perfusion and dobutamine stress wall motion imaging. Circulation 2007;115(13):1769–76.

66. Ingkanisorn WP, Kwong RY, Bohme NS, et al. Prognosis of negative adenosine stress magnetic resonance in patients presenting to an emergency department with chest pain. J Am Coll Cardiol 2006;47(7):1427–32.

67. Klem I, Heitner JF, Shah DJ, et al. Improved detection of coronary artery disease by stress perfusion cardiovascular magnetic resonance with the use of delayed enhancement infarction imaging. J Am Coll Cardiol 2006;47(8):1630–8.

68. Bekkers SC, Yazdani SK, Virmani R, et al. Microvascular obstruction: underlying pathophysiology and clinical diagnosis. J Am Coll Cardiol 2010;55(16): 1649–60.

69. Kidambi A, Mather AN, Motwani M, et al. The effect of microvascular obstruction and intramyocardial hemorrhage on contractile recovery in reperfused myocardial infarction: insights from cardiovascular magnetic resonance. J Cardiovasc Magn Reson 2013;15(1):58.

70. Gerber BL, Rochitte CE, Melin JA, et al. Microvascular obstruction and left ventricular remodeling early after acute myocardial infarction. Circulation 2000;101(23):2734–41.

71. Nijveldt R, Beek AM, Hirsch A, et al. Functional recovery after acute myocardial infarction: comparison

between angiography, electrocardiography, and cardiovascular magnetic resonance measures of microvascular injury. J Am Coll Cardiol 2008;52(3):181–9.

72. Ito H, Maruyama A, Iwakura K, et al. Clinical implications of the 'no reflow' phenomenon. A predictor of complications and left ventricular remodeling in reperfused anterior wall myocardial infarction. Circulation 1996;93(2):223–8.

73. de Waha S, Desch S, Eitel I, et al. Relationship and prognostic value of microvascular obstruction and infarct size in ST-elevation myocardial infarction as visualized by magnetic resonance imaging. Clin Res Cardiol 2012;101(6):487–95.

74. Weinsaft JW, Kim HW, Shah DJ, et al. Detection of left ventricular thrombus by delayed-enhancement cardiovascular magnetic resonance prevalence and markers in patients with systolic dysfunction. J Am Coll Cardiol 2008;52(2):148–57.

75. Fuster V, Halperin JL. Left ventricular thrombi and cerebral embolism. N Engl J Med 1989;320(6):392–4.

76. Greaves SC, Zhi G, Lee RT, et al. Incidence and natural history of left ventricular thrombus following anterior wall acute myocardial infarction. Am J Cardiol 1997;80(4):442–8.

77. Schmidt A, Azevedo CF, Cheng A, et al. Infarct tissue heterogeneity by magnetic resonance imaging identifies enhanced cardiac arrhythmia susceptibility in patients with left ventricular dysfunction. Circulation 2007;115(15):2006–14.

78. Heidary S, Patel H, Chung J, et al. Quantitative tissue characterization of infarct core and border zone in patients with ischemic cardiomyopathy by magnetic resonance is associated with future cardiovascular events. J Am Coll Cardiol 2010;55(24):2762–8.

79. Sciagra R, Bisi G, Santoro GM, et al. Comparison of baseline-nitrate technetium-99m sestamibi with rest-redistribution thallium-201 tomography in detecting viable hibernating myocardium and predicting post-revascularization recovery. J Am Coll Cardiol 1997;30(2):384–91.

80. Bax JJ, Cornel JH, Visser FC, et al. Prediction of improvement of contractile function in patients with ischemic ventricular dysfunction after revascularization by fluorine-18 fluorodeoxyglucose single-photon emission computed tomography. J Am Coll Cardiol 1997;30(2):377–83.

81. Klein C, Nekolla SG, Bengel FM, et al. Assessment of myocardial viability with contrast-enhanced magnetic resonance imaging: comparison with positron emission tomography. Circulation 2002;105(2):162–7.

82. Heijenbrok-Kal MH, Fleischmann KE, Hunink MG. Stress echocardiography, stress single-photon-emission computed tomography and electron beam computed tomography for the assessment of coronary artery disease: a meta-analysis of diagnostic performance. Am Heart J 2007;154(3):415–23.

83. Baer FM, Theissen P, Crnac J, et al. Head to head comparison of dobutamine-transoesophageal echocardiography and dobutamine-magnetic resonance imaging for the prediction of left ventricular functional recovery in patients with chronic coronary artery disease. Eur Heart J 2000;21(12):981–91.

84. Sandstede JJ, Bertsch G, Beer M, et al. Detection of myocardial viability by low-dose dobutamine cine MR imaging. Magn Reson Imaging 1999;17(10):1437–43.

85. Cwajg JM, Cwajg E, Nagueh SF, et al. End-diastolic wall thickness as a predictor of recovery of function in myocardial hibernation: relation to rest-redistribution T1-201 tomography and dobutamine stress echocardiography. J Am Coll Cardiol 2000;35(5):1152–61.

86. Koyama Y, Matsuoka H, Mochizuki T, et al. Assessment of reperfused acute myocardial infarction with two-phase contrast-enhanced helical CT: prediction of left ventricular function and wall thickness. Radiology 2005;235(3):804–11.

87. Gerber BL, Belge B, Legros GJ, et al. Characterization of acute and chronic myocardial infarcts by multidetector computed tomography: comparison with contrast-enhanced magnetic resonance. Circulation 2006;113(6):823–33.

88. Deseive S, Bauer RW, Lehmann R, et al. Dual-energy computed tomography for the detection of late enhancement in reperfused chronic infarction: a comparison to magnetic resonance imaging and histopathology in a porcine model. Invest Radiol 2011;46(7):450–6.

89. Kartje JK, Schmidt B, Bruners P, et al. Dual energy CT with nonlinear image blending improves visualization of delayed myocardial contrast enhancement in acute myocardial infarction. Invest Radiol 2013;48(1):41–5.

90. Wichmann JL, Bauer RW, Doss M, et al. Diagnostic accuracy of late iodine-enhancement dual-energy computed tomography for the detection of chronic myocardial infarction compared with late gadolinium-enhancement 3-T magnetic resonance imaging. Invest Radiol 2013;48(12):851–6.

91. Wichmann JL, Hu X, Kerl JM, et al. Non-linear blending of dual-energy CT data improves depiction of late iodine enhancement in chronic myocardial infarction. Int J Cardiovasc Imaging 2014;30:1145–50.

92. Nensa F, Poeppel TD, Beiderwellen K, et al. Hybrid PET/MR imaging of the heart: feasibility and initial results. Radiology 2013;268(2):366–73.

Tissue Characterization of the Myocardium
State of the Art Characterization by Magnetic Resonance and Computed Tomography Imaging

Puskar Pattanayak, MD[a], David A. Bleumke, MD, PhD[b],*

KEYWORDS

- Characterization • Myocardium • Magnetic resonance • Computed tomography • T1 mapping
- Late gadolinium enhancement • Extracellular volume fraction

KEY POINTS

- Late gadolinium enhancement (LGE) is a simple, robust, well-validated method for the assessment of scar in acute and chronic myocardial infarction.
- LGE is useful for distinguishing between ischemic and nonischemic cardiomyopathy. Specific LGE patterns are seen in nonischemic cardiomyopathy.
- Patient studies using T1 mapping have varied in study, design, and acquisition sequences.
- Despite the differences in technique, a clear pattern that has been seen is that in cardiac disease postcontrast T1 times are shorter.
- Extracellular volume fraction measured with cardiac computed tomography represents a new approach to the clinical assessment of diffuse myocardial fibrosis by evaluating the distribution of iodinated contrast.

INTRODUCTION

Fibrosis is a feature of many cardiomyopathies and the failing heart and is a major independent predictor of adverse cardiac outcomes. Replacement fibrosis is typically the result of myocardial infarction (MI). Diffuse interstitial fibrosis results from common cardiovascular risk factors; interstitial fibrosis has been shown to be reversible and treatable with early intervention. Noninvasive imaging methods to detect fibrosis are in development. Recent advances have been made in cardiac magnetic resonance (MR) imaging (CMR), computed tomography (CT), and nuclear medicine. This article focuses on CMR and the techniques of late gadolinium enhancement (LGE) and T1 mapping, which are useful in the detection of myocardial scar and diffuse myocardial fibrosis respectively.

PATHOLOGIC BASIS OF FIBROSIS

The extracellular matrix (ECM) is a dynamic molecular network that is essential in giving strength to the heart and in coordinated signaling between cells in the tissue. It anchors cardiac muscle cells (myocytes), regulates tissue mechanics, and stores growth factors.[1-3] The ECM is composed of collagens and elastic fibers buried in a gel of proteoglycans, polysaccharides, and glycoproteins. Aberrant healing processes result in the common pathologic feature called fibrosis. Fibrosis forms from an increased amount of collagen (fibrosis)

[a] Laboratory of Diagnostic Radiology Research, National Institutes of Health, 10 Center Drive, Bethesda, MD 20814, USA; [b] Radiology and Imaging Sciences, National Institutes of Health, Bethesda, MD 20814, USA
* Corresponding author.
E-mail address: bluemked@nih.gov

Radiol Clin N Am 53 (2015) 413–423
http://dx.doi.org/10.1016/j.rcl.2014.11.005
0033-8389/15/$ – see front matter Published by Elsevier Inc.

resulting from altered collagen turnover, in which net collagen deposition exceeds net collagen breakdown. Diffuse myocardial fibrosis is known to increase with age and other cardiovascular risk factors.[4] At a molecular level, matrix metalloproteinases also play a key role in the development of myocardial fibrosis.

Increased myocardial collagen deposition is the common end point for a wide variety of cardiomyopathies. Collagen deposition results in abnormal myocardial stiffness and contractility, which leads to progression of heart failure and disruption of the intercellular signaling. These disruptive processes may lead to malignant arrhythmias and sudden death. Multiple clinical studies have shown fibrosis to be a major independent predictor of adverse cardiac outcomes.[5–8] It is always present in end-stage heart failure.[9] Diastolic function is initially affected and is followed by deterioration of systolic function.[10]

The 2 distinct types of fibrosis in the heart are replacement fibrosis and interstitial fibrosis. Replacement fibrosis is focal development of scar that replaces dead cardiomyocytes from injury and is only seen when the integrity of the cell wall is affected.[11] Depending on the cause, both regional and diffuse patterns can be seen. Scarring from MI is the most common cause of replacement fibrosis. Hypertrophic cardiomyopathy, sarcoidosis, myocarditis, chronic renal insufficiency, and toxic cardiomyopathies are other conditions associated with this type of fibrosis.[12,13]

Interstitial fibrosis is generally a diffuse process. It has 2 subtypes: reactive and infiltrative interstitial. Reactive fibrosis is present in a variety of common conditions, including aging and hypertension. It is caused by an increase in collagen production and deposition by stimulated myofibroblasts. Infiltrative interstitial fibrosis is much rarer and is caused by progressive deposition of insoluble proteins or glycosphingolipids in the interstitium. Examples of infiltrative fibrosis include amyloidosis and Anderson-Fabry disease.[14,15] Both interstitial and infiltrative fibrosis eventually lead to cardiomyocyte apoptosis and replacement fibrosis.[10] Unlike replacement fibrosis, interstitial fibrosis may be reversible and is a target for treatment.[16,17]

The ability to noninvasively image fibrosis could be useful for diagnostic and therapeutic purposes in cardiomyopathy treatment. Tissue biopsy has been the gold standard for fibrosis assessment, but it is invasive and prone to sampling error. The emergence of noninvasive imaging modalities like CMR imaging and CT has led to the development of novel imaging methods for a range of cardiomyopathies.

DETECTION OF FIBROSIS WITH ENDOMYOCARDIAL BIOPSY

The gold standard for the detection of myocardial fibrosis is endomyocardial fibrosis. A small (<1 mm³) sample is taken, typically from the right ventricular side of the distal myocardial septum. The sample is assessed using Masson trichrome staining. Quantitative absolute assessment of the collagen volume fraction in tissue samples is measured by quantitative morphometry with picrosirius red.

Being an invasive technique, this carries a risk of complications. In cases of localized fibrosis, sampling error restricts the accuracy. It is also not possible to determine fibrotic involvement of the whole left ventricle.

DETECTION OF REPLACEMENT/FOCAL FIBROSIS WITH LATE GADOLINIUM ENHANCEMENT CARDIAC MAGNETIC RESONANCE

CMR provides safe, high-resolution imaging without ionizing radiation. CMR is well established as a standard of reference for the evaluation of myocardial structure and function. Pixel signal intensity of CMR images is based on the magnetic properties of hydrogen nuclei in the magnetic field. The 2 most common parameters from CMR are longitudinal relaxation time (T1), and transverse relaxation time (T2).

A unique clinical role of CMR (compared with echocardiography) is the use of LGE to define the presence of focal fibrosis or myocardial scar. For example, for the evaluation of focal fibrosis from MI, LGE imaging has been a gold standard for visualization and quantification of scar. **Fig. 1** shows scar from an inferior wall MI.

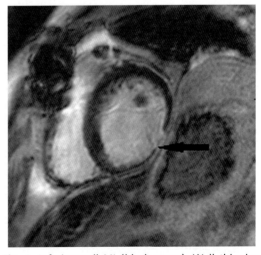

Fig. 1. Inferior wall MI (*black arrow*). Wall thinning and LGE is seen.

Myocardial scar is most commonly observed as a result of MI. However, nonischemic cardiomyopathies are also frequently associated with LGE. CMR can be used to classify patients with myocardial dysfunction as ischemic versus nonischemic based on LGE images. This distinction is meaningful for clinical treatment. **Fig. 2** shows LGE at the inferior right ventricular insertion point, which is a typical location for scar in patients with hypertrophic cardiomyopathy.

The physiologic basis of the LGE of myocardial fibrosis is based on the combination of an increased volume of distribution for the contrast agent and a prolonged washout related to the decreased capillary density within the myocardial fibrotic tissue.[18,19]

Late Gadolinium Enhancement Cardiac Magnetic Resonance Technique

The LGE technique to detect myocardial scar has a major advantage in its simplicity and robustness: an inversion pulse is used to suppress normal myocardium, followed by a standard gated T1-weighted gradient echo acquisition.

LGE sequences are based on distribution difference of the gadolinium-based contrast agent in normal and fibrotic tissue. In areas of high gadolinium chelate concentration, T1 time is shorter than in adjacent issue and shows high signal intensity on LGE images.

The discrimination between scarred/fibrotic myocardium and normal myocardium relies on contrast concentration differences combined with the chosen setting of the inversion-recovery sequence parameters. These parameters are set to null the normal myocardial signal that appears

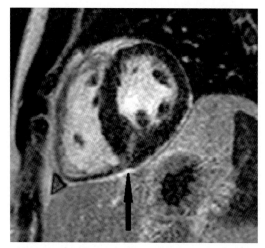

Fig. 2. Delayed postcontrast image showing LGE (*black arrow*) at the inferior right ventricular insertion point in a patient with hypertrophic cardiomyopathy.

dark in the final image relative to the bright signal of the scarred/fibrotic myocardium.

Given various specific properties of the tissue, the T1 shortening induced by the gadolinium contrast agent generates specific differences in signal intensity. The major tissue parameters that influence the final voxel signal intensity in the contrast-enhanced images are local perfusion; extracellular volume of distribution; water exchange rates among the vascular, interstitial, and cellular spaces; and wash-in and washout kinetics of the contrast agent.[18,20]

The myocardial gray zone is increasingly being defined on LGE clinical studies. The gray zone has been conceptually defined as myocardium with intermediate signal intensity enhancement between normal and scarred/fibrotic myocardium.[21] This area reflects tissue heterogeneity within the infarct periphery and has been shown to correlate strongly with ventricular arrhythmia inducibility and post-MI mortality in ischemic cardiomyopathy.[21,22]

Late Gadolinium Enhancement Cardiac Magnetic Resonance: Clinical Applications

LGE CMR has become a first-line noninvasive examination for assessment of the cause of new-onset myocardial dysfunction.[13,23] LGE with CMR came to the clinical forefront in the setting of ischemic cardiomyopathy. Subendocardial or transmural LGE is the typical pattern seen in myocardial infarcts using LGE CMR.

Kim and colleagues[24] showed that regional differences in signal intensity were correlated with the extent and severity of myocardial injury. They subsequently reported in experimental studies that the spatial extent of hyperenhancement was the same as the spatial extent of the collagenous scar at 8 weeks, with highly significant correlations. In ischemic cardiomyopathy, the transmural extent of LGE is predictive of myocardial wall recovery after revascularization, but it is also predictive of adverse LV remodeling.[25,26]

LGE CMR also provides prognostic information in nonischemic cardiomyopathies. LGE is significantly and independently associated with adverse cardiac events in patients with cardiac amyloidosis[27] and in patients undergoing aortic valve replacement.[28] In hypertrophic cardiomyopathy, Rubinshtein and colleagues[29] and Kwon and colleagues[30] reported that LGE was strongly associated with arrhythmia and subsequent sudden cardiac death.

Different patterns of enhancement have been reported according to the underlying cause, whether ischemic or nonischemic.[31]

Late Gadolinium Enhancement Cardiac Magnetic Resonance Limitations

The CMR community has recently come to realize a disadvantage of the LGE method: the normal myocardium that is suppressed by the inversion pulse contains low levels of diffuse fibrotic tissue in many diseases. Although LGE CMR is well validated and clinically accepted for the evaluation of focal myocardial scar, it has inherent disadvantages for assessment of diffuse myocardial fibrosis. LGE relies on the differences in signal intensity between scarred and adjacent normal myocardium to generate image contrast. Because this method needs a normal myocardium reference value, the LGE CMR method is unlikely to detect the presence of fibrosis in diffuse cases in which there is no clear distinction between fibrotic tissue and normal myocardium.

There are limitations of the LGE CMR method in its precise classification of myocardial fibrosis as present or absent. With conventional LGE imaging sequences, signal intensity is expressed on an arbitrary scale that differs from one imaging study to another and therefore is challenging to assess for direct signal quantification in cross-sectional or longitudinal comparisons. The late gadolinium-enhanced myocardial fibrotic tissue is influenced not only by technical parameters set during image acquisition (eg, inversion time,[32] slice thickness) but also according to the intensity threshold that is arbitrarily set during postprocessing to differentiate normal from fibrotic myocardium.[33] At present, there is no single consensus on the intensity threshold settings to use for clinical assessment of myocardial fibrosis.

Various methods have been reported to define late enhanced myocardium, with significantly different results,[33] perhaps explaining the variation in frequency of myocardial fibrosis by LGE CMR in different studies.[34] Although the LGE CMR method has been widely adopted in the clinical setting, wide variation in quantification of focal fibrosis and lack of detection of diffuse myocardial fibrosis have therefore led to additional CMR approaches.

DETECTION OF DIFFUSE FIBROSIS WITH CARDIAC MAGNETIC RESONANCE BY T1 MAPPING

T1 mapping is an imaging method that can provide a quantitative assessment of tissue characterization on CMR.[35] T1 mapping enables identification of early myocardial fibrosis at a treatable stage, when it cannot be otherwise detected by circulating biomarkers.[36] There is now a growing body of evidence that T1 mapping can detect early fibrosis that is not otherwise detectable by the LGE method.[37]

Compared with LGE images, T1 mapping reduces the influences of windowing and variations in signal enhancement by directly measuring the underlying T1 relaxation times. T1 relaxation time is measured in milliseconds, and represents a magnetic property of the tissue, also referred to as longitudinal or spin lattice relaxation. The T1 relaxation time of the normal myocardium is on the order of 1000 milliseconds. In the presence of an MR imaging contrast agent, the T1 relaxation time can be substantially reduced and thus the T1 time reflects the concentration of the MR imaging contrast agent in the tissue. The T1 times of each element of the myocardium are determined on a pixel-by-pixel basis.

Before gadolinium contrast agent administration (native T1 values), areas of diffuse myocardial fibrosis have greater T1 values (by about 10%–20%) than normal tissue. After gadolinium administration, T1 values are lower than normal in diffuse myocardial fibrosis. The expanded extracellular space in diffuse fibrosis accumulates more gadolinium-based contrast than healthy tissue, which is compact with myocytes. However, reduction in T1 values is not specific for diffuse myocardial fibrosis. T1 time reduction may also occur with cardiomyopathies in which the extracellular space is expanded, such as with amyloid depositions.[38]

T1 Mapping Technique

By reconstructing a sequence of images, T1 maps are generated in which every pixel represents T1 relaxation time of the corresponding section of myocardium. The modified Look-Locker inversion-recovery (MOLLI) sequence, described by Messroghli and colleagues[39–42] is a frequently used T1 mapping sequence. A currently favored approach to T1 mapping is a short MOLLI (ShMOLLI) sequence. Using the ShMOLLI sequence, the average breath hold decreases from 18 to 9.1 seconds, and the number of required heartbeats decreases from 17 to 9,[43] which is particularly useful for dyspneic patients.

High-resolution native and postcontrast T1 maps may be obtained within a single breath hold. This MOLLI sequence has been thoroughly described, optimized, and tested in phantom studies, on healthy volunteers, and patients with ischemic cardiomyopathy. Electrocardiogram-gated images are acquired at end-diastole. Images from multiple consecutive inversion-recovery acquisitions are then merged into 1 data set. A T1 map of the myocardium is created, which is a parametric reconstructed image.

T1 maps can be obtained before or after gadolinium contrast administration. The precontrast T1 map is a baseline reference. The postcontrast T1 maps are assessed at different time points after contrast administration. A T1 distribution histogram may be created to analyze the composition of each myocardial slice. A curve of myocardial T1 recovery that reflects the contrast agent washout can be obtained using postcontrast maps.[44] The MOLLI technique is sensitive to heart rate extreme values. It may also underestimate T1 times before gadolinium (native T1) and is best used for postgadolinium images. However, it does produce highly reproducible and fast T1 maps of the heart. Intraobserver and interobserver agreement level range is on the order of 10%.[44]

Besides MOLLI and ShMOLLI T1 mapping, other CMR techniques are also available to obtain CMR T1 maps.[39,42,45–47] These T1 mapping variants have been designed to have varying sensitivities to motion artifacts, heart rate, and intrinsic T1 value ranges.[42] The accuracy and reproducibility of the final T1 measurements is directly affected by the acquisition sequence. When comparing results of different studies it is thus important to note the particular technique used. **Fig. 3** shows gray scale images of precontrast and 25-minute postcontrast T1 maps in a healthy volunteer acquired using the ShMOLLI technique.

Quantifying T1 Mapping Results: Parameters Available from T1 Maps

There are 3 general approaches to obtaining T1 values to describe the tissue composition of the myocardium: native T1 values (no gadolinium contrast administered), postgadolinium T1 time,

and normalized values (such as extracellular volume fraction [ECV] or partition coefficient). Postgadolinium T1 times vary, depending on renal excretion of the contrast agent and delay time in measurement after gadolinium administration. The impact of those confounding variables might be reduced by calculating relative T1 mapping indices, including the partition coefficient (λ) and ECV; both parameters are derived from the ratio of T1 change in blood and myocardium[45,48] and are expressed as percentages. Calculation of ECV requires concurrent measurement of hematocrit (HCT). The ECV and λ are calculated using the following formulas[49]:

$$\Delta R1_{myo} = 1/T1_{myo\text{-}post} - 1/T1_{myo\text{-}pre}$$

$$\Delta R1_{blood} = 1/T1_{blood\text{-}post} - 1/T1_{blood\text{-}pre}$$

$$\lambda = \Delta R1_{myo}/\Delta R1_{blood}$$

$$ECV = \lambda \times (1 - HCT)$$

$T1_{myo\text{-}pre}$, pre contrast myocardial T1 value; $T1_{myo\text{-}post}$, post contrast myocardial T1 value; $T1_{blood\text{-}pre}$, pre contrast blood T1 value; $T1_{blood\text{-}post}$, post contrast blood T1 value.

The ECV expresses the proportion of the myocardium representing interstitial space versus cellular space. With greater fibrosis, the interstitial component increases relative to the cellular space. Gadolinium distributes only to the extracellular space and appears to be retained preferentially in areas of collagen/scar. Thus in the presence of disease, native T1 is increased, postgadolinium T1 is decreased, and ECV is increased. ECV maps can be created from coregistration of T1 maps to locate the diffuse fibrosis.[50,51]

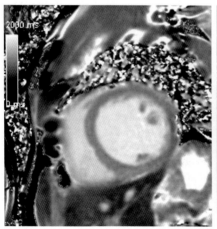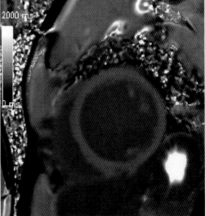

Fig. 3. Gray scale images of precontrast (*left*) and 25-minute postcontrast (*right*) T1 maps acquired using the ShMOLLI technique in a healthy volunteer.

A small number of studies are available to identify the best T1 parameter (eg, native T1, postgadolinium T1, or ECV) to detect various disease states. ECV has been a particularly attractive variable to quantify myocardial fibrosis because it normalizes for blood pool and HCT. However, ECV incorporates 5 different variables into its computation, each with an associated measurement error. If the errors in these variables accumulate, ECV could be insensitive for disease detection.

T1 Mapping: Clinical Applications

Patient studies using T1 mapping have varied in study and design. The acquisition sequences have varied. Some studies have evaluated both native and postcontrast T1 maps, whereas others have only evaluated native T1 maps. Despite the differences in technique, a clear pattern is that in cardiac disease postcontrast T1 times are shorter. Table 1 summarizes 10 key articles that have assessed cardiovascular diseases with T1 mapping.

Multiple studies have also examined the use of ECV and cardiovascular diseases. A concern is that ECV has a wide range of normal values, ranging from about 23% to 30%.[37] This range may overlap with ECV values in early disease. Although ECV is less likely to be useful as a single cutoff value to identify abnormal versus normal patients, change in ECV within an individual may be a more promising approach to assess, for example, a therapeutic response.

The accuracy of myocardial T1 mapping has been recorded in a few studies. Bauner and colleagues[52] and Messroghli and colleagues[42] found sensitivities and specificities to be greater than 95% for detection of chronic MI using contrast-enhanced T1 mapping. Ferreira and colleagues[53] reported that, in 21 patients with acute regional myocardial edema and no infarction and 21 healthy patients, unenhanced T1 mapping had sensitivity and specificity of 92%.

T1 Mapping Validation

Few validation studies have been performed comparing histology with T1 mapping values. Iles and colleagues[47] studied a symptomatic heterogeneous heart failure population using postcontrast MOLLI. On myocardial biopsy of transplanted hearts, they showed an inverse correlation of T1 values with percentage fibrosis. They also found a reduction in T1 time with worsening diastolic function. Sibley and colleagues[54] used a postcontrast Look-Locker technique. They also showed an inverse correlation between T1 time and histologic fibrosis on biopsy in patients with a broad range of cardiomyopathies.

A few other studies using postcontrast Look-Locker, MOLLI, and other T1 techniques have shown a correlation between T1 values and percentage myocardial fibrosis. Noncontrast T1 mapping techniques have been less well validated.

T1 mapping can accurately differentiate both interstitial and replacement fibrosis from normal myocardium, as shown by Kehr and colleagues.[55] They performed an in vitro MR study of selected human myocardium samples, and postcontrast T1 values for both diffuse and replacement fibrosis were significantly different from T1 values for normal myocardium. However, there was no significant difference between the diffuse fibrosis and replacement fibrosis T1 values.

T1 Mapping Limitations

T1 mapping of the heart is technically demanding and standardization of the methodology is required.

The accuracy is sensitive to several confounding factors.[35] These factors include the gadolinium myocardial washout rate (affected by glomerular filtration rate) and the properties of the gadolinium contrast agent (dose, concentration, injection rate, relaxivity, water exchange rate). The time delay after gadolinium administration by which postcontrast times are measured and the type of acquisition sequence used should be recorded because they significantly affect the final T1 value. Areas of LGE significantly affect the mean slice T1 value and interfere with diagnosing diffuse fibrosis. These areas therefore need to be accounted for. Myocardial T1 distribution can be significantly scattered, and this might limit its sensitivity for disease states with less severe fibrosis. T1 maps are usually created at the midventricular level. If the fibrosis is not homogeneous, areas of disease may not be measured.

COMPUTED TOMOGRAPHY

CT scanning has increasingly widespread clinical application for evaluation of coronary artery disease. The utility of cardiac CT for the evaluation of coronary artery stenosis has already been shown in large, multicenter clinical trials.[56–59] Given the significant clinical advantages of coronary CT angiography for coronary artery lesion evaluation, it would be highly desirable for CT also to be used for characterization of myocardial tissue abnormalities as well as myocardial function.

CT thus far has shown initial utility primarily for the evaluation of myocardial scar. Lardo and

Table 1 Clinical studies using T1 mapping to evaluate myocardial fibrosis				
Author and Date	Disease	Technique	Sample Size (Cases/Controls)	Conclusions
Messroghli et al,[42] 2007	Acute or chronic	MOLLI	24/24	In acute and chronic infarction, precontrast T1 values were higher than T1 values in remote myocardium
Maceira et al,[46] 2005	Amyloidosis	LL	22/16	Subepicardial postcontrast T1 values were significantly reduced in amyloid compared with controls
Broberg et al,[64] 2010	Adult congenital heart disease	LL	50/14	Cases of adult congenital heart disease had increased fibrosis index
Flett et al,[65] 2010	Aortic stenosis/HCM	LL	18/8 (aortic stenosis), 8/8 (HCM)	A high correlation was seen between T1 mapping with equilibrium contrast cardiac imaging and histologic samples of aortic stenosis and HCM
Gai et al,[66] 2011	Type 1 diabetes	LL	19/13	A significant difference was seen in postcontrast T1 values between those at low risk for diabetes compared with those at high risk
Ugander et al,[49] 2012	NICM/prior MI	MOLLI	30/11, 36/11	ECV is increased in those with prior MI and NICM
Bauner et al,[52] 2012	Chronic MI	MOLLI	26/26	A significant difference is seen in postcontrast T1 values in chronically infarcted myocardium compared with healthy myocardium
Turkbey et al,[67] 2012	Myotonic muscular dystrophy	LL	33/13	Lower postcontrast T values were seen in myotonic muscular dystrophy than in controls
Dass et al,[68] 2012	HCM/DCM	ShMOLLI	28/12 (HCM), 18/12 (DCM)	Cases with HCM or DCM had higher precontrast T1 times than controls
Messroghli et al,[41] 2003	Acute MI	LL	8/8	Postcontrast T1 values in acute MI were significantly reduced compared with normal myocardium

Abbreviations: DCM, dilated cardiomyopathy; HCM, hypertrophic cardiomyopathy; LL, Look-Locker; NICM, nonischemic cardiomyopathy.

colleagues[60] showed in an animal study that the spatial extent of acute and healed MI could be determined and quantified accurately with contrast-enhanced CT. The CT findings were compared with histology. In a cohort of patients with intermediate to high pretest probability, Bettencourt and colleagues found that CT delayed enhancement had good accuracy (90%) for ischemic scar detection with low sensitivity (53%) but excellent specificity (98%).

The use of multi-detector CT (MDCT) for diffuse abnormalities of myocardial tissue is significantly more challenging than the evaluation of focal myocardial scar because of the low contrast resolution of CT scanning. The distribution of iodinated contrast agent in the myocardium may be used to assess the degree of fibrosis. Several new studies highlight the potential of MDCT in this regard.

ECV measured with cardiac CT represents a new approach to the clinical assessment of diffuse myocardial fibrosis. Nacif and colleagues[61] found good correlation between myocardial ECV measured at cardiac CT and that measured at T1 mapping cardiac MR imaging in 24 subjects. A combination of healthy subjects and patients with heart failure was studied. ECV was higher in patients with heart failure than in healthy control subjects for both cardiac CT and cardiac MR imaging, as expected. For both cardiac MR imaging and cardiac CT, ECV was positively associated with end-diastolic and end-systolic volume and inversely related to ejection fraction. Fig. 4 shows precontrast and postcontrast MR and CT images. The anterolateral segment was used because this segment was most reliably identified on the precontrast CT.

The results of Nacif and colleagues[61] were confirmed in a subsequent study by Bandula and colleagues[62] who showed that ECV measured using an equilibrium CT technique in 24 patients with aortic stenosis correlated well with histologic quantification of myocardial fibrosis and with ECV derived by using equilibrium MR imaging.

In terms of clinical application, Langer and colleagues[63] studied patients with hypertrophic cardiomyopathy with MDCT. CT was able to reliably detect myocardial fibrosis as shown by late enhancement. Patient-based and segment-based sensitivity was 100% and 68% respectively compared with LGE CMR. This technique can therefore potentially be used in cases with CMR contraindications.

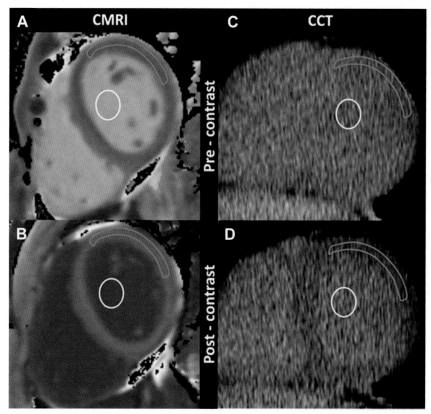

Fig. 4. Cardiac MR imaging region of interest measurements obtained (A) before and (B) after gadolinium chelate administration, and reformatted cardiac CT region of interest measurements obtained (C) before and (D) after administration of an iodinated contrast agent. Orange outline indicates myocardium; white circle indicates blood pool. (From Nacif MS, Kawel N, Lee JJ, et al. Interstitial myocardial fibrosis assessed as extracellular volume fraction with low-radiation-dose cardiac CT. Radiology 2012;264(3):878; with permission.)

SUMMARY AND FUTURE PERSPECTIVES

CMR methods to identify diffuse myocardial fibrosis noninvasively have great potential to characterize and quantify early disease. Myocardial fibrosis is a common end point of many chronic myocardial and systemic diseases and is not identifiable by other noninvasive tests. T1 mapping adds to the information provided by LGE CMR and further improves the knowledge and the clinical assessment of myocardial diffuse fibrosis. This technique might help clinicians to better stratify patient populations that are much larger and at lower cardiovascular risk (diabetics, hypertensive), detecting subclinical myocardial changes before the onset of diastolic and systolic dysfunction.

However, the clinical value of T1 mapping remains to be seen. Two especially interesting applications for T1 mapping are amyloidosis and hypertrophic cardiomyopathy. In both cases, the extent of disease is otherwise difficult to quantify.

Further work is ongoing to determine which disease processes may benefit by T1 mapping, and which parameters (eg, native T1, postgadolinium T1, ECV) are most sensitive and specific to identify the presence or absence of disease and its extent. Studies with large groups of patients and prospective studies are needed using standardized imaging protocols.

REFERENCES

1. Libby P, Lee RT. Matrix matters. Circulation 2000; 102(16):1874–6.
2. Speiser B, Riess CF, Schaper J. The extracellular matrix in human myocardium: part I: Collagens I, III, IV, and VI. Cardioscience 1991;2(4):225–32.
3. Speiser B, Weihrauch D, Riess CF, et al. The extracellular matrix in human cardiac tissue. Part II: Vimentin, laminin, and fibronectin. Cardioscience 1992;3(1):41–9.
4. Caspari PG, Gibson K, Harris P. Changes in myocardial collagen in normal development and after beta blockade. Recent Adv Stud Cardiac Struct Metab 1975;7:99–104.
5. Kwong RY, Chan AK, Brown KA, et al. Impact of unrecognized myocardial scar detected by cardiac magnetic resonance imaging on event-free survival in patients presenting with signs or symptoms of coronary artery disease. Circulation 2006;113(23):2733–43.
6. Kwong RY, Sattar H, Wu H, et al. Incidence and prognostic implication of unrecognized myocardial scar characterized by cardiac magnetic resonance in diabetic patients without clinical evidence of myocardial infarction. Circulation 2008;118(10):1011–20.
7. Assomull RG, Prasad SK, Lyne J, et al. Cardiovascular magnetic resonance, fibrosis, and prognosis in dilated cardiomyopathy. J Am Coll Cardiol 2006; 48(10):1977–85.
8. Dweck MR, Joshi S, Murigu T, et al. Midwall fibrosis is an independent predictor of mortality in patients with aortic stenosis. J Am Coll Cardiol 2011;58(12): 1271–9.
9. Schaper J, Speiser B. The extracellular matrix in the failing human heart. Basic Res Cardiol 1992; 87(Suppl 1):303–9.
10. Weber KT, Brilla CG. Pathological hypertrophy and cardiac interstitium. Fibrosis and renin-angiotensin-aldosterone system. Circulation 1991;83(6):1849–65.
11. Sutton MG, Sharpe N. Left ventricular remodeling after myocardial infarction: pathophysiology and therapy. Circulation 2000;101(25):2981–8.
12. Bohl S, Wassmuth R, Abdel-Aty H, et al. Delayed enhancement cardiac magnetic resonance imaging reveals typical patterns of myocardial injury in patients with various forms of non-ischemic heart disease. Int J Cardiovasc Imaging 2008;24(6):597–607.
13. Karamitsos TD, Francis JM, Myerson S, et al. The role of cardiovascular magnetic resonance imaging in heart failure. J Am Coll Cardiol 2009;54(15): 1407–24.
14. Hosch W, Kristen AV, Libicher M, et al. Late enhancement in cardiac amyloidosis: correlation of MRI enhancement pattern with histopathological findings. Amyloid 2008;15(3):196–204.
15. Moon JC, Sachdev B, Elkington AG, et al. Gadolinium enhanced cardiovascular magnetic resonance in Anderson-Fabry disease. Evidence for a disease specific abnormality of the myocardial interstitium. Eur Heart J 2003;24(23):2151–5.
16. Pitt B, Zannad F, Remme WJ, et al. The effect of spironolactone on morbidity and mortality in patients with severe heart failure. Randomized Aldactone Evaluation Study Investigators. N Engl J Med 1999;341(10):709–17.
17. Zannad F, Alla F, Dousset B, et al. Limitation of excessive extracellular matrix turnover may contribute to survival benefit of spironolactone therapy in patients with congestive heart failure: insights from the Randomized Aldactone Evaluation Study (RALES). Rales Investigators. Circulation 2000; 102(22):2700–6.
18. Croisille P, Revel D, Saeed M. Contrast agents and cardiac MR imaging of myocardial ischemia: from bench to bedside. Eur Radiol 2006;16(9):1951–63.
19. Kim RJ, Chen EL, Lima JA, et al. Myocardial Gd-DTPA kinetics determine MRI contrast enhancement and reflect the extent and severity of myocardial injury after acute reperfused infarction. Circulation 1996;94(12):3318–26.
20. Judd RM, Atalay MK, Rottman GA, et al. Effects of myocardial water exchange on T1 enhancement during bolus administration of MR contrast agents. Magn Reson Med 1995;33(2):215–23.

21. Yan AT, Shayne AJ, Brown KA, et al. Characterization of the peri-infarct zone by contrast-enhanced cardiac magnetic resonance imaging is a powerful predictor of post-myocardial infarction mortality. Circulation 2006;114(1):32–9.

22. Schmidt A, Azevedo CF, Cheng A, et al. Infarct tissue heterogeneity by magnetic resonance imaging identifies enhanced cardiac arrhythmia susceptibility in patients with left ventricular dysfunction. Circulation 2007;115(15):2006–14.

23. Mahrholdt H, Wagner A, Judd RM, et al. Delayed enhancement cardiovascular magnetic resonance assessment of non-ischaemic cardiomyopathies. Eur Heart J 2005;26(15):1461–74.

24. Kim RJ, Fieno DS, Parrish TB, et al. Relationship of MRI delayed contrast enhancement to irreversible injury, infarct age, and contractile function. Circulation 1999;100(19):1992–2002.

25. Kim RJ, Wu E, Rafael A, et al. The use of contrast-enhanced magnetic resonance imaging to identify reversible myocardial dysfunction. N Engl J Med 2000;343(20):1445–53.

26. Orn S, Manhenke C, Anand IS, et al. Effect of left ventricular scar size, location, and transmurality on left ventricular remodeling with healed myocardial infarction. Am J Cardiol 2007;99(8):1109–14.

27. Austin BA, Tang WH, Rodriguez ER, et al. Delayed hyper-enhancement magnetic resonance imaging provides incremental diagnostic and prognostic utility in suspected cardiac amyloidosis. JACC Cardiovasc Imaging 2009;2(12):1369–77.

28. Azevedo CF, Nigri M, Higuchi ML, et al. Prognostic significance of myocardial fibrosis quantification by histopathology and magnetic resonance imaging in patients with severe aortic valve disease. J Am Coll Cardiol 2010;56(4):278–87.

29. Rubinshtein R, Glockner JF, Ommen SR, et al. Characteristics and clinical significance of late gadolinium enhancement by contrast-enhanced magnetic resonance imaging in patients with hypertrophic cardiomyopathy. Circ Heart Fail 2010;3(1):51–8.

30. Kwon DH, Smedira NG, Rodriguez ER, et al. Cardiac magnetic resonance detection of myocardial scarring in hypertrophic cardiomyopathy: correlation with histopathology and prevalence of ventricular tachycardia. J Am Coll Cardiol 2009;54(3):242–9.

31. Cummings KW, Bhalla S, Javidan-Nejad C, et al. A pattern-based approach to assessment of delayed enhancement in nonischemic cardiomyopathy at MR imaging. Radiographics 2009;29(1):89–103.

32. Simonetti OP, Kim RJ, Fieno DS, et al. An improved MR imaging technique for the visualization of myocardial infarction. Radiology 2001;218(1):215–23.

33. Spiewak M, Malek LA, Misko J, et al. Comparison of different quantification methods of late gadolinium enhancement in patients with hypertrophic cardiomyopathy. Eur J Radiol 2010;74(3):e149–53.

34. Amado LC, Gerber BL, Gupta SN, et al. Accurate and objective infarct sizing by contrast-enhanced magnetic resonance imaging in a canine myocardial infarction model. J Am Coll Cardiol 2004;44(12):2383–9.

35. Mewton N, Liu CY, Croisille P, et al. Assessment of myocardial fibrosis with cardiovascular magnetic resonance. J Am Coll Cardiol 2011;57(8):891–903.

36. Wynn TA. Cellular and molecular mechanisms of fibrosis. J Pathol 2008;214(2):199–210.

37. Liu S, Han J, Nacif MS, et al. Diffuse myocardial fibrosis evaluation using cardiac magnetic resonance T1 mapping: sample size considerations for clinical trials. J Cardiovasc Magn Reson 2012;14:90.

38. Robbers LF, Baars EN, Brouwer WP, et al. T1 mapping shows increased extracellular matrix size in the myocardium due to amyloid depositions. Circ Cardiovasc Imaging 2012;5(3):423–6.

39. Messroghli DR, Radjenovic A, Kozerke S, et al. Modified Look-Locker inversion recovery (MOLLI) for high-resolution T1 mapping of the heart. Magn Reson Med 2004;52(1):141–6.

40. Messroghli DR, Greiser A, Frohlich M, et al. Optimization and validation of a fully-integrated pulse sequence for modified look-locker inversion-recovery (MOLLI) T1 mapping of the heart. J Magn Reson Imaging 2007;26(4):1081–6.

41. Messroghli DR, Niendorf T, Schulz-Menger J, et al. T1 mapping in patients with acute myocardial infarction. J Cardiovasc Magn Reson 2003;5(2):353–9.

42. Messroghli DR, Walters K, Plein S, et al. Myocardial T1 mapping: application to patients with acute and chronic myocardial infarction. Magn Reson Med 2007;58(1):34–40.

43. Piechnik SK, Ferreira VM, Dall'Armellina E, et al. Shortened Modified Look-Locker Inversion recovery (ShMOLLI) for clinical myocardial T1-mapping at 1.5 and 3 T within a 9 heartbeat breathhold. J Cardiovasc Magn Reson 2010;12:69.

44. Messroghli DR, Plein S, Higgins DM, et al. Human myocardium: single-breath-hold MR T1 mapping with high spatial resolution–reproducibility study. Radiology 2006;238(3):1004–12.

45. Flacke SJ, Fischer SE, Lorenz CH. Measurement of the gadopentetate dimeglumine partition coefficient in human myocardium in vivo: normal distribution and elevation in acute and chronic infarction. Radiology 2001;218(3):703–10.

46. Maceira AM, Joshi J, Prasad SK, et al. Cardiovascular magnetic resonance in cardiac amyloidosis. Circulation 2005;111(2):186–93.

47. Iles L, Pfluger H, Phrommintikul A, et al. Evaluation of diffuse myocardial fibrosis in heart failure with cardiac magnetic resonance contrast-enhanced T1 mapping. J Am Coll Cardiol 2008;52(19):1574–80.

48. Jerosch-Herold M, Sheridan DC, Kushner JD, et al. Cardiac magnetic resonance imaging of myocardial

contrast uptake and blood flow in patients affected with idiopathic or familial dilated cardiomyopathy. Am J Physiol Heart Circ Physiol 2008;295(3): H1234–42.

49. Ugander M, Oki AJ, Hsu LY, et al. Extracellular volume imaging by magnetic resonance imaging provides insights into overt and sub-clinical myocardial pathology. Eur Heart J 2012;33(10):1268–78.

50. Kellman P, Wilson JR, Xue H, et al. Extracellular volume fraction mapping in the myocardium, part 1: evaluation of an automated method. J Cardiovasc Magn Reson 2012;14:63.

51. Kellman P, Wilson JR, Xue H, et al. Extracellular volume fraction mapping in the myocardium, part 2: initial clinical experience. J Cardiovasc Magn Reson 2012;14:64.

52. Bauner KU, Biffar A, Theisen D, et al. Extracellular volume fractions in chronic myocardial infarction. Invest Radiol 2012;47(9):538–45.

53. Ferreira VM, Piechnik SK, Dall'Armellina E, et al. Non-contrast T1-mapping detects acute myocardial edema with high diagnostic accuracy: a comparison to T2-weighted cardiovascular magnetic resonance. J Cardiovasc Magn Reson 2012;14:42.

54. Sibley CT, Noureldin RA, Gai N, et al. T1 mapping in cardiomyopathy at cardiac MR: comparison with endomyocardial biopsy. Radiology 2012;265(3): 724–32.

55. Kehr E, Sono M, Chugh SS, et al. Gadolinium-enhanced magnetic resonance imaging for detection and quantification of fibrosis in human myocardium in vitro. Int J Cardiovasc Imaging 2008;24(1):61–8.

56. Miller JM, Dewey M, Vavere AL, et al. Coronary CT angiography using 64 detector rows: methods and design of the multi-centre trial CORE-64. Eur Radiol 2009;19(4):816–28.

57. Meijboom WB, Meijs MF, Schuijf JD, et al. Diagnostic accuracy of 64-slice computed tomography coronary angiography: a prospective, multicenter, multivendor study. J Am Coll Cardiol 2008;52(25): 2135–44.

58. Budoff MJ, Dowe D, Jollis JG, et al. Diagnostic performance of 64-multidetector row coronary computed tomographic angiography for evaluation of coronary artery stenosis in individuals without known coronary artery disease: results from the prospective multicenter ACCURACY (Assessment by Coronary Computed Tomographic Angiography of Individuals Undergoing Invasive Coronary Angiography) trial. J Am Coll Cardiol 2008;52(21):1724–32.

59. Hausleiter J, Meyer T, Hadamitzky M, et al. Non-invasive coronary computed tomographic angiography for patients with suspected coronary artery disease: the Coronary Angiography by Computed Tomography with the Use of a Submillimeter resolution (CACTUS) trial. Eur Heart J 2007;28(24): 3034–41.

60. Lardo AC, Cordeiro MA, Silva C, et al. Contrast-enhanced multidetector computed tomography viability imaging after myocardial infarction: characterization of myocyte death, microvascular obstruction, and chronic scar. Circulation 2006;113(3): 394–404.

61. Nacif MS, Kawel N, Lee JJ, et al. Interstitial myocardial fibrosis assessed as extracellular volume fraction with low-radiation-dose cardiac CT. Radiology 2012;264(3):876–83.

62. Bandula S, White SK, Flett AS, et al. Measurement of myocardial extracellular volume fraction by using equilibrium contrast-enhanced CT: validation against histologic findings. Radiology 2013;269(2): 396–403.

63. Langer C, Lutz M, Eden M, et al. Hypertrophic cardiomyopathy in cardiac CT: a validation study on the detection of intramyocardial fibrosis in consecutive patients. Int J Cardiovasc Imaging 2014;30(3): 659–67.

64. Broberg CS, Chugh SS, Conklin C, et al. Quantification of diffuse myocardial fibrosis and its association with myocardial dysfunction in congenital heart disease. Circ Cardiovasc Imaging 2010;3(6): 727–34.

65. Flett AS, Hayward MP, Ashworth MT, et al. Equilibrium contrast cardiovascular magnetic resonance for the measurement of diffuse myocardial fibrosis: preliminary validation in humans. Circulation 2010; 122(2):138–44.

66. Gai N, Turkbey EB, Nazarian S, et al. T1 mapping of the gadolinium-enhanced myocardium: adjustment for factors affecting interpatient comparison. Magn Reson Med 2011;65(5):1407–15.

67. Turkbey EB, Gai N, Lima JA, et al. Assessment of cardiac involvement in myotonic muscular dystrophy by T1 mapping on magnetic resonance imaging. Heart Rhythm 2012;9(10):1691–7.

68. Dass S, Suttie JJ, Piechnik SK, et al. Myocardial tissue characterization using magnetic resonance non-contrast t1 mapping in hypertrophic and dilated cardiomyopathy. Circ Cardiovasc Imaging 2012; 5(6):726–33.

Index

Note: Page numbers of article titles are in **boldface** type.

A

AAR (area at risk), stress cardiac MRI for, 358
Acute cardiac ischemia (ACI), stress cardiac MRI for, 357–358
Acute coronary syndromes (ACSs), CCTA for, key points of, 289, 292
  diagnostic workup for, 298, 303
  lesion severity and, 265
  pathobiology of, high-risk plaques in, 293, 297–298, 308
    significant stenosis in, 297–298
  plaque vulnerability and, 264, 298
  prognosis of, 262
  spatial plaque distribution and, 266
  stress cardiac MRI for, 357–358
  subdiagnoses of, 298
  triage of, CCTA costs for, 300, 302
    in emergency department, 302–303
    traditional, 298
Acute myocardial infarction (AMI), CMR imaging of, 376, 378–379
    with LGE, 400, 402
  risk stratification for, 400
  stress cardiac MRI for, 357–358
Adenosine stress test, for stress cardiac MRI, 358, 361–364
  myocardial, dynamic CT perfusion imaging and, 280
    static CT perfusion imaging and, 326–327
Agatston score, for coronary calcifications, 272
Age, in ACS risk stratification, 302
Allograft vasculopathy, in heart transplant recipients, CTA surveillance of, 290
Amyloidosis, fibrosis associated with, 414
Angina pectoris, acute. See *Acute coronary syndromes (ACSs).*
  stable. See *Stable chest pain syndrome.*
  unstable, ACS and, 298
Angiography, coronary, invasive. See *Coronary catheter angiography.*
  noninvasive, with CT. See *Coronary CT angiography (CCTA).*
    with MRI. See *MR angiography (MRA).*
    with x-ray, 346, 348
Angioplasty, complications of, stress cardiac MRI detection of, 361
Anomalies, cardiovascular, CMR imaging of, 372
  CTA for, 290–291

Aortic opacification, corresponding descending, in TAG, 329–330
Area at risk (AAR), stress cardiac MRI for, 358
Arrhythmias, CTA evaluation of, 276, 290
  myocardial fibrosis and, 414
  with CMR imaging, 338, 370, 372
  with static CT perfusion imaging, 327
Asymptomatic individuals, CTA for, 289–290
Atherogenesis, in CAD, 262–263
    macroscopic cross-section of coronary artery showing, 262
    mechanisms of disease, 262–263
    plaque development with, 263–267. See also *Atherosclerotic plaque.*
    risk factors for, 262
Atherosclerotic plaque, coronary, CT imaging of, **307–315**
    for assessment and outcomes, 311–312
    for characterization, 309–310
    for intracoronary characterization, 310–311
    for vulnerability, 307, 310–312
    future directions for, 312
    introduction to, 307–308
    invasive modalities vs., 263, 308–309
    key points of, 307
    summary of, 313
  effects on myocardial function. See *Functional assessment.*
  in CAD, 263–267
    Agatston score for, 272
    CCTA referral for, 291–292
      in ACS, 299, 303
    high-risk, CCTA considerations of, 293
      CT imaging of, 308–312
      pathobiology of, 297–298, 308
    ischemic cascade and, 266–267
    lesion severity and, 264–265
    microscopic cross-section of vessel displaying, 263
    molecular imaging of, 263
    morphologic features of, 263
    myocardial ischemia linked to, 266. See also *Ischemic heart disease (IHD).*
    spatial distribution of, 266
    vascular remodeling and, 263–264
      MR angiography of, 348–349
    vulnerability concept of, 264–266
      ACS and, 298

Radiol Clin N Am 53 (2015) 425–439
http://dx.doi.org/10.1016/S0033-8389(15)00012-3
0033-8389/15/$ – see front matter © 2015 Elsevier Inc. All rights reserved.

Moving?

Make sure your subscription moves with you!

To notify us of your new address, find your **Clinics Account Number** (located on your mailing label above your name), and contact customer service at:

Email: journalscustomerservice-usa@elsevier.com

800-654-2452 (subscribers in the U.S. & Canada)
314-447-8871 (subscribers outside of the U.S. & Canada)

Fax number: 314-447-8029

Elsevier Health Sciences Division
Subscription Customer Service
3251 Riverport Lane
Maryland Heights, MO 63043

*To ensure uninterrupted delivery of your subscription, please notify us at least 4 weeks in advance of move.